Fourth Edition

Network
Protocols
Handbook

TCP/IP

Ethernet ATM

Frame Relay WAN LAN

SS7/C7 VOIP Security

MAN WLAN IEEE IETF ISO

VLAN IBM

VPN SAN ANSI Novell

ITU-T Apple Microsoft

Cisco

Javvin Technologies, Inc.

Network Protocols Handbook

4th Edition.

13485 Old Oak Way
Saratoga CA 95070 USA
408-872-3881
handbook@javvin.com

Warning and Disclaimer

This book is designed to provide information about the current network communication protocols. Best effort has been made to make this book as complete and accurate as possible, but no warranty or fitness is implied. The infomation is provided on an "as is" basis. The author, publisher and distributor shall not have liability nor responsibility to anyone or group with respect to any loss arising from the information contained in this book and associated materials.

Table of Contents

Wide Area Network and Wan Protocols ·· 133

Table of Figures

Preface

We are living in the IT(Information Technologies) times. The IT provides us many powerful tools that have significantly changed our way of life, work and business operations. Among all the IT advancements, Internet has the most impact in every aspect of our society for the past 20 years. From Internet, people can get instant news, communicate with others, use it as a super-encyclopedia and find anything that they are interested in via search engines at their finger tips; Company can conduct business to business(B2B), business to consumer(B2C), with great efficiency; Government can announce polices, publicize regulations, and provide administrative information and services to the general public. Internet not only provides unprecedented convenience to our daily life, but also opens up new areas of disciplines and commercial opportunities that have boosted overall economy by creating many new jobs. It is reported that Internet will become a $20 trillion industry in the near future.

The Internet has also made significant progress and rapid adoption in China. According to the 14th Statistical Survey Report on the Internet Development in China announced on Jul 20, 2004 by CNNIC(China Internet Network Information Center), there are about 87 million Internet users as counted by the end of June 30, 2004, in mainland China, second only to the US; There are about 36 million computer hosts; The number of domain names registered under CN is 382216; The number of "www" websites is 626,600. It should be also noted that China has started its CNGI(China Next Generation Internet) project at the beginning of 2000, right after US and Europe started the similar initiatives. China now is becoming one of the most important and influential members not only in the World Trade Organization, but also within the Internet community.

To build the Internet and many other networks, engineers and organizations around the world have created many technologies over the past 20 years, in which network protocol is one of the key technology areas. After years of development on the communication standards and generations of networking architecture, network communication protocols have become a very complex subject. Various standard organizations have defined many communication protocols and all major vendors have their own proprietary technologies. Yet, people in the industry are continuously proposing and designing new protocols to address new problems in the network communications. It has become a huge challenge for IT and network professionals at all levels to understand the overall picture of communication protocols and to keep up with the pace of its on-going evolutions.

Javvin Company, based on Silicon Valley in California, USA, is a network software provider. This book is one of its contributions to provide an overview of network protocols and to serve as a reference and handbook for IT and network professionals.. The book fully explains and reviews all commonly used network communication protocols, including TCP/IP, security, VOIP, WAN, LAN , MAN, SAN and ISO protocols. It also covers Cisco, Novell, IBM, Microsoft, Apple and DEC network protocols. Hundreds of hyperlinks of references for further reading and studies are available in the book. It is an excellent reference for Internet programmers, network professionals and college students who are majoring IT and networking technology. It is also useful for individuals who want to know more details about the technologies underneath the Internet. I highly recommend this book to our readers.

Ke Yan, Ph.D.
Chief Architect of Juniper Networks
Founder of NetScreen Technologies

Network Communication Architecture and Protocols

A network architecture is a blueprint of the complete computer communication network, which provides a framework and technology foundation for designing, building and managing a communication network. It typically has a layered structure. Layering is a modern network design principle which divides the communication tasks into a number of smaller parts, each part accomplishing a particular sub-task and interacting with the other parts in a small number of well-defined ways. Layering allows the parts of a communication to be designed and tested without a combinatorial explosion of cases, keeping each design relatively simple.

If a network architecture is open, no single vendor owns the technology and controls its definition and development. Anyone is free to design hardware and software based on the network architecture. The TCP/IP network architecture, which the Internet is based on, is such an open network architecture and it is adopted as a worldwide network standard and widely deployed in local area network (LAN), wide area network (WAN), small and large enterprises, and last but not the least, the Internet.

Open Systems Interconnection (OSI) network architecture, developed by International Organization for Standardization (ISO), is an open standard for communication in the network across different equipment and applications by different vendors. Though not widely deployed, the OSI 7 layer model is considered the primary network architectural model for inter-computing and inter-networking communications.

In addition to the OSI network architecture model, there exist other network architecture models by many vendors, such as IBM SNA (Systems Network Architecture), Digital Equipment Corporation (DEC; now part of HP) DNA (Digital Network Architecture), Apple computer's AppleTalk, and Novell's NetWare. Actually, the TCP/IP architecture does not exactly match the OSI model. Unfortunately, there is no universal agreement regarding how to describe TCP/IP with a layered model. It is generally agreed that TCP/IP has fewer levels (from three to five layers) than the seven layers of the OSI model.

Network architecture provides only a conceptual framework for communications between computers. The model itself does not provide specific methods of communication. Actual communication is defined by various communication protocols.

OSI Network Architecture 7 Layers Model

Open Systems Interconnection (OSI) model is a reference model developed by ISO (International Organization for Standardization) in 1984, as a conceptual framework of standards for communication in the network across different equipment and applications by different vendors. It is now considered the primary architectural model for inter-computing and internetworking communications. Most of the network communication protocols used today have a structure based on the OSI model. The OSI model defines the communications process into 7 layers, dividing the tasks involved with moving information between networked computers into seven smaller, more manageable task groups. A task or group of tasks is then assigned to each of the seven OSI layers. Each layer is reasonably self-contained so that the tasks assigned to each layer can be implemented independently. This enables the solutions offered by one layer to be updated without adversely affecting the other layers.

The OSI 7 layers model has clear characteristics at each layer. Basically, layers 7 through 4 deal with end-to-end communications between data source and destinations, while layers 3 to 1 deal with communications between network devices. On the other hand, the seven layers of the OSI model can be divided into two groups: upper layers (layers 7, 6 & 5) and lower layers (layers 4, 3, 2, 1). The upper layers of the OSI model deal with application issues and generally are implemented only in software. The highest layer, the application layer, is closest to the end user. The lower layers of the OSI model handle data transport issues. The physical layer and the data link layer are implemented in hardware and software. The lowest layer, the physical layer, is closest to the physical network medium (the wires, for example) and is responsible for placing data on the medium.

The specific description for each layer is as follows:

Layer 7: Application Layer
• Defines interface to user processes for communication and data transfer in network
• Provides standardized services such as virtual terminal, file and job transfer and operations

Layer 6: Presentation Layer
• Masks the differences of data formats between dissimilar systems
• Specifies architecture-independent data transfer format
• Encodes and decodes data; encrypts and decrypts data; compresses and decompresses data

Layer 5: Session Layer
• Manages user sessions and dialogues
• Controls establishment and termination of logic links between users
• Reports upper layer errors

Layer 4: Transport Layer
• Manages end-to-end message delivery in network
• Provides reliable and sequential packet delivery through error recovery and flow control mechanisms
• Provides connectionless-oriented packet delivery

Layer 3: Network Layer
• Determines how data are transferred between network devices
• Routes packets according to unique network device addresses
• Provides flow and congestion control to prevent network resource depletion

Layer 2: Data Link Layer
• Defines procedures for operating the communication links
• Frames packets
• Detects and corrects packets transmit errors

Layer 1: Physical Layer
• Defines physical means of sending data over network devices
• Interfaces between network medium and devices
• Defines optical, electrical and mechanical characteristics

Information being transferred from a software application in one computer to an application in another proceeds through the OSI layers. For example, if a software application in computer A has information to pass to a software application in computer B, the application program in computer A need to pass the information to the application layer (Layer 7) of computer A, which then passes the information to the presentation layer (Layer 6), which relays the data to the session layer (Layer 5), and so on all the way down to the physical layer (Layer 1). At the physical layer, the data is placed on the physical network medium and is sent across the medium to computer B. The physical layer of computer B receives the data from the physical medium, and then its physical layer passes the information up to the data link layer (Layer 2), which relays it to the network layer (Layer 3), and so on, until it reaches the application layer (Layer 7) of computer B. Finally, the application layer of computer B passes the information to the recipient application program to complete the communication process.

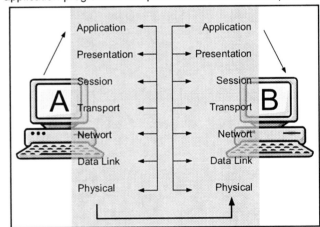

The following diagram illustrated this process.
Figure 1-1: Communication between computers in a network

The seven OSI layers use various forms of control information to communicate with their peer layers in other computer systems. This control information consists of specific requests and instructions that are exchanged between peer OSI layers.

Headers and Trailers of data at each layer are the two basic forms to carry the control information.

Headers are prepended to data that has been passed down from upper layers. Trailers are appended to data that has been passed down from upper layers. An OSI layer is not required to attach a header or a trailer to data from upper layers.

Each layer may add a Header and a Trailer to its Data, which consists of the upper layer's Header, Trailer and Data as it proceeds through the layers. The Headers contain information that specifically addresses layer-to-layer communication.

Headers, trailers and data are relative concepts, depending on the layer that analyzes the information unit. For example, the Transport Header (TH) contains information that only the Transport layer sees. All other layers below the Transport layer pass the Transport Header as part of their Data. At the network layer, an information unit consists of a Layer 3 header (NH) and data. At the data link layer, however, all the information passed down by the network layer (the Layer 3 header and the data) is treated as data. In other words, the data portion of an information unit at a given OSI layer potentially can contain headers, trailers, and data from all the higher layers. This is known as encapsulation.

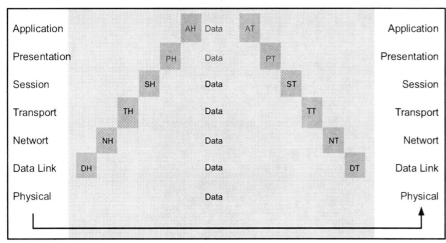

Figure 1-2: Data encapsulation at each layer

For example, if computer A has data from a software application to send to computer B, the data is passed to the application layer. The application layer in computer A then communicates any control information required by the application layer in computer B by prepending a header to the data. The resulting message unit, which includes a header, the data and maybe a trailer, is passed to the presentation layer, which prepends its own header containing control information intended for the presentation layer in computer B. The message unit grows in size as each layer prepends its own header and trailer containing control information to be used by its peer layer in computer B. At the physical layer, the entire information unit is transmitted through the network medium.

The physical layer in computer B receives the information unit and passes it to the data link layer. The data link layer in computer B then reads the control information contained in the header prepended by the data link layer in computer A. The header and the trailer are then removed, and the remainder of the information unit is passed to the network layer. Each layer performs the same actions: The layer reads the header and trailer from its peer layer, strips it off, and passes the remaining information unit to the next higher layer. After the application layer performs these actions, the data is passed to the recipient software application in computer B, in exactly the form in which it was transmitted by the application in computer A.

One OSI layer communicates with another layer to make use of the services provided by the second layer. The services provided by adjacent layers help a given OSI layer communicate with its peer layer in other computer systems. A given layer in the OSI model generally communicates with three other OSI layers: the layer directly above it, the layer directly below it and

its peer layer in other networked computer systems. The data link layer in computer A, for example, communicates with the network layer of computer A, the physical layer of computer A and the data link layer in computer B. The following chart illustrates this example.

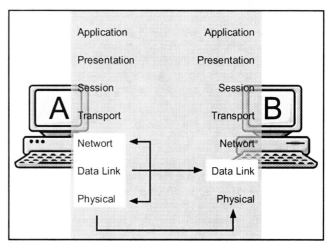

Figure 1-3: Data communication between peer layers

TCP/IP Four Layers Architecture Model

TCP/IP architecture does not exactly follow the OSI model. Unfortunately, there is no universal agreement regarding how to describe TCP/IP with a layered model. It is generally agreed that TCP/IP has fewer levels (from three to five layers) than the seven layers of the OSI model. We adopt a four layers model for the TCP/IP architecture.

TCP/IP architecture omits some features found under the OSI model, combines the features of some adjacent OSI layers and splits other layers apart. The 4-layer structure of TCP/IP is built as information is passed down from applications to the physical network layer. When data is sent, each layer treats all of the information it receives from the upper layer as data, adds control information (header) to the front of that data and then pass it to the lower layer. When data is received, the opposite procedure takes place as each layer processes and removes its header before passing the data to the upper layer.

The TCP/IP 4-layer model and the key functions of each layer is described below:

Application Layer

The Application Layer in TCP/IP groups the functions of OSI Application, Presentation Layer and Session Layer. Therefore any process above the transport layer is called an Application in the TCP/IP architecture. In TCP/IP socket and port are used to describe the path over which applications communicate. Most application level protocols are associated with one or more port number.

Transport Layer

In TCP/IP architecture, there are two Transport Layer protocols. The Transmission Control Protocol (TCP) guarantees information transmission. The User Datagram Protocol (UDP) transports datagram swithout end-to-end reliability checking. Both protocols are useful for different applications.

Network Layer

The Internet Protocol (IP) is the primary protocol in the TCP/IP Network Layer. All upper and lower layer communications must travel through IP as they are passed through the TCP/IP protocol stack. In addition, there are many supporting protocols in the Network Layer, such as ICMP, to facilitate and manage the routing process.

Network Access Layer

In the TCP/IP architecture, the Data Link Layer and Physical Layer are normally grouped together to become the Network Access layer. TCP/IP makes use of existing Data Link and Physical Layer standards rather than defining its own. Many RFCs describe how IP utilizes and interfaces with the existing data link protocols such as Ethernet, Token Ring, FDDI, HSSI, and ATM. The physical layer, which defines the hardware communication properties, is not often directly interfaced with the

TCP/IP protocols in the network layer and above.

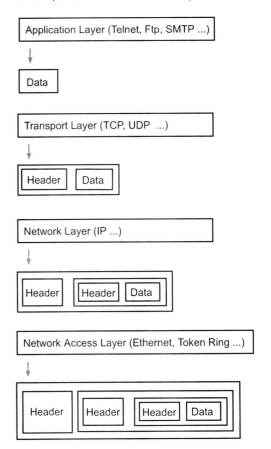

Figure 1-4: TCP/IP Protocol Stack 4 Layer Model

In this book, however, we present TCP/IP protocols into the OSI 7 layers structure for comparison purpose.

Other Network Architecture Models: IBM SNA

In addition to the open architectural models such as OSI 7 layers model and the TCP/IP model, there exist a few popular vendor specific network communication models, such as IBM SNA (Systems Network Architecture), Digital Equipment Corporation's (DEC, now part of HP) DNA (Digital Network Architecture). We will only provide details on the IBM SNA here.

Although it is now considered a legacy networking architecture, the IBM SNA is still widely deployed. SNA was designed around the host-to-terminal communication model that IBM's mainframes use. IBM expanded the SNA protocol to support peer-to-peer networking. This expansion was deemed Advanced Peer-to-Peer Networking (APPN) and Advanced Program-to-Program Communication (APPC). Advanced Peer-to-Peer Networking (APPN) represents IBM's second-generation SNA. In creating APPN, IBM moved SNA from a hierarchical, mainframe-centric environment to a peer-based networking environment. At the heart of APPN is an IBM architecture that supports peer-based communications, directory services, and routing between two or more APPC systems that are not directly attached.

SNA has many similarities with the OSI 7 layers reference model. However, the SNA model has only six layers and it does not define specific protocols for its physical control layer. The physical control layer is assumed to be implemented via other standards. The functions of each SNA component are described as follows:

• Data Link Control (DLC) -- Defines several protocols, including the Synchronous Data Link Control (SDLC) protocol for hierarchical communication, and the Token Ring Network communication protocol for LAN communication between peers. SDLC provided a foundation for ISO HDSL and IEEE 802.2.
• Path control -- Performs many OSI network layer functions, including routing and datagram segmentation and reassembly (SAR)
• Transmission control -- Provides a reliable end-to-end connection service (similar to TCP), as well as encrypting and decrypting services
• Data flow control -- Manages request and response processing, determines whose turn it is to communicate, groups messages and interrupts data flow on request
• Presentation services -- Specifies data-transformation algorithms that translate data from one format to another, coordinate resource sharing and synchronize transaction operations
• Transaction services -- Provides application services in the form of programs that implement distributed processing or management services

The following figure illustrates how the IBM SNA model maps to the ISO OSI reference model.

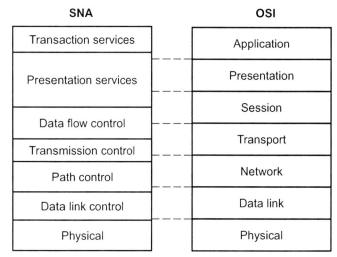

SNA	OSI
Transaction services	Application
Presentation services	Presentation
	Session
Data flow control	Transport
Transmission control	
Path control	Network
Data link control	Data link
Physical	Physical

Figure 1-5: SNA vs. OSI model

A typical SNA network topology:

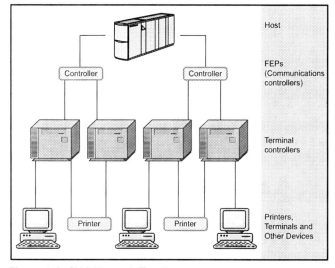

Figure 1-6: SNA Network Topology

SNA supports the following types of networks:

• A subarea network is a hierarchically organized network consisting of subarea nodes and peripheral nodes. Subarea nodes, such as hosts and communication controllers, handle general network routing. Peripheral nodes, such as terminals, attach to the network without awareness of general network routing.
• A peer network is a cooperatively organized network consisting of peer nodes that all participate in general network routing.
• A mixed network is a network that supports both host-controlled communications and peer communications.

In SNA networks, programs that exchange information across the SNA network are called transaction programs (TPs). Communication between a TP and the SNA network occurs through network accessible units or NAUs (formerly called "network addressable units"), which are unique network resources that can be accessed (through unique local addresses) by other network resources. There are three types of NAU: Physical

Unit, Logic Units and Control Points.

Communication between Transaction Programs (TP) and Logic Units (LU) is shown as follows:

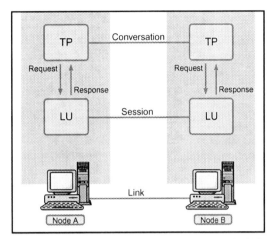

Figure 1-7: Communication between TP and LU in SNA

Network Protocol: Definition and Overview

The OSI model, and any other network communication model, provide only a conceptual framework for communication between computers, but the model itself does not provide specific methods of communication. Actual communication is defined by various communication protocols. In the context of data communication, a protocol is a formal set of rules, conventions and data structure that governs how computers and other network devices exchange information over a network. In other words, a protocol is a standard procedure and format that two data communication devices must understand, accept and use to be able to talk to each other.

In modern protocol design, protocols are "layered" according to the OSI 7 layer model or a similar layered model. Layering is a design principle which divides the protocol design into a number of smaller parts, each part accomplishing a particular sub-task, and interacting with the other parts of the protocol only in a small number of well-defined ways. Layering allows the parts of a protocol to be designed and tested without a combinatorial explosion of cases, keeping each design relatively simple. Layering also permits familiar protocols to be adapted to unusual circumstances.

The header and/or trailer at each layer reflect the structure of the protocol. Detailed rules and procedures of a protocol or protocol stack are often defined by a lengthy document. For example, IETF uses RFCs (Request for Comments) to define protocols and updates to the protocols.

A wide variety of communication protocols exist. These protocols are defined by many standard organizations throughout the world and by technology vendors over years of technology evolution and development. One of the most popular protocol suites is TCP/IP, which is the heart of Internetworking communications. The IP, the Internet Protocol, is responsible for exchanging information between routers so that the routers can select the proper path for network traffic, while TCP is responsible for ensuring the data packets are transmitted across the network reliably and error free. LAN and WAN protocols are also critical protocols in network communications. The LAN protocols suite is for the physical and data link layers communications over various LAN media such as Ethernet wires and wireless waves. The WAN protocol suite is for the lowest three layers and defines communication over various wide-area media, such as fiber optic and copper cable.

Network communication has gradually evolved – Today's new technologies are based on accumulation over years of technologies, which may be still existing or obsolete. Because of this, the protocols which define the network communication, are highly inter-related. Many protocols rely on others for operation. For example, many routing protocols use other network protocols to exchange information between routers.

In addition to standards for individual protocols in transmission, there are now also interface standards for different layers to talk to the ones above or below (usually operating-system-specific). For example: Winsock and Berkeley sockets between layers 4 and 5, NDIS and ODI between layers 2 and 3.

The protocols for data communication cover all areas as defined in the OSI model. However, the OSI model is only loosely defined. A protocol may perform the functions of one or more of the OSI layers, which introduces complexity to understand protocols relevant to the OSI 7 layer model. In real-world protocols, there is some argument as to where the distinctions between layers are drawn; there is no one black and white answer.

To develop a complete technology that is useful for the industry, very often a group of protocols is required in the same layer or across many different layers. Different protocols often describe different aspects of a single communication; taken together, these form a protocol suite. For example, Voice over IP (VOIP), a group of protocols developed by many vendors and standard organizations, has many protocols across the 4 top layers in the OSI model.

Protocols can be implemented either in hardware or software, or a mixture of both. Typically, the lower layers are implemented in hardware, with the higher layers being implemented in software.

Protocols could be grouped into suites (or families, or stacks) by their technical functions, or origin of the protocol introduction, or both. A protocol may belong to one or multiple protocol suites, depending on how you categorize it. For example, the Gigabit Ethernet protocol IEEE 802.3z is a LAN (Local Area Network) protocol and it can also be used in MAN (Metropolitan Area Network) communications.

Most recent protocols are designed by the IETF for Internetworking communications, and the IEEE for local area networking (LAN) and metropolitan area networking (MAN). The ITU-T contributes mostly to wide area networking (WAN) and telecommunications protocols. ISO has its own suite of protocols for internetworking communications, which is mainly deployed in European countries.

Protocols Guide

TCP/IP Protocols

The TCP/IP protocol suite establishes the technical foundation of the Internet. Development of the TCP/IP started as DOD projects. Now, most protocols in the suite are developed by the Internet Engineering Task Force (IETF) under the Internet Architecture Board (IAB), an organization initially sponsored by the US government and now an open and autonomous organization. The IAB provides the coordination for the R&D underlying the TCP/IP protocols and guides the evolution of the Internet. The TCP/IP protocols are well documented in the Request For Comments (RFC), which are drafted, discussed, circulated and approved by the IETF committees. All documents are open and free and can be found online in the IETF site listed in the reference.

TCP/IP architecture does not exactly match the OSI model. Unfortunately, there is no universal agreement regarding how to describe TCP/IP with a layered model. It is generally agreed that TCP/IP has fewer levels (from three to five layers) than the seven layers of the OSI model. In this document, we force TCP/IP protocols into the OSI 7 layers structure for comparison purpose.

The TCP/IP suite's core functions are addressing and routing (IP/IPv6 in the networking layer) and transportation control (TCP, UDP in the transport layer).

IP - Internet Protocol

Addressing of network components is a critical issue for information routing and transmission in network communications. Each technology has its own convention for transmitting messages between two machines within the same network. On a LAN, messages are sent between machines by supplying the six bytes unique identifier (the "MAC" address). In an SNA network, every machine has Logical Units with their own network addresses. DECNET, AppleTalk, and Novell IPX all have a scheme for assigning numbers to each local network and to each workstation attached to the network.

On top of these local or vendor specific network addresses, IP assigns a unique number to every network device in the world, which is called an IP address. This IP address is a four-byte value in IPv4 that, by convention, is expressed by converting each byte into a decimal number (0 to 255) and separating the bytes with a period. In IPv6, the IP address has been increased to 16 bytes. Details of the IP and IPv6 protocols are presented in separate documents.

TCP - Transmission Control Protocol

TCP provides a reliable stream delivery and virtual connection service to applications through the use of sequenced acknowledgment with retransmission of packets when necessary. TCP provides stream data transfer, transportation reliability, efficient flow control, full-duplex operation, and multiplexing. Check the TCP section for more details.

In the follwoing TCP/IP protocol stack table, we list all the protocols according to their functions in mapping to the OSI 7 layers network communication reference model. However, the TCP/IP architecture does not follow the OSI model closely, for example, most TCP/IP applications directly run on top of the transport layer protocols, TCP and UDP, without the presentation and session layers in between.

TCP/IP Protocol Stack

Application Layer

BOOTP: Bootstrap Protocol
DCAP: Data Link Switching Client Access Protocol
DHCP: Dynamic Host Configuration Protocol
DNS: Domain Name Systems
FTP: File Transfer Protocol
Finger: User Information Protocol
HTTP: Hypertext Transfer Protocol
S-HTTP: Secure Hypertext Transfer Protocol (S-HTTP)
IMAP & IMAP4: Internet Message Access Protocol
IPDC: IP Device Control
IRCP (IRC): Internet Relay Chat Protocol
LDAP: Lightweighted Directory Access Protocol
MIME (S-MIME): Multipurpose Internet Mail Extensions (Secure MIME)
NAT: Network Address Translation
NNTP: Network News Transfer Protocol
NTP: Network Time Protocol
POP & POP3: Post Office Protocol (version 3)
rlogin: Remote Login in Unix
RMON: Remote Monitoring MIBs in SNMP
SLP: Service Location Protocol
SMTP: Simple Mail Transfer Protocol
SNMP: Simple Network Management Protocol
SNTP: Simple Network Time Protocol
Syslog Protocol
TELNET: TCP/IP Terminal Emulation Protocol
TFTP: Trivial File Transfer Protocol
URL: Uniform Resource Locator
XMPP: Extensible Messaging and Presence Protocol
X-Window: X Window or X Protocol or X System

Presentation Layer
LPP: Lightweight Presentation Protocol

Session Layer
RPC: Remote Procedure Call protocol

Transport Layer
ITOT: ISO Transport Over TCP/IP
RDP: Reliable Data Protocol
RUDP: Reliable UDP
TALI: Transport Adapter Layer Interface
TCP: Transmission Control Protocol
UDP: User Datagram Protocol
Van Jacobson: Compressed TCP

Network Layer
Routing
BGP/BGP-4: Border Gateway Protocol
EGP: Exterior Gateway Protocol
IP: Internet Protocol
IPv6: Internet Protocol version 6
ICMP/ICMPv6: Internet Control Message Protocol
IRDP: ICMP Router Discovery Protocol
Mobile IP: IP Mobility Support Protocol for IPv4 & IPv6
NARP: NBMA Address Resolution Protocol
NHRP: Next Hop Resolution Protocol
OSPF: Open Shortest Path First
RIP (RIP2): Routing Information Protocol
RIPng: RIP for IPv6
RSVP: Resource ReSerVation Protocol

VRRP: Virtual Router Redundancy Protocol
Multicast
BGMP: Border Gateway Multicast Protocol
DVMRP: Distance Vector Multicast Routing Protocol
IGMP: Internet Group Management Protocol
MARS: Multicast Address Resolution Server
MBGP: Multiprotocol BGP
MOSPF: Multicast OSPF
MSDP: Multicast Source Discovery Protocol
MZAP: Multicast-Scope Zone Announcement Protocol
PGM: Pragmatic General Multicast Protocol
PIM-DM: Protocol Independent Multicast - Dense Mode
PIM-SM: Protocol Independent Multicast - Sparse Mode
MPLS Protocols
MPLS: Multi-Protocol Label Switching
CR-LDP: Constraint-Based Label Distribution Protocol
LDP: Label Distribution Protocol
RSVP-TE: Resource ReSerVation Protocol-Traffic Engineering
GMPLS: Generalized Multi-Protocol Lable Switching

Data Link Layer
ARP and InARP: Address Resolution Protocol and Inverse ARP
IPCP and IPv6CP: IP Control Protocol and IPv6 Control Protocol
RARP: Reverse Address Resolution Protocol
SLIP: Serial Line IP

Related protocol suites
LAN, MAN, WAN, SAN, Security/VPN

Sponsor Source
IETF, DARPA, ISO

BOOTP: Bootstrap Protocol

Protocol Description

The Bootstrap Protocol (BOOTP) is an UDP/IP-based protocol which allows a booting host to configure itself dynamically and without user supervision. BOOTP provides a means to notify a host of its assigned IP address, the IP address of a boot server host and the name of a file to be loaded into memory and executed. Other configuration information such as the local subnet mask, the local time offset, the addresses of default routers and the addresses of various Internet servers, can also be communicated to a host using BOOTP.

BOOTP uses two different well-known port numbers. UDP port number 67 is used for the server and UDP port number 68 is used for the BOOTP client. The BOOTP client broadcasts a single packet called a BOOTREQUEST packet that contains the client's physical network address and optionally, its IP address if known. The client could send the broadcast using the address 255.255.255.255, which is a special address called the limited broadcast address. The client waits for a response from the server. If a response is not received within a specified time interval, the client retransmits the request.

The server responds to the client's request with a BOOTREPLY packet. The request can (optionally) contain the 'generic' filename to be booted, for example, 'unix' or 'ethertip'. When the server sends the bootreply, it replaces this field with the fully qualified path name of the appropriate boot file. In determining this name, the server may consult its own database correlating the client's address and filename request, with a particular boot file customized for that client. If the bootrequest filename is a null string, then the server returns a filename field indicating the 'default' file to be loaded for that client.

In the case of clients which do not know their IP addresses, the server must also have a database relating hardware address to IP address. This client IP address is then placed into a field in the bootreply.

BOOTP is an alternative to RARP, which operates at the Data Link Layer for LAN only. BOOTP, a UDP/IP based configuration protocol, provides much more configuration information and allows dynamic configuration for an entire IP network. BOOTP and its extensions became the basis for the Dynamic Host Configuration Protocol (DHCP).

Protocol Structure

	8	16	24	32bit
Op	Htype	Hlen	Hops	
Xid				
Secs		Flags		
Ciaddr				
Yiaddr				
Siaddr				
Giaddr				
Chaddr (16 bytes)				

Sname (64 bytes)
File (128 bytes)
Option (variable)

Op -- The message operation code. Messages can be either BOOTREQUEST or BOOTREPLY.
Htype -- The hardware address type.
Hlen -- The hardware address length.
Xid -- The transaction ID.
Secs -- The seconds elapsed since the client began the address acquisition or renewal process.
Flags -- The flags.
Ciaddr -- The client IP address.
Yiaddr -- The "Your" (client) IP address.
Siaddr -- The IP address of the next server to use in bootstrap.
Giaddr -- The relay agent IP address used in booting via a relay agent.
Chaddr -- The client hardware address.
Sname -- Optional server host name, null terminated string
File -- Boot file name, null terminated string; generic name or null in DHCPDISCOVER, fully qualified directory-path name in DHCPOFFER.
Options -- Optional parameters field.

Related Protocols
IP, UDP, DHCP, RARP

Sponsor Source
BOOTP is defined by IETF (http://www.ietf.org) RFC951 and RFC 1542.

Reference
http://www.javvin.com/protocol/rfc951.pdf
BOOTSTRAP PROTOCOL (BOOTP)
http://www.javvin.com/protocol/rfc1542.pdf
Clarifications and Extensions for the Bootstrap Protocol
http://www.javvin.com/protocol/rfc2132.pdf
DHCP Options and BOOTP Vendor Extensions
http://www.javvin.com/protocol/rfc3396.pdf
Encoding Long Options in the (DHCPv4)

DCAP: Data Link Switching Client Access Protocol

Protocol Description

The Data Link Switching Client Access Protocol (DCAP) is an application layer protocol used between workstations and routers to transport SNA/NetBIOS traffic over TCP sessions.

DCAP was introduced to address a few deficiencies in the Data Link Switching Protocol (DLSw). The implementation of the Data Link Switching Protocol (DLSw) on a large number of workstations raises the important issues of scalability and efficiency. Since DLSw is a switch-to-switch protocol, it is not efficient when implemented on workstations. DCAP addresses these issues. It introduces a hierarchical structure to resolve the scalability problems. All workstations are clients to the router (server) rather than peers to the router. This creates a client/server model. It also provides a more efficient protocol between the workstation (client) and the router (server).

In a DLSw network, each workstation needs a MAC address to communicate with an FEP attached to a LAN. When DLSw is implemented on a workstation, it does not always have a MAC address defined. For example, when a workstation connects to a router through a modem via PPP, it only consists of an IP address. In this case, the user must define a virtual MAC address. This is administratively intensive since each workstation must have a unique MAC address. DCAP uses the Dynamic Address Resolution protocol to solve this problem. The Dynamic Address Resolution protocol permits the server to dynamically assign a MAC address to a client without complex configuration.

Protocol Structure

4	8	16bit
Protocol ID	Version Number	Message Type
Packet Length		

Protocol ID -- The Protocol ID is set to 1000.
Version number -- The Version number is set to 0001.
Message type -- The message type is the DCAP message type.
Packet length -- The total packet length is the length of the packet including the DCAP header, DCAP data and user data. The minimum size of the packet is 4, which is the length of the header.

Related Protocols
TCP, DLSw, NetBIOS

Sponsor Source
DCAP is defined by IETF (http://www.ietf.org) in RFC 2114.

Reference
http://www.javvin.com/protocol/rfc2114.pdf
Data Link Switching Client Access Protocol

DHCP: Dynamic Host Configuration Protocol

Protocol Description

Dynamic Host Configuration Protocol (DHCP) is a communications protocol enabling network administrators manage centrally and to automate the assignment of IP addresses in a network. In an IP network, each device connecting to the Internet needs a unique IP address. DHCP lets a network administrator supervise and distribute IP addresses from a central point and automatically sends a new IP address when a computer is plugged into a different place in the network.

DHCP uses the concept of a "lease" or amount of time that a given IP address will be valid for a computer. The lease time can vary depending on how long a user is likely to require the Internet connection at a particular location. It's especially useful in education and other environments where users change frequently. Using very short leases, DHCP can dynamically reconfigure networks in which there are more computers than there are available IP addresses.

DHCP supports static addresses for computers containing Web servers that need a permanent IP address.

DHCP is an alternative to another network IP management protocol, Bootstrap Protocol (BOOTP). DHCP is a more advanced protocol but both configuration management protocols are commonly used. Some operating systems, including Windows NT/2000, come with DHCP servers. A DHCP or BOOTP client is a program that is located in each computer so that it can be configured.

Protocol Structure

8	16	24	32bit
Op	Htype	Hlen	Hops
Xid			
Secs		Flags	
Ciaddr			
Yiaddr			
Siaddr			
Giaddr			
Chaddr (16 bytes)			
Sname (64 bytes)			
File (128 bytes)			
Option (variable)			

Op -- The message operation code. Messages can be either BOOTREQUEST or BOOTREPLY.
Htype -- The hardware address type.
Hlen -- The hardware address length.
Xid -- The transaction ID.
Secs -- The seconds elapsed since the client began the address acquisition or renewal process.
Flags -- The flags.
Ciaddr -- The client IP address.

Yiaddr -- The "Your" (client) IP address.

Siaddr -- The IP address of the next server to use in bootstrap.

Giaddr -- The relay agent IP address used in booting via a relay agent.

Chaddr -- The client hardware address.

Sname -- Optional server host name, null terminated string

File -- Boot file name, null terminated string; generic name or null in DHCPDISCOVER, fully qualified directory-path name in DHCPOFFER.

Options -- Optional parameters field. See the options documents for a list of defined options.

Related Protocols

IP, BOOTP, UDP, TCP, RARP

Sponsor Source

DHCP is defined by IETF (http://www.ietf.org) RFC2131 and RFC 3396.

Reference

http://www.javvin.com/protocol/rfc2131.pdf
Dynamic Host Configuration Protocol
http://www.javvin.com/protocol/rfc3396.pdf
Encoding Long Options in the (DHCPv4)

DNS: Domain Name System (Service) protocol

Protocol Description

Domain Name System (DNS) is a distributed Internet directory service. DNS is used mostly to translate between domain names and IP addresses and to control Internet email delivery. Most Internet services rely on DNS to work, and if DNS fails, web sites cannot be located and email delivery stalls.

DNS has two independent aspects:
1. It specifies the name syntax and rules for delegating authority over names. The basic syntax is: local.group.site
2. It specifies the implementation of a distributed computing system that efficiently maps names to addresses.

In the DNS naming scheme, a decentralized and hierarchical mechanism is used by the delegating authority for parts of the namespace and distributing responsibility for mapping names and addresses. The naming scheme of DNS is used to assign network device names globally and is implemented by geographically distributed sets of severs to names to addresses.

In theory, the domain name standard in DNS protocol specifies an abstract hierarchical namespace with arbitrary values for labels. Any group can build an instance of the domain system to choose labels for all parts of its hierarchy. However most users of the DNS protocols follow the hierarchical labels used by the official Internet domain system. Some of the top level domains are: COM, EDU, GOV, NET, ORG, BIZ ... plus many country codes.

The distributed scheme of DNS allows efficient and reliable mapping of names to IP addresses. Most names can be mapped locally and a set of servers operating at multiple sites cooperatively solve the mapping problem of a large network. Because of the distributing nature, no single machine failure will prevent the DNS from operating correctly.

Protocol Structure

16	21			28			32bit
ID	Q	Query	A	T	R	V	B	Rcode
Question count	Answer count						
Authority count	Additional count						

ID -- 16-bit field used to correlate queries and responses.

Q -- 1-bit field that identifies the message as a query or response.

Query -- 4-bit field that describes the type of message: 0 Standard query (name to address); 1 Inverse query; 2 Server status request.

A -- Authoritative Answer. 1-bit field. When set to 1, identifies the response as one made by an authoritative name server.

T -- Truncation. 1-bit field. When set to 1, indicates the message has been truncated.

R -- 1-bit field. Set to 1 by the resolve to request recursive service by the name server.

V -- 1-bit field. Signals the availability of recursive service by the name server.

B -- 3-bit field. Reserved for future use. Must be set to 0.

Rcode -- Response Code. 4-bit field that is set by the name server to identify the status of the query.

Question count -- 16-bit field that defines the number of entries in the question section.

Answer count -- 16-bit field that defines the number of resource records in the answer section.

Authority count -- 16-bit field that defines the number of name server resource records in the authority section.

Additional count -- 16-bit field that defines the number of resource records in the additional records section.

Related Protocols
IP, TCP, IGMP, ICMP, SNMP, TFTP and NFS

Sponsor Source
DNS is defined by IETF (http://www.ietf.org) RFC1034 and updated by 1035, 1101, 1183, 1348, 1876, 1982, 2181, 2308, 2535

Reference
http://www.javvin.com/protocol/rfc1034.pdf

Domain Names – Concept and Facilities

Finger: User Information Protocol

Protocol Description
The Finger user information protocol provides an interface to a remote user information program (RUIP). Finger, based on the Transmission Control Protocol, is a protocol for the exchange of user information using TCP port 79. The local host opens a TCP connection to a remote host on the Finger port. An RUIP becomes available on the remote end of the connection to process the request. The local host sends the RUIP a one line query based upon the Finger query specification and waits for the RUIP to respond. The RUIP receives and processes the query, returns an answer, then initiates the close of the connection. The local host receives the answer and the close signal and then proceeds to close its end of the connection.

Finger discloses information about users; moreover, such information may be considered sensitive. Security administrators should make explicit decisions about whether to run Finger and what information should be provided in responses. One existing implementation provides the time the user last logged in, the time he last read mail, whether unread mail was waiting for him and who the most recent unread mail was from! This makes it possible to track conversations in progress and see where someone's attention was focused. Sites that are information-security conscious should not run Finger without an explicit understanding of how much information it is giving away.

Implementations should be tested against various forms of attack. In particular, an RUIP SHOULD protect itself against malformed inputs. Vendors providing Finger with the operating system or network software should subject their implementations to penetration testing. Finger is one of the avenues for direct penetration. Like Telnet, FTP and SMTP, Finger is one of the protocols at the security perimeter of a host. Accordingly, the soundness of the implementation is paramount. The implementation should receive just as much security scrutiny during design, implementation, and testing as Telnet, FTP, or SMTP.

Protocol Structure
Any data transferred between two Finger hosts MUST be in ASCII format, with no parity, and with lines ending in CRLF (ASCII 13 followed by ASCII 10). This excludes other character formats such as EBCDIC, etc. This also means that any characters between ASCII 128 and ASCII 255 should truly be international data, not 7-bit ASCII with the parity bit set.

The Finger query specification is defined:

```
{Q1}    ::= [{W}|{W}{S}{U}]{C}
{Q2}    ::= [{W}{S}][{U}]{H}{C}
{U}     ::= username
{H}     ::= @hostname | @hostname{H}
{W}     ::= /W
{W}     ::= /W
{S}     ::= <SP> | <SP>{S}
{C}     ::= <CRLF>
```

Related Protocols
TCP, TELNET, SMTP, FTP

Sponsor Source
Finger is defined by IETF (http://www.ietf.org) in RFC 1288.

Reference
http://www.javvin.com/protocol/rfc1288.pdf
FILE TRANSFER PROTOCOL (FTP)

FTP: File Transfer Protocol

Protocol Description
File Transfer Protocol (FTP) enables file sharing between hosts. FTP uses TCP to create a virtual connection for control information and then creates a separate TCP connection for data transfers. The control connection uses an image of the TELNET protocol to exchange commands and messages between hosts.

The key functions of FTP are:

1) to promote sharing of files (computer programs and/or data);
2) to encourage indirect or implicit (via programs) use of remote computers;
3) to shield a user from variations in file storage systems among hosts; and
4) to transfer data reliably and efficiently.

FTP, though usable directly by a user at a terminal, is designed mainly for use by programs. FTP control frames are TELNET exchanges and can contain TELNET commands and option negotiation. However, most FTP control frames are simple ASCII text and can be classified as FTP commands or FTP messages. FTP messages are responses to FTP commands and consist of a response code followed by explanatory text.

FTP has little security protection when performing file transfer: both user password and the data are exposed to public. To make the file transfer more secure, some enhancements have been made on the FTP, including SFTP, SSH protected FTP and BBFTP.

• SFTP encrypts the data that is transferred. It should only be used to transfer small (1-10KB) files containing sensitive data. Large files that do not contain sensitive information should be transferred via a method that does not encrypt data.
• SSH protected FTP: This transfer method encrypts the password information but does NOT encrypt the data being transferred. As a result, it should only be used to transfer files that do NOT contain sensitive information. Files that contain sensitive information should be transferred with SFTP.
• BBFTP: BBFTP only encrypts usernames and passwords. It does NOT encrypt the data being transferred. BBFTP is a non-interactive FTP-like system that supports parallel TCP streams for data transfers, allowing it to achieve bandwidths that are greater than normal FTP. Because of these characteristics, it is the preferred method for transferring large data files over network.

Protocol Structure

Command	Description
ABOR	Abort data connection process.
ACCT <account>	Account for system privileges.
ALLO <bytes>	Allocate bytes for file storage on server.
APPE <filename>	Append file to file of same name on server.

CDUP <dir path>	Change to parent directory on server.
CWD <dir path>	Change working directory on server.
DELE <filename>	Delete specified file on server.
HELP <command>	Return information on specified command.
LIST <name>	List information if name is a file or list files if name is a directory.
MODE <mode>	Transfer mode (S=stream, B=block, C=compressed).
MKD <directory>	Create specified directory on server.
NLST <directory>	List contents of specified directory.
NOOP	Cause no action other than acknowledgement from server.
PASS <password>	Password for system log-in.
PASV	Request server wait for data connection.
PORT <address>	IP address and two-byte system port ID.
PWD	Display current working directory.
QUIT	Log off from the FTP server.
REIN	Reinitialize connection to log-in status.
REST <offset>	Restart file transfer from given offset.
RETR <filename>	Retrieve (copy) file from server.
RMD <directory>	Remove specified directory on server.
RNFR <old path>	Rename from old path.
RNTO <new path>	Rename to new path.
SITE <params>	Site specific parameters provided by server.
SMNT <pathname>	Mount the specified file structure.
STAT <directory>	Return information on current process or directory.
STOR <filename>	Store (copy) file to server.
STOU <filename>	Store file to server name.
STRU <type>	Data structure (F=file, R=record, P=page).
SYST	Return operating system used by server.
TYPE <data type>	Data type (A=ASCII, E=EBCDIC, I=binary).
USER <username>	User name for system log-in.

Standard FTP messages are as follows:

Response Code	Explanatory Text
110	Restart marker at MARK yyyy=mmmm (new file pointers).
120	Service ready in nnn minutes.
125	Data connection open, transfer starting.

150	Open connection.
200	OK.
202	Command not implemented.
211	(System status reply).
212	(Directory status reply).
213	(File status reply).
214	(Help message reply).
215	(System type reply).
220	Service ready.
221	Log off network.
225	Data connection open.
226	Close data connection.
227	Enter passive mode (IP address, port ID).
230	Log on network.
250	File action completed.
257	Path name created.
331	Password required.
332	Account name required.
350	File action pending.
421	Service shutting down.
425	Cannot open data connection.
426	Connection closed.
450	File unavailable.
451	Local error encountered.
452	Insufficient disk space.
500	Invalid command.
501	Bad parameter.
502	Command not implemented.
503	Bad command sequence.
504	Parameter invalid for command.
530	Not logged onto network.
532	Need account for storing files.
550	File unavailable.
551	Page type unknown.
552	Storage allocation exceeded.
553	File name not allowed.

Related Protocols
TELNET, SFTP, SSH, BBFTP

Sponsor Source
FTP is defined by IETF (http://www.ietf.org) in RFC 959 and updated by 2228, 2640 and 2773.

Reference
http://www.javvin.com/protocol/rfc959.pdf
FILE TRANSFER PROTOCOL (FTP)

HTTP: Hypertext Transfer Protocol

Protocol Description

The Hypertext Transfer Protocol (HTTP) is an application-level protocol with the lightness and speed necessary for distributed, collaborative, hypermedia information systems. HTTP has been in use by the World-Wide Web global information initiative since 1990.

HTTP allows an open-ended set of methods to be used to indicate the purpose of a request. It builds on the discipline of reference provided by the Uniform Resource Identifier (URI), as a location (URL) or name (URN), for indicating the resource on which a method is to be applied. Messages are passed in a format similar to that used by Internet Mail and the Multipurpose Internet Mail Extensions (MIME).

HTTP is also used as a generic protocol for communication between user agents and proxies/gateways to other Internet protocols, such as SMTP, NNTP, FTP, Gopher and WAIS, allowing basic hypermedia access to resources available from diverse applications and simplifying the implementation of user agents.

The HTTP protocol is a request/response protocol. A client sends a request to the server in the form of a request method, URI, and protocol version, followed by a MIME-like message containing request modifiers, client information, and possible body content over a connection with a server. The server responds with a status line, including the message's protocol version and a success or error code, followed by a MIME-like message containing server information, entity meta information, and possible entity-body content.

The first version of HTTP, referred to as HTTP/0.9, was a simple protocol for raw data transfer across the Internet. HTTP/1.0, as defined by RFC 1945, improved the protocol by allowing messages to be in the format of MIME-like messages, containing meta information about the data transferred and modifiers on the request/response semantics. However, HTTP/1.0 does not sufficiently take into consideration the effects of hierarchical proxies, caching, the need for persistent connections, or virtual hosts. "HTTP/1.1" includes more stringent requirements than HTTP/1.0 in order to ensure reliable implementation of its features. There is a secure version of HTTP (S-HTTP) specification, which will be discussed in a separate document.

Protocol Structure

HTTP messages consist of requests from client to server and responses from server to client.

The request message has the following format:

Request Line	General header	Request header	Entity header	Message Body

The Request-Line begins with a method token, followed by the Request-URI and the protocol version, and ends with CRLF. The elements are separated by SP characters. No CR or LF is allowed except in the final CRLF sequence. The details of the general header, request header and entity header can be found in the reference documents.

The response message has the following format:

Status Line	General header	Response header	Entity header	Message Body

The Status-Code element is a 3-digit integer result code of the attempt to understand and satisfy the request. The Reason-Phrase is intended to give a short textual description of the Status-Code. The Status-Code is intended for use by automata and the Reason-Phrase is intended for the human user. The client is not required to examine or display the Reason-Phrase. The details of the general header, response header and entity header could be found in the reference documents.

Related Protocols

WWW, FTP, SMTP, NNTP, Gopher, WAIS, DNS, S-HTTP

Sponsor Source

HTTP is defined by IETF (http://www.ietf.org) in RFC 1945 and 2616.

Reference

http://www.javvin.com/protocol/rfc1945.pdf
Hypertext Transfer Protocol -- HTTP 1.0
http://www.javvin.com/protocol/rfc2616.pdf
Hypertext Transfer Protocol -- HTTP 1.1

S-HTTP: Secure Hypertext Transfer Protocol

Protocol Description

Secure HTTP (S-HTTP) is a secure message-oriented communications protocol designed for use in conjunction with HTTP. S-HTTP is designed to coexist with HTTP's messaging model and to be easily integrated with HTTP applications.

Secure HTTP provides a variety of security mechanisms to HTTP clients and servers, providing the security service options appropriate to the wide range of potential end uses possible for the World-Wide Web (WWW). S-HTTP provides symmetric capabilities to both client and server (in that equal treatment is given to both requests and replies, as well as for the preferences of both parties) while preserving the transaction model and implementation characteristics of HTTP.

Several cryptographic message format standards may be incorporated into S-HTTP clients and servers. S-HTTP supports interoperation among a variety of implementations and is compatible with HTTP. S-HTTP aware clients can communicate with S-HTTP oblivious servers and vice-versa, although such transactions obviously would not use S-HTTP security features.

S-HTTP does not require client-side public key certificates (or public keys), as it supports symmetric key-only operation modes. This is significant because it means that spontaneous private transactions can occur without requiring individual users to have an established public key. While S-HTTP is able to take advantage of ubiquitous certification infrastructures, its deployment does not require it.

S-HTTP supports end-to-end secure transactions. Clients may be "primed" to initiate a secure transaction (typically using information supplied in message headers); this may be used to support encryption of fill-out forms, for example. With S-HTTP, no sensitive data need ever be sent over the network in the clear.

S-HTTP provides full flexibility of cryptographic algorithms, modes and parameters. Option negotiation is used to allow clients and servers to agree on transaction modes, cryptographic algorithms (RSA vs. DSA for signing, DES vs. RC2 for encrypting, etc.) and certificate selection.

S-HTTP attempts to avoid presuming a particular trust model, although its designers admit to a conscious effort to facilitate multiply-rooted hierarchical trust, and anticipate that principals may have many public key certificates. S-HTTP differs from Digest-Authentication in that it provides support for public key cryptography and consequently digital signature capability, as well as providing confidentiality. Another popular technology for secured web communication is HTTPS, which is HTTP running on top of TLS and SSL for secured web transactions.

Protocol Structure

Syntactically, Secure HTTP messages are the same as HTTP, consisting of a request or status line followed by headers and a body. However, the range of headers is different and the bodies are typically cryptographically enhanced.

S-HTTP messages, just as HTTP messages, consist of requests from client to server and responses from server to client.

The request message has the following format:

Request Line	General header	Request header	Entity header	Message Body

In order to differentiate S-HTTP messages from HTTP messages and allow for special processing, the request line should use the special "Secure" method and use the protocol designator "Secure-HTTP/1.4". Consequently, Secure-HTTP and HTTP processing can be intermixed on the same TCP port, e.g. port 80. In order to prevent leakage of potentially sensitive information Request-URI should be "*".

S-HTTP responses should use the protocol designator "Secure-HTTP/1.4".

The response message has the following format:

Status Line	General header	Response header	Entity header	Message Body

Note that the status in the Secure HTTP response line does not indicate anything about the success or failure of the unwrapped HTTP request. Servers should always use 200 OK provided that the Secure HTTP processing is successful. This prevents analysis of success or failure for any request, which the correct recipient can determine from the encapsulated data. All case variations should be accepted.

For details of the S-HTTP messages, please check the reference documents.

Related Protocols
WWW, FTP, SMTP, NNTP, Gopher, WAIS, HTTP, DNS, HTTPS

Sponsor Source
S-HTTP is defined by IETF (http://www.ietf.org) in RFC 2660.

Reference
http://www.javvin.com/protocol/rfc2660.pdf
The Secure HyperText Transfer Protocol
http://www.javvin.com/protocol/rfc2818.pdf
HTTP Over TLS

IMAP & IMAP4: Internet Message Access Protocol (version 4)

Protocol Description

Internet Message Access Protocol (IMAP) is a method of accessing electronic mail or bulletin board messages that are kept on a mail server. IMAP permits a "client" email program to access remote message stores as if they were local. Email stored on an IMAP server can be manipulated from a desktop computer remotely, without the need to transfer messages or files back and forth between these computers.

There are several different technologies and approaches to building a distributed electronic mail infrastructure: POP (Post Office Protocol), DMSP (Distributed Mail System Protocol) and IMAP (Internet Message Access Protocol) among them. Of the three, POP is the oldest and consequently the best known. DMSP is largely limited to a single application, PCMAIL, and is known primarily for its excellent support of "disconnected" operation. IMAP offers a superset of POP and DMSP capabilities, and provides good support for all three modes of remote mailbox access: offline, online, and disconnected.

In the online mode, the IMAP mail client does not copy mails in a shared server all at once and then delete them. It is an interactive client-server model, where the client can ask the server for headers or the bodies of specified messages, or to search for messages meeting certain criteria. Messages in the mail repository can be marked with various status flags (e.g. "deleted" or "answered") and they stay in the repository until explicitly removed by the user. IMAP is designed to permit manipulation of remote mailboxes as if they were local. Depending on the IMAP client implementation and the mail architecture desired by the system manager, the user may save messages directly on the client machine or save them on the server, or be given the choice of doing either.

IMAP includes operations for creating, deleting and renaming mailboxes; checking for new messages; permanently removing messages; setting and clearing flags; server-based and MIME parsing, and searching; and selective fetching of message attributes, texts, and portions thereof for efficiency. IMAP allows clients to access messages (both new and saved) from more than one computer. This feature has become extremely important as reliance on electronic messaging and use of multiple computers has increased.

The current version of IMAP is version 4 revision 1(IMAP4 rev1). Key features for IMAP4 include:

• Fully compatible with Internet messaging standards, e.g. MIME.
• Allows message access and management from more than one computer.
• Allows access without reliance on less efficient file access protocols.
• Provides support for "online", "offline", and "disconnected" access modes.

• Supports concurrent access to shared mailboxes.
• Client software needs no knowledge about the server's file store format.

Protocol Structure

IMAP key commands:

APPEND
AUTHENTICATE
CAPABILITY
CHECK
CLOSE
COPY
CREATE
DELETE
DELETEACL
EXAMINE
EXPUNGE
FETCH
GETACL
GETQUOTA
GETQUOTAROOT
LIST
LISTRIGHTS
LOGIN
LOGOUT
LSUB
MYRIGHTS
NOOP
RENAME
SEARCH
SELECT
SETACL
SETQUOTA
STARTTLS
STATUS
STORE
SUBSCRIBE
UID
UNSELECT
UNSUBSCRIBE
X<atom>

Related Protocols

SMTP, TCP, POP, POP3, MIME, DMSP

Sponsor Source

IMAP is defined by IETF (http://www.ietf.org)

Reference

http://www.javvin.com/protocol/rfc3501.pdf
INTERNET MESSAGE ACCESS PROTOCOL - VERSION 4rev1

IRCP: Internet Relay Chat Protocol

Protocol Description

Internet Relay Chat Protocol (IRCP), which is well-suited to running on many machines in a distributed fashion, enables teleconferencing on the Internet. The IRC protocol has been developed on systems using the TCP/IP network protocol, although there is no requirement that this remain the only environment in which it operates. The IRC protocol is a text-based protocol, with the simplest client being any socket program capable of connecting to the server.

A typical setup in IRCP involves a single process (the server) forming a central point for clients (or other servers) to connect to, performing the required message delivery/multiplexing and other functions. The server forms the backbone of IRC, providing a point to which clients may connect to talk to each other, and a point for other servers to connect to, forming an IRC network. The only network configuration allowed for IRC servers is that of a spanning tree where each server acts as a central node for the rest of the net it sees.

To allow a reasonable amount of order to be kept within the IRC network, a special class of clients (operators) is allowed to perform general maintenance functions on the network. Another concept in the IRCP is a channel, which is a named group of one or more clients which will all receive messages addressed to that channel.

IRCP allows communications between two clients, one to many(all) clients, client to server, and server to server. This protocol provides the technical foundation for most of the Internet instant message and chat systems.

Protocol Structure

IRCP is a text-based protocol with many commands. The key commands are:

USER <username> <hostname> <servername> <realname>: is used at the beginning of connection to specify the username, hostname, servername and realname of a new user.
PASS <password>: is used to set a 'connection password'.
NICK <nickname> <hopcount>: is used to give user a nickname or change the previous one.
SERVER <servername> <hopcount> <info>: is used to tell a server that the other end of a new connection is a server.
OPER <user> <password>: request to get operator privileges.
QUIT <quit message>: a client session is ended with a quit message.
SQUIT <server> <comment>: is needed to tell about quitting or dead servers.
JOIN <channel>: is used by client to start listening to a specific channel.
PART <channel>: causes the client sending the message to be removed from the list of active users for the channels in the parameter.
MODE <channel> or <nickname>: allows both usernames and channels to have their mode changed.
TOPIC <channel>: is used to change or view the topic of a channel.
NAMES <channel>: is used to list all nicknames that are visible to a user on any channel.
LIST <channel>: is used to list channels and their topics.
INVITE <nickname> <channel>: is used to invite users to a channel.
KICK <channel> <user> <comment>: can be used to forcibly remove a user from a channel.

Related Protocols
IP, IPv6, TCP

Sponsor Source
IRCP is defined by IETF (http://www.ietf.org) in RFC 1459 and updated by RFC 2810, 2811, 2812, 2813.

Reference
http://www.javvin.com/protocol/rfc1459.pdf
Internet Relay Chat Protocol.

LDAP: Lightweight Directory Access Protocol (version 3)

Protocol Description

Lightweight Directory Access Protocol (LDAP)is designed to provide access to the X.500 Directory while not incurring the resource requirements of the Directory Access Protocol (DAP). LDAP is specifically targeted at simple management applications and browser applications that provide simple read/write interactive access to the X.500 Directory, and is intended to be a complement to the DAP itself.

Key aspects of LDAP version 3 are:

• All protocol elements of LDAPv2 are supported.
• The protocol is carried directly over TCP or other transport, bypassing much of the session/presentation overhead of X.500 DAP.
• Most protocol data elements can be encoded as ordinary strings.
• Referrals to other servers may be returned.
• SASL mechanisms may be used with LDAP to provide association security services.
• Attribute values and Distinguished Names have been internationalized through the use of the ISO 10646 character set.
• The protocol can be extended to support new operations, and controls may be used to extend existing operations.
• The schema is published in the directory for use by clients.

The general model adopted by LDAP is one of clients performing protocol operations against servers. In this model, a client transmits a protocol request to a server, describing the operation to be performed. The server is then responsible for performing the necessary operation(s) in the directory. Upon completion of the operation(s), the server returns a response, containing any results or errors to the requesting client.

In LDAP versions 1 and 2, no provision was made for protocol servers returning referrals to clients. However, for improved performance and distribution LDAP v3 permits servers to return to clients referrals to other servers. This allows servers to offload the work of contacting other servers to progress operations.

Protocol Structure

LDAP messages are PDUs mapped directly onto the TCP byte stream and use port 389. The LDAP messages do not have their own header and are text messages based on ANS.1. For the purposes of protocol exchanges, all protocol operations are encapsulated in a common envelope, the LDAP Message.

The function of the LDAPMessage is to provide an envelope containing common fields required in all protocol exchanges. At this time, the only common fields are the message ID and the controls.

Related Protocols
TCP, DAP

Sponsor Source

LDAP is defined by IETF (http://www.ietf.org) in RFC 2251, 2252, 2253, 2254, 2255, 2256, 2829, 2830 and 3377.

Reference
http://www.javvin.com/protocol/rfc2251.pdf
Lightweight Directory Access Protocol (v3) The specification of the LDAP on-the-wire protocol
http://www.javvin.com/protocol/rfc2252.pdf
Lightweight Directory Access Protocol (v3): Attribute Syntax Definitions
http://www.javvin.com/protocol/rfc2253.pdf
Lightweight Directory Access Protocol (v3): UTF-8 String Representation of Distinguished Names
http://www.javvin.com/protocol/rfc2254.pdf
The String Representation of LDAP Search Filters
http://www.javvin.com/protocol/rfc2255.pdf
The LDAP URL Format
http://www.javvin.com/protocol/rfc2256.pdf
A Summary of the X.500(96) User Schema for use with LDAPv3
http://www.javvin.com/protocol/rfc2829.pdf
Authentication Methods for LDAP
http://www.javvin.com/protocol/rfc2830.pdf
Lightweight Directory Access Protocol (v3): Extension for Transport Layer Security
http://www.javvin.com/protocol/rfc3377.pdf
Lightweight Directory Access Protocol (v3): Technical Specification

MIME (S-MIME): Multipurpose Internet Mail Extensions and Secure MIME

Protocol Description

MIME, an acronym for Multipurpose Internet Mail Extensions, specifies how messages must be formatted so that they can be exchanged between different email systems. MIME is a very flexible format, permitting one to include virtually any type of file or document in an email message. MIME messages can contain text, images, audio, video, or other application-specific data. Specifically, MIME allows mail messages to contain:

- Multiple objects in a single message.
- Text having unlimited line length or overall length.
- Character sets other than ASCII, allowing non-English language messages.
- Multi-font messages.
- Binary or application-specific files.
- Images, Audio, Video and multi-media messages.

A MIME multipart message contains a boundary in the Content-type: header; this boundary, which must not occur in any of the parts, is placed between the parts, and at the beginning and end of the body of the message.

A secure version of MIME, S/MIME (Secure/Multipurpose Internet Mail Extensions), is defined to support encryption of email messages. Based on the MIME standard, S/MIME provides the following cryptographic security services for electronic messaging applications: authentication, message integrity and non-repudiation of origin and privacy and data security.

S/MIME can be used by traditional mail user agents (MUAs) to add cryptographic security services to mail that is sent, and to interpret cryptographic security services in mail that is received. However, S/MIME is not restricted to mail; it can be used with any transport mechanism that transports MIME data, such as HTTP. As such, S/MIME takes advantage of the object-based features of MIME and allows secure messages to be exchanged in mixed-transport systems.

Further, S/MIME can be used in automated message transfer agents that use cryptographic security services that do not require any human intervention, such as the signing of software-generated documents and the encryption of FAX messages sent over the Internet.

Protocol Structure

Definition of MIME header fields is as follows:

```
entity-headers := [ content CRLF ]
             [ encoding CRLF ]
             [ id CRLF ]
             [ description CRLF ]
             *( MIME-extension-field CRLF )

MIME-message-headers := entity-headers
             fields
```

```
          version CRLF
          ; The ordering of the header
          ; fields implied by this BNF
          ; definition should be ignored.

MIME-part-headers := entity-headers
             [ fields ]
             ; Any field not beginning with
             ; "content-" can have no defined
             ; meaning and may be ignored.
             ; The ordering of the header
             ; fields implied by this BNF
             ; definition should be ignored.
```

The message format and procedure of S/MIME can be found in the reference documents.

Related Protocols

POP3, SMTP

Sponsor Source

MIME is defined by IETF (http://www.ietf.org) in RFC 2045, 2046, 2047, 2048, 2049. S/MIME version 3 is defined in RFC 2632, 2633 etc.

Reference

http://www.javvin.com/protocol/rfc2045.pdf
Multipurpose Internet Mail Extensions (MIME) Part One: Format of Internet Message Bodies
http://www.javvin.com/protocol/rfc2046.pdf
Multipurpose Internet Mail Extensions (MIME) Part Two: Media Types
http://www.javvin.com/protocol/rfc2047.pdf
MIME (Multipurpose Internet Mail Extensions) Part Three: Message Header Extensions for Non-ASCII Text
http://www.javvin.com/protocol/rfc2048.pdf
Multipurpose Internet Mail Extensions (MIME) Part Four: Registration Procedures.
http://www.javvin.com/protocol/rfc2049.pdf
Multipurpose Internet Mail Extensions
http://www.javvin.com/protocol/rfc2632.pdf
S/MIME Version 3 Certificate Handling
http://www.javvin.com/protocol/rfc2633.pdf
S/MIME Version 3 Message Specification

NAT: Network Address Translation

Protocol Description

Basic Network Address Translation (Basic NAT) is a method by which IP addresses are mapped from one group to another, transparent to end users. Network Address Port Translation, or NAPT, is a method by which many network addresses and their TCP/UDP ports are translated into a single network address and its TCP/UDP ports. Together, these two operations, referred to as traditional NAT, provide a mechanism to connect a realm with private addresses to an external realm with globally unique registered addresses.

The need for IP Address translation arises when a network's internal IP addresses cannot be used outside the network either for privacy reasons or because they are invalid for use outside the network. Network topology outside a local domain can change in many ways. Customers may change providers, company backbones may be reorganized, or providers may merge or split. Whenever external topology changes with time, address assignment for nodes within the local domain must also change to reflect the external changes. Changes of this type can be hidden from users within the domain by centralizing changes to a single address translation router. Basic Address Translation allows hosts in a private network to transparently access the external network and enable access to selected local hosts from the outside. Organizations with a network setup predominantly for internal use and with a need for occasional external access are good candidates for this scheme.

There are limitations to using the translation method. It is mandatory that all requests and responses pertaining to a session be routed via the same NAT router. One way to ascertain this would be to have NAT based on a border router that is unique to a stub domain, where all IP packets either originated from the domain or are destined for the domain. There are other ways to ensure this with multiple NAT devices.

The NAT solution has the disadvantage of taking away the end-to-end significance of an IP address, and making up for this with an increased state in the network. As a result, with a NAT device enroute, end-to-end IP network level security assured by IPsec cannot be assumed to apply to end hosts. The advantage of this approach, however, is that it can be installed without changes to hosts or routers.

Protocol Structure

NAT is a procedure, not a structured protocol.

Related Protocols

IP, IPv6, TCP, UDP, NATP

Sponsor Source

NAT is defined by IETF (http://www.ietf.org) in RFC 3022.

Reference

http://www.javvin.com/protocol/rfc3022.pdf
Traditional IP Network Address Translator (Traditional NAT).

NNTP: Network News Transfer Protocol

Protocol Description

Network News Transfer Protocol (NNTP) specifies a protocol for the distribution, inquiry, retrieval, and posting of news articles using a reliable stream (such as TCP port 119) server-client model. NNTP is designed so that news articles need only be stored on one (presumably central) server host, and subscribers on other hosts attached to the network may read news articles using stream connections to the news host. The Network News Transfer Protocol (NNTP) established the technical foundation for the widely used Newsgroups.

NNTP is modeled after the USENET news system. However, NNTP makes few demands upon the structure, content or storage of news articles and thus it can easily be adapted to other non-USENET news systems. Using NNTP, hosts exchanging news articles have an interactive mechanism for deciding which articles are to be transmitted.

A host desiring new news or has new news to send, will typically contact one or more of its neighbors using NNTP. The client host will then inquire as to which new articles have arrived in all or some of the newsgroups that it desires to receive, using the NEWNEWS command. It will receive a list of new articles from the server, and can request transmission of those articles that it desires and does not already have. Finally, the client can advise the server of those new articles which the client has recently received. The server will indicate those articles that it has already obtained copies of and which articles should be sent to add to its collection. In this manner, only those articles which are not duplicates and which are desired are transferred.

Protocol Structure

NNTP uses commands and responses for communications. Commands consist of a command word, which, in some cases, may be followed by a parameter. NNTP has many commands.

The following are the key commands:

• ARTICLE <message ID> -- Displays the header, a blank line, then the body (text) of the specified article by the message ID.
• HEAD -- Identical to the ARTICLE command except that it returns only the header lines.
• STAT -- Similar to the ARTICLE command except that no text is returned.
• GROUP <ggg> -- Returns the article numbers of the first and last articles in the group<ggg>, and an estimate of the number of articles on file in the group.The required parameter <ggg> is the name of the newsgroup to be selected.
• BODY -- Identical to the ARTICLE command except that it returns only the text body of the article.
• LIST- Returns a list of valid newsgroups and associated information.
• NEWSGROUPS data time -- A list of newsgroups created since <date and time> will be listed in the same format as the

LIST command.
• NEWNEWS newsgroups date time -- A list of message-ids of articles posted to or received by the specified newsgroup since "date and time" will be listed.
• NEXT -- The internally maintained "current article pointer" is advanced to the next article in the current newsgroup.
• POST -- Posting articles to the server. The article should be presented in the format specified by RFC850. A response code will be returned to indicate success or failure of the posting attempt.
• QUIT -- The server process acknowledges the QUIT command and then closes the connection to the client.
• HELP -- Provides a short summary of commands that are understood by this implementation of the server.
• IHAVE <messageid> -- Informs the server that the client has an article whose id is <messageid>.
• LAST -- Sets the "current article pointer" to the previous article in the current newsgroup.
• SLAVE -- Indicates to the server that this client connection is to a slave server, rather than a user.

Related Protocols
TCP

Sponsor Source
NNTP is defined by IETF (http://www.ietf.org) in RFC 977.

Reference
http://www.javvin.com/protocol/rfc977.pdf
Network News Transfer Protocol
http://www.javvin.com/protocol/rfc850.pdf
Standard for interchange of USENET messages

NTP: Network Time Protocol

Protocol Description
Network Time Protocol (NTP) is a time synchronization system for computer clocks through the Internet network. It provides the mechanisms to synchronize time and coordinate time distribution in a large, diverse internet operating at rates from mundane to light wave. It uses a returnable time design in which a distributed sub network of time servers, operating in a self-organizing, hierarchical master-slave configuration, synchronizes logical clocks within the sub network and to national time standards via wire or radio. The servers can also redistribute reference time via local routing algorithms and time daemons.

NTP is designed to produce three products: clock offset, roundtrip delay and dispersion, all of which are relative to a selected reference clock. Clock offset represents the amount to adjust the local clock to bring it into correspondence with the reference clock. Roundtrip delay provides the capability to launch a message to arrive at the reference clock at a specified time. Dispersion represents the maximum error of the local clock relative to the reference clock. Since most host time servers will synchronize via another peer time server, there are two components in each of these three products, those determined by the peer relative to the primary reference source of standard time and those measured by the host relative to the peer. Each of these components is maintained separately in the protocol in order to facilitate error control and management of the subnet itself. They provide not only precision measurements of offset and delay, but also definitive maximum error bounds, so that the user interface can determine not only the time, but the quality of the time as well.

NTP evolved from the Time Protocol and the ICMP Timestamp message but is specifically designed to maintain accuracy and robustness, even when used over typical Internet paths involving multiple gateways, highly dispersive delays and unreliable nets. NTP version 3 is the current version but previous superseded versions are compatible.

Protocol Structure

2	5	8	16	24	32bit
LI	VN	Mode	Stratum	Poll	Precision
Root Delay					
Root Dispersion					
Reference Identifier					
Reference timestamp (64)					
Originate Timestamp (64)					
Receive Timestamp (64)					
Transmit Timestamp (64)					
Key Identifier (optional) (32)					
Message digest (optional) (128)					

LI -- Leap Indicator warning of impending leap-second to be inserted at the end of the last day of the current month.
VN -- Version number indicating the version number

Mode -- The mode: This field can contain the following values:

      0 -- Reserved.
      1 -- Symmetric active.
      3 -- Client.
      4 -- Server.
      5 -- Broadcast.
      6 -- NTP control message.

Stratum -- An integer identifying the stratum level of the local clock.

Poll -- Signed integer indicating the maximum interval between successive messages, in seconds to the nearest power of 2.

Precision -- Signed integer indicating the precision of the local clock, in seconds to the nearest power of 2.

Root Delay -- Signed fixed-point number indicating the total roundtrip delay to the primary reference source, in seconds with fraction point between bits 15 and 16.

Root Dispersion -- Unsigned fixed-point number indicating the nominal error relative to the primary reference source, in seconds with fraction point between bits 15 and 16.

Reference Identifier -- Identifying the particular reference source.

Originate Timestamp -- This is the time at which the request departed the client for the server, in 64-bit timestamp format.

Receive Timestamp -- This is the time at which the request arrived at the server, in 64-bit timestamp format.

Transmit Timestamp -- This is the time at which the reply departed the server for the client, in 64-bit timestamp format.

Authenticator (optional) -- When the NTP authentication scheme is implemented, the Key Identifier and Message Digest fields contain the message authentication code (MAC) information defined.

Related Protocols
ICMP, SNTP

Sponsor Source
NTP is defined by IETF (http://www.ietf.org) in RFC 1305.

Reference
http://www.javvin.com/protocol/rfc1305.pdf
Network Time Protocol (Version 3) Specification, Implementation.

POP and POP3: Post Office Protocol (version 3)

Protocol Description
The Post Office Protocol (POP) is designed to allow a workstation with an email client to dynamically access a mail drop on a server host over the TCP/IP network. POP3 is the version 3 (the latest version) of the Post Office Protocol, which has obsoleted the earlier versions of the POP protocol: POP1 and POP2. POP3 transmissions appear as data messages between stations. The messages are either command or reply messages.

There are several different technologies and approaches to building a distributed electronic mail infrastructure: POP (Post Office Protocol), DMSP (Distributed Mail System Protocol), and IMAP (Internet Message Access Protocol) among them. Of the three, POP is the oldest and consequently the best known. DMSP is largely limited to a single application, PCMAIL, and is known primarily for its excellent support of "disconnected" operation. IMAP offers a superset of POP and DMSP capabilities, and provides good support for all three modes of remote mailbox access: offline, online, and disconnected.

POP was designed to support "offline" mail processing, in which mail is delivered to a server, and a personal computer user periodically invokes a mail "client" program that connects to the server and downloads all of the pending mails the user's own machine. The offline access mode is a kind of store-and-forward service, intended to move mail (on demand) from the mail server (drop point) to a single destination machine, usually a PC or Mac. Once delivered to the PC or Mac, the messages are then deleted from the mail server.

POP3 is not designed to provide extensive manipulation operations of mail on the server; which are done by a more advanced (and complex) protocol IMAP4. POP3 uses TCP as the transport protocol.

Protocol Structure
POP3 messages are ASCII messages sent between client and servers. POP3 Command Summary:

Commands	Description
USER	Name of user
PASS	User's password
STAT	Information on messages in the server
RETR	Number of message to get
DELE	Number of message to delete
LIST	Number of message to show
TOP <messageID> <nombredelignes>	Print X lines of the message starting from the beginning (header included)
QUIT	Exit to POP3's server

Optional POP3 Commands:
APOP name digest -- valid in the AUTHORIZATION state

TOP msg n -- valid in the TRANSACTION state UIDL [msg]

POP3 Replies:
+OK
-ERR

Related Protocols
SMTP, IMAP4, TCP, POP

Sponsor Source
POP3 is defined by IETF (http://www.ietf.org) in RFC 1939.

Reference
http://www.javvin.com/protocol/rfc1939.pdf
Post Office Protocol - Version 3

rlogin: Remote Login to UNIX Systems

Protocol Description
rlogin (remote login) is a UNIX command that allows an authorized user to login to other UNIX machines (hosts) on a network and to interact as if the user were physically at the host computer. Once logged in to the host, the user can do anything that the host has given permission for, such as read, edit, or delete files.

Each remote machine may have a file named /etc/hosts.equiv containing a list of trusted hostnames with which it shares usernames. Users with the same username on both the local and remote machine may rlogin from the machines listed in the remote machine's /etc/hosts.equiv file without supplying a password. Individual users may set up a similar private equivalence list with the file .rhosts in their home directories. Each line in this file contains two names: a host name and a username separated by a space. An entry in a remote user's .rhosts file permits the user named username who is logged into hostname to log in to the remote machine as the remote user without supplying a password. If the name of the local host is not found in the /etc/hosts.equiv file on the remote machine and the local username and hostname are not found in the remote user's .rhosts file, then the remote machine will prompt for a password. Hostnames listed in /etc/hosts.equiv and .rhosts files must be the official hostnames listed in the host's database; nicknames may not be used in either of these files. For security reasons, the .rhosts file must be owned by either the remote user or by root.

The remote terminal type is the same as your local terminal type (as given in your environment TERM variable). The terminal or window size is also copied to the remote system if the server supports the option, and changes in size are reflected as well. All echoing takes place at the remote site, so that (except for delays) the remote login is transparent. Flow control using <CTRL-S> and <CTRL-Q> and flushing of input and output on interrupts are handled properly.

A secure version of rlogin (slogin) was combined with two other UNIX utilities, ssh and scp, in the Secure Shell suite, an interface and protocol created to replace the earlier utilities.

Protocol Structure
rlogin command is:

rlogin [-8EL] [-ec] [-l username] hostname

OPTION Flags

-8EL	Allows an 8-bit data path at all times. Otherwise, unless the start and stop characters on the remote host are not Ctrl-S and Ctrl-Q, the rlogin command uses a 7-bit data path and parity bits are stripped.
-e Character	Changes the escape character. Substitute the character you choose for Character.

-f	Causes the credentials to be forwarded. This flag will be ignored if Kerberos 5 is not the current authentication method. Authentication will fail if the current DCE credentials are not marked forwardable.
-F	Causes the credentials to be forwarded. In addition, the credentials on the remote system will be marked forwardable (allowing them to be passed to another remote system). This flag will be ignored if Kerberos 5 is not the current authentication method. Authentication will fail if the current DCE credentials are not marked forwardable.
-k realm	Allows the user to specify the realm of the remote station if it is different from the local systems realm. For these purposes, a realm is synonymous with a DCE cell. This flag will be ignored if Kerberos 5 is not the current authentication method.
-l User	Changes the remote user name to the one you specify. Otherwise, your local user name is used at the remote host.

Hostname - The remote machine on which rlogin establishes the remote login session.

Related Protocols
FTP, TELNET

Sponsor Source
rlogin is a UNIX command.

Reference
http://www.javvin.com/protocol/rfc1282.pdf
BSD Rlogin

RMON: Remote Monitoring MIBs (RMON1 and RMON2)

Protocol Description
Remote Monitoring (RMON) is a standard monitoring specification that enables various network monitors and console systems to exchange network-monitoring data. RMON provides network administrators with more freedom in selecting network-monitoring probes and consoles with features that meet their particular networking needs.

RMON was originally developed to address the problem of managing LAN segments and remote sites from a central location. The RMON is an extension of the SNMP MIB. Within an RMON network monitoring data is defined by a set of statistics and functions and exchanged between various different monitors and console systems. Resultant data is used to monitor network utilization for network planning and performance-tuning, as well as assisting in network fault diagnosis.

There are 2 versions of RMON: RMONv1 and RMONv2. RMONv1, which can now be found on most modern network hardware, defined 9 MIB groups for basic network monitoring. RMON2 is an extension of RMON that focuses on higher layers of traffic above the medium access-control(MAC) layer. RMON2 has an emphasis on IP traffic and application-level traffic. RMON2 allows network management applications to monitor packets on all network layers. This is different from RMONv1, which only allows network monitoring at MAC layer or below.

RMON solutions are comprised of two components: a probe (or an agent or a monitor), and a management station. Agents store network information within their RMON MIB and are normally found as embedded software on network hardware such as routers and switches although they can be a program running on a PC. Agents can only see the traffic that flows through them so they must be placed on each LAN segment or WAN link that is to be monitored. Clients, or management stations, communicate with the RMON agent or probe, using SNMP to obtain and correlate RMON data.

There are a number of variations to the RMON MIB. For example, the Token Ring RMON MIB provides objects specific to managing Token Ring networks. The SMON MIB extends RMON by providing RMON analysis for switched networks.

Protocol Structure
The monitoring focus of RMON1 and RMON 2 in the network layers:

OSI Model

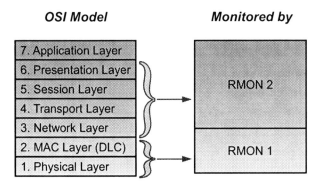

Figure 2-1: RMON Monitoring Layers

Token Ring	Support of Token Ring	(not used often)

RMON 1 MIB Group	Function	Elements
Statistics	Contains statistics measured by the probe for each monitored interface on this device.	Packets dropped, packets sent, bytes sent (octets), broadcast packets, multicast packets, CRC errors, runts, giants, fragments, jabbers, collisions, and counters for packets ranging from 64 to 128, 128 to 256, 256 to 512, 512 to 1024, and 1024 to 1518 bytes.
History	Records periodic statistical samples from a network and stores for retrieval.	Sample period, number of samples, items sampled.
Alarm	Periodically takes statistical samples and compares them with set thresholds for events generation.	Includes the alarm table and requires the implementation of the event group. Alarm type, interval, starting threshold, stop threshold.
Host	Contains statistics associated with each host discovered on the network.	Host address, packets, bytes received and transmitted, as well as broadcast, multicast, and error packets.
HostTopN	Prepares tables that describe the top hosts.	Statistics, host(s), sample start and stop periods, rate base, duration.
Matrix	Stores and retrieves statistics for conversations between sets of two addresses.	Source and destination address pairs and packets, bytes, and errors for each pair.
Filters	Enables packets to be matched by a filter equation for capturing or events.	Bit-filter type (mask or not mask), filter expression (bit level), conditional expression (and, or not) to other filters.
Packet Capture	Enables packets to be captured after they flow through a channel.	Size of buffer for captured packets, full status (alarm), number of captured packets.
Events	Controls the generation and notification of events from this device.	Event type, description, last time event sent

RMON 2 MIB Group	Functions
Protocol Directory	The Protocol Directory is a simple and interoperable way for an RMON2 application to establish which protocols a particular RMON2 agent implements. This is especially important when the application and the agent are from different vendors
Protocol Distribution	Mapping the data collected by a probe to the correct protocol name that can then be displayed to the network manager.
Address mapping	Address translation between MAC-layer addresses and network-layer addresses which are much easier to read and remember. Address translation not only helps the network manager, it supports the SNMP management platform and will lead to improved topology maps.
Network Layer host	Network host (IP layer) statistics
Network layer matrix	Stores and retrieves network layer (IP layer) statistics for conversations between sets of two addresses.
Application layer host	Application host statistic
Application layer matrix	Stores and retrieves application layer statistics for conversations between sets of two addresses.
User history	This feature enables the network manager to configure history studies of any counter in the system, such as a specific history on a particular file server or a router-to-router connection.
Probe configuration	This RMON2 feature enables one vendor's RMON application to remotely configure another vendor's RMON probe.

Related Protocols
SNMP, SMI

Sponsor Source
RMON is defined by IETF (http://www.ietf.org) with a group of RFCs shown in the reference links.

Reference
http://www.javvin.com/protocol/rfc2819.pdf
Remote Network Monitoring Management Information Base
http://www.javvin.com/protocol/rfc2021.pdf
Remote Network Monitoring Management Information Base Version 2 using SMIv2
http://www.javvin.com/protocol/rfc1157.pdf
A Simple Network Management Protocol

SLP: Service Location Protocol

Protocol Description

The Service Location Protocol (SLP) provides a scalable framework for the discovery and selection of network services. Using this protocol, computers using the Internet no longer need so much static configuration for network services for network-based applications. This is especially important as computers become more portable and users less tolerant or less able to fulfill the demands of network system administration.

Traditionally, users find services by using the name of a network host (a human readable text string), which is an alias for a network address. SLP (Service Location Protocol) eliminates the need for a user to know the name of a network host supporting a service. Rather, the user names the service and supplies a set of attributes, which describe the service. SLP (Service Location Protocol) allows the user to bind this description to the network address of the service.

SLP (Service Location Protocol) provides a dynamic configuration mechanism for applications in local area networks. It is not a global resolution system for the entire Internet; rather it is intended to serve enterprise networks with shared services. Applications are modeled as clients that need to find servers attached to the enterprise network at a possibly distant location. For cases where there are many different clients and/or services available, the protocol is adapted to make use of nearby Directory Agents that offer a centralized repository for advertised services.

The basic operation in SLP is that a client attempts to discover the location for a service. In small installations, each service is configured to respond individually to each client. In larger installations, each service will register its service with one or more directory agents and clients contact the directory agent to fulfill a request for service location information. This is intended to be similar to URL specifications and make use of URL technology.

Protocol Structure

Service Location Protocol Header

8	16	32bit
Version	Function	Length
O M U A F rsvd	Dialect	Language Code
Char encoding		XID

Version - The current version is version 1
Function - The function field describes the operation of the Service location datagram. The following message types exist:

Function Value	Message Type	Abbreviation
1	Service Request	SrvReq
2	Service Reply	SrvRply
3	Service Registration	SrvReg
4	Service Deregister	SrvDereg
5	Service Acknowledge	SrvAck
6	Attribute Request	AttrRgst
7	Attribute Reply	AttrRply
8	DA Advertisement	DAADvert
9	Service Type Request	SrvTypeRqst
10	Service Type Reply	SrvTypeRply

Length - Number of bytes in the message including the Service location header.
O - The overflow bit.
M - The monolingual bit.
U - RL Authentication bit present.
A - Attribute authentication bit present.
F - If the F bit is set in a Service Acknowledgement, the directory agent has registered the service as a new entry.
Rsvd - These bits are reserved and must have a value of 0.
Dialect - To be use by future versions of the SLP. Must be set to zero.
Language Code - The language encoded in this field indicates the language in which the remainder of the message should be interpreted.
Character Encoding - The characters making up strings within the remainder of this message may be encoded in any standardized encoding
XID - Transaction Identifier. Allows matching replies to individual requests.

Related Protocols
TCP, UDP, DHCP

Sponsor Source
SLP is defined by IETF (http://www.ietf.org) in RFC 2165.

Reference
http://www.javvin.com/protocol/rfc2165.pdf
Service Location Protocol

SMTP: Simple Mail Transfer Protocol

Protocol Description

Simple Mail Transfer Protocol (SMTP) is a protocol designed to transfer electronic mail reliably and efficiently. SMTP is a mail service modeled on the FTP file transfer service. SMTP transfers mail messages between systems and provides notification regarding incoming mail.

SMTP is independent of the particular transmission subsystem and requires only a reliable ordered data stream channel. An important feature of SMTP is its capability to transport mail across networks, usually referred to as "SMTP mail relaying". A network consists of the mutually-TCP-accessible hosts on the public Internet, the mutually-TCP-accessible hosts on a firewall-isolated TCP/IP Intranet, or hosts in some other LAN or WAN environment utilizing a non-TCP transport-level protocol. Using SMTP, a process can transfer mail to another process on the same network or to some other network via a relay or gateway process accessible to both networks.

In this way, a mail message may pass through a number of intermediate relay or gateway hosts on its path from sender to ultimate recipient. The Mail eXchanger mechanisms of the domain name system are used to identify the appropriate next-hop destination for a message being transported.

Protocol Structure

SMTP commands are ASCII messages sent between SMTP hosts. Possible commands are as follows:

Command	Description
DATA	Begins message composition.
EXPN <string>	Returns names on the specified mail list.
HELO <domain>	Returns identity of mail server.
HELP <command>	Returns information on the specified command.
MAIL FROM <host>	Initiates a mail session from host.
NOOP	Causes no action, except acknowledgement from server.
QUIT	Terminates the mail session.
RCPT TO <user>	Designates who receives mail.
RSET	Resets mail connection.
SAML FROM <host>	Sends mail to user terminal and mailbox.
SEND FROM <host>	Sends mail to user terminal.
SOML FROM <host>	Sends mail to user terminal or mailbox.
TURN	Switches role of receiver and sender.
VRFY <user>	Verifies the identity of a user.

Related Protocols
POP3, IMAP4, TCP, POP, FTP

Sponsor Source
SMTP is defined by IETF (http://www.ietf.org) in RFC 2821.

Reference
http://www.javvin.com/protocol/rfc2821.pdf
Simple Mail Transfer Protocol

SNMP: Simple Network Management Protocol

Protocol Description

Simple Network Management Protocol (SNMP) is the standard protocol developed to manage nodes (servers, workstations, routers, switches and hubs, etc.) on an IP network. SNMP enables network administrators to manage network performance, find and solve network problems, and plan for network growth. Network management systems learn of problems by receiving traps or change notices from network devices implementing SNMP.

An SNMP managed network consists of three key components:

managed devices, agents, and network-management systems (NMSs). A managed device is a network node that contains an SNMP agent and that resides on a managed network. Managed devices collect and store management information and make this information available to NMSs using SNMP. Managed devices, sometimes called network elements, can be routers and access servers, switches and bridges, hubs, computer hosts, or printers. An agent is a network management software module that resides in a managed device. An agent has local knowledge of management information and translates that information into a form compatible with SNMP. An NMS executes applications that monitor and control managed devices. NMSs provide the bulk of the processing and memory resources required for network management. One or more NMSs must exist on any managed network. The following picture illustrates the SNMP architecture:

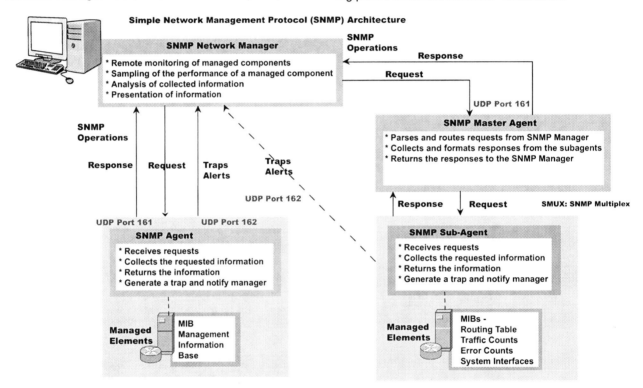

Figure 2-2: Simple Network Management Protocol (SNMP) Architecture

Currently, there are three versions of Simple Network Management Protocols defined: SNMP v1, SNMP v2 and SNMP v3. The following table provides the summary of the operations and features of the different versions of SNMP:

SNMP v1	Basic Operations and Features
Get	Used by the NMS to retrieve the value of one or more object instances from an agent
GetNext	Used by the NMS to retrieve the value of the next object instance in a table or a list within an agent
Set	Used by the NMS to set the values of object instances within an agent.
Trap	Used by agents to asynchronously inform the NMS of a significant event.
SNMP v2	Additional Operations and Features

GetBulk	Used by the NMS to efficiently retrieve large blocks of data.
Inform	Allows one NMS to send trap information to another NMS and to then receive a response.
SNMP v3	Security Enhancement
	User-based Security Model (USM) for SNMP message security.
	View-based Access Control Model (VACM) for access control.
	Dynamically configure the SNMP agents using SNMP SET commands.

To solve the incompatible issues among different versions of SNMP, RFC 3584 defines the coexistence strategies.

SNMP also includes a group of extensions as defined by RMON, RMON 2, MIB, MIB2, SMI, OIDs, and Enterprise

OIDs.

Protocol Structure

SNMP is an application protocol, which is encapsulated in UDP. The general SNMP message format for all versions is shown below:

Version	Community	PDU

• Version -- SNMP version number. Both the manager and agent must use the same version of SNMP. Messages containing different version numbers are discarded without further processing.
• Community -- Community name used for authenticating the manager before allowing access to the agent.
• PDU (Protocol Data Unit) -- The PDU types and formats for SNMPv1, v2 and v3 will be explained in the corresponding sections.

Related Protocols

SNMPv1, SNMPv2, SNMPv3, UDP, RMON, SMI, OIDs

Sponsor Source

SNMP is defined by IETF (http://www.ietf.org) with a group of RFCs shown in the reference links.

Reference

http://www.javvin.com/protocol/rfc1155.pdf
Structure and Identification of Management Information for TCP/IP based internets
http://www.javvin.com/protocol/rfc1156.pdf
Management Information Base Network
http://www.javvin.com/protocol/rfc1157.pdf
A Simple Network Management Protocol
http://www.javvin.com/protocol/rfc1441.pdf
Introduction to SNMPv2
http://www.javvin.com/protocol/rfc2579.pdf
Textual Conventions for SNMPv2
http://www.javvin.com/protocol/rfc2580.pdf
Conformance Statements for SNMPv2
http://www.javvin.com/protocol/rfc2578.pdf
Structure of Management Information for SNMPv2
http://www.javvin.com/protocol/rfc3416.pdf
Protocol Operations for SNMPv2
http://www.javvin.com/protocol/rfc3417.pdf
Transport Mappings for SNMPv2
http://www.javvin.com/protocol/rfc3418.pdf
Management Information Base for SNMPv2
http://www.javvin.com/protocol/rfc3410.pdf
Introduction and Applicability Statements for Internet Standard Management Framework
http://www.javvin.com/protocol/rfc3411.pdf
Architecture for Describing SNMP Frameworks
http://www.javvin.com/protocol/rfc3412.pdf
Message Processing and Dispatching for the SNMP
http://www.javvin.com/protocol/rfc3413.pdf
SNMP Applications
http://www.javvin.com/protocol/rfc3414.pdf
User-based Security Model (USM) for SNMPv3
http://www.javvin.com/protocol/rfc3415.pdf
View-based Access Control Model for the SNMP
http://www.javvin.com/protocol/rfc3584.pdf
Coexistence between SNMP v1, v2 and v3

SNMPv1: Simple Network Management Protocol version one

Protocol Description

Simple Network Management Protocol (SNMP) is the protocol developed to manage nodes (servers, workstations, routers, switches and hubs etc.) on an IP network. SNMP enables network administrators to manage network performance, find and solve network problems and plan for network growth. Network management systems learn of problems by receiving traps or change notices from network devices implementing SNMP.

Currently, there are three versions of SNMP defined: SNMP v1, SNMP v2 and SNMP v3. In this document, we provide information primarily on the SNMPv1. SNMPv1 is a simple request/response protocol. The network-management system issues a request, and managed devices return responses. This behavior is implemented by using one of four protocol operations: Get, GetNext, Set, and Trap. The Get operation is used by the NMS to retrieve the value of one or more object instances from an agent. If the agent responding to the Get operation cannot provide values for all the object instances in a list, it does not provide any values. The GetNext operation is used by the NMS to retrieve the value of the next object instance in a table or a list within an agent. The Set operation is used by the NMS to set the values of object instances within an agent. The trap operation is used by agents to asynchronously inform the NMS of a significant event.

For information on the SNMP overview, SNMPv2 and SNMPv3, please check the corresponding pages.

Protocol Structure

SNMP is an application protocol, which is encapsulated in UDP. The general SNMP message format for all versions is shown below:

Version	Community	PDU

• Version -- SNMP version number. Both the manager and agent must use the same version of SNMP. Messages containing different version numbers are discarded without further processing.
• Community -- Community name used for authenticating the manager before allowing access to the agent.
• PDU for SNMPv1 -- There are five different PDU types: GetRequest, GetNextRequest, GetResponse, SetRequest, and Trap. A general description of each of these is given in the next section.

The format for GetRequest, GetNext Request, GetResponse and SetRequest PDUs is shown here.

PDU type	Request ID	Error status	Error index	Object 1, value 1	Object 2, value 2	...

• PDU type -- Specifies the type of PDU transmitted: 0 GetRequest, 1 GetNextRequest, 2 GetResponse and 3 SetRequest.
• Request ID -- Associates SNMP requests with responses.
• Error status -- Indicates one of a number of errors and error types. Only the response operation sets this field. Other operations set this field to zero.
• Error index -- Associates an error with a particular object instance. Only the response operation sets this field. Other operations set this field to zero.
• Variable bindings -- Serves as the data field of the SNMPv1 PDU. Each variable binding associates a particular object instance with its current value (with the exception of Get and GetNext requests, for which the value is ignored).

The format of the Trap PDU is shown below:

PDU type	En-terp	Agent Addr	Gen Trap	Spec Trap	Time Stamp	Obj 1, Val 1	Obj 1, Val 1	...

• PDU type --Specifies the type of PDU (4=Trap).
• Enterprise -- Identifies the management enterprise under whose registration authority the trap was defined.
• Agent address- - IP address of the agent, used for further identification.
• Generic trap type -- Field describing the event being reported.
• Specific trap type -- Used to identify a non-generic trap when the Generic Trap Type is enterprise specific.
• Timestamp -- Value of the sysUpTime object, representing the amount of time elapsed between the last (re-)initialization and the generation of that Trap.

Related Protocols
SNMPv1, SNMPv2, SNMPv3, UDP, RMON, SMI, OIDs

Sponsor Source
SNMPv1 is defined by IETF (http://www.ietf.org) in RFC 1157 plus a few supporting RFCs shown in the reference links.

Reference
http://www.javvin.com/protocol/rfc1157.pdf
A Simple Network Management Protocol
http://www.javvin.com/protocol/rfc1155.pdf
Structure and Identification of Management Information for TCP/IP based internets
http://www.javvin.com/protocol/rfc1156.pdf
Management Information Base Network

SNMPv2: Simple Network Management Protocol version two

Protocol Description
Simple Network Management Protocol (SNMP) is the protocol developed to manage nodes (servers, workstations, routers, switches and hubs etc.) on an IP network. SNMP enables network administrators to manage network performance, find and solve network problems, and plan for network growth. Network management systems learn of problems by receiving traps or change notices from network devices implementing SNMP.

Currently, there are three versions of SNMP defined: SNMP v1, SNMP v2 and SNMP v3. In this document, we provide information primarily on the SNMPv2. SNMP version 2 (SNMPv2) is an evolution of SNMPv1. The Get, GetNext, and Set operations used in SNMPv1 are exactly the same as those used in SNMPv2. However, SNMPv2 adds and enhances some protocol operations. The SNMPv2 Trap operation, for example, serves the same function as that used in SNMPv1 but uses a different message format and is designed to replace the SNMPv1 Trap.

SNMPv2 also defines two new operations: GetBulk and Inform. The GetBulk operation is used by the NMS to efficiently retrieve large blocks of data, such as multiple rows in a table. GetBulk fills a response message with as much of the requested data as will fit. The Inform operation allows one NMS to send trap information to another NMS and to then receive a response. In SNMPv2, if the agent responding to GetBulk operations cannot provide values for all the variables in a list, it provides partial results.

For information on the SNMP overview, SNMPv1 and SNMPv3, please check the corresponding pages.

Protocol Structure
SNMP is an application protocol, which is encapsulated in UDP. The general SNMP message format for all versions is shown below:

Version	Community	PDU

• Version -- SNMP version number. Both the manager and agent must use the same version of SNMP. Messages containing different version numbers are discarded without further processing.
• Community -- Community name used for authenticating the manager before allowing access to the agent.
• PDU (Protocol Data Unit) - The PDU types and formats are different for SNMPv1, v2 and v3, which will be explained in the corresponding sections.

For SNMPv2, Get, GetNext, Inform, Response, Set, and Trap PDUs have the following format:

PDU type	Re-quest ID	Error status	Er-ror in-dex	Object 1, value 1	Object 2, value 2	...

• PDU type -- Identifies the type of PDU transmitted (Get, Get-Next, Inform, Response, Set, or Trap).
• Request ID -- Associates SNMP requests with responses.
• Error status -- Indicates one of a number of errors and error types. Only the response operation sets this field. Other operations set this field to zero.
• Error index -- Associates an error with a particular object instance. Only the response operation sets this field. Other operations set this field to zero.
• Variable bindings -- Serves as the data field (value 1, value 2...) of the SNMPv2 PDU. Each variable binding associates a particular object instance with its current value (with the exception of Get and GetNext requests, for which the value is ignored).

SNMPv2 GetBulk PDU Format

PDU type	Re-quest ID	Non repeat-ers	Max repeti-tions	Obj 1, Val 1	Obj 1, Val 1	...

• PDU type -- Identifies the PDU as a GetBulk operation.
• Request ID -- Associates SNMP requests with responses.
• Non repeaters -- Specifies the number of object instances in the variable bindings field that should be retrieved no more than once from the beginning of the request. This field is used when some of the instances are scalar objects with only one variable.
• Max repetitions -- Defines the maximum number of times that other variables beyond those specified by the Non repeaters field should be retrieved.
• Variable bindings -- Serves as the data field (Obj 1, Obj 2 ...) of the SNMPv2 PDU. Each variable binding associates a particular object instance with its current value (with the exception of Get and GetNext requests, for which the value is ignored).

Related Protocols
SNMPv1, SNMPv2, SNMPv3, UDP, RMON, SMI, OIDs

Sponsor Source
SNMPv2 is defined by IETF (http://www.ietf.org) in RFC 1441 originally plus by a group of supporting and updating RFCs shown in the list below.

Reference
http://www.javvin.com/protocol/rfc1441.pdf
Introduction to SNMPv2
http://www.javvin.com/protocol/rfc2579.pdf
Textual Conventions for SNMPv2
http://www.javvin.com/protocol/rfc2580.pdf
Conformance Statements for SNMPv2
http://www.javvin.com/protocol/rfc2578.pdf
Structure of Management Information for SNMPv2
http://www.javvin.com/protocol/rfc3416.pdf
Protocol Operations for SNMPv2
http://www.javvin.com/protocol/rfc3417.pdf

Transport Mappings for SNMPv2
http://www.javvin.com/protocol/rfc3418.pdf
Management Information Base for SNMPv2

SNMPv3: Simple Network Management Protocol version three

Protocol Description

Simple Network Management Protocol (SNMP) is the protocol developed to manage nodes (servers, workstations, routers, switches and hubs etc.) on an IP network. SNMP enables network administrators to manage network performance, find and solve network problems and plan for network growth. Network management systems learn of problems by receiving traps or change notices from network devices implementing SNMP. Currently, there are three versions of SNMP defined: SNMP v1, SNMP v2 and SNMP v3. In this document, we provide information primarily on the SNMPv3.

SNMP Version 3 (SNMPv3) adds security and remote configuration capabilities to the previous versions. The SNMPv3 architecture introduces the User-based Security Model (USM) for message security and the View-based Access Control Model (VACM) for access control. The architecture supports the concurrent use of different security, access control and message processing models. More specifically:

Security
• authentication and privacy
• authorization and access control

Administrative Framework
• naming of entities
• people and policies
• usernames and key management
• notification destinations
• proxy relationships
r• emotely configurable via SNMP operations

SNMPv3 also introduces the ability to dynamically configure the SNMP agent using SNMP SET commands against the MIB objects that represent the agent's configuration. This dynamic configuration function enables addition, deletion, and modification of configuration entries either locally or remotely.

For information on the SNMP overview, SNMPv1 and SNMPv2, please check the corresponding pages.

Protocol Structure

SNMPv3 message format:

Msg Processed by MPM (Msg Processing Model)				
Version	ID	Msg Size	Msg Flag	Security Model
Msg Processed by USM (User Security Module)				
Authoritative Engin ID	Authoritative Boots	Authoritative Engine Time	User name	Authentication parameters	Privacy Parameter
Scoped PDU				

Context engine ID	Context name	PDU

• Version -- snmv3(3).
• ID -- A unique identifier used between two SNMP entities to coordinate request and response messages
• Msg Size -- Maximum size of a message in octets supported by the sender of the message
• Msg Flags -- An octet string containing three flags in the least significant three bits: reportableFlag, privFlag, authFlag.
• Security Model -- An identifier to indicate which security model was used by the sender and therefore which security model must be used by the receiver to process this message.
• AuthoritativeEngineID -- The snmpEngineID of the authoritative SNMP engine involved in the exchange of this message. Thus, this value refers to the source for a Trap, Response, or Report, and to the destination for a Get, GetNext, GetBulk, Set, or Inform.
• AuthoritativeEngineBoots -- The snmpEngineBoots value of the authoritative SNMP engine involved in the exchange of this message.
• AuthoritativeEngineTime -- The snmpEngineTime value of the authoritative SNMP engine involved in the exchange of this message.
• User Name --The user (principal) on whose behalf the message is being exchanged.
• AuthenticationParameters -- Null if authentication is not being used for this exchange. Otherwise, this is an authentication parameter.
• PrivacyParameters -- Null if privacy is not being used for this exchange. Otherwise, this is a privacy parameter.
• PDU (Protocol Data Unit) -- The PDU types for SNMPv3 are the same as for SNMPv2.

Related Protocols
SNMPv1, SNMPv2, SNMPv3, UDP, RMON, SMI, OIDs

Sponsor Source
SNMPv3 is defined by IETF (http://www.ietf.org) in RFC 3411 plus a group of supporting RFCs shown in the reference links.

Reference
http://www.javvin.com/protocol/rfc3410.pdf
Introduction and Applicability Statements for Internet Standard Management Framework
http://www.javvin.com/protocol/rfc3411.pdf
Architecture for Describing SNMP Frameworks
http://www.javvin.com/protocol/rfc3412.pdf
Message Processing and Dispatching for the SNMP
http://www.javvin.com/protocol/rfc3413.pdf
SNMP Applications
http://www.javvin.com/protocol/rfc3414.pdf
User-based Security Model (USM) for SNMPv3
http://www.javvin.com/protocol/rfc3415.pdf
View-based Access Control Model for the SNMP
http://www.javvin.com/protocol/rfc3584.pdf
Coexistence between SNMP v1, v2 and v3

SNTP: Simple Network Time Protocol

Protocol Description

The Simple Network Time Protocol (SNTP) Version 4 is an adaptation of the Network Time Protocol (NTP) used to synchronize computer clocks in the Internet. SNTP can be used when the ultimate performance of the full NTP implementation is not needed or justified. When operating with current and previous NTP and SNTP versions, SNTP Version 4 involves no changes to the NTP specification or known implementations, but rather a clarification of certain design features of NTP which allow operation in a simple, stateless remote-procedure call (RPC) mode with accuracy and reliability expectations similar to the UDP/TIME protocol.

It is strongly recommended that SNTP be used only at the extremities of the synchronization subnet. SNTP clients should operate only at the leaves (highest stratum) of the subnet and in configurations where no NTP or SNTP client is dependent on another SNTP client for synchronization. SNTP servers should operate only at the root (stratum 1) of the subnet and then only in configurations where no other source of synchronization other than a reliable radio or modem time service is available. The full degree of reliability ordinarily expected of primary servers is possible only using the redundant sources, diverse subnet paths and crafted algorithms of a full NTP implementation. This extends to the primary source of synchronization itself in the form of multiple radio or modem sources and backup paths to other primary servers should all sources fail or the majority delivers incorrect time. Therefore, the use of SNTP rather than NTP in primary servers should be carefully considered.

The only significant protocol change in SNTP Version 4 over previous versions of NTP and SNTP is a modified header interpretation to accommodate Internet Protocol Version 6 (IPv6) and OSI addressing. However, SNTP Version 4 includes certain optional extensions to the basic Version 3 model, including an anycast mode and an authentication scheme designed specifically for multicast and anycast modes.

Protocol Structure

SNTP message has the same format as the NTP:

2	5	8	16	24	32bit
LI	VN	Mode	Stratum	Poll	Precision
Root Delay					
Root Dispersion					
Reference Identifier					
Reference timestamp (64)					
Originate Timestamp (64)					
Receive Timestamp (64)					
Transmit Timestamp (64)					
Key Identifier (optional) (32)					
Message digest (optional) (128)					

LI -- Leap Indicator warning of impending leap-second to be inserted at the end of the last day of the current month.
VN -- Version number indicating the version number.
Mode -- This field can contain the following values:
    0 -- Reserved.
    1 -- Symmetric active.
    3 -- Client.
    4 -- Server.
    5 -- Broadcast.
    6 -- NTP control message.
Stratum -- An integer identifying the stratum level of the local clock.
Poll -- Signed integer indicating the maximum interval between successive messages, in seconds to the nearest power of 2.
Precision -- Signed integer indicating the precision of the local clock, in seconds to the nearest power of 2.
Root Delay -- Signed fixed-point number indicating the total roundtrip delay to the primary reference source, in seconds with fraction point between bits 15 and 16.
Root Dispersion -- Unsigned fixed-point number indicating the nominal error relative to the primary reference source, in seconds with fraction point between bits 15 and 16.
Reference Identifier -- Identifying the particular reference source.
Originate Timestamp -- This is the time at which the request departed the client for the server, in 64-bit timestamp format.
Receive Timestamp -- This is the time at which the request arrived at the server, in 64-bit timestamp format.
Transmit Timestamp -- This is the time at which the reply departed the server for the client, in 64-bit timestamp format.
Authenticator (optional) -- When the NTP authentication scheme is implemented, the Key Identifier and Message Digest fields contain the message authentication code (MAC) information defined.

Related Protocols
NTP, UDP

Sponsor Source
SNTP is defined by IETF (http://www.ietf.org) in RFC 2030.

Reference
http://www.javvin.com/protocol/rfc2030.pdf
Simple Network Time Protocol (SNTP) Version 4 for IPv4, IPv6 and OSI.

Syslog Protocol

Protocol Description

Syslog protocol is a standard to send event notification messages across IP networks to event message collectors - also known as "syslogd", "syslog daemon" or "syslog servers". The term "syslog" is often used for both the actual syslog protocol, as well as the application or library sending syslog messages. Syslog is a simple protocol typically used for computer system management and security auditing. While it has a number of shortcomings, syslog is supported by a wide variety of devices and receivers across multiple platforms and operating systems. Because of this, syslog can be used to integrate log data from many different types of systems into a central repository.

Since each process, application and operating system was written somewhat independently, there is little uniformity to the content of syslog messages. For this reason, no assumption is made upon the formatting or contents of the messages. The protocol is simply designed to transport these event messages. In all cases, there is one device that originates the message. The syslog process on that machine may send the message to a collector. No acknowledgement of the receipt is made. Syslog uses the user datagram protocol (UDP) as its underlying transport layer mechanism. The UDP port that has been assigned to syslog is 514. Often the data is sent in cleartext, however, an SSL wrapper such as Stunnel, sslio or sslwrap can be used to provide for a layer of encryption through SSL/TLS.

One of the fundamental tenets of the syslog protocol and process is its simplicity. No stringent coordination is required between the transmitters and the receivers. Indeed, the transmission of syslog messages may be started on a device without a receiver being configured, or even actually physically present. Conversely, many devices will most likely be able to receive messages without explicit configuration or definitions. This simplicity has greatly aided the acceptance and deployment of syslog.

Protocol Structure

Sample syslog architecture:

No assumption is made upon the formatting or contents of the syslog messages. The syslog packet size is limited to 1024 bytes and carries the following information:

• Facility -- integers indicate the categories of sources that generate the syslog messages. These sources can be the operating system, the process, or an application.
• Severity -- single digit integers indicate the severity of the message,
• Hostname -- The hostname field consists of the host name (as configured on the host itself) or the IP address. In devices such as routers or firewalls, which use multiple interfaces, syslog uses the IP address of the interface from which the message is transmitted.
• Timestamp -- The timestamp is the local time, in MMM DD HH:MM:SS format, of the device when the message was generated.
• Message -- This is the text of the syslog message, along with

some additional information about the process that generated the message.

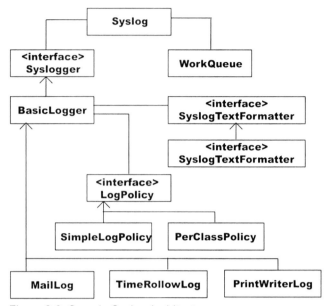

Figure 2-3: Sample Syslog Architecture

Related Protocols
IP, UDP

Sponsor Source
Syslog is defined by IETF (http://www.ietf.org) in RFC 3164.

Reference
http://www.javvin.com/protocol/rfc3164.pdf:
The BSD Syslog Protocol

TELNET: Terminal emulation protocol of TCP/IP

Protocol Description

TELNET is the terminal emulation protocol in a TCP/IP environment for the remote access of a terminal (client) to a server. TELNET uses the TCP as the transport protocol to establish connection between server and client. After connecting, TELNET server and client enter a phase of option negotiation that determines the options that each side can support for the connection. Each connected system can negotiate new options or renegotiate old options at any time. In general, each end of the TELNET connection attempts to implement all options that maximize performance for the systems involved.

When a TELNET connection is first established, each end is assumed to originate and terminate at a "Network Virtual Terminal", or NVT. An NVT is an imaginary device which provides a standard, network-wide, intermediate representation of a canonical terminal. This eliminates the need for "server" and "user" hosts to keep information about the characteristics of each other's terminals and terminal handling conventions.

The principle of negotiated options takes cognizance of the fact that many hosts will wish to provide additional services over and above those available within an NVT and many users will have sophisticated terminals and would like to have elegant, rather than minimal, services.

Option requests are likely to flurry back and forth when a TELNET connection is first established, as each party attempts to get the best possible service from the other party. Beyond that, however, options can be used to dynamically modify the characteristics of the connection to suit changing local conditions.

Modern TELNET application system provides versatile terminal emulation functions due to the many options that have evolved over the past twenty years. Options give TELNET the ability to transfer binary data, support byte macros, emulate graphics terminals and convey information to support centralized terminal management.

Protocol Structure

TELNET commands are ASCII text. The following are the TELNET commands:

Commands	Code No. Dec Hex		Description
data			All terminal input/output data.
End sub-Neg	240	FO	End of option subnegotiation command.
No Operation	241	F1	No operation command.
Data Mark	242	F2	End of urgent data stream.
Break	243	F3	Operator pressed the Break key or the Attention key.
Int process	244	F4	Interrupt current process.
Abort output	245	F5	Cancel output from current process.
You there?	246	F6	Request acknowledgment.
Erase char	247	F7	Request that operator erase the previous character.
Erase line	248	F8	Request that operator erase the previous line.
Go ahead!	249	F9	End of input for half-duplex connections.
SubNegotiate	230	FA	Begin option subnegotiation.
Will Use	231	FB	Agreement to use the specified option.
Won't Use	232	FC	Reject the proposed option.
Start use	233	FD	Request to start using specified option.
Stop Use	234	FE	Demand to stop using specified option.
LAC	235	FF	Interpret as command.

Related Protocols

TCP, IP, SMTP, FTP

Sponsor Source

TELNET is defined by IETF (http://www.ietf.org) in RFC 854.

Reference

http://www.javvin.com/protocol/rfc854.pdf
TELNET Protocol Specification

TFTP: Trivial File Transfer Protocol

Protocol Description
Trivial File Transfer Protocol (TFTP) is a simple protocol to transfer files. It has been implemented on top of the User Datagram Protocol (UDP) using port number 69. TFTP is designed to be small and easy to implement and, therefore, lacks most of the features of a regular FTP. TFTP only reads and writes files (or mail) from/to a remote server. It cannot list directories, and currently has no provisions for user authentication.

Three modes of transfer are currently supported by TFPT: netASCII, that is 8 bit ASCII; octet (this replaces the "binary" mode of previous versions of this document.) i.e. raw 8-bit bytes; mail, netASCII characters sent to a user rather than a file. Additional modes can be defined by pairs of cooperating hosts.

In TFTP, any transfer begins with a request to read or write a file, which also serves to request a connection. If the server grants the request, the connection is opened and the file is sent in fixed length blocks of 512 bytes. Each data packet contains one block of data and must be acknowledged by an acknowledgment packet before the next packet can be sent. A data packet of less than 512 bytes signals termination of a transfer. If a packet gets lost in the network, the intended recipient will timeout and may retransmit his last packet (which may be data or an acknowledgment), thus causing the sender of the lost packet to retransmit that lost packet. The sender has to keep just one packet on hand for retransmission, since the lock step acknowledgment guarantees that all older packets have been received. Notice that both machines involved in a transfer are considered senders and receivers. One sends data and receives acknowledgments, the other sends acknowledgments and receives data.

The current version of TFTP is version 2.

Protocol Structure
The header structures of the TFTP messages/packets:

RRQ/WRQ packet:

2 bytes	String	1 byte	String	1 byte
Opcode	Filename	0	Mode	0

Opcode -- Operation code or commands. The following are TFTP commands:

Opcode	Command	Description
1	Read Request	Request to read a file.
2	Write Request	Request to write to a file.
3	File Data	Transfer of file data.
4	Data Acknowledge	Acknowledgement of file data.
5	Error	Error indication.

Filename -- the name of file to be transferred.

Mode -- Datamode. The format of the file data that the protocol is to transfer. It could be NetASCII Standard ASCII, Octet Eight-bit binary data, or Mail Standard ASCII.

Data packet:

2 bytes	2 bytes	0 - 512 bytes
Opcode	Block #	Data

The opcode is 3.

Block # -- Block numbers on data packets begin with one and increase by one for each new block of data.
Data -- Data field range from 0 to 512 bytes.

ACK packet:

2 bytes	2 bytes
Opcode	Block #

The Opcode is 4.

Block# -- Block number echoes the block number of the DATA packet being acknowledged.

A WRQ is acknowledged with an ACK packet having a block number of zero.

Error Packet:

2 bytes	2 bytes	String	1 byte
Opcode	Error Code	ErrMsg	0

The Opcode is 5.

Error code -- an integer indicating the nature of the error.
  0 -- Not defined, see error message (if any).
  1 -- File not found.
  2 -- Access violation.
  3 -- Disk full or allocation exceeded.
  4 -- Illegal TFTP operation.
  5 -- Unknown transfer ID.
  6 -- File already exists.
  7 -- No such user.
ErrMSG -- Error message is intended for human consumption, and should be in netascii. It is terminated with a zero byte.

Related Protocols
UDP, FTP

Sponsor Source
TFTP is defined by IETF (http://www.ietf.org) in RFC 1350.

Reference
http://www.javvin.com/protocol/rfc1350.pdf
The TFTP Protocol (Revision 2).

URL: Uniform Resource Locator

Protocol Description
Uniform Resource Locator (URL) is the syntax and semantics for a compact string representation of a resource available via the Internet. For example, we use URL to locate web addresses and FTP site addresses. The generic syntax for URLs provides a framework for new schemes to be established using protocols other than those defined in this document.

URLs are used to `locate' resources, by providing an abstract identification of the resource location. Having located a resource, a system may perform a variety of operations on the resource, as might be characterized by such words as `access', `update', `replace', `find attributes'. In general, only the `access' method needs to be specified for any URL scheme.

Protocol Structure
URLs are sequences of characters, i.e., letters, digits, and special characters. URLs are written as follows:

  <scheme>:<scheme-specific-part>

A URL contains the name of the scheme being used (<scheme>) followed by a colon and then a string (the <scheme-specific-part>) whose interpretation depends on the scheme.

Scheme names consist of a sequence of characters. The lower case letters "a"--"z", digits, and the characters plus ("+"), period ("."), and hyphen ("-") are allowed. For resiliency, programs interpreting URLs should treat upper case letters as equivalent to lower case in scheme names (e.g., allow "HTTP" as well as "http").

Related Protocols
http, www, FTP

Sponsor Source
URL is defined by IETF (http://www.ietf.org) in RFC 1738.

Reference
http://www.javvin.com/protocol/rfc1738.pdf
Uniform Resource Locators (URL).

Whois (and RWhois): Remote Directory Access Protocol

Protocol Description
The whois protocol retrieves information about domain names from a central registry. The whois service is provided by the organizations that run the Internet. Whois is often used to retrieve registration information about an Internet domain or server. It can tell who owns the domain, how their technical contact can be reached, along with other information.

The original Whois function was to be a central directory of resources and people on ARPANET. However, it could not adequately meet the needs of the expanded Internet. RWhois extends and enhances the Whois concept in a hierarchical and scaleable fashion. In accordance with this, RWhois focuses primarily on the distribution of "network objects", or the data representing Internet resources or people, and uses the inherently hierarchical nature of these network objects (domain names, Internet Protocol (IP) networks, email addresses) to more accurately discover the requested information.

The RWhois defines both a directory access protocol and a directory architecture. As a directory service, RWhois is a distributed database, where data is split across multiple servers to keep database sizes manageable.

On the Internet, two such types of data are widely used: domain names and IP networks. Domain names are organized via a label-dot system, reading from a more specific label to a more general label left to right. IP networks are also lexically hierarchical labels using the Classless Inter-Domain Routing (CIDR) notation but their hierarchy is not easily determined with simple text manipulation. Instead, an IP network's hierarchy is determined by converting the network to binary notation and applying successively shorter bit masks.

RWhois directs clients toward the appropriate authority area by generating referrals. Referrals are pointers to other servers that are presumed to be closer to the desired data. The client uses this referral to contact the next server and ask the same question. The next server may respond with data, an error, or another referral (or referrals). By following this chain of referrals, the client will eventually reach the server with the appropriate authority area.

Protocol Structure
The entire RWhois protocol can be defined as a series of directives, responses, queries, and results.

```
rwhois-protocol = client-sends / server-returns
client-sends = *(directives / rwhois-query)
server-returns = *(responses / rwhois-query-result)
```

Related Protocols
TCP, SMTP, FTP, Finger, DNS

Sponsor Source
Whois and RWhois are defined by IETF (http://www.ietf.org) in RFC 954 and RFC 2167.

Reference

http://www.javvin.com/protocol/rfc954.pdf
Nickname/Whois
http://www.javvin.com/protocol/rfc2167.pdf
Referral Whois (RWhois) Protocol V1.5

XMPP: Extensible Messaging and Presence Protocol

Protocol Description

Extensible Messaging and Presence Protocol (XMPP) is designed to stream XML elements for near-real-time messaging, presence, and request-response services. XMPP is based on the Jabber protocol, an open and popular protocol for instant messaging.

Although XMPP is not wedded to any specific network architecture, it usually has been implemented via a client-server architecture wherein a client utilizing XMPP accesses a server over a TCP connection, and servers also communicate with each other over TCP connections. A server acts as an intelligent abstraction layer for XMPP communications. Most clients connect directly to a server over a TCP connection and use XMPP to take full advantage of the functionality provided by a server and any associated services. Multiple resources may connect simultaneously to a server on behalf of each authorized client. The recommended port for connections between a client and a server is 5222. A gateway is a special-purpose server-side service whose primary function is to translate XMPP into the protocol used by a foreign (non-XMPP) messaging system, as well as to translate the return data back into XMPP. Examples are gateways to email, Internet Relay Chat (IRC), SIMPLE, Short Message Service (SMS), and legacy instant messaging services such as AIM, ICQ, MSN Messenger, and Yahoo! Instant Messenger.

Two fundamental concepts make possible the rapid, asynchronous exchange of relatively small payloads of structured information between presence-aware entities: XML streams and XML stanzas. An XML stream is a container for the exchange of XML elements between any two entities over a network. An XML stanza is a discrete semantic unit of structured information that is sent from one entity to another over an XML stream.

XMPP includes a method for securing the stream from tampering and eavesdropping. This channel encryption method makes use of the Transport Layer Security (TLS) protocol [TLS], along with a "STARTTLS" extension that is modelled after similar extensions for the IMAP [IMAP], POP3 [POP3], and ACAP [ACAP] protocols. XMPP includes a method for authenticating a stream by means of an XMPP-specific profile of the Simple Authentication and Security Layer (SASL) protocol [SASL].

Protocol Structure

An XML stream acts as an envelope for all the XML stanzas sent during a session. We can represent this in a simplistic fashion as follows:

<stream>
<presence>   <show/> </presence>

```
<message to='foo'>
  <body/>
</message>
```

```
<iq to='bar'>
  <query/>
</iq>
```

```
...
```

```
</stream>
```

Stream attributes:

	initiating to receiving	receiving to initiating
to	hostname of receiver	silently ignored
from	silently ignored	hostname of receiver
id	silently ignored	session key
xml:lang	default language	default language
version	signals XMPP 1.0 support	signals XMPP 1.0 support

Related Protocols
SIMPLE, XML, SMS, IRCP

Sponsor Source
XMPP is defined by IETF (http://www.ietf.org) in RFC 3920, REC 3921, RFC 3922 and RFC 3923.

Reference
http://www.javvin.com/protocol/rfc3920.pdf
Extensible Messaging and Presence Protocol (XMPP): Core
http://www.javvin.com/protocol/rfc3921.pdf
Extensible Messaging and Presence Protocol (XMPP): Instant Messaging and Presence
http://www.javvin.com/protocol/rfc3922.pdf
Mapping the Extensible Messaging and Presence Protocol (XMPP) to Common Presence and Instant Messaging (CPIM)
http://www.javvin.com/protocol/rfc3923.pdf
End-to-End Signing and Object Encryption for the Extensible Messaging and Presence Protocol (XMPP)

X Window/X Protocol: X Window System Protocol

Protocol Description
The X Window System Protocol, also known as X Window or X Protocol, is a graphics architecture used as the graphical system on UNIX systems (primarily) and Linux systems. The X Window System is also used, less commonly, on VMS, MVS, and MS-Windows systems. X Window System (X Protocol) provides an inherently client/server oriented base for displaying windowed graphics. X Window provides a public protocol by which client programs can query and update information on X servers. X Window (X Protocol) allows processes on various computers on a network to display contents on display devices elsewhere on the network.

X Window System (X Protocol) defines the Client and Server roles as follows:

• An X server is a program that runs on a user's desktop to manage a video system including "interactive" I/O devices such as mice, keyboards, and some more unusual devices. The key functions are: 1) displays drawing requests on the screen. 2) replies to information requests. 3) reports an error in a request. 4) manages the keyboard, mouse and display device. 5) multiplexes keyboard and mouse input onto the network (or via local IPC) to the respective X clients. (X events) 6) creates, maps and destroys windows and 7) writes and draws in windows.
• X client is an application program that often runs on another host which connect to an X Server in order to display things. The client is often on a powerful Unix/Linux box that would commonly be known as a "server." The key functions are: 1) sends requests to the server. 2) receives events from server. 3) receives errors from the server.

X systems separate out the various components as separate subsystems. The key components in the X Window System (X Protocol) architecture are:

• Window manager -- controls what happens when the mouse pointer is pointing outside of screen areas controlled by specific applications.
• Program/File manager -- which is commonly a program that displays icons representing applications, and allows the user to run those applications.
• Inter-application interfaces -- The standard scheme for X Window clients to communicate is commonly termed ICCCM. CORBA is also used to provide more sophisticated ways for X Window clients to communicate. The communications are based on TCP/IP network.

X Window System (X Protocol) has two primary versions: X10 and X11.

Protocol Structure
The X Protocol has the following key communication messages between the Client and Server:

Requests
• X clients make requests to the X server for a certain action to

take place. i.e.: Create Window
• To enhance performance, the X client normally does not expect nor wait for a response. The request is typically left to the reliable network layer to deliver.
• X requests are any multiple of 4 bytes.

Replies
• The X server will respond to certain X client requests that require a reply. As noted, not all requests require a reply.
• X replies are any multiple of 4 bytes with a minimum of 32 bytes.

Events
• The X server will forward to the X client an event that the application is expecting. This could include keyboard or mouse input. To minimize network traffic, only expected events are sent to X clients.
• X events are 32 bytes

Errors
• The X server will report errors in requests to the X client. Errors are like an event but are handled differently.
• X errors are the same size as events to simplify their handling. They are sent to the error handling routine of the X client. (32 bytes)

Related Protocols
IP, TCP, CORBA

Sponsor Source
X Window/ X Protocol is currently developed by X.ORG. (http://www.ietf.org).

Reference
http://www.x.org/X11_protocol.html
The X Protocol

LPP: Lightweight Presentation Protocol

Protocol Description
Lightweight Presentation Protocol (LPP) describes an approach for providing "stream-lined" support of OSI application services on top of TCP/IP-based network for some constrained environments. LPP was initially derived from a requirement to run the ISO Common Management Information Protocol (CMIP) in TCP/IP-based networks.

LPP is designed for a particular class of OSI applications, namely those entities whose application context contains only an Association Control Service Element (ACSE) and a Remote Operations Service Element (ROSE). In addition, a Directory Services Element (DSE) is assumed for use by the application-entity, but only in a very limited sense. LPP is not applicable to entities whose application context is more extensive (e.g., contains a Reliable Transfer Service Element).

If one wants to implement ISO applications in a TCP/IP based network without constrains, the ITOT mechanisms (specified in RFC 2126) should be used.

Protocol Structure
The service provider is in one of the following states:IDLE, WAIT1, WAIT2, DATA, WAIT3 or WAIT4

The possible events are:

• PS-user
  • P-CONNECT.REQUEST
  • P-CONNECT.RESPONSE
  • P-RELEASE.REQUEST
  • P-RELEASE.RESPONSE
  • P-DATA.REQUEST
  • P-U-ABORT.REQUEST
• network
  • TCP closed or errored(*)
  • receive ConnectRequest PDU
  • receive ConnectResponse PDU
  • receive ReleaseRequest PDU
  • receive ReleaseResponse PDU
  • receive UserData(*) or CL-UserData(**) PDU
  • receive user-initiated Abort PDU
  • receive provider-initiated Abort PDU
  • timer expires(**)
The possible actions are:

• PS-user
  • P-CONNECT.INDICATION
  • P-CONNECT.CONFIRMATION
  • P-RELEASE.INDICATION
  • P-RELEASE.CONFIRMATION
  • P-DATA.INDICATION
  • P-U-ABORT.INDICATION
  • P-P-ABORT.INDICATION
• network
  • open TCP(*)

- close TCP(*)
- send ConnectRequest PDU
- send ConnectResponse PDU
- send ReleaseRequest PDU
- send ReleaseResponse PDU
- send UserData(*) or CL-UserData(**) PDU
- send user-initiated Abort PDU
- send provider-initiated Abort PDU
- set timer(**)

(*) tcp-based service only
(**) udp-based service only

Related Protocols
TCP, UDP, IP, CMIP, CMOT, CMIS, ACSE, ROSE, CMISE, ITOT

Sponsor Source
LPP is defined by ISO (http://www.iso.org) and IETF (http://www.ietf.org).

Reference
http://www.javvin.com/protocol/rfc1085.pdf
ISO Presentation Services on top of TCP/IP-based internets
http://www.javvin.com/protocol/rfc2126.pdf
ISO Transport Service on top of TCP (ITOT)

RPC: Remote Procedure Call protocol

Protocol Description
Remote Procedure Call (RPC) is a protocol for requesting a service from a program located in a remote computer through a network, without having to understand the under layer network technologies. RPC presumes the existence of a low-level transport protocol, such as TCP or UDP, for carrying the message data between communicating programs. RPC spans the Transport layer and the Application layer in the Open Systems Interconnection (OSI) model of network communication. RPC makes it easier to develop an application that includes multiple programs distributed in a network.

RPC uses the client/server model. The requesting program is a client and the service-providing program is the server. First, the caller process sends a call message that includes the procedure parameters to the server process. Then, the caller process waits for a reply message (blocks). Next, a process on the server side, which is dormant until the arrival of the call message, extracts the procedure parameters, computes the results, and sends a reply message. The server waits for the next call message. Finally, a process on the caller receives the reply message, extracts the results of the procedure, and the caller resumes execution.

There are several RPC models and implementations. Sun Microsystem originally introduced the RPC. IETF ONC charter modified the Sun version and made the ONC PRC protocol, an IETF standard protocol. A popular model and implementation is the Open Software Foundation's Distributed Computing Environment (DCE).

Protocol Structure
The Remote Procedure Call (RPC) message protocol consists of two distinct structures: the call message and the reply message. The message flows are displayed as follows:

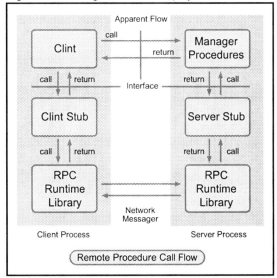

Figure 2-4: Remote Procedure Call Flow

RPC Call Message: Each remote procedure call message contains the following unsigned integer fields to uniquely identify the remote procedure:

- Program number
- Program version number
- Procedure number

The body of an RPC call message takes the following form:

```
struct call_body {
    unsigned int rpcvers;
    unsigned int prog;
    unsigned int vers;
    unsigned int proc;
    opaque_auth cred;
    opaque_auth verf;
    1 parameter
    2 parameter . . .
};
```

RPC Reply Message: The RPC protocol for a reply message varies depending on whether the call message is accepted or rejected by the network server. The reply message to a request contains information to distinguish the following conditions:

- RPC executed the call message successfully.
- The remote implementation of RPC is not protocol version 2. The lowest and highest supported RPC version numbers are returned.
- The remote program is not available on the remote system.
- The remote program does not support the requested version number. The lowest and highest supported remote program version numbers are returned.
- The requested procedure number does not exist. This is usually a caller-side protocol or programming error.

The RPC reply message takes the following form:

```
enum reply_stat stat {
    MSG_ACCEPTED = 0,
    MSG_DENIED   = 1
};
```

Related Protocols
NFS, NIS, RPC Mount

Sponsor Source
Sun Microsystems and IETF

Reference
http://www.javvin.com/protocol/rfc1831.pdf
RPC: Remote Procedure Call Protocol Specification Version 2 (ONC version)
http://www.javvin.com/protocol/rfc1057.pdf
RPC: Remote Procedure Call Protocol Specification Version 2 (Sun version)
The IEEE defines RPC in its ISO Remote Procedure Call Specification, ISO/IEC CD 11578 N6561, ISO/IEC, November 1991.

ITOT: ISO Transport Service on top of TCP

Protocol Description
ISO Transport Service on top of TCP (ITOT) is a mechanism that enables ISO applications to be ported to a TCP/IP network. There are two basic approaches which can be taken when "porting" ISO applications to TCP/IP (and IPv6) environments. One approach is to port each individual application separately, developing local protocols on top of TCP. A second approach is based on the notion of layering the ISO Transport Service over TCP/IP. This approach solves the problem for all applications which use the ISO Transport Service.

ITOT is a Transport Service which is identical to the Services and Interfaces offered by the ISO Transport Service Definition [ISO8072], but which will in fact implement the ISO Transport Protocol [ISO8073] on top of TCP/IP (IPv4 or IPv6), rather than the ISO Network Service [ISO8348]. The 'well known' TCP port 102 is reserved for hosts which implement the ITOT Protocol. Two variants of the ITOT protocol are defined, "Class 0 over TCP" and "Class 2 over TCP", which are based closely on the ISO Transport Class 0 and 2 Protocol. Class 0 provides the functions needed for connection establishment with negotiation, data transfer with segmentation, and protocol error reporting. It provides Transport Connection with flow control based on that of the NS-provider (TCP). It provides Transport Disconnection based on the NS-provider Disconnection. Class 0 is suitable for data transfer with no Explicit Transport Disconnection.

Class 2 provides the functions needed for connection establishment with negotiation, data transfer with segmentation and protocol error reporting. It provides Transport Connection with flow control based on that of the NS-provider TCP. It provides Explicit Transport Disconnection. Class 2 is suitable when independence of Normal and Expedited Data channels is required or when Explicit Transport Disconnection is needed.

Protocol Structure

8	16	32bit	Variable
Version	Reserved	Packet Length	TPDU
Message Length			

- Protocol Version: Value: 3
- Reserved - Value: 0
- Packet Length - Value: Length of the entire TPKT in octets, including Packet Header
- TPDU - ISO Transport TPDU as defined in ISO 8073.

Mapping parameters between the TCP service and the ISO 8348 CONS service is done as follow:

ISO Network Service	TCP
CONNECTION ESTABLISHMENT	
Called address	Server's IPv4 or IPv6 address and TCP port number.

Calling address	Client's IPv4 or IPv6 address
All other parameters	Ignored
DATA TRANSFER	
NS User Data (NSDU)	DATA
CONNECTION RELEASE	
All parameters	Ignored

Related Protocols
TCP, UDP, IP, CMIP, CMOT, CMIS, ACSE, ROSE, CMISE, ITOT

Sponsor Source
LPP is defined by ISO (http://www.iso.org) and IETF (http://www.ietf.org).

Reference
http://www.javvin.com/protocol/rfc1085.pdf
ISO Presentation Services on top of TCP/IP-based internets
http://www.javvin.com/protocol/rfc2126.pdf
ISO Transport Service on top of TCP (ITOT)

RDP : Reliable Data Protocol

Protocol Description
Reliable Data Protocol (RDP) is a connection-oriented transport protocol designed to efficiently support the bulk transfer of data for such host monitoring and control applications as loading/dumping and remote debugging. It attempts to provide only those services necessary, in order to be efficient in operation and small in size. The key functions of RDP are as follows:

• RDP will provide a full-duplex communications channel between the two ports of each transport connection.
• RDP will attempt to reliably deliver all user messages and will report a failure to the user if it cannot deliver a message. RDP extends the datagram service of IP to include reliable delivery.
• RDP will attempt to detect and discard all damaged and duplicate segments. It will use a checksum and sequence number in each segment header to achieve this goal.
• RDP will optionally provide sequenced delivery of segments. Sequenced delivery of segments must be specified when the connection is established.
• RDP will acknowledge segments received out of sequence, as they arrive. This will free up resources on the sending side.

RDP supports a much simpler set of functions than TCP. The flow control, buffering, and connection management schemes of RDP are considerably simpler. The goal is a protocol that can be easily and efficiently implemented and that will serve a range of applications.

RDP functions can also be subset to further reduce the size of a particular implementation. For example, a target processor requiring down-loading from another host might implement an RDP module supporting only the passive Open function and a single connection. The module might also choose not to implement out-of-sequence acknowledgements.

Protocol Structure

1	2	3	4	5	6	8	16bit
SYN	ACK	EAK	RST	NUL	0	Ver No	Header Length
Source Port							
Destination Port							
Data Length							
Sequence Number							
Acknowledgement Number							
Checksum							
Variable header area …							

Control flags - The 8 control bits are divided as follows:
• SYN -- The SYN bit indicates a synchronization segment is present.
• ACK -- The ACK bit indicates the acknowledgment number in the header is valid.
• EACK -- The EACK bit indicates an extended ac knowledge segment is present.
• RST -- The RST bit indicates the packet is a reset segment.

• NUL -- The NUL bit indicates the packet is a null segment.
• 0 -- The value of this field must be zero.
• Ver no -- version number; current version is 2.
Header length -- The length of the RDP header.
Source Ports -- Source address to identify the processes that originated the communication. The combination of the port identifiers with the source and destination addresses in the network access protocol header serves to fully qualify the connection and constitutes the connection identifier. This permits RDP to distinguish multiple connections between two hosts.
Destination Ports -- Destination address to identify the processes targeted in the communication.
Data Length -- The length in octets of the data in this segment. The data length does not include the RDP header.
Sequence number -- The sequence number of this segment.
Acknowledgement number -- If the ACK bit is set in the header, this is the sequence number of the segment that the sender of this segment last received correctly and in sequence. Once a connection is established this should always be sent.
Checksum -- The checksum to ensure integrity
Variable Header Area -- This area is used to transmit parameters for the SYN and EACK segments.

Related Protocols
UDP, RUDP, IP, TCP, ICMP

Sponsor Source
RDP is defined by IETF (http://www.ietf.org) in RFC 908 and updated by RFC 1151.

Reference
http://www.javvin.com/protocol/rfc908.pdf
Reliable Data Protocol (RDP)
http://www.javvin.com/protocol/rfc1151.pdf
Version 2 of the Reliable Data Protocol (RDP)

RUDP: Reliable User Datagram Protocol (Reliable UDP)

Protocol Description
Reliable UDP (RUDP) is a simple packet based transport protocol which was intended as a reliable transport protocol to transport telephony signalling across IP networks. RUDP is designed to allow characteristics of each connection to be individually configured so that a number of protocols with different transport requirement can be implemented simultaneously not on the same platform. It is layered on the UDP/IP protocols and provides reliable in-order delivery (up to a maximum number of retransmissions) for virtual connections. RUDP has a very flexible design that makes it suitable for a variety of transport uses. One such use would be to transport telecommunication-signalling protocols.

Reliable UDP is a set of quality of service enhancements, such as congestion control tuning improvements, retransmit, and thinning server algorithms, that improves the ability to present a good quality RTP stream to RTP clients even in the presence of packet loss and network congestion. Reliable UDP's congestion control mechanisms allow streams to behave in a TCP-friendly fashion without disturbing the real-time nature of the protocol.

To work well with TCP traffic on the Internet, Reliable UDP uses retransmission and congestion control algorithms similar to the algorithms used by TCP. Additionally, these algorithms are time-tested to utilize available bandwidth optimally.

Reliable UDP features include:

• Client acknowledgment of packets sent by the server to the client
• Windowing and congestion control so the server does not exceed the currently available bandwidth
• Server retransmission to the client in the event of packet loss
• Faster than real-time streaming known as "overbuffering"

Protocol Structure
The basic TFTP header structure:

1	2	3	4	5	6	7	8	16bit
SYN	ACK	EAK	RST	NUL	CHK	TCS	0	Header Length
Sequence number								Ack number
Checksum								

Control bits -- Indicate what is present in the packet. Details as follows:
• SYN -- The SYN bit indicates a synchronization segment is present.
• ACK -- The ACK bit indicates the acknowledgment number in the header is valid.

• EACK -- The EACK bit indicates an extended acknowledge segment is present.
• RST -- The RST bit indicates the packet is a reset segment.
• NUL -- The NUL bit indicates the packet is a null segment.
• CHK -- The CHK bit indicates whether the Checksum field contains the checksum of just the header or the header and the body (data).
• TCS -- The TCS bit indicates the packet is a transfer connection state segment.
• 0 -- The value of this field must be zero.
Header length -- Indicates where user data begins in the packet.
Sequence number -- When a connection is first opened, each peer randomly picks an initial sequence number. This sequence number is used in the SYN segments to open the connection. Each transmitter increments the sequence number before sending a data, null, or reset segment.
Acknowledgement number -- This field indicates to a transmitter the last in- sequence packet the receiver has received.
Checksum - The checksum is always calculated on the RUDP header to ensure integrity. The checksum here is the same algorithm used in UDP and TCP headers.

Related Protocols
UDP, RDP, IP, TCP

Sponsor Source
RUDP is discussed in IETF (http://www.ietf.org) as documented in a memo.

Reference
http://www.javvin.com/protocol/reliable-UDP.pdf
Reliable UDP protocol
http://www.javvin.com/protocol/rfc908.pdf
Reliable Data Protocol (RDP)
http://www.javvin.com/protocol/rfc1151.pdf
Version 2 of the Reliable Data Protocol (RDP)

TALI: Tekelec's Transport Adapter Layer Interface

Protocol Description
Tekelec's Transport Adapter Layer Interface (TALI) is the interface of a Signalling Gateway, which provides interworking between the Switched Circuit Network (SCN) and an IP network. Since the Gateway is the central point of signalling information, not only does it provide transportation of signalling from one network to another, but can also provide additional functions such as protocol translation, security screening, routing information, and seamless access to Intelligent Network (IN) services on both networks.

The Transport Adapter Layer Interface (TALI) protocol provides TCAP, ISUP, and MTP messaging over TCP/IP and is used to support reliable communication between the SS7 Signalling Network and applications residing within the IP network.

This version of TALI provides 3 SS7 signalling transport methods and provides functionality for MTP over TCP/IP, SCCP/TCAP over TCP/IP and ISUP over TCP/IP.

Protocol Structure
The basic TFTP header structure:

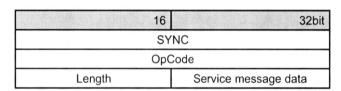

16	32bit
SYNC	
OpCode	
Length	Service message data

SYNC - Four bytes must be (54 41 4C 49) TALI in ASCII.
OpCode -- Operation code are specified as follows:
• Type of frame
• Test Service on this Socket test
• Allow Service messages on this socket allo
• Prohibit Service messages on this socket proh
• Prohibit Service messages Ack proa
• Monitor Socket message on this socket moni
• Monitor Socket message Ack mona
• SCCP Service message sccp
• ISUP Service message isot
• MTP3 Service message mtp3
• MTP Primitives mtpp
• SCCP Primitives scpp
• Routing Key Registration rkrg
• Routing Key De-Registration rkdr
• Special Service Message spcl
Length -- The length of the frame. Non-zero if message contains a Service or Monitor Socket message.
Service message data -- The service message data.

Related Protocols
TCAP, ISUP, SCCP, TCP, IP, MTP, SS7

Sponsor Source
TALI is defined by IETF (http://www.ietf.org) in RFC 3094.

Reference

TCP: Transmission Control Protocol

Protocol Description

Transmission Control Protocol (TCP) is the transport layer protocol in the TCP/IP suite, which provides a reliable stream delivery and virtual connection service to applications through the use of sequenced acknowledgment with retransmission of packets when necessary. Along with the Internet Protocol (IP), TCP represents the heart of the Internet protocols.

Since many network applications may be running on the same machine with one single IP address, computers need something to make sure that the correct software application on the destination computer gets the data packets from the source machine and the replies get routed back to the correct application on the source computer. This is accomplished through the use of the TCP "port numbers". The combination of IP address of a network station and its port number is known as a "socket" or an "endpoint". TCP establishes connections or virtual circuits between two "sockets" or "endpoints" for reliable communications. Details of TCP port numbers can be found in the Appendix and the reference documents.

Among the services TCP provides are stream data transfer, reliability, efficient flow control, full-duplex operation, and multiplexing.

With stream data transfer, TCP delivers an unstructured stream of bytes identified by sequence numbers. This service benefits applications because the application does not have to chop data into blocks before handing it off to TCP. TCP can group bytes into segments and pass them to IP for delivery.

TCP offers reliability by providing connection-oriented, end-to-end reliable packet delivery. It does this by sequencing bytes with a forwarding acknowledgment number that indicates to the destination the next byte the source expects to receive. Bytes not acknowledged within a specified time period are retransmitted. The reliability mechanism of TCP allows devices to deal with lost, delayed, duplicate, or misread packets. A time-out mechanism allows devices to detect lost packets and request retransmission.

TCP offers efficient flow control - When sending acknowledgments back to the source, the receiving TCP process indicates the highest sequence number it can receive without overflowing its internal buffers.

Full-duplex operation: TCP processes can both send and receive packets at the same time.

Multiplexing in TCP: Numerous simultaneous upper-layer conversations can be multiplexed over a single connection.

Protocol Structure

	16		32bit
Source port		Destination port	
Sequence number			

Acknowledgement number								
Offset	Re-served	U	A	P	R	S	F	Window
Checksum							Urgent pointer	
Option + Padding								
Data								

• Source port -- Identifies points at which upper-layer source process receives TCP services.
• Destination port -- Identifies points at which upper-layer Destination process receives TCP services.
• Sequence number -- Usually specifies the number assigned to the first byte of data in the current message. In the connection-establishment phase, this field also can be used to identify an initial sequence number to be used in an upcoming transmission.
• Acknowledgment number – Contains the sequence number of the next byte of data the sender of the packet expects to receive. Once a connection is established, this value is always sent.
• Data offset -- The number of 32-bit words in the TCP header indicates where the data begins.
• Reserved -- Reserved for future use. Must be zero.
• Control bits (Flags) -- Carry a variety of control information. The control bits may be:
  • U (URG) -- Urgent pointer field significant.
  • A (ACK) -- Acknowledgment field significant.
  • P (PSH) -- Push function.
  • R (RST) -- Reset the connection.
  • S (SYN) -- Synchronize sequence numbers.
  • F (FIN) -- No more data from sender.
• Window -- Specifies the size of the sender's receive window, that is, the buffer space available in octets for incoming data.
• Checksum -- Indicates whether the header was damaged in transit.
• Urgent Pointer -- Points to the first urgent data byte in the packet.
• Option + Paddling – Specifies various TCP options.
  • 0 -- End of Option List
  • 1 -- No operation (pad)
  • 2 -- Maximum segment size
  • 3 -- Window scale
  • 4 -- Selective ACK ok
  • 8 -- Timestamp
• Data -- Contains upper-layer information.

Related Protocols
IP, UDP, ICMP, SNMP, FTP, TELNET, SMTP, RPC, XDR, and NFS

Sponsor Source
TCP is defined by IETF (http://www.ietf.org) RFC793.

Reference
http://www.javvin.com/protocol/rfc793.pdf
TCP Specifications
http://www.javvin.com/protocol/rfc3168.pdf
The Addition of Explicit Congestion Notification (ECN) to IP
http://www.iana.org/assignments/port-numbers
TCP and UDP port numbers

UDP: User Datagram Protocol

Protocol Description
User Datagram Protocol (UDP) is a connectionless transport layer (layer 4) protocol in the OSI model which provides a simple and unreliable message service for transaction-oriented services. UDP is basically an interface between IP and upper-layer processes. UDP protocol ports distinguish multiple applications running on a single device from one another.

Since many network applications may be running on the same machine, computers need something to make sure the correct software application on the destination computer gets the data packets from the source machine and some way to make sure replies get routed to the correct application on the source computer. This is accomplished through the use of the UDP "port numbers". For example, if a station wished to use a Domain Name System (DNS) on the station 128.1.123.1, it would address the packet to station 128.1.123.1 and insert destination port number 53 in the UDP header. The source port number identifies the application on the local station that requested domain name server, and all response packets generated by the destination station should be addressed to that port number on the source station. Details of UDP port numbers can be found in the Appendix and the reference documents.

Unlike TCP, UDP adds no reliability, flow-control, or error-recovery functions to IP. Because of UDP's simplicity, UDP headers contain fewer bytes and consume less network overhead than TCP.

UDP is useful in situations where the reliability mechanisms of TCP are not necessary, such as in cases where a higher-layer protocol or application might provide error and flow control.

UDP is the transport protocol for several well-known application-layer protocols, including Network File System (NFS), Simple Network Management Protocol (SNMP), Domain Name System (DNS), and Trivial File Transfer Protocol (TFTP).

Protocol Structure

16	32bit
Source port	Destination port
Length	Checksum
Data	

• Source port -- An optional field. When used, it indicates the port of the sending process and may be assumed to be the port to which a reply should be addressed in the absence of any other information. If not used, a value of zero is inserted.
• Destination port -- Identifies points at which upper-layer Destination process receives UDP services
 • Length -- It is the length in octets of the entire user datagram, including header and data. The minimum value of the length is eight octets.
• Checksum -- The sum of a pseudo-header of information from the IP header, the UDP header and the data, padded with zero octets at the end, if necessary, to make a multiple of two

octets.
• Data -- Contains upper-level data information.

Related Protocols
IP, TCP, ICMP, SNMP, DNS, TFTP and NFS

Sponsor Source
UDP is defined by IETF (http://www.ietf.org) RFC768.

Reference
http://www.javvin.com/protocol/rfc768.pdf
User Datagram Protocol (UDP) Specifications
http://www.iana.org/assignments/port-numbers
UDP and TCP port numbers

Van Jacobson: Compressed TCP protocol

Protocol Description
Van Jacobson is a compressed TCP protocol which improves the TCP/IP performance over low speed (300 to 19,200 bps) serial links and to solves problems in link-level framing, address assignment, routing, authentication and performance.

The compression proposed in the Van Jacobson protocol is similar in spirit to the Thinwire-II protocol. However, this protocol compresses more effectively (the average compressed header is 3 bytes compared to 13 in Thinwire-II) and is both efficient and simple to implement. Van Jacobson compression is specific to TCP/IP datagrams.

Protocol Structure
The format of the compressed TCP is as follows:

	C	I	P	S	A	W	U
Connection number (C)							
TCP checksum							
Urgent pointer (U)							
D Window (W)							
D Ack (A)							
D Sequence (S)							
D IP ID (I)							
data							

C, I, P, S, A, W, U -- Change mask. Identifies which of the fields expected to change per-packet actually changed.
Connection number -- Used to locate the saved copy of the last packet for this TCP connection.
TCP checksum -- Included so that the end-to-end data integrity check will still be valid.
Urgent pointer -- This is sent if URG is set.
D values for each field -- Represent the amount the associated field changed from the original TCP (for each field specified in the change mask).

Related Protocols
TCP

Sponsor Source
Van Jacobson is defined by IETF (http://www.ietf.org) in RFC 1144.

Reference
http://www.javvin.com/protocol/rfc1144.pdf
Compressing TCP/IP Headers for Low-Speed Serial Links

Network Layer Protocols
Routing Protocals

BGP (BGP4): Border Gateway Protocol

Protocol Description

The Border Gateway Protocol (BGP), runs over TCP and is an inter-Autonomous System routing protocol. BGP is the only protocol that is designed to deal with a network of the Internet's size, and the only protocol that can deal well with having multiple connections to unrelated routing domains. It is built on experience gained with Exterior Gateway Protocol (EGP). The primary function of a BGP system is to exchange network reachability information with other BGP systems. This network reachability information includes information on the list of Autonomous Systems (ASs) that reachability information traverses. This information is sufficient to construct a graph of AS connectivity from which routing loops may be pruned and some policy decisions at the AS level may be enforced.

BGP version 4 (BGP-4), the latest version of BGP, provides a new set of mechanisms for supporting classless interdomain routing (CIDR). These mechanisms include support for advertising an IP prefix and eliminate the concept of network "class" within BGP. BGP-4 also introduces mechanisms which allow aggregation of routes, including aggregation of AS paths. These changes provide support for the proposed supernetting scheme.

Protocol Structure

Marker (16 bytes)	Length (2 bytes)	Type (1 byte)

Marker -- Message containing a value predictable by the receiver of the message.
Length -- The length of the message including the header.
Type -- The message type. Possible messages are: Open, Update, Notification, KeepAlive.

After a transport protocol connection is established, the first message sent by each side is an OPEN message. If the OPEN message is acceptable, a KEEPALIVE message confirming the OPEN is sent back. Once the OPEN is confirmed, UPDATE, KEEPALIVE, and NOTIFICATION messages may be exchanged. The format of each type of messages could be found in the reference documents.

Related Protocols
IP, TCP, EGP

Sponsor Source
BGP is defined by IETF (http://www.ietf.org) RFC 4271.

Reference
http://www.javvin.com/protocolrfc4271.pdf
A Border Gateway Protocol 4 (BGP-4)

EGP: Exterior Gateway Protocol

Protocol Description

Exterior Gateway Protocol (EGP) is for exchanging routing information between two neighbor gateway hosts in a network of autonomous systems. EGP is commonly used between hosts on the Internet to exchange routing table information. The protocol is based on periodic polling using Hello/I-Heard-You (I-H-U) message exchanges to monitor neighbor reachability and Poll commands to solicit Update responses. The routing table contains a list of known routers, the addresses they can reach, and a cost metric associated with the path to each router so that the best available route is chosen. Each router polls its neighbor at intervals between 120 to 480 seconds and the neighbor responds by sending its complete routing table. EGP-2 is the latest version of EGP.

A more recent exterior gateway protocol, the Border Gateway Protocol (BGP), provides additional capabilities.

Protocol Structure
Here are the EGP message types:

Name	Function
Request	request acquisition of neighbor and/or initialize polling variables
Confirm	confirm acquisition of neighbor and/or initialize polling variables
Refuse	refuse acquisition of neighbor
Cease	request de-acquisition of neighbor
Cease-ack	confirm de-acquisition of neighbor
Hello	request neighbor reachability
I-H-U	confirm neighbor reachability
Poll	request net-reachability update
Update	net-reachability update
Error	error

The common portion of the message format:

8	16	24	32bit
Version	Type	Code	Status
Checksum		Autonomous System number	
Sequence number		(Different for different messages)	

• Version -- The version number. This version is version 2.
• Type -- Identifies the message type.
• Code -- Identifies the message code.
• Status -- Contains message-dependent status information.
• Checksum -- The EGP checksum is the 16-bit one's complement of the one's complement sum of the EGP message starting with the EGP version number field. When computing the checksum the checksum field itself should be zero.
• Autonomous System Number -- Assigned number identifying

the particular autonomous system.
• Sequence Number -- Send state variable (commands) or receive state variable (responses and indications).

Related Protocols
IP, TCP, BGP, IGP

Sponsor Source
EGP is defined by IETF (http://www.ietf.org) RFC904.

Reference
http://www.javvin.com/protocol/rfc904.pdf
Exterior Gateway Protocol formal specification

ICMP & ICMPv6: Internet Message Control Protocol for IP and IPv6

Protocol Description
Internet Control Message Protocol (ICMP) is an integrated part of the IP suite. ICMP messages, delivered in IP packets, are used for out-of-band messages related to network operation or mis-operation. ICMP packet delivery is unreliable, so hosts can't count on receiving ICMP packets for any network problems. The key ICMP functions are:

• Announce network errors, such as a host or entire portion of the network being unreachable, due to some type of failure. A TCP or UDP packet directed at a port number with no receiver attached is also reported via ICMP.
• Announce network congestion. When a router begins buffering too many packets, due to an inability to transmit them as fast as they are being received, it will generate ICMP Source Quench messages. Directed at the sender, these messages should cause the rate of packet transmission to be slowed. Of course, generating too many Source Quench messages would cause even more network congestion, so they are used sparingly.
• Assist Troubleshooting. ICMP supports an Echo function, which just sends a packet on a round--trip between two hosts. Ping, a common network management tool, is based on this feature. Ping will transmit a series of packets, measuring average round--trip times and computing loss percentages.
• Announce Timeouts. If an IP packet's TTL field drops to zero, the router discarding the packet will often generate an ICMP packet announcing this fact. TraceRoute is a tool which maps network routes by sending packets with small TTL values and watching the ICMP timeout announcements.

The Internet Control Message Protocol (ICMP) was revised during the definition of IPv6. ICMPv6 is used by IPv6 nodes to report errors encountered in processing packets, and to perform other internet-layer functions, such as diagnostics (ICMPv6 "ping"). ICMPv6 is an integral part of IPv6 and must be fully implemented by every IPv6 node. In addition, the multicast control functions of the IPv4 Group Membership Protocol (IGMP) are now incorporated in the ICMPv6.

Protocol Structure

8	16	32bit
Type	Code	Checksum
Message Body		

• Type -- Messages can be error or informational messages.
• Code -- For each type of message several different codes are defined. The following table displays the ICMP message types and codes:

Type	Code
0 Echo Reply	0

3 Destination Unreachable	0 Net Unreachable 1 Host Unreachable 2 Protocol Unreachable 3 Port Unreachable 4 Fragmentation Needed & DF Set 5 Source Route Failed 6 Destination Network Unknown 7 Destination Host Unknown 8 Source Host Isolated 9 Network Administratively Prohibited 10 Host Administratively Prohibited 11 Network Unreachable for TOS 12 Host Unreachable for TOS 13 Communication Administratively Prohibited
4 Source Quench	0
5 Redirect	0 Redirect Datagram for the Network 1 Redirect Datagram for the Host 2 Redirect Datagram for the TOS & Network 3 Redirect Datagram for the TOS & Host
8 Echo	0
9 Router Advertisement	0
10 Router Selection	0
11 Time Exceeded	0 Time to Live exceeded in Transit 1 Fragment Reassembly Time Exceeded
12 Parameter Problem	0 Pointer indicates the error 1 Missing a Required Option 2 Bad Length
13 Timestamp	0
14 Timestamp Reply	0
15 Information Request	0
16 Information Reply	0
17 Address Mask Request	0
18 Address Mask Reply	0
30 Traceroute	0

• Checksum -- Complement sum of the ICMP message starting with the ICMP Type. For computing the checksum, the checksum field should be zero.

For original ICMP, three additional fields in the message body:

• Identifier -- A 16 bits field to aid in matching quest/replies. Maybe zero.

• Sequence number -- A 16 bits field to aid in matching request/replies. Maybe zero.
• Address mask -- A 32 bits mask.

ICMPv6 messages are grouped into two classes: error messages and informational messages. Error messages are identified as such by having a zero in the high-order bit of their message Type field values. Thus, error messages have message Types from 0 to 127; informational messages have message Types from 128 to 255.

ICMPv6 error messages:

• 1 -- Destination Unreachable
• 2 -- Packet Too Big
• 3 -- Time Exceeded
• 4 -- Parameter Problem

ICMPv6 informational messages:

• 128 -- Echo Request
• 129 -- Echo Reply

For ICMPv6, the value of the type field determines the format of the remaining data. The code field depends on the message type. It is used to create an additional level of message granularity.

Related Protocols
IP, TCP, IGMP, SNMP, DNS, TFTP and NFS

Sponsor Source
ICMP is defined by IETF (http://www.ietf.org) RFC792 and 950; ICMPv6 is defined by RFC 2461, 2463.

Reference
http://www.javvin.com/protocol/rfc792.pdf
Internet Control Message Protocol
http://www.javvin.com/protocol/rfc950.pdf
Internet Standard Subnetting Procedure
http://www.javvin.com/protocol/rfc2461.pdf
Neighbor Discovery for IP Version 6 (IPv6).
http://www.javvin.com/protocol/rfc2463.pdf
ICMPv6 for the Internet Protocol Version 6 (IPv6) Specification

IP: Internet Protocol (IPv4)

Protocol Description

The Internet Protocol (IP) is a network-layer (Layer 3 in the OSI model) protocol that contains addressing information and some control information to enable packets to be routed in a network. IP is the primary network-layer protocol in the TCP/IP protocol suite. Along with the Transmission Control Protocol (TCP), IP represents the heart of the Internet protocols. IP is equally well suited for both LAN and WAN communications.

IP has two primary responsibilities: providing connectionless, best-effort delivery of datagrams through a network; and providing fragmentation and reassembly of datagrams to support data links with different maximum-transmission unit (MTU) sizes. The IP addressing scheme is integral to the process of routing IP datagrams through an internetwork. Each IP address has specific components and follows a basic format. These IP addresses can be subdivided and used to create addresses for subnetworks. Each computer (known as a host) on a TCP/IP network is assigned a unique 32-bit logical address that is divided into two main parts: the network number and the host number. The network number identifies a network and must be assigned by the Internet Network Information Center (InterNIC) if the network is to be part of the Internet. An Internet Service Provider (ISP) can obtain blocks of network addresses from the InterNIC and can itself assign address space as necessary. The host number identifies a host on a network and is assigned by the local network administrator.

When you send or receive data (for example, an e-mail note or a Web page), the message gets divided into little chunks called packets. Each of these packets contains both the sender's Internet address and the receiver's address. Because a message is divided into a number of packets, each packet can, if necessary, be sent by a different route across the Internet. Packets can arrive in a different order than the order they were sent in. The Internet Protocol just delivers them. It's up to another protocol, the Transmission Control Protocol (TCP) to put them back in the right order.

All other protocols within the TCP/IP suite, except ARP and RARP, use IP to route frames from host to host. There are two basic IP versions, IPv4 and IPv6. This document describes the IPv4 details. The IPv6 details are described in a separate document.

Protocol Structure

4	8	16	32bit
Version	IHL	Type of service	Total length
Identification		Flags	Fragment offset
Time to live	Protocol	Header checksum	
Source address			
Destination address			
Option + Padding			
Data			

• Version -- indicates the version of IP currently used (4 for IPv4).
• IP Header Length (IHL) -- is the datagram header length in 32-bit words. Points to the beginning of the data. Minimum value is 5 (20bytes) and maximum value is 15 (60 bytes).
• Type-of-Service -- indicates the quality of service desired by specifying how an upper-layer protocol would like a current datagram to be handled and assigns datagrams various levels of importance. These 8 bits fields are used for the assignment of Precedence, Delay, Throughput and Reliability.

Type of service	Differentiated Services
Precedence (000 – 111)	000
D (1 = minimize delay)	0
T (1 = maximize throughout)	0
R (1 = maximize reliability)	0
C (1 = minimize cost)	1 = ENC capable
x (reserved and set to 0)	1 = congestion experienced

• Total Length -- specifies the length, in bytes, of the entire IP packet, including the data and header. The maximum length is 65,535 bytes. Typically, hosts are prepared to accept datagrams up to 576 bytes.
• Identification -- contains an integer that identifies the current datagram. This field is assigned by sender to help receiver to assemble the datagram fragments.
• Flags -- consists of a 3-bit field of which the two low-order (least-significant) bits control fragmentation.
  • X (reserved and set to 0
  • D (1 = don't fragment)
  • M (1 = more fragment)
• Fragment Offset -- This 13-bits field indicates the position of the fragment's data relative to the beginning of the data in the original datagram, which allows the destination IP process to properly reconstruct the original datagram.
• Time-to-Live -- is a counter that gradually decrements down to zero, at which point the datagram is discarded. This keeps packets from looping endlessly.
• Protocol -- indicates which upper-layer protocol receives incoming packets after IP processing is complete. Some sample protocols:

• 1 -- ICMP	• 2 -- IGMP	• 6 -- TCP
• 9 -- IGRP	• 17 -- UDP	• 47 --GRE
• 50 -- ESP	• 51 -- AH	• 57 -- SKIP
• 88 -- EIGRP	• 89 -- OSPF	• 115 -- L2TP

• Header Checksum -- helps ensure IP header integrity. Since some header fields change, e.g., Time to Live, this is recomputed and verified at each point the Internet header is processed.
• Source Address -- specifies the sending node.
• Destination Address -- specifies the receiving node.
• Options -- allows IP to support various options.
  • 0 -- End of option list
  • 1 -- No operation (PAD)
  • 7 -- Record route
  • 68 -- timestamp
  • 131 -- Loose source route
  • 137 -- Strict source route
• Data -- contains upper-layer information.

Related Protocols

IPv6, TCP, UDP, ICMP, SNMP, FTP, TELNET, SMTP, ARP, RARP, RPC, XDR, and NFS

Sponsor Source
The Internet Protocol is defined by IETF (http://www.ietf.org) RFC 791.

Reference
http://www.javvin.com/protocol/rfc791.pdf
Internet Protocol Specifications
http://www.cisco.com/univercd/cc/td/doc/cisintwk/ito_doc/ip.htm
IP Overview

IPv6: Internet Protocol version 6

Protocol Description
Internet Protocol version 6 (IPv6) is the new version of Internet Protocol (IP) based on IPv4. It is a network-layer (Layer 3) protocol that contains addressing information and some control information enabling packets to be routed in the network. IPv6 is also called the next generation IP or IPng.

The most significant change in IPv6 is increasing the IP address size from 32 bits in IPv4 to 128 bits, to support more levels of addressing hierarchy, a much greater number of addressable nodes, and simpler auto-configuration of addresses. There are three types of IP addresses in IPv6: Unicast, Multicast and Anycast. Broadcast no longer exists in IPv6, which becomes a special form of multicast. IPv6 addresses are expressed in hexadecimal format (base 16), which allows not only numerals (0-9) but a few characters as well (a-f).
IPv6 fixes many shortages in IPv4 in addition to the limited number of available IPv4 addresses. IPv6 has enhanced network layer routing in two main areas: 1) Improved support for extensions and options; 2) Flow labeling capability to differenciate the packets at network layer. The key benefits of introducing IPv6 are:

• 340 undecillion IP addresses for the whole world network devices
• Plug and Play configuration with or without DHCP
• Better network bandwidth efficiency using multicast and anycast without broadcast
• Better QOS support for all types of applications
• Improved support for extensions and options with better routing efficiency
• Native information security framework for both data and control packets
• Enhanced mobility with fast handover, better route optimization and hierarchical mobility

The following table compares the key characters of IPv6 vs. IPv4:

Subjects	IPv4	IPv6	IPv6 Advantages
Address Space	4 Billion Addresses	3.4 x 1038 addresses	79 Octillion times the IPv4 address space
Configuration	Manual or use DHCP	Universal Plug and Play (UPnP) with or without DHCP	Lower Operation Expenses and less error
Broadcast / Multicast	Both	Broadcast is a form of multicast	Better bandwidth efficiency

Anycast	Not part of the original protocol	Explicit support of anycast	Allows for newer applications in mobility, data center, etc.
Routing efficiency	Need to process Option and Checksum by every router	No checksum; Extended header for options.	Flexible extensions and options; better routing efficiency.
Network Reconfiguration	Mostly manual & Labor intensive	By design; Facilitate the re-numbering of hosts and routers	Lower operation expenses and facilitate migration
QoS support	ToS using DIFFServ	Flow classes and flow labels	More Granular control of QoS
Security	IPsec for data packet protection	IPsec is the native technology to protect data and control packets	Unified framework for security and more secure computing environment
Mobility	Mobile IPv4	Mobile IPv6	Better efficiency and scalability; Work with the latest 3G mobile technologies and beyond.

Few in the industry would argue with the principle that IPv6 represents a major leap forward for the Internet and the users. However, given the magnitude of a migration that affects so many millions of network devices, it is clear that IPv4 and IPv6 will coexist for a long period of time.

Protocol Structure

4	12	16	24	32 bit
Version	Traffic Class	Flow label		
Payload length			Next header type	Hop limit
Source address (128 bits)				
Destination address (128 bits)				
Next header	Extension Header Information (optional and variable length)			
Data (Variable Length)				

• Version -- Internet Protocol Version number (For IPv6 it is 6).

• Traffic Class -- enables a source to identify the desired delivery priority of the packets. Priority values are divided into ranges: traffic where the source provides congestion control and non-congestion control traffic.
• Flow label -- used by a source to label those packets for special handling by the IPv6 router. The flow is uniquely identified by the combination of a source address and a non-zero flow label.
• Payload length -- the length of the data portion of the packet.
• Next headertype -- identifies the type of header immediately following the IPv6 header. Hop limit specifies the maximum number of routers (hops) through which a packet can traverse before discarded. It is decremented by one by each node that forwards the packet. Source address – 128-bit address of the originator of the packet.Destination address – 128-bit address of the intended recipient of the packet (possibly not the ultimate recipient, if a Routing header is present). Extension Header Information – an optional field with variable length. The following IPv6 extension headers are currently defined.

    • Routing -- Extended routing, like IPv4 loose source route

    • Fragmentation -- Fragmentation and reassembly
    • Authentication -- Integrity and authentication, security

    • Encapsulation -- Confidentiality
    • Hop-by-Hop Option -- Special options that require hop-by-hop processing
    • Destination Options -- Optional information to be examined by the destination node

The format of IPv6 address is:

16 bits	16 bits	16 bits	16 bits	16 bits	16 bits	16 bits	16 bits
aaaa	aaaa	aaaa	aaaa	aaaa	aaaa	aaaa	aaaa

IPv6 address is classified in three types: Unicast, Multicast and Anycast. Unicast Address is applied to one network interface. The common global unicast address divisions:

Global Routing Prefix (N bits)	Subnet ID (64-N bits)	Interface ID (64 bits)

Link-local unicast address divisions:

1111111010 (10 bits)	0x00...0 (54bits)	Interface ID (64 bits)

Site-local unicast address divisions:

1111111011 (10 bits)	0x00...0	SLA	Interface ID (64 bits)

(Interface ID is based on hardware MAC address.)

Multicast Address: applied for multiple network interfaces, and communication is conducted with all hosts with the same address.

0xFF (8 bits)	Flag (4bits)	Scope(4bits)	Group ID (64 bits)

Anycast Address: applied for multiple network interfaces, but actual communication is conducted with one of them. It has the same format as the Unicast.

IPv4 mapped to IPv6 address:

0x00...0 (80 bits)	0x00...0 (16 bits)	IPv4 Address (32 bits)

IPv4-compatible IPv6 address:

0x00...0 (80 bits)	0x0000 (16 bits)	IPv4 Address (32 bits)

Related Protocols
IPv4, TCP, UDP, ICMPv6, Mobile IPv6, OSPFv3, BGP-MP, IPsec, RIPng

Sponsor Source
IPv6 is defined by IETF (http://www.ietf.org) RFC 1883 (original) and RFC 2460 (latest).

Reference
http://www.javvin.com/protocol/rfc1883.pdf
IPv6 Specifications (original)
http://www.javvin.com/protocol/rfc2460.pdf
IPv6 specifications (the latest)
http://www.ipv6forum.com
A good informational site

IRDP: ICMP Router Discovery Protocol

Protocol Description
ICMP Router Discovery Protocol (IRDP) enables a host to determine the address of a router that it can use as a default gateway. IRDP is an alternative router discovery method using a pair of ICMP messages, for use on multicast links. IRDP eliminates the need for manual configuration of router addresses and is independent of any specific routing protocol. IRDP is similar to ES-IS in an ISO network but it is used with the IP-based network.

Hosts must discover routers before they can send IP datagrams outside their subnet. Typically, this is accomplished by reading a list of one or more router addresses from a (possibly remote) configuration file at startup time. On multicast links, some hosts also discover router addresses by listening to routing protocol traffic. Both of these methods have serious drawbacks: configuration files must be maintained manually - a significant administrative burden -- and are unable to track dynamic changes in router availability; eavesdropping on routing traffic requires that hosts recognize the particular routing protocols in use, which vary from subnet to subnet and which are subject to change at any time. ICMP Router discovery Protocol uses Internet Control Message Protocol (ICMP) router advertisements and router solicitation messages to allow a host to discover the addresses of operational routers on the subnet. Each router periodically multicasts a router advertisement from each of its multicast interfaces, announcing the IP address of that interface. Hosts listen for advertisements to discover the addresses of their neighboring routers. When a host attached to a multicast link starts up, it can send a multicast router solicitation to ask for immediate advertisements, rather than waiting for the next periodic ones to arrive; if (and only if) no advertisements are forthcoming, the host may retransmit the solicitation a small number of times, but then must desist from sending any more solicitations. Any routers that subsequently start up, or that were not discovered because of packet loss or temporary link partitioning, are eventually discovered by reception of their periodic (unsolicited) advertisements. (Links that suffer high packet loss rates or frequent partitioning are accommodated by increasing the rate of advertisements, rather than increasing the number of solicitations that hosts are permitted to send.)

The ICMP router discovery messages do not constitute a routing protocol. They enable hosts to discover the existence of neighboring routers but do not determine which router is best to reach a particular destination. If a host chooses a poor first-hop router for a particular destination, it should receive an ICMP Redirect from that router, identifying a better one.

Protocol Structure
ICMP Router Advertisement Message

8	16	32bit
Type	Code	Checksum
Num addrs	Addr Entry Size	Life Time

Router address 1
Preference Level 1
...

IP Fields:
• Source Address -- An IP address belonging to the interface from which this message is sent.
• Destination Address -- The configured Advertisement Address or the IP address of a neighboring host.
• Time-to-Live -- 1 if the Destination Address is an IP multicast address; at least 1 otherwise.

ICMP Fields:
• Type -- 9
• Code -- 0
• Checksum -- The 16-bit one's complement of the one's complement sum of the ICMP message, starting with the ICMP Type. For computing the checksum, the Checksum field is set to 0.
• Num Addrs -- The number of router addresses advertised in this message.
• Addr Entry Size -- The number of 32-bit words of information per each router address (2, in the version of the protocol described here).
• Lifetime -- The maximum number of seconds that the router addresses may be considered valid.
• Router Address[i] -- The sending router's IP address(es) on the i = 1..Num Addrs interface from which this message is sent.
• Preference Level[i] -- The preferability of each Router Address[i] i = 1..Num Addrs as a default router address, relative to other router addresses on the same subnet.

ICMP Router Solicitation Message:

8	16	32bit
Type	Code	Checksum
Reserved		

P Fields:
• Source Address -- An IP address belonging to the interface from which this message is sent, or 0.
• Destination Address -- The configured SolicitationAddress.
• Time-to-Live -- 1 if the Destination Address is an IP multicast address; at least 1 otherwise.

ICMP Fields:
• Type -- 10
• Code -- 0
• Checksum -- The 16-bit one's complement of the one's complement sum of the ICMP message, starting with the ICMP Type. For computing the checksum, the Checksum field is set to 0.
• Reserved -- Sent as 0; ignored on reception.

Related Protocols
IP, TCP, IGMP, ICMP

Sponsor Source
IRDP is defined by IETF (http://www.ietf.org) RFC 1256.

Reference
http://www.javvin.com/protocol/rfc1256.pdf
ICMP Router Discovery Messages
http://www.javvin.com/protocol/rfc792.pdf
Internet Control Message Protocol
http://www.javvin.com/protocol/rfc2463.pdf
ICMPv6 for the Internet Protocol Version 6 (IPv6) Specification

Mobile IP: IP Mobility Support Protocol for IPv4 & IPv6

Protocol Description

Mobile IP is the key protocol to enable mobile computing and networking, which brings together two of the world's most powerful technologies, the Internet and mobile communication. In Mobile IP, two IP addresses are provided for each computer: home IP address which is fixed and care-of IP address which is changing as the computer moves. When the mobile moves to a new location, it must send its new address to an agent at home so that the agent can tunnel all communications to its new address timely.

The main components defined in the Mobile IPv6 architecture are shown as follows:

• Mobile node -- A mobile unit that can change links, and therefore addresses, and maintain reachability using its home address.
• Home link -- The link from which the mobile node originates.
• Home address -- An address assigned to the mobile node when it is attached to the home link and through which the mobile node is always reachable, regardless of its location on an IPv6 network.
• Home agent -- A router on the home link that maintains registrations of mobile nodes that are away from home and their current addresses.
• Foreign link -- A link that is not the mobile node's home link.
• Care-of address -- An address used by a mobile node while it is attached to a foreign link. The association of a home address with a care-of address for a mobile node is known as a binding.
• Correspondent node A node that communicates with a mobile node. A correspondent node does not have to be Mobile IPv6-capable.

There are two versions of Mobile IP: Mobile IP for IPv4 and IPv6. The major differences are summarized as follows:

Key Features	Mobile IPv4	Mobile IPv6
Special router as foreign agent	Yes	No
Support for route optimization	Part of the protocol	In Extensions
Ensure symmetric reachability between mobile nodes and its router at current location	No	Yes
Routing bandwidth overhead	More	Less
Decouple from Link Layer	No	Yes
Need to manage "Tunnel soft state"	Yes	No
Dynamic home agent address discovery	No	Yes

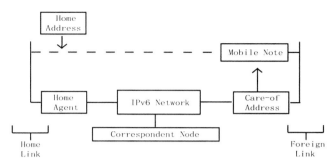

Figure 2-5: Mobile IP Functional Flow Chart

Protocol Structure

Mobility IPv6 Protocol header structure:

8	16	24	32bit
Next Header	Length	Type	reserved
Checksum		Data :::	

• Next Header -- Identifies the protocol following this header.
• Length -- 8 bits unsigned. Size of the header in units of 8 bytes excluding the first 8 bytes.
• Type -- Mobility message types.

Type	Description
0	BRR, Binding Refresh Request.
1	HoTI, Home Test Init.
2	CoTI, Care-of Test Init.
3	HoT, Home Test.
4	CoT, Care-of Test.
5	BU, Binding Update.
6	Binding Acknowledgement.
7	BE, Binding Error.

• Reserved -- MUST be cleared to zero by the sender and MUST be ignored by the receiver.
• Checksum -- Checksum of the Mobility Header.
• Data -- Variable length.

Related Protocols

IP, UDP, IGMP, ICMP, Correspondent Node, Care-of Address, Destination Address, Home Agent, Mobility Internet Protocol, Mobile Node

Sponsor Source

Mobile IP is defined by IETF (http://www.ietf.org) RFC 3344 and 3775.

Reference

http://www.javvin.com/protocol/rfc3344.pdf
IP Mobility Support for IPv4
http://www.javvin.com/protocol/rfc3775.pdf
IP Mobility Support of IPv6

NARP: NBMA Address Resolution Protocol

Protocol Description

The NBMA Address Resolution Protocol (NARP) allows a source terminal (a host or router), wishing to communicate over a Non-Broadcast, Multi-Access (NBMA) link layer network, to find out the NBMA addresses of a destination terminal if the destination terminal is connected to the same NBMA network as the source.

A conventional address resolution protocol, such as ARP for IP, may not be sufficient to resolve the NBMA address of the destination terminal, since it only applies to terminals belonging to the same IP subnetwork, whereas an NBMA network can consist of multiple logically independent IP subnets.

Once the NBMA address of the destination terminal is resolved, the source may either start sending IP packets to the destination (in a connectionless NBMA network such as SMDS) or may first establish a connection to the destination with the desired bandwidth and QOS characteristics (in a connection-oriented NBMA network such as ATM).

An NBMA network can be non-broadcast either because it technically doesn't support broadcasting (e.g., an X.25 network) or because broadcasting is not feasible for one reason or another (e.g., an SMDS broadcast group or an extended Ethernet would be too large).

Protocol Structure

8	16	32bit
Version	Hop Count	Checksum
Type	Code	Unused
Destination IP address		
Source IP address		
NBMA Len.	NBMA address (variable length)	

• Version -- NARP version number. Currently this value is 1.
• Hop Count -- Indicates the maximum number of NASs that a request or reply is allowed to traverse before being discarded.
• Checksum -- Standard IP checksum over the entire NARP packet (starting with the fixed header).
• Type -- NARP packet type. The NARP Request has a type code 1; NARP Reply has a type code 2.
• Code -- A response to an NARP request may contain cached information. If an authoritative answer is desired, then code 2.
• Source and Destination IP Address -- Respectively, these are the IP addresses of the NARP requestor and the target terminal for which the NBMA address is destined.
• NBMA Length and NBMA Address -- The NBMA length field is the length of the NBMA address of the source terminal in bits.

Related Protocols
ARP

Sponsor Source

NARP is defined by IETF (http://www.ietf.org) in RFC 1735.

Reference
http://www.javvin.com/protocol/rfc1735.pdf
NBMA Address Resolution Protocol (NARP)

NHRP: Next Hop Resolution Protocol

Protocol Description

NBMA Next Hop Resolution Protocol (NHRP) is used by a source station (host or router) connected to a Non-Broadcast, Multi-Access (NBMA) subnetwork to determine the internetworking layer address and NBMA subnetwork addresses of the "NBMA next hop" towards a destination station. If the destination is connected to the NBMA subnetwork, then the NBMA next hop is the destination station itself. Otherwise, the NBMA next hop is the egress router from the NBMA subnetwork that is "nearest" to the destination station. NHRP is intended for use in a multiprotocol internetworking layer environment over NBMA subnetworks.

NHRP Resolution Requests traverse one or more hops within an NBMA subnetwork before reaching the station that is expected to generate a response. Each station, including the source station, chooses a neighboring NHS to which it will forward the NHRP Resolution Request. The NHS selection procedure typically involves applying a destination protocol layer address to the protocol layer routing table which causes a routing decision to be returned. This routing decision is then used to forward the NHRP Resolution Request to the downstream NHS. The destination protocol layer address previously mentioned is carried within the NHRP Resolution Request packet. Note that even though a protocol layer address was used to acquire a routing decision, NHRP packets are not encapsulated within a protocol layer header but rather are carried at the NBMA layer using the encapsulation described in its own header.

Protocol Structure

8	16	24	32 bit
ar$afn		ar$pro.type	
ar$pro.snap			
ar$pro.snap	ar$hopcnt	ar$pkstz	
ar$chksum		ar$extoff	
ar$op.version	ar$op.type	ar$shtl	ar$sstl

• ar$afn -- Defines the type of link layer address being carried.
• ar$pro.type -- This field is an unsigned integer reserved for various uses.
• ar$pro.snap -- Where a protocol has an assigned number in the ar$pro.type space (excluding 0x0080) the short form MUST be used when transmitting NHRP messages. If both Ethertype and NLPID codings exist then when transmitting NHRP messages, the Ethertype coding MUST be used. When ar$pro.type has a value of 0x0080, a snap encoded extension is being used to encode the protocol type.
• ar$hopcnt -- The hop count. This indicates the maximum number of NHSs that an NHRP packet is allowed to traverse before being discarded.
• ar$pktsz -- The total length of the NHRP packet in octets.
• ar$chksum -- The standard IP checksum over the entire NHRP packet.

• ar$extoff -- This field identifies the existence and location of NHRP extensions.
• ar$op.version -- This field indicates what version of generic address mapping and management protocol is represented by this message.
• ar$op.type -- If the ar$op.version is 1 then this field represents the NHRP packet type. Possible values for packet types are:

    1 -- NHRP Resolution Request.
    2 -- NHRP Resolution Reply.
    3 -- NHRP Registration Request.
    4 -- NHRP Registration Reply.
    5 -- NHRP Purge Request.
    6 -- NHRP Purge Reply.
    7 -- NHRP Error Indication.

• ar$shtl -- The type and length of the source NBMA address interpreted in the context of the address family number.
• ar$sstl -- The type and length of the source NBMA subaddress interpreted in the context of the "address family number".

Related Protocols
ARP, NARP

Sponsor Source
NHRP is defined by IETF (http://www.ietf.org) in RFC 2332.

Reference
http://www.javvin.com/protocol/rfc2332.pdf
NBMA Next Hop Resolution Protocol (NHRP)

OSPF: Open Shortest Path First protocol

Protocol Description

Open Shortest Path First (OSPF) is an interior gateway protocol which is used for routing between routers belonging to a single Autonomous System. OSPF uses link-state technology in which routers send each other information about the direct connections and links which they have to other routers. Each OSPF router maintains an identical database describing the Autonomous System's topology. From this database, a routing table is calculated by constructing a shortest- path tree. OSPF recalculates routes quickly in the face of topological changes, utilizing a minimum of routing protocol traffic. OSPF provides support for equal-cost multi-path. An area routing capability is provided, enabling an additional level of routing protection and a reduction in routing protocol traffic. In addition, all OSPF routing protocol exchanges are authenticated.

OSPF routes IP packets based solely on the destination IP address found in the IP packet header. IP packets are routed "as is"; they are not encapsulated in any further protocol headers as they transit the Autonomous System.

OSPF allows sets of networks to be grouped together. Such a grouping is called an area. The topology of an area is hidden from the rest of the Autonomous System. This information hiding enables a significant reduction in routing traffic. Also, routing within the area is determined only by the area's own topology, lending the area protection from bad routing data.

OSPF version 2 (OSPFv2) has been designed expressly for the IPv4 internet environment, including explicit support for CIDR and the tagging of externally-derived routing information. OSPFv2 also provides for the authentication of routing updates and utilizes IP multicast when sending/receiving the updates.

OSPFv2 enables the flexible configuration of IP subnets. Each route distributed by OSPF has a destination and mask. Two different subnets of the same IP network number may have different sizes (i.e., different masks). This is commonly referred to as variable length subnetting. A packet is routed to the best (i.e., longest or most specific) match.

Open Shortest Path First version 3 (OSPFv3), also known as OSPF for IPv6, is the modification of the widely deployed OS-PFv2 (for IPv4) for IPv6 based networks. OSPFv3 has maintained fundamental mechanisms of OSPFv2. Changes between OSPFv2 for IPv4 and OSPFv3 include the following:

1) Addressing semantics have been removed from OSPF packets and the basic LSAs.
2) New LSAs have been created to carry IPv6 addresses and prefixes.
3) OSPF now runs on a per-link basis, instead of on a per-IP-subnet basis.
4) Flooding scope for LSAs has been generalized.
5) Authentication has been removed from the OSPF protocol itself, instead relying on IPv6's Authentication Header and Encapsulating Security Payload.

Protocol Structure

OPSFv2 packet header:

8	16	32bit
Version No.	Packet Type	Packet length
Router ID		
Area ID		
Checksum		AuType
Authentication (64 bits)		

- Version number -- Protocol version number
- Packet type -- Valid types are as follows:
  1 Hello
  2 Database Description
  3 Link State Request
  4 Link State Update
  5 Link State Acknowledgment.
- Packet length -- The length of the protocol packet in bytes. This length includes the standard OSPF header.
- Router ID -- The router ID of the packet's source. In OSPF, the source and destination of a routing protocol packet are the two ends of a (potential) adjacency.
- Area ID -- identifying the area that this packet belongs to. All OSPF packets are associated with a single area. Most travel a single hop only.
- Checksum -- The standard IP checksum of the entire contents of the packet, starting with the OSPF packet header but excluding the 64-bit authentication field.
- AuType -- Identifies the authentication scheme to be used for the packet.
- Authentication -- A 64-bit field for use by the authentication scheme.

OPSFv3 packet header:

8	16	32bit
Version No.	Packet Type	Packet length
Router ID		
Area ID		
Checksum		Instance ID	0

- Version number -- Protocol version number.
- Packet type -- Valid types are as follows:
  1 Hello
  2 Database Description
  3 Link State Request
  4 Link State Update
  5 Link State Acknowledgment.
- Packet length -- The length of the protocol packet in bytes. This length includes the standard OSPF header.
- Router ID -- The router ID of the packet's source. In OSPF, the source and destination of a routing protocol packet are the two ends of a (potential) adjacency.
- Area ID -- Identifying the area that this packet belongs to. All OSPF packets are associated with a single area. Most travel a single hop only.
- Checksum -- The standard IP checksum of the entire contents of the packet, starting with the OSPF packet header but

excluding the 64-bit authentication field.
• Instance ID -- Enables multiple instances of OSPF to be run over a single link.

Related Protocols
IP, IPv4, IPv6, TCP, OSPFv2, OSPFv3

Sponsor Source
OSPF is defined by IETF (http://www.ietf.org) in RFC 2328 (OSPFv2) and RFC 2740 (OSPFv3).

Reference
http://www.javvin.com/protocol/rfc2328.pdf
OSPF (Open Shortest Path First) version 2
http://www.javvin.com/protocol/rfc2740.pdf
OSPF for IPv6 (OSPFv3)

RIP: Routing Information Protocol (RIP2)

Protocol Description
Routing Information Protocol (RIP) is a standard for exchange of routing information among gateways and hosts. This protocol is most useful as an "interior gateway protocol". In a nationwide network such as the current Internet, there are many routing protocols used for the whole network. The network will be organized as a collection of "autonomous systems". Each autonomous system will have its own routing technology, which may well be different for different autonomous systems. The routing protocol used within an autonomous system is referred to as an interior gateway protocol, or "IGP". A separate protocol is used to interface among the autonomous systems. The earliest such protocol, still used in the Internet, is "EGP" (exterior gateway protocol). Such protocols are now usually referred to as inter-AS routing protocols. RIP is designed to work with moderate-size networks using reasonably homogeneous technology. Thus it is suitable as an IGP for many campuses and for regional networks using serial lines whose speeds do not vary widely. It is not intended for use in more complex environments.

RIP2 is an extension of the Routing Information Protocol (RIP) intended to expand the amount of useful information carried in the RIP2 messages and to add a measure of security. RIP2 is an UDP-based protocol. Each host that uses RIP2 has a routing process that sends and receives datagrams on UDP port number 520.

RIP and RIP2 are for the IPv4 network while the RIPng is designed for the IPv6 network, which will be discussed in a separate document.

Protocol Structure

8	16	32bit
Command	Version	Unused
Address family identifier		Route tag (only for RIP2; 0 for RIP)
IP address		
Subnet mask (only for RIP2; 0 for RIP)		
Next hop (only for RIP2; 0 for RIP)		
Metric		

• Command -- The command field is used to specify the purpose of the datagram. There are five commands: Request, Response, Traceon (obsolete), Traceoff (Obsolete) and Reserved.
• Version -- The RIP version number. The current version is 2.
• Address family identifier -- Indicates what type of address is specified in this particular entry. This is used because RIP2 may carry routing information for several different protocols. The address family identifier for IP is 2.
• Route tag -- Attribute assigned to a route which must be preserved and readvertised with a route. The route tag provides a method of separating internal RIP routes (routes for networks within the RIP routing domain) from external RIP routes, which

may have been imported from an EGP or another IGP.
• IP address -- The destination IP address.
• Subnet mask -- Value applied to the IP address to yield the non-host portion of the address. If zero, then no subnet mask has been included for this entry.
• Next hop -- Immediate next hop IP address to which packets to the destination specified by this route entry should be forwarded.
• Metric -- Represents the total cost of getting a datagram from the host to that destination. This metric is the sum of the costs associated with the networks that would be traversed in getting to the destination.

Related Protocols
IP, IPv6, IGP, EGP, RIPng, UDP, TCP

Sponsor Source
RIP is defined by IETF (http://www.ietf.org) RFC1058, RFC2453.

Reference
http://www.javvin.com/protocol/rfc1058.pdf
Routing Information Protocol Specification (Version 1)
http://www.javvin.com/protocol/rfc2453.pdf
RIP Version 2 Specification.

RIPng: Routing Information Protocol next generation for IPv6

Protocol Description
Routing Information Protocol next generation (RIPng), an information routing protocol for the IPv6, is based on protocols and algorithms used extensively in the IPv4 Internet. In an international network, such as the Internet, there are many routing protocols used for the entire network. The network will be organized as a collection of Autonomous Systems (AS). Each AS will have its own routing technology, which may differ among AS's. The routing protocol used within an AS is referred to as an Interior Gateway Protocol (IGP). A separate protocol, called an Exterior Gateway Protocol (EGP), is used to transfer routing information among the AS's. RIPng was designed to work as an IGP in moderate-size AS's. It is not intended for use in more complex environments.

RIPng is one of a class of algorithms known as Distance Vector algorithms. The basic algorithms used by this protocol were used in computer routing as early as 1969 in the ARPANET. However, the specific ancestry of this protocol is within the Xerox network protocols. The PUP protocols used the Gateway Information Protocol to exchange routing information. A somewhat updated version of this protocol was adopted for the Xerox Network Systems (XNS) architecture, with the name Routing Information Protocol (RIP). Berkeley's routed is largely the same as the Routing Information Protocol, with XNS addresses replaced by a more general address format capable of handling IPv4 and other types of address, and with routing updates limited to one every 30 seconds. Because of this similarity, the term Routing Information Protocol (or just RIP) is used to refer to both the XNS protocol and the protocol used by routed.

For the IPv4 network, the corresponding routing information protocols are RIP and RIP2, which are described in a separate document.

Protocol Structure

Command (1 byte)	Version (1 byte)	0 (2 bytes)
Route table entry 1 (20 bytes)		
. .		
Route table entry N (20 bytes)		

• Command -- Two commands are:
    Request -- A request for the responding system to send all or part of its routing table
    Response -- A message containing all or part of the sender's routing table.
• Version -- The version of the protocol. The current version is version 1.
• Route table entry -- Each route table entry contains a destination prefix, the number of significant bits in the prefix and the cost of reaching that destination.

Related Protocols

RIP, RIP2, IP, UDP, TCP, EGP, IGP

Sponsor Source
RIPng is defined by IETF (http://www.ietf.org) RFC2080.

Reference
http://www.javvin.com/protocol/rfc2080.pdf
RIPng for IPv6

RSVP: Resource ReSerVation Protocol

Protocol Description

Resource ReSerVation Protocol (RSVP) is a resource reservation setup protocol designed for quality integrated services over the Internet. RSVP is used by a host to request specific qualities of service from the network for particular application data streams or flows. RSVP is also used by routers to deliver quality-of-service (QoS) requests to all nodes along the path(s) of the flows and to establish and maintain state to provide the requested service. RSVP requests will generally result in resources being reserved in each node along the data path.

RSVP requests resources in only one direction. Therefore, RSVP treats a sender as logically distinct from a receiver, although the same application process may act as both a sender and a receiver at the same time. RSVP operates on top of IPv4 or IPv6, occupying the place of a transport protocol in the protocol stack. However, RSVP does not transport application data but is rather an Internet control protocol, like ICMP, IGMP, or routing protocols. Like the implementations of routing and management protocols, an implementation of RSVP will typically execute in the background, not in the data forwarding path.

RSVP is not a routing protocol by itself; RSVP is designed to operate with current and future unicast and multicast routing protocols. An RSVP process consults the local routing database(s) to obtain routes. In the multicast case, for example, a host sends IGMP messages to join a multicast group and then sends RSVP messages to reserve resources along the delivery path(s) of that group. Routing protocols determine where packets get forwarded; RSVP is only concerned with the QoS of those packets that are forwarded in accordance with routing. In order to efficiently accommodate large groups, dynamic group membership, and heterogeneous receiver requirements, RSVP makes receivers responsible for requesting a specific QoS [RSVP93]. A QoS request from a receiver host application is passed to the local RSVP process. The RSVP protocol then carries the request to all the nodes (routers and hosts) along the reverse data path(s) to the data source(s), but only as far as the router where the receiver's data path joins the multicast distribution tree. As a result, RSVP's reservation overhead is in general logarithmic rather than linear in the number of receivers.

Protocol Structure

4	8	16	32 bit
Version	Flags	Message type	RSVP checksum
Send TTL		(Reserved)	RSVP length

• Version -- The protocol version number, the current version is 1.
• Flags -- No flag bits are defined yet.
• Message type -- Possible values are: 1 Path, 2 Resv, 3 PathErr, 4 ResvErr,, 5 PathTear, 6 ResvTear, 7 ResvConf.
• RSVP checksum -- The checksum for message errors.

• Send TTL -- The IP TTL value with which the message was sent.
• RSVP length -- The total length of the RSVP message in bytes, including the common header and the variable length objects that follow.

Related Protocols
IP, TCP, UDP, RSVP-TE

Sponsor Source
RSVP is defined by IETF (http://www.ietf.org) RFC2205 with an update RFC2750.

Reference
http://www.javvin.com/protocol/rfc2205.pdf
RSVP Functional Specification
http://www.javvin.com/protocol/rfc2750.pdf
RSVP Extensions for Policy Control

VRRP: Virtual Router Redundancy Protocol

Protocol Description
Virtual Router Dedundancy Protocol (VRRP) specifies an election protocol that dynamically assigns responsibility for a virtual router to one of the VRRP routers on a LAN. The VRRP router controlling the IP address(es) associated with a virtual router is called the Master, and forwards packets sent to these IP addresses. The election process provides dynamic fail over in the forwarding responsibility should the Master become unavailable. This allows any of the virtual router IP addresses on the LAN to be used as the default first hop router by end-hosts. The advantage of using VRRP is a higher availability default path without requiring configuration of dynamic routing or router discovery protocols on every end-host. VRRP packets are sent encapsulated in IP packets.

Using VRRP, a virtual IP address can be specified manually or with Dynamic Host Configuration Protocol (DHCP) as a default. A virtual IP address is shared among the routers, with one designated as the master router and the others as backups. In case, the master fails, the virtual IP address is mapped to a backup router's IP address. (This backup becomes the master router.) VRRP can also be used for load balancing. VRRP is part of both IPv4 and IPv6.

Protocol Structure

4	8	16	24	32bit
Version	Type	Virtual Rtr ID	Priority	Count IP Addrs
Auth Type		Advet Int	Checksum	
IP Address 1				
....				
IP Address n				
Authentication Data 1				
Authentication Data 2				

• Version -- The version field specifies the VRRP protocol version of this packet. This version is version 2.
• Type -- The type field specifies the type of this VRRP packet. The only packet type defined in this version of the protocol is: 1 ADVERTISEMENT.
• Virtual Rtr ID -- The Virtual Router Identifier (VRID) field identifies the virtual router this packet is reporting status for.
• Priority -- Specifies the sending VRRP router's priority for the virtual router. VRRP routers backing up a virtual router MUST use priority values between 1 to 254 (decimal).
• Count IP Addresses --The number of IP addresses contained in this VRRP advertisement.
• Auth Type -- Identifies the authentication method being utilized.
• Advertisement Interval -- Indicates the time interval (in seconds) between advertisements.
• Checksum – 16 bit field used to detect data corruption in the VRRP message.
• IP Address(es) -- One or more IP addresses that are associated with the virtual router. The number of addresses included

is specified in the "Count IP Addrs" field. These fields are used for troubleshooting misconfigured routers.

• Authentication Data -- The authentication string is currently only utilized for simple text authentication, similar to the simple text authentication found in the Open Shortest Path First routing protocol (OSPF). It is up to 8 characters of plain text.

Related Protocols
IP, IPv6, DHCP, TCP

Sponsor Source
VRRP is defined by IETF (http://www.ietf.org) RFC2338.

Reference
http://www.javvin.com/protocol/rfc2338.pdf
VRRP Specification

BGMP: Border Gateway Multicast Protocol

Protocol Description
Border Gateway Multicast Protocol (BGMP) is a protocol for inter-domain multicast routing. BGMP natively supports "source-specific multicast" (SSM). To also support "any-source multicast" (ASM), BGMP builds shared trees for active multicast groups, and allows domains to build source-specific, inter-domain, distribution branches where needed. Building upon concepts from PIM-SM and CBT, BGMP requires that each global multicast group be associated with a single root. However, in BGMP, the root is an entire exchange or domain, rather than a single router.

For non-source-specific groups, BGMP assumes that ranges of the multicast address space have been associated with selected domains. Each such domain then becomes the root of the shared domain-trees for all groups in its range. An address allocator will generally achieve better distribution trees if it takes its multicast addresses from its own domain's part of the space, thereby causing the root domain to be local.

BGMP uses TCP as its transport protocol. This eliminates the need to implement message fragmentation, retransmission, acknowledgement, and sequencing. BGMP uses TCP port 264 for establishing its connections. This port is distinct from BGP's port to provide protocol independence, and to facilitate distinguishing between protocol packets.

Two BGMP peers form a TCP connection between one another, and exchange messages to open and confirm the connection parameters. They then send incremental Join/Prune Updates as group memberships change. BGMP does not require periodic refresh of individual entries. KeepAlive messages are sent periodically to ensure the liveness of the connection. Notification messages are sent in response to errors or special conditions. If a connection encounters an error condition, a notification message is sent and the connection is closed if the error is a fatal one.

Protocol Structure

16	24	32bit
Length	Type	Reserved

• Length -- The total length of the message including the header in octets. It allows one to locate in the transport-level stream the start of the next message.

• Type -- The type code of the message. The following type codes are available:

1 OPEN	2 UPDATE
3 NOTIFICATION	4 KEEPALIVE

After a transport protocol connection is established, the first message sent by each side is an OPEN message. If the OPEN message is acceptable, a KEEPALIVE message confirming the OPEN is sent back. Once the OPEN is confirmed, UPDATE, KEEPALIVE, and NOTIFICATION messages may be exchanged.

The format of each message type is different.

Related Protocols
IP, TCP, BGP, PIM-SM

Sponsor Source
BGMP is defined by IETF (http://www.ietf.org).

Reference
http://www.javvin.com/protocol/rfc3913.pdf
Border Gateway Multicast Protocol (BGMP): Protocol Specification

DVMRP: Distance Vector Multicast Routing Protocol

Protocol Description
Distance Vector Multicast Routing Protocol (DVMRP) is an Internet routing protocol that provides an efficient mechanism for connectionless message multicast to a group of hosts across an internetwork. DVMRP is an "interior gateway protocol" (IGP); suitable for use within an autonomous system, but not between different autonomous systems. DVMRP is not currently developed for use in routing non-multicast datagrams, so a router that routes both multicast and unicast datagrams must run two separate routing processes.

DVMRP is developed based upon RIP. DVMRP combines many of the features of RIP with the Truncated Reverse Path Broadcasting (TRPB) algorithm. In addition, to allow experiments to traverse networks that do not support multicasting, a mechanism called tunneling was developed. The key differences of DVMRP from RIP are: RIP routes and forwards datagrams to a particular destination. The purpose of DVMRP is to keep track of the return paths to the source of multicast datagrams.

DVMRP packets are encapsulated in IP datagrams, with an IP protocol number of 2 (the same as IGMP).

Protocol Structure
DVMRP uses the IGMP to exchange routing datagrams. DVMRP datagrams are composed of two portions: a small, fixed length IGMP header, and a stream of tagged data.

4	8	16	24	32 bit
Version	Type	Sub-Type	Checksum	
DVMRP Data stream				

• Version -- It is 1.
• Type -- DVMRP type is 3.
• Sub-type -- The subtype is one of:
　　　1 = Response; the message provides routes to some destination(s).
　　　2 = Request; the message requests routes to some destination(s).
　　　3 = Non-membership report; the message provides non-membership report(s).
　　　4 = Non-membership cancellation; the message cancels previous non-membership report(s).
• Checksum -- One's complement of the one's complement sum of the DVMRP message. The checksum must be calculated upon transmission and must be validated on reception of a packet. The checksum of the DVMRP message should be calculated with the checksum field set to zero.

Related Protocols
IP, IGMP, RIP

Sponsor Source
DVMRP is defined by IETF (http://www.ietf.org) in RFC 1075.

Reference
http://www.javvin.com/protocol/rfc1075.pdf
Distance Vector Multicast Routing Protocol

IGMP: Internet Group Management Protocol

Protocol Description

Internet Group Management Protocol (IGMP), a multicasting protocol in the internet protocols family, is used by IP hosts to report their host group memberships to any immediately neighboring multicast routers. IGMP messages are encapsulated in IP datagrams, with an IP protocol number of 2. IGMP has versions IGMP v1, v2 and v3.

• IGMPv1 -- Hosts can join multicast groups. There are no leave messages. Routers use a time-out based mechanism to discover the groups that are of no interest to the members.
• IGMPv2 -- Leave messages were added to the protocol, allowing group membership termination to be quickly reported to the routing protocol, which is important for high-bandwidth multicast groups and/or subnets with highly volatile group membership.
• IGMPv3 -- A major revision of the protocol allows hosts to specify the list of hosts from which they want to receive traffic. Traffic from other hosts is blocked inside the network. It also allows hosts to block inside the network packets that come from sources that send unwanted traffic.

The variant protocols of IGMP are:
• DVMRP -- Distance Vector Multicast Routing Protocol.
• IGAP -- IGMP for user Authentication Protocol.
• RGMP -- Router-port Group Management Protocol.

Protocol Structure

There are basically 5 types of messages that must be implemented for IGMP v3 to function properly and be compatible with previous versions:

0x11: membership query
0x22: version 3 membership report
0x12: version 1 membership report
0x16: version 2 membership report
0x17 version 2 leave group

As an example, the message format for 0x11 (membership query) is displayed:

8	16	32 bit
Type	Max response time	Checksum
Group address		
RSV	S	QRV	QQIC	Number of Source
Source Address (1)		
...		
Source Address (N)		

• Type -- The message type: 0x11 (Membership query).
• Max Response Time -- Used only in Membership query messages. Specifies the maximum time allowed, in units of 1/10 second, before sending a responding report. In all other messages, it is set to 0 by the sender and ignored by the receiver.

• Checksum -- The checksum for message errors
• Group Address -- The Group address is set to 0 when sending a general query. It is set to the group address being queried, when sending a group specific query or group-and-source-specific query. In a membership report of a leave group message, it holds the IP multicast group address of the group being reported or left.
• RSV -- Reserved; Set to zero on transmission, and ignored on reception.
• QQIC -- Querier's Query Interval Code
• Number of Source (N) -- The number of source addresses in this message.
• Source Address -- The vector of the IP unicast address

The details of other message types can be found in the reference RFC 1112, 2236 and 3376.

Related Protocols
IP, TCP, DVMRP, IGAP, RGMP

Sponsor Source
IGMP is defined by IETF (http://www.ietf.org) RFC1112, RFC2236 and RFC3376.

Reference
http://www.javvin.com/protocol/rfc1112.pdf
IGMP version 1 specification
http://www.javvin.com/protocol/rfc2236.pdf
IGMP version 2 specification
http://www.javvin.com/protocol/rfc3376.pdf
IGMP version 3 specification

MARS: Multicast Address Resolution Server

Protocol Description
Multicast Address Resolution Server (MARS) is a mechanism for supporting IP multicast over an ATM network. A MARS serves a group of nodes (known as a cluster); each node in the cluster is configured with the ATM address of the MARS. The MARS supports multicast through multicast messages of overlaid point-to-multipoint connections or through multicast servers. ATM-based IP hosts and routers use a MARS to support IP multicast over the ATM Forum's UNI 3.0/3.1 point-to-multipoint connection service. Clusters of endpoints share a MARS and use it to track and disseminate information identifying the nodes listed as receivers for given multicast groups.

The MARS protocol has two broad goals: to define a group address registration and membership distribution mechanism that allows UNI 3.0/3.1-based networks to support the multicast service of protocols and to define specific endpoint behaviors for managing point to multipoint VCs to achieve multicasting of layer 3 packets. MARS is an extended analog of the ATM ARP Server. It acts as a registry, associating layer 3 multicast group identifiers with the ATM interfaces representing the group's members. MARS messages support the distribution of multicast group membership information between MARS and endpoints (hosts or routers). Endpoint address resolution entities query the MARS when a layer 3 address needs to be resolved to the set of ATM endpoints making up the group at any one time. Endpoints keep the MARS informed when they need to join or leave particular layer 3 groups. To provide for asynchronous notification of group membership changes, the MARS manages a point to multipoint VC out to all endpoints desiring multicast support. Each MARS manages a cluster of ATM-attached endpoints.

Protocol Structure

Address family (2 bytes)	Protocol identification (7 bytes)		Reserved (3 bytes)

Check-sum (2 bytes)	Exten-sions offset (2 bytes)	Oper-ation code (2 bytes)	Type & length of source ATM Num-ber (1 byte)	Type & length of source ATM subad-dress (1 byte)

• Address family -- Defines the type of link layer addresses being carried.
• Protocol ID -- Contains 2 subfields: 16 bits, protocol type; 40 bits, optional SNAP extension to protocol type.
• Reserved -- This reserved field may be subdivided and assigned specific meanings for other control protocols indicated by the version number.
• Checksum -- This field carries a standard IP checksum calculated across the entire message.
• Extension offset -- This field identifies the existence and loca-

tion of an optional supplementary parameters list.
• Operation code -- This field is divided into 2 subfields: version and type. Version indicates the operation being performed, within the context of the control protocol version indicated by mar$op.version.
• Type and length of ATM source number -- Information regarding the source hardware address.
• Type and length of ATM source subaddress -- Information regarding the source hardware subaddress.

Related Protocols
ATM, UNI, IP

Sponsor Source
MARS is defined by IETF (http://www.ietf.org) RFC2022.

Reference
http://www.javvin.com/protocol/rfc2022.pdf
Support for Multicast over UNI 3.0/3.1 based ATM Networks

MBGP: Multiprotocol BGP

Protocol Description
The multiprotocol BGP (MBGP) feature adds capabilities to BGP to enable multicast routing policy throughout the Internet and to connect multicast topologies within and between BGP autonomous systems. In other words, multiprotocol BGP (MBGP) is an enhanced BGP that carries IP multicast routes. BGP carries two sets of routes, one set for unicast routing and one set for multicast routing. The routes associated with multicast routing are used by the Protocol Independent Multicast (PIM) to build data distribution trees.

Multiprotocol BGP is useful when a link is required to be dedicated to multicast traffic, perhaps to limit which resources are used for which traffic, or if all multicast traffic exchange at one network access point (NAP) is required. Multiprotocol BGP allows a unicast routing topology different from a multicast routing topology.

The only three pieces of information carried by BGP-4 that are IPv4 specific are: (a) the NEXT_HOP attribute (expressed as an IPv4 address); (b) AGGREGATOR (contains an IPv4 address); and (c) Network Layer Reachability Information (NLRI: expressed as IPv4 address prefixes and subnet mask). Any network device implemented with BGPand MBGP, has to have an IPv4 address, which will be used, among other things, in the AGGREGATOR attribute. To enable BGP-4 to support routing for multiple Network Layer protocols, the only two things that have to be added to BGP-4 are: (a) the ability to associate a particular Network Layer protocol with the next hop information; and (b) the ability to associate a particular Network Layer protocol with NLRI.

There are two attributes defined in the MBGP regarding NLRI: 1) MP_REACH_NLRI for the purpose of advertising a feasible route to a peer, permitting a route to advertise the network layer address of the router to be used as the next hop and allowing a given router to report some or all of the subnetwork points of attachment (SNPAs) and 2) MP_UNREACH_NLRI for the purpose of withdrawing multiple unfeasible routes from service.

To provide backward compatibility, as well as to simplify introduction of the multiprotocol capabilities into BGP-4, two new attributes, Multiprotocol Reachable NLRI (MP_REACH_NLRI), and Multiprotocol Unreachable NLRI (MP_UNREACH_NLRI) are used in the MBGP. MP_REACH_NLRI is used to carry the set of reachable destinations together with the next hop information to be used for forwarding to these destinations. MP_UNREACH_NLRI is used to carry the set of unreachable destinations. Both of these attributes are optional and non-transitive. This way a BGP speaker that doesn't support the multiprotocol capabilities will just ignore the information carried in these attributes, and will not pass it to other BGP speakers.
Protocol Structure

Multiprotocol Reachable NLRI - MP_REACH_NLRI (Type Code 14): The attribute is encoded as follows:

2 Bytes	1Byte	1Byte

Address Family Identifier	Subsequent Address Family Identifier	Length of Next Hop Network Address
Network Address of Next Hop (variable)		
Number of SNPAs	Length of first SNPA	First SNPA (variable)	Length of second SNPA (1 Byte)
Second SNPA (variable)	Length of Last SNPA (1 Byte)	Last SNPA (variable)	Network Layer Reachability Information (variable)

• Address Family Identifier -- carries the identity of the Network Layer protocol associated with the Network Address that follows.
• Subsequent Address Family Identifier -- provides additional information about the type of the Network Layer Reachability Information carried in the attribute.
• Length of Next Hop Network Address -- expresses the length of the "Network Address of Next Hop" field as measured in octets.
• Network Address of Next Hop -- a variable length field that contains the Network Address of the next router on the path to the destination system.
• Number of SNPAs -- contains the number of distinct SNPAs to be listed in the following fields. The value 0 may be used to indicate that no SNPAs are listed in this attribute.
• Length of Nth SNPA -- expresses the length of the "Nth SNPA of Next Hop" field as measured in semi-octets
• Nth SNPA of Next Hop -- contains an SNPA of the router whose Network Address is contained in the "Network Address of Next Hop" field.
• Network Layer Reachability Information -- lists NLRI for the feasible routes that are being advertised in this attribute.
Multiprotocol Unreachable NLRI -- MP_UNREACH_NLRI: The attribute is encoded as follows:

Address Family Identifier (2 Bytes)	Subsequent Address Family Identifier (1 Byte)	Withdrawn Routes (variable)

• Address Family Identifier -- carries the identity of the Network Layer protocol associated with the NLRI that follows.
• Subsequent Address Family Identifier -- provides additional information about the type of the Network Layer Reachability Information carried in the attribute.
• Withdrawn Routes -- lists NLRI for the routes that are being withdrawn from service.

Related Protocols
IP, TCP, BGP

Sponsor Source
MBGP is defined by IETF (http://www.ietf.org) RFC2858.

Reference
http://www.javvin.com/protocol/rfc2858.pdf
Multiprotocol Extensions for BGP-4

MOSPF: Multicast Extensions to OSPF

Protocol Description
Multicast Extensions to OSPF (MOSPF) provides enhancements to OSPF Version 2 to support IP multicast routing. The enhancements have been added in a backward-compatible fashion; routers running the multicast additions will interoperate with non-multicast OSPF routers when forwarding regular (unicast) IP data traffic.

MOSPF works by including multicast information in OSPF link state advertisements. An MOSPF router learns which multicast groups are active on which LANs. MOSPF builds a distribution tree for each source/group pair and computes a tree for active sources sending to the group. The tree state is cached, and trees must be recomputed when a link state change occurs or when the cache times out.

MOSPF provides the ability to forward multicast datagrams from one IP network to another through internet routers. MOSPF forwards a multicast datagram on the basis of both the datagram's source and destination. The OSPF link state database provides a complete description of the Autonomous System's topology. By adding a new type of link state advertisement, the group-membership-LSA, the location of all multicast group members is pinpointed in the database. The path of a multicast datagram can then be calculated by building a shortest-path tree rooted at the datagram's source. All branches not containing multicast members are pruned from the tree. These pruned shortest-path trees are initially built when the first datagram is received. The results of the shortest path calculation are then cached for use by subsequent datagrams having the same source and destination.
MOSPF is used internal to a single Autonomous System. When supporting IP multicast over the entire Internet, MOSPF would have to be used in concert with an inter-AS multicast routing protocol such as DVMRP.

Routers running MOSPF works only in internetworks that are using MOSPF but can be intermixed with non-multicast OSPF routers. Both types of routers can interoperate when forwarding regular (unicast) IP data traffic. In MOSPF, just as in the base OSPF protocol, datagrams (multicast or unicast) are routed "as is"; they are not further encapsulated or decapsulated as they transit the Autonomous System.

Protocol Structure
The MOSPF packet formats are the same as for OSPF Version 2. One additional option has been added to the Options field that appears in OSPF Hello packets, Database Description packets and all link state advertisements. This new option indicates a router's/network's multicast capability. The presence of this new option is ignored by all non-multicast routers.

1	2	3	4	5	6	7	8bit
*	*	*	*	*	MC	E	T

• T-bit -- describes the router's TOS capability.
• E-bit -- AS external link advertisements are not flooded into/

through OSPF stub areas. The E-bit ensures that all members of a stub area agree on that area's configuration.
• MC-bit -- describes the multicast capability of the various pieces of the OSPF routing domain.

To support MOSPF, one of OSPF's link state advertisements has been modified, and a new link state advertisement has been added. The format of the router-LSA has been modified to include a new flag indicating whether the router is a wild-card multicast receiver.

The rtype field in the router LSA:

1	2	3	4	5	6	7	8bit
*	*	*	*	W	V	E	B

• bit B -- B is for border . When set, the router is an area border router. These routers forward unicast data traffic between OSPF areas.
• bit E -- E is for external. When set, the router is an AS boundary router (). These routers forward unicast data traffic between Autonomous Systems.
• bit V -- V is for virtual. When set, the router is an endpoint of an active virtual link which uses the described area as its Transit area.
• bit W -- When set, the router is a wild-card multicast receiver. These routers receive all multicast datagrams, regardless of destination. Inter-area multicast forwarders and inter-AS multicast forwarders are sometimes wild-card multicast receivers.

A new link state advertisement, called the group-membership-LSA, has been added to pinpoint multicast group members in the link state database. This new advertisement is neither flooded nor processed by non-multicast routers.

Related Protocols
IP, TCP, OSPF, IGMP

Sponsor Source
MOSPF is defined by IETF (http://www.ietf.org) in RFC 1584.

Reference
http://www.javvin.com/protocol/rfc1584.pdf
Multicast Extensions to OSPF
http://www.javvin.com/protocol/rfc1585.pdf
MOSPF: Analysis and Experience

MSDP: Multicast Source Discovery Protocol

Protocol Description
The Multicast Source Discovery Protocol (MSDP) describes a mechanism to connect multiple PIM Sparse-Mode (PIM-SM) domains together. Each PIM-SM domain uses its own independent RP(s) and does not have to depend on RPs in other domains. Advantages of this approach include:

No Third-party resource dependencies on a domain's RP PIM-SM domains can rely on their own RPs only.

Receiver only Domains: Domains with only receivers get data without globally advertising group membership.

MSDP may be used with protocols other than PIM-SM.

MSDP-speaking routers in a PIM-SM domain have an MSDP peering relationship with MSDP peers in another domain. The peering relationship is made up of a TCP connection in which control information is exchanged. Each domain has one or more connections to this virtual topology.

The purpose of this topology is to allow domains to discover multicast sources from other domains. If the multicast sources are of interest to a domain which has receivers, the normal source-tree building mechanism in PIM-SM will be used to deliver multicast data over an inter-domain distribution tree.

Protocol Structure
MSDP TLV format

8	24bit	Variable
Type	Length	Value

• Type -- Describes the format of the Value field. The following TLV Types are defined:

Code	Type
1	IPv4 Source-Active
2	IPv4 Source-Active Request
3	IPv4 Source-Active Response
4	KeepAlive
5	Reserved (Previously: Notification)
6	MSDP traceroute in progress
7	MSDP traceroute reply

• Length -- Length of Type, Length, and Value fields in octets. Minimum length required is 4 octets, except for Keepalive messages. The maximum TLV length is 9192.
• Value (variable length) -- Format is based on the Type value. The length of the value field is Length field minus 3. All reserved fields in the Value field MUST be transmitted as zeros and ignored on receipt.

Related Protocols

IP, TCP, BGP, PIM-SM, PIM-DM

Sponsor Source
MSDP is circulated by IETF (http://www.ietf.org) as an experimental protocol.

Reference
http://www.javvin.com/protocol/rfc3618.pdf
Multicast Source Discovery Protocol

MZAP: Multicast-Scope Zone Announcement Protocol

Protocol Description
Multicast-Scope Zone Announcement Protocol (MZAP) is for the discovery of the multicast administrative scope zones that are relevant at a particular location. MZAP also provides mechanisms to discover common misconfigurations of administrative scope zones.

The use of administratively-scoped IP multicast allows packets to be addressed to a specific range of multicast addresses such that the packets will not cross configured administrative boundaries, and also allows such addresses to be locally assigned and hence are not required to across administrative boundaries.

The range of administratively-scoped addresses can be subdivided by administrators so that multiple levels of administrative boundaries can be simultaneously supported. As a result, a "multicast scope" is defined as a particular range of addresses which has been given some topological meaning.

Multicast Scope Zone Announcement Protocol (MZAP) allows an entity to learn what scope zones it is within. Typically servers will cache the information learned from MZAP and can then provide this information to applications in a timely fashion upon request using other means, e.g., via MADCAP. MZAP also provides diagnostic information to the boundary routers themselves that enables misconfigured scope zones to be detected.

All MZAP messages are sent over UDP, with a destination port of [MZAP-PORT] and an IPv4 TTL or IPv6 Hop Limit of 255.

Protocol Structure

8	9	16	24	32bit
Version	B	PTYPE	Address Family	NameCount
Message Origin				
Zone ID Address				
Zone Start Address				
Zone End Address				
Encoded Zone Name-1 (variable length)				
...				
Encoded Zone Name-N (variable length)				
			Padding (if needed)	

• Version -- The version number; currently defined as 0.
• B -- Big Scope bit. 0 Indicates that the addresses in the scoped range are not subdividable, and that address allocators may utilize the entire range. If 1, address allocators should not use the entire range, but should learn an appropriate subrange via another mechanism.
Packet Type -- The packet types defined are:
        0 -- Zone Announcement Message (ZAM)
        1 -- Zone Limit Exceeded (ZLE)

2 -- Zone Convexity Message (ZCM)
3 -- Not-Inside Message (NIM)
• Address Family -- Identifies the address family for all addresses in the packet. The families defined for IP are: 1: IPv4; 2: IPv6.
• Name Count -- The number of encoded zone name blocks in this packet. The count may be zero.
• Message Origin -- The IP address of the interface that originated the message.
• Zone Start Address -- The start address for the scope zone boundary. For example, if the zone is a boundary for 239.1.0.0 to 239.1.0.255, then the Zone Start Address is 239.1.0.0.
• Zone End Address -- The ending address for the scope zone boundary. For example, if the zone is a boundary for 239.1.0.0 to 239.1.0.255, then the Zone End Address is 239.1.0.255.
• Zone ID Address -- The lowest IP address of a boundary router that has been observed in the zone originating the message. Together with the Zone Start Address and Zone End Address, it forms a unique ID for the zone. Note that this ID is usually different from the ID of the Local Scope zone in which the origin resides.
• Encoded Zone Name -- Combined from the next fields: D, LangLen, Language Tag, NameLen, Zone Name.

Related Protocols
IP, IPv6, UDP

Sponsor Source
MZAP is defined by IETF (http://www.ietf.org) in RFC 2776.

Reference
http://www.javvin.com/protocol/rfc2776.pdf
Multicast-Scope Zone Announcement Protocol (MZAP)

PGM: Pragmatic General Multicast Protocol

Protocol Description
Pragmatic General Multicast (PGM) is a reliable transport protocol for applications that require ordered or unordered, duplicate-free, multicast data delivery from multiple sources to multiple receivers.

PGM is specifically intended as a workable solution for multicast applications with basic reliability requirements rather than as a comprehensive solution for multicast applications with sophisticated ordering, agreement, and robustness requirements. Its central design goal is simplicity of operation with due regard for scalability and network efficiency.

PGM has no notion of group membership. It simply provides reliable multicast data delivery within a transmit window advanced by a source according to a purely local strategy. Reliable delivery is provided within a source's transmit window from the time a receiver joins the group until it departs. PGM guarantees that a receiver in the group either receives all data packets from transmissions and repairs, or is able to detect unrecoverable data packet loss. PGM supports any number of sources within a multicast group, each fully identified by a globally unique Transport Session Identifier (TSI), but since these sources/sessions operate entirely independently of each other, this specification is phrased in terms of a single source and extends without modification to multiple sources.

More specifically, PGM is not intended for use with applications that depend either upon acknowledged delivery to a known group of recipients, or upon total ordering amongst multiple sources. Rather, PGM is best suited to those applications in which members may join and leave at any time, and that are either insensitive to unrecoverable data packet loss or are prepared to resort to application recovery in the event. Through its optional extensions, PGM provides specific mechanisms to support applications as disparate as stock and news updates, data conferencing, low-delay real-time video transfer, and bulk data transfer.

Protocol Structure
PGM header:

16	32bit
Source Port	Destination Port
Flags	Options	Checksum
Global Source ID	
Global Source ID	TSDU Length
Data :::	

• Source Port -- Data-Destination Port
• Destination Port. Data -- Source Port
• Flags -- Here are the bits definitions:

1	2	3	4	5	6	7	8

Version	0	0	Type

- Version -- PGM version number.
- Type -- Type of message
- Options -- Here are the bits definitions:

1	2	3	4	5	6	7	8
E	N					T	P

    E -- Option Extensions. 1 bit.

    N -- Options are network-significant. 1 bit.

    T -- Packet is a parity packet for a transmission group of variable sized packets. 1 bit.

    P -- Packet is a parity packet. 1 bit.

- Checksum -- Error checking.
- Global Source ID -- A globally unique source identifier.
- TSDU Length -- The length in bytes of the transport data unit exclusive of the transport header.
- Data -- Variable length.

Related Protocols
IP, TCP

Sponsor Source
PGM is circulated by IETF (http://www.ietf.org) as an experimental protocol.

Reference
http://www.javvin.com/protocol/rfc3208.pdf
PGM Reliable Transport Protocol Specification

PIM-DM: Protocol Independent Multicast – Dense Mode

Protocol Description
Protocol Independent Multicast (PIM) refers to a group of multicast routing protocols, each optimized for a different environment. There are two main PIM protocols, PIM Sparse Mode and PIM Dense Mode. A third PIM protocol, Bi-directional PIM (BIDIR-PIM), is still in drafting. All PIM protocols share a common control message format. PIM control messages are sent as raw IP datagrams, either multicast to the link-local ALL PIM ROUTERS multicast group, or unicast to a specific destination. We focus on the Dense Mode in this document.

PIM-DM is mainly designed for multicast LAN applications, while the PIM-SM is for wide area, inter-domain networks. PIM-DM implements the same flood-and-prune mechanism that Distance Vector Multicast Routing Protocol (DVMRP) and other dense mode routing protocols employ. The main difference between DVMRP and PIM-DM is that PIM-DM introduces the concept of protocol independence. PIM-DM can use the routing table populated by any underlying unicast routing protocol to perform reverse path forwarding (RPF) checks.

ISPs typically appreciate the ability to use any underlying unicast routing protocol with PIM-DM because they need not introduce and manage a separate routing protocol just for RPF checks. Unicast routing protocols extended as Multiprotocol Extensions to BGP (MBGP) and Multitopology Routing for IS-IS (M-ISIS) were later employed to build special tables to perform RPF checks, but PIM-DM does not require them.

PIM-DM can use the unicast routing table populated by OSPF, IS-IS, BGP, and so on, or PIM-DM can be configured to use a special multicast RPF table populated by MBGP or M-ISIS when performing RPF checks.

Protocol Structure
The protocol format of PIM-DM is the same as that of PIM-SM:

PIM version	Type	Reserved (Address length)	Checksum

- PIM version -- The current PIM version is 2.
- Type -- Types for specific PIM messages.
- Address length -- Address length in bytes. The length of the address field throughout, in the specific message.
- Reserved -- The value of this field is set to 0, ignore on receipt
- Checksum -- The 16-bit field is the one's complement sum of the entire PIM message.

Related Protocols
PIM-SM, BIDIR-PIM, ICMP, RIP, OSPF, DVMRP, IS-IS, BGP, IGRP, EIGRP

Sponsor Source
PIM-DM is defined by IETF (http://www.ietf.org) in RFC 3973.

Reference
http://www.javvin.com/protocol/rfc3973.pdf
Protocol Independent Multicast - Dense Mode (PIM-DM): Protocol Specification (Revised)

PIM-SM: Protocol Independent Multicast-Sparse Mode

Protocol Description

Protocol Independent Multicast (PIM) refers to a group of multicast routing protocols, each optimized for a different environment. There are two main PIM protocols, PIM Sparse Mode and PIM Dense Mode. A third PIM protocol, Bi-directional PIM (BIDIR-PIM), is still in drafting. All PIM protocols share a common control message format. PIM control messages are sent as raw IP datagrams, either multicast to the link-local ALL PIM ROUTERS multicast group, or unicast to a specific destination. We focus on the Sparse Mode in this document.

PIM-SM is a protocol for efficiently routing to multicast groups that may span wide-area (WAN and inter-domain) internets, while PIM-DM is mainly for LAN. The protocol is not dependent on any particular unicast routing protocol, and is designed to support sparse groups. It uses the traditional IP multicast model of receiver-initiated membership, supports both shared and shortest-path trees, and uses soft-state mechanisms to adapt to changing network conditions. It can use the route information that any routing protocol enters into the multicast Routing Information Base (RIB). Examples of these routing protocols include unicast protocols such as the Routing Information Protocol (RIP) and Open Shortest Path First (OSPF), but multicast protocols that populate the routing tables—such as the Distance Vector Multicast Routing Protocol (DVMRP)—can also be used.

PIM-SM was designed to support the following goals:

• Maintain the traditional IP multicast service model of receiver-initiated multicast group membership. In this model, sources simply put packets on the first-hop Ethernet, without any signaling. Receivers signal to routers in order to join the multicast group that will receive the data.
• Leave the host model unchanged. PIM-SM is a router-to-router protocol, which means that hosts don't have to be upgraded, but that PIM-SM-enabled routers must be deployed in the network.
• Support both shared and source distribution trees. For shared trees, PIM-SM uses a central router, called the Rendezvous Point (RP), as the root of the shared tree. All source hosts send their multicast traffic to the RP, which in turn forwards the packets through a common tree to all the members of the group. Source trees directly connect sources to receivers. There is a separate tree for every source. Source trees are considered shortest-path trees from the perspective of the unicast routing tables. PIM-SM can use either type of tree or both simultaneously.
• Maintain independence from any specific unicast routing protocol (see above).
• Use soft-state mechanisms to adapt to changing network conditions and multicast group dynamics. Soft-state means that, unless it is refreshed, the router's state configuration is short-term and expires after a certain amount of time.

Currently, there are two versions of PIM-SM. We focus on version 2, which is widely deployed.

Protocol Structure
The protocol format of PIM-DM is the same as that of PIM-SM:

PIM version	Type	Reserved (Address length)	Checksum

- PIM version -- The current PIM version is 2.
- Type -- Types for specific PIM messages.
- Address length -- Address length in bytes. The length of the address field throughout, in the specific message.
- Reserved -- The value of this field is set to 0, ignore on receipt
- Checksum -- The 16-bit field is the one's complement sum of the entire PIM message.

Related Protocols
PIM-DM, BIDIR-PIM, ICMP, RIP, OSPF, DVMRP, IS-IS, BGP, IGRP, EIGRP

Sponsor Source
PIM-SM is defined by IETF (http://www.ietf.org) RFC2362.

Reference
http://www.javvin.com/protocol/rfc2362.pdf
PIM-SM: Protocol Specification

MPLS: Multiprotocol Label Switching

Protocol Description
Multiprotocol Label Switching (MPLS) is an architecture for fast packet switching and routing, which operates independent of the layer 2 and layer 3 protocols. MPLS provides a means to map IP addresses to simple, fixed-length labels used by different packet-forwarding and packet-switching technologies. It interfaces to existing routing and switching protocols, such as IP, ATM, Frame Relay, PPP and Ethernet. High-speed switching of data using MPLS is possible because the fixed-length labels are inserted at the very beginning of the packet or cell and can be used by hardware to switch packets quickly between links.In MPLS, data transmission occurs on Label-Switched Paths (LSPs). LSPs are virtual tunnels that are formed by a sequence of labels at each and every node along the path from the source to the destination. Martini proposed "two-label" approach in which two labels are prepended at the ingress Label Switch Router (LSR) to carry Protocol Data Unit (PDU) forward across the entire MPLS network and finally removed at the engress LSR. The first label, called a Tunnel Label, decides which LSP will be used to get packets from the ingress LSR to the engress LSR. The second label, called a VC Label, provides Layer 2 forwarding information at egress LSR. Martini method is the most popular way for encapsulating of layer 2 protocols such as Frame Relay, ATM, or Ethernet.

MPLS utilizes existing IP routing protocols such as Border Gateway Protocol (BGP), Resource ReSerVation Protocol (RSVP) and Open Shortest Path First (OSPF), etc. MPLS has also defined a new set of protocols such as LDP, CR-LDP, RSVP-TE for more effective signaling and routing. The industry is developing more new standards such as VPLS, HVPLS and GMPLS, to fully extend its capabilities.

MPLS has mechanisms to manage traffic flows of various granularities for the purpose of traffic management and QoS. Specifically, MPLS provides a rich set of traffic management capabilities in the areas of traffic policing, congestion management, traffic shapping and priority queuing.

In summary, MPLS is designed to address many current network problems such as networks speed, scalability, quality of service (QoS) management and traffic engineering. With its powerful new features and abilities to interface with legacy technologies, MPLS has become a solution for the next generation backbone networks for multiple services such as data, voice and video over the same network.
Generalized MPLS (GMPLS), a newer standard, extends the MPLS capabilities to cover multiple underlay traffic technologies such as TDM, FDM, Fiber, Optical etc. with better management and provisioning schemes. In this section, we focus on the MPLS framework. Other protocols in the MPLS suite and GMPLS will be discussed in separate documents.

Protocol Structure
MPLS label structure:

	20	23	24	32bit

Label	Exp	S	TTL

• Label -- Label Value carries the actual value of the Label. When a labeled packet is received, the label value at the top of the stack is looked up and the system learns:

    a) the next hop to which the packet is to be forwarded;

    b) the operation to be performed on the label stack before forwarding; this operation may be to replace the top label stack entry with another, or to pop an entry off the label stack, or to replace the top label stack entry and then to push one or more additional entries on the label stack.

• Exp -- Experimental Use: Reserved for experimental use.
• S -- Bottom of Stack: This bit is set to one for the last entry in the label stack, and zero for all other label stack entries
• TTL -- Time to Live field is used to encode a time-to-live value.

The MPLS architecture protocol family includes:

• MPLS related Routing and Signaling Protocols, such as OSPF, RSVP, IS-IS, BGP, ATM PNNI, etc.
• LDP: Label Distribution Protocol.
• CR-LDP: Constraint-Based LDP
• RSVP-TE: Resource Reservation Protocol – Traffic Engineering

The following figure shows the MPLS protocol stack:

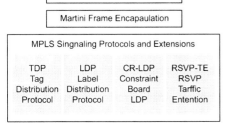

Figure 2-6: MPLS protocol stack

The structure of each protocol will be discussed in separate documents.

Related Protocols
LDP, CR-LDP, RSVP-TE, IP, ATM, RSVP, OSPF, GMPLS

Sponsor Source
MPLS is defined by IETF (http://www.ietf.org) RFC3031 and RFC 3032.

Reference
http://www.javvin.com/protocol/rfc3031.pdf
Multiprotocol Label Switching Architecture
http://www.javvin.com/protocol/rfc3032.pdf

MPLS Label Stack Encoding
http://www.javvin.com/protocol/rfc3443.pdf
Time To Live (TTL) Processing in Multi-Protocol Label Switching (MPLS) Networks
http://www.javvin.com/protocol/rfc3036.pdf
LDP Specification
http://www.javvin.com/protocol/rfc3209.pdf
RSVP-TE: Extensions to RSVP for LSP Tunnels
http://www.javvin.com/protocol/rfc3212.pdf
Constraint-Based LSP Setup using LDP
http://www.javvin.com/protocol/rfc3213.pdf
Applicability Statement for CR-LDP
http://www.faqs.org/ftp/pub/internet-drafts/draft-martini-l2circuit-encap-mpls-12.txt
Encapsulation Methods for Transport of Layer 2 Frames Over IP and MPLS Networks

GMPLS: Generalized Multi-protocol Label Switching

Protocol Description

Generalized Multiprotocol Label Switching (GMPLS) enhances MPLS architecture by the complete separation of the control and data planes of various networking layers. GMPLS enables a seamless interconnection and convergence of new and legacy networks by allowing end-to-end provisioning, control and traffic engineering even when the start and the end nodes belong to heterogeneous networks.

GMPLS is based on the IP routing and addressing models. This assumes that IPv4 and/or IPv6 addresses are used to identify interfaces but also that traditional (distributed) IP routing protocols are reused. The common control plane promises to simplify network operation and management by automating end-to-end provisioning of connections, managing network resources, and providing the level of QoS that is expected in the new applications.

While the technology used by the GMPLS control plane remains IP-based, the data plane (traffic plane) can now diversify to include more varieties of traffic (TDM, Lambda, packet, and fiber, etc). Generalized MPLS (GMPLS) supports multiple types of switching, i.e., the addition of support for TDM, lambda, and fiber (port) switching. In summary, GMPLS extends MPLS functionality by establishing and provisioning paths for:

- TDM paths, where time slots are the labels (SONET).
- FDM paths, where electromagnetic frequency is the label (light waves).
- Space division multiplexed paths, where the label indicates the physical position of data (Photonic Cross-connect).

GMPLS is based on the Traffic Engineering (TE) extensions to MPLS(MPLS-TE). The biggest addition in the GMPLS protocol suite is a new signaling protocol, Link Management Protocol (LMP), to establish, release and manage connections between two adjacent GMPLS-capable nodes. Other protocols RSVP-TE, OSPF-TE, CR-LDP-TE and IS-IS-TE, where OSPF-TE and IS-IS-TE are extended from the original protocols for GMPLS, are used in the GMPLS architecture.

Protocol Structure

GMPLS Protocol Suite Overview:

Protocols		Description
Routing	OSPF–TE, IS–IS–TE	Routing protocols for the auto-discovery of network topology, advertise resource availability.
Signaling	RSVP–TE, CR–LDP-TE	Signaling protocols for the establishment of traffic-engineered LSPs.
Link Management	LMP	Control-Channel Management Link-Connectivity Verification Link-Property Correlation Fault Isolation

GMPLS Protocol Stack Diagram

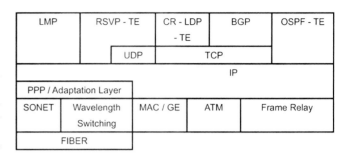

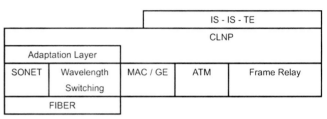

Figure 2-7: GMPLS Protocol Stack Diagram

Related Protocols

MPLS, LDP, CR-LDP, RSVP-TE, IP, ATM, RSVP, OSPF-TE, IS-IS-TE, LMP

Sponsor Source

GMPLS architecture is defined by IETF (http://www.ietf.org) RFC3945.

Reference

http://www.ietf.org/html.charters/ccamp-charter.html
GMPLS Charter
http://www.javvin.com/protocol/rfc3031.pdf
Multiprotocol Label Switching Architecture
http://www.javvin.com/protocol/rfc3945.pdf
Generalized Multi-Protocol Label Switching (GMPLS) Architecture

CR-LDP : Constraint-based LDP

Protocol Description

Constraint-based LDP (CR-LDP), is one of the protocols in the MPLS architecture. It contains extensions for LDP to extend its capabilities such as setup paths beyond what is available for the routing protocol. For instance, an LSP (Label Switched Path) can be setup based on explicit route constraints, QoS constraints, and other constraints. Constraint-based routing (CR) is a mechanism used to meet Traffic Engineering requirements. These requirements are met by extending LDP for support of constraint-based routed label switched paths (CR-LSPs). Other uses for CR-LSPs include MPLS-based VPNs.

Protocol Structure

CR-LDP has the same structure as LDP except for the following additional TLV parameters.

Value	Parameter
821	LSPID
822	ResCls
503	Optical Session Parameters
800	Explicit Route
801-804	ER-Hop TLVS
810	Traffic Parameters
820	Preemption
823	Route Pinning
910	Optical Interface Type
920	Optical Trail Desc
930	Optical Label
940	Lambada Set

Related Protocols

MPLS, LDP, RSVP-TE, IP, ATM, RSVP, OSPF

Sponsor Source

CR-LDP is specified by IETF (http://www.ietf.org) RFC3212.

Reference

http://www.javvin.com/protocol/rfc3031.pdf
Multiprotocol Label Switching Architecture
http://www.javvin.com/protocol/rfc3036.pdf
LDP Specification
http://www.javvin.com/protocol/rfc3212.pdf
Constraint-Based LSP Setup using LDP
http://www.javvin.com/protocol/rfc3213.pdf
Applicability Statement for CR-LDP

LDP: Label Distribution Protocol

Protocol Description

Label Distribution Protocol (LDP) is a key protocol in the MPLS (Multi Protocol Label Switching) architecture. In the MPLS network, 2 label switching routers (LSR) must agree on the meaning of the labels used to forward traffic between and through them. LDP defines a set of procedures and messages by which one LSR (Label Switched Router) informs another of the label bindings it has made. The LSR uses this protocol to establish label switched paths through a network by mapping network layer routing information directly to data-link layer switched paths.

Two LSRs (Label Switched Routers) which use LDP to exchange label mapping information are known as LDP peers and they have an LDP session between them. In a single session, each peer is able to learn about the others label mappings, in other words, the protocol is bi-directional.

Protocol Structure

2 bytes	2 bytes
Version	PDU Length
LDP Identifier (6 bytes)	
LDP Messages	

• Version -- The protocol version number. The present number is 1.
• PDU Length -- The total length of the PDU excluding the version and the PDU length field.
• LDP identifier -- This field uniquely identifies the label space of the sending LSR for which this PDU applies. The first 4 octets encode the IP address assigned to the LSR. The lst 2 indicate a label space within the LSR.
LDP messages -- All LDP messages have the following format:

U	Message type	Message length
Message ID		
Parameters		

• U -- The U bit is an unknown message bit.
• Message type -- The type of message. The following message types exist: Notification, Hello, Initialization, Keep Alive, Address, Address Withdraw, Label Request, Label Withdraw, Label Release, and Unknown Message name.
• Message length -- The length in octets of the message ID, mandatory parameters and optional parameters
• Message ID -- 32-bit value used to identify the message.
• Parameters -- The parameters contain the TLVs. There are both mandatory and optional parameters. Some messages have no mandatory parameters, and some have no optional parameters.

TLV format:

U	F	Type	Length
Value			

```
                TLV format
```

- U -- The U bit is an unknown TLV bit.
- F -- Forward unknown TLV bit.
- Type -- Encodes how the Value field is to be interpreted.
- Length -- Specifies the length of the Value field in octets
- Value -- Octet string of Length octets that encodes information to be interpreted as specified by the Type field.

Related Protocols
MPLS, CR-LDP, RSVP-TE, IP, ATM, RSVP, OSPF

Sponsor Source
LDP is specified by IETF (http://www.ietf.org) RFC3036.

Reference
http://www.javvin.com/protocol/rfc3031.pdf
Multiprotocol Label Switching Architecture
http://www.javvin.com/protocol/rfc3036.pdf
LDP Specification

RSVP-TE: Resource Reservation Protocol - Traffic Extension

Protocol Description
The Resource Reservation Protocol – Traffic Extension (RSVP-TE) is an addition to the RSVP protocol for establishing label switched paths (LSPs) in MPLS networks. The extended RSVP protocol supports the instantiation of explicitly routed LSPs, with or without resource reservations. It also supports smooth rerouting of LSPs, preemption, and loop detection.

The RSVP protocol defines a session as a data flow with a particular destination and transport-layer protocol. However, when RSVP and MPLS are combined, a flow or session can be defined with greater flexibility and generality. The ingress node of an LSP (Label Switched Path) uses a number of methods to determine which packets are assigned a particular label. Once a label is assigned to a set of packets, the label effectively defines the flow through the LSP. We refer to such an LSP as an LSP tunnel because the traffic through it is opaque to intermediate nodes along the label switched path. New RSVP Session, Sender and Filter Spec objects, called LSP Tunnel IPv4 and LSP Tunnel IPv6 have been defined to support the LSP tunnel feature. The semantics of these objects, from the perspective of a node along the label switched path, is that traffic belonging to the LSP tunnel is identified solely on the basis of packets arriving from the "previous hop" (PHOP) with the particular label value(s) assigned by this node to upstream senders to the session. In fact, the IPv4(v6) that appears in the object name only denotes that the destination address is an IPv4(v6) address. When referring to these objects generically, the qualifier LSP Tunnel is used.

In some applications it is useful to associate sets of LSP tunnels, such as during reroute operations or in spreading a traffic trunk over multiple paths, such sets are called TE tunnels. To enable the identification and association of the LSP tunnels, two identifiers are carried. A tunnel ID is part of the Session object. The Session object uniquely defines a traffic engineered tunnel. The Sender and Filter Spec objects carry an LSP ID. The Sender (or Filter Spec) object, together with the Session object, uniquely identifies an LSP tunnel.

Protocol Structure
Apart from the existing message types listed in RSVP an additional message type is available:

Value	Message type
14	Hello

In addition, the following additional Protocol Object Types exist:

Value	Message type
16	Label
19	Optical

20	Explicit Route
21	Record Route
22	Hello
207	Attribute Session

Related Protocols
MPLS, LDP, CR-LDP, IP, ATM, RSVP, OSPF

Sponsor Source
RSVP-TE is defined by IETF (http://www.ietf.org) RFC3209.

Reference
http://www.javvin.com/protocol/rfc3031.pdf
Multiprotocol Label Switching Architecture
http://www.javvin.com/protocol/rfc3209.pdf
RSVP-TE: Extensions to RSVP for LSP Tunnels

ARP and InARP: Address Resolution Protocol and Inverse ARP

Protocol Description
Address Resolution Protocol (ARP) performs mapping of an IP address to a physical machine address (MAC address for Ethernet) that is recognized in the local network. For example, in IP Version 4, an address is 32 bits long. In an Ethernet local area network, however, addresses for attached devices are 48 bits long. A table, usually called the ARP cache, is used to maintain a correlation between each MAC address and its corresponding IP address. ARP provides the rules for making this correlation and providing address conversion in both directions.

Since protocol details differ for each type of local area network, there are separate ARP specifications for Ethernet, Frame Relay, ATM, Fiber Distributed-Data Interface, HIPPI, and other protocols.

Inverse Address Resolution Protocol (InARP) is an addition to ARP to provide address mapping in Frame Relay environment. Basic InARP operates essentially the same as ARP with the exception that InARP does not broadcast requests, since the hardware address of the destination station is already known in the Frame Relay network.

There is a Reverse ARP (RARP) for host machines that don't know their IP address. RARP enables them to request their IP address from the gateway's ARP cache. Details of RARP are presented in a separate document.

Protocol Structure
ARP and InARP have the same structure:

16		32 bit
Hardware Type		Protocol Type
HLen	Plen	Operation
Sender Hardware Address		
Sender Protocol Address		
Target Hardware Address		
Target Protocol Address		

• Hardware type -- Specifies a hardware interface type for which the sender requires a response.
• Protocol type -- Specifies the type of high-level protocol address the sender has supplied.
• Hlen -- Hardware address length.
• Plen -- Protocol address length.
• Operation -- The values are as follows:
      1 -- ARP request.
      2 -- ARP response.
      3 -- RARP request.
      4 -- RARP response.
      5 -- Dynamic RARP request.

6 -- Dynamic RARP reply.
7 -- Dynamic RARP error.
8 -- InARP request.
9 -- InARP reply.
• Sender hardware address -- HLen bytes in length.
• Sender protocol address -- PLen bytes in length.
• Target hardware address -- HLen bytes in length.
• Target protocol address -- PLen bytes in length.

Related Protocols
ARP, RARP, InARP

Sponsor Source
ARP and InARP are defined by IETF (http://www.ietf.org) in RFC 826, 2390, 2625.

Reference
http://www.javvin.com/protocol/rfc826.pdf
An Ethernet Address Resolution Protocol
http://www.javvin.com/protocol/rfc2390.pdf
Inverse Address Resolution Protocol (Frame Relay)
http://www.javvin.com/protocol/rfc2625.pdf
IP and ARP over Fibre Channel

IPCP and IPv6CP: IP Control Protocol and IPv6 Control Protocol

Protocol Description
IP Control Protocol (IPCP) and IPv6 Control Protocol (IPv6CP) define the Network Control Protocol for establishing and configuring the Internet Protocol or IPv6 over PPP, and a method to negotiate and use Van Jacobson TCP/IP header compression with PPP.

IPCP is responsible for configuring, enabling, and disabling the IP protocol modules on both ends of the point-to-point link. IPCP uses the same packet exchange mechanism as the Link Control Protocol (LCP). IPCP packets may not be exchanged until PPP has reached the Network-Layer Protocol phase. IPCP packets received before this phase is reached should be silently discarded.

Before any IP packets may be communicated, PPP must reach the Network-Layer Protocol phase, and the IP Control Protocol must reach the Opened state.

Van Jacobson TCP/IP header compression reduces the size of the TCP/IP headers to as few as three bytes. This can be a significant improvement on slow serial lines, particularly for interactive traffic.

The IP Compression Protocol Configuration Option is used to indicate the ability to receive compressed packets. Each end of the link must separately request this option if bidirectional compression is desired.

IPv6CP is responsible for configuring, enabling, and disabling the IPv6 protocol modules on both ends of the point-to-point link. IPv6CP uses the same packet exchange mechanism as the Link Control Protocol (LCP). IPv6CP packets may not be exchanged until PPP has reached the Network-Layer Protocol phase. IPv6CP packets received before this phase is reached should be silently discarded.

Protocol Structure
IPCP and IPv6CP configuration option packet header:

8	16	32bit
Type	Length	Configuration Option

• Type – 1 for IP-Address, 2 for IP-Compression Protocol, and 3 for IP-Address
• Length >= 4
• Configuration Option - The field is two octets and indicates one of the following options:
 For IPCP:
  Type 1: IP-Addresses
  Type 2: IP-Compression Protocol
  Type 3: IP-Address.
 For IPv6CP:
  Type 1: Interface – Identifier
  Type 2: IPv6-Compression Protocol
IPCP and IPv6CP header structure:

8	16	32bit
Code	Identifier	Length
Data (variable)		

- Code -- Specifies the function to be performed.
- Identifier -- Used to match requests and replies.
- Length -- Size of the packet including the header.
- Data -- Zero or more bytes of data as indicated by the Length. This field may contain one or more Options.

Related Protocols
IP, IPv6, PPP, TCP, Van Jacobson

Sponsor Source
IPCP is defined by IETF (http://www.ietf.org) in RFC 1332 and IPv6CP is defined in RFC 2472.

Reference
http://www.javvin.com/protocol/rfc1332.pdf
The PPP Internet Protocol Control Protocol (IPCP).
http://www.javvin.com/protocol/rfc2472.pdf
IP Version 6 over PPP
http://www.javvin.com/protocol/rfc3241.pdf
Robust Header Compression (ROHC) over PPP.
http://www.javvin.com/protocol/rfc3544.pdf
IP Header Compression over PPP.

RARP: Reverse Address Resolution Protocol

Protocol Description
Reverse Address Resolution Protocol (RARP) allows a physical machine in a local area network to request its IP address from a gateway server's Address Resolution Protocol (ARP) table or cache. A network administrator creates a table in a local area network's gateway router that maps the physical machines' (or Media Access Control - MAC) addresses to corresponding Internet Protocol addresses. When a new machine is set up, its RARP client program requests its IP address from the RARP server on the router. Assuming that an entry has been set up in the router table, the RARP server will return the IP address to the machine, which can store it for future use.
RARP is available for Ethernet, Fiber Distributed-Data Interface, and Token Ring LANs. It is now obsoleted by BOOTP, which has richer features than RARP.

Protocol Structure
The protocol header for RARP is the same as for ARP:

	16	32bit
Hardware Type		Protocol Type
Hlen	Plen	Operation
Sender Hardware Address		
Sender Protocol Address		
Target Hardware Address		
Target Protocol Address		

- Hardware type -- Specifies a hardware interface type for which the sender requires a response.
- Protocol type -- Specifies the type of high-level protocol address the sender has supplied.
- Hlen -- Hardware address length.
- Plen -- Protocol address length.
- Operation -- The values are as follows:
  - 1 -- ARP request.
  - 2 -- ARP response.
  - 3 -- RARP request.
  - 4 -- RARP response.
  - 5 -- Dynamic RARP request.
  - 6 -- Dynamic RARP reply.
  - 7 -- Dynamic RARP error.
  - 8 -- InARP request.
  - 9 -- InARP reply.
- Sender hardware address -- HLen bytes in length.
- Sender protocol address -- PLen bytes in length.
- Target hardware address -- HLen bytes in length.
- Target protocol address -- PLen bytes in length.

Related Protocols
ARP, InARP, BOOTP

Sponsor Source
RARP is defined by IETF (http://www.ietf.org) in RFC 903.

Reference

http://www.javvin.com/protocol/rfc903.pdf
Reverse Address Resolution Protocol

SLIP: Serial Line IP

Protocol Description

Serial Line IP (SLIP) is used for point-to-point serial connections running TCP/IP. SLIP is commonly used on dedicated serial links and sometimes for dialup purposes, and is usually used with line speeds between 1200bps and 19.2Kbps. SLIP is useful for allowing mixes of hosts and routers to communicate with one another (host-host, host-router and router-router are all common SLIP network configurations).

SLIP is merely a packet framing protocol: SLIP defines a sequence of characters that frame IP packets on a serial line. It does not provide addressing, packet type identification, error detection/correction or compression mechanisms.

The SLIP protocol defines two special characters: END and ESC. END is octal 300 (decimal 192) and ESC is octal 333 (decimal 219). To send a packet, a SLIP host simply starts sending the data in the packet. If a data byte is the same code as the END character, a two byte sequence of ESC and octal 334 (decimal 220) is sent instead. If it the same as an ESC character, a two byte sequence of ESC and octal 335 (decimal 221) is sent instead. When the last byte in the packet has been sent, an END character is then transmitted.

Because there is no 'standard' SLIP specification, there is no real defined maximum packet size for SLIP. It is probably best to accept the maximum packet size used by the Berkeley UNIX SLIP drivers: 1006 bytes including the IP and transport protocol headers (not including the framing characters).

Compressed Serial Line IP (CSLIP) performs the Van Jacobson header compression on outgoing IP packets. This compression improves throughput for interactive sessions noticeably.

Today, SLIP is largely replaced by the Point–to-Point Protocol (PPP), which is more feature rich and flexible.

Related Protocols
IP, TCP, PPP, Van Jacobson

Sponsor Source
SLIP is defined by IETF (http://www.ietf.org) in RFC 1055.

Reference
http://www.javvin.com/protocol/rfc1055.pdf
A Nonstandard for Transmission of IP Datagramsover serial Lines: SLIP

Network Security Technologies and Protocols

Description

Network security covers such issues as network communication privacy, information confidentiality and integrity over network, controlled access to restricted network domains and sensitive information, and using the public network such as Internet for private communications. To address these issues, various network and information security technologies have been developed by various organizations and technology vendors. Here is a summary of the technologies:

AAA: Authorization, Authentication and Accounting is a technology for intelligently controlling access to network resources, enforcing policies, auditing usage, and providing the information necessary to bill for services. Authentication provides a way of identifying a user, typically by having the user enter a valid user name and valid password before access is granted. The authorization process determines whether the user has the authority to access certain information or some network sub-domains. Accounting measures the resources a user consumes while using the network, which includes the amount of system time or the amount of data a user has sent and/or received during a session, which could be used for authorization control, billing, trend analysis, resource utilization, and capacity planning activities. A dedicated AAA server or a program that performs these functions often provides authentication, authorization, and accounting services.

VPN: Virtual Private Network is a technology allowing private communications by business and individuals, such as remote access to a corporate network or using a public telecommunication infrastructure, such as the Internet. A virtual private network can also be a specially configured network over the public network infrastructure that is only used by one organization. Various network-tunneling technologies such as L2TP have been developed to reach this goal. Using encryption technologies such as IPsec could further enhance information privacy over network and virtual private networks.

Firewall: Firewall is a software program or hardware device that filters the information coming through the Internet connection into a private network or computer system. Firewalls use one or more of three methods to control traffic flowing in and out the network:

• Packet filtering - Packets are analyzed against a set of filters. Packets that make it through the filters are sent to the requesting system and all others are discarded.
• Proxy service - Information from the Internet is retrieved by the firewall and then sent to the requesting system and vice versa.
• Stateful inspection - compares certain key parts of packets passing through with a database of trusted information. Outgoing information from inside the firewall is monitored for specific defining characteristics, and incoming information is then compared with these characteristics. If the comparison yields a reasonable match, the information is allowed through. Otherwise it is discarded.

Protocols

The key protocols for AAA and VPN:

Authentication Authorization Accounting	Kerberos: Network Authentication Protocol
	RADIUS: Remote Authentication Dial In User Service
	SSH: Secure Shell Protocol
	TACACS: Terminal Access Controller Access Control Protocol (and TACACS+)

Tunneling	L2F: Level 2 Forwarding protocol
	L2TP: Layer 2 Tunneling Protocol
	PPTP: Point to Point Tunneling Protocol
Secured Routing	DiffServ: Differentiated Service
	GRE: Generic Routing Encapsulation
	IPsec: Security Architecture for IP network
	IPsec AH: IPsec Authentication Header
	IPsec ESP: IPsecEncapsulating Security Payload
	IPsec IKE: Internet Key Exchange Protocol
	IPsec ISAKMP: Internet Security Association and Key Management Protocol
	TLS: Transport Layer Security Protocol
Others	Socks: Protocol for sessions traversal across firewall securely

Reference

http://www.cisco.com/univercd/cc/td/doc/cisintwk/ito_doc/security.htm
Securities Technologies

Kerberos: Network Authentication Protocol

Protocol Description

Kerberos is a network authentication protocol. Kerberos is designed to provide strong authentication for client/server applications by using secret-key cryptography. This is accomplished without relying on authentication by the host operating system, without basing trust on host addresses, without requiring physical security of all the hosts on the network, and under the assumption that packets traveling along the network can be read, modified, and inserted at will. Kerberos performs authentication under these conditions as a trusted third-party authentication service by using conventional cryptography, i.e., shared secret key.

The authentication process proceeds as follows: A client sends a request to the authentication server (AS) requesting "credentials" for a given server. The AS responds with these credentials, encrypted in the client's key. The credentials consist of 1) a "ticket" for the server and 2) a temporary encryption key (often called a "session key"). The client transmits the ticket (which contains the client's identity and a copy of the session key, both encrypted in the server's key) to the server. The session key (now shared by the client and server) is used to authenticate the client, and may optionally be used to authenticate the server. It may also be used to encrypt further communication between the two parties or to exchange a separate sub-session key to be used to encrypt further communication. The authentication exchanges mentioned above require read-only access to the Kerberos database. Sometimes, however, the entries in the database must be modified, such as when adding new principals or changing a principal's key. This is done using a protocol between a client and a third Kerberos server, the Kerberos Administration Server (KADM). The administration protocol is not described in this document. There is also a protocol for maintaining multiple copies of the Kerberos database, but this can be considered an implementation detail and may vary to support different database technologies.

Protocol Structure

Kerberos messages:

• The Client/Server Authentication Exchange

Message direction	Message type
Client to Kerberos	KRB_AS_REQ
Kerberos to client	KRB_AS_REP or KRB_ERROR

• The Client/Server Authentication Exchange

Message direction	Message type
Client to Application server	KRB_AP_REQ
[optional] Application server to client	KRB_AP_REP or KRB_ERROR

• The Ticket-Granting Service (TGS) Exchange

Message direction	Message type
Client to Kerberos	KRB_TGS_REQ
Kerberos to client	KRB_TGS_REP or KRB_ERROR

• The KRB_SAFE Exchange
• The KRB_PRIV Exchange
• The KRB_CRED Exchange

Related Protocols

RADIUS, TACACS+

Sponsor Source

Kerberos is defined by MIT.

Reference

http://www.javvin.com/protocol/rfc1510.pdf
The Kerberos Network Authentication Service (V5)
http://www.javvin.com/protocol/rfc1964.pdf
The Kerberos Version 5 GSS-API Mechanism
http://web.mit.edu/kerberos/www/
Kerberos: The Network Authentication Protocol

RADIUS: Remote Authentication Dial In User Service

Protocol Description

Remote Authentication Dial In User Service (RADIUS) is a protocol for carrying authentication, authorization, and configuration information between a Network Access Server which desires to authenticate its links and a shared Authentication Server. RADIUS uses UDP as the transport protocol. RADIUS also carries accounting information between a Network Access Server and a shared Accounting Server.

Key features of RADIUS are:

Client/Server Model: A Network Access Server (NAS) operates as a client of RADIUS. The client is responsible for passing user information to designated RADIUS servers, and then acting on the response which is returned. RADIUS servers are responsible for receiving user connection requests, authenticating the user, and then returning all configuration information necessary for the client to deliver service to the user. A RADIUS server can act as a proxy client to other RADIUS servers or other kinds of authentication servers.

Network Security: Transactions between the client and RADIUS server are authenticated through the use of a shared secret, which is never sent over the network. In addition, any user passwords are sent encrypted between the client and RADIUS server, to eliminate the possibility that someone snooping on an insecure network could determine a user's password.

Flexible Authentication Mechanisms: The RADIUS server can support a variety of methods to authenticate a user. When it is provided with the user name and original password given by the user, it can support PPP PAP or CHAP, UNIX login, and other authentication mechanisms.

Extensible Protocol: All transactions are comprised of variable length Attribute-Length-Value 3-tuples. New attribute values can be added without disturbing existing implementations of the protocol.

Protocol Structure

8	16	32 bit
Code	Identifier	Length
Authenticator (16 bytes)		

• Code -- The message types are described as follows:
    1 -- Access-Request
    2 -- Access-Accept
    3 -- Access-Reject
    4 -- Accounting-Request
    5 -- Accounting-Response
    11 -- Access-Challenge
    12 -- Status-Server (experimental)
    13 -- Status-Client (experimental)
    255 -- Reserved
• Identifier -- The identifier matches requests and replies.
• Length -- The message length including the header.

• Authenticator -- A field used to authenticate the reply from the radius server and in the password hiding algorithm.

Related Protocols
UDP, CHAP, RAP

Sponsor Source
RADIUS is defined by IETF (http://www.ietf.org) in RFC 2865 and 2866.

Reference
http://www.javvin.com/protocol/rfc2865.pdf
Remote Authentication Dial In User Service (RADIUS)
http://www.javvin.com/protocol/rfc2866.pdf
RADIUS Accounting

SSH: Secure Shell Protocol

Protocol Description
Secure Shell Protocol (SSH) is a protocol for secure remote login and other secure network services over an insecure network. SSH consists of three major components:

The Transport Layer Protocol [SSH-TRANS] provides server authentication, confidentiality, and integrity. It may optionally also provide compression. The transport layer will typically be run over a TCP/IP connection, but might also be used on top of any other reliable data stream. SSH-Trans provides strong encryption, cryptographic host authentication, and integrity protection. Authentication in this protocol level is host-based; this protocol does not perform user authentication. A higher level protocol for user authentication can be designed on top of this protocol.

The User Authentication Protocol [SSH-USERAUTH] authenticates the client-side user to the server. It runs over the transport layer protocol SSH-TRANS. When SSH-USERAUTH starts, it receives the session identifier from the lower-level protocol (this is the exchange hash H from the first key exchange). The session identifier uniquely identifies this session and is suitable for signing in order to prove ownership of a private key. SSH-USERAUTH also needs to know whether the lower-level protocol provides confidentiality protection.

The Connection Protocol [SSH-CONNECT] multiplexes the encrypted tunnel into several logical channels. It runs over the user authentication protocol. It provides interactive login sessions, remote execution of commands, forwarded TCP/IP connections, and forwarded X11 connections.

The client sends a service request once a secure transport layer connection has been established. A second service request is sent after user authentication is complete. This allows new protocols to be defined and coexist with the protocols listed above. The connection protocol provides channels that can be used for a wide range of purposes. Standard methods are provided for setting up secure interactive shell sessions and for forwarding ("tunneling") arbitrary TCP/IP ports and X11 connections.

Protocol Structure
Secure Shell (SSH) protocols have many messages and each message may have different formats. For details of the message formats, please refer to the Reference documents listed below.

Related Protocols
TCP

Sponsor Source
SSH is defined by IETF (http://www.ietf.org) in RFC 4251, 4252, 4253, 4254, etc.

Reference
http://www.javvin.com/protocol/rfc4251.pdf
SSH Protocol Architecture

Tunneling Protocols

L2F: Layer 2 Forwarding Protocol

Protocol Description

The Layer 2 Forwarding protocol (L2F) is used to establish a secure tunnel across a public infrastructure (such as the Internet) that connects an ISP POP to an enterprise home gateway. This tunnel creates a virtual point-to-point connection between the user and the enterprise customer's network.

Layer Two Forwarding protocol (L2F) permits the tunneling of the link layer (i.e., HDLC, async HDLC, or SLIP frames) of higher level protocols. Using such tunnels, it is possible to divorce the location of the initial dial-up server from the location at which the dial-up protocol connection is terminated and access to the network provided.

L2F allows encapsulation of PPP/SLIP packets within L2F. The ISP NAS and the Home gateway require a common understanding of the encapsulation protocol so that SLIP/PPP packets can be successfully transmitted and received across the Internet.

Protocol Structure

1	1	1	1	1	1	1	1	1	1	1	1	1	16	24	32bit
F	K	P	S	0	0	0	0	0	0	0	0	C	Version	Protocol	Sequence
Multiplex ID														Client ID	
Length														Offset	
Key															

• Version -- The major version of the L2F software creating the packet.
• Protocol -- The protocol field specifies the protocol carried within the L2F packet.
• Sequence -- The sequence number is present if the S bit in the L2F header is set to 1.
• Multiplex ID -- The packet multiplex ID identifies a particular connection within a tunnel.
• Client ID -- The client ID (CLID) assists endpoints in demultiplexing tunnels.
• Length -- The length is the size in octets of the entire packet, including the header, all the fields and the payload.
• Offset -- This field specifies the number of bytes past the L2F header at which the payload data is expected to start. This field is present if the F bit in the L2F header is set to 1.
• Key -- The key field is present if the K bit is set in the L2F header. This is part of the authentication process.
• Checksum -- The checksum of the packet. The checksum field is present if the C bit in the L2F header is set to 1.

Related Protocols

GRE, PPP, L2TP, PPTP, SLIP

Sponsor Source

L2F is defined by Cisco.

Reference

http://www.javvin.com/protocol/rfc2341.pdf
Cisco Layer Two Forwarding (Protocol) "L2F"

L2TP: Layer 2 Tunneling Protocol

Protocol Description

The Layer 2 Tunneling Protocol (L2TP) Protocol is used for integrating multi-protocol dial-up services into existing Internet Service Providers Point of Presence. PPP defines an encapsulation mechanism for transporting multiprotocol packets across layer 2 (L2) point-to-point links. Typically, a user obtains a L2 connection to a Network Access Server (NAS) using one of a number of techniques (e.g., dialup POTS, ISDN, ADSL, etc.) and then runs PPP over that connection. In such a configuration, the L2 termination point and PPP session endpoint reside on the same physical device (i.e., the NAS).

L2TP extends the PPP model by allowing the L2 and PPP endpoints to reside on different devices interconnected by a packet-switched network. With L2TP, a user has an L2 connection to an access concentrator (e.g., modem bank, ADSL DSLAM, etc.), and the concentrator then tunnels individual PPP frames to the NAS. This allows the actual processing of PPP packets to be divorced from the termination of the L2 circuit.

One obvious benefit of such a separation is that instead of requiring the L2 connection to terminate at the NAS, the connection may terminate at a (local) circuit concentrator, which then extends the logical PPP session over a shared infrastructure such as a frame relay circuit or the Internet. From the user's perspective, there is no functional difference between having the L2 circuit terminate in an NAS directly and using L2TP. This protocol may also be used to solve the "multilink hunt-group splitting" problem. Multilink PPP, often used to aggregate ISDN B channels, requires that all channels composing a multilink bundle be grouped at a single Network Access Server (NAS). Because L2TP makes a PPP session appear at a location other than the physical point at which the session was physically received, it can be used to make all channels appear at a single NAS, allowing for a multilink operation even when the physical calls are spread across distinct physical NASs.

L2TP utilizes two types of messages, control messages and data messages. Control messages are used in the establishment, maintenance and clearing of tunnels and calls. Data messages are used to encapsulate PPP frames being carried through the tunnel. Control messages utilize a reliable Control Channel within L2TP to guarantee delivery (see section 5.1 for details). Data messages are not retransmitted when packet loss occurs.

Protocol Structure

L2TP Common header:

12											16	32 bit
T	L	X	X	S	X	O	P	X	X	X	X	VER	Length
Tunnel ID													Session ID
Ns (opt)													Nr (opt)

Offset size (opt)	Offset pad (opt)

- T -- The T bit indicates the type of message. It is set to 0 for data messages and 1 for control messages.
- L -- When set, this indicates that the Length field is present, indicating the total length of the received packet. Must be set for control messages.
- X -- The X bits are reserved for future extensions. All reserved bits are set to 0 on outgoing messages and are ignored on incoming messages.
- S -- If the S bit is set, both the Nr and Ns fields are present. S must be set for control messages.
- O -- When set, this field indicates that the Offset Size field is present in payload messages. This bit is set to 0 for control messages.
- P -- If the Priority (P) bit is 1, this data message receives preferential treatment in its local queuing and transmission.
- Ver -- The value of the ver bit is always 002. This indicates a version 1 L2TP message.
- Length -- Overall length of the message, including header, message type AVP, plus any additional AVP's associated with a given control message type.
- Tunnel ID -- Identifies the tunnel to which a control message applies. If an Assigned Tunnel ID has not yet been received from the peer, Tunnel ID must be set to 0. Once an Assigned Tunnel ID is received, all further packets must be sent with Tunnel ID set to the indicated value.
- Call ID -- Identifies the user session within a tunnel to which a control message applies. If a control message does not apply to a single user session within the tunnel (for instance, a Stop-Control-Connection-Notification message), Call ID must be set to 0.
- Nr -- The sequence number expected in the next control message to be received.
- Ns -- The sequence number for this data or control message.
- Offset size & pad -- This field specifies the number of bytes past the L2TP header at which the payload data is expected to start. Actual data within the offset padding is undefined. If the offset field is present, the L2TP header ends after the last octet of the offset padding.

Related Protocols

PPP, PPTP, L2F, ATM, Frame Relay, UDP

Sponsor Source

L2TP is defined by IETF (http://www.ietf.org) in RFC 2661.

Reference

http://www.javvin.com/protocol/rfc2661.pdf
Layer Two Tunneling Protocol "L2TP"

PPTP: Point-to-Point Tunneling Protocol

Protocol Description

Point-to-Point-Tunneling Protocol (PPTP) is a networking technology that supports multiprotocol virtual private networks (VPN), enabling remote users to access corporate networks securely across the Microsoft Windows NT® Workstation, Windows® 95, and Windows 98 operating systems and other point-to-point protocol (PPP)-enabled systems to dial into a local Internet service provider to connect securely to their corporate network through the Internet.

PPTP can also be used to tunnel a PPP session over an IP network. In this configuration the PPTP tunnel and the PPP session run between the same two machines with the caller acting as a PNS. PPTP uses a client-server architecture to decouple functions which exist in current Network Access Servers and support Virtual Private Networks. PPTP specifies a call-control and management protocol which allows the server to control access for dial-in circuit switched calls originating from a PSTN or ISDN, or to initiate outbound circuit switched connections.

PPTP is implemented only by the PAC and PNS. No other systems need to be aware of PPTP. Dial networks may be connected to a PAC without being aware of PPTP. Standard PPP client software should continue to operate on tunneled PPP links.

PPTP uses an extended version of GRE to carry user PPP packets. These enhancements allow for low-level congestion and flow control to be provided on the tunnels used to carry user data between PAC and PNS. This mechanism allows for efficient use of the bandwidth available for the tunnels and avoids unnecessary retransmissions and buffer overruns. PPTP does not dictate the particular algorithms to be used for this low level control but it does define the parameters that must be communicated in order to allow such algorithms to work.

Protocol Structure

16	32 bit
Length	PPTP message type
Magic cookie	
Control message type	Reserved 0
Protocol Version	Reserved 1
Framing capability	
Bearing capability	
Maximum channels	Firmware revision
Host name (64 Octets)	
Vendor string (64 Octets)	

- Length -- Total length in octets of this PPTP message including the entire PPTP header.
- Magic cookie -- The magic cookie is always sent as the con-

stant 0x1A2B3C4D. Its basic purpose is to allow the receiver to ensure that it is properly synchronized with the TCP data stream.
• Control Message Type -- Values may be:

     Control Connection Management - 1 Start-Control-Connection-Request; 2 Start-Control-Connection-Reply; 3 Stop-Control-Connection-Request; 4 Stop-Control-Connection-Reply; 5 Echo-Request; 6 Echo-Reply.

     Call Management - 7 Outgoing-Call-Request; 8 Outgoing-Call-Reply; 9 Incoming-Call-Request; 10 Incoming-Call-Reply; 11 Incoming-Call-Connected; 12 Call-Clear-Request; 13 Call-Disconnect-Notify

     Error Reporting - 14 WAN-Error-Notify
     PPP Session Control - 15 Set-Link-Info.
• Reserved 0 & 1 -- Must be set to 0.
• Protocol version -- PPTP version number
• Framing Capabilities -- Indicating the type of framing that the sender of this message can provide: 1 - Asynchronous Framing supported; 2 - Synchronous Framing supported
• Bearer Capabilities -- Indicating the bearer capabilities that the sender of this message can provide: 1 - Analog access supported; 2 - Digital access supported
• Maximum Channels -- The total number of individual PPP sessions this PAC can support.
• Firmware Revision -- Contains the firmware revision number of the issuing PAC, when issued by the PAC, or the version of the PNS PPTP driver if issued by the PNS.
• Host Name -- Containing the DNS name of the issuing PAC or PNS.
• Vendor Name -- Containing a vendor specific string describing the type of PAC being used, or the type of PNS software being used if this request is issued by the PNS.

Related Protocols
GRE, PPP, L2TP, L2F

Sponsor Source
PPTP is defined by PPTP forum led by Microsoft and circulated among IETF community.

Reference
http://www.javvin.com/protocol/rfc2637.pdf
Point to Point Tunneling Protocol (PPTP)

DiffServ: Differentiated Service Architecture

Protocol Description
Differentiated Service Architecture (DiffServ) defines an architecture for implementing scalable service differentiation in the Internet. A "Service" defines some significant characteristics of packet transmission in one direction across a set of one or more paths within a network. These characteristics may be specified in quantitative or statistical terms of throughput, delay, jitter, and/or loss, or may otherwise be specified in terms of some relative priority of access to network resources. Service differentiation is desired to accommodate heterogeneous application requirements and user expectations, and to permit differentiated pricing of Internet service.

DiffServ architecture is composed of a number of functional elements implemented in network nodes, including a small set of per-hop forwarding behaviors, packet classification functions, and traffic conditioning functions including metering, marking, shaping, and policing. This architecture achieves scalability by implementing complex classification and conditioning functions only at network boundary nodes, and by applying per-hop behaviors to aggregates of traffic which have been appropriately marked using the DS field in the IPv4 or IPv6 headers [DSFIELD]. Per-hop behaviors are defined to permit a reasonably granular means of allocating buffer and bandwidth resources at each node among competing traffic streams. Per-application flow or per-customer forwarding state need not be maintained within the core of the network.

The differentiated services architecture is based on a simple model where traffic entering a network is classified and possibly conditioned at the boundaries of the network, and assigned to different behavior aggregates. Each behavior aggregate is identified by a single DS codepoint. Within the core of the network, packets are forwarded according to the per-hop behavior associated with the DS codepoint. In this section, we discuss the key components within a differentiated services region, traffic classification and conditioning functions, and how differentiated services are achieved through the combination of traffic conditioning and PHB-based forwarding.

Protocol Structure
In DiffServ, a replacement header field, called the DS field, is defined, which is intended to supersede the existing definitions of the IPv4 TOS octet and the IPv6 Traffic Class octet. The format of the header as follows:

	6	8bit
	DSCP	CU

• DSCP -- differentiated services codepoint to select the PHB a packet experiences at each node
• CU -- currently unused

Related Protocols
IP, IPv6

Sponsor Source

DiffServ is defined by IETF (http://www.ietf.org) in RFC 2474 and 2475.

Reference

http://www.javvin.com/protocol/rfc2475.pdf
An Architecture for Differentiated Services
http://www.javvin.com/protocol/rfc2475.pdf
Differentiated Services Field

GRE: Generic Routing Encapsulation

Protocol Description

Generic Routing Encapsulation (GRE) is a protocol for encapsulation of an arbitrary network layer protocol over another arbitrary network layer protocol.

In the most general case, a system has a packet, namely a payload, which needs to be encapsulated and delivered to some destination. The payload is first encapsulated in a GRE packet. The resulting GRE packet can then be encapsulated in some other protocol and then forwarded. This outer protocol is called the delivery protocol.

When IPv4 is being carried as the GRE payload, the Protocol Type field MUST be set to 0x800. When a tunnel endpoint decapsulates a GRE packet which has an IPv4 packet as the payload, the destination address in the IPv4 payload packet header MUST be used to forward the packet and the TTL of the payload packet MUST be decremented. Care should be taken when forwarding such a packet, since if the destination address of the payload packet is the encapsulator of the packet (i.e., the other end of the tunnel), looping can occur. In this case, the packet MUST be discarded. The IPv4 protocol 47 is used when GRE packets are encapsulated in IPv4.

Security in a network using GRE should be relatively similar to security in a normal IPv4 network, as routing using GRE follows the same routing that IPv4 uses natively. Route filtering will remain unchanged. However packet filtering requires either that a firewall look inside the GRE packet or that the filtering is done at the GRE tunnel endpoints. In those environments in which this is considered to be a security issue it may be desirable to terminate the tunnel at the firewall.

Protocol Structure

In DiffServ, a replacement header field, called the DS field, is defined, which is intended to supersede the existing definitions of the IPv4 TOS octet and the IPv6 Traffic Class octet. The format of the header as follows:

1	13	16	32bit
C	Reserved 0&1	Ver	Protocol type
Checksum (optional)			Reserved

• C -- Checksum Present.
• Reserved 0 & 1 -- reserved for future use.
• Ver -- version number; must be zero.
• Protocol Type -- contains the protocol type of the payload packet.
• Checksum -- contains the IP checksum sum of the all the 16 bit words in the GRE header and the payload packet.

Related Protocols

IPv4

Sponsor Source

GRE is defined by IETF (http://www.ietf.org) in RFC 2784.

Reference

http://www.javvin.com/protocol/rfc2784.pdf
Generic Routing Encapsulation (GRE)

IPsec: Internet Protocol Security Architecture

Protocol Description

Internet Protocol Security (IPsec) defines the security services at the network layer by enabling a system to select required security protocols, determine the algorithm(s) to use for the service(s), and put in place any cryptographic keys required to provide the requested services. IPsec can be used to protect one or more "paths" between a pair of hosts, between a pair of security gateways, or between a security gateway and a host. The set of security services that IPsec can provide includes access control, connectionless integrity, data origin authentication, rejection of replayed packets (a form of partial sequence integrity), confidentiality (encryption), and limited traffic flow confidentiality. Because these services are provided at the IP layer, they can be used by any higher layer protocol, e.g., TCP, UDP, ICMP, BGP, etc.

These objectives are met through the use of two traffic security protocols, the Authentication Header (AH) and the Encapsulating Security Payload (ESP), and through the use of cryptographic key management procedures and protocols. The set of IPsec protocols employed in any context, and the ways in which they are employed, will be determined by the security and system requirements of users, applications, and/or sites/organizations.

When these mechanisms are correctly implemented and deployed, they ought not to adversely affect users, hosts, and other Internet components that do not employ these security mechanisms for protection of their traffic. These mechanisms also are designed to be algorithm-independent. This modularity permits selection of different sets of algorithms without affecting the other parts of the implementation. For example, different user communities may select different sets of algorithms (creating cliques) if required.

A standard set of default algorithms is specified to facilitate interoperability in the global Internet. The use of these algorithms, in conjunction with IPsec traffic protection and key management protocols, is intended to permit system and application developers to deploy high quality, Internet layer, cryptographic security technology.

Protocol Structure

IPsec Architecture includes many protocols and algorithms. The relationship of these protocols is displayed as follows:

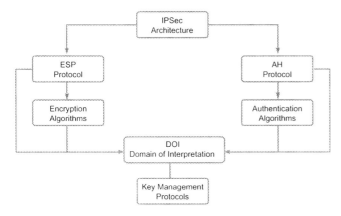

Figure 2-8: IPsec Protocol Stack Structure

The details of each protocol will be presented in separate documents.

Related Protocols

ESP, AH, DES, AES, IKE, DOI, HMAC, HMAC-MD5, HMAC-SHA, PKI, IP, IPv6, ICMP

Sponsor Source

IPsec is defined by IETF (http://www.ietf.org).

Reference

http://www.javvin.com/protocol/rfc2401.pdf
Security Architecture for the Internet Protocol
http://www.javvin.com/protocol/rfc2411.pdf
IP Security Document Roadmap

IPsec AH: IPsec Authentication Header

Protocol Description

IP Authentication Header (AH), a key protocol in the IPsec (Internet Security) architecture, is used to provide connectionless integrity and data origin authentication for IP datagrams, and to provide protection against replays. This protection service against replay is an optional service to be selected by the receiver when a Security Association is established. AH provides authentication for as much of the IP header as possible, as well as for upper level protocol data. However, some IP header fields may change in transit and the value of these fields, when the packet arrives at the receiver, may not be predictable by the sender. The values of such fields cannot be protected by AH. Thus the protection provided to the IP header by AH is only partial in some cases.

AH may be applied alone, in combination with the IP Encapsulating Security Payload (ESP), or in a nested fashion through the use of tunnel mode. Security services can be provided between a pair of communicating hosts, between a pair of communicating security gateways, or between a security gateway and a host. ESP may be used to provide the same security services, and it also provides a confidentiality (encryption) service. The primary difference between the authentications provided by ESP and by AH is the extent of the coverage. Specifically, ESP does not protect any IP header fields unless those fields are encapsulated by ESP. For more details on how to use AH and ESP in various network environments, see the reference documents.

When used with IPv6, the Authentication Header normally appears after the IPv6 Hop-by-Hop Header and before the IPv6 Destination Options. When used with IPv4, the Authentication Header normally follows the main IPv4 header.

Protocol Structure

8	16	32bit
Next Header	Payload Length	Reserved
Security parameters index (SPI)		
Sequence Number Field		
Authentication data (variable)		

• Next header -- identifies the type of the next payload after the Authentication Header.
• Payload Length -- specifies the length of AH in 32-bit words (4-byte units), minus "2".
• SPI -- an arbitrary 32-bit value that, in combination with the destination IP address and security protocol (AH), uniquely identifies the Security Association for this datagram.
• Sequence Number -- contains a monotonically increasing counter value and is mandatory and is always present even if the receiver does not elect to enable the anti-replay service for a specific SA.
• Authentication Data -- a variable-length field containing an Integrity Check Value (ICV) computed over the ESP packet minus the Authentication Data.

Related Protocols

IPsec, ESP, DES, AES, IKE, DOI, HMAC, HMAC-MD5, HMAC-SHA, PKI, IP, IPv6, ICMP

Sponsor Source

IPsec AH is defined by IETF (http://www.ietf.org)in RFC 2402.

Reference

http://www.javvin.com/protocol/rfc2402.pdf
IP Authentication Header

IPsec ESP: IPsec Encapsulating Security Payload

Protocol Description

Encapsulating Security Payload (ESP), a key protocol in the IPsec (Internet Security) architecture, is designed to provide a mix of security services in IPv4 and IPv6. The IP Encapsulating Security Payload (ESP) seeks to provide confidentiality and integrity by encrypting data to be protected and placing the encrypted data in the data portion of the IP ESP. Depending on the user's security requirements, this mechanism may be used to encrypt either a transport-layer segment (e.g., TCP, UDP, ICMP, IGMP) or an entire IP datagram. Encapsulating the protected data is necessary to provide confidentiality for the entire original datagram.

The ESP header is inserted after the IP header and before the upper layer protocol header (transport mode) or before an encapsulated IP header (tunnel mode). The Internet Assigned Numbers Authority has assigned Protocol Number 50 to ESP. The header immediately preceding an ESP header will always contain the value 50 in its Next Header (IPv6) or Protocol (IPv4) field. ESP consists of an unencrypted header followed by encrypted data. The encrypted data includes both the protected ESP header fields and the protected user data, which is either an entire IP datagram or an upper-layer protocol frame (e.g., TCP or UDP).

ESP is used to provide confidentiality, data origin authentication, connectionless integrity, an anti-replay service, and limited traffic flow confidentiality. The set of services provided depends on options selected at the time of Security Association establishment and on the placement of the implementation. Confidentiality may be selected independent of all other services. However, use of confidentiality without integrity/authentication (either in ESP or separately in AH) may subject traffic to certain forms of active attacks that could undermine the confidentiality service. Data origin authentication and connectionless integrity are joint services and are offered as an option in conjunction with (optional) confidentiality. The anti-replay service may be selected only if data origin authentication is selected, and its election is solely at the discretion of the receiver.

Protocol Structure

16	24	32bit
Security association identifier (SPI)		
Sequence Number		
Payload data (variable length)		
Padding (0-255 bytes)		
	Pad Length	Next Header
Authentication Data (variable)		

• Security association identifier -- a pseudo-random value identifying the security association for this datagram.
• Sequence Number -- contains a monotonically increasing counter value and is mandatory and is always present even if the receiver does not elect to enable the anti-replay service

for a specific SA.
• Payload Data -- a variable-length field containing data described by the Next Header field.
• Padding -- padding for encryption.
• Pad length -- indicates the number of pad bytes immediately preceding it.
• Next header -- identifies the type of data contained in the Payload Data field, e.g., an extension header in IPv6 or an upper layer protocol identifier.
• Authentication Data -- a variable-length field containing an Integrity Check Value (ICV) computed over the ESP packet minus the Authentication Data.

Related Protocols

IPsec, AH, DES, AES, IKE, DOI, HMAC, HMAC-MD5, HMAC-SHA, PKI, IP, IPv6, ICMP

Sponsor Source

ESP is defined by IETF (http://www.ietf.org) in RFC 2406.

Reference

http://www.javvin.com/protocol/rfc2406.pdf
IP Encapsulating Security Payload (ESP)

IPsec IKE: Internet Key Exchange Protocol

Protocol Description

Internet Key Exchange (IKE) Protocol, a key protocol in the IPsec architecture, is a hybrid protocol using part of Oakley and part of SKEME in conjunction with ISAKMP to obtain authenticated keying material for use with ISAKMP, and for other security associations such as AH and ESP for the IPsec DOI. ISAKMP provides a framework for authentication and key exchange but does not define them. ISAKMP is designed to be key exchange independent and supports many different key exchanges. The Internet Key Exchange (IKE) is one of a series of key exchanges—called "modes".

IKE processes can be used for negotiating virtual private networks (VPNs) and also for providing a remote user from a remote site (whose IP address need not be known beforehand) access to a secure host or network. Client negotiation is supported. Client mode is where the negotiating parties are not the endpoints for which security association negotiation is taking place. When used in client mode, the identities of the end parties remain hidden.

IKE implementations support the following attribute values:

• DES in CBC mode with a weak, and semi-weak, key check
• MD5 and SHA.
• Authentication via pre-shared keys.
• MODP over default group number one.

In addition, IKE implementations support: 3DES for encryption; Tiger for hash; the Digital Signature Standard, RSA signatures and authentication with RSA public key encryption; and MODP group number 2. IKE implementations MAY support any additional encryption algorithms and MAY support ECP and EC2N groups.

The IKE modes must be implemented whenever the IPsec DOI is implemented. Other DOIs MAY use the modes described here.

Protocol Structure

IKE messages are a combination of ISAKMP header and SKEME and Oakley fields. The specific message format depends on the message phases and modes. For more details, see the reference documents.

Related Protocols

IPsec, ESP, AH, DES, AES, DOI, HMAC, HMAC-MD5, HMAC-SHA, PKI, IP, IPv6, ICMP

Sponsor Source

IP IKE is defined by IETF (http://www.ietf.org) in RFC 2409.

Reference

http://www.javvin.com/protocol/rfc2409.pdf
The Internet Key Exchange (IKE)

IPsec ISAKMP: Internet Security Association and Key Management Protocol

Protocol Description

The Internet Security Association and Key Management Protocol (ISAKMP), a key protocol in the IPsec (Internet Security) architecture, combines the security concepts of authentication, key management, and security associations to establish the required security for government, commercial, and private communications on the Internet.

ISAKMP defines procedures and packet formats to establish, negotiate, modify and delete Security Associations (SAs). SAs contain all the information required for execution of various network security services, such as the IP layer services (such as header authentication and payload encapsulation), transport or application layer services, or self-protection of negotiation traffic. ISAKMP defines payloads for exchanging key generation and authentication data. These formats provide a consistent framework for transferring key and authentication data independent of the key generation technique, encryption algorithm and authentication mechanism.

ISAKMP is distinct from key exchange protocols in order to clearly separate the details of security association management (and key management) from the details of key exchange. There may be many different key exchange protocols, each with different security properties. However, a common framework is required for agreeing to the format of SA attributes, and for negotiating, modifying, and deleting SAs. ISAKMP serves as this common framework.

Separating the functionality into three parts adds complexity to the security analysis of a complete ISAKMP implementation. However, the separation is critical for interoperability between systems with differing security requirements, and should also simplify the analysis of further evolution of an ISAKMP server. ISAKMP is intended to support the negotiation of SAs for security protocols at all layers of the network stack (e.g., IPSEC, TLS, TLSP, OSPF, etc.). By centralizing the management of the security associations, ISAKMP reduces the amount of duplicated functionality within each security protocol. ISAKMP can also reduce connection setup time, by negotiating a whole stack of services at once.

Within ISAKMP, a Domain of Interpretation (DOI) is used to group related protocols using ISAKMP to negotiate security associations. Security protocols sharing a DOI choose security protocol and cryptographic transforms from a common namespace and share key exchange protocol identifiers. They also share a common interpretation of DOI-specific payload data content, including the Security Association and Identification payloads.

Overall, ISAKMP places requirements on a DOI definition to define the following:

• Naming scheme for DOI-specific protocol identifiers
• Interpretation for the Situation field
• Set of applicable security policies
• Syntax for DOI-specific SA Attributes (Phase II)
• Syntax for DOI-specific payload contents
• Additional Key Exchange types, if needed
• Additional Notification Message types, if needed

Protocol Structure

8	12	16	24	32 bit
Initiator Cookie				
Responder Cookie				
Next Pay-load	MjVer	Mn-Ver	Exchange Type	Flags
Message ID				
Length				

• Initiator Cookie -- The Initiator Cookie: Cookie of the entity that initiated SA establishment, SA notification, or SA deletion
• Responder Cookie -- The Responder Cookie: Cookie of the entity that is responding to an SA establishment request, SA notification, or SA deletion.
• Next Payload -- The type of the next payload in the message.
• Major Version -- The major version of the ISAKMP protocol in use.
• Minor Version -- The minor version of the ISAKMP protocol in use.
• Exchange Type -- The type of exchange being used
• Flags -- Various options that are set for the ISAKMP exchange.
• Message ID -- A Unique Message Identifier used to identify protocol state during Phase 2 negotiations.
• Length -- Length of total message (header + payloads) in octets.

Related Protocols

IPsec, ESP, AH, DES, AES, IKE, DOI, HMAC, HMAC-MD5, HMAC-SHA, PKI, IP, IPv6, ICMP

Sponsor Source

ISAKMP is defined by IETF (http://www.ietf.org) in RFC 2408.

Reference

http://www.javvin.com/protocol/rfc2408.pdf
Internet Security Association and Key Management Protocol (ISAKMP)

SSL/TLS: Secure Socket Layer and Transport Layer Security Protocol

Protocol Description

Secure Socket Layer (SSL) and Transport Layer Security (TLS) Protocol provide privacy and data integrity between two communicating applications. The protocol is composed of two layers: the TLS Record Protocol and the TLS Handshake Protocol. At the lowest level, layered on top of some reliable transport protocol (TCP) is the TLS Record Protocol. The TLS Record Protocol provides connection security that has two basic properties:

• Private - Symmetric cryptography is used for data encryption (DES, RC4, etc.) The keys for this symmetric encryption are generated uniquely for each connection and are based on a secret negotiated by another protocol (such as the TLS Handshake Protocol). The Record Protocol can also be used without encryption.
• Reliable - Message transport includes a message integrity check using a keyed MAC. Secure hash functions (SHA, MD5, etc.) are used for MAC computations. The Record Protocol can operate without a MAC, but is generally only used in this mode while another protocol is using the Record Protocol as a transport for negotiating security parameters.

The TLS Record Protocol is used for encapsulation of various higher level protocols. One such encapsulated protocol, the TLS Handshake Protocol, allows the server and client to authenticate each other and to negotiate an encryption algorithm and cryptographic keys before the application protocol transmits or receives its first byte of data. The TLS Handshake Protocol provides connection security that has three basic properties:

• The peer's identity can be authenticated using asymmetric, or public key, cryptography (RSA, DSS, etc.). This authentication can be made optional, but is generally required for at least one of the peers.
• The negotiation of a shared secret is secure: The negotiated secret is unavailable to eavesdroppers, and for any authenticated connection the secret cannot be obtained, even by an attacker who can place himself in the middle of the connection.
• The negotiation is reliable: no attacker can modify the negotiation communication without being detected by the parties to the communication.

TLS is based on the Secure Socket Layer (SSL), a protocol originally created by Netscape. One advantage of TLS is that it is application protocol independent. The TLS protocol runs above TCP/IP and below application protocols such as HTTP or IMAP. The HTTP running on top of TLS or SSL is often called HTTPS. The TLS standard does not specify how protocols add security with TLS; the decisions on how to initiate TLS handshaking and how to interpret the authentication certificates exchanged are left up to the judgment of the designers and implementers of protocols which run on top of TLS.

SSL/TLS, a popular protocol to handle secure web traffic, is increasingly used to secure non-web application protocols (such as SMTP, LDAP, POP, IMAP, and TELNET). When used as a VPN technology, SSL/TLS can carry any TCP traffic, and some can handle UDP as well. Because SSL is a transport-layer service, an SSL VPN has the advantage of being able to apply this access control at transport- and application-layers, providing greater granularity of control.

Protocol Structure

TLS protocol includes two protocol groups: TLS Record Protocol and TLS Handshake Protocols, which have many messages with different formats. We only summarize the protocols here without details, which can be found in the reference documents.

TLS Record Protocol is a layered protocol. At each layer, messages may include fields for length, description, and content. The Record Protocol takes messages to be transmitted, fragments the data into manageable blocks, optionally compresses the data, applies a MAC, encrypts, and transmits the result. Received data is decrypted, verified, decompressed, and reassembled, then delivered to higher level clients.

TLS connection state is the operating environment of the TLS Record Protocol. It specifies a compression algorithm, encryption algorithm, and MAC algorithm.

TLS Record Layer receives uninterrupted data from higher layers in non-empty blocks of arbitrary size. Key calculation: The Record Protocol requires an algorithm to generate keys, IVs, and MAC secrets from the security parameters provided by the handshake protocol.

TLS Handshake Protocol: consists of a suite of three sub-protocols which are used to allow peers to agree upon security parameters for the record layer, authenticate themselves, instantiate negotiated security parameters, and report error conditions to each other.

• Change cipher spec protocol
• Alert protocol
• Handshake protocol

Related Protocols

GRE, PPP, L2TP, PPTP, RSA, SSL

Sponsor Source

TLS is defined by IETF (http://www.ietf.org) in RFC 2246 and updated in RFC 3546.
SSL is defined by Netscape Communication.

Reference

http://www.javvin.com/protocol/rfc2246.pdf
The TLS Protocol Version 1.0.
http://wp.netscape.com/eng/ssl3/ssl-toc.html
The SSL Protocol (version 3.0)

SOCKS v5: Protocol for Sessions Traversal Across Firewall Securely

Protocol Description

The SOCKS protocol, also known as authenticated firewall traversal (AFT), provides a framework for client-server applications in both the TCP and UDP domains to conveniently and securely use the services of a network firewall. The protocol is conceptually a "shim-layer" between the application layer and the transport layer, and as such does not provide network layer gateway services, such as forwarding of ICMP messages.

The use of network firewalls, systems that effectively isolate an organizations internal network structure from an exterior network, such as the Internet is becoming increasingly popular. These firewall systems typically act as application-layer gateways between networks, usually offering controlled TELNET, FTP, and SMTP access. SOCKS provides a general framework for these protocols to transparently and securely traverse a firewall.

SOCKS version 5, also, provides strong authentication of such traversal, while SOCKS Version 4 provides only unsecured firewall traversal for TCP-based client-server applications, including TELNET, FTP, and protocols such as HTTP, WAIS and GOPHER. SOCKS version 5 extends the SOCKS Version 4 model to include UDP, and extends the framework to include provisions for generalized strong authentication schemes. It also adapts the addressing scheme to encompass domain-name and IPv6 addresses.

The implementation of the SOCKS protocol typically involves the recompilation or relinking of TCP-based client applications to use the appropriate encapsulation routines in the SOCKS library.

Protocol Structure

SOCKS v5 has a few types of messages with different formats.

Version identifier/method selection message:

1 byte	1 byte	1-225 bytes
Version	NMethods	Methods

The SOCKS request message:

1 byte	1 byte	Value of 0	1 byte	Variable	2 bytes
Version	CMD	Rsv	ATYP	DST addr	DST Port

The method selection message:

1 byte	1 byte
Version	Method

The reply message:

1 byte	1 byte	Value of 0	1 byte	Variable	2 bytes
Version	REP	RSV	ATYP	BND addr	BND Port

UDP request header:

2 bytes	1 byte	1 byte	Variable	2 bytes	Variable
RSV	FRAG	ATYP	DST Addr	DST Port	Data

Related Protocols

TCP, UDP, ICMP, HTTP, Gopher, TELNET, FTP

Sponsor Source

SOCKS is defined by IETF (http://www.ietf.org) in RFC 1928.

Reference

http://www.javvin.com/protocol/rfc1928.pdf
SOCKS Protocol Version 5

Voice over IP and VOIP Protocols

Description

Voice over IP (VOIP) uses the Internet Protocol (IP) to transmit voice as packets over an IP network. Using VOIP protocols, voice communications can be achieved on any IP network regardless whether it is Internet, Intranet or Local Area Networks (LAN). In a VOIP enabled network, the voice signal is digitized, compressed and converted to IP packets and then transmitted over the IP network. VOIP signaling protocols are used to set up and tear down calls, carry information required to locate users and negotiate capabilities. The key benefits of Internet telephony (Voice over IP) are the very low cost, the integration of data, voice and video on one network, the new services created on the converged network and simplified management of end user and terminals.

There are a few VOIP protocol stacks which are derived by various standard bodies and vendors, namely H.323, SIP, MEGACO and MGCP.

H.323 is the ITU-T's standard, which was originally developed for multimedia conferencing on LANs, but was later extended to cover Voice over IP. The standard encompasses both point to point communications and multipoint conferences. H.323 defines four logical components: Terminals, Gateways, Gatekeepers and Multipoint Control Units (MCUs). Terminals, gateways and MCUs are known as endpoints.

Session Initiation Protocol (SIP) is the IETF's standard for establishing VOIP connections. SIP is an application layer control protocol for creating, modifying and terminating sessions with one or more participants. The architecture of SIP is similar to that of HTTP (client-server protocol). Requests are generated by the client and sent to the server. The server processes the requests and then sends a response to the client. A request and the responses for that request make a transaction.

Media Gateway Control Protocol (MGCP), an IETF standard based on Cisco and Telcordia proposals, defines communication between call control elements (Call Agents or Media Gateway) and telephony gateways. MGCP is a control protocol, allowing a central coordinator to monitor events in IP phones and gateways and instruct them to send media to specific addresses. In the MGCP architecture, the call control intelligence is located outside the gateways and is handled by the call control elements (the Call Agent). Also, the call control elements (Call Agents) will synchronize with each other to send coherent commands to the gateways under their control. CableLab has adopted the MGCP for its PacketCable embbed clients in VOIP applications and the resulted protocol is called Network Based Signaling Protocol (NCS).

The Media Gateway Control Protocol (Megaco) is a result of joint efforts of the IETF and the ITU-T (ITU-T Recommendation H.248). Megaco/H.248 is a protocol for the control of elements in a physically decomposed multimedia gateway, which enables separation of call control from media conversion. Megaco/H.248 addresses the relationship between the Media Gateway (MG), which converts circuit-switched voice to packet-based traffic, and the Media Gateway Controller, which dictates the service logic of that traffic. Megaco/H.248 instructs an MG to connect streams coming from outside a packet or cell data network onto a packet or cell stream such as the Real-Time Transport Protocol (RTP). Megaco/H.248 is essentially quite similar to MGCP from an architectural standpoint and the controller-to-gateway relationship, but Megaco/H.248 supports a broader range of networks.

The SS7/C7 is the traditional signaling protocol for the circuit switched voice networks. To integrate the SS7/C7 network with the IP network, a group of protocols are defined, namely SIGTRAN (Signaling Transpor protocol). The key transport protocol in the SIGTRAN stack, the Stream Control Transmission Protocol (SCTP), has been applied in a much broader base after its creation.

In the past few years, the VOIP industry has been working on addressing the following key issues:

Quality of voice -- As IP was designed for carrying data, it does not provide real time guarantees but only provides best effort service. For voice communications over IP to become acceptable to users, the packet delay and getter needs to be less than a threshold value.

Interoperability -- In a public network environment, products from different vendors need to operate with each other for Voice over IP to become common among users.

Security -- Encryption (such as SSL) and tunneling (L2TP) technologies have been developed to protect VOIP signaling and bear traffic.

Integration with Public Switched Telephone Network(PSTN) -- While Internet telephony is being introduced, it will need to work in conjunction with PSTN in the foreseeable future. Gateway technologies are being developed to bridge the two networks.

Scalability -- VOIP systems need to be flexible enough to grow to the large user market for both private and public services. Many network management and user management technologies and products are being developed to address the issue.

Key VOIP Protocols

Signaling	
ITU-T H.323	H.323: Packet-based multimedia communications (VoIP) architecture
	H.225: Call Signaling and RAS in H.323 VOIP Architecture
	H.235: Security for H.323 based systems and communications
	H.245: Control Protocol for Multimedia Communication
	T.120: Multipoint Data Conferencing Protocol Suite
IETF	Megaco / H.248: Media Gateway Control protocol
	MGCP: Media Gateway Control Protocol
	RTSP: Real Time Streaming Protocol
	SIP: Session Initiation Protocol
	SDP: Session Description Protocol
	SAP: Session Announcement Protocol
CableLab	NCS: Netowrk-based Call Signaling Protocol
Cisco Skinny	SCCP: Skinny Client Control Protocol

Media/CODEC	G.7xx: Audio (Voice) Compression Protocols (G.711, G.721, G.722, G.723, G.726, G.727. G.728, G.729)
	H.261: Video CODEC for Low Quality Videoconferencing
	H.263: Video CODEC for Medium Quality Videoconferencing
	H.264 / MPEG-4: Video CODEC for High Quality Video Streaming
	Video CODEC for Medium Quality Video-conferencingRTP: Real Time Transport Protocol
	RTCP: RTP Control Protocol
Others	COPS: Common Open Policy Service
	SIGTRAN: Signaling Transport protocol stack for SS7/C7 over IP
	SCTP: Stream Control Transmission Protocol
	TRIP: Telephony Routing Over IP

Sponsor Source

VOIP protocols are defined by IETF, ITU-T and some vendors.

Reference

http://www.cis.ohio-state.edu/~jain/refs/ref_voip.htm
Voice Over IP and IP Telephony References

H.323: ITU-T VOIP Protocols

Protocol Description

H.323, a protocol suite defined by ITU-T, is for voice transmission over internet (Voice over IP or VOIP). In addition to voice applications, H.323 provides mechanisms for video communication and data collaboration, in combination with the ITU-T T.120 series standards. H.323 is one of the major VOIP standards, on a par with Megaco and SIP.

H.323 is an umbrella specification, because it includes various other ITU standards. The components under H.323 architecture are terminal, gateway, gatekeeper and multipoint control units (MCUs).

Terminal represents the end device of every connection. It provides real time two way communications with another H.323 terminal, GW or MSU. This communication consists of speech, speech and data, speech, and video, or a combination of speech, data and video.

Gateways establish the connection between the terminals in the H.323 network and the terminals belonging to networks with different protocol stacks such as the traditional PSTN network or SIP or Megaco end points.

Gatekeepers are responsible for translating between telephone number and IP addresses. They also manage the bandwidth and provide a mechanism for terminal registration and authentication. Gatekeepers also provide services such as call transfer, call forwarding etc.

MCUs take care of establishing multipoint conferences. An MCU consists of a mandatory Multipoint Control, which is for call signaling and conference control, and an optional Multipoint Processor, which is for switching/mixing of the media stream and sometimes real-time transcoding of the received audio/video streams.

There are five types of information exchange enabled in the H.323 architecture:

• Audio (digitized) voice
• Video (digitized)
• Data (files or image)
• Communication control (exchange of supported functions, controlling logic channels, etc.)
• Controlling connections and sessions (setup and tear down)

The H.323 was first published in 1996 and the latest version (v5) was completed in 2003.

Protocol Structure

The protocols in the H.323 protocol suite are:

• Call control and signaling
• H.225.0: Call signaling protocols and media stream packetization (uses a subset of Q.931 signaling protocol)
• H.225.0/RAS: Registration, Admission and Status
• H.245: Control protocol for multimedia communication

Audio processing:

• G.711: Pulse code modulation of voice frequencies
• G.722: 7 kHz audio coding within 64 kb/s
• G.723.1: Dual rate speech coders for multimedia communication transmitting at 5.3 and 6.3 kb/s
• G.728: Coding of speech at 16 kb/s using low-delay code excited linear prediction
• G.729: Coding of speech at 8kb/s using conjugate-structure algebraic-code-excited linear-prediction

Video processing:

• H.261: Video codecs for audiovisual services at Px64kps. (Low quality)
• H.263: Video coding for low bit rate communication.(Medium Quality)
• H.264 / MPEG-4: Video CODEC for high quality video streaming

Data conferencing:

• T.120: This is a protocol suite for data transmission between end points. It can be used for various applications in the field of Collaboration Work, such as white-boarding, application sharing, and joint document management. T.120 utilizes layer architecture similar to the OSI model. The top layers (T.126, T.127) are based on the services of lower layers (T.121, T.125).

Media transportation:

• RTP: Real time Transport Protocol
• RTCP: RTP Control Protocol

Security:

• H.235: Security and encryption for H.series multimedia terminals.

Supplementary services:

• H.450.1: Generic functions for the control of supplementary services in H.323
• H.450.2: Call transfer
• H.450.3: Call diversion
• H.450.4: Call hold
• H.450.5: Call park and pick up
• H.450.6: Call waiting
• H.450.7: Message waiting indication
• H.450.8: Names Identification services
• H.450.9: Call completion services for H.323 networks

The following figure illustrates the structure of the key protocol in the H.323 architecture. Details of each protocols will be discussed in separate documents.

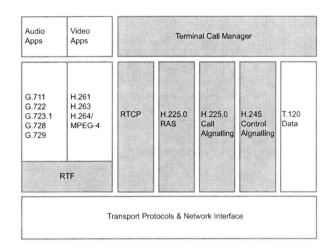

Figure 2-9: H.323 Protocol Stack Structure

Related Protocols

RTP, RTSP, SIP, Megaco, H.248, Q.931, H.225

Sponsor Source

H.323 is a ITU-T (http://www.itu.int/ITU-T/) standard.

Reference

http://www.h323forum.org/papers/
H.323 papers and documents

H.225.0: Call signalling protocols and media stream packetization for packet-based multimedia communication systems

Protocol Description

H.225.0, a key protocol in the H.323 VOIP architecture defined by ITU-T, is a standard to cover narrow-band visual telephone services defined in H.200/AV.120-Series Recommendations. It specifically deals with those situations where the transmission path includes one or more packet based networks, each of which is configured and managed to provide a non-guaranteed QoS, which is not equivalent to that of N-ISDN, such that additional protection or recovery mechanisms beyond those mandated by Rec. H.320 are necessary in the terminals. H.225.0 describes how audio, video, data and control information on a packet based network can be managed to provide conversational services in H.323 equipment. H.225 has two major parts: Call signaling and RAS (Registration, Admission and Status).

H.225 call control signaling is used to setup connections between H.323 endpoints. This is achieved by exchanging H.225 protocol messages on the call-signaling channel. The call-signaling channel is opened between two H.323 endpoints or between an endpoint and the gatekeeper. The ITU H.225 recommendation specifies the use and support of Q.931 signaling messages. A reliable (TCP) call control channel is created across an IP network on TCP port 1720. This port initiates the Q.931 call control messages for the purpose of connecting, maintaining, and disconnecting calls. When a gateway is present in the network zone, H.225 call setup messages are exchanged either via Direct Call Signaling or Gatekeeper-Routed Call Signaling (GKRCS). The gatekeeper decides the method chosen during the RAS admission message exchange. If no gatekeeper is present, H.225 messages are exchanged directly between the endpoints.

H.225/RAS (Registration, Admission and Status) is the protocol between endpoints (terminals and gateways) and gatekeepers. The RAS is used to perform registration, admission control, bandwidth changes, status, and disengage procedures between endpoints and gatekeepers. An RAS channel is used to exchange RAS messages. This signaling channel is opened between an endpoint and a gatekeeper prior to the establishment of any other channel.

Protocol Structure

1	2	3	4	8bit
Protocol Discriminator				
0	0	0	0	Length of call reference bits
Call reference value				
0	Message type			
Information Elements				

• Protocol discriminator -- Distinguishes messages for user-network call control from other messages.
• Length of call ref -- The length of the call reference value.
• Call reference value -- Identifies the call or facility registration/cancellation request at the local user-network interface to which the particular message applies. May be up to 2 octets in length.
• Message type -- Identifies the function of the message sent.
• Information elements -- Two categories of information elements are defined: single octet information elements and variable length information elements, as shown in the following illustrations.

1	4	8bit
1	IEI	Contents of IE

1	8bit
1	IE Identifier

1	8bit
1	IEI
Length of contents of IE	
Contents of IE (variable)	

Key RAS messages:

Message	Function
RegistrationRequest (RRQ)	Request from a terminal or gateway to register with a gatekeeper. Gatekeeper either confirms or rejects (RCF or RRJ).
AdmissionRequest (ARQ)	Request for access to packet network from terminal to gatekeeper. Gatekeeper either confirms or rejects (ACF or ARJ).
BandwidthRequest (BRQ)	Request for changed bandwidth allocation, from terminal to gatekeeper. Gatekeeper either confirms or rejects (BCF or BRJ).
DisengageRequest (DRQ)	If sent from endpoint to gatekeeper, DRQ informs gatekeeper that endpoint is being dropped; if sent from gatekeeper to endpoint, DRQ forces call to be dropped. Gatekeeper either confirms or rejects (DCF or DRJ). If DRQ sent by gatekeeper, endpoint must reply with DCF.
InfoRequest (IRQ)	Request for status information from gatekeeper to terminal.
InfoRequest-Response (IRR)	Response to IRQ. May be sent unsolicited by terminal to gatekeeper at predetermined intervals.
RAS timers and Request in Progress (RIP)	Recommended default timeout values for response to RAS messages and subsequent retry counts if response is not received.

Related Protocols
RTP, RTSP, SIP, Megaco, H.248, Q.931, H.323, H.245

Sponsor Source
H.225 is an ITU-T (http://www.itu.int/ITU-T/) standard.

Reference
http://www.javvin.com/protocol/H225v5.pdf
Call signalling protocols and media stream packetization for packet-based multimedia communication systems" Version 5.
http://www.h323forum.org/papers/
H.323 papers and documents

H.235: Security and encryption for H-series (H.323 and other H.245-based) multimedia terminals

Protocol Description

H.235 is the security recommendation for the H.3xx series systems. In particular, H.235 provides security procedures for H.323-, H.225.0-, H.245- and H.460-based systems. H.235 is applicable to both simple point-to-point and multipoint conferences for any terminals which utilize H.245 as a control protocol.

The scope of H.235 is to provide authentication, privacy and integrity for H.xxx based systems. H.235 provides a means for a person, rather than a device, to be identified. The security profiles include: 1) a simple, password-based security profile; 2) a profile using digital certificates and dependent on a fully-deployed public-key infrastructure; and 3) combines features of both 1) and 2). Use of these security profiles is optional.

H.235 includes the ability to negotiate services and functionality in a generic manner, and to be selective concerning cryptographic techniques and capabilities utilized. The specific manner in which these are used relates to systems capabilities, application requirements and specific security policy constraints. H.235 supports varied cryptographic algorithms, with varied options appropriate for different purposes; e.g. key lengths. Certain cryptographic algorithms may be allocated to specific security services.H.235 supports signalling of well-known algorithms in addition to signalling non standardized or proprietary cryptographic algorithms. There are no specifically mandated algorithms; however, it is strongly suggested in H.235 that endpoints support as many of the applicable algorithms as possible in order to achieve interoperability. This parallels the concept that the support of H.245 does not guarantee the interoperability between two entities' codecs.

Protocol Structure

H.235 recommends many messages, procedures, structures and algorithms for the security concerns of signaling, control and media communications under H.323 architecture. Here is a summary of the definitions:

1) The call signalling channel may be secured using TLS or IPSEC on a secure well-known port (H.225.0).
2) Users may be authenticated either during the initial call connection, in the process of securing the H.245 channel and/or by exchanging certificates on the H.245 channel.
3) The encryption capabilities of a media channel are determined by extensions to the existing capability negotiation mechanism.
4) Initial distribution of key material from the master is via H.245 OpenLogicalChannel or OpenLogicalChannelAck messages.
5) Re-keying may be accomplished by H.245 commands: EncryptionUpdateCommand, EncryptionUpdateRequest, EncryptionUpdate and EncryptionUpdateAck.
6) Key material distribution is protected either by operating the H.245 channel as a private channel or by specifically protecting the key material using the selected exchanged certificates.
7) The security protocols presented conform either to ISO published standards or to IETF proposed standards.

The following is a sample flow chart in the H.235 recommendations of encryption for media security.

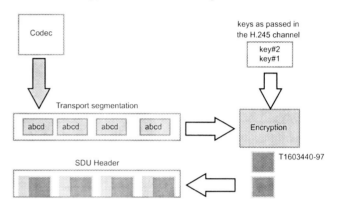

Figure 2-10: H.235 – Encryption of media

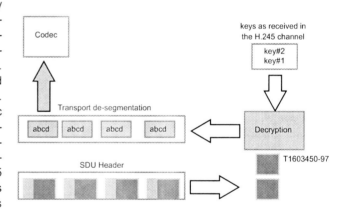

Figure 2-11: H.235 – Decryption of media

Related Protocols

RTP, RTSP, H.225, Q.931, H.323, H.245

Sponsor Source

H.235 is an ITU-T (http://www.itu.int/ITU-T/) standard.

Reference

http://www.javvin.com/protocol/H235v3.pdf
Security and encryption for H-series (H.323 and other H.245-based) multimedia terminals
http://www.h323forum.org/papers/
H.323 papers and documents

H.245: Control Protocol for Multimedia Communication

Protocol Description

H.245, a control signaling protocol in the H.323 multimedia communication architecture, is for of the exchange of end-to-end H.245 messages between communicating H.323 endpoints/terminals. The H.245 control messages are carried over H.245 control channels. The H.245 control channel is the logical channel 0 and is permanently open, unlike the media channels. The messages carried include messages to exchange capabilities of terminals and to open and close logical channels.

After a connection has been set up via the call signaling procedure, the H.245 call control protocol is used to resolve the call media type and establish the media flow, before the call can be established. It also manages the call after it has been established. The steps involved are:

• Master-slave determination process. This is used to determine the master of the call and is useful for avoiding conflicts during call control operations.
• Capability exchange procedure. Each endpoint notifies the other what kind of information it is capable of receiving and transmitting through the receive-and-transmit capabilities.
• Logical channel procedures. Used for opening and closing logical channels, which are multiplexed paths between the endpoints used for data transfer.
• Request mode command. Using this command, at any point during the conference, the receiving endpoint can request a change in mode of the transmitted information provided the mode is in the transmit capability of the transmitter.
• Control flow command. This can be used by the receiver to fix an upper limit for the transmitter bit rate on any logical channel.
• Communication mode messages. Used by the multipoint controller for selecting a common mode of operation in a multipoint conference.
• Conference request and response messages. Used for controlling a multipoint conference, e.g. password requests, conference chair control.
• Round-trip delay commands. Used for measuring the round-trip delay between two endpoints on the control channel.
• Video fast update command. Used for requesting updates for video frames, in case of data loss.
• End session command. After this command the endpoints close all logical channels, drop the call and inform the gatekeeper about the end of the call.

Protocol Structure

H.245 messages are in ASN.1 syntax. MultimediaSystemControlMessage types can be defined as request, response, command and indication messages. Key H.245 messages are as follows:

Message	Function

Master-Slave Determination	Determines which terminal is the master and which is the slave. Possible replies: Acknowledge, Reject, Release (in case of a time out).
Terminal Capability Set	Contains information about a terminal's capability to transmit and receive multimedia streams. Possible replies: Acknowledge, Reject, Release.
Open Logical Channel	Opens a logical channel for transport of audiovisual and data information. Possible replies: Acknowledge, Reject, Confirm.
Close Logical Channel	Closes a logical channel between two endpoints. Possible replies: Acknowledge
Request Mode	Used by a receive terminal to request particular modes of transmission from a transmit terminal. General mode types include VideoMode, AudioMode, DataMode and Encryption Mode. Possible replies: Acknowledge, Reject, Release.
Send Terminal Capability Set	Commands the far-end terminal to indicate its transmit-and-receive capabilities by sending one or more Terminal Capability Sets.
End Session Command	Indicates the end of the H.245 session. After transmission, the terminal will not send any more H.245 messages.

Related Protocols

RTP, RTSP, SIP, Megaco, H.248, Q.931, H.323, H.225, H.235

Sponsor Source

H.245 is an ITU-T (http://www.itu.int/ITU-T/) standard.

Reference

http://www.javvin.com/protocol/H245v9.pdf
Control Protocol for Multimedia Communication (version 9)
http://www.h323forum.org/papers/
H.323 papers and documents

Megaco/H.248: Media Gateway Control Protocol

Protocol Description

Megaco/H.248, the Media Gateway Control Protocol, is for the control of elements in a physically decomposed multimedia gateway, enabling the separation of call control from media conversion. The Media Gateway Control Protocol (Megaco) is a result of joint efforts of the IETF and the ITU-T Study Group 16. Therefore, the IETF defined Megaco is the same as ITU-T Recommendation H.248.

Megaco/H.248 addresses the relationship between the Media Gateway (MG), which converts circuit-switched voice to packet-based traffic, and the Media Gateway Controller (MGC, sometimes called a call agent or softswitch, which dictates the service logic of that traffic). Megaco/H.248 instructs an MG to connect streams coming from outside a packet or cell data network onto a packet or cell stream such as the Real-Time Transport Protocol (RTP). Megaco/H.248 is essentially quite similar to MGCP from an architectural standpoint and the controller-to-gateway relationship, but Megaco/H.248 supports a broader range of networks, such as ATM.

There are two basic components in Megaco/H.248: terminations and contexts. Terminations represent streams entering or leaving the MG (for example, analog telephone lines, RTP streams, or MP3 streams). Terminations have properties, such as the maximum size of a jitter buffer, which can be inspected and modified by the MGC.

Terminations may be placed into contexts, which are defined as occuring when two or more termination streams are mixed and connected together. The normal, "active" context might have a physical termination (say, one DS0 in a DS3) and one ephemeral one (the RTP stream connecting the gateway to the network). Contexts are created and released by the MG under command of the MGC. A context is created by adding the first termination, and is released by removing (subtracting) the last termination.

A termination may have more than one stream, and therefore a context may be a multistream context. Audio, video, and data streams may exist in a context among several terminations.

Protocol Structure

All Megaco/H.248 messages are in the format of ASN.1 text messages. Megaco/H.248 uses a series of commands to manipulate terminations, contexts, events, and signals. The following is a list of the commands:

1. Add. -- The Add command adds a termination to a context. The Add command on the first Termination in a Context is used to create a Context.
2. Modify -- The Modify command modifies the properties, events and signals of a termination.
3. Subtract -- The Subtract command disconnects a Termination from its Context and returns statistics on the Termination's participation in the Context. The Subtract command on the last Termination in a Context deletes the Context.

4. Move -- The Move command automatically moves a Termination to another context.
5. AuditValue -- The AuditValue command returns the current state of properties, events, signals and statistics of Terminations.
6. AuditCapabilities -- The AuditCapabilities command returns all the possible values for Termination properties, events and signals allowed by the Media Gateway.
7. Notify -- The Notify command allows the Media Gateway to inform the Media Gateway Controller of the occurrence of events in the Media Gateway.
8. ServiceChange -- The ServiceChange Command allows the Media Gateway to notify the Media Gateway Controller that a Termination or group of Terminations is about to be taken out of service or has just been returned to service. ServiceChange is also used by the MG to announce its availability to an MGC (registration), and to notify the MGC of impending or completed restart of the MG. The MGC may announce a handover to the MG by sending it ServiceChange command. The MGC may also use ServiceChange to instruct the MG to take a Termination or group of Terminations in or out of service.

All of these commands are sent from the MGC to the MG, although ServiceChange can also be sent by the MG. The Notify command, with which the MG informs the MGC that one of the events the MGC was interested in has occurred, is sent by the MG to the MGC.

Related Protocols

RTP, RTSP, SIP, H.323, MGCP

Sponsor Source

Megaco/H.248 v1 is defined by IETF (www.ietf.org) and ITU-T. Megaco/H.248 version 2 and version 3 are in drafting.

Reference

http://www.javvin.com/protocol/rfc3525.pdf
Gateway Control Protocol Version 1
http://www.javvin.com/protocol/megaco-h248v2.pdf
The Megaco/H.248 Gateway Control Protocol, version 2
http://www.javvin.com/protocol/h248v3-draft.pdf
Recommendation H.248.1 v3 "Gateway Control Protocol: Version 3"

MGCP: Media Gateway Control Protocol

Protocol Description

Media Gateway Control Protocol (MGCP) is a VOIP protocol used between elements of a decomposed multimedia gateway which consists of a Call Agent, containing the call control "intelligence", and a media gateway containing the media functions, e.g., conversion from TDM voice to Voice over IP.

Media gateways contain endpoints on which the Call Agent can create, modify and delete connections in order to establish and control media sessions with other multimedia endpoints. A media gateway is typically a network element that provides conversion between the audio signals carried on telephone circuits and data packets carried over the Internet or over other packet networks. The Call Agent can instruct the endpoints to detect certain events and generate signals. The endpoints automatically communicate changes in service state to the Call Agent. Furthermore, the Call Agent can audit endpoints as well as the connections on endpoints.

MGCP assumes a call control architecture where the call control "intelligence" is outside the gateways and handled by Call Agents. It assumes that Call Agents will synchronize with each other to send coherent commands and responses to the gateways under their control. MGCP does not define a mechanism for synchronizing Call Agents. MGCP is, in essence, a master/slave protocol, where the gateways are expected to execute commands sent by the Call Agents.

MGCP assumes a connection model where the basic constructs are endpoints and connections. Endpoints are sources and/or sinks of data and can be physical or virtual. Creation of physical endpoints requires hardware installation, while creation of virtual endpoints can be done by software. Connections may be either point to point or multipoint. A point to point connection is an association between two endpoints with the purpose of transmitting data between these endpoints. Once this association is established for both endpoints, data transfer between these endpoints can take place. A multipoint connection is established by connecting the endpoint to a multipoint session. Connections can be established over several types of bearer networks.

In the MGCP model, the gateways focus on the audio signal translation function, while the Call Agent handles the call signaling and call processing functions. As a consequence, the Call Agent implements the "signaling" layers of the H.323 standard, and presents itself as an "H.323 Gatekeeper" or as one or more "H.323 Endpoints" to the H.323 systems.

Protocol Structure

The MGCP is a text based protocol. The transactions are composed of a command and a mandatory response. There are eight types of commands:

MGC --> MG	CreateConnection: Creates a connection between two endpoints; uses SDP to define the receive capabilities of the participating endpoints.
MGC --> MG	ModifyConnection: Modifies the properties of a connection; has nearly the same parameters as the CreateConnection command.
MGC <--> MG	DeleteConnection: Terminates a connection and collects statistics on the execution of the connection.
MGC --> MG	NotificationRequest: Requests the media gateway to send notifications on the occurrence of specified events in an endpoint.
MGC <-- MG	Notify: Informs the media gateway controller when observed events occur.
MGC --> MG	AuditEndpoint: Determines the status of an endpoint.
MGC --> MG	AuditConnection: Retrieves the parameters related to a connection.
MGC <-- MG	RestartInProgress: Signals that an endpoint or group of endpoints is taken in or out of service.

Related Protocols

RTP, RTSP, SIP, H.323, Megaco, H.248

Sponsor Source

MGCP is an IETF standard based on Cisco SGCP.

Reference

http://www.javvin.com/protocol/rfc3435.pdf
Media Gateway Control Protocol (MGCP) Version 1.0.
http://www.javvin.com/protocol/rfc3661.pdf
Media Gateway Control Protocol (MGCP) Return Code Usage

NCS: Network-Based Call Signaling Protocol

Protocol Description

Network-based Call Signaling, based on the Media Gateway Control Protocol (MGCP), is the VOIP signaling protocol adobted by the CableLab as a standard for PacketCable embbed clients, which is a network element that provides:

• Two or more traditional analog (RJ11) access lines to a voice-over-IP (VoIP) network.
• Optionally, one or more video lines to a VoIP network

MGCP is a call signaling protocol for use in a centralized call control architecture, and assumes relatively simple client devices. The call signaling protocol is one layer of the overall PacketCable suite of specifications and relies upon companion protocol specifications to provide complete end-to-end PacketCable functionality.

NCS provides a PacketCable profile of an application programming interface (MGCI), and a corresponding protocol (MGCP) for controlling voice-over-IP (VoIP) embedded clients from external call control elements. MGCI functions provide for connection control, endpoint control, auditing, and status reporting. They each use the same system model and the same naming conventions.

Thr NCS profile of MGCP has been modified from the MGCP 1.0 in the following ways:
• The NCS protocol only aims at supporting PacketCable-embedded clients. Functionality present in the MGCP 1.0 protocol, which was superfluous to NCS, has been removed.
• The NCS protocol contains extensions and modifications to MGCP. However, the MGCP architecture, and all of the MGCP constructs relevant to embedded clients, are preserved in NCS.
• The NCS protocol contains minor simplifications from MGCP 1.0

The relations between MGCP/NCS and other VOIP standards such as H.323 and SIP are displayed as follows:

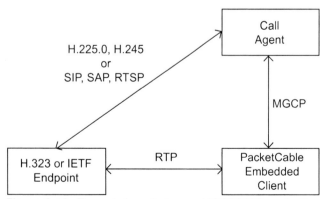

Figure 2-12: The relations between MGCP/NCS and other VOIP standards

Protocol Structure

NCS uses the same protocol format as the MGCP, which is a text-based protocol. The transactions are composed of a command and a mandatory response. There are eight types of commands:

MGC --> MG	CreateConnection: Creates a connection between two endpoints; uses SDP to define the receive capabilities of the participating endpoints.
MGC --> MG	ModifyConnection: Modifies the properties of a connection; has nearly the same parameters as the CreateConnection command.
MGC <--> MG	DeleteConnection: Terminates a connection and collects statistics on the execution of the connection.
MGC --> MG	NotificationRequest: Requests the media gateway to send notifications on the occurrence of specified events in an endpoint.
MGC <-- MG	Notify: Informs the media gateway controller when observed events occur.
MGC --> MG	AuditEndpoint: Determines the status of an endpoint.
MGC --> MG	AuditConnection: Retrieves the parameters related to a connection.
MGC <-- MG	RestartInProgress: Signals that an endpoint or group of endpoints is taken in or out of service.

Related Protocols

MGCP, RTP, RTSP, SIP, H.323, Megaco, H.248

Sponsor Source

NCS is a CableLab defined standard based on MGCP.

Reference

http://www.packetcable.com/downloads/specs/PKT-SP-NCS1.5-I01-050128.pdf
Network Based Signaling Protocol
http://www.javvin.com/protocol/rfc3435.pdf
Media Gateway Control Protocol (MGCP) Version 1.0.

RTSP: Real-Time Streaming Protocol

Protocol Description

The Real-Time Streaming Protocol (RTSP) establishes and controls either a single or several time-synchronized streams of continuous media such as audio and video. RTSP does not typically deliver the continuous streams itself, although interleaving of the continuous media stream with the control stream is possible. In other words, RTSP acts as a "network remote control" for multimedia servers. RTSP provides an extensible framework to enable controlled, on-demand delivery of real-time data, such as audio and video. Sources of data can include both live data feeds and stored clips. RTSP is intended to control multiple data delivery sessions, provide a means for choosing delivery channels, such as UDP, multicast UDP and TCP, and provide a means for choosing delivery mechanisms based upon RTP.

There is no notion of an RTSP connection; instead, a server maintains a session labeled by an identifier. An RTSP session is in no way tied to a transport-level connection such as a TCP connection. During an RTSP session, an RTSP client may open and close many reliable transport connections to the server to issue RTSP requests. Alternatively, it may use a connectionless transport protocol such as UDP.

The streams controlled by RTSP may use RTP, but the operation of RTSP does not depend on the transport mechanism used to carry continuous media. RTSP is intentionally similar in syntax and operation to HTTP/1.1 so that extension mechanisms to HTTP can in most cases also be added to RTSP. However, RTSP differs in a number of important aspects from HTTP:

• RTSP introduces a number of new methods and has a different protocol identifier.
• An RTSP server needs to maintain state by default in almost all cases, as opposed to the stateless nature of HTTP.
• Both an RTSP server and client can issue requests.
• Data is carried out-of-band by a different protocol, in most cases.
• RTSP is defined to use ISO 10646 (UTF-8) rather than ISO 8859-1, consistent with current HTML internationalization efforts.
• The Request-URI always contains the absolute URI. Because of backward compatibility with a historical blunder, HTTP/1.1 carries only the absolute path in the request and puts the host name in a separate header field.

The protocol supports the following operations:

• Retrieval of media from a media server: The client can request a presentation description via HTTP or some other method.
• Invitation of a media server to a conference: A media server can be "invited" to join an existing conference, either to play back media into the presentation or to record all or a subset of the media in a presentation.
• Addition of media to an existing presentation: Particularly for live presentations, it is useful if the server can tell the client about additional media becoming available.

Protocol Structure

RTSP is a text-based protocol and uses the ISO 10646 character set in UTF-8 encoding. Lines are terminated by CRLF, but receivers should be prepared to also interpret CR and LF by themselves as line terminators. The header fields are summarized as follows:

Header	Type	Support	Methods
Accept	R	opt.	entity
Accept-Encoding	R	opt.	entity
Accept-Language	R	opt.	all
Allow	R	opt.	all
Authorization	R	opt.	all
Bandwidth	R	opt.	all
Blocksize	R	opt.	All but OPTIONS, TEARDOWN
Cache-Control	G	opt.	SETUP
Conference	R	opt.	SETUP
Connection	G	req.	all
Content-Base	E	opt.	entity
Content-Encoding	E	req.	SET_PARAMETER
Content-Encoding	E	req.	DESCRIBE, AN-NOUNCE
Content-Language	E	req.	DESCRIBE, AN-NOUNCE
Content-Length	E	req.	SET_PARAMETER, ANNOUNCE
Content-Length	E	req.	entity
Content-Location	E	opt.	entity
Content-Type	E	req.	SET_PARAMETER, ANNOUNCE
Content-Type	R	req.	entity
CSeq	G	req.	all
Date	G	opt.	all
Expires	E	opt.	DESCRIBE, AN-NOUNCE
From	R	opt.	all
If-Modified-Since	R	opt.	DESCRIBE, SETUP
Last-Modified	E	opt.	entity
Proxy-Authenticate			
Proxy-Require	R	req.	all
Public	R	opt.	all
Range	R	opt.	PLAY, PAUSE, RECORD
Range	R	opt.	PLAY, PAUSE, RECORD
Referer	R	opt.	all

Require	R	req.	all
Retry-After	r	opt.	all
RTP-Infor	R	req.	PLAY
Scale	Rr	opt.	PLAY, RECORD
Session	Rr	req.	All but SETUP, OPTIONS
Server	R	opt.	all
Speed	Rr	opt.	PLAY
Transport	Rr	req.	SETUP
Unsupported	R	req.	all
User-Agent	R	opt.	all
Via	G	opt.	all
WWW-Authenticate	R	opt.	all

Type "g" designates general request headers to be found in both requests and responses, type "R" designates request headers, type "r" designates response headers, and type "e" designates entity header fields. Fields marked with "req." in the column labeled "support" MUST be implemented by the recipient for a particular method, while fields marked "opt." are optional. Note that not all fields marked "req." will be sent in every request of this type. The "req." means only that client (for response headers) and server (for request headers) MUST implement the fields. The last column lists the method for which this header field is meaningful; the designation "entity" refers to all methods that return a message body.

Related Protocols

UDP, TCP, HTTP, S-HTTP, RTP

Sponsor Source

RTSP is defined by IETF (www.ietf.org) in RFC 2326.

Reference

http://www.javvin.com/protocol/rfc2326.pdf
Real Time Streaming Protocol

SAP: Session Announcement Protocol

Protocol Description

Session Announcement Protocol (SAP) is an announcement protocol that is used to assist the advertisement of multicast multimedia conferences and other multicast sessions, and to communicate the relevant session setup information to prospective participants.

A SAP announcer periodically multicasts an announcement packet to a well-known multicast address and port. The announcement is multicast with the same scope as the session it is announcing, ensuring that the recipients of the announcement can also be potential recipients of the session the announcement describes (bandwidth and other such constraints permitting). This is also important for the scalability of the protocol, as it keeps local session announcements local.

A SAP listener learns of the multicast scopes it is within (for example, using the Multicast-Scope Zone Announcement Protocol) and listens on the well-known SAP address and port for those scopes. In this manner, it will eventually learn of all the sessions being announced, allowing those sessions to be joined.

It is to be expected that sessions may be announced by a number of different mechanisms, not only SAP. For example, a session description may be placed on a web page, sent by email or conveyed in a session initiation protocol. To increase interoperability with these other mechanisms, application level security is employed, rather than using IPsec authentication headers.

Protocol Structure

3	4	5	6	7	8	16	32bit
V=1	A	R	T	E	C	Auth len	Msg ID hash
Originating source (32 or 128 bits)							
Optional Authentication Data							
Optional timeout							
Optional payload type							
						0	
Payload							

• V -- Version Number field is three bits and MUST be set to 1.
• A -- Address Type can have a value of 0 or 1:
    0 -- The originating source field contains a 32-bit IPv4 address.
    1 -- The originating source contains a 128-bit IPv6 address.
• R -- Reserved. SAP announcers set this to 0. SAP listeners ignore the contents of this field.
• T -- Message Type can have a value of 0 or 1:
    0 -- Session announcement packet
    1 -- Session deletion packet.
• E -- Encryption Bit bit may be 0 or 1.

1 -- The payload of the SAP packet is encrypted and the timeout field must be added to the packet header.

0 -- The packet is not encrypted and the timeout must not be present.

• C -- Compressed Bit. If the compressed bit is set to 1, the payload is compressed.

• Authentication Length -- An 8 bits unsigned quantity following the main SAP header contains authentication data. If it is zero, no authentication header is present.

• Message Identifier Hash -- used in combination with the originating source, provides a globally unique identifier indicating the precise version of this announcement.

• Originating Source -- This field contains the IP address of the original source of the message. This is an IPv4 address if the A field is set to zero; otherwise, it is an IPv6 address. The address is stored in network byte order.

• Timeout -- When the session payload is encrypted, the detailed timing fields in the payload are not available to listeners not trusted with the decryption key. Under such circumstances, the header includes an additional 32-bit timestamp field stating when the session should be timed out. The value is an unsigned quantity giving the NTP time in seconds at which time the session is timed out. It is in network byte order.

• Payload Type -- The payload type field is a MIME content type specifier, describing the format of the payload. This is a variable length ASCII text string, followed by a single zero byte (ASCII NUL).

• Payload -- The Payload field includes various subfields.

Related Protocols

RTP, RTSP, SIP, SDP

Sponsor Source

SAP is defined by IETF (www.ietf.org) in RFC 2974.

Reference

http://www.javvin.com/protocol/rfc2974.pdf
SAP Session Announcement Protocol

SDP: Session Description Protocol

Protocol Description

The Session Description Protocol (SDP) describes multimedia sessions for the purpose of session announcement, session invitation and other forms of multimedia session initiation.

Session directories assist the advertisement of conference sessions and communicate the relevant conference setup information to prospective participants. SDP is designed to convey such information to recipients. SDP is purely a format for session description - it does not incorporate a transport protocol, and is intended to use different transport protocols as appropriate including the Session Announcement Protocol (SAP), Session Initiation Protocol (SIP), Real-Time Streaming Protocol (RTSP), electronic mail using the MIME extensions, and the Hypertext Transport Protocol (HTTP).

SDP is intended to be general purpose so that it can be used for a wider range of network environments and applications than just multicast session directories. However, it is not intended to support negotiation of session content or media encodings.

On Internet Multicast backbone (Mbone) a session directory tool is used to advertise multimedia conferences and communicate the conference addresses and conference tool-specific information necessary for participation. The SDP does this. It communicates the existence of a session and conveys sufficient information to enable participation in the session. Many of the SDP messages are sent by periodically multicasting an announcement packet to a well-known multicast address and port using SAP (Session Announcement Protocol). These messages are UDP packets with a SAP header and a text payload. The text payload is the SDP session description. Messages can also be sent using email or the WWW (World Wide Web).

The SDP text messages include:

• Session name and purpose
• Time the session is active
• Media comprising the session
• Information to receive the media (address etc.)

Protocol Structure

SDP messages are text messages using the ISO 10646 character set in UTF-8 encoding. SDP Session description (optional fields have an *) is:

v= (protocol version)
o= (owner/creator and session identifier).
s= (session name)
i=* (session information)
u=* (URI of description)
e=* (email address)
p=* (phone number)
c=* (connection information - not required if included in all media)
b=* (bandwidth information)

One or more time descriptions (see below)
z=* (time zone adjustments)
k=* (encryption key)
a=* (zero or more session attribute lines)
Zero or more media descriptions (see below)

Time description

t= (time the session is active)
r=* (zero or more repeat times)

Media description

m= (media name and transport address)
i=* (media title)
c=* (connection information - optional if included at session-level)
b=* (bandwidth information)
k=* (encryption key)
a=* (zero or more media attribute lines)

Related Protocols

UDP, TCP, SIP, SAP, RTSP, RTP, H.320, MPEG, H.261, HTTP, MIME

Sponsor Source

SDP is defined by IETF (www.ietf.org) in RFC 2327.

Reference

http://www.javvin.com/protocol/rfc2327.pdf
Session Description Protocol

SIP: Session Initiation Protocol

Protocol Description

Session Initiation Protocol (SIP) is an application-layer control protocol that can establish, modify, and terminate multimedia sessions such as Internet telephony calls. SIP can also invite participants to already existing sessions, such as multicast conferences. Media can be added to (and removed from) an existing session. SIP transparently supports name mapping and redirection services, which supports personal mobility - users can maintain a single externally visible identifier regardless of their network location.

SIP supports five facets of establishing and terminating multimedia communications:

• User location: determination of the end system to be used for communication;
• User availability: determination of the willingness of the called party to engage in communications;
• User capabilities: determination of the media and media parameters to be used;
• Session setup: "ringing", establishment of session parameters at both called and calling party;
• Session management: including transfer and termination of sessions, modifying session parameters, and invoking services.

SIP is a component that can be used with other IETF protocols to build a complete multimedia architecture, such as the Real-time Transport Protocol (RTP) for transporting real-time data and providing QoS feedback, the Real-Time streaming protocol (RTSP) for controlling delivery of streaming media, the Media Gateway Control Protocol (MEGACO) for controlling gateways to the Public Switched Telephone Network (PSTN), and the Session Description Protocol (SDP) for describing multimedia sessions. Therefore, SIP should be used in conjunction with other protocols in order to provide complete services to the users. However, the basic functionality and operation of SIP does not depend on any of these protocols.

SIP provides a suite of security services, which include denial-of-service prevention, authentication (both user-to-user and proxy-to-user), integrity protection, and encryption and privacy services.

SIP works with both IPv4 and IPv6. For Internet telephony sessions, SIP works as follows:

Callers and callees are identified by SIP addresses. When making a SIP call, a caller first locates the appropriate server and then sends a SIP request. The most common SIP operation is the invitation. Instead of directly reaching the intended callee, a SIP request may be redirected or may trigger a chain of new SIP requests by proxies. Users can register their location(s) with SIP servers. SIP addresses (URLs) can be embedded in Web pages and therefore can be integrated as part of such powerful implementations as Click to talk.
To facilitate the interconnection of the PSTN with IP, SIP-T

(SIP for telephones) is defined by IETF in RFC 3372. SIP-T allows traditional IN-type services to be seamlessly handled in the Internet environment. It is essential that SS7 information be available at the points of PSTN interconnection to ensure transparency of features not otherwise supported in SIP. SS7 information should be available in its entirety and without any loss to the SIP network across the PSTN-IP interface. SIP-T defines SIP functions that map to ISUP interconnection requirements.

Protocol Structure

SIP messages can be transmitted either over TCP or UDP SIP messages are text-based and use the ISO 10646 character set in UTF-8 encoding. Lines must be terminated with CRLF. Much of the message syntax and header field are similar to HTTP. Messages can be request messages or response messages.

A request message has the following format:

Method	Request URI	SIP version

• Method -- The method to be performed on the resource. Possible methods are Invite, Ack, Options, Bye, Cancel, Register.
• Request-URI -- A SIP URL or a general Uniform Resource Identifier; this is the user or service to which this request is being addressed.
• SIP version -- The SIP version being used.

The format of the Response message header is shown in the following illustration:

SIP version	Status code	Reason phrase

• SIP version -- The SIP version being used.
• Status-code -- A 3-digit integer result code of the attempt to understand and satisfy the request.
• Reason-phrase -- A textual description of the status code.

Related Protocols

SIP-T, UDP, TCP, IP, RTSP, RTP, HTTP, SDP, MEGACO

Sponsor Source

SIP is defined by IETF (www.ietf.org) in RFC 3261, 3262, 3263, 3264, and 3265.

Reference

http://www.javvin.com/protocol/rfc3261.pdf
Session Initiation Protocol.
http://www.javvin.com/protocol/rfc3262.pdf
Reliability of Provisional Responses in the Session Initiation Protocol (SIP)
http://www.javvin.com/protocol/rfc3263.pdf
Session Initiation Protocol (SIP): Locating SIP Servers
http://www.javvin.com/protocol/rfc3264.pdf
An Offer/Answer Model with the Session Description Protocol (SDP)
http://www.javvin.com/protocol/rfc3265.pdf
Session Initiation Protocol (SIP)-Specific Event Notification
http://www.javvin.com/protocol/rfc3372.pdf

Session Initiation Protocol for Telephones (SIP-T)

SCCP (Skinny): Cisco Skinny Client Control Protocol

Protocol Description

Skinny Client Control Protocol (SCCP or Skinny) is a Cisco proprietary protocol used between Cisco Call Manager and Cisco VOIP phones. It is also supported by some other vendors.

For VOIP solutions, the end station of a LAN or IP- based PBX must be simple to use, familiar and relatively cheap. SCCP defines a simple and easy to use architecture, while the H.323 recommendations produce quite an expensive system. An H.323 proxy can be used to communicate with the Skinny Client using the SCCP. In such a case the telephone is a skinny client over IP, in the context of H.323. A proxy is used for the H.225 and H.245 signalling.

With the SCCP architecture, the vast majority of the H.323 processing power resides in an H.323 proxy known as the Cisco Call Manager. The end stations (telephones) run what is called the Skinny Client, which consumes less processing overhead. The Client communicates with the Call Manager using connection-oriented (TCP/IP-based) communication to establish a call with another H.323-compliant end station. Once the Call Manager has established the call, the two H.323 end stations use connectionless (UDP/IP-based) communication for audio transmissions. Costs and overhead are thus reduced by confining the complexities of H.323 call setup to the Call Manager, and using the Skinny protocol for the actual audio communication into and out of the end stations.

Protocol Structure

The skinny client (i.e. an Ethernet Phone) uses TCP/IP to transmit and receive calls and RTP/UDP/IP to/from a Skinny Client or H.323 terminal for audio. Skinny messages are carried above TCP and use port 2000. The message types are as follows:

Code	Station Message ID Message
0x0000	Keep Alive Message
0x0001	Station Register Message
0x0002	Station IP Port Message
0x0003	Station Key Pad Button Message
0x0004	Station Enbloc Call Message
0x0005	Station Stimulus Message
0x0006	Station Off Hook Message
0x0007	Station On Hook Message
0x0008	Station Hook Flash Message
0x0009	Station Forward Status Request Message
0x11	Station Media Port List Message
0x000A	Station Speed Dial Status Request Message
0x000B	Station Line Status Request Message
0x000C	Station Configuration Status Request Message
0x000D	Station Time Date Request Message
0x000E	Station Button Template Request Message
0x000F	Station Version Request Message
0x0010	Station Capabilities Response Message
0x0012	Station Server Request Message
0x0020	Station Alarm Message

0x0021	Station Multicast Media Reception Ack Message
0x0024	Station Off Hook With Calling Party Number Message
0x22	Station Open Receive Channel Ack Message
0x23	Station Connection Statistics Response Message
0x25	Station Soft Key Template Request Message
0x26	Station Soft Key Set Request Message
0x27	Station Soft Key Event Message
0x28	Station Unregister Message
0x0081	Station Keep Alive Message
0x0082	Station Start Tone Message
0x0083	Station Stop Tone Message
0x0085	Station Set Ringer Message
0x0086	Station Set Lamp Message
0x0087	Station Set Hook Flash Detect Message
0x0088	Station Set Speaker Mode Message
0x0089	Station Set Microphone Mode Message
0x008A	Station Start Media Transmission
0x008B	Station Stop Media Transmission
0x008F	Station Call Information Message
0x009D	Station Register Reject Message
0x009F	Station Reset Message
0x0090	Station Forward Status Message
0x0091	Station Speed Dial Status Message
0x0092	Station Line Status Message
0x0093	Station Configuration Status Message
0x0094	Station Define Time & Date Message
0x0095	Station Start Session Transmission Message
0x0096	Station Stop Session Transmission Message
0x0097	Station Button Template Message
0x0098	Station Version Message
0x0099	Station Display Text Message
0x009A	Station Clear Display Message
0x009B	Station Capabilities Request Message
0x009C	Station Enunciator Command Message
0x009E	Station Server Respond Message
0x0101	Station Start Multicast Media Reception Message
0x0102	Station Start Multicast Media Transmission Message
0x0103	Station Stop Multicast Media Reception Message
0x0104	Station Stop Multicast Media Transmission Message
0x105	Station Open Receive Channel Message
0x0106	Station Close Receive Channel Message
0x107	Station Connection Statistics Request Message
0x0108	Station Soft Key Template Respond Message
0x109	Station Soft Key Set Respond Message
0x0110	Station Select Soft Keys Message
0x0111	Station Call State Message
0x0112	Station Display Prompt Message
0x0113	Station Clear Prompt Message
0x0114	Station Display Notify Message
0x0115	Station Clear Notify Message
0x0116	Station Activate Call Plane Message
0x0117	Station Deactivate Call Plane Message
0x118	Station Unregister Ack Message

Related Protocols

RTP, RTSP, SIP, H.323, Megaco, H.248

Sponsor Source

SCCP/Skinny is a Cisco protocol.

T.120: Multipoint Data Conferencing and Real Time Communication Protocols

Protocol Description

The ITU T.120 standard is made up of a suite of communication and application protocols. T.120 protocols are designed for multipoint Data Conferencing and real time communication including multilayer protocols which considerably enhance multimedia, MCU and codec control capabilities. Depending on the type of T.120 implementations, the resulting product can make connections, transmit and receive data, and collaborate using compatible data conferencing features, such as program sharing, whiteboard conferencing, and file transfer. The key functionalities of T.120 are:

• Establish and maintain conferences without any platform dependence.
• Manage multiple participants and programs.
• Send and receive data accurately and securely over a variety of supported networking connections.

The T.120 protocol suite includes the following protocols:

T.121 provides a template for T.120 resource management that developers should use as a guide for building application protocols. T.121 is mandatory for standardized application protocols and is highly recommended for non-standard application protocols. The template ensures consistency and reduces the potential for unforeseen interaction between different protocol implementations.

T.122 defines the multi-point services available to the developer. Together with T.125, it forms MCS, the multi-point "engine" of the T.120 conference. MCS relies on T.123 to actually deliver the data. MCS is a powerful tool that can be used to solve virtually any multi-point application design requirement. MCS is an elegant abstraction of a rather complex organism. Learning to use MCS effectively is the key to successfully developing real-time applications.

T.123 specifies transport profiles for each of the following: 1) Public Switched Telephone Networks (PSTN) 2) Integrated Switched Digital Networks (ISDN); 3) Circuit Switched Digital Networks (CSDN); 4)Packet Switched Digital Networks (PSDN); 5) Novell Netware IPX (via reference profile); and 6) TCP/IP (via reference profile). T.120 applications expect the underlying transport to provide reliable delivery of its Protocol Data Units (PDUs) and to segment and sequence that data.

T.124 specifies the Generic Conference Control (GCC), which provides a comprehensive set of facilities for establishing and managing the multi-point conference. It is with GCC that we first see features that are specific to the electronic meeting.

T.125 describes the Multipoint Communication Service Protocol (MCS). It defines: 1) Procedures for a single protocol for the transfer of data and control information from one MCS provider to a peer MCS provider; and 2) The structure and encoding of the MCS protocol data units used for the transfer of data and control information.

T.126 defines a protocol for viewing and annotating still images transmitted between two or more applications. This capability is often referred to as document conferencing or shared whiteboarding.

T.127 specifies a means for applications to transmit files between multiple endpoints in a conference. Files can be transferred to all participants in the conference or to a specified subset of the conference. Multiple file transfer operations may occur simultaneously in any given conference and developers can specify priority levels for the file delivery. Finally, T.127 provides options for compressing files before delivering the data.

Protocol Structure

The T.120 architecture relies on a multi-layered approach with defined protocols and service definitions between layers. Each layer presumes the existence of all layers below. The lower level layers (T.122, T.123, T.124, and T.125) specify an application-independent mechanism for providing multi-point data communications services to any application that can use these facilities. The upper level layers (T.126 and T.127) define protocols for specific conferencing applications, such as shared whiteboarding and binary file transfer. These "standardized applications" can co-exist in the same conference with "non-standardized" applications such as a business card exchange program or a textual chat application. The following figure represent the architecture of the T.120.

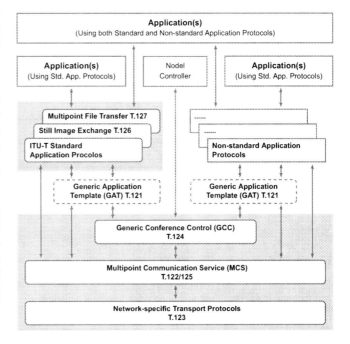

Figure 2-13: T.120 Data Conferencing Protocol Structure

Related Protocols

RTP, RTSP, SIP, Megaco, H.248, Q.931, H.323, H.225

Sponsor Source

T.120, T.121, T.122, T.123, T.124, T.125, T.126, T.127 are ITU-T (http://www.itu.int/ITU-T/) standards.

Reference

http://www.packetizer.com/conf/t120/primer/
A Primer on the T.120 Series Standard

Media / CODEC

G.7xx: Audio (Voice) Compression Protocols

Protocol Description

G.7xx is a suite of ITU-T standards for audio compression and de-commpressions. It is primarily used in telephony. In telephony, there are 2 main algorithms defined in the standard, mu-law algorithm (used in America) and a-law algorithm (used in Europe and the rest of the world). Both are logarithmic, but the later a-law was specifically designed to be simpler for a computer to process. The G.7xx protocol suite is composed of the following protocols:

G.711 -- Pulse code modulation (PCM) of voice frequencies on a 64 kbps channel
G.721 -- 32 kbit/s adaptive differential pulse code modulation (ADPCM)
G.722 -- 7 kHz audio-coding within 64 kbit/s
G.722.1 -- Coding at 24 and 32 kbit/s for hands-free operation in systems with low frame loss
G.722.2 -- Wideband coding of speech at around 16 kbit/s using adaptive multi-rate wideband (AMR-WB)
G.726 -- 40, 32, 24, 16 kbit/s adaptive differential pulse code modulation (ADPCM)
G.727 -- 5-, 4-, 3- and 2-bit/sample embedded adaptive differential pulse code modulation (ADPCM)
G.728 -- Coding of speech at 16 kbit/s using low-delay code excited linear prediction
G.729 -- Coding of speech at 8 kbit/s using conjugate-structure algebraic-code-excited linear-prediction (CS-ACELP)

Protocol Structure

Name	standard-ized by	description	bit rate (kb/s)	sampling rate (kHz)	frame size (ms)	remarks
(ADPCM) DVI	Intel, IMA	ADPCM	32	8	sample	
G.711	ITU-T	Pulse code modulation (PCM)	64	8	sample	mu-law (US, Japan) and A-law (Europe) companding
G.721	ITU-T	Adaptive differential pulse code modulation (ADPCM)	32	8	sample	Now described in G.726; obsolete.
G.722	ITU-T	7 kHz audio-coding within 64 kbit/s	64	16	sample	Subband-codec that divides 16 kHz band into two subbands, each coded using ADPCM
G.722.1	ITU-T	Coding at 24 and 32 kbit/s for hands-free operation in systems with low frame loss	24/32	16	20	
G.723	ITU-T	Extensions of Recommendation G.721 adaptive differential pulse code modulation to 24 and 40 kbit/s for digital circuit multiplication equipment application	24/40	8	sample	Superceded by G.726; obsolete. This is a completely different codec than G.723.1.

G.723.1	ITU-T	Dual rate speech coder for multi-media communications transmitting at 5.3 and 6.3 kbit/s	5.6/6.3	8	30	Part of H.324 video conferencing. It encodes speech or other audio signals in frames using linear predictive analysis-by-synthesis coding. The excitation signal for the high rate coder is Multipulse Maximum Likelihood Quantization (MP-MLQ) and for the low rate coder is Algebraic-Code-Excited Linear-Prediction (ACELP).
G.726	ITU-T	40, 32, 24, 16 kbit/s adaptive differential pulse code modulation (ADPCM)	16 / 24 / 32 / 40	8	sample	ADPCM; replaces G.721 and G.723.
G.727	ITU-T	5-, 4-, 3- and 2-bit/sample embedded adaptive differential pulse code modulation (ADPCM)	var.	?	sample	ADPCM. Related to G.726.
G.728	ITU-T	Coding of speech at 16 kbit/s using low-delay code excited linear prediction	16	8		CELP. Annex J offers variable-bit rate operation for DCME.
G.729	ITU-T	Coding of speech at 8 kbit/s using conjugate-structure algebraic-code-excited linear-prediction (CS-ACELP)	8	8	10	Low delay (15 ms)
GSM 06.10	ETSI	Regular Pulse Excitation Long Term Predictor (RPE-LTP)	13	8	22.5	Used for GSM cellular telephony.

Related Protocols

RTP, RTSP, H.323, H.225

Sponsor Source

G.7xx is a suite of ITU-T (http://www.itu.int/ITU-T/) standards.

Reference

http://www.h323forum.org/papers/
H.323 papers and documents

H.261: Video CODEC for Low Quality Videoconferencing

Protocol Description

H.261 is the video coding standard of the ITU. It was designed for data rates which are multiples of 64Kbit/s and is sometimes called p x 64Kbit/s (p is in the range 1-30). These data rates suit ISDN lines, for which this video codec was originally designed. H.261 transports a video stream using the real-time transport protocol, RTP, with any of the underlying protocols that carry RTP.

The coding algorithm is a hybrid of inter-picture prediction, transform coding and motion compensation. The data rate of the coding algorithm was designed to be able to be set to between 40 Kbits/s and 2 Mbits/s. INTRA coding encodes blocks of 8x8 pixels each only with reference to themselves and sends them directly to the block transformation process. On the other hand, INTER coding frames are encoded with respect to another reference frame. The inter-picture prediction removes temporal redundancy. The transform coding removes the spatial redundancy. Motion vectors are used to help the codec compensate for motion. To remove any further redundancy in the transmitted bitstream, variable length coding is used.

H261 supports motion compensation in the encoder as an option. In motion compensation a search area is constructed in the previous (recovered) frame to determine the best reference macroblock.

H261 supports two image resolutions, QCIF (Quarter Common Interchange format) which is (144x176 pixels) and CIF (Common Interchange format), which is (288x352).

The video multiplexer structures the compressed data into a hierarchical bitstream that can be universally interpreted. The hierarchy has four layers:

1. Picture layer: corresponds to one video picture (frame)
2. Group of blocks: corresponds to 1/12 of CIF pictures or 1/3 of QCIF
3. Macroblocks : corresponds to 16x16 pixels of luminance and the two spatially corresponding 8x8 chrominance components
4. Blocks: corresponds to 8x8 pixels

Protocol Structure

H.261 Header Structure:

3	6	7	8	12	17	22	27	32bit
SBIT	EBIT	I	V	GOBN	MBAP	QUANT	HMVD	VMVD

• SBIT -- Start bit. Number of most significant bits that are to be ignored in the first data octet.
• EBIT -- End bit. Number of least significant bits that are to be ignored in the last data octet.
• I -- INTRA-frame encoded data field. Set to 1 if this stream contains only INTRA-frame coded blocks and to 0 if this stream may or may not contain INTRA-frame coded blocks.
• V -- Motion Vector flag. Set to 0 if motion vectors are not used in this stream and to 1 if motion vectors may or may not be used in this stream.
• GOBN -- GOB number. Encodes the GOB number in effect at the start of the packet. Set to 0 if the packet begins with a GOB header.
• MBAP -- Macroblock address predictor. Encodes the macroblock address predictor (i.e., the last MBA encoded in the previous packet). This predictor ranges from 0 to 32 (to predict the valid MBAs 1-33), but because the bit stream cannot be fragmented between a GOB header and MB 1, the predictor at the start of the packet can never be 0.
• QUANT -- Quantizer field. Shows the Quantizer value (MQUANT or GQUANT) in effect prior to the start of this packet. Set to 0 if the packet begins with a GOB header.
• HMVD -- Horizontal motion vector data field. Represents the reference horizontal motion vector data (MVD). Set to 0 if V flag is 0 or if the packet begins with a GOB header, or when the MTYPE of the last MB encoded in the previous packet was not MC.
• VMVD -- Vertical motion vector data (VMVD). Reference vertical motion vector data (MVD). Set to 0 if V flag is 0 or if the packet begins with a GOB header, or when the MTYPE of the last MB encoded in the previous packet was not MC.

Related Protocols

RTP, RTSP, H.248, H.323, H.225, H.245, H.263, H.264, MPEG-4

Sponsor Source

H.261 is an ITU-T (http://www.itu.int/ITU-T/) standards.

Reference

http://www.javvin.com/protocol/rfc2032.pdf
RTP Payload Format for H.261 Video Streams
http://www.h323forum.org/papers/
H.323 papers and documents

H.263: Video CODEC for Medium Quality Videoconferencing

Protocol Description

The H.263, by the International Telecommunications Union (ITU), supports video compression (coding) for video-conferencing and video-telephony applications. H.263 was developed to stream video at bandwidths as low as 20K to 24K bit/sec and was based on the H.261 codec. As a general rule, H.263 requires half the bandwidth to achieve the same video quality as in the H.261. As a result, H.263 has largely replaced H.261. H.263 uses RTP to transport video streams.

The coding algorithm of H.263 is similar to that used by H.261, however with some improvements and changes to improve performance and error recovery. Half pixel precision is used for motion compensation whereas H.261 used full pixel precision and a loop filter. Some parts of the hierarchical structure of the datastream are now optional, so the codec can be configured for a lower datarate or better error recovery. There are now four optional negotiable options included to improve performance: Unrestricted Motion Vectors, Syntax-based arithmetic coding, Advance prediction, and forward-and-backward frame prediction similar to MPEG called P-B frames.

H.263 supports five resolutions. In addition to QCIF and CIF that were supported by H.261 there are SQCIF, 4CIF, and 16CIF. SQCIF is approximately half the resolution of QCIF. 4CIF and 16CIF are 4 and 16 times the resolution of CIF respectively. The support of 4CIF and 16CIF means the codec can compete with other higher bitrate video coding standards such as the MPEG standards.

The differences between the H.261 and H.263 coding algorithms are listed as follows:

Picture format	Luminance pixels	Luminance lines	H.261 support	H.263 support	Uncompressed bit rate (Mbits/s)			
					10 frames/s		30 frames/s	
					Grey	Color	Grey	Color
SQCIF	128	96		Yes	1.0	1.5	3.0	4.4
QCIF	176	144	Yes	Yes	2.0	3.0	6.1	9.1
CIF	352	288	Optional	Optional	8.1	12.2	24.3	36.5
4CIF	704	576		Optional	32.4	48.7	97.3	146.0
16CIF	1408	1152		Optional	129.8	194.6	389.3	583.9

H.263 video streams need to be packetized for transportion over networks. The transport protocol for H.263 streams is the Real Time Transport Protocol (RTP).

Protocol Structure

The Real Time Transport Protocol (RTP) is used for the transportation of H.263 video streams. Three formats (mode A, mode B and mode C) are defined for the H.263 payload

header . In mode A, an H.263 payload header of four bytes is present before the actual compressed H.263 video bitstream. It allows fragmentation at GOB boundaries. In mode B, an 8-byte H.263 payload header is used and each packet starts at MB boundaries without the PB-frames option. Finally, a 12-byte H.263 payload header is defined in mode C to support fragmentation at MB boundaries for frames that are coded with the PB-frames option.

The format of the header for mode A is shown in the following illustration:

1	2	5	8	11	12	13	14	15	16bit
F	P	SBIT	EBIT	SRC	I	U	S	A	R
R (cont.)		DBQ	TRB	TR					

- F -- Flag bit indicates the mode of the payload header. Values are as follows:
  - 0 -- mode A.
  - 1 -- mode B or mode C depending on P bit.
- P -- P bit specifies the optional PB-frames mode.
- SBIT -- Start bit position specifies number of most significant bits that are ignored in the first data byte.
- EBIT -- End bit position specifies number of least significant bits that are ignored in the last data byte.
- SRC -- Source format (bit 6,7 and 8 in PTYPE in the standard H.263 compressed bitstream) specifies the resolution of the current picture.
- I -- Picture coding type (bit 9 in PTYPE in the standard H.263 compressed bitstream).
- U -- Set to 1 if the Unrestricted Motion Vector option (bit 10 in PTYPE in the standard H.263 compressed bitstream) was set to 1 in the current picture header, otherwise 0.
- S -- Set to 1 if the Syntax-based Arithmetic Coding option (bit 11 in PTYPE in the standard H.263 compressed bitstream) was set to 1 for the current picture header, otherwise 0.
- A -- Set to 1 if the Advanced Prediction option (bit 12 in PTYPE in the standard H.263 compressed bitstream) was set to 1 for current picture header, otherwise 0.
- R -- Reserved; set to zero.
- DBQ -- Differential quantization parameter used to calculate quantizer for the B frame based on quantizer for the P frame, when PB-frames option is used. The value should be the same as DBQUANT in the standard H.263 compressed bitstream. Set to zero if PB-frames option is not used.
- TRB -- Temporal Reference for the B frame in the standard H.263 compressed bitstream. Set to zero if PB-frames option is not used.
- TR -- Temporal Reference for the P frame in the standard H.263 compressed bitstream. Set to zero if the PB-frames option is not used.

The format of the header for mode B is shown here:

1	2	5	8	11	16bit
F	P	SBIT	EBIT	SRC	QUANT
GOBN			MBR		R
I	U	S	A	HMV1	VMV1	HMV2	VMV2

• F, P, SBIT, EBIT, SRC, I, U, S and A are defined the same as in mode A.

• QUANT -- Quantization value for the first MB coded at the starting of the packet. Set to 0 if the packet begins with a GOB header.

• GOBN -- GOB number in effect at the start of the packet. GOB number is specified differently for different resolutions.

• MBA -- The address within the GOB of the first MB in the packet, counting from zero in scan order. For example, the third MB in any GOB is given MBA=2.

• R -- Reserved, set to zero.

• HMV1, VMV1 -- Horizontal and vertical motion vector predictors for the first MB in this packet. When four motion vectors are used for the current MB with advanced prediction option, they are the motion vector predictors for block number 1 in the MB. Each 7-bit field encodes a motion vector predictor in half pixel resolution as a 2's complement number.

• HMV2, VMV2 -- Horizontal and vertical motion vector predictors for block number 3 in the first MB in this packet when four motion vectors are used with the advanced prediction option. This is needed because block number 3 in the MB needs different motion vector predictors from other blocks in the MB. These two fields are not used when the MB only has one motion vector. Each 7 bits field encodes a motion vector predictor in half pixel resolution as a 2's complement number.

The format of the header for mode C is shown here:

1	2		5		8		11			16bit
F	P	SBIT		EBIT		SRC		QUANT		
GOBN			MBR							R
I	U	S	A	HMV1		VMV1		HMV2		VMV2
RR										
RR(c)		DBR		TRB		TR				

• F, P, SBIT, EBIT, SRC, I, U, S, A, DBQ, TRB and TR are defined as in mode A. QUANT, GOBN, MBA, HMV1, VMV1, HMV2, VNV2 are defined the same as in mode B.

• RR -- Reserved, set to zero (19 bits).

Related Protocols

RTP, RTSP, H.245, H.323, H.225, H.261, H.264, MPEG-4

Sponsor Source

H.263 is an ITU-T (http://www.itu.int/ITU-T/) standards.

Reference

http://www.javvin.com/protocol/rfc2190.pdf
RTP Payload Format for H.263 Video Streams
http://www.h323forum.org/papers/
H.323 papers and documents

H.264/MPEG-4: Video CODEC For High Quality Video Streaming

Protocol Description

The H.264 and the MPEG-4 Part 10, also named Advanced Video Coding (AVC), is jointly developed by ITU and ISO. H.264/MPEG-4 supports video compression (coding) for video-conferencing and video-telephony applications. The H.264 video codec has a very broad rang of applications that covers all forms of digital compressed video from, low bit-rate Internet streaming applications to HDTV broadcast and Digital Cinema applications with nearly lossless coding. H.264/MPEG-4 is designed as a simple and straightforward video coding, with enhanced compression performance, and to provide a "network-friendly" video representation. H.264/MPEG-4 has achieved a significant improvement in the rate-distortion efficiency –providing a factor of two in bit-rate savings compared with MPEG-2 Video, which is the most common standard used for video storage and transmission. The coding gain of H.264 over H.263 is in the range of 25% to 50%, depends on the types of applications.

The H.264/MPEG-4 design covers a Video Coding Layer (VCL), which efficiently represents the video content, and a Network Abstraction Layer (NAL), which formats the VCL representation of the video and provides header information in a manner appropriate for conveyance by particular transport layers (such as Real Time Transport Protocol) or storage media. All data are contained in NAL units, each of which contains an integer number of bytes. A NAL unit specifies a generic format for use in both packet-oriented and bitstream systems. The format of NAL units for both packet-oriented transport and bitstream delivery is identical - except that each NAL unit can be preceded by a start code prefix in a bitstream-oriented transport layer.

H.264/MPEG-4 video streams need to be packetized for transportion over networks. The transport protocol for H.264/MPEG-4 streams is the Real Time Transport Protocol (RTP).

The following table lists the H.264/MPEG-4 key features and benefits:

Feature	Benefit
Quarter-sample-accurate motion compensation	H.264 codec uses quarter-sample-accurate motion compensation as in H.263 with further enhancements and reduced complexity.
Display order and referencing independency	The decoder may choose the most efficient way of displaying pictures for motion compensation referencing improving overall performance.
Weighted prediction	Motion-compensated prediction signal may be weighted and offset by the encoder, improving performance in scenes containing fades.

Small block-size transform	H.264 is based primarily on 4x4 transform, which positively influences the quality of certain scenes.
Hierarchical block-size transform	Even though the default block-size transform is 4x4, the standard is flexible enough for bigger block-size transforms, such as 8x8 or 16x16, for improved performance in certain scenes.
Short word-length transform	H.264 reduces computation complexity requiring only 16-bit processing.
Exact-match inverse transform	As opposed to most previous standards, all decoders processing video stream encoded using H.264 will produce exactly the same picture.
Arithmetic and context-adaptive entropy coding	H.264 codec uses advanced entropy coding methods improving overall performance.
Parameter set structure	The separation of the parameter set structure from the remaining data and special handling makes it less prone to information loss.

Protocol Structure

The Network Abstraction Layer (NAL) unit type octet has the following format:The format of the header for mode A is shown in the following illustration:

1	3	8 bit
F	NRI	Type

• F: Forbidden_zero_bit. The H.264 specification declares a value of 1 as a syntax violation.
• NRI: nal_ref_idc. 00: the content of the NAL unit is not used to reconstruct reference pictures for inter picture prediction. Other values: the decoding of the NAL unit is required to maintain the integrity of the reference pictures.
• Type: nal_unit_payload type.

Type	Packet	Type Name
0	undefined	
1-23	NAL unit	Single NAL unit packet per H.264
24	STAP-A	Single-time aggregation packet
25	STAP-B	Single-time aggregation packet
26	MTAP16	Multi-time aggregation packet
27	MTAP24	Multi-time aggregation packet
28	FU-A	Fragmentation unit
29	FU-B	Fragmentation unit
30-31	undefined	

Since the Real Time Transport Protocol (RTP) is the transport protocol for H.264/MPEG-4 video streams, the H.264 / MPEG-4 pakects are encapsulated by RTP frames.

Related Protocols
RTP, RTSP, H.245, H.323, H.225, H.261, H.263, MPEG-2

Sponsor Source

H.264/MPEG-4 is developed jointly by ITU (http://www.itu.int) ISO (http://www.iso.org).

Reference
http://www.javvin.com/protocol/rfc3984.pdf
RTP Payload Format for H.264 Video
http://www.vcodex.com/h264.html
H.264 / MPEG-4 Part 10 Tutorials

RTP: Real-Time Transport Protocol

Protocol Description

The Real-time Transport Protocol (RTP) provides end-to-end delivery services for data with real-time characteristics, such as interactive audio and video or simulation data, over multicast or unicast network services. Applications typically run RTP on top of UDP to make use of its multiplexing and checksum services; both protocols contribute parts of the transport protocol functionality. However, RTP may be used with other suitable underlying network or transport protocols. RTP supports data transfer to multiple destinations using multicast distribution if provided by the underlying network.

RTP itself does not provide any mechanism to ensure timely delivery or provide other quality-of-service guarantees but relies on lower-layer services to do so. It does not guarantee delivery or prevent out-of-order delivery, nor does it assume that the underlying network is reliable. It delivers packets in sequence. The sequence numbers included in RTP allow the receiver to reconstruct the sender's packet sequence but sequence numbers might also be used to determine the proper location of a packet, for example in video decoding, without necessarily decoding packets in sequence.

RTP consists of two closely-linked parts:

The real-time transport protocol (RTP), to carry data that has real-time properties.

The RTP control protocol (RTCP), to monitor the quality of service and to convey information about the participants in an on-going session. The latter aspect of RTCP may be sufficient for "loosely controlled" sessions, i.e., where there is no explicit membership control and set-up, but it is not necessarily intended to support all of an application's control communication requirements.

Protocol Structure

2	3	4	8	9	16bit	32bit
V	P	X	CSRC count	M	Payload type	Sequence number
Timestamp						
SSRC: Synchronization source						
CSRC: Contributing source (variable 0 – 15 items 32bits each)						

• V -- Version. Identifies the RTP version.
• P -- Padding. When set, the packet contains one or more additional padding octets at the end which are not part of the payload.
• X -- Extension bit. When set, the fixed header is followed by exactly one header extension, with a defined format.
• CSRC count -- Contains the number of CSRC identifiers that follow the fixed header.
• M -- Marker. The interpretation of the marker is defined by a profile. It is intended to allow significant events such as frame boundaries to be marked in the packet stream.
• Payload type -- Identifies the format of the RTP payload and determines its interpretation by the application. A profile specifies a default static mapping of payload type codes to payload formats. Additional payload type codes may be defined dynamically through non-RTP means.
• Sequence number -- Increments by one for each RTP data packet sent, and may be used by the receiver to detect packet loss and to restore packet sequence.
• Timestamp -- Reflects the sampling instant of the first octet in the RTP data packet. The sampling instant must be derived from a clock that increments monotonically and linearly in time to allow synchronization and jitter calculations.
• SSRC -- Synchronization source. This identifier is chosen randomly, with the intent that no two synchronization sources within the same RTP session will have the same SSRC identifier.
• CSRC -- Contributing source identifiers list. Identifies the contributing sources for the payload contained in this packet.

Related Protocols

RTCP, RTSP, UDP, TCP, IP

Sponsor Source

RTP is defined by IETF (www.ietf.org) in RFC 3550 and 3551.

Reference

http://www.javvin.com/protocol/rfc3550.pdf
RTP: A Transport Protocol for Real-Time Applications
http://www.javvin.com/protocol/rfc3551.pdf
RTP Profile for Audio and Video Conferences with Minimal Control

RTCP: RTP Control Protocol

Protocol Description

The RTP control protocol (RTCP) is based on the periodic transmission of control packets to all participants in the session, using the same distribution mechanism as the data packets. The underlying protocol must provide multiplexing of the data and control packets, for example using separate port numbers with UDP. RTCP performs four functions:

1. RTCP provides feedback on the quality of the data distribution. This is an integral part of the RTP's role as a transport protocol and is related to the flow and congestion control functions of other transport protocols.

2. RTCP carries a persistent transport-level identifier for an RTP source called the canonical name or CNAME. Since the SSRC identifier may change if a conflict is discovered or a program is restarted, receivers require the CNAME to keep track of each participant. Receivers may also require the CNAME to associate multiple data streams from a given participant in a set of related RTP sessions, for example, to synchronize audio and video.

3. The first two functions require that all participants send RTCP packets, therefore the rate must be controlled in order for RTP to scale up to a large number of participants. By having each participant send its control packets to all the others, each can independently observe the number of participants. This number is used to calculate the rate at which the packets are sent.

4. An OPTIONAL function is to convey minimal session control information, for example, participant identification to be displayed in the user interface. This is most likely to be useful in "loosely controlled" sessions where participants enter and leave without membership control or parameter negotiation.

Functions 1-3 SHOULD be used in all environments, but particularly in the IP multicast environment. RTP application designers SHOULD avoid mechanisms that can only work in unicast mode and will not scale to larger numbers. Transmission of RTCP MAY be controlled separately for senders and receivers for cases such as unidirectional links where feedback from receivers is not possible.

Protocol Structure

2	3	8	16bit
Version	P	RC	Packet type
Length			

• Version -- Identifies the RTP version which is the same in RTCP packets as in RTP data packets. The version defined by this specification is two (2).

• P -- Padding. When set, this RTCP packet contains some additional padding octets at the end which are not part of the control information. The last octet of the padding is a count of how many padding octets should be ignored. Padding may be needed by some encryption algorithms with fixed block sizes. In a compound RTCP packet, padding should only be required on the last individual packet because the compound packet is encrypted as a whole.

• RC -- Reception report count, the number of reception report blocks contained in this packet. A value of zero is valid. Packet type Contains the constant 200 to identify this as an RTCP SR packet.

• Length -- The length of this RTCP packet in 32-bit words minus one, including the header and any padding. (The offset of one makes zero a valid length and avoids a possible infinite loop in scanning a compound RTCP packet, while counting 32-bit words avoids a validity check for a multiple of 4.)

Related Protocols

RTP, RTSP, UDP, TCP, IP

Sponsor Source

RTCP is defined by IETF (www.ietf.org) in RFC 3550.

Reference

http://www.javvin.com/protocol/rfc3550.pdf
RTP: A Transport Protocol for Real-Time Applications

Other Protocols

COPS: Common Open Policy Service

Protocol Description

The Common Open Policy Service (COPS) protocol is a simple query and response protocol that can be used to exchange policy information between a policy server (Policy Decision Point or PDP) and its clients (Policy Enforcement Points or PEPs). One example of a policy client is an RSVP router that must exercise policy-based admission control over RSVP usage. At least one policy server exists in each controlled administrative domain. The COPS protocol has a simple but extensible design. The main characteristics of the COPS protocol include:

1. COPS employs a client/server model where the PEP sends requests, updates, and deletes to the remote PDP and the PDP returns decisions back to the PEP.
2. COPS uses TCP as its transport protocol for reliable exchange of messages between policy clients and a server.
3. COPS is extensible in that it is designed to leverage off self-identifying objects and can support diverse client specific information without requiring modifications to the COPS protocol itself. COPS was created for the general administration, configuration, and enforcement of policies.
4. COPS provides message level security for authentication, replay protection, and message integrity. COPS can also re-use existing protocols for security such as IPsec or TLS to authenticate and secure the channel between the PEP and the PDP.
5. COPS is stateful in two main aspects: (1) Request/Decision state is shared between client and server and (2) State from various events (Request/Decision pairs) may be inter-associated.
6. Additionally, COPS is stateful in that it allows the server to push configuration information to the client, and then allows the server to remove such state from the client when it is no longer applicable.

Protocol Structure

COPS common header:

4	8	16	32bit
Version	Flags	Op Code	Client-type
Message Length			

• Version -- The version field specifies the COPS version number. The current version is 1.
• Flags -- The defined flag values is 1 a Solicited Message Flag Bit. This flag is set when the message is solicited by another COPS message. (All other flags MUST be set to 0).
• Op Code -- Code identifying the COPS operations: 1 Request (REQ); 2 Decision (DEC); 3 Report State (RPT); 4 Delete Request State (DRQ); 5 Synchronize State Req (SSQ); 6 Client-Open (OPN); 7 Client-Accept (CAT); 8 Client-Close (CC); 9 Keep-Alive (KA); 10 Synchronize Complete (SSC)
• Client-type -- The Client-type identifies the policy client. Interpretation of all encapsulated objects is relative to the client-type.
• Message length -- Size of message in octets, which includes the standard COPS header and all encapsulated objects.

Related Protocols

TCP, RSVP

Sponsor Source

COPS is defined by IETF (www.ietf.org) in RFC 2748.

Reference

http://www.javvin.com/protocol/rfc2748.pdf
The COPS (Common Open Policy Service) Protocol

SIGTRAN: Signaling Transport Protocol Stack

Protocol Description

Signaling Transport (SIGTRAN) refers to a protocol stack for the transport of Switched Circuit Network (SCN) signaling protocols (such as SS7/C7 and Q.931) over an IP network. SIGTRAN, an evolution of the PSTN signaling, defines adaptors and a core transport capabilities that blend SS7 and packet protocols to provide users with the best both technologies have to offer. Applications of SIGTRAN include:Internet dial-up remote access, IP telephony interworking with PSTN and other services as identified.

The key components in the SIGTRAN achitecture are as follows:

• MGC -- Media Gateway Controller, responsible for mediating call control (between the SG and MG) and controlling access from the IP world to/from the PSTN.
• SG -- Signaling Gateway, responsible for interfacing to the SS7 network and passing signaling messages to the IP nodes.
• MG -- Media Gateway, responsible for packetization of voice traffic and transmitting the traffic towards the destination.
• IP SCP -- an IP-enabled Service Control Point (SCP). This exists wholly within the IP network,but is addressable from the SS7 network.
• IP Phone -- generically referred to as a "terminal."

The interfaces pertaining to signaling transport include SG to MGC, SG to SG. Signaling transport may potentially be applied to the MGC to MGC or MG to MGC interfaces as well, depending on requirements for transport of the associated signaling protocol.

For interworking with SS7-controlled SCN networks, the SG terminates the SS7 link and transfers the signaling information to the MGC using signaling transport. The MG terminates the interswitch trunk and controls the trunk based on the control signaling it receives from the MGC. For interworking with PSTN (Public Switched Telephone Network), IP networks will need to transport signaling such as Q.931 or SS7 ISUP messages between IP nodes such as a Signaling Gateway and Media Gateway Controller or Media Gateway.

Stream Control Transmission Protocol (SCTP), a core protocol in the SIGTRAN protocol stack, provides transport layer services over IP. Examples of such transport include: transport of signaling between a Signaling Gateway and Media Gateway or Media Gateway Controller; transport of signaling ("back-haul") from a Media Gateway to a Media Gateway Controller; transport of TCAP between a Signaling Gateway and other IP nodes. SCTP is used by one of the following User Adaptation layer protocols.

• SUA -- Signalling Connection Control Part User Adaptation Layer
• IUA -- ISDN Q.921-User Adaptation Layer
• M3UA -- SS7 Message Transfer Part 3 (MTP3) User Adaptation layer

• M2UA -- SS7 Message Transfer Part 2 (MTP2) User Adaptation layer
• M2PA -- MTP2 Peer-to-peer user Adaptation layer
• V5UA -- V5.2-User Adaptation Layer

For each, the SS7 stack is substituted at one of its well-defined layers with a packet transport replacement. By moving up to higher layers in the stack, more of the legacy SS7 concepts can be eliminated and replaced with flexible packet and IP protocol routing capabilities. Because SIGTRAN is an industry standard, it allows customers to interoperate in a multi-vendor environment.

Protocol Structure

SIGTRAN Architecture:

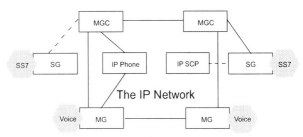

Figure 2-14: SIGTRAN Architecute

SIGTRAN Protocol Stack:

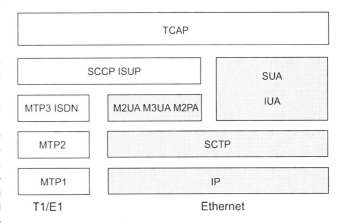

Figure 2-15: SIGTRAN Protocol Stack

Related Protocols

SS7, ISUP, MTP, SCCP, TCAP, SCTP, SUA, IUA, M2UA, M3UA, M3PA, Q.931

Sponsor Source

SIGTRAN protocols are defined by the IETF – SIGTRAN committee.

Reference

http://www.javvin.com/protocol/rfc2719.pdf
Architectural Framework for Signaling Transport
http://www.javvin.com/protocol/rfc2960.pdf
Stream Control Transmission Protocol
http://www.javvin.com/protocol/rfc3057.pdf
ISDN Q.921-User Adaptation Layer

http://www.javvin.com/protocol/rfc3331.pdf
Signaling System 7 (SS7) Message Transfer Part (MTP)2 - User Adaptation Layer
http://www.javvin.com/protocol/rfc3332.pdf
SS7 MTP3-User Adaptation Layer (M3UA)
http://www.javvin.com/protocol/rfc3788.pdf
Security Considerations for SIGTRAN Protocols
http://www.javvin.com/protocol/rfc3807.pdf
V5.2-User Adaptation Layer (V5UA)
http://www.javvin.com/protocol/rfc3873.pdf
Stream Control Transmission Protocol Management Information Base
http://www.javvin.com/protocol/rfc3868.pdf
Signalling Connection Control Part User Adaptation Layer (SUA)
http://www.javvin.com/protocol/rfc4165.pdf
Signaling System 7 (SS7) Message Transfer Part 2 (MTP2) - User Peer-to-Peer Adaptation Layer (M2PA)

SCTP: Stream Control Transmission Protocol

Protocol Description

Stream Control Transmission Protocol (SCTP), a key protocol in the Signalling Transport (SIGTRAN) protocol family, was originally designed to transport PSTN signaling messages (SS7/C7) over IP networks. Similar to TCP, SCTP is a reliable transport protocol operating on top of a connectionless packet network such as IP. SCTP is designed to address the limitations and complexity of TCP while transporting real time signaling and data such as SS7/C7 over an IP network. Due to its advantages, broader applications are found for the SCTP in other signaling and non-signaling transportations.

SCTP offers the following core services:

• acknowledged error-free non-duplicated transfer of user data;
• data fragmentation to conform to discovered path MTU size;
• sequenced delivery of user messages within multiple streams, with an option for order-of-arrival delivery of individual user messages;
• optional bundling of multiple user messages into a single SCTP packet; and
• network-level fault tolerance through supporting of multi homing at either or both ends of an association.

The design of SCTP includes appropriate congestion avoidance behavior and resistance to flooding and masquerade attacks. The SCTP datagram is comprised of a common header and chunks. The chunks contain either control information or user data.

Stream Control Transmission Protocol, working with other protocols in the SIGTRAN protocol stack, provides transport layer services over IP for SS7/C7. Examples of such transport include: transport of signaling between a Signaling Gateway and Media Gateway or Media Gateway Controller; transport of signaling ("backhaul") from a Media Gateway to a Media Gateway Controller; transport of TCAP between a Signaling Gateway and other IP nodes.

SCTP can also be used to provide the transport services to the Session Initiation Protocol (SIP), which is used to initiate and manage interactive sessions on the Internet. SCTP has also other non-signalling applications such as:

• Transport of Authentication, Authorization and Accounting (AAA) information.
• Transport of Block Storage traffic (for example, SCSI, Fibre Channel...)
• Transport of Remote Direct Data Placement traffic.
• Transport of Reliable Server pooling traffic.
• Transport of IP Flow information export traffic.

Protocol Structure

SCTP Common Header Structure:

16	32bit

Source Port Number	Destination Port Number
Verification Tag	
Checksum	

• Source Port Number -- SCTP sender's port number. It can be used by the receiver, in combination with the source IP Address, to identify the association to which this datagram belongs.
• Destination Port Number -- Destination port number where SCTP datagram is intended to go. The receiving host will use this port number to de-multiplex the SCTP datagram to the correct receiving endpoint/application.
• Verification Tag -- The receiver uses the Verification tag to identify the association. On transmit, the value of this Verification tag must be set to the value of the Initiate tag received from the peer endpoint during the association initialization.
• Checksum -- This field contains an Adler-32 checksum on this SCTP datagram.

The field format for the chunks to be transmitted in the SCTP packet:

8	16	32bit
Chunk Type	Chunk Flag	Chunk Length
Chunk value (Variable length)		

• Chunk Type -- Identifies the type of information contained in the Chunk Value field. It takes a value from 0 to 254.
• Chunk Flags -- The usage of these bits depends on the chunk type as given by the Chunk Type. Unless otherwise specified, they are set to zero on transmit and are ignored on receipt.
• Chunk Length -- Represents the size of the chunk in bytes including the Chunk Type, Chunk Flags, Chunk Length, and Chunk Value fields. Therefore, if the Chunk Value field is zero-length, the Length field will be set to 4. The Chunk Length field does not count any padding.
• Chunk Value -- Contains the actual information to be transferred in the chunk. The usage and format of this field is dependent on the Chunk Type.

The total length of a chunk (including Type, Length and Value fields) MUST be a multiple of 4 bytes. If the length of the chunk is not a multiple of 4 bytes, the sender MUST pad the chunk with all zero bytes and this padding is not included in the chunk length field. The sender should never pad with more than 3 bytes. The receiver MUST ignore the padding bytes.

Related Protocols
TCP, IP, SS7/C7, SIGTRAN, SIP

Sponsor Source
SCTP is defined by IETF (www.ietf.org) in RFC 2960 and updated in RFC 3309.

Reference
http://www.javvin.com/protocol/rfc2960.pdf
Stream Control Transmission Protocol
http://www.javvin.com/protocol/rfc4168.pdf
The Stream Control Transmission Protocol (SCTP) as a Transport for the Session Initiation Protocol (SIP)

TRIP: Telephony Routing over IP

Protocol Description

Telephony Routing over IP (TRIP) is a policy driven inter-administrative domain protocol for advertising the reachability of telephony destinations between location servers and for advertising attributes of the routes to those destinations. TRIP's operation is independent of any signaling protocol; hence TRIP can serve as the telephony routing protocol for any signaling protocol.

The primary function of a TRIP speaker, called a location server (LS), is to exchange information with other LSs. This information includes the reachability of telephony destinations, the routes towards these destinations, and information about gateways towards those telephony destinations residing in the PSTN. LSs exchange sufficient routing information to construct a graph of ITAD connectivity so that routing loops may be prevented. In addition, TRIP can be used to exchange attributes necessary to enforce policies and to select routes based on path or gateway characteristics. This specification defines TRIP's transport and synchronization mechanisms, its finite state machine, and the TRIP data. This specification defines the basic attributes of TRIP. The TRIP attribute set is extendible, so additional attributes may be defined in future documents.

TRIP, used to distribute telephony routing information between telephony administrative domains, is modeled after the Border Gateway Protocol 4, which is used to distribute routing information between administrative domains. TRIP is enhanced with some link state features, as in the Open Shortest Path First (OSPF) protocol, IS-IS, and the Server Cache Synchronization Protocol (SCSP). TRIP uses BGP's inter-domain transport mechanism, BGP's peer communication, BGP's finite state machine, and similar formats and attributes to BGP. Unlike BGP however, TRIP permits generic intra-domain LS topologies, which simplifies configuration and increases scalability in contrast to BGP's full mesh requirement of internal BGP speakers. TRIP uses an intra-domain flooding mechanism similar to that used in OSPF, IS-IS, and SCSP.

TRIP runs over a reliable transport protocol. This eliminates the need to implement explicit fragmentation, retransmission, acknowledgment, and sequencing. The error notification mechanism used in TRIP assumes that the transport protocol supports a graceful close, i.e., that all outstanding data will be delivered before the connection is closed.

TRIP's operation is independent of any particular telephony signaling protocol. Therefore, TRIP can be used as the routing protocol for any of these protocols, e.g., H.323 and SIP.

The LS peering topology is independent of the physical topology of the network. In addition, the boundaries of an ITAD are independent of the boundaries of the layer 3 routing autonomous systems. Neither internal nor external TRIP peers need to be physically adjacent.

Protocol Structure

Each TRIP message has a fixed-size header. There may or may not be a data portion following the header, depending on the message type.

16	24bit
Length	Type

• Length -- unsigned integer indicating the total length of the message, including the header, in octets. Thus, it allows one to locate, in the transport-level stream, the beginning of the next message. The value of the Length field must always be at least 3 and no greater than 4096, and may be further constrained depending on the message type. No padding of extra data after the message is allowed, so the Length field must have the smallest value possible given the rest of the message.
• Type -- unsigned integer indicating the type code of the message. The following type codes are defined:
     1 -- OPEN
     2 -- UPDATE
     3 -- NOTIFICATION
     4 -- KEEPALIVE

Related Protocols

BGP-4, H.323, SIP, SCSP

Sponsor Source

TRIP is defined by IETF (www.ietf.org) in RFC 3219.

Reference

http://www.javvin.com/protocol/rfc3219.pdf
Telephony Routing over IP (TRIP)

Wide Area Network and WAN Protocols

Description

A Wide Area Network (WAN) is a computer network covering multiple distance areas, which may spread across the entire world. WANs often connect multiple smaller networks, such as local area networks (LANs) or metro area networks (MANs). The world's most popular WAN is the Internet. Some segments of the Internet are also WANs in themselves. A wide area network may be privately owned or rented from a service provider, but the term usually connotes the inclusion of public (shared user) networks.

A virtual private network (VPN) riding on the public switched data network (PSDN) is often used by organizations for their private and secured communications. VPN uses encryption and other techniques to make it appear that the organisation has a dedicated network while making use of the shared infrastructure of the WAN.

WANs generally utilize different networking technologies and equipment than do LANs. Key technologies often found in WANs include SONET, Frame Relay, X.25, ATM, and PPP.

WAN technologies and protocols are mostly data link layer (layer 2) protocols which are defined by many organizations over time. The key organizations in this space are IETF for PPP, ITU-T for ATM, Frame Relay, ISO for X.25 and SONET.

Key Protocols

The key WAN protocols are listed as follows:

WAN	Wide Area Network
ATM	ATM: Asynchronous Transfer Mode Reference Model
	ATM Layer
	AAL: ATM Adaptation Layer Type 0-5 reserved for variable bit rate video transfer.
	ATM UNI: ATM Signaling User-to-Network Interface
	LANE-NNI: LAN Emulation - Network to Network Interface
	LANE-UNI: LAN Emulation - User to Network Interface
	MPOA: Multi Protocol Over ATM
	PNNI: Private Network-to-Network Interface
	Q.2931: ATM Signalling User Interface
SONET/SDH	Synchronous Optical Network and Synchronous Digital Hierarchy
	EoS: Ethernet over SONET/SDH

Broadband Access	DOCSIS: Data Over Cable Service Interface Specification
	BISDN: Broadband Integrade Service Digital Network
	ISDN: Integrated Services Digital Network
	Q.931: ISDN network layer interface protocol
	LAPD: ISDN Link Access Protocol Channel D (Q.921)
	xDSL: Digital Subscriber Line Technologies (DSL, IDSL, ADSL, HDSL, SDSL, VDSL, G.Lite)
PPP	PPP: Point-to-Point Protocols
	BAP: PPP Bandwidth Allocation Protocol
	BACP: PPP Bandwidth Allocation Control Protocol
	BCP: PPP Bridging Control Protocol
	CHAP: Challenge Handshake Authentication Protocol
	EAP: PPP Extensible Authentication Protocol
	LCP: PPP Link Control Protocol
	MultiPPP: MultiLink PPP (MP)
	NCP: PPP Network Control Protocol
	PAP: Password Authentication Protocol
	PPPoE: PPP over Ethernet
	PPPoA: PPP over ATM AAL5
	PoS: Packet Over SONET/SDH
X.25	HDLC: High Level Data Link Control protocol
	LAPB: Link Access Procedure Balanced for x.25
	X.25: ITU-T WAN communication protocol
Frame Relay	Frame Relay: WAN protocol for internetworking at layer 2
	LAPF: Link Access Procedure/Protocol (ITU Q.922)
Other	IBM SDLC: Synchronous Data Link Control protocol

Related protocols
LAN, MAN, TCP/IP

ATM: Asynchronous Transfer Mode Reference Model and Protocols

Protocol Description

The Asynchronous Transfer Mode (ATM) comprises a protocol suite under the ATM reference model which establishes a mechanism to carry all traffic on a stream of fixed 53-byte packets (cells). A fixed-size packet can ensure that the switching and multiplexing function could be carried out quickly and easily. ATM is a connection-oriented technology, i.e. two systems on the network should inform all intermediate switches about their service requirements and traffic parameters in order to establish communication.

The ATM reference model present three planes and each plane has three layers. The following diagram illustrates the ATM reference model:

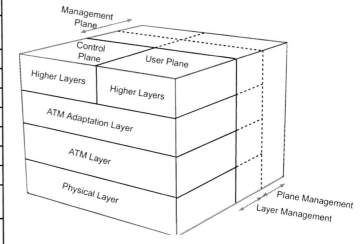

Figure 2-16: ATM Asynchronous Transfer Mode

The management plane performs two functions: layer management and plane management. The plane management provides management facilities for the systems as a whole. The layer management provides information and control facilities for the protocol entities that exists in each individual layer. This includes operation and maintenance (OAM) functions for each layer. The protocols in the ATM management plane are presented in separate articles.

The control plane is responsible for the supervision of connections, including call set-up, call release and maintenance. The protocols in the ATM control plane are presented in separate articles.

The user plane provides for the transfer of user information. It also includes mechanisms to perform error recovery, flow control etc. The ATM user plane is divided into three layers: the ATM adaptation layer (AAL), the ATM layer, and the physical layer. The AAL interfaces the higher layer protocols to the ATM Layer, which relays ATM cells both from the upper layers to the ATM Layer and vice versa. When relaying information received from the higher layers, the AAL segments the data into ATM cells. When relaying information received from the ATM Layer, the AAL must reassemble the payloads into a format the higher layers can understand. This is called Segmentation and Reassembly (SAR). Different AALs are defined in supporting different types of traffic or service expected to be used on ATM networks.

The ATM layer is responsible for relaying cells from the AAL to the physical layer for transmission and from the physical layer to the AAL for use at the end systems. It determines where the incoming cells should be forwarded to, resets the corresponding connection identifiers and forwards the cells to the next link, buffers cells and handles various traffic management functions such as cell loss priority marking, congestion indication, and generic flow control access. It also monitors the transmission rate and conformance to the service contract (traffic policing).

The physical layer of ATM defines the bit timing and other characteristics for encoding and decoding the data into suitable electrical/optical waveforms for transmission and reception on the specific physical media used. In addition, it also provides a frame adaptation function, which includes cell delineation, header error check (HEC) generation and processing, performance monitoring, and payload rate matching of the different transport formats used at this layer. SONET, DS3, Fiber, and twisted-pair are a few of the media often used at the physical layer.

The following table lists the main protocols in the ATM stack in the user plane:

ATM Protocol Stack	
Data Link Layers	
ATM Adaptation Layer (AAL)	Convergence Sublayer (CS) Segmentation and Reassembly (SAR) Sublayer
ATM Layer	Generic flow control (GFC) Cell header creation and verification Cell virtual path identifier (VPI) and virtual channel identifier (VCI) translation Cell multiplex and demultiplex
Physical Layers	
Transmission Convergence (TC) Sublayer	Header error control (HEC) generation and verification Cell delineation Cell-rate decoupling Transmission adaptation
Physical Medium Dependent (PMD) Sublayer	Bit timing (time recover) Line coding for physical medium

Protocol Structure

ATM Cell Format:

HEADER	GFC or VPI		VPI	
	VPI		VCI	
	VCI			
	VCI		PT (3 Bit)	CLP
	HEC			
IE	Cell Payload (48 Bytes)			

• Header -- (5 Bytes) Generic flow control, VPI/VCI, and other control header.
• IE -- (48 Bytes) Cell Payload.

Physical Layer Specification – Private UNI:

Frame Format	Bit Rate/Line Rate	Media
Cell Stream	25.6 Mbps/ 32 Mbaud	UTP-3
STS-1	51.84 Mbps	UTP-3
FDDI	100 Mbps/ 125 Mbaud	Multimode Fiber
STS-3c, STM-1	155.52 Mbps	UTP-5
STS-3c, STM-1	155.52 Mbps	Single-Mode Fiber, Multimode Fiber, Coax pair
Cell Stream	155.52 Mbps/ 194.4Mbaud	Multimode Fiber, STP
STS-3c, STM-1	155.52 Mbps	UTP-3
STS-12, STM-4	622.08 Mbps	SMF, MMF

Physical Layer Specification – Public UNI:

Frame Format	Bit Rate/Line Rate	Media
DS1	1.544 Mbp	Twisted pair
DS3	44.736 Mbps	Coax pair
STS-3c, STM-1	155.520 Mbps	Single-mode Fiber
E1	2.048 Mbps	Twisted pair, Coax pair
E3	34.368 Mbps	Coax pair
J2	6.312 Mbps	Coax pair
N × T1	N × 1.544 Mbps	Twisted pair

Related Protocols

SONET, AAL0-AAL5, LAN Emulation, CES, PNNI and MPOA, Q.2931

Sponsor Source

The ATM protocol reference model is based on standards developed by the ITU.

Reference

ITU-T Recommendation I.363, "B-ISDN ATM Adaptation Layer (AAL) Specification"
http://www.cisco.com/univercd/cc/td/doc/cisintwk/ito_doc/atm.htm
ATM Overview

ATM Layer: Asynchronous Transfer Mode Layer

Protocol Description

The ATM layer, the layer 2 in the ATM reference model, provides an interface between the ATM adaptation layer (AAL) and the physical layer. This layer is responsible for relaying cells from the AAL to the physical layer, such as SONET, for transmission and from the physical layer to the AAL for use at the end systems. It determines where the incoming cells should be forwarded to, resets the corresponding connection identifiers and forwards the cells to the next link, buffers incoming and outgoing cells and handles various traffic management functions, such as cell loss priority marking, congestion indication and generic flow control access. It also monitors the transmission rate and conformance to the service contract (traffic policing).

The fields in the ATM header define the functionality of the ATM layer. The format of the header for ATM cells has two different forms, one for use at the user-to-network interface (UNI) and the other for use internal to the network, the network-to-node interface (NNI).

Protocol Structure

UNI Structure:

8	7	6	5	4	3	2	1
GFC				VPI			
VPI				VCI			
VCI							
VCI			PT (3 Bit)			CLP	
HEC							
Information (48 Bytes)							

• GFC -- generic flow control, used to limit the amount of data entering the network during periods of congestion.
• VPI -- Virtual Path Identifier.
• VCI -- Virtual Channel Identifier. The VPI and the virtual channel identifier (VCI) together form the routing field, also called VPCI, which associates each cell with a particular channel or circuit. The VCI is a single-channel identifier. The VPI allows grouping of VCs with different VCIs and allows the group to be switched together as an entity. However, the VPIs and VCIs have significance only on the local link; the contents of the routing field will generally change as the cell traverses from link to link. These fields, in UNI, can support up to 16 million desks (users) to network sessions.
• PT -- Payload Type.
• CLP -- Cell Loss Priority.
• HEC -- Header Error Control.

NNI Structure:

8	7	6	5	4	3	2	1
VPI							

VPI	VCI	
VCI		
VCI	PT (3 Bit)	CLP
HEC		
Information (48 Bytes)		

• VPI -- Virtual Path Identifier.
• VCI -- Virtual Channel Identifier. See above for VPCI detail definition. These fields, which allows 268 millions NNI sessions, represent the network-to-node routing information within the ATM cell.
• PT -- Payload Type.
• CLP -- Cell Loss Priority.
• HEC -- Header Error Control.

Related Protocols

ATM, SONET, AAL0-AAL5, LAN Emulation (LANE), CES, UNI, NNI and Q.2931

Sponsor Source

The ATM protocols is based on standards developed by the ITU.

Reference

ITU-T Recommendation I.363, "B-ISDN ATM Adaptation Layer (AAL) Specification"
http://www.cisco.com/univercd/cc/td/doc/cisintwk/ito_doc/atm.htm
ATM Overview

AAL: ATM Adaptation Layers (AAL1, AAL2, AAL3/4, AAL5)

Protocol Description

The ATM Adaptation Layer (AAL) relays the ATM cells between ATM Layer and higher layers. When relaying information received from the higher layers, it segments the data into ATM cells. When relaying information received from the ATM Layer, it must reassemble the payloads into a format the higher layers can understand. This operation, which is called Segmentation and Reassembly (SAR), is the main task of AAL. Different AALs were defined in supporting different traffic or services expected to be used. The service classes and the corresponding types of AALs are as follows:

Class A -- Constant Bit Rate (CBR) service: AAL1 supports a connection-oriented service in which the bit rate is constant. Examples of this service include 64 Kbit/sec voice, fixed-rate uncompressed video and leased lines for private data networks.

Class B -- Variable Bit Rate (VBR) service: AAL2 supports a connection-oriented service in which the bit rate is variable but requires a bounded delay for delivery. Examples of this service include compressed packetized voice or video. The bounded delay for delivery is necessary for the receiver to reconstruct the original uncompressed voice or video.

Class C -- Connection-oriented data service: For connection-oriented file transfer and in general, data network applications where a connection is set up before data is transferred. This type of service has variable bit rate and does not require bounded delay for delivery. Two AAL protocols were defined to support this service class, and have been merged into a single type, called AAL3/4. However, with its high complexity, the AAL5 protocol is often used to support this class of service.

Class D -- Connectionless data service: Examples of this service include datagram traffic and in general, data network applications where no connection is set up before data is transferred. Either AAL3/4 or AAL5 can be used to support this class of service.

Operation Administration and Maintenance (OA&M) - OA&M is defined for supervision, testing, and performance monitoring. It uses loop-back for maintenance and ITU TS standard CMIP, with organization into 5 hierarchical levels: Virtual Channel (F5 - Between VC endpoints), Virtual Path (F4- Between VP endpoints), Transmission Path (F3- Between elements that perform assembling, and disassembling of payload, header, or control), Digital Section (F2 Between section end-points, performs frame synchronization) and Regenerator Section (F1- Between regeneration sections).

Protocol Structure

AAL0 PDU: AAL0 payload, also referred as raw cells, consists of 48 bytes without special fields.

AAL1 PDU: AAL1 is used for connection-oriented, delay-sensitive services requiring constant bit rates (CBR), such as video and voice traffic.

1	3 bits	3 bits	1	47 Bytes
SN		SNP		SAR
CSI	SC	CRC	P	Payload

• SN -- Sequence number. Numbers the stream of SAR PDUs of a CPCS PDU (modulo 16).
• CSI -- Convergence sublayer indicator. Used for residual time stamp for clocking.
• SC -- Sequence count.
• NP -- Sequence number protection.
• CRC -- Cyclic redundancy check calculated over the SAR header.
• P -- Parity calculated over the CRC.
• SAR PDU payload -- 47-byte user information field.

AAL2 PDU: AAL2, with compression, silent and idle channel suppression, is perfect for low-rate voice traffic. AAL2 is subdivided into the Common Part Sublayer (CPS) and the Service Specific Convergence Sublayer (SSCS).

AAL2 CPS Packet

The CPS packet consists of a 3 octet header followed by a payload. The structure of the AAL2 CPS packet is shown in the following illustration.

8bits	6bits	5bits	5bits	1-45/64 bytes
CID	LI	UUI	HEC	Information payload
AAL2 CPS packet				

• CID -- Channel identification.
• LI -- Length indicator: the length of the packet payload associated with each individual user. Value is one less than the packet payload and has a default value of 45 bytes (may be set to 64 bytes).
• UUI -- User-to-user indication. Provides a link between the CPS and an appropriate SSCS that satisfies the higher layer application.
• HEC -- Header error control.
• Information payload -- Contains the CPS/SSCS PDU.

AAL2 CPS PDU

The structure of the AAL2 CPS PDU is shown as follows:

6bits	1bit	1bit	0-47 bytes	0-47 bytes
OSF	SN	P	AAL2 PDU payload	PAD
AAL2 CPS PDU				

• OSF -- Offset field. Identifies the location of the start of the next CPS packet within the CPS-PDU.
• SN -- Sequence number. Protects data integrity.
• P -- Parity. Protects the start field from errors.
• SAR PDU payload -- Information field of the SAR PDU.
• PAD -- Padding.
AAL2 SSCS Packet

The SSCS conveys narrowband calls consisting of voice, voiceband data or circuit mode data. SSCS packets are transported as CPS packets over AAL2 connections. The CPS packet contains a SSCS payload. There are 3 SSCS packet types: Type 1 Unprotected (This is used by default); Type 2 Partially protected; and Type 3 Fully protected (The entire payload is protected by a 10-bit CRC which is computed as for OAM cells. The remaining 2 bits of the 2-octet trailer consist of the message type field).

AAL2 SSCS Type 3 Packets:

The AAL2 type 3 packets are used for Dialed digits, Channel associated signalling bits, Facsimile demodulated control data, Alarms and User state control operations. The general structure of AAL2 SSCS Type 3 PDUs is shown as follows. The format varies according to the actual message type.

2bits	14bits	16bits	6bits	10bits
Redundancy	Time stamp	Message dependant information	Message type	CRC-10
AAL2 SSCS Type 3 PDU – General Structure				

• Redundancy -- Packets are sent 3 times to ensure error correction. The value in this field signifies the transmission number.
• Time stamp -- Counters packet delay variation and allows a receiver to accurately reproduce the relative timing of successive events separated by a short interval.
• Message dependant information -- Packet content that varies, depending on the message type.
• Message type -- The message type code.
• CRC-10 -- The 10-bit CRC.

AAL3/4 PDU: AAL 3/4 supports both connectionless and connection-oriented links, but is primarily used for the transmission of SMDS packets over ATM networks.

2	4	10 bits	44 Bytes	6 bits	10 bits
ST	SN	MID	PDU Payload	LI	CRC

• ST -- Segment Type: BOM (Beginning of Message), COM (Continuation of Message), EOM (End of Message), SSM (Single Segment Message).
• SN -- Sequence number. Numbers the stream of SAR PDUs of a CPCS PDU (modulo 16).
• MID -- Multiplexing Indication
• PDU payload -- 44-byte user information field.
• LI -- Length indicator.
• CRC -- Cyclic redundancy check calculated over the SAR header.

AAL3/4 CS PDU:

1	1	2 bits	40 Bytes	1	1	2 bits
CPI	BTag	BA-size	PDU Payload + PAD	AL	ETag	LEN

• CPI -- Common Part Indication

- BTag -- Beginning Tag
- BAsize -- Buffer Allocation Size
- PDU payload -- Variable length user information field up to 40 Bytes
- PAD -- Padding (up to 3 bytes) used to cell align the trailer.
- AL -- Alignment. A filling byte coded with zero
- ETag -- End Tag.
- LEN -- Length of Information Field

AAL5 CS PDU: AAL5 supports connection-oriented VBR services. AAL5 is used predominantly for the transfer of classic IP over ATM and LANE traffic. AAL5 uses SEAL and is the least complex of the current AAL recommendations. AAL5 has no per-cell length or per-cell CRC fields. And offers low bandwidth overhead and simpler processing requirements in exchange for reduced bandwidth capacity and error-recovery capability.

0-48 Bytes	0-47	1	1	2	4 Bytes
PDU payload	PAD	UU	CPI	LI	CRC-32

- PDU payload -- Variable length user information field
- PAD -- Padding used to cell align the trailer which may be between 0 and 47 bytes long.
- UU -- CPCS user-to-user indication to transfer one byte of user information
- CPI -- Common Part Indication
- LI -- Length indicator.

For OA&M cells, there are pre-defined (reserved) VPI/VCI numbers:

- 0/0 Unassigned or Idle
- 0/1 Meta-signaling
- 0/3 Segment F4 Flow
- 0/4 End-to-end F4 flow
- 0/5 Signaling
- 0/15 SMDS
- 0/16 Interim Layer Management Interface (ILMI)

F4/F5 OA&M PDU format:

4 bits	4 bits	45 Bytes	6 bits	10 bits
OAM Type	Function Type	Function Spec	Re-serve	CRC-10

- OAM type / Function type -- The possible values for OAM type and function type are defined for Fault, Performance, Activation/Deactivation
- CRC-10 -- Cyclic redundancy check calculated over the SAR header. $G(x) = x^{10}+x^9+x^5+x^4+x+1$

Related Protocols

SONET, AAL0-AAL5, LAN Emulation, CES, PNNI and MPOA, Q.2931

Sponsor Source

ATM Adaptation Layers (AALs) are defined by ITU in document I.366.2.

Reference

http://www.cisco.com/univercd/cc/td/doc/cisintwk/ito_doc/atm.htm
ATM Overview

ATM UNI: ATM Signaling User-to-Network Interface

Protocol Description

Signalling is the process by which ATM users and the network exchange the control of information, request the use of network resources, or negotiate for the use of circuit parameters. The VPI/VCI pair and requested bandwidth are allocated as a result of a successful signalling exchange. These messages are sent over the Signalling ATM Adaptation Layer (SAAL), which ensures their reliable delivery. The SAAL is divided into a Service Specific Part and a Common Part. The Service Specific Part is further divided into a Service Specific Coordination Function (SSCF), which interfaces with the SSCF user; and a Service Specific Connection-Oriented Protocol (SSCOP), which assures reliable delivery.

The UNI signaling protocols within the SAAL are responsible for ATM call and connection control, including call establishment, call clearing, status enquiry and point-to-multipoint control between ATM end users and a private ATM switch, or between a private ATM switch and the public carrier ATM network. ATM UNI signaling message uses the Q.931 message format, which is made up of a message header and a variable number of Information Elements.

The VPI/VCI pair and requested bandwidth are allocated as a result of a successful signalling exchange. Two levels of virtual connections can be supported at the UNI:

1) a point-to-point or point-to-multipoint Virtual Channel Connection (VCC), which consists of a single connection established between two ATM VCC end-points;

2) a point-to-point or point-to-multipoint Virtual Path Connection (VPC), which consists of a bundle of VCCs carried transparently between two ATM VPC end-points.

For VPC at the Public UNI, traffic monitoring and throughput enforcement will be performed across all cells carried on the same VPI independently of the VCI values.

Protocol Structure

SAAL protocol stacks illustrated below support UNI connection control signaling:

	User-Network Signalling
	UNI SSCF
SAAL	SSCOP
	AAL Type 5 Common Part
	ATM Layer
	Physical Layer

UNI Signaling Message:

8	7	6	5	4	3	2	1	bit/Octet
Protocol discriminator								1

0	0	0	0	Length of call reference value		2
Flag	Call reference value					3
Call reference value (continued)						4
						5
Message type						6
Message type (continued)						7
Message length						8
Message length (continued)						9
Variable length Information Elements as required						etc.

• Protocol discriminator -- Distinguishes Messages for user-network call control from other messages. (9 for Q.2931 messages)

• Call reference -- Unique number for every ATM connection which serves to link all signalling messages relating to the same connection. It is comprised of the call reference value and the call reference flag. The call reference flag indicates who allocated the call reference value.

• Message type -- The message may be of the following types:

    1. Call establishment messages: such as CALL PROCEEDING, sent by the called user to the network or by the network to the calling user to indicate initiation of the requested call. CONNECT, sent by the called user to the network and by the network to the calling user to indicate that the called user accepted the call. CONNECT ACKNOWLEDGE, sent by the network to the called user to indicate that the call was awarded and by the calling user to the network; and SETUP, sent by the calling user to the network and by the network to the calling user to initiate a call.

    2. Call clearing messages: such as RELEASE, sent by the user to request that the network clear the connection or sent by the network to indicate that the connection has cleared. RELEASE COMPLETE, sent by either the user or the network to indicate that the originator has released the call reference and virtual channel. RESTART, sent by the user or the network to restart the indicated virtual channel. RESTART ACKNOWLEDGE, sent to acknowledge the receipt of the RESTART message.

    3. Miscellaneous messages: such as STATUS, sent by the user or network in response to a STATUS ENQUIRY message. STATUS ENQUIRY, sent by the user or the network to solicit a STATUS message.

    4. Point-to-Multipoint messages: such as ADD PARTY, which adds a party to an existing connection. ADD PARTY ACKNOWLEDGE, which acknowledges a successful ADD PARTY. ADD PARTY REJECT, which indicates an unsuccessful ADD PARTY. DROP PARTY, which drops a party from an existing point-to-multipoint connection. DROP PARTY ACKNOWLEDGE, which acknowledges a successful DROP PARTY.

• Message length -- The length of the contents of a message.

• Information Elements -- There are several types of information elements. Some may appear only once in the message; others may appear more than once. Depending on the message type, some information elements are mandatory and some are optional. The order of the information elements does not matter to the signalling protocol. The information elements in UNI 3.0 are listed in the following table:

IE	Description	Max. No.
Cause	Gives the reason for certain messages. For example, the Cause IE is part of the release message, indicating why the call was released.	2
Call state	Indicates the current state of the call.	1
Endpoint reference	Identifies individual endpoints in a point-to-multipoint call.	1
Endpoint state	Indicates the state of an endpoint in a point-to-multipoint call.	1
AAL parameters	Includes requested AAL type and other AAL parameters.	1
ATM user cell rate	Specifies traffic parameters.	1
Connection identifier	Identifies the ATM connection and gives the VPI and VCI values.	1
Quality of Service parameter	Indicates the required Quality of Service class for the connection.	1
Broadband high-layer information	Gives information about the high-layer protocols for compatibility purposes.	1
Broadband bearer capacity	Requests a service from the network (such as CBR or VBR link, point-to-point and point-to-multipoint link).	1
Broadband low-layer information	Checks compatibility with layer 2 and 3 protocols.	3
Broadband locking shift	Indicates a new active codeset.	-
Broadband non-locking shift	Indicates a temporary codeset shift.	-
Broadband sending complete	Indicates the competition of sending the called party number.	1
Broadband repeat indicator	Indicates how IEs which are repeated in the message should be handled.	1

Calling party number	Origin of the call.	1
Calling party sub-address	Subaddress of calling party.	1
Called party number	Destination of the call.	1
Called party sub-address	Subaddress of the called party.	1
Transit network selection	Identifies one requested transit network.	1
Restart indicator	Identifies which facilities should be restarted (e.g., one VC, all VCs).	1

Related Protocols

ATM, AAL0-AAL5, LAN Emulation (LANE), CES, PNNI, MPOA, NNI and Q.2931.

Sponsor Source

The ATM protocols are based on standards developed by the ITU.

Reference

ITU-T Recommendation I.363, "B-ISDN ATM Adaptation Layer (AAL) Specification"

http://www.cisco.com/univercd/cc/td/doc/cisintwk/ito_doc/atm.htm

ATM Overview

LANE NNI: ATM LAN Emulation NNI

Protocol Description

The ATM LAN Emulation (LANE) enables the implementation of emulated LANs over an ATM network. An emulated LAN provides communication of user data frames among all its users, similar to a physical LAN. One or more emulated LANs could run on the same ATM network. However, each of the emulated LANs is logically independent of the others. Communication between emulated LANs requires some type of interconnection device (bridge, router, etc.), even though direct ATM connections between emulated LANs are explicitly allowed in some circumstances. The LAN Emulation LUNI defines the protocols and interactions between LAN Emulation Clients (LE Clients) and the LAN Emulation Service. Each LE Client connects across the LUNI to a single LES and BUS, may connect to a single LECS, and may have connections to multiple SMSs.

The LAN Emulation NNI (LNNI) defines the behavior of these LANE service components as seen by each other, the procedures necessary to provide a distributed and reliable LAN Emulation Service. A single ELAN may be served by multiple LECSs, LESs, BUSs and SMSs. Each LES, BUS, and SMS serves a single ELAN, while an LECS may serve multiple ELANs. LANE service components interconnect with multiple VCCs for Configuration, Status, Database Synchronization, Control and Data forwarding. The LNNI specification provides multivendor interoperability among the components serving an ELAN so that consumers may mix and match the LANE Service implementations of different vendors.

LANE service consists of four major components:

• LAN emulation client (LEC) -- located in ATM end systems, implements the LUNI interface, serves as a proxy for LAN systems to perform data forwarding and address resolution, provides a MAC level emulated Ethernet/IEEE 802.3 or IEEE 802.5 service interface to higher level software.
• LAN emulation server (LES) -- supports the address resolution protocol (LE-ARP), and is used to determine the ATM address of the target LEC responsible for a certain destination MAC address. An LE Client is connected to only one LE Server. An LE Client may register LAN Destinations it represents and/or multicast MAC addresses it wishes to receive with its LE Server. An LE Client will also query its LE Server to resolve a MAC address or route descriptor of an ATM address.
• Broadcast/Unknown Server (BUS) -- handles all multicast traffic forwarding to all attached LECs. An LE Client sees a single Broadcast and Unknown Server.
• Selective Multicast Server (SMS) -- may be used to offload much of the multicast processing from the BUSs, which also have to forward broadcast frames and frames for unresolved LAN destinations, to efficiently forwaqrd multicast frames.

The multiple LANE Service entities serving an ELAN need to co-operate and communicate in order to provide a distributed and reliable LAN Emulation Service. The communications required for LNNI may be partitioned as follows:

a) Control Plane

• Configuration and Status Communications -- LESs and SMSs obtain configuration information from an LECS over Configuration Direct VCCs. LECSs obtain the status of LESs and SMSs over the same connection.
• LANE Control Communications -- Each LES is responsible for distributing LE_ARP requests for unregistered destinations from local LE Clients to local LE Clients and to other LESs. LESs must also forward LE_ARP responses back to the originator. Additionally, LESs must be able to forward LE_FLUSH responses and LE_TOPOLOGY requests to the correct destination(s).

b) Synchronization Plane

• LECS Synchronization -- A particular LECS may not directly receive status from all service components. Thus, LECSs must exchange LES and SMS status information among themselves. In order to distribute this status information, all LECSs participating in an ELAN must maintains an LECS Synchronization VCC to all other LECSs in the network.
• LES-SMS Database Synchronization -— LESs and SMSs use SCSP to synchronize their databases.

c) Data Plane

• BUS Data Communications -- Each BUS is assumed to be logically paired with an LES, and the BUS is assumed to have access to the registration database maintained by the LES, which includes the ATM address of all BUSs. No protocol is defined between a paired LES and BUS.
• SMS Data Communications -- Every SMS (and LES) obtains a complete copy of the registration database for the entire ELAN via SCSP, so every SMS knows of every other SMS and BUS. When an LE client uses LE_ARPs for a multicast address, the LES should assign the client to an SMS as a sender if an SMS is available for that destination, otherwise a BUS's ATM address is returned in the LE_ARP response. An ELAN, and hence all the ELAN's SMSs, may operate in either distributed or stand-alone mode, as determined by the network administrator.

Protocol Structure

LANE Data Frames:

The LNNI Control frame format is shown below:

0	LLC = X"AAAA03"		OUI
4	OUI	Frame Type	
8	ELAN-ID		

LANE Control Frame	12	REQUESTER-LECID		FLAGS
	16	SOURCE-LAN-DESTINATION		
	24	TARGET-LAN-DESTINATION		
	32	SOURCE-ATM-ADDRESS		
	52	LAN-Type	MAX-Frame-Size	Number-TLVS	ELAN-Name-Size
	56	TARGET-ATM-ADDRESS		
	76	ELAN-NAME		
	108	TLVs BEGIN		

• LLC -- Logical Link Control: The Control Coordinate VCCs are all LLC encapsulated.
• OUI -- Organizationally Unique Identifier = X"00A03E" which indicates ATM Forum.
• FRAME -- TYPE = X"000F"
• ELAN-ID -- Emulated LAN ID
• OP-CODE (2 Bytes) -- Control frame Operation type. Some defined OP-Code are:

OP-CODE Value	OP-CODE Function
X"000b"	LNNI_CONFIGURE_TRIGGER
X"000C"	LNNI_LECS_SYNC_REQUEST
X"000d"	LNNI_KEEP_ALIVE_REQUEST
X"000d"	LNNI_KEEP_ALIVE_RESPONSE
X"000e"	LNNI_VALIDATE_REQUEST
X"000e"	LNNI_VALIDATE_RESPONSE

• Status -- (2 Bytes) Control frame Operation status.
• TLV -- Type/ Length / Value Encoded Parameter, Examples of LNNI TLVs are:

Item	Type	LEN	Description
ServerId	00-A0-3E-14	2	Unique identifier for a server within an ELAN
Server-GroupId	00-A0-3E-15	2	Uniquely correlates to an ELAN-ID. Required for SCSP.
Synchro-nization-PeerServer	00-A0-3E-16	20	Multiplexed ATM Address of ES or SMS to synchronize DB using SCSP.
SmsMode-OfOpera-tion	00-A0-3E-19	1	Indicates SMS operational mode. 0 = STAND_ALONE 1 = DISTRIBUTED

Related Protocols

ATM, SONET, AAL0-AAL5, LAN Emulation (LANE), CES, UNI, NNI and Q.2931.

Sponsor Source

The ATM protocols are based on standards developed by the ITU.

Reference

ITU-T Recommendation I.363, "B-ISDN ATM Adaptation Layer (AAL) Specification"
http://www.cisco.com/univercd/cc/td/doc/cisintwk/ito_doc/atm.htm
ATM Overview

LANE UNI: ATM LAN Emulation UNI

Protocol Description

The ATM LAN emulation (LANE) specification defines how an ATM network can emulate a sufficient set of the medium access control (MAC) services of existing LAN technologies such as Ethernet and Token Ring, so that higher layer protocols can be used without modification. An emulated LAN (ELAN), which provides the appearance of either an Ethernet or Token-Ring LAN segment over a switched ATM network, is composed of a collection of LE Clients and a set of co-operating service entities: LAN Emulation Configuration Servers (LECSs), LAN Emulation Servers (LESs), Broadcast and Unknown Servers (BUSs), and Selective Multicast Servers (SMSs).

The LAN Emulation LUNI defines the protocols and interactions between LAN Emulation Clients (LE Clients) and the LAN Emulation Service, including initialization, registration, address resolution, and data transfer procedures. Each LE Client connects across the LUNI to a single LES and BUS, may connect to a single LECS, and may have connections to multiple SMSs.

Communication among LE Clients and between LE Clients and the LE Service is performed over ATM virtual channel connections (VCCs). Each LE Client must communicate with the LE Service over control and data VCCs. LANE assumes the availability of point-to-point and point-to-multipoint Switched Virtual Circuits (SVCs). Multicast Forward and Control Distribute flows are carried on point-to-multipoint VCCs. Data Direct, Control Direct, Configure Direct, Default Multicast Send and Selective Multicast Send flows are carried on point-to-point VCCs. Only Data Direct flows may be LLC-multiplexed. All other flows are non-multiplexed.

LAN Emulation encompasses both Ethernet and Token Ring emulation. In Ethernet emulation, a LAN Emulation component need examine only a data frame's destination MAC address in order to direct the frame towards its ultimate destinations. In Token Ring emulation, however, a LAN emulation component may have to use a "Route Descriptor" extracted from the data frame's Routing Information Field (RIF) in order to properly direct the frame over the Emulated LAN.

Most LAN emulation services would be implemented as device drivers below the network layer in ATM-to-legacy LAN bridges and ATM end systems. In LANE, the bandwidth management capability is currently supported by the "available bit rate" (ABR) service.

Protocol Structure

LE Data Frames:

1) For 802.3 (Ethernet) Frame – Non-multiplexed data frame:

0	LE Header	Destination Address
4	Destination Address	
8	Source Address	

12	Source Address	Type / Length
16 and on	User Info	

2) For 802.5 (Token Ring) Frame– Non-multiplexed data frame:

0	LE Header	AC PAD	FC
4	Destination Address		
8	Destination Address	Source Address	
12	Source Address	Type / Length	
16-46	Routing Information Field		
	User Info		

• LE Header -- LAN Emulation header which contains either the LAN Emulation client identifier value, the sending client, or X'0000'.

LE Control Frame:

Except for LLC multiplexed Data with Direct VCCs, all LAN Emulation control frames, such as LE_FLUSH_REQUESTs, READY_IND and READY_QUERY, use the format described below:

0	MARKER = X"FF00"	PROTO-COL = X"01"	VERSION = X"01"
4	OP-CODE	STATUS	
8	TRANSACTION-ID		
12	REQUESTER-LECID	FLAGS	
16	SOURCE-LAN-DESTINATION		
24	TARGET-LAN-DESTINATION		
32	SOURCE-ATM-ADDRESS		
52	LAN-Type	MAX-Frame-Size	Number-TLVS	ELAN-Name-Size
56	TARGET-ATM-ADDRESS		
76	ELAN-NAME		
108	TLVs BEGIN		

• OP-CODE – (2 Bytes) Control frame Operation type. Some defined OP-Code are:

OP-CODE Value	OP-CODE Function
X"0001" & X"0101"	LE_CONFIGURE_REQUEST & LE_CONFIGURE_RESPONSE
X"0002" & X"0102"	LE_JOIN_REQUEST & LE_JOIN_RESPONSE
X"0003" & X"0103"	READY_QUERY & READY_IND

X"0004" & X"0104"	LE_REGISTER_REQUEST & LE_REG-ISTER_RESPONSE
X"0005" & X"0105"	LE_UNREGISTER_REQUEST & LE_UN-REGISTER_RESPONSE
X"0006" & X"0106"	LE_ARP_REQUEST & LE_ARP_RE-SPONSE
X"0007" & X"0107"	LE_FLUSH_REQUEST LE_FLUSH_RE-SPONSE
X"0008" & X"0108"	LE_NARP_REQUEST & Undefined
X"0009" & X"0109"	LE_TOPOLOGY_REQUEST & Undefined
X"000A" & X"010A"	LE_VERIFY_REQUEST & LE_VERIFY_RESPONSE

• Status -- (2 Bytes) Control frame Operation status. Some defined Status codes are:

Code (dec)	Name	Code (dec)	Name
0	Success	1	Version Not Supported
2	Invalid request parameters	4	Duplicate LAN Destination registration
5	Duplicate ATM address	6	Insufficient resources to grant request
7	Access denied	8	Invalid REQUESTOR-ID
9	Invalid LAN Destination	10	Invalid ATM Address
20	No Configuration	21	LE_CONFIGURE Error
22	Insufficient Information	24	TLV Not Found

• TLV -- Type / Length / Value Encoded Parameter.

LANE LLC-multiplexed Frame - has a 12-octet LLC multiplexing header:

0	LLC-X"AA"	LLC-X"AA"	LLC X"03"	OUI-X"00"
4	OUI-X"A0"	OUI-X"3E"	Frame-Type	
8	ELAN-ID			
12-28/58	LANE Data Frame Header (802.3 or 802.5)			
	User Info			

LLC field is three octets, containing the constant value X"AAAA03", indicating that an OUI follows.

OUI field is three octets, containing the constant value X"00A03E", indicating "ATM Forum".

The next two octets are a FRAME-TYPE field containing the value X"000C" for IEEE 802.3 data frame, X"000D" for IEEE 802.5 data frame, X"000E" for for LANE LLC-multiplexed READY_IND and READY_QUERY control frames.

The ELAN-ID field identifies the emulated LAN for this data frame.

Related Protocols
ATM, SONET, AAL0-AAL5, LAN Emulation (LANE), CES, UNI, NNI and Q.2931.

Sponsor Source
The ATM protocols is based on standards developed by the ITU.

Reference
ITU-T Recommendation I.363, "B-ISDN ATM Adaptation Layer (AAL) Specification"
http://www.cisco.com/univercd/cc/td/doc/cisintwk/ito_doc/atm.htm
ATM Overview

MPOA: Multi-Protocol Over ATM

Protocol Description

The Multi Protocol Over ATM (MPOA) deals with the efficient transfer of inter-subnet unicast data in a LANE environment. MPOA integrates LANE and NHRP to preserve the benefits of LAN Emulation, while allowing inter-subnet, internetwork layer protocol communication over ATM VCCs without requiring routers in the data path. MPOA provides a framework for effectively synthesizing bridging and routing with ATM in an environment of diverse protocols, network technologies, and IEEE 802.1 virtual LANs. MPOA is capable of using both routing and bridging information to locate the optimal exit from the ATM cloud. It allows the physical separation of internetwork layer route calculation and forwarding, a technique known as virtual routing.

Based on ATM UNI signaling, LAN Emulation, and Next Hop Resolution Protocol (NHRP), MPOA defines two components: MPOA Clients (MPCs) and MPOA Servers (MPSs), and the protocols that are required to communicate and receive services.

The MPS is a component of a router, and is only useful in a router that has a Next Hop Server (NHS) and interfaces to one or more LAN Emulation Clients (LECs). The data and control path from the router through the LEC(s) to LANE is unaltered by MPOA. The MPS does, however, interact with the router, its LEC(s), the NHS, and other MPOA components. A LEC is associated with a single MPS.

MPOA uses a protocol based on the Next Hop Resolution Protocol [NHRP] to manage caches and establish shortcuts. It performs the following operations:

• Configuration -- Obtaining the appropriate configuration information.
• Discovery -- MPCs and MPSs learning of each others' existence.
• Target Resolution -- Determining the mapping of a Target to an egress ATM address, an optional Tag, and a set of parameters used to set up a Shortcut Virtual Channel Connection (VCC) to forward packets across subnet boundaries.
• Connection Management -- VCCs creating, maintaining, and terminating for the purpose of transferring control information and data.
• Data Transfer -- Forwarding internetwork layer data across a Shortcut.

MPOA components must support the use of Logic Link Control (LLC/SNAP) encapsulation for all PDUs. By default VCCs must be signaled to use LLC encapsulation. An MPOA component must be capable of establishing, receiving and maintaining a VCC to any entity that conforms to the connection management procedures, whether or not that entity is an MPOA component.

Protocol Structure

MPOA tagged encapsulation format:

0	LLC-X"AA"	LLC-X"AA"	LLC X"03"	OUI-X"00"
4 bytes	OUI-X"00"	OUI-X"00"	Frame-Type = 0x884C	
8 bytes	MPOA Tag			
12-n bytes	Internetwork Layer PDU (up to 2^16 - 13 octets)			

Three bytes of Logic Link Control (LLC) header with proper value as indicated must be used and three bytes of SNAP header with the Organizational Unique Identifier (OUI) must be used, which should be filled with "0s" in this case.

MPOA Control Frame – MPOA tagged encapsulation format:

0	LLC-X"AA"	LLC-X"AA"	LLC X"03"	OUI-X"00"
4	OUI-X"00"	OUI-X"5E"	Frame-Type = 0x0003	
8-n bytes	MPOA PDU (up to 2^16 - 9 octets)			

Again, three bytes of Logic Link Control header with proper value as indicated must be used and three bytes of SNAP header with the Organizational Unique Identifier (OUI) with proper value as indicated must be used.

By default, MPOA uses LLC encapsulation for all control flows as defined in [NHRP], with the same fixed header as an NHRP packet described below:

0	ar$afn		ar$pro.type	
4	ar$pro.snap			
8	ar$pro.snap	ar$hopcnt	ar$pkstz	
12	ar$chksum		ar$extoff	
16	ar$op.version	ar$op.type	ar$shtl	ar$sstl

• ar$afn -- Defines the type of "link layer" address being carried.
• ar$pro.type -- Protocol Type. This field is a 16-bit unsigned integer.
• ar$pro.snap -- When ar$pro.type field equals to 0x0080, a snap encoded extension, which is placed in the ar$pro.snap field. is used to encode the protocol type. By default this field should be set to 0.
• ar$hopcnt -- Hop count- the maximum number of NHSs that an MPOA packet is allowed to traverse.
• ar$pktsz -- The total length of the MPOA packet in octets.
• ar$chksum -- The standard IP 16-bit checksum over the entire MPOA packet.
• ar$extoff -- This field identifies the existence and location of MPOA extensions.
• ar$op.version -- Version of generic address mapping and management protocol, set to X"01" NHRP
• ar$op.type -- The MPOA packet type. Some values for packet types are:

128	MPOA Cache Imposition Request.	129	MPOA Cache Imposition Reply.
130	MPOA Egress Cache Purge Request.	131	MPOA Egress Cache Purge Reply.
132	MPOA Keep-Alive.	133	MPOA Trigger.
134	MPOA Resolution Request.	135	MPOA Resolution Reply.
136	MPOA Error Indicator		

• ar$shtl -- The type and length of the source NBMA address interpreted.
• ar$sstl -- The type and length of the source NBMA subaddress interpreted.

Related Protocols

ATM, AAL0-AAL5, LAN Emulation (LANE), NHRP, LLC, SNAP, UNI and NNI

Sponsor Source

The MPOA is jointly defined by ITU-T and IETF.

Reference

http://www.javvin.com/protocol/rfc2332.pdf
NBMA Next Hop Resolution Protocol (NHRP)
http://www.javvin.com/protocol/rfc2684.pdf
Multiprotocol Encapsulation over ATM Adaptation Layer 5
http://www.cisco.com/univercd/cc/td/doc/cisintwk/ito_doc/atm.htm
ATM Overview

ATM PNNI: ATM Private Network-to-Network Interface

Protocol Description

The ATM Private Network-Node Interface (PNNI), an ATM network-to-network signaling protocol, provides mechanisms to support scalable, QoS-based ATM routing and switch-to-switch switched virtual connection (SVC) interoperability.

The PNNI is a hierarchical, dynamic link-state routing protocol. It is designed to support large-scale ATM networks. The PNNI protocol uses VPI/VCI 0 and 18 for its messages. In addition, it uses signalling messages to support connection establishment across multiple networks. PNNI is based on UNI 4.0 and Q.2931. Specific information elements were added to UNI 4.0 in order to support the routing process of PNNI. PNNI Signalling contains the procedure to dynamically establish, maintain and clear ATM connections at the private network-to-network interface or network node interface between 2 ATM networks or 2 ATM network nodes. The PNNI signalling protocol is based on the ATM forum UNI specification and on Q.2931.

PNNI Messages include:

ALERTING, CALL PROCEEDING, CONNECT, SETUP, RELEASE, RELEASE COMPLETE, NOTIFY, STATUS, STATUS ENQUIRY, RESTART, RESTART ACKNOWLEDGE, STATUS, ADD PARTY, ADD PARTY ACKNOWLEDGE, PARTY ALERTING, ADD PARTY REJECT, DROP PARTY, DROP PARTY ACKNOWLEDGE

Protocol Structure

The structure of the PNNI header is shown in the following illustration:

2 bytes	2 bytes	1 byte	1 byte	1 byte	1 byte
Packet type	Packet length	Prot ver	Newest ver	Oldest ver	Reserved

• Packet type -- The following packet types are defined:
    1. Hello -- Sent by each node to identify neighbor nodes belonging to the same peer group.
    2. PTSP -- PNNI Topology State Packet. Passes topology information between groups.
    3. PTSE -- PNNI Topology State Element (Request and Ack). Conveys topology parameters such as active links, their available bandwidth, etc.
    4. Database Summary -- Used during the original database exchange between two neighboring peers.
• Packet length -- The length of the packet.
• Prot ver -- Protocol Version. The version according to which this packet was formatted.
• Newest ver / Oldest ver -- Newest version supported / oldest version supported. The newest version supported and the oldest version supported fields are included in order for nodes to negotiate the most recent protocol version that can be understood by both nodes exchanging a particular type of packet.

Related Protocols

ATM, BISDN, SONET, AAL0-AAL5, LAN Emulation (LANE), CES, UNI, NNI, MPOA and Q.2931

Sponsor Source

The ATM protocols are based on standards developed by the ITU.
http://www-comm.itsi.disa.mil/atmf/sig.html#af10.1
UNI 4.0 Specification

Reference

http://www.cisco.com/univercd/cc/td/doc/cisintwk/ito_doc/atm.htm
ATM Overview

Q.2931: ATM Signaling for B-ISDN

Protocol Description

Signaling is the process by which ATM users and the network exchange the control of information, request the use of network resources or negotiate for the use of circuit parameters. Q.2931, based on Q.931, is a signaling protocol, which specifies the procedures for the establishment, maintenance and clearing of network connections at the B-ISDN user network interface. The PNNI and the UNI specifications are based on Q.2931. The procedures are defined in terms of messages exchanged.

The basic capabilities supported by Q.2931 Signaling are as follows:

• Demand (switched virtual) channel connections.
• Point-to-point switched channel connections.
• Connections with symmetric or asymmetric bandwidth requirements.
• Single-connection (point-to-point) calls.
• Basic signalling functions via protocol messages, information elements and procedures.
• Class X, Class A and Class C ATM transport services.
• Request and indication of signalling parameters.
• VCI negotiation.
• Out-of-band signalling for all signalling messages.
• Error recovery.
• Public UNI addressing formats for unique identification of ATM endpoints.
• End-to-end compatibility parameter identification.
• Signalling interworking with N-ISDN and provision of N-ISDN services.
• Forward compatibility.

The message types for Q.2931 are the same as in UNI, with a few exceptions, such as point-to-multipoint messages (which are not supported in version 3.0/3.1) and SETUP ACKNOWLEDGE and INFORMATION in version 4.0. New signaling messages specific to Q.2931 are ALERTING, PROGRESS, SETUP ACKNOWLEDGE, INFORMATION, and NOTIFY.

The VPI/VCI pair and requested bandwidth are allocated as a result of a successful signalling exchange. These messages are sent over the Signalling ATM Adaptation Layer (SAAL), which ensures their reliable delivery.

Protocol Structure

Protocol stacks illustrated below support User Networking connection control signaling:

	User-Network Signalling
	UNI SSCF
SAAL	SSCOP
	AAL Type 5 Common Part
	ATM Layer

Physical Layer

Q.2931Signaling Message:

8	7	6	5	4	3	2	1	bit/Octet
Protocol discriminator								1
0	0	0	0	Length of call reference value				2
Flag	Call reference value							3
Call reference value (continued)								4
								5
Message type								6
Message type (continued)								7
Message length								8
Message length (continued)								9
Variable length Information Elements as required								etc.

• Protocol discriminator -- Distinguishes Messages for user-network call control from other messages. (9 for Q.2931 messages)

• Call reference -- Unique number for every ATM connection which serves to link all signalling messages relating to the same connection. It is comprised of the call reference value and the call reference flag. The call reference flag indicates who allocated the call reference value.

• Message type -- Connection control message types.

• Message length -- The length of the contents of a message.

• Information Elements -- There are several types of information elements. Some may appear only once in the message; others may appear more than once. Depending on the message type, some information elements are mandatory and some are optional. The order of the information elements does not matter to the signalling protocol. Information elements defined in Q.2931 are as follows:

    - Called party number.
    - Called party sub-address.
    - Transit network selection.
    - Restart indicator.
    - Narrow-band low layer compatibility.
    - Narrow-band high layer compatibility.
    - Broadband locking shift.
    - Broadband non-locking shift.
    - Broadband sending complete.
    - Broadband repeat indicator.
    - Calling party number.
    - Calling party sub-address.
    - ATM adaptation layer parameters.
    - ATM traffic descriptor.
    - Connection identifier.
    - OAM traffic descriptor.
    - Quality of Service parameter.
    - Broadband bearer capability.
    - Broadband Low Layer Information (B-LLI).
    - Broadband High Layer Information (B-HLI).
    - End-to-end transit delay.
    - Notification indicator.
    - Call state.
    - Progress indicator.
    - Narrow-band bearer capability.
    - Cause

Related Protocols

ATM, BISDN, PNNI, SONET, AAL0-AAL5, Q.931, LAN Emulation (LANE), CES, UNI, NNI and MPOA

Sponsor Source

The ATM protocols are based on standards developed by the ITU-T.
http://www-comm.itsi.disa.mil/atmf/sig.html#af10.1
UNI 4.0 Specification

Reference

http://members.tripod.com/ATM_protocols/PtoP/Q_2931.html
Q.2931 Recommendation
http://www.cisco.com/univercd/cc/td/doc/cisintwk/ito_doc/atm.htm
ATM Overview

SONET/SDH: Synchronous Optical Network and Synchronous Digital Hierarchy

Protocol Description

The Synchronous Optical Network (SONET), also calledand Synchronous Digital Hierarchy (SDH), are a set of related standards for synchronous data transmission over fiber optic networks that are often used for framing and synchronization at the physical layer. SONET is the United States version of the standard published by the American National Standards Institutue (ANSI). SDH is the international version of the standard published by the International Telecommunications Union (ITU).

SONET/SDH can be used in an ATM or non-ATM environment. Packet Over SONET/SDH (POS) maps IP datagrams into the SONET frame payload using Point-to-Point Protocol (PPP). In the ATM enviroment, connections to SONET/SDH lines may be via multi-mode, single-mode or UTP.

SONET is based on transmission at speeds of multiples of 51.840 Mbps (STS-1) and SDH is based on STM-1 which has a data rate of 155.52 Mbps, equivalent to STS-3.

The following table lists the hierarchy of the most common SONET/SDH data rates:

SONET Signal	Bit Rate (Mbp)	SDH Signal	SONET Capacity	SDH Capacity
STS-1/ OC-1	51.840	STM-0	28 DS1 or DS3	21 E1s
STS-3/ OC-3	155.520	STM-1	84 DS1s or 3 DS3s	63 E1s or E4
STS-12/ OC-12	622.080	STM-4	336 DS1s or 12 DS3s	252 E1s or 4 E4s
STS-48 / OC-48	2.488.32	STM-16	1,344 DS1s or 48 DS3s	1,008 E1s or 16 E4s
STS-192/ OC-192	9,953.280	STM-64	5,376 DS1s or 192 DS3s	4,032 E1s or 64 E4s
STS-768/ OC-768	39,813.120	STM-256	21,504 DSs or 786 DS3	16,128 E1s or 256 E4s

Other rates such as OC-9, OC-18, OC-24, OC-36, OC-96 and OC-768 are referenced in some of the standards documents but were not widely implemented. Higher rate maybe defined for future implementations.

Protocol Structure

The frame structure of STS and STM is different. We only display the details of the STS-1 frame structure here. The STS-1 frame is composed of octets which are nine rows high and 90 columns wide. The first three columns are used by the Transport Overhead (TOH) and contain framing, error monitoring, management and payload pointer information. The data (Payload) uses the remaining 87 columns, of which the first column is used for Path Overhead (POH). A pointer in the TOH identifies the start of the payload, which is referred to as the Synchronous Payload Envelope or SPE.

9 Columns	POH	260 Columns						
	J1							
	B3							
	C2							
	G1							
	F2							9 Rows
	H4							
	Z3							
	Z4							
	Z5							

• SOH -- Section Overhead.

A1, A2 -- Frame alignment. These octets contain the value of 0xF628. The receiver searches for these values in the incoming bit stream. These bytes are not scrambled.

C1 -- STS-1 identification. Since OC-3c and STM-1 contain three STS-1 streams, the three C1 bytes contain 0x01, 0x02 and 0x03, respectively.

B1 -- Section error monitoring. Contains BIP-8 of all bits in the previous frame using even parity, before scrambling.

• LOH -- Line Overhead

B2 -- Line error monitoring. Contains BIP-24 calculated over all bits of the line overhead of the previous frame with even parity.

H1 (bits 1-4) -- New data flag (specifies when the pointer has changed), path AIS.

H1 and H2 (bits 7-16) -- Pointer value, path AIS. These bytes specify the offset between the pointer and the first payload byte. A change in this value is ignored until received at least three consecutive times.

H1* and H2* -- Concatenation indication, path AIS.

H3 -- Pointer action (used for frequency justification), path AIS.

K2 (bits 6-8) -- Line AIS, line FERF, removal of line FERF.

Z2 -- Line FEBE. This contains the number of B2 (BIP-24) errors detected in the previous interval.

• POH -- Path Overhead

J1 -- STS path trace. This byte is used repetitively to transmit a 64-byte fixed string so that the receiving terminal in a path can verify its continued connection to the transmitter. Its contents are unspecified.

B3 -- Path error monitoring. Path BIP-8 over all bits of the payload of the previous frame, using even parity before scrambling.

C2 -- Path signal level indicator. Contains one of two codes:

Code 0: indicates STS payload unequipped: no path originating equipment.

Code 1: indicates STS payload equipped:

nonspecific payload for payloads that need no further differentiation.

    G1 (bits 1-4) -- Path FEBE. Allows monitoring of complete full-duplex path at any point along a complex path.

    G1 (bit 5) -- Path yellow alarm, path RDI (Remote Defect Indicator).

Related Protocols

ATM, STS, STM

Sponsor Source

SONET is an ANSI standard defined in documents T1.105. xx and T1.119.xx and SDH is defined by ITU-T in documents G.707, G.781, G.782, G.783 and G.803.

Reference

http://www.iec.org/online/tutorials/sonet/
Synchronous Optical Network (SONET)

EoS: Ethernet over SONET/SDH

Protocol Description

EoS represents a group of industry standard specifications for optimal transport of Ethernet through SONET/SDH. Ethernet and SONET/SDH are the two primary link technologies used in the network communications while Ethernet in the LAN and SONET/SDH in the Telco/PTT WAN. However, Ethernet rates do not match SONET/SDH rates and Ethernet traffic can not be effectively carried over the SONET/SDH network directly. Ethernet over SONET/SDH (EoS) technologies address this problem and turn the Sonet/SDH MAN/WAN infrastructure backbone into a transparent Ethernet segment for attached servers and clients. Packet over SONET/SDH (PoS), the traditional transmission of IP data over Sonet frames via PPP, is gradually replaced by EoS in many cases.

EoS specifications account for the mapping, aligning, bandwidth management, sequencing and delay compensation of the individual channels. The core technologies in the EoS architectures are the encapsulation schemes to match Ethernet and SONET/SDH rates effectively and manage bandwidth usage. Currently, there are a few encapsulation techniques used: virtual concatenation (VC) and the link capacity adjustment scheme (LCAS) techniques, the generic framing procedure (GFP) and link access procedure for SDH (LAPS) techniques. Virtual Concatenation (VC): VC allows for non-standard SONET/SDH multiplexing in order to address the bandwidth mismatch problem between Ethernet and SONET/SDH. Using virtual concatenation, the SONET/SDH transport pipes may be "right-sized" for Ethernet transport. Virtual Concatenation allows SONET channels to be multiplexed together in arbitrary arrangements, which permits custom-sized SONET pipes to be created that are any multiple of the basic rates. Virtual concatenation is valid for STS-1 rates as well as for Virtual Tributary (VT) rates. All the intelligence to handle virtual concatenation is located at the endpoints of the connections, so each SONET channel may be routed independently through the network without it requiring any knowledge of the virtual concatenation. In this manner, virtually concatenated channels may be deployed on the existing SONET/SDH network with a simple endpoint upgrade. All the equipment currently in the center of the network need not be aware of the virtual concatenation.

Link Capacity Adjustment Scheme (LCAS): a supporting technology to the Virtual Concatenation, LCAS dynamically changes the amount a bandwidth used for a virtual concatenated channel and provides "tuning" of the allocated bandwidth depends on customer needs. LCAS is also useful for fault tolerance and protection since the protocol has the ability to remove failed links from the Virtually Concatenated Group (VCG). Using Link Capacity Adjustment Scheme (LCAS), signaling messages are exchanged within the SONET overhead in order to change the number of tributaries being used by a VCG. The number of tributaries may be either reduced or increased, and the resulting bandwidth change may be applied without loss of data in the absence of network errors.

Link Access Procedure for SDH (LAPS): a type of high-level

data link controller (HDLC), LAPS includes data link service and protocol specification used in transporting IP packets over SDH networks. LAPS provides a point-to-point unacknowledged connectionless service over SONET/SDH. LAPS enables the encapsulation of IPv6, IPv4, PPP, and other higher-layer protocols.

Generic Framing Procedure (GFP): another key encapsulation scheme in EoS and more robust technology than LAPS, GFP maps Ethernet packet data into an octet-synchronous transport such as SONET. GFP has adapted the cell delineation protocol used by ATM to encapsulate variable length packets. A fixed amount of overhead is required by the GFP encapsulation that is independent of the contents of the packets. In contrast to LAPS/HDLC whose overhead is data dependent, the fixed amount of overhead per packet allows deterministic matching of bandwidth between the Ethernet stream and the virtually concatenated SONET stream. Within GFP, there are two different mapping modes defined: frame based mapping and transparent mapping. Each mode is optimized for providing different services.

Protocol Structure

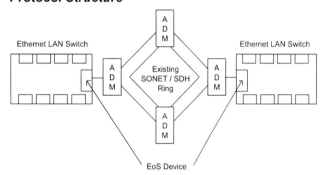

Figure 2-17: EoS Protocol Structure

Related Protocols

EoS, Ethernet over SONET/SDH, POS: Packet Over SONET/SDH, Ethernet, SONET, SDH, Generic Framing Procedure (GFP), Virtual Concatenation, LAPS, LCAS

Sponsor Source

EoS protocols are mainly defined by ITU-T

Reference

Related ITU-T documents:
1. ITU-T G.707/Y.1322, October 2000: Network Node Interface for the Synchronous Digital Hierarchy ([G707])
2. ITU-T G.783, October 2000: Characteristics of SDH Equipment Functional Blocks ([G783])
3. ITU-T G.803, March 2000: Architecture of Transport Networks Based on SDH. ([G803])
4. T G.805, March 2000: Generic Functional Architecture of Transport Networks ([G805])
5. T G.7041/Y1303, January 2002: Generic Framing Procedure ([G7041])
6. T G.7042/Y1305, November 2001: LCAS for Virtually Concatenated Signals ([G7042])
7. T Recommendation X.85/Y.1321, March 2001: IP over SDH Using LAPS

8. T Recommendation X.86, February 2001: Ethernet over LAPS

BISDN: Broadband Integrated Services Digital Network (Broadband ISDN)

Protocol Description

Broadband Integrated Services Digital Network (BISDN or Broadband ISDN) is designed to handle high-bandwidth applications. BISDN currently uses ATM technology over SONET-based transmission circuits to provide data rates from 155 to 622Mbps and beyond, contrast with the traditional narrowband ISDN (or N-ISDN), which is only 64 kps basically and up to 2 Mbps maximum.

The designed Broadband ISDN (BISDN) services can be categorised as follows:

• Conversational services such as telephone-like services, which are also supported by N-ISDN. The additional bandwidth offered also allows such services as video telephony, video conferencing and high-volume, high-speed data transfer.
• Messaging services, which are mainly store-and-forward services. Applications include voice and video mail, as well as multi-media mail and traditional electronic mail.
• Retrieval services which provide access to (public) information stores, information being sent to the user on demand only.
• No user control of presentation. This would be for instance, a TV broadcast, where the user can choose simply either to view or not.
• User controlled presentation. This would apply to broadcast information that the user can partially control.

The B-ISDN is designed to offer both connection oriented and connectionless services. In both cases, the broadband information transfer is provided by the use of asynchronous transfer mode (ATM), using end-to-end logical connections or virtual circuits. Broadband ISDN uses out-of-band signaling (as does N-ISDN). Instead of using a D Channel as in N-ISDN, a special virtual circuit channel can be used for signaling. However, B-ISDN has not widely been deployed so far.

Protocol Structure

Broadband ISDN protocol reference model is based on the ATM reference model.

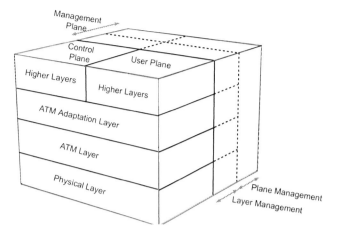

Figure 2-18: ATM Reference Model

ATM adaptation layer (AAL). This layer is responsible for mapping the service offered by ATM to the service expected by the higher layers. It has two sublayers.

ATM Layer. This layer is independent of the physical medium over which transmission is to take place. It has those functions: Generic flow control (GFC) function, Cell header generation and extraction, Cell multiplex and demultiplex.

Physical layer. This consists of two sublayers: Transport Convergence (TC) and Physical medium (PM)

The management plane consists of two functions to perform layer management and plane management. The plane management is not layered as the other layers are. This is because it needs information on all aspects of the system to provide management facilities for the systems as a whole. The layer management provides information and control facilities for the protocol entities that exists in each individual layer. This includes operation and maintenance (OAM) functions for each layer.

The control plane is responsible for the supervision of connections, including call set-up, call release and maintenance.

The user plane provides for the transfer of user information. It also includes mechanisms to perform error recovery, flow control etc.

Related Protocols

ISDN, ATM, B-ICI

Sponsor Source

BISDN protocol is defined by ITU-T.

Reference

http://www.cs.ucl.ac.uk/staff/S.Bhatti/D51-notes/node35.html
Broadband ISDN

ISDN: Integrated Services Digital Network

Protocol Description

Integrated Services Digital Network (ISDN) is a system with digitized phone connections. For decades, telephony has used purely analogue connections. ISDN is the first protocol to define a digital communications line that allows for the transmission of voice, data, video and graphics, at high speeds, over standard communication lines. The various media are simultaneously carried by bearer channels (B channels) occupying a bandwidth of 64 kbits per second (some switches limit bandwidth to 56 kb/s). A defined data channel (D channel) handles signaling at 16 kb/s or 64 kb/s, depending on the service type. ISDN is not restricted to public telephone networks alone; it may be transmitted via packet switched networks, telex, CATV networks, etc. There are two basic types of ISDN service:

• Basic Rate Interface (BRI) -- consists of two 64 kb/s B channels and one 16 kb/s D channel for a total of 144 kb/s. This basic service is intended to meet the needs of most individual users. The U interface provided by the telco for BRI is a 2-wire, 160 kb/s digital connection. Echo cancellation is used to reduce noise, and data encoding schemes (2B1Q in North America, 4B3T in Europe) permit this relatively high data rate over ordinary single-pair local loops.
• Primary Rate Interface (PRI) is intended for users with greater capacity requirements. Typically the channel structure is 23 B channels plus one 64 kb/s D channel for a total of 1536 kb/s. In Europe, PRI consists of 30 B channels plus one 64 kb/s D channel for a total of 1984 kb/s. It is also possible to support multiple PRI lines with one 64 kb/s D channel using Non-Facility Associated Signaling (NFAS).

The CCITT (now ITU-T) study group responsible for ISDN first published a set of ISDN recommendations in 1984. Prior to this publication, various geographical areas had developed different versions of ISDN. The use of nation-specific information elements is enabled by using the Codeset mechanism which allows different areas to use their own information elements within the data frames. A common nation-specific ISDN variant is National ISDN by Bellcore, used in the USA. It has four network-specific message types. It does not have any single octet information elements. Other changes are the addition of the SEGMENT, FACILITY and REGISTER message types and the Segmented Message and Extended Facility information elements. Also, some meanings of field values have changed and some new accepted field values have been added.

Due to its limitation of bandwidth and services, this traditional ISDN is called narrowband ISDN, in contrast to the BISDN (Broadband ISDN).

Protocol Structure

Below is the general structure of the ISDN frame:

8	7	6	5	4	3	2	1
Protocol discriminator							
0	0	0	0	Length of reference call value			

Flag	Call reference value
0	Message type
Other information elements as required	

• Protocol discriminator -- The protocol used to encode the remainder of the Layer.
• Length of call reference value -- Defines the length of the next field. The Call reference may be one or two octets long depending on the size of the value being encoded.
• Flag -- Set to zero for messages sent by the party that allocated the call reference value; otherwise set to one.
• Call reference value -- An arbitrary value that is allocated for the duration of the specific session, which identifies the call between the device maintaining the call and the ISDN switch.
• Message type -- Defines the primary purpose of the frame. The message type may be one octet or two octets (for network specific messages). When there is more than one octet, the first octet is coded as eight zeros. A complete list of message types is given in ISDN Message Types below.
• ISDN Information Elements -- There are two types of information elements: single octet and variable length.
• Single octet information elements -- The single octet information element appears as follows:

8	7	6	5	4	3	2	1
1	Information element identifier				Information element		

• Variable length information elements -- The following is the format for the variable length information element:

8	7	6	5	4	3	2	1
0	Information element identifier						
Length of information elements							
Information elements (multiple bytes)							

• The information element identifier identifies the chosen element and is unique only within the given Codeset. The length of the information element informs the receiver as to the amount of the following octets belonging to each information element.
• ISDN Message Types -- The possible ISDN message types are: Call Establishment, Call Information Phase, Call Clearing, and Miscellaneous.
• Codeset -- Three main Codesets are defined. In each Codeset, a section of the information elements are defined by the associated variant of the protocol:

Codeset 0	The default code, referring to the CCITT set of information elements.
Codeset 5	The national specific Codeset.
Codeset 6	The network specific Codeset.

• CPE -- Customer Premises Equipment; Refers to all ISDN compatible equipment connected at the user site. Examples of devices are telephone, PC, Telex, Facsimile, etc. The exception is the FCC definition of NT1. The FCC views the NT1 as a CPE because it is on the customer site, but the CCITT views NT1 as part of the network. Consequently the network reference point of the network boundary is dependent on the variant in use.
• ISDN Channels B, D and H -- The three logical digital com-

munication channels of ISDN perform the following functions:

B-Channel	Carries user service information including: digital data, video, and voice.
D-Channel	Carries signals and data packets between the user and the network
H-Channel	Performs the same function as B-Channel, but operates at rates exceeding DS-0 (64 Kbps). They are implemented as H0 (384 kb/s (6 B channels), H10 (1472 kb/s -23 B channels), H11 (1536 kb/s; 24 B channels), and H12 (1920 kb/s for International -E1 only).

Related Protocols

LAP-D, BRI, PRI, Q.920-Q.923, LAP-B, X.25, Q.931, ATM

Sponsor Source

ISDN protocol is defined by ITU I-series and G-series documents (Physical Layer) and Q-series documents (Data-link and Network layers).

Reference

http://www.nationalisdncouncil.com/isdnassistance
The National ISDN Council (NIC) specification
http://www.catcouncil.org/isdn/index
The Council for Access Technologies (CAT formerly NIC) specification and documents.

LAP-D: ISDN Link Access Protocol-Channel D

Protocol Description

ISDN Link Access Protocol – Channel D (LAP-D or LAPD), a layer 2 protocol in the ISDN suite, is used to do call setup and other signaling over the D Channel. Data transmissions take place on B channels. LAP-D is almost identical to the X.25 LAP-B protocol. The three logical digital communication channels of ISDN perform the following functions:

- B-Channel -- Carries user service information including: digital data, video, and voice.
- D-Channel -- Carries signals and data packets between the user and the network.
- H-Channel -- Performs the same function as B-Channels, but operates at rates exceeding DS-0 (64 Kbps).

The Link Establishment process in ISDN performed by LAP-D is as follows:

1. The TE (Terminal Endpoint) and the Network initially exchange Receive Ready (RR) frames, listening for someone to initiate a connection.
2. The TE sends an Unnumbered Information (UI) frame with a SAPI of 63 (management procedure, query network) and TEI of 127 (broadcast).
3. The Network assigns anavailable TEI(in the range 64-126).
4. The TE sends a Set Asynchronous Balanced Mode (SABME) frame with a SAPI of 0 (call control, used to initiate a SETUP) and a TEI of the value assigned by the network.
5. The network responds with an Unnumbered Acknowledgement (UA), SAPI=0, TEI=assigned.

The LAPD is defined in CCITT Q.920/921. LAPD works in the Asynchronous Balanced Mode (ABM). This mode is totally balanced (i.e., no master/slave relationship). Each station may initialize, supervise, recover from errors, and send frames at any time. The protocol treats the DTE and DCE as equals.

Protocol Structure

The format of a standard LAPD frame is as follows:

Flag	Address field	Control field	Informa-tion	FCS	Flag

- Flag -- The value of the flag is always (0x7E)." Bit Stuffing" technique is used in order to ensure that the bit pattern of the frame delimiter flag does not appear in the data field of the frame.
- Address field -- The first two bytes of the frame after the header flag are known as the address field. The format of the address field is as follows:

1	2	3	4	5	6	7	8
SAPI (6 bits)						C/R	EA0
TEI (7 bits)							EA1

- SAPI (Service access point identifier), 6-bits (see below)
- C/R (Command/Response) bit indicates if the frame

is a command or a response
> • EA0 (Address Extension) bit indicates whether this is the final octet of the address or not
> • TEI (Terminal Endpoint Identifier) 7-bit device identifier (see below)
> • EA1 (Address Extension) bit, same as EA0

• Control field -- The field following the Address Field is called the Control Field and serves to identify the type of the frame. In addition, it includes sequence numbers, control features and error tracking according to frame type. The following are the Supervisory Frame Types defined in LAPD:

RR	Information frame acknowledgement and indication to receive more.
REJ	Request for retransmission of all frames after a given sequence number.
RNR	Indicates a state of temporary occupation of station (e.g., window full).

Some Unnumbered Frame Types supported in LAPD are DISC (Request disconnection), UA (Acknowledgement frame), DM (Response to DISC indicating disconnected mode), FRMR (Frame reject), SABM, SABME, UI and XID.

• FCS -- The Frame Check Sequence (FCS) enables a high-level of physical error control by allowing the integrity of the transmitted frame data to be checked. The sequence is first calculated by the transmitter using an algorithm based on the values of all the bits in the frame. The receiver then performs the same calculation on the received frame and compares its value to the CRC.

• Window size -- LAPD supports an extended window size (modulo 128) where the number of possible outstanding frames for acknowledgement is raised from 8 to 128. This extension is generally used for satellite transmissions where the acknowledgement delay is significantly greater than the frame transmission time. The type of the link initialization frame determines the modulo of the session and an "E" is added to the basic frame type name (e.g., SABM becomes SABME).

Related Protocols

LAP-D, BRI, PRI, Q.920-Q.923, LAP-B, X.25, Q.931, ATM

Sponsor Source

The LAP-D protocol is based on standards developed by the ITU Q-series documents.

Reference

http://www.nationalisdncouncil.com/isdnassistance
The National ISDN Council (NIC) specification
http://www.catcouncil.org/isdn/index
The Council for Access Technologies (CAT formerly NIC) specification and documents.

Q.931: ISDN Network Layer Protocol for Signaling

Protocol Description

Q.931, the Network Layer (layer 3) protocol in the telecommunication architecture, is used in ISDN for call establishment and the maintenance, and termination of logical network connections between two devices. Q.931 is one of the layer 3 protocols in the telecommunication architecture specified by ITU in Q series documents Q.930 to Q.939.

During the layer 3 call setup, messages sent and received among three parties: 1) the Caller, 2) the ISDN Switch, and 3) the Receiver. Following is an example of call setup steps:

• Caller sends a SETUP to the Switch.
• If the SETUP is OK, the switch sends a CALL PROCeeding to the Caller, and then a SETUP to the Receiver.
• The Receiver gets the SETUP. If it is OK, it rings the phone and sends an ALERTING message to the Switch.
• The Switch forwards the ALERTING message to the Caller.
• When the receiver answers the call, it sends a CONNECT message to the Switch
• The Switch forwards the CONNECT message to the Caller.
• The Caller sends a CONNECT ACKnowledge message to the Switch
• The Switch forwards the CONNECT ACK message to the Receiver.
• Done. The connection is now up.

What services and features the telco switch provides to the attached ISDN device are specified in the optional field - Service Profile IDs (SPIDs); when they are used, they are only accessed at device initialization time, before the call is set up. The format of the SPID is usually the 10-digit phone number of the ISDN line, plus a prefix and a suffix that are sometimes used to identify features on the line but can be whatever the Telco decides they should be. Details can be found in the Q series documents.

Protocol Structure

Information Field Structure -- The Information Field is a variable length field that contains the Q.931 protocol data:

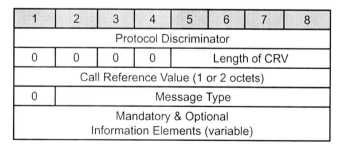

1	2	3	4	5	6	7	8
Protocol Discriminator							
0	0	0	0	Length of CRV			
Call Reference Value (1 or 2 octets)							
0	Message Type						
Mandatory & Optional Information Elements (variable)							

• Protocol Discriminator (1 octet) -- identifies the Layer 3 protocol. If this is a Q.931 header, this value is always 0816.
• Length(1 octet) - indicates the length of the next field, the CRV.
• Call Reference Value (CRV) (1 or 2 octets) -- used to uniquely identify each call on the user-network interface. This value is assigned at the beginning of a call and becomes available for

another call when the call is cleared.

• Message Type (1 octet) -- identifies the message type (i.e., SETUP, CONNECT, etc.). This determines what additional information is required and allowed.

• Mandatory and Optional Information Elements (variable length) -- are options that are set depending on the Message Type.

Related Protocols

LAP-D, BRI, PRI, Q.920-Q.923, LAP-B, X.25, Q.931, ATM

Sponsor Source

The Q.931 protocol is based on standards developed by the ITU Q-series documents.

Reference

http://www.nationalisdncouncil.com/isdnassistance
The National ISDN Council (NIC) specification
http://www.catcouncil.org/isdn/index
The Council for Access Technologies (CAT formerly NIC) specification and documents.

DOCSIS: Data Over Cable Service Interface Specification

Protocol Description

Data Over Cable Service Interface Specification(DOCSIS), developed by CableLabs and approved by the ITU, defines interface requirements for cable modems involved in a high-speed data distribution (both MPEG and IP data) over cable television system networks. Other devices that recognize and support the DOCSIS standard include HDTVs and Web enabled set-top boxes for regular televisions.

There are two key components in the DOCSIS architecture: a Cable Modem (CM) which is located at the customer's premise, and the Cable Modem Termination System (CMTS), which is located at the head end of the service provider and used to aggregate traffic from multiple Cable Modems and then communicate with the backbone network. DOCSIS specifies modulation schemes and the protocol for exchanging bidirectional signals between these two components over cable.

Three versions of DOCSIS are now implemented and deployed:

• DOCSIS 1.0 -- High Speed Internet Access. Key features: Downstream traffic transfer rates between 27 and 36 Mbps over a radio frequency (RF) path in the 50 MHz to 750+ MHz range, and upstream traffic transfer rates between 320 Kbps and 10 Mbps (average 5 Mbps) over an RF path between 5 and 42 MHz. However, because data over cable travels on a shared loop, individuals will see transfer rates drop as more users gain access.

• DOCSIS 1.1 -- Data, Voice, Gaming and Streaming. Key features: DOSCIS 1.1 is interoperable with DOCSIS 1.0. It provides enhanced QoS for multiple services such as voice and streaming; improved security over DOCSIS 1.0; and more robust upstream data transmission (average 10 Mbps).

• DOCSIS 2.0 -- Has added capacity for symmetric services by operating at 64 QAM and having new 6.4 MHz wide channel. It has increased bandwidth for IP traffic by using enhanced modulation and improved error correction. The result for upstream transmission is 30 Mbps, which is 3 times better than DOCSIS 1.1 and 6 times than DOSCIS 1.0. DOSCIS 2.0 is interoperable and backward compatible with DOCSIS 1.x.

The latest DOCSIS specification eDOCSIS has been published to the industry. eDOCSIS, embedded DOCSIS, provides a subordinate function at the core chip level to the host device. Rather than leveraging a home networking protocol, an embedded DOCSIS device feeds directly into a cable network's DOCSIS channel. eDOCSIS is intended to solve end device (and traffic) management, configuration and security issues, to significantly reduce cost in the service operation and to improve speed and quality of end customer services.

Protocol Structure

The specifications of the various DOCSIS versions can be found in the attached reference documents.

Related Protocols

IP, MPEG, DOCSIS 1.0, DOCSIS 1.1, DOCSIS 2.0, eDOCSIS

Sponsor Source

DOCSIS is defined by CableLabs (http://www.cablemodem.com/) and approved by ITU.

Reference

http://www.cablemodem.com/downloads/specs/SP_CMTS_NSII01-960702.pdf
DOCSIS - CMTS Network Site Interface Specification
http://www.cablemodem.com/downloads/specs/SP-CMCI-I09-030730.pdf
DOCSIS 1.1 Specification
http://www.cablemodem.com/downloads/specs/SP-RFIv2.0-I04-030730.pdf
DOCSIS 2.0 - Radio Frequency Interface Specification
http://www.cablemodem.com/downloads/specs/SP-OSSIv2.0-I04-030730.pdf
DOCSIS 2.0 - Operation Support System Interface Specification
http://www.cablemodem.com/downloads/specs/SP-eDOCSIS-I02-031117.pdf
eDOCSIS Specification

xDSL: Digital Subscriber Line Technologies (DSL, IDSL, ADSL, HDSL, SDSL, VDSL, G.Lite)

Protocol Description

DSL (Digital Subscriber Line) is a modem technology for broadband data access over ordinary copper telephone lines (POTS) from homes and businesses. xDSL refers collectively to all types of DSL, such as ADSL (and G.Lite), HDSL, SDSL, IDSL and VDSL etc. They are sometimes referred to as last-mile (or first mile) technologies because they are used only for connections from a telephone switching station to a home or office, not between switching stations.

xDSL is similar to ISDN in as much as both operate over existing copper telephone lines (POTS) using sophisticated modulation schemes and both require short runs to a central telephone office (usually less than 20,000 feet). However, xDSL offers much higher speeds - up to 32 Mbps for upstream traffic, and from 32 Kbps to over 1 Mbps for downstream traffic.

Several modulation technologies are used by various kinds of DSL:

• Discrete Multitone Technology (DMT)
• Simple Line Code (SLC)
• Carrierless Amplitude Modulation (CAP)
• Multiple Virtual Line (MVL)
• Discrete Wavelet Multitone (DWMT).

To interconnect multiple DSL users to a high-speed backbone network, the telephone company uses a Digital Subscriber Line Access Multiplexer (DSLAM). The DSLAM aggregates data transmission from all access DSL lines and then connects to an asynchronous transfer mode (ATM) network. At the other end of each transmission, a DSLAM demultiplexes the signals and forwards them to appropriate individual DSL connections. Most DSL technologies require that a signal splitter be installed at a customer's premises. However, it is possible to manage the splitting remotely from the central office. This is known as splitterless DSL, "DSL Lite," G.Lite, or Universal ADSL.

Protocol Structure

The following table provides a summary of various DSL specifications.

Type	Description	Data Rate	Mode	Distance	Applications
IDSL	ISDN Digital Subscriber Line	128 kbps	Duplex	18k ft on 24 gauge wire	ISDN service Voice and data communication

	High data rate Digital Subscriber Line	1.544 Mbps to 42.048 Mbps	Duplex	12k ft on 24 gauge wire	T1/E1 service Feeder plant, WAN, LAN access, server access
HDSL					
SDSL	Single Line Digital Subscriber Line	1.544 Mbps to 2.048 Mbps	Duplex	12k ft on 24 gauge wire	Same as HDSL plus premises access for symmetric services
ADSL	Asymmetric Digital Subscriber Line	1.5 to 9 Mbps 16 to 640 kbps	Down Up	Up to 18k ft on 24 gauge wire	Internet access, video on-demand, simplex video, remote LAN access, interactive multimedia
DSL Lite (G.Lite)	"Splitterless" DSL	1.544 Mbps to 6 Mbps 16 to 640 kbps	Down Up	18k ft on 24 gauge wire	The standard ADSL; sacrifices speed for not having to install a splitter at the user's premises.
VDSL	Very high data rate Digital Subscriber Line	13 to 52 Mbps 1.5 to 2.3 Mbps	Down Up	1k to 4.5k ft depending on data rate	Same as ADSL plus HDTV

Related Protocols

ISDN, DSL, ADSL, HDSL, VDSL, SDSL, G.Lite, IDSL, ATM

Sponsor Source

DSL is defined by ITU-T (www.itu.org) and DSL Forum (www.dslforum.org)

Reference

http://www.dslforum.org/
Educate yourself about DSL
http://www.cisco.com/univercd/cc/td/doc/cisintwk/ito_doc/adsl.htm
Digital Subscriber Line

PPP: Point-to-Point Protocols

Protocol Description

The Point-to-Point Protocol (PPP) suite provides a standard method for transporting multi-protocol datagrams over point-to-point links. PPP was originally devised as an encapsulation protocol for transporting IP traffic between two peers. It is a data link layer protocol (layer 2 in the OSI model) in the TCP-IP protocol suite over synchronous modem links, as a replacement for the non-standard layer 2 protocol SLIP. However, other protocols other than IP can also be carried over PPP, including DECnet and Novell's Internetwork Packet Exchange (IPX).

PPP is comprised of the following main components:

• Encapsulation -- A method for encapsulating multi-protocol datagrams. The PPP encapsulation provides for multiplexing of different network-layer protocols simultaneously over the same link. The PPP encapsulation has been carefully designed to retain compatibility with most commonly used supporting hardware.
• Link Control Protocol -- The LCP provided by PPP is versatile and portable to a wide variety of environments. The LCP is used to automatically agree upon the encapsulation format options, handle varying limits on sizes of packets, detect a looped-back link and other common misconfiguration errors, and terminate the link. Other optional facilities provided are authentication of the identity of its peer on the link, and determination when a link is functioning properly and when it is failing.
• Network Control Protocol -- An extensible Link Control Protocol (LCP) for establishing, configuring, and testing and managing the data-link connections.
• Configuration -- Easy and self configuration mechanisms using Link Control Protocol. This mechanism is also used by other control protocols such as Network Control Protocols (NCPs).

In order to establish communications over a point-to-point link, each end of the PPP link must first send LCP packets to configure and test the data link. After the link has been established and optional facilities have been negotiated as needed by the LCP, PPP must send NCP packets to choose and configure one or more network-layer protocols. Once each of the chosen network-layer protocols has been configured, datagrams from each network-layer protocol can be sent over the link.

The link will remain configured for communications until explicit LCP or NCP packets close the link down, or until some external event occurs (an inactivity timer expires or network administrator intervention).

Protocol Structure

1byte	2bytes	3bytes	5bytes	Variable ...	2 – 4 bytes
Flag	Address	Control	Protocol	Information	FCS

• Flag -- indicates the beginning or end of a frame, consists of the binary sequence 01111110.
• Address -- contains the binary sequence 11111111, the standard broadcast address. (Note: PPP does not assign individual station addresses.)
• Control -- contains the binary sequence 00000011, which calls for transmission of user data in an unsequenced frame.
• Protocol -- identifies the protocol encapsulated in the information field of the frame.
• Information -- zero or more octet(s) contains the datagram for the protocol specified in the protocol field.
• FCS -- Frame Check Sequence (FCS) Field, normally 16 bits. By prior agreement, consenting PPP implementations can use a 32-bit FCS for improved error detection.

Related Protocols

PPPoE, PPPoA, SLIP, CHAP, HDLC, LCP, NCP, L2TP, CHAP, PAS, IPCP, IPv6CP, IPX, DECNet

Sponsor Source

PPP is defined by IETF (http://www.ietf.org) RFC1661 with an update RFC2153.

Reference

http://www.javvin.com/protocol/rfc1661.pdf
The Point-to-Point Protocol (PPP)
http://www.javvin.com/protocol/rfc2153.pdf
PPP Vendor Extensions

BAP: PPP Bandwidth Allocation Protocol and BACP: Bandwidth Allocation Control Protocol

Protocol Description

The Bandwidth Allocation Protocol (BAP) and the Bandwidth Allocation Control Protocol (BACP), provide Multilink PPP peers with the ability to manage link utilization and bandwidth on demand. Once connection between peers is successfully negotiated using BACP, peer nodes can use the Bandwidth Allocation Protocol (BAP) to negotiate bandwidth allocation.

BACP can operate over any physical interface that is PPP multilink capable and has a dial capability. Initially, BACP supports ISDN and asynchronous serial interfaces. BACP allows multilink implementations to interoperate by providing call control through the use of link types, speeds, and telephone numbers, and links being brought up and removed quickly. BACP informs both ends of the link when links are added or removed from a multilink bundle.

BAP defines packets, parameters and negotiation procedures to allow two endpoints to negotiate adding and dropping links from a multilink bundle, which allows dynamic bandwidth allocation. BAP also specifies which peer is responsible for various decisions regarding managing bandwidth during a multi-link connection. After BACP reaches the opened state, either peer MAY request another link be added to the bundle by sending a BAP Call- or Callback-Request packet. A Call-Request packet is sent if the implementation wishes to originate the call for the new link, and a Callback-Request packet is sent if the implementation wishes its peer to originate the call for the new link. The implementation receiving a Call- or Callback-Request MUST respond with a Call- or Callback-Response with a valid Response Code. The removal of a link is controlled by a link drop message in BAP.

Protocol Structure

BAP Packet structure:

8	16bit	Variable
Type	Length	Data

• Type -- Indicates the type of the BAP Datagram Option. This field is binary coded Hexadecimal.

BACP packet structure:

8	16	32bit	Variable
Code	Identifier	Length	Data

• Code -- Decimal value which indicates the type of BACP packet.
• Identifier -- Decimal value which aids in matching requests and replies.
• Length -- Length of the BACP packet, including the Code,

Identifier, Length and Data fields.
• Data -- Variable length field which may contain one or more configuration options.

Related Protocols
PPP, Multi PPP, SLIP, CHAP, HDLC, ISDN

Sponsor Source
BAP and BACP are defined by IETF (http://www.ietf.org) .

Reference
http://www.javvin.com/protocol/rfc2125.pdf
The PPP Bandwidth Allocation Protocol (BAP) / The PPP Bandwidth Allocation Control Protocol (BACP)

BCP: PPP Bridging Control Protocol

Protocol Description
The Bridging Control Protocol (BCP) is responsible for configuring the bridging protocol parameters on both ends of the point-to-point link. BCP uses the same packet exchange mechanism as the Link Control Protocol. BCP packets can not be exchanged until PPP has reached the Network-Layer Protocol phase. BCP packets received before this phase is reached are discarded.

The Point-to-Point Protocol (PPP) provides a standard method for transporting multi-protocol datagrams over point-to-point links. PPP defines an extensible Link Control Protocol (LCP) and proposes a family of Network Control Protocols (NCP) for establishing and configuring different network-layer protocols. This document defines the NCP for establishing and configuring Remote Bridging for PPP links.

BCP compares the configurations of two devices and seeks to negotiate an acceptable subset of their intersection so as to enable correct interoperation even in the presence of minor configuration or implementation differences. In the event that a major misconfiguration is detected, the negotiation will not complete successfully, resulting in the link coming down or not coming up. It is possible that if a bridged link comes up with a rogue peer, network information may be learned from forwarded multicast traffic, or denial of service attacks may be created by closing loops that should be detected and isolated or by offering rogue load.

Such attacks are not isolated to BCP. Any PPP NCP is subject to attack when connecting to a foreign or compromised device. However, no situations arise which are not common to all NCPs; any NCP that comes up with a rogue peer is subject to snooping and other attacks. Therefore, it is recommended that links on which this may happen should be configured to use PPP authentication during the LCP start-up phase.

Protocol Structure

8	16	32bit	Variable
Code	Identifier	Length	Data

• Code -- Decimal value which indicates the type of BCP packet.
• Identifier -- Decimal value which aids in matching requests and replies.
• Length -- Length of the BCP packet, including the Code, Identifier, Length and Data fields.
• Data -- Variable length field which may contain one or more configuration options. The following is a list of BCP configuration options:
> • Bridge-Identification
> • Line-Identification
> • MAC-Support
> • Tinygram-Compression
> • MAC-Address
> • Spanning Tree Protocol (old formatted)

- IEEE-802-Tagged-Frame
- Management-Inline
- Bridge-Control-Packet-Indicator

Related Protocols
PPP, PPPoE, PPPoA, SLIP, CHAP, HDLC, LCP, NCP

Sponsor Source
BCP is defined by IETF (http://www.ietf.org) .

Reference
http://www.javvin.com/protocol/rfc3518.pdf
Point-to-Point Protocol (PPP) Bridging Control Protocol (BCP)

EAP: PPP Extensible Authentication Protocol

Protocol Description
The PPP Extensible Authentication Protocol (EAP) is for PPP authentication. EAP supports multiple authentication mechanisms. EAP does not select a specific authentication mechanism at Link Control Phase, but rather postpones this until the Authentication Phase. This allows the authenticator to request more information before determining the specific authentication mechanism. This also permits the use of a "back-end" server which actually implements the various mechanisms while the PPP authenticator merely passes through the authentication exchange.

1. After the Link Establishment phase is complete, the authenticator sends one or more Requests to authenticate the peer. The Request has a type field to indicate what is being requested. Examples of Request types include Identity, MD5-challenge, One-Time Passwords, Generic Token Card, etc. The MD5-challenge type corresponds closely to the CHAP authentication protocol. Typically, the authenticator will send an initial Identity Request followed by one or more Requests for authentication information. However, an initial Identity Request is not required, and MAY be bypassed in cases where the identity is presumed (leased lines, dedicated dial-ups, etc.).
2. The peer sends a Response packet in reply to each Request. The Response packet contains a type field which corresponds to the type field of the Request.
3. The authenticator ends the authentication phase with a Success or Failure packet.

The EAP protocol can support multiple authentication mechanisms without having to pre-negotiate a particular one during LCP Phase. Certain devices (e.g. an NAS) do not necessarily have to understand each request type and may be able to simply act as a passthrough agent for a "back-end" server on a host. The device only need look for the success/failure code to terminate the authentication phase.

However, EAP does require the addition of a new authentication type to LCP and thus PPP implementations will need to be modified to use it. It also strays from the previous PPP authentication model of negotiating a specific authentication mechanism during LCP.

Protocol Structure
The Authentication-Protocol Configuration Option format to negotiate the EAP Authentication Protocol is shown below:

8	16	32bit	Variable
Type	Length	Authentication-Protocol	Data

- Type -- 3
- Length -- 4
- Authentication-Protocol -- C227 (Hex) for PPP Extensible Authentication Protocol (EAP)

One PPP EAP packet is encapsulated in the Information field

of a PPP Data Link Layer frame where the protocol field indicates type hex C227 (PPP EAP). The EAP packet format is shown below:

8	16	32bit	Variable
Code	Identifier	Length	Data

• Code -- The Code field identifies the type of EAP packet.
• EAP Codes are assigned as follows: 1 Request; 2 Response; 3 Success; 4 Failure.
• Identifier -- The Identifier field aids in matching responses with requests.
• Length -- The Length field indicates the length of the EAP packet including the Code, Identifier, Length and Data fields.
• Data -- The format of the Data field is determined by the Code field.

Related Protocols

PPP, CHAP

Sponsor Source

EAP is defined by IETF (http://www.ietf.org) .

Reference

http://www.javvin.com/protocol/rfc2284.pdf
PPP Extensible Authentication Protocol (EAP)

CHAP: Challenge Handshake Authentication Protocol

Protocol Description

Challenge Handshake Authentication Protocol (CHAP) is used to periodically verify the identity of the peer using a 3-way handshake. This is done upon initial link establishment and may be repeated any time after the link has been established.
• After the Link Establishment phase is complete, the authenticator sends a "challenge" message to the peer.
• The peer responds with a value calculated using a "one-way hash" function.
• The authenticator checks the response against its own calculation of the expected hash value. If the values match, the authentication is acknowledged; otherwise the connection SHOULD be terminated.
• At random intervals, the authenticator sends a new challenge to the peer and the three steps above are repeated.

CHAP provides protection against playback attack by the peer through the use of an incrementally changing identifier and a variable challenge value. The use of repeated challenges is intended to limit the time of exposure to any single attack. The authenticator is in control of the frequency and timing of the challenges.

This authentication method depends upon a "secret" known only to the authenticator and that peer. The secret is not sent over the link.

Although the authentication is only one-way, by negotiating CHAP in both directions the same secret set may easily be used for mutual authentication.

Since CHAP may be used to authenticate many different systems, name fields may be used as an index to locate the proper secret in a large table of secrets. This also makes it possible to support more than one name/secret pair per system, and to change the secret in use at any time during the session.

CHAP requires that the secret be available in plaintext form. Irreversably encrypted password databases commonly available cannot be used. It is not as useful for large installations, since every possible secret is maintained at both ends of the link.

Protocol Structure

Configuration Option format for CHAP:

8	16	32	40bit
Type	Length	Authentication-Protocol	Algorithm

• Type -- 3
• Length -- 5
• Authentication-Protocol -- C223 (Hex) for CHAP
• Algorithm The Algorithm field is one octet and indicates the authentication method to be used.

The structure of the CHAP packet is shown in the following

illustration.

8	16	32bit	Variable
Code	Identifier	Length	Data ...

• Code -- Identifies the type of CHAP packet. CHAP codes are assigned as follows:

    1 Challenge
    2 Response
    3 Success
    4 Failure

• Identifier -- Aids in matching challenges, responses and replies.
• Length -- Length of the CHAP packet including the Code, Identifier, Length and Data fields.
• Data -- Zero or more octets, the format of which is determined by the Code field. For Success and Failure, the data field contains a variable message field which is implementation dependent.

Related Protocols

PPP, PPPoE, PPPoA, LCP, NCP, PAP

Sponsor Source

CHAP is defined by IETF (http://www.ietf.org) .

Reference

http://www.javvin.com/protocol/rfc1994.pdf
PPP Challenge Handshake Authentication Protocol (CHAP)

LCP: PPP Link Control Protocol

Protocol Description

The Link Control Protocol (LCP) is used to automatically agree upon the encapsulation format options, handle varying limits on sizes of packets, detect a looped-back link and other common misconfiguration errors, and terminate the link. Other optional facilities provided are authentication of the identity of its peer on the link, and determination when a link is functioning properly and when it is failing. The Link Control Protocol LCP in PPP is versatile and portable to a wide variety of environment.

There are three classes of LCP packets:

1. Link Configuration packets used to establish and configure a link (Configure-Request, Configure-Ack, Configure-Nak and Configure-Reject).
2. Link Termination packets used to terminate a link (Terminate-Request and Terminate-Ack).
3. Link Maintenance packets used to manage and debug a link (Code-Reject, Protocol-Reject, Echo-Request, Echo-Reply, and Discard-Request).

In the interest of simplicity, there is no version field in the LCP packet. A correctly functioning LCP implementation will always respond to unknown Protocols and Codes with an easily recognizable LCP packet, thus providing a deterministic fallback mechanism for implementations of other versions.

Regardless of which Configuration Options are enabled, all LCP Link Configuration, Link Termination, and Code-Reject packets (codes 1 through 7) are always sent as if no Configuration Options were negotiated. In particular, each Configuration Option specifies a default value. This ensures that such LCP packets are always recognizable, even when one end of the link mistakenly believes the link to be open.

Exactly one LCP packet is encapsulated in the PPP Information field, where the PPP Protocol field indicates type hex c021 (Link Control Protocol).

Protocol Structure

8	16	32bit	Variable
Code	Identifier	Length	Data

• Code -- Decimal value which indicates the type of LCP packet:

    1 Configure-Request.
    2 Configure-Ack.
    3 Configure-Nak.
    4 Configure-Reject.
    5 Terminate-Request.
    6 Terminate-Ack.
    7 Code-Reject.
    8 Protocol-Reject.
    9 Echo-Request.
    10 Echo-Reply.

11 Discard-Request.
12 Link-Quality Report.
• Identifier -- Decimal value which aids in matching requests and replies.
• Length -- Length of the LCP packet, including the Code, Identifier, Length and Data fields.
• Data -- Variable length field which may contain one or more configuration options.

Related Protocols

PPP, PPPoE, PPPoA, SLIP, CHAP, HDLC, NCP

Sponsor Source

LCP is defined by IETF (http://www.ietf.org) .

Reference

http://www.javvin.com/protocol/rfc1570.pdf
PPP LCP Extensions.
http://www.javvin.com/protocol/rfc1661.pdf
The Point-to-Point Protocol (PPP)

MP: MultiLink Point to Point Protocol (MultiPPP)

Protocol Description

MultiLink Point to Point Protocol (MultiPPP or MPPP) is a method for splitting, recombining and sequencing datagrams across multiple logical data links. PPP MultiLink (MP) protocol is based on an LCP option negotiation that permits a system to indicate to its peer that it is capable of combining multiple physical links into a "bundle". Multilink is negotiated during the initial LCP option negotiation. A system indicates to its peer that it is willing to do multilink by sending the multilink option as part of the initial LCP option negotiation.

Once multilink has been successfully negotiated, the sending system is free to send PDUs encapsulated and/or fragmented with the multilink header. To establish communications over a point-to-point link, each end of the PPP link must first send LCP packets to configure the data link during Link Establishment phase. After the link has been established, there is an Authentication phase in which the Authentication protocols can be used to determine identifiers associated with each system connected by the link.

Multilink coordinates multiple independent links between a fixed pair of systems, providing a virtual link with greater bandwidth than any of the constituent members. The aggregate link, or bundle, is named by the pair of identifiers for two systems connected by the multiple links. A system identifier may include information provided by PPP Authentication and information provided by LCP negotiation. The bundled links can be different physical links, as in multiple async lines, but may also be instances of multiplexed links, such as ISDN, X.25 or Frame Relay. The links can be of different kinds, such as pairing dialup async links with leased synchronous links.

Multilink operation is moduled as a virtual PPP link-layer entity where packets received over different physical link-layer entities are identified as belonging to a separate PPP network protocol (the Multilink Protocol, or MP) and recombined and sequenced according to information present in a multilink fragmentation header. All packets received over links identified as belonging to the multilink arrangement are presented to the same network-layer protocol processing machine, whether they have multilink headers or not.

Network protocol packets to be transmitted using the multilink procedure are first encapsulated (but not framed) according to normal PPP procedures, and large packets are broken up into multiple segments sized appropriately for the multiple physical links. A new PPP header consisting of the Multilink Protocol Identifier, and the Multilink header is inserted before each section.

Protocol Structure

The header of MP can either be in Long Sequence Number Fragment format or in Short Sequence Number Fragment Format.

Long Sequence Number Fragment Format

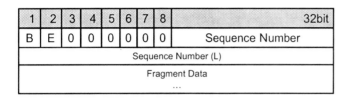

Short Sequence Number Fragment Format

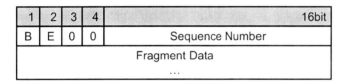

• Address, Control -- Compressed fields for the Address, the control field and the Protocol ID.
• PID (L), PID (H) -- Protocol Identifier for PPP MultiLink; this is 0x00-0x3d
• B(egining) Bit -- One bit field set to 1 on the first fragment derived from a PPP packet and set to 0 for all other fragments from the same PPP packet.
• E(nd) Bit -- A one bit field set to 1 on the last fragment and set to 0 for all other fragments.
• 00 -- Reserved field with the value of 0
• Sequence Number -- The sequence field is a 24-bit or 12-bit number that is incremented for every fragment transmitted.
• Fragment Data -- The data itself.

Related Protocols

PPP, PPPoE, PPPoA, SLIP, CHAP, HDLC, LCP, NCP

Sponsor Source

MP (MultiPPP) is defined by IETF (http://www.ietf.org) .

Reference

http://www.javvin.com/protocol/rfc1990.pdf
The PPP Multilink Protocol (MP).
http://www.javvin.com/protocol/rfc1661.pdf
The Point-to-Point Protocol (PPP)

PPP NCP: Point to Point Protocol Network Control Protocols

Protocol Description

The Network Control Protocol (NCP), a protocol in the Point to Point Protocol (PPP) suite, provides services in the PPP link connection process to establish and configure different network-layer protocols such as IP, IPX or AppleTalk. After a NCP has reached the opened state, PPP will carry the corresponding network-layer protocol packets. Any supported networklayer protocol packets received when the corresponding NCP is not in the Opened state must be silently discarded.

During this phase, link traffic consists of any possible combination of LCP, NCP and network layer protocol packets.

The most common network layer (layer 3) protocol negotiated is for the Internet Protocol (IP). The routers exchange IP Control Protocol (IPCP) messages negotiating options specific to the protocol. In other words, IPCP is the most commonly used Network Control Protocol. The corresponding network control protocol for IPv6 is IPv6CP.

IPCP negotiates two options: compression and IP address assignments. However, IPCP is also used to pass network-related information, such as primary and backup Windows Name Service (WINS) and Domain Name System (DNS) servers.

Protocol Structure

Network Control Protocols such as IPCP and IPv6CP use the same packet format as the Link Control Protocols.

Configuration Option format:

8	16	32bit
Type	Length	Configuration Option

Packet format:

8	16	32bit	Variable
Code	Identifier	Length	Data

• Code -- The Code field is one octet and identifies the type of the packet.
• Identifier -- The Identifier field is one octet and aids in matching requests and replies.
• Length -- The Length field is two octets and indicates the length of the packet.
• Data -- The Data field is zero or more octets. The format of the Data field is determined by the Code field.

Related Protocols

PPP, NCP, IPCP, IPv6CP, LCP, IP, IPX, DECnet, AppleTalk

Sponsor Source

PPP Network Control Protocols are defined by IETF (http://

www.ietf.org) .

Reference

http://www.javvin.com/protocol/rfc1661.pdf
The Point-to-Point Protocol (PPP)
http://www.javvin.com/protocol/rfc1332.pdf
The PPP Internet Protocol Control Protocol (IPCP).
http://www.javvin.com/protocol/rfc2472.pdf
IP Version 6 over PPP
http://www.javvin.com/protocol/rfc3241.pdf
Robust Header Compression (ROHC) over PPP.
http://www.javvin.com/protocol/rfc3544.pdf
IP Header Compression over PPP.

PAP: Password Authentication Protocol

Protocol Description

The Password Authentication Protocol (PAP), a Link Control Protocol in the PPP suite, provides a simple method for the peer to establish its identity using a 2-way handshake. This is done only upon initial link establishment.

After the Link Establishment phase is complete, an ID/Password pair is repeatedly sent by the peer to the authenticator until authentication is acknowledged or the connection is terminated.

PAP is not a strong authentication method. Passwords are sent over the circuit in text format, and there is no protection from sniffing, playback or repeated trial and error attacks. The peer is in control of the frequency and timing of the attempts. Any implementations which include a stronger authentication method (such as CHAP) MUST offer to negotiate that method prior to PAP.

This authentication method is most appropriately used where a plaintext password must be available to simulate a login at a remote host. In such a use, this method provides a similar level of security to the usual user login at the remote host.

Protocol Structure

Configuration Option format for Password Authentication Protocol:

8	16	32bit
Type	Length	Authentication-Protocol

• Type -- 3
• Length -- 4
• Authentication-Protocol -- C023 (Hex) for Password Authentication Protocol

Password Authentication Protocol (PAP) packet format:

8	16	32bits	Variable
Code	Identifier	Length	Data

• Code -- The Code field is one octet and identifies the type of PAP packet. PAP Codes are assigned as follows:

    1 Authenticate-Request
    2 Authenticate-Ack
    3 Authenticate-Nak

• Identifier -- The Identifier field is one octet and aids in matching requests and replies.
• Length -- The Length field is two octets and indicates the length of the PAP packet including the Code, Identifier, Length and Data fields. Octets outside the range of the Length field should be treated as Data Link Layer padding and should be ignored on reception.
• Data -- The Data field is zero or more octets. The format of the Data field is determined by the Code field.

Related Protocols

PPP, CHAP, LCP, NCP

Sponsor Source

PAP is defined by IETF (http://www.ietf.org) RFC 1334; now replaced by RFC 1994.

Reference

http://www.javvin.com/protocol/rfc1334.pdf
PPP Authentication Protocols
http://www.javvin.com/protocol/rfc1994.pdf
PPP Challenge Handshake Authentication Protocol (CHAP)

PoS: Packet over SONET/SDH

Protocol Description

Packet Over SONET/SDH (PoS), also known as PPP over SONET/SDH, refers to the scheme of using PPP encapsulation to map IP datagrams into the SONET/SDH frame payload. Since SONET/SDH is a point-to-point circuit, PPP is well suited to use over these links. PoS is a highly scalable protocol that overcomes many of the inefficiencies of ATM, while providing legacy support to internetworks with existing SONET/SDH architectures.

PoS provides a mechanism to carry packets directly within the SONET/SDH synchronous payload envelope (SPE) using a small amount of High-Level Data Link Control (HDLC) or PPP framing. PoS can be viewed as three layers:

• Top layer -- IP encapsulation into PPP
• Mid layer -- Framing of PPP with HDLC
• Bottom layer -- Mapping into SONET/SDH

The bottom layer, mapping into SONET, is the unique part defined by IETF in RFC 2615 for PoS. It contains the following characters:

• High-order containment -- PoS frames must be placed in the required synchronous transport signals used in SONET. PPP in HDLC-like framing presents an octet interface to the physical layer.
• Octet alignment -- This refers to the alignment of the data packet octet boundaries to the STS octet boundaries. The octet stream is mapped into the SONET STS-SPE/SDH Higher Order VC, with the octet boundaries aligned with the SONET STS-SPE/SDH Higher Order VC octet boundaries.
• Payload scrambling -- Scrambling is the process of encoding digital 1s and 0s onto a line in such a way that provides an adequate number for 1s requirement. Scrambling is performed during insertion into the SONET STS-SPE/SDH Higher Order VC to provide adequate transparency and protect against potential security threats. For PPP over SONET/SDH, the entire SONET/SDH payload (SONET STS-SPE/SDH Higher Order VC minus the path overhead and any fixed stuff) is scrambled using a self-synchronous scrambler of polynomial $X^{**}43 + 1$.

The proper order of operation of PoS is:

When transmitting:

IP -> PPP -> FCS generation -> Byte stuffing -> Scrambling -> SONET/SDH framing

When receiving:

SONET/SDH framing -> Descrambling -> Byte destuffing -> FCS detection -> PPP -> IP

Protocol Structure

Packet over SONET/SDH:

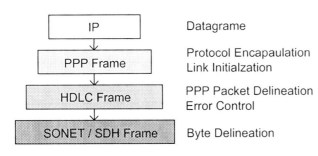

IP — Datagrame

PPP Frame — Protocol Encapaulation
Link Initialzation

HDLC Frame — PPP Packet Delineation
Error Control

SONET / SDH Frame — Byte Delineation

Figure 2-19: Packet over SONET/SDH

Encapsulating IP into a SONET/SDH frame:

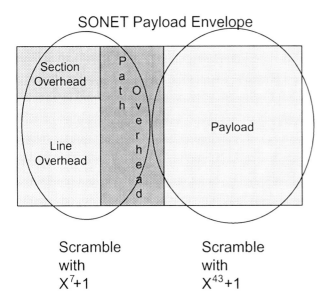

Figure 2-20: Encapsulating IP into a SONET/SDH frame

Related Protocols
ATM, IP, SONET/SDH, PPP, HDLC

Sponsor Source
Packet over SONET/SDH specification is defined by IETF.

Reference
http://www.javvin.com/rfc1661.pdf
The Point-to-Point Protocol, July 1994
http://www.javvin.com/rfc1662.pdf
PPP in HDLC-like Framing, July 1994
http://www.javvin.com/rfc2615.pdf
PPP over SONET/SDH, June 1999

PPPoA: PPP over ATM AAL5

Protocol Description
PPP over ATM AAL5 (PPPoA) describes the use of ATM Adaptation Layer 5 (AAL5) for framing PPP encapsulated packets.

The Point-to-Point Protocol (PPP) provides a standard method for transporting multi-protocol datagrams over point-to-point links.
The ATM AAL5 protocol is designed to provide virtual connections between end stations attached to the same network. These connections offer a packet delivery service that includes error detection, but does not do error correction.

Most existing implementations of PPP use ISO 3309 HDLC as a basis for their framing.

When an ATM network is configured with point-to-point connections, PPP can use AAL5 as a framing mechanism.

The PPP layer treats the underlying ATM AAL5 layer service as a bit-synchronous point-to-point link. In this context, the PPP link corresponds to an ATM AAL5 virtual connection. The virtual connection MUST be full-duplex, point to point, and it MAY be either dedicated (i.e. permanent, set up by provisioning) or switched (set up on demand). LLC encapsulated PPP over AAL5 is the alternative technique to VC-multiplexed PPP over AAL5.

When transporting a PPP payload over AAL5, an implementation:

1. MUST support virtual circuit multiplexed PPP payloads as described in section 5 below by mutual configuration or negotiation of both end points. This technique is referred to as "VC-multiplexed PPP".
2. MUST support LLC encapsulated PPP payloads on PVCs, as described in section 6 below by mutual configuration or negotiation of both end points. This technique is referred to as "LLC encapsulated PPP".
3. For SVC set up, an implementation MUST negotiate using the Q.2931 [9] Annex C procedure, encoding the Broadband Lower Layer Interface (B-LLI) information element to signal either VC- multiplexed PPP or LLC encapsulated PPP.

Protocol Structure
Virtual Circuit Multiplexed PPP Over AAL5. The AAL5 PDU format is shown below:

AAL5 CPCS-PDU Format

1 byte	0-47 bytes	1 byte	1 byte	2 bytes	4 bytes
CPCS-PDU	PAD	CPCS-UU	CPI	Length	CRC
			CPCS-PDU Trailer		

The AAL5 CPCS-PDU payload field is encoded as shown below:
1. LLC header: 2 bytes encoded to specify a source SAP and destination SAP of routed OSI PDU (values 0xFE 0xFE), fol-

lowed by an Un-numbered Information (UI) frame type (value 0x03).

2. Network Layer Protocol IDentifier (NLPID) representing PPP, (value 0xCF).

3. The PPP protocol identifier field, which can be either 1 or 2 octets long.

4. Followed by the PPP information field.

Destination SAP	Source SAP	Frame type	LLC Header	
NLPID = PPP				
Protocol ID	PPP Info	Padding	PPP Payload	
PAD (0 – 47 bytes)				
CPCS-UU	CPI	Length	CRC	CPCS-PDU Trailer

Related Protocols

PPP, 802.3, ATM

Sponsor Source

PPPoA is defined by IETF (http://www.ietf.org) RFC 2364.

Reference

http://www.javvin.com/protocol/rfc2364.pdf
PPP Over AAL5

PPPoE: PPP over Ethernet

Protocol Description

PPP over Ethernet (PPPoE) provides the ability to connect a network of hosts over a simple bridging access device to a remote Access Concentrator. With this model, each host utilizes its own PPP stack and the user is presented with a familiar user interface. Access control, billing and type of service can be done on a per-user, rather than per-site, basis.

To provide a point-to-point connection over Ethernet, each PPP session must learn the Ethernet address of the remote peer, as well as establish a unique session identifier. PPPoE includes a discovery protocol that provides this.

PPPoE has two distinct stages. There is a Discovery stage and a PPP Session stage. When a Host wishes to initiate a PPPoE session, it must first perform Discovery to identify the Ethernet MAC address of the peer and establish a PPPoE SESSION_ID. While PPP defines a peer-to-peer relationship, Discovery is inherently a client-server relationship. In the Discovery process, a Host (the client) discovers an Access Concentrator (the server). Based on the network topology, there may be more than one Access Concentrator that the Host can communicate with. The Discovery stage allows the Host to discover all Access Concentrators and then select one. When Discovery completes successfully, both the Host and the selected Access Concentrator have the information they will use to build their point-to-point connection over Ethernet.

The Discovery stage remains stateless until a PPP session is established. Once a PPP session is established, both the Host and the Access Concentrator MUST allocate the resources for a PPP virtual interface.

Protocol Structure

The Ethernet payload for PPPoE is as follows:

4	8	16	32bit
Ver	Type	Code	Session-ID
Length		Payload	

• VER -- version of PPPOE MUST be set to 0x1.
• TYPE -- MUST be set to 0x1.
• CODE -- is defined below for the Discovery and PPP Session stages.
• SESSION_ID -- is an unsigned value in network byte order. It's value is defined below for Discovery packets. The value is fixed for a given PPP session and, in fact, defines a PPP session along with the Ethernet SOURCE_ADDR and DESTINATION_ADDR. A value of 0xffff is reserved for future use and MUST NOT be used
• LENGTH -- The value, in network byte order, indicates the length of the PPPoE payload. It does not include the length of the Ethernet or PPPoE headers.

Related Protocols

PPP, 802.3

Sponsor Source

PPPoE is defined by IETF (http://www.ietf.org) RFC 2516.

Reference

http://www.javvin.com/protocol/rfc2516.pdf
A Method for Transmitting PPP Over Ethernet (PPPoE)

Other WAN Protocols

Frame Relay: WAN Protocol for Internetworking

Protocol Description

Frame Relay is a WAN protocol for LAN internetworking which operates at the physical and data link layer to provide a fast and efficient method of transmitting information from a user device to another across multiple switches and routers.

Frame Relay is based on packet-switched technologies similar to x.25, which enables end stations to dynamically share the network medium and the available bandwidth. It employs the following two packet techniques: a) Variable-length packets and b) Statistical multiplexing. It does not guarantee data integrity and discard packets when there is network congestion. In reality, it still delivers data with high reliability.

The Frame Relay frame is transmitted to its destination through virtual circuits, which are logical paths from an originating point in the network to a destination point. Virtual circuits provide bidirectional communication paths from one terminal device to another and are uniquely identified by a data-link connection identifier (DLCI). A number of virtual circuits can be multiplexed into a single physical circuit for transmission across the network. This capability often can reduce the equipment and network complexity required to connect multiple terminal devices. A virtual circuit can pass through any number of intermediate switches located within the Frame Relay packet switched network.

There are permanent virtual circuits (PVCs) and switched virtual circuits (SVCs). PVCs are set up administratively by the network manager for a dedicated point-to-point connection; SVCs are set up on a call-by-call basis using the same signaling as for ISDN set up.

Due to its bandwidth efficiency and high reliability, Frame Relay offers an attractive alternative to both dedicated lines and X.25 networks for the inter-connecting of LANs through switches and routers.

Protocol Structure

The Frame Relay (LAPF Q.922 based) frame structure is as follows:

1byte	2 bytes	Variable	2 bytes	1byte
Flags	Address	Data	FCS	Flags

• Flags --Delimits the beginning and end of the frame. The value of this field is always the same and is represented either as the hexadecimal number 7E or as the binary number 01111110.
• Address -- Contains the following information:

6	7	8	12	13	14	15	16bit
DLCI	C/R	E	DLCI	FECN	BECN	DE	EA

　　　　• DLCI -- Datalink Connection Identifier field repre-

sents the address of the frame and corresponds to a PVC.
    • C/R -- Designates whether the frame is a command or response.
    • EA -- Extended Address field signifies up to two additional bytes in the Frame Relay header, thus greatly expanding the number of possible addresses.
    • FECN -- Forward Explicit Congestion Notification (see ECN below).
    • BECN -- Backward Explicit Congestion Notification (see ECN below).
    • DE -- Discard Eligibility.
• Data -- Contains encapsulated upper-layer data. Each frame in this variable-length field includes a user data or payload field that will vary in length up to 16,000 octets. This field serves to transport the higher-layer protocol packet (PDU) through a Frame Relay network.
• Frame Check Sequence -- Ensures the integrity of transmitted data. This value is computed by the source device and verified by the receiver to ensure integrity of transmission.

Frame Relay frames that conform to the LMI specifications consist of the fields as follows:

1 byte	2 bytes	1 byte	1 byte	1 byte	1 byte
Flags	LMI DLCI	I-Indicator	Proto-col Dis	Call Ref	M-Type
Information Elements (Variable)			FCS		Flags

• Flags -- Delimits the beginning and end of the frame.
• LMI DLCI -- Identifies the frame as an LMI frame instead of a basic Frame Relay frame. The LMI-specific DLCI value defined in the LMI consortium specification is DLCI = 1023.
• Unnumbered Information Indicator -- Sets the poll/final bit to zero.
• Protocol Discriminator -- Always contains a value indicating that the frame is an LMI frame.
• Call Reference -- Always contains zeros. This field currently is not used for any purpose.
• Message Type -- Labels the frame as one of the following message types:
    • Status-inquiry message -- Allows a user device to inquire about the status of the network.
    • Status message -- Responds to status-inquiry messages. Status messages include keepalives and PVC status messages.
• Information Elements -- Contains a variable number of individual information elements (IEs). IEs consist of the following fields:
    • IE Identifier -- Uniquely identifies the IE.
    • IE Length -- Indicates the length of the IE.
    • Data -- Consists of 1 or more bytes containing encapsulated upper-layer data.
• Frame Check Sequence (FCS) -- Ensures the integrity of transmitted data.

Related Protocols

LAPD, ISDN, X.25, LAPF

Sponsor Source

Frame Relay is defined by ITU-T (http://www.itu.org), ANSI (http://www.ansi.org) in the ANSI T1.618 and ANSI t1.617.

Reference

http://www.cisco.com/univercd/cc/td/doc/cisintwk/ito_doc/frame.htm
Understand Frame Relay

LAPF: Link Access Procedure for Frame Mode Services

Protocol Description

Link Access Procedure for Frame Mode Services (LAPF), as defined in ITU Q.922, is an enhanced LAPD (Q.921) with congestion control capabilities for Frame Mode Services in the Frame Relay network. LADF is used in the Frame Relay network for end-to-end signaling. LAPF conveys data link service data units between DL-service users in the User Plane for frame mode bearer services across the ISDN user-network interface on B-, D- or H-channels. The core functions of LAPF are:

- Frame delimiting, alignment, and flag transparency
- Virtual circuit multiplexing and de-multiplexing
- Octet alignment: Integer number of octets before zero-bit insertion
- Checking minimum and maximum frame sizes
- Error detection, Sequence and non-duplication
- Congestion control

Frame mode bearer connections are established using either procedures specified in Recommendation Q.933 or (for permanent virtual circuits) by subscription. LAPF uses a physical layer service and allows for statistical multiplexing of one or more frame mode bearer connections over a single ISDN B-, D- or H-channel by use of LAPF and compatible HDLC procedures.

Protocol Structure

LAPF is similar to LAPD and its address format is as follows:

6	7	8	12	13	14	15	16bit
DLCI	C/R	E	DLCI	FECN	BECN	DE	EA

- DLCI -- Datalink Connection Identifier field represents the address of the frame and corresponds to a PVC.
- C/R -- Designates whether the frame is a command or response.
- EA -- Extended Address field signifies up to two additional bytes in the Frame Relay header, thus greatly expanding the number of possible addresses.
- FECN -- Forward Explicit Congestion Notification (see ECN below).
- BECN -- Backward Explicit Congestion Notification (see ECN below).
- DE -- Discard Eligibility.

LAPF control field format:

Control field bits (Modulo 128)	8	7	6	5	4	3	2	1

I Format	N(S)							0
	N(R)							P/F
S Format	X	X	X	X	Su	Su	0	1
	N(R)							P/F
U Format	M	M	M	P/F	M	M	1	1

- N(S) -- Transmitter send sequence number.
- N(R) -- Transmitter receive sequence number.
- P/F -- Poll bit when used as a command, final bit when used as a response.
- X -- Reserved and set to 0.
- Su -- Supervisory function bit.
- M -- Modifier function bit.

Related Protocols

LAPD, ISDN, X.25, Frame Relay

Sponsor Source

LAPF is defined by ITU-T (http://www.itu.org) Q.922: ISDN Data Link Layer Specification for Frame Mode Bearer Services

Reference

http://www.cisco.com/univercd/cc/td/doc/cisintwk/ito_doc/frame.htm
Understand Frame Relay

HDLC: High Level Data Link Control

Protocol Description

The High Level Data Link Control (HDLC) protocol, an ISO data link layer protocol based on the IBM SDLC, ensures that data passed up to the next layer has been received exactly as transmitted (i.e. error free, without loss and in the correct order). Another important function of HDLC is flow control, which ensures that data is transmitted only as fast as the receiver can receive it. There are two distinct HDLC implementations: HDLC NRM (also known as SDLC) and HDLC Link Access Procedure Balanced (LAPB). The later is the more popular implementation. HDLC is part of the X.25 stack.

LAPB is a bit-oriented synchronous protocol that provides complete data transparency in a full-duplex point-to-point operation. It supports a peer-to-peer link in which neither end of the link plays the role of the permanent master station. HDLC NRM, on the other hand, has a permanent primary station with one or more secondary stations.

HDLC LAPB is a very efficient protocol, which requires a minimum of overhead to ensure flow control, error detection and recovery. If data is flowing in both directions (full duplex), the data frames themselves carry all the information required to ensure data integrity.

The concept of a frame window is used to send multiple frames before receiving confirmation that the first frame has been correctly received. This means that data can continue to flow in situations where there may be long "turn-around" time lags without stopping to wait for an acknowledgement. This kind of situation occurs, for instance in satellite communication.

There are three categories of frames:

• Information frames transport data across the link and may encapsulate the higher layers of the OSI architecture.
• Supervisory frames perform the flow control and error recovery functions.
• Unnumbered frames provide the link initialization and termination.

Protocol Structure

1 byte	1-2 bytes	1 byte	variable	2 bytes	1 byte
Flag	Address field	Control field	Information	FCS	Flag

• Flag -- The value of the flag is always (0x7E).
• Address field -- Defines the address of the secondary station which is sending the frame or the destination of the frame sent by the primary station. It contains Service Access Point (6bits), a Command/Response bit to indicate whether the frame relates to information frames (I-frames) being sent from the node or received by the node, and an address extension bit which is usually set to true to indicate that the address is of length one byte. When set to false it indicates that an additional byte follows.

• Extended address -- HDLC provides another type of extension to the basic format. The address field may be extended to more than one byte by agreement between the involved parties.
• Control field -- Serves to identify the type of the frame. In addition, it includes sequence numbers, control features and error tracking according to the frame type.
• FCS -- The Frame Check Sequence (FCS) enables a high-level of physical error control by allowing the integrity of the transmitted frame data to be checked.

Related Protocols

LAPB, X.25, Frame Relay, SDLC

Sponsor Source

HDLC is defined by ISO (http://www.iso.org).

Reference

http://www2.rad.com/networks/1994/hdlc/hdlc.htm
High Level Data Link Control

LAPB: Link Access Procedure, Balanced

Protocol Description

Link Access Procedure, Balanced (LAPB) is a data link layer protocol used to manage communication and packet framing between data terminal equipment (DTE) and the data circuit-terminating equipment (DCE) devices in the X.25 protocol stack. LAPB, a bit-oriented protocol derived from HDLC, is actually the HDLC in BAC (Balanced Asynchronous Class) mode. LAPB makes sure that frames are error free and properly sequenced.

LAPB shares the same frame format, frame types, and field functions as SDLC and HDLC. Unlike either of these, however, LAPB is restricted to the Asynchronous Balanced Mode (ABM) transfer mode and is appropriate only for combined stations. Also, LAPB circuits can be established by either the DTE or DCE. The station initiating the call is determined to be the primary, and the responding station the secondary. Finally, LAPB use of the P/F bit is somewhat different from that of the other protocols.

In LAPB, since there is no master/slave relationship, the sender uses the Poll bit to insist on an immediate response. In the response frame this same bit becomes the receivers Final bit. The receiver always turns on the Final bit in its response to a command from the sender with the Poll bit set. The P/F bit is generally used when either end becomes unsure about proper frame sequencing because of a possible missing acknowledgement, and it is necessary to re-establish a point of reference.

LAPB's Frame Types:

• I-Frames (Information frames): Carry upper-layer information and some control information. I-frame functions include sequencing, flow control, and error detection and recovery. I-frames carry send-and-receive sequence numbers.
• S-Frames (Supervisory Frames): Carry control information. S-frame functions include requesting and suspending transmissions, reporting on status, and acknowledging the receipt of I-frames. S-frames carry only receive sequence numbers.
• U-Frames (Unnumbered Frames): Carry control information. U-frame functions include link setup and disconnection, as well as error reporting. U-frames carry no sequence numbers.

Protocol Structure

The format of an LAPB frame is as follows:

1 byte	1 byte	1-2 bytes	variable	2 byte	1 byte
Flag	Address field	Control field	Informa-tion	FCS	Flag

• Flag -- The value of the flag is always (0x7E). In order to ensure that the bit pattern of the frame delimiter flag does not appear in the data field of the frame (and therefore cause frame misalignment), a technique known as Bit Stuffing is used by both the transmitter and the receiver.

• Address field -- In LAPB, the address field has no meaning since the protocol works in a point to point mode and the DTE network address is represented in the layer 3 packets.
• Control field -- Serves to identify the type of the frame. In addition, it includes sequence numbers, control features and error tracking according to the frame type.
• Modes of operation -- LAPB works in the Asynchronous Balanced Mode (ABM). This mode is totally balanced (i.e., no master/slave relationship) and is signified by the SABM(E) frame. Each station may initialize, supervise, recover from errors, and send frames at any time. The DTE and DCE are treated as equals.
• FCS -- The Frame Check Sequence enables a high-level of physical error control by allowing the integrity of the transmitted frame data to be checked.
• Window size -- LAPB supports an extended window size (modulo 128) where the number of possible outstanding frames for acknowledgement is raised from 8 to 128.

Related Protocols

LAPD, ISDN, X.25, Frame Relay, HDLC, SDLC

Sponsor Source

LAPB is defined by ISO (http://www.iso.org).

Reference

http://www.cisco.com/univercd/cc/td/doc/cisintwk/ito_doc/x25.htm
X.25
http://www2.rad.com/networks/1994/hdlc/hdlc.htm
High Level Data Link Control

X.25: ISO/ITU-T Protocol for WAN Communications

Protocol Description

X.25, an ISO and ITU-T protocol for WAN communications, is a packet switched data network protocol which defines the exchange of data as well as control information between a user device, called Data Terminal Equipment (DTE) and a network node, called Data Circuit Terminating Equipment (DCE).

X.25 is designed to operate effectively regardless of the type of systems connected to the network. X.25 is typically used in the packet-switched networks (PSNs) of common carriers, such as the telephone companies. Subscribers are charged based on their use of the network. X.25 utilizes a Connection-Oriented service which insures that packets are transmitted in order.

X.25 sessions are established when one DTE device contacts another to request a communication session. The DTE device that receives the request can either accept or refuse the connection. If the request is accepted, the two systems begin full-duplex information transfer. Either DTE device can terminate the connection. After the session is terminated, any further communication requires the establishment of a new session. X.25 uses virtual circuits for packets communications. Both switched and permanent virtual circuits are used.

The X.25 protocol suite comes with three levels based on the first three layers of the OSI seven layers architecture.

The Physical Level: describes the interface with the physical environment. There are three protocols in this group: 1) X.21 interface operates over eight interchange circuits; 2) X.21bis defines the analogue interface to allow access to the digital circuit switched network using an analogue circuit; 3) V.24 provides procedures which enable the DTE to operate over a leased analogue circuit connecting it to a packet switching node or concentrator.

The Link Level is responsible for reliable communication between the DTE and the DCE. There are four protocols in this group: 1) LAPB, derived from HDLC and the most commonly used, has all the characteristics of HDLC and also enables the formatition of a logical link connection; 2) Link Access Protocol (LAP) is an earlier version of LAPB and is seldom used today; and 3) LAPD, derived from LAPB and used for ISDN, enables data transmission between DTEs through D channel, especially between a DTE and an ISDN node; 4) Logical Link Control (LLC), an IEEE 802 LAN protocol, enables X.25 packets to be transmitted through a LAN channel.

The Packet Layer Protocol (PLP): describes the data transfer protocol in the packet switched network at the network layer (layer 3). PLP manages packet exchanges between DTE devices across virtual circuits. PLPs also can run over Logical Link Control 2 implementations on LANs as well as over ISDN interfaces running LAPD. The PLP operates in five distinct modes: call setup, data transfer, idle, call clearing, and restarting.

- Call setup mode is used to establish SVCs between DTE devices.
- Data transfer mode is used for transferring data between two DTE devices across a virtual circuit.
- Idle mode is used when a virtual circuit is established but data transfer is not occurring.
- Call clearing mode is used to end communication sessions between DTE devices and to terminate SVCs.
- Restarting mode is used to synchronize transmission between a DTE device and a locally connected DCE device.

X.75 is the signaling protocol for X.25, which defines the signaling system between two PDNs. X.75 is essentially a Network-to-Network Interface (NNI).

We focus on the X.25 PLP; other protocols will be discussed separately.

Protocol Structure

X.25 PLP has many control messages. The control packet as well as all X.25 packets begins with a 3-byte header. Bytes 1 and 2 contain the Group and the Channel fields that together form a 12 bit virtual circuit number. The additional information for each message is different.

1. Control Packet

1	2	3	4	8	16	23	24bit
0	0	0	1	Group	Channel	Type	C
Additional Information (Variable)							

2. The additional information of the Call Request Packet is as follows:

4bits	4bits	Variable	2bits	6bits	Variable
Length Calling address	Length Called address	Calling & Called address	00	Facility length	Facilities
Data (Variable)					

Other Control Packets are:

- The CALL ACCEPTED packet is sent by the callee DTE if it accepts the call.
- The CLEAR REQUEST is sent for various reasons. The fourth byte of the packet tells why the connection is being cleared. It is acknowledged by a CLEAR REQUEST CONFIRMATION packet.
- The INTERRUPT packet allows a short (32 bytes) signal to be sent out of sequence. It is acknowledged by an INTERRUPT CONFIRMATION packet.
- The RECEIVE READY (RR) packet is used to send separate acknowledgments where there is no reverse traffic. The ppp field (three first bits of the type field) tells which packet is expected next.
- The RECEIVE NOT READY (RNR) packet allows a DTE to tell the other side to stop sending packets to it for a while.
- The REJECT packet allows a DTE to request retransmission of a series of packets. The ppp field gives the first sequence number desired.
- The RESET and RESTART packets are used to recover from

varying degrees of trouble. Both are acknowledged by RESET CONFIRMATION and RESTART CONFIRMATION respectively.

• The DIAGNOSTIC packet is also provided, to allow the network to inform the user of problems.

3. The format of the data packet is as follows:

1	2	4	8	16	23	24	31	32bit
Q	D	Mod-ulo	Group	Chan-nel	Pig-gy-back	M	se-quence	C
Data (Variable)								

Related Protocols

LAPB, X.25, Frame Relay, HDLC, ISDN, LLC, LAPD

Sponsor Source

X.25 protocol stack is defined by ISO (http://www.iso.org) and ITU-T (http://www.itu.org).

Reference

http://www.cisco.com/univercd/cc/td/doc/cisintwk/ito_doc/x25.htm
X.25 Overview
http://www2.rad.com/networks/1996/x25/x25.htm
X.25 Protocols

Local Area Network and LAN Protocols

Description

Local Area Network (LAN) is a data communications network connecting terminals, computers and printers within a building or other geographically limited areas. These devices may be connected through wired cables or wireless links. Ethernet, Token Ring and Wireless LAN using IEEE 802.11 are examples of standard LAN technologies.

Ethernet is by far the most commonly used LAN technology. Token Ring technology is still used by some companies. FDDI is sometimes used as a backbone LAN interconnecting Ethernet or Token Ring LANs. WLAN using IEEE 802.11 technologies is rapidly becoming the new leading LAN technology because of its mobility and easy to use features.

Local Area Networks can be interconnected using Wide Area Network (WAN) or Metropolitan Area Network (MAN) technologies. The common WAN technologies include TCP/IP, ATM, Frame Relay etc. The common MAN technologies include SMDS and 10 Gigabit Ethernet.

LANs are traditionally used to connect a group of people who are in the same local area. However, working groups are becoming more geographically distributed in today's working environment. In these cases, virtual LAN (VLAN) technologies are defined for people in different places to share the same networking resource.
Local Area Network protocols are mostly at the data link layer (layer 2). IEEE is the leading organization defining LAN standards. There are some vendor specific LAN protocols such as Novell Netware, AppleTalk etc. which are discussed in seperate sections.

Key Protocols

Ethernet	Ethernet LAN protocols as defined in IEEE 802.3 suite
	Fast Ethernet: Ethernet LAN at data rate 100Mbps (IEEE 802.3u)
	Gigabit Ethernet: Ethernet at data rate 1000Mbps (IEEE 802.3z, 802.3ab)
	10Gigabit Ethernet: Ethernet at data rate 10 Gbps (IEEE 802.3ae)
VLAN	802.1Q: Virtual LAN Bridging Switching Protocol
	GARP: Generic Attribute Registration Protocol (802.1P)
	GMRP: GARP Multicast Registration Protocol (802.1P)
	GVRP: GARP VLAN Registration Protocol (802.1P, 802.1Q)
	IEEE 802.1P: LAN Layer 2 QoS/CoS Protocol
WLAN and WPAN	WLAN: Wireless LAN Defined by IEEE 802.11
	IEEE 802.11i: WLAN Security Standards
	IEEE 802.1X: WLAN Authentication & Key Management
	WPAN: Wireless Personal Area Network Communication Protocols
	IEEE 802.15.1 and the Bluetooth for WPAN Communications
Token Ring	Token Ring: IEEE 802.5 LAN protocol
FDDI	FDDI: Fiber Distributed Data Interface
Others	LLC: Logic Link Control (IEEE 802.2)
	SNAP: SubNetwork Access Protocol
	STP: Spanning Tree Protocol (IEEE 802.1D)

Ethernet: IEEE 802.3 Local Area Network protocols

Protocol Description

Ethernet protocols refer to the family of local-area networks (LAN) covered by a group of IEEE 802.3 standards. In the Ethernet standard, there are two modes of operation: half-duplex and full-duplex. In the half-duplex mode, data are transmitted using the popular Carrier-Sense Multiple Access/Collision Detection (CSMA/CD) protocol on a shared medium. The main disadvantages of the half-duplex are the efficiency and distance limitation, in which the link distance is limited by the minimum MAC frame size. This restriction reduces the efficiency drastically for high-rate transmission. Therefore, the carrier extension technique is used to ensure the minimum frame size of 512 bytes in Gigabit Ethernet to achieve a reasonable link distance.

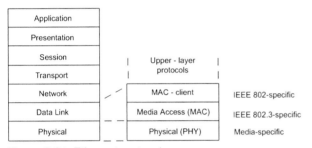

Figure 2-21: Ethernet protocols

Four data rates are currently defined for operation over optical fiber and twisted-pair cables:

• 10 Mbps -- Ethernet 10Base-T(802.3i), 10Base2 and 10Base5 (IEEE 802.3) and 10BaseF (802.3j)
• 100 Mbps -- Fast Ethernet 100BaseX: 100Base-T, 100Base-F (IEEE 802.3u)
• 1000 Mbps -- Gigabit Ethernet 1000BaseX: 1000Base-T (IEEE 802.3ab), 1000Base-F, 1000Base-LX, LH, SX, CX (IEEE 802.3z)
• 10 Gbps -- 10 Gigabit Ethernet 10GbaseE, 10GbaseL and 10GBaseS(IEEE 802.3ae); 10GbaseCX4 (IEEE 802.3ak) and 10GBaseT (IEEE 802.3an)

In this document, we discuss the general aspects of the Ethernet. The specific issues on fast Ethernet, Gigabit and 10 Gigabit Ethernet will be discussed in separate documents.

The Ethernet system consists of three basic elements: 1) the physical medium used to carry Ethernet signals between computers, 2) a set of medium access control rules embedded in each Ethernet interface that allows multiple computers to fairly arbitrate access to the shared Ethernet channel, and 3) an Ethernet frame that consists of a standardized set of bits used to carry data over the system.

As with all IEEE 802 protocols, the ISO data link layer is divided into two IEEE 802 sublayers, the Media Access Control (MAC) sub-layer and the MAC-client sublayer. The IEEE 802.3 physical layer corresponds to the ISO physical layer.

The MAC sublayer has two primary responsibilities:

• Data encapsulation, including frame assembly before transmission, and frame parsing/error detection during and after reception
• Media access control, including initiation of frame transmission and recovery from transmission failure

The MAC-client sublayer may be one of the following:

• Logical Link Control (LLC), which provides the interface between the Ethernet MAC and the upper layers in the protocol stack of the end station. The LLC sublayer is defined by IEEE 802.2 standards.
• Bridge entity, which provides LAN-to-LAN interfaces between LANs that use the same protocol (for example, Ethernet to Ethernet) and also between different protocols (for example, Ethernet to Token Ring). Bridge entities are defined by IEEE 802.1 standards.

Each Ethernet-equipped computer operates independently of all other stations on the network: there is no central controller. All stations attached to an Ethernet are connected to a shared signaling system, also called the medium. To send data a station first listens to the channel and, when the channel is idle then transmits its data in the form of an Ethernet frame, or packet.

After each frame transmission, all stations on the network must contend equally for the next frame transmission opportunity. Access to the shared channel is determined by the medium access control (MAC) mechanism embedded in the Ethernet interface located in each station. The medium access control mechanism is based on a system called Carrier Sense Multiple Access with Collision Detection (CSMA/CD). As each Ethernet frame is sent onto the shared signal channel, all Ethernet interfaces look at the destination address. If the destination address of the frame matches with the interface address, the frame will be read entirely and be delivered to the networking software running on that computer. All other network interfaces will stop reading the frame when they discover that the destination address does not match their own address.

When it comes to how signals flow over the set of media segments that make up an Ethernet system, it helps to understand the topology of the system. The signal topology of the Ethernet is also known as the logical topology, to distinguish it from the actual physical layout of the media cables. The logical topology of an Ethernet provides a single channel (or bus) that carries Ethernet signals to all stations.

Multiple Ethernet segments can be linked together to form a larger Ethernet LAN using a signal amplifying and retiming device called a repeater. Through the use of repeaters, a given Ethernet system of multiple segments can grow as a "non-rooted branching tree." "Non-rooted" means that the resulting system of linked segments may grow in any direction, and does not have a specific root segment. Most importantly, segments must never be connected in a loop. Every segment in the system must have two ends, since the Ethernet system will not operate correctly in the presence of loop paths.

Even though the media segments may be physically connected in a star pattern, with multiple segments attached to a repeater, the logical topology is still that of a single Ethernet channel that carries signals to all stations.

Protocol Structure

The basic IEEE 802.3 MAC Data Frame for 10/100Mbps Ethernet:

7	1	6	6	2	46-1500bytes	4bytes
Pre	SFD	DA	SA	Length Type	Data unit + pad	FCS

• Preamble (Pre) -- 7 bytes. The PRE is an alternating pattern of ones and zeros that tells receiving stations that a frame is coming, and that provides a means to synchronize the frame-reception portions of receiving physical layers with the incoming bit stream.
• Start-of-frame delimiter (SFD) -- 1 byte. The SOF is an alternating pattern of ones and zeros, ending with two consecutive 1-bits indicating that the next bit is the left-most bit in the left-most byte of the destination address.
• Destination address (DA) -- 6 bytes. The DA field identifies which station(s) should receive the frame.
• Source addresses (SA) -- 6 bytes. The SA field identifies the sending station.
• Length/Type -- 2 bytes. This field indicates either the number of MAC-client data bytes that are contained in the data field of the frame, or the frame type ID if the frame is assembled using an optional format.
• Data -- Is a sequence of n bytes (46=< n =<1500) of any value. The total frame minimum is 64bytes.
• Frame check sequence (FCS) -- 4 bytes. This sequence contains a 32-bit cyclic redundancy check (CRC) value, which is created by the sending MAC and is recalculated by the receiving MAC to check for damaged frames.

MAC Frame with Gigabit Carrier Extension:

1000Base-X has a minimum frame size of 416bytes, and 1000Base-T has a minimum frame size of 520bytes. An extension field is used to fill the frames that are shorter than the minimum length.

7	1	6	6	2	46=< n =<1500	4bytes	Variable
Pre	SFD	DA	SA	Length Type	Data unit + pad	FCS	Ext

Related Protocols

IEEE 802.3, 802.3u, 802.3z, 802.3ab, 802.2, 802.1, 802.3ae, 802.1D, 802.1G, 802.1Q, 802.1p

Sponsor Source

Ethernet standards are defined by IEEE (http://www.ieee.org) in 802.3 specifications.

Reference

http://standards.ieee.org/getieee802/download/802.3-2002.pdf
Carrier sense multiple access with collision detection (CSMA/CD) access method and physical layer specification.
http://www.cisco.com/univercd/cc/td/doc/cisintwk/ito_doc/ethernet.htm
Ethernet Technologies
http://www.cisco.com/warp/public/cc/techno/media/lan/gig/tech/gigbt_tc.htm
Introduction to gigabit Ethernet

Fast Ethernet: 100Mbps Ethernet (IEEE 802.3u)

Protocol Description

Fast Ethernet (100BASE-T) offers a speed increase ten times that of the 10BaseT Ethernet specification, while preserving such qualities as frame format, MAC mechanisms, and MTU. Such similarities allow the use of existing 10BaseT applications and network management tools on Fast Ethernet networks. Officially, the 100BASE-T standard is IEEE 802.3u.

Like Ethernet, 100BASE-T is based on the CSMA/CD LAN access method. There are several different cabling schemes that can be used with 100BASE-T, including:

100BASE-TX: two pairs of high-quality twisted-pair wires
100BASE-T4: four pairs of normal-quality twisted-pair wires
100BASE-FX: fiber optic cables

The Fast Ethernet specifications include mechanisms for Auto-Negotiation of the media speed. This makes it possible for vendors to provide dual-speed Ethernet interfaces that can be installed and run at either 10-Mbps or 100-Mbps automatically. The IEEE identifiers include three pieces of information. The first item, "100", stands for the media speed of 100-Mbps. The "BASE" stands for "baseband," which is a type of signaling. Baseband signaling simply means that Ethernet signals are the only signals carried over the media system.

The third part of the identifier provides an indication of the segment type. The "T4" segment type is a twisted-pair segment that uses four pairs of telephone-grade twisted-pair wires. The "TX" segment type is a twisted-pair segment that uses two pairs of wires and is based on the data grade twisted-pair physical medium standard developed by ANSI. The "FX" segment type is a fiber optic link segment based on the fiber optic physical medium standard developed by ANSI and uses two strands of fiber cable. The TX and FX medium standards are collectively known as 100BASE-X.

The 100BASE-TX and 100BASE-FX media standards used in Fast Ethernet are both adopted from physical media standards first developed by ANSI, the American National Standards Institute. The ANSI physical media standards were originally developed for the Fiber Distributed Data Interface (FDDI) LAN standard (ANSI standard X3T9.5), and are widely used in FDDI LANs.

Protocol Structure

Fast Ethernet has a minimum frame of 64 bytes and maximum up to 1518bytes, just as for Ethernet 802.3.

7	1	6	6	2	46=< n =<1500	4bytes
Pre	SFD	DA	SA	Length Type	Data unit + pad	FCS

• Preamble (Pre) -- 7 bytes. The PRE is an alternating pattern of ones and zeros that tells receiving stations that a frame is coming, and that provides a means to synchronize the frame-reception portions of receiving physical layers with the incoming bit stream.
• Start-of-frame delimiter (SFD) -- 1 byte. The SOF is an alternating pattern of ones and zeros, ending with two consecutive 1-bits indicating that the next bit is the left-most bit in the left-most byte of the destination address.
• Destination address (DA) -- 6 bytes. The DA field identifies which station(s) should receive the frame..
• Source addresses (SA) -- 6 bytes. The SA field identifies the sending station.
• Length/Type -- 2 bytes. This field indicates either the number of MAC-client data bytes that are contained in the data field of the frame, or the frame type ID if the frame is assembled using an optional format.
• Data -- Is a sequence of n bytes (46=< n =<1500) of any value. The total frame minimum is 64bytes.
• Frame check sequence (FCS) -- 4 bytes. This sequence contains a 32-bit cyclic redundancy check (CRC) value, which is created by the sending MAC and is recalculated by the receiving MAC to check for damaged frames.

Related Protocols

IEEE 802.3, 802.3u, 802.3z, 802.3ab, 802.2, 802.1, 802.3ae, 802.1D, 802.1G, 802.1Q, 802.1p, 802.1w

Sponsor Source

Fast Ethernet standard is defined by IEEE (http://www.ieee.org) in 802.3u.

Reference

http://www.ethermanage.com/ethernet/descript-100quickref.html
Fast Ethernet Quick Guide

Gigabit (1000 Mbps) Ethernet: IEEE 802.3z (1000Base-X) and 802.3ab (1000Base-T)

Protocol Description

Ethernet protocols refer to the family of local-area network (LAN) covered by the IEEE 802.3 standard. The Gigabit Ethernet protocol is based on the Ethernet protocol but has ten-fold speed increase over Fast Ethernet, using shorter frames with carrier Extension. It is published as the IEEE 802.3z and 802.3ab supplements to the IEEE 802.3 base standards.

Carrier Extension is a simple solution, but it wastes bandwidth. Packet Bursting is "Carrier Extension plus a burst of packets". Burst mode is a feature that allows a MAC to send a short sequence (a burst) of frames equal to approximately 5.4 maximum-length frames without having to relinquish control of the medium.

The Gigabit Ethernet standards are fully compatible with Ethernet and Fast Ethernet installations. They retain Carrier Sense Multiple Access/Collision Detection (CSMA/CD) as the access method. Full-duplex as well as half duplex modes of operation are supported, as are single-mode and multi mode fiber and short-haul coaxial cable, and twisted pair cables. The Gigabit Ethernet architecture is displayed in the following figure:

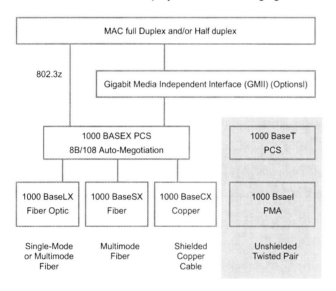

Figure 2-22: Gigabit Ethernet Protocol Stack

IEEE 802.3z defines the Gigabit Ethernet over fiber and cable and has the physical media standard 1000Base-X, which include: 1000BaseLX, 1000BaseSX, 1000BaseCX and 1000BaseLH. Basically, all standards included in 1000BaseX uses 8B/10B coding scheme with 8 bits of data and 2 bits of error-correction data. Each specification allows various cable (fiber or copper) lengthes, uses different cable media. IEEE 802.3ab defines the Gigabit Ethernet over the unshielded twisted pair wire (1000Base-T, covering up to 75m).

The Gigabit interface converter (GBIC) allows network managers to configure each gigabit port on a port-by-port basis for short-wave (SX), long-wave (LX), long-haul (LH), and copper physical interfaces (CX). LH GBICs extend the single-mode fiber distance from the standard 5 km to 10 km.

Protocol Structure

1000Base-X has a minimum frame size of 416bytes, and 1000Base-T has a minimum frame size of 520bytes. An extension field is used to fill the frames that are shorter than the minimum length.

7	1	6	6	2	46=< n =<1500	4bytes	Variable
Pre	SFD	DA	SA	Length Type	Data unit + pad	FCS	Ext

• Preamble (Pre) -- 7 bytes. The Pre is an alternating pattern of ones and zeros that tells receiving stations that a frame is coming, and that provides a means to synchronize the frame-reception portions of receiving physical layers with the incoming bit stream.
• Start-of-frame delimiter (SFD) -- 1 byte. The SOF is an alternating pattern of ones and zeros, ending with two consecutive 1-bits indicating that the next bit is the left-most bit in the left-most byte of the destination address.
• Destination address (DA -- 6 bytes. The DA field identifies which station(s) should receive the frame..
• Source addresses (SA) -- 6 bytes. The SA field identifies the sending station.
• Length/Type -- 2 bytes. This field indicates either the number of MAC-client data bytes that are contained in the data field of the frame, or the frame type ID if the frame is assembled using an optional format.
• Data -- Is a sequence of n bytes (46=< n =<1500) of any value. The total frame minimum is 64bytes.
• Frame check sequence (FCS) -- 4 bytes. This sequence contains a 32-bit cyclic redundancy check (CRC) value, which is created by the sending MAC and is recalculated by the receiving MAC to check for damaged frames.
• Ext -- Extension, which is a non-data variable extension field for frames that are shorter than the minimum length.

Packet Bursting Mode:

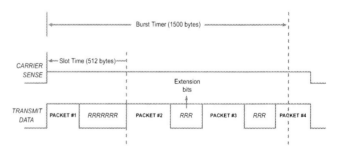

Figure 2-23: Packet Bursting Mode in Gigabit Ethernet

Related Protocols

IEEE 802.3, 802.3u, 802.3z, 802.3ab, 802.2, 802.1, 802.3ae, 802.1D, 802.1G, 802.1Q, 802.1p, 802.1w

Sponsor Source

Gigabit Ethernet standards are defined by IEEE (http://www.

ieee.org) 802.3z (1000BaseX) and 802.3ab(1000BaseT).

Reference

http://www.cisco.com/univercd/cc/td/doc/cisintwk/ito_doc/ethernet.htm
Ethernet Technologies
http://www.cis.ohio-state.edu/~jain/cis788-97/ftp/gigabit_ethernet/index.htm
Gigabit Ethernet
http://www.cis.ohio-state.edu/~jain/refs/gbe_refs.htm
Links and reference regarding Ethernet

10-Gigabit Ethernet: IEEE 802.3ae and 802.3an

Protocol Description

10-Gigabit Ethernet, standardized in IEEE 802.3ae and 802.3an, offers data speeds up to 10 billion bits per second. Built on the Ethernet technology used in most of today's local area networks (LANs), it offers similar benefits to those of the preceding Ethernet standard. 10-Gigabit Ethernet is used to interconnect local area networks (LANs), wide area networks (WANs), and metropolitan area networks (MANs). 10-Gigabit Ethernet uses the familiar IEEE 802.3 Ethernet media access control (MAC) protocol and its frame format and size. However, it supports full-duplex, but not half-duplex, mode for both optical fiber (802.3ae) and unshielded twisted pair cables (802.3an). The 10-Gigabit Ethernet architecture is displayed as follows:

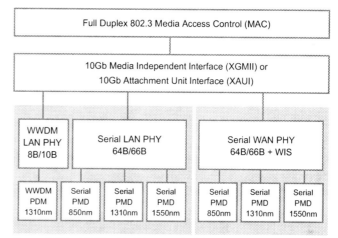

Figure 2-24: 10 Gigabit Ethernet Architecture

The 10-Gigabit specifications, contained in the IEEE 802.3ae and 802.3an, provide support to extend the 802.3 protocol and MAC specification to an operating speed of 10 Gb/s. In addition to the data rate of 10 Gb/s, 10-Gigabit Ethernet is able to accommodate slower date rates, such as 9.584640 Gb/s (OC-192), through its "WAN interface sublayer" (WIS), which allows 10 Gigabit Ethernet equipment to be compatible with the Synchronous Optical Network (SONET) STS-192c transmission format.

The 10GBASE-SR and 10GBASE-SW media types are designed for use over short wavelength (850 nm) multimode fiber (MMF), which covers a fiber distance from 2 meters to 300 meters.. The 10GBASE-SR media type is designed for use over dark fiber, meaning a fiber optic cable that is not in use and that is not connected to any other equipment. The 10GBASE-SW media type is designed to connect to SONET equipment, which is typically used to provide long distance data communications.

The 10GBASE-LR and 10GBASE-LW media types are designed for use over long wavelength (1310 nm) single-mode fiber (SMF), which covers a fiber distance from 2 meters to 10 kilometers (32,808 feet). The 10GBASE-LR media type is designed for use over dark fiber, while the 10GBASE-LW media type is designed to connect to SONET equipment.

The 10GBASE-ER and 10GBASE-EW media types are designed for use over extra long wavelength (1550 nm) single-mode fiber (SMF), which covers a fiber distance from 2 meters up to 40 kilometers (131,233 feet). The 10GBASE-ER media type is designed for use over dark fiber, while the 10GBASE-EW media type is designed to connect to SONET equipment. The 10GBASE-LX4 media type uses wave division multiplexing technology to send signals over four wavelengths of light carried over a single pair of fiber optic cables. The 10GBASE-LX4 system is designed to operate at 1310 nm over multimode or single-mode dark fiber. The design goal for this media system is from 2 meters up to 300 meters over multimode fiber or from 2 meters up to 10 kilometers over single-mode fiber.

Finally, there is the 10Gbase-T, a standard proposed by the IEEE 802.3an committee to provide 10 Gigabit/second connections over conventional unshielded twisted pair cables (Category 5e or Category 6 or Category 7 cables). 10GBASE-T allows the conventional RJ-45 used for ethernet LANs. 10GBASE-T can support signal transmision at the full 100m distance specified for LAN wiring.

Protocol Structure

10 gigabit Ethernet has a minimum frame of 64 bytes and maximum up to 1518bytes, as for the Ethernet 802.3.

7	1	6	6	2	46=< n =<1500	4bytes
Pre	SFD	DA	SA	Length Type	Data unit + pad	FCS

• Preamble (Pre) -- 7 bytes. The Pre is an alternating pattern of ones and zeros that tells receiving stations that a frame is coming, and that provides a means to synchronize the frame-reception portions of receiving physical layers with the incoming bit stream.
• Start-of-frame delimiter (SFD) -- 1 byte. The SFD is an alternating pattern of ones and zeros, ending with two consecutive 1-bits indicating that the next bit is the left-most bit in the left-most byte of the destination address.
• Destination address (DA) -- 6 bytes. The DA field identifies which station(s) should receive the frame.
• Source address (SA) -- 6 bytes. The SA field identifies the sending station.
• Length/Type -- 2 bytes. This field indicates either the number of MAC-client data bytes that are contained in the data field of the frame, or the frame type ID if the frame is assembled using an optional format.
• Data -- Is a sequence of n bytes (46=< n =<1500) of any value. The total frame minimum is 64bytes.
• Frame check sequence (FCS) -- 4 bytes. This sequence contains a 32-bit cyclic redundancy check (CRC) value, which is created by the sending MAC and is recalculated by the receiving MAC to check for damaged frames.

Related Protocols

IEEE 802.3, 802.3u, 802.3z, 802.3ab, 802.2, 802.1, 802.3ae, 802.1D, 802.1G, 802.1Q, 802.1p, 802.1w

Sponsor Source

10-Gigabit Ethernet standard is defined by IEEE (http://www.ieee.org) 802.3ae and 802.3an.

Reference

http://www.10gea.org/10GEA%20White%20Paper_0502.pdf
10 Gigabit Ethernet Technology White Paper
http://www.intel.com/network/connectivity/resources/doc_library/white_papers/pro10gbe_lr_sa_wp.pdf
10 Gigabit Ethernet technology Overview
http://www.ieee802.org/3/an/
IEEE 802.3an Task Force website.

VLAN: Virtual Local Area Network and the IEEE 802.1Q

Protocol Description

Virtual LAN (VLAN) refers to a group of logically networked devices on one or more local area networks (LANs) that are configured so that they can communicate as if they were attached to the same LAN, when in fact they are located on a number of different LAN segments. Because VLANs are based on logical, instead of physical, connections, they are very flexible for user/host management, bandwidth allocation and resource optimization.

There are the following types of Virtual LANs:

1. Port-Based VLAN: Each physical switch port is configured with an access list specifying membership in a set of VLANs.
2. MAC-based VLAN: A switch is configured with an access list mapping individual MAC addresses to VLAN membership.
3. Protocol-based VLAN: A switch is configured with a list of mapping layer 3 protocol types to VLAN membership – thereby filtering IP traffic from nearby end-stations using a particular protocol such as IPX.
4. ATM VLAN – uses LAN Emulation (LANE) protocol to map Ethernet packets into ATM cells and deliver them to their destination by converting an Ethernet MAC address into an ATM address.

The IEEE 802.1Q specification establishes a standard method for tagging Ethernet frames with VLAN membership information. The IEEE 802.1Q standard defines the operation of VLAN Bridges that permit the definition, operation and administration of Virtual LAN topologies within a Bridged LAN infrastructure. The 802.1Q standard is intended to address the problem of how to break large networks into smaller parts so broadcast and multicast traffic will not grab more bandwidth than necessary. The standard also helps provide a higher level of security between segments of internal networks.

The key for the IEEE 802.1Q to perform the above functions is in its tags. 802.1Q-compliant switch ports can be configured to transmit tagged or untagged frames. A tag field containing VLAN (and/or 802.1p priority) information can be inserted into an Ethernet frame. If a port has an 802.1Q-compliant device attached (such as another switch), these tagged frames can carry VLAN membership information between switches, thus letting a VLAN span multiple switches. However, it is important to ensure ports with non-802.1Q-compliant devices attached are configured to transmit untagged frames. Many NICs for PCs and printers are not 802.1Q-compliant. If they receive a tagged frame, they will not understand the VLAN tag and will drop the frame. Also, the maximum legal Ethernet frame size for tagged frames was increased in 802.1Q (and its companion, 802.3ac) from 1,518 to 1,522 bytes. This could cause network interface cards and older switches to drop tagged frames as "oversized."

Protocol Structure

IEEE 802.1Q Tagged Frame for Ethernet:

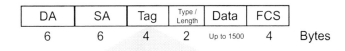

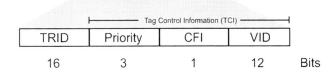

Figure 2-25: IEEE 802.1Q Tagged Frame for Ethernet

• TPID -- defined value of 8100 in hex. When a frame has the EtherType equal to 8100, this frame carries the tag IEEE 802.1Q/802.1P.
• TCI -- Tag Control Information field including user priority, Canonical format indicator and VLAN ID.
• Priority -- Defines user priority, giving eight priority levels. IEEE 802.1P defines the operation for these 3 user priority bits.
• CFI -- Canonical Format Indicator is always set to zero for Ethernet switches. CFI is used for compatibility reasons between an Ethernet type network and a Token Ring type network. If a frame received at an Ethernet port has a CFI set to 1, then that frame should not be forwarded, as it is to an untagged port.
• VID -- VLAN ID is the identification of the VLAN, which is basically used by the standard 802.1Q. It has 12 bits and allows the identification of 4096 (2^12) VLANs. Of the 4096 possible VIDs, a VID of 0 is used to identify priority frames and value 4095 (FFF) is reserved, so the maximum possible VLAN configurations are 4,094.

Related Protocols

IEEE 802.3, 802.2, 802.1, 802.1D, 802.1G, 802.1Q, 802.1p

Sponsor Source

VLAN standard is defined by IEEE (http://www.ieee.org) 802.1Q.

Reference

http://standards.ieee.org/getieee802/download/802.1Q-2003.pdf
IEEE 802.1Q-2003 Standard

IEEE 802.1P: LAN Layer 2 QoS/CoS Protocol for Traffic Prioritization

Protocol Description

IEEE 802.1p specification enables Layer 2 switches to prioritize traffic and perform dynamic multicast filtering. The prioritization specification works at the media access control (MAC) framing layer (OSI model layer 2). The 802.1p standard also offers provisions to filter multicast traffic to ensure it does not proliferate over layer 2-switched networks.

The 802.1p header includes a three-bit field for prioritization, which allows packets to be grouped into various traffic classes. The IEEE has made broad recommendations concerning how network managers can implement these traffic classes, but it stops short of mandating the use of its recommended traffic class definitions. It can also be defined as best-effort QoS (Quality of Service) or CoS (Class of Service) at Layer 2 and is implemented in network adapters and switches without involving any reservation setup. 802.1P traffic is simply classified and sent to the destination; no bandwidth reservations are established.

The IEEE 802.1p is an extension of the IEEE 802.1Q (VLANs tagging) standard and the two standards work in tandem. The 802.1Q standard specifies a tag that appends to an Ethernet MAC frame. The VLAN tag has two parts: the VLAN ID (12-bit) and Prioritization (3-bit). The prioritization field was not defined and used in the 802.1Q VLAN standard. The 802.1P defines this prioritization field.

IEEE 802.1p establishes eight levels of priority. Although network managers must determine actual mappings, IEEE has made broad recommendations. The highest priority is seven, which might go to network-critical traffic such as Routing Information Protocol (RIP) and Open Shortest Path First (OSPF) table updates. Values five and six might be for delay-sensitive applications such as interactive video and voice. Data classes four through one range from controlled-load applications such as streaming multimedia and business-critical traffic - SAP data, for instance - down to "loss eligible" traffic. The zero value is used as a best-effort default, invoked automatically when no other value has been set.

Protocol Structure

IEEE 802.1Q Tagged Frame for Ethernet – modified format from Ethernet (802.3) frame:

7	1	6	6	2	2	2	42-1496	4bytes
Pre-amble	SFD	DA	SA	TPID	TCI	Length Type	Data	CRC

• Preamble (Pre) -- 7 bytes. The Pre is an alternating pattern of ones and zeros that tells receiving stations that a frame is coming, and that provides a means to synchronize the frame-reception portions of receiving physical layers with the incoming bit stream.
• Start-of-frame delimiter (SFD) -- 1 byte. The SFD is an alternating pattern of ones and zeros, ending with two consecutive 1-bits indicating that the next bit is the left-most bit in the left-most byte of the destination address.
• Destination address (DA) -- 6 bytes. The DA field identifies which station(s) should receive the frame.
• Source address (SA) -- 6 bytes. The SA field identifies the sending station.
• TPID -- defined value of 8100 in hex. When a frame has the EtherType equal to 8100, this frame carries the tag IEEE 802.1Q / 802.1P.
• TCI -- Tag Control Information field including user priority, Canonical format indicator and VLAN ID.

3	1	12bits
User Priority	CFI	Bits of VLAN ID (VIDI) to identify possible VLANs

• User Priority -- Defines user priority, giving eight priority levels. IEEE 802.1P defines the operation for these 3 user priority bits.
• CFI -- Canonical Format Indicator is always set to zero for Ethernet switches. CFI is used for compatibility reasons between an Ethernet type network and a Token Ring type network. If a frame received at an Ethernet port has a CFI set to 1, then that frame should not be forwarded as it is to an untagged port.
• VID -- VLAN ID is the identification of the VLAN, which is basically used by the standard 802.1Q. It has 12 bits and allows the identification of 4096 (2^12) VLANs. Of the 4096 possible VIDs, a VID of 0 is used to identify priority frames and value 4095 (FFF) is reserved, so the maximum possible VLAN configurations are 4,094.
• Length/Type -- 2 bytes. This field indicates either the number of MAC-client data bytes that are contained in the data field of the frame, or the frame type ID if the frame is assembled using an optional format.
• Data -- Is a sequence of n bytes (42=< n =<1496) of any value. The total frame minimum is 64bytes.
• Frame check sequence (FCS) -- 4 bytes. This sequence contains a 32-bit cyclic redundancy check (CRC) value, which is created by the sending MAC and is recalculated by the receiving MAC to check for damaged frames.

Related Protocols

IEEE 802.2, 802.3, 802.1D, 802.1Q

Sponsor Source

802.1P is an IEEE (http://www.ieee.org) protocol.

Reference

http://standards.ieee.org/getieee802/download/802.1Q-2003.pdf
IEEE 802.1Q-2003 Standard

GARP: Generic Attribute Registration Protocol

Protocol Description

The Generic Attribute Registration Protocol (GARP) provides a generic framework whereby devices in a bridged LAN, e.g. end stations and switches, can register and de-register attribute values, such as VLAN Identifiers, with each other. In doing so, the attributes are propagated to devices in the bridged LAN, and these devices form a "reachability" tree that is a subset of an active topology. GARP defines the architecture, rules of operation, state machines and variables for the registration and de-registration of attribute values.

A GARP participation in a switch or an end station consists of a GARP application component, and a GARP Information Declaration (GID) component associated with each port or switch. The propagation of information between GARP participants for the same application in a bridge is carried out by the GARP Information Propagation (GIP) component. Protocol exchanges take place between GARP participants by means of LLC Type 1 services, using the group MAC address and PDU format defined for the GARP application concerned.

GARP is part of the IEEE 802.1p extension to the 802.1d (spanning tree) specification. It includes:

• GARP Information Declaration (GID): The part of GARP that generates data.
• GARP Information Propagation (GIP): The part of GARP that distributes data.
• GARP Multicast Registration Protocol (GMRP): Provides a mechanism that allows participants to dynamically register and de-register information with the Media Access Control (MAC) bridges attached to the same local-area network (LAN) segment.

Protocol Structure

GARP PDU structure

2 bytes	
Protocol ID	Message

GARP message structure

1 byte				
Attribute type	Attribute 1	...	Attribute n	End mark

GARP attribute structure

1 byte	1 byte	n bytes
Attribute length	Attribute event	Attribute value

• Protocol ID -- Identifies the GARP protocol.
• Identifier -- Decimal value which aids in matching requests and replies.
• Attribute type -- Defines the attribute. Values may be: 1 Group attribute; 2 Service Requirement attribute.
• Attribute length -- Length of the Attribute.
• Attribute event -- The values of the attribute event can be:

0 Leave_all
1 Join_Empty operator
2 Join_In operator
3 Leave_Empty operator
4 Leave_In operator
5 Empty operator

• Attribute value -- This is encoded in accordance with the specification for the Attribute Type. The number of bytes depends on the specific application.
• End mark -- Coded as 0.

Related Protocols

IEEE 802.1D, 802.1G, 802.1Q, 802.3ac, 802.1P, VTP, GVRP, GMRP

Sponsor Source

GARP standard is defined by IEEE (http://www.ieee.org) 802.1P.

Reference

http://www.alliedtelesyn.co.nz/documentation/at8700/261/pdf/garp.pdf
Overview of Generic Attribute Registration Protocol

GMRP: GARP Multicast Registration Protocol

Protocol Description

GARP Multicast Registration Protocol (GMRP) is a Generic Attribute Registration Protocol (GARP) application that provides a constrained multicast flooding facility similar to IGMP snooping. GMRP and GARP are industry-standard protocols defined by the IEEE 802.1P.

GMRP provides a mechanism that allows bridges and end stations to dynamically register group membership information with the MAC bridges attached to the same LAN segment and for that information to be disseminated across all bridges in a Bridged LAN that supports extended filtering services. The operation of GMRP relies upon the services provided by the GARP.

GMRP software components run on both the switch and the host. On the host, GMRP is typically used with IGMP: The host GMRP software spawns Layer 2 GMRP versions of the host's Layer 3 IGMP control packets. The switch receives both the Layer 2 GMRP and the Layer 3 IGMP traffic from the host. The switch uses the received GMRP traffic to constrain multicasts at Layer 2 in the host's VLAN. In all cases, you can use IGMP snooping to constrain multicasts at Layer 2 without the need to install or configure software on hosts.

When a host wants to join an IP multicast group, it sends an IGMP join message, which spawns a GMRP join message. Upon receipt of the GMRP join message, the switch adds the port through which the join message was received to the appropriate multicast group. The switch propagates the GMRP join message to all other hosts in the VLAN, one of which is typically the multicast source. When the source is multicasting to the group, the switch forwards the multicast only to the ports from which it has received join messages for the group. The switch sends periodic GMRP queries. If a host wants to remain in a multicast group, it responds to the query. In this case, the switch does nothing. If a host does not want to remain in the multicast group, it can either send a leave message or not respond to the periodic queries from the switch. If the switch receives a leave message or receives no response from the host for the duration of the leaveall timer, it removes the host from the multicast group.

Protocol Structure

GMRP messages have the same structure as GARP with the attribute type specific to GMRP:

This can be as follows: 1. Group Attribute Type; 2. Service Requirement Attribute Type.

GARP PDU Format:

2 bytes	
Protocol ID	Message

GARP message structure

1 byte				
Attribute type	Attribute 1	...	Attribute n	End mark

GARP attribute structure

1 byte	1 byte	1 byte
Attribute length	Attribute event	Attribute value

• Protocol ID -- Identifies the GARP protocol.
• Identifier -- Decimal value which aids in matching requests and replies.
• Attribute type -- Defines the attribute. Values may be: 1 Group attribute; 2 Service Requirement attribute.
• Attribute length -- Length of the Attribute.
• Attribute event -- The values of the attribute event can be:
> 0 Leave_all
> 1 Join_Empty operator
> 2 Join_In operator
> 3 Leave_Empty operator
> 4 Leave_In operator
> 5 Empty operator

• Attribute value -- This is encoded in accordance with the specification for the Attribute Type.
• End mark -- Coded as 0.

Related Protocols

IEEE 802.1D, 802.1G, 802.1Q, 802.1P, 802.1ac, VTP, GVRP, GARP

Sponsor Source

GMRP standard is defined by IEEE (http://www.ieee.org) 802.1P.

Reference

http://www.alliedtelesyn.co.nz/documentation/at8700/261/pdf/garp.pdf
Overview of Generic Attribute Registration Protocol

GVRP: GARP VLAN Registration Protocol

Protocol Description

The GARP (Generic Attribute Registration Protocol) VLAN Registration Protocol (GVRP) defines a GARP application that provides 802.1Q-compliant VLAN pruning and dynamic VLAN creation on 802.1Q trunk ports. GVRP is an application, defined in the IEEE 802.1P standard, which allows for the control of 802.1Q VLANs.

With GVRP, the switch can exchange VLAN configuration information with other GVRP switches, prune unnecessary broadcast and unknown unicast traffic, and dynamically create and manage VLANs on switches connected through 802.1Q trunk ports.

GVRP makes use of GID and GIP, which provide the common state machine descriptions and the common information propagation mechanisms defined for use in GARP-based applications. GVRP runs only on 802.1Q trunk links. GVRP prunes trunk links so that only active VLANs will be sent across trunk connections. GVRP expects to hear join messages from the switches before it will add a VLAN to the trunk. GVRP updates and hold timers can be altered. GVRP ports run in various modes to control how they will prune VLANs. GVRP can be configured to dynamically add and manage VLANS to the VLAN database for trunking purposes.

In other words, GVRP allows the propagation of VLAN information from device to device. With GVRP, a single switch is manually configured with all the desired VLANs for the network, and all other switches on the network learn those VLANs dynamically. An endnode can be plugged into any switch and be connected to that endnode's desired VLAN. For endnodes to make use of GVRP, they need GVRP-aware Network Interface Cards (NICs). The GVRP-aware NIC is configured with the desired VLAN or VLANs, then connected to a GVRP-enabled switch. The NIC communicates with the switch, and VLAN connectivity is established between the NIC and switch.

Protocol Structure

GVRP messages have the same structure as GARP with the attribute type pecific to GVRP: 1 VID Group Attribute Type.

GARP PDU Format:

2 bytes	
Protocol ID	Message

GARP message structure:

1 byte				
Attribute type	Attribute 1	...	Attribute n	End mark

GARP attribute structure

1 byte	1 byte	2 bytes
Attribute length	Attribute event	Attribute value

• Protocol ID -- Identifies the GARP protocol.
• Identifier -- Decimal value which aids in matching requests and replies.
• Attribute type -- Defines the attribute. Values may be: 1 Group attribute; 2 Service Requirement attribute.
• Attribute length -- Length of the Attribute.
• Attribute event -- The values of the attribute event can be:
    0 Leave_all
    1 Join_Empty operator
    2 Join_In operator
    3 Leave_Empty operator
    4 Leave_In operator
    5 Empty operator
• Attribute value -- This is encoded in accordance with the specification for the Attribute Type. In case of GVRP, it has two bytes with the VLAN ID value.
• End mark -- Coded as 0.

Related Protocols

IEEE 802.1D, 802.1Q, 802.1P, GMRP, GARP

Sponsor Source

GVRP standard is defined by IEEE (http://www.ieee.org) 802.1Q.

Reference

http://standards.ieee.org/getieee802/download/802.1Q-2003.pdf
IEEE 802.1Q-2003 Standard

WLAN: Wireless LAN by IEEE 802.11 protocols

Protocol Description

The Wireless Local Area Network (WLAN) technology is defined by the IEEE 802.11 family of specifications. There are currently five specifications in the family: 802.11, 802.11a, 802.11b 802.11g and 802.11n. All use the Ethernet protocol and CSMA/CA (carrier sense multiple access with collision avoidance; instead of CSMA/CD) for path sharing.

• 802.11 -- applies to wireless LANs and provides 1 or 2 Mbps transmission in the 2.4 GHz band using either frequency hopping spread spectrum (FHSS) or direct sequence spread spectrum (DSSS).
• 802.11a -- an extension to 802.11 that applies to wireless LANs and provides up to 54 Mbps in the 5GHz band. 802.11a uses an orthogonal frequency division multiplexing (OFDM) encoding scheme rather than FHSS or DSSS. The 802.11a specification applies to wireless ATM systems and is used in access hubs.
• 802.11b (also referred to as 802.11 High Rate or Wi-Fi) -- an extension to 802.11 that applies to wireless LANS and provides 11 Mbps transmission (with a fallback to 5.5, 2 and 1 Mbps) in the 2.4 GHz band. 802.11b uses only DSSS. 802.11b is a modification of the original 802.11 standard, allowing wireless functionality comparable to Ethernet.
• 802.11g -- offers wireless transmission over relatively short distances at 20 – 54 Mbps in the 2.4 GHz band. 802.11g also uses the OFDM encoding scheme.
• 802.11n - builds upon previous 802.11 standards by adding MIMO (multiple-input multiple-output). 802.11n offers high throughput wireless transmission at 100Mbps – 200 Mbps.

The modulation used in 802.11 has historically been phase-shift keying (PSK). The modulation method selected for 802.11b is known as complementary code keying (CCK), which allows higher data speeds and is less susceptible to multipath-propagation interference. 802.11a uses a modulation scheme known as orthogonal frequency-division multiplexing (OFDM) that makes possible data speeds as high as 54 Mbps, but most commonly, communications takes place at 6 Mbps, 12 Mbps, or 24 Mbps. The 802.11 stack structure is as figure 2-26.

For short range and low power wireless (less than 10 meters) communications among personal devices such as PDA, Bluetooth and subsequent IEEE standards (802.15) are taking effects. For long range wireless communications in the metropolitan areas, WiMax as defined in the IEEE 802.16 is the standard.

Protocol Structure

801.11 protocol family MAC frame structure:

2	2	6	6	6	2	6	0-2312	4bytes
Frame Control	Duration	Address 1	Address 2	Address 3	Seq	Address 4	Data	Check sum

• Frame Control Structure:

2 bits	2 bits	4 bits	1 bit	1 bit	1 bit	1 bit	1 bit	1 bit	1 bit	1 bit
Version	Type	Subtype	To DS	From DS	MF	Retry	Pwr	More	W	O

• Protocol Version -- indicates the version of IEEE 802.11 standard.
• Type -- Frame type: Management, Control and Data.
• Subtype -- Frame subtype: Authentication frame, Deauthentication frame; Association request frame; Association response frame; Reassociation request frame; Reassociation response frame; Disassociation frame; Beacon frame; Probe frame; Probe request frame or Probe response frame.
• To DS -- is set to 1 when the frame is sent to Distribution System (DS)
• From DS -- is set to 1 when the frame is received from the Distribution System (DS)
• MF -- More Fragment is set to 1 when there are more fragments belonging to the same frame following the current fragment ment

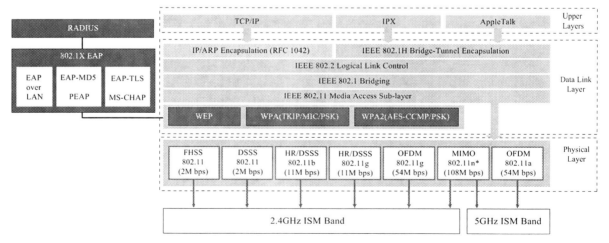

IEEE 802.11 Protocol Stack

Figure 2-26: IEEE 802.11 WLAN Protocol Stack

• Retry indicates that this fragment is a retransmission of a previously transmitted fragment. (For receiver to recognize duplicate transmissions of frames)
• Pwr - Power Management indicates the power management mode that the station will be in after the transmission of the frame.
• More -- More Data indicates that there are more frames buffered to this station.
• W -- WEP indicates that the frame body is encrypted according to the WEP (wired equivalent privacy) algorithm.
• O -- Order indicates that the frame is being sent using the Stritly-Ordered service class.
• Duration/ID (ID)
    • Station ID is used for Power-Save poll message frame type.
    • The duration value is used for the Network Allocation Vector (NAV) calculation.
• Address fields (1-4) -- contain up to 4 addresses (source, destination, transmitter and receiver addresses) depending on the frame control field (the ToDS and FromDS bits).
• Sequence Control -- consists of fragment number and sequence number. It is used to represent the order of different fragments belonging to the same frame and to recognize packet duplications.
• Data -- is information that is transmitted or received.
• CRC -- contains a 32-bit Cyclic Redundancy Check (CRC).

Related Protocols

IEEE 802.2, 802.3, 802.11, 802.11a, 802.11b, 802.11g, 802.11n, Bluetooth 802.15, WiMax 802.16

Sponsor Source

WLAN protocols are defined by IEEE (http://www.ieee.org) 802.11 specifications.

Reference

http://standards.ieee.org/getieee802/download/802.11-1999.
pdf
Wireless LAN Media Access Control (MAC) and Physical Control Specifications
http://standards.ieee.org/getieee802/download/802.11a-1999.
pdf
Wireless LAN MAC: High-speed physical layer in the 5 GHz Band.
http://standards.ieee.org/getieee802/download/802.11b-
1999_Cor1-2001.pdf
Wireless LAN MAC: Higher-speed physical layer extension in the 2.4 GHz band.
http://standards.ieee.org/getieee802/download/802.11g-2003.
pdf
Wireless LAN specifications - Amendment 4: Further Higher-Speed Physical Layer Extension in the 2.4 GHz Band

IEEE 802.11i: WLAN Security Standard

Protocol Description

The standard IEEE 802.11i is designed to provide secured communication of wireless LAN as defined by all the IEEE 802.11 specifications. IEEE 802.11i enhances the WEP (Wireline Equivalent Privacy), a technology used for many years for the WLAN security, in the areas of encryption, authentication and key management. IEEE 802.11i, also called WPA 2, is based on the Wi-Fi Protected Access (WPA), which was a quick fix of the WEB weaknesses.

The IEEE 802.11i has the following key components:

1. Temporal Key Integrity Protocol (TKIP): a method for periodically ratating encryption key to improve the security of products that implemented WEP. TKIP uses a message integrity code called Michael, which enables devices to authenticate that the packets are coming from the claimed source. Also TKIP uses a mixing function to defeat weak-key attacks, which enabled attackers to decrypt traffic.
2. Counter-Mode/CBC-MAC Protocol (CCMP): a data-confidentiality protocol that handles packet authentication as well as encryption. For confidentiality, CCMP uses AES in counter mode. For authentication and integrity, CCMP uses Cipher Block Chaining Message Authentication Code (CBC-MAC). In IEEE 802.11i, CCMP uses a 128-bit key. CCMP protects some fields that aren't encrypted. The additional parts of the IEEE 802.11 frame that get protected are known as additional authentication data (AAD). AAD includes the packets source and destination and protects against attackers replaying packets to different destinations.
3. IEEE 802.1x: offers an effective framework for authenticating and controlling user traffic to a protected network, as well as dynamically varying encryption keys. 802.1X ties a protocol called EAP (Extensible Authentication Protocol) to both the wired and wireless LAN media and supports multiple authentication methods.
4. EAP encapsulation over LANs (EAPOL)– it is the key protocol in IEEE 802.1x for key exchange. Two main EAPOL-key exchanges are defined in IEEE 802.11i. The first is referred to as the 4-way handshake and the second is the group key handshake.

Because IEEE 802.11i has more than one data-confidentiality protocol, IEEE 802.11i provides an algorithm for the IEEE 802.11i client card and access point to negotiate which protocol to use during specific traffic circumstances and to discover any unknown security parameters.

Protocol Structure

IEEE 802.11i Components:

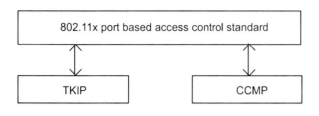

Figure 2-27: IEEE 802.11i Components

CCMP MPDU Format

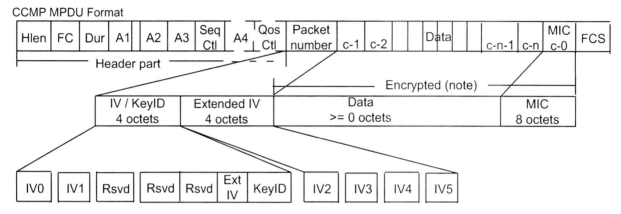

Figure 2-28: CCMP MPDU Format

CCMP CBC-MAC IV

CCMP CTR

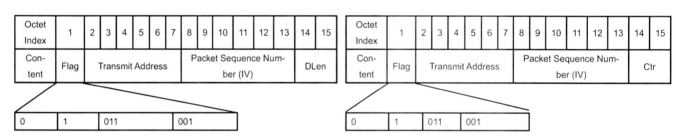

Reserved MIC Hdr MIC size=64 bits Dlen=16 octets

Figure 2-29: CCMP CBC-MAC IV

Reserved No Hdr No MIC Ctr size=16 bits

Figure 2-30: CCMP CTR

TKIP MPDU Format

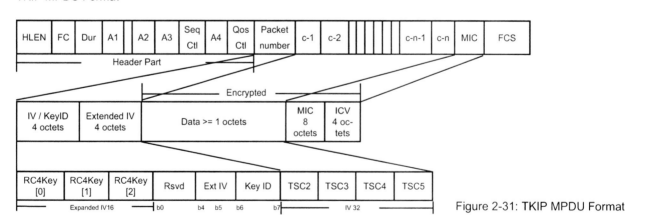

Figure 2-31: TKIP MPDU Format

Related Protocols

IEEE 802.11a, IEEE802.11b, IEEE 802.11g, IEEE 802.11n, WEP, WPA, 802.1x, EAP, EAPoL, TKIP

Sponsor Source

IEEE 802.11i is defined by IEEE (http://www.ieee.org) 802.11 working group.

Reference

http://standards.ieee.org/getieee802/download/802.11i-2004.pdf

Wireless LAN specifications - Amendment 6: Medium Access Control (MAC) Security Enhancements

IEEE 802.1X: EAP over LAN (EAPOL) for LAN/WLAN Authentication and Key Management

Protocol Description

802.1x is an IEEE standard for port-based network access control, particularly useful for securing 802.11 wireless local area networks (WLANs). The IEEE 802.1X offers an effective framework for authenticating and controlling user traffic to a protected network, as well as dynamically varying encryption keys. 802.1X ties a protocol called EAP (Extensible Authentication Protocol) to both the wired and wireless LAN media and supports multiple authentication methods, such as token cards, Kerberos, one-time passwords, certificates, and public key authentication.

In the 802.1x architecture, there are three key components: 1) Supplicant: the user or client that wants to be authenticated; 2) the authentication server, typically a RADIUS server; and 3) the authenticator: the device in between, such as a wireless access point, which can be simple and dumb.

The key protocol in 802.1x is called EAP encapsulation over LANs (EAPOL). It is currently defined for Ethernet-like LANs including 802.11 wireless, as well as token ring LANs (including FDDI). The operation process in 802.1X is as follows:

1. The supplicant (such as a client wireless card) sends an "EAP-Response/Identity" packet to the authenticator (such as an 802.11 access point), which is then passed on to the authentication server (RADIUS server which is located at the wired side of the access point).
2. The authentication server sends back a challenge to the authenticator. The authenticator unpacks this from IP and re-packages it into EAPOL and sends it to the supplicant.
3. The supplicant responds to the challenge via the authenticator and passes the response onto the authentication server. The authentication server uses a specific authentication algorithm to verify the client's identity. This could be through the use of digital certificates or other EAP authentication type.
4. If the supplicant provides proper identity, the authentication server responds with a success message, which is then passed onto the supplicant. The authenticator now opens port for the supplicant to access the LAN based on attributes that came back from the authentication server.

The 802.1X (EAPOL) protocol provides effective authentication regardless of whether 802.11 WEP keys are implemented or there is no encryption at all. If configured to implement dynamic key exchange, the 802.1X authentication server can return session keys to the access point along with the accept message. The access point uses the session keys to build, sign and encrypt an EAP key message that is sent to the client immediately after sending the success message. The client can then use contents of the key message to define applicable encryption keys.
802.1X (EAPOL) is a delivery mechanism and does not provide the actual authentication mechanisms. When utilizing 802.1X,

an EAP type, such as Transport Layer Security (EAP-TLS) or EAP Tunneled Transport Layer Security (EAP-TTLS), which defines how the authentication takes place, must be chosen. The specific EAP type resides on the authentication server and within the operating system or application software on the client devices. The access point acts as a "pass through" for 802.1X messages, which means that any EAP type can be specifie without an 802.1X-compliant access point needing to be upgraded.

Protocol Structure

EAPOL Frame Format for 802.3/Ethernet:

2 bytes	1 byte	1 byte	2 bytes	Variable
PAE Ethernet Type	Protocol version	Packet type	Packet Body length	Packet Body

• PAE Ethernet type -- PAE (Port Access Entity) Ethernet type contains the Ethernet Type value assigned for use by the PAE.
• Protocol version -- an unsigned binary number, the value of which is the version of the EAPOL protocol.
• Packet type -- an unsigned binary number, the value of which determines the type of the packet as follows: a) EAP-packet; b) EAPOL-Start; c) EAPOL-Logoff; d) EAPOL-Key; e) EAPOL-Encapsulated-ASF-Alert
• Packet body length -- an unsigned binary, the value of which defines the length in octets of the packet body field.
• Packet Body -- This field is presented if the packet type contains the value EAP-Packet, EAPOL-Key, or EAP-Encapsulated-ASF-Alert, otherwise, it is not presented.

EAPOL Frame Format for Token Ring /FDDI:

8 bytes	1 byte	1 byte	2 bytes	Variable
SNAP Ethernet Type	Protocol version	Packet type	Packet Body length	Packet Body

• SNAP Ethernet Type -- contains the SNAP-encoded Ethernet type encoded in the SNAP format as follows: 1-3 bytes carry the standard SNAP header; 4-6 bytes carry the SNAP PID; 7-8 bytes carry the PAE Ethernet Type value.

Related Protocols

Ethernet, EAP, EAPoL, RADIUS, Token Ring, IEEE802.11i, IEEE 802.11a, 802.11b, 802.11g, 802.11n

Sponsor Source

EAPOL (802.1X) is defined by IEEE (http://www.ieee.org).

Reference

http://standards.ieee.org/getieee802/download/802.1X-2001.pdf
Port based Network Access Control

WPAN: Wireless Personal Area Network Communication Protocols

Protocol Description

Wireless Personal Area Network (WPAN) is a small area network using wireless technologies as physical connections. The reach of a WPAN is typically within a few meters. Technologies enabling WPAN include Bluetooth, ZigBee, Ultra-wideband (UWB), IrDA, HomeRF, etc., in which the Bluetooth is the most widely used technology for the WPAN communication. Each technology is optimized for specific usage, applications, or domains. Although in some respects, certain technologies might be viewed as competing in the WPAN space, but they are often complementary to each other.

The IEEE 802.15 Working Group is the most notable organization to define the WPAN technologies. Firstly IEEE802.15 working group made the IEEE802.15.1 based on the Bluetooth technology for communication among devices such as telephones, computer and its accessories, as well as personal digital assistants, within a short range. In addition, IEEE proposed two additional categories of WPAN technologies in the 802.15 family: the low rate 802.15.4 (also known as ZigBee) and the high rate 802.15.3 (also known as Ultra-wideband or UWB). ZigBee provides data speeds of 20 Kbps or 250 Kbps, for home and building control type of low power and low cost solutions. UWB supports data speeds ranging from 20 Mbps to 1Gbps, for multi-media data transfer applications.

In the following table, the main characters of the WPAN technologies as specified in the IEEE 802.15 are compared:

Param-eters	Bluetooth (IEEE 802.15.1)	UWB (IEEE 802.15.3)	ZigBee (IEEE 802.15.4)
Applica-tions	Computer and accessory devices Computer to compute Computer with other digital devices	Multimedia content transfer, High-resolution radar, Ground-penetrating radar, Wireless sensor network, Radio locations systems	Home control Building automation Industrial automation Home security Medical monitoring
Frequency Band	2.4 – 2.48GHz	3.1-10.6GHz	868MHz 902-928MHz 2.4-2.48GHZ
Range	~10 meters	~10 meters	~100 meters
Maximum Data transfer rate	3 Mbps	1 Gbps	20 Kbps 40 Kbps 250 Kbps
Modulation	GFSK, 2PSK, DQSP, 8PSK	OPSK, BPSK	BPSK (868/928MHz) OPSK (2.4GHz)

WPAN, WLAN and WMAN technologies are complementary to each other and each play a unique role in today's wireless communications. The following table outlines the three technologies:

Param-eters	WMAN (IEEE802.16 WiMAX)	WLAN (IEEE802.11)	WPAN (IEEE802.15)
Frequency Band	2-66GHz	2.4 – 5.8GHz	868 – 10.6GHz
Range	~31 miles	~100 meters	~10meters (Bluetooth and UWB) ~100 meters (ZigBee)
Maximum data transfer rate	134 Mbps	55 Mbps	3Mbps (Bluetooth) 250 Kbps (ZigBee) 1Gbps (UWB)
Number of users	Thousands	Dozens	Dozens

Related Protocols

WLAN, WMAN, WiMAX, IEEE 802.11, IEEE 802.16, BlueTooth, ZigBee, UWB, IrDA, HomeRF, IEEE802.15, IEEE802.15.1, IEEE802.15.3, IEEE802.15.4

Sponsor Source

Bluetooth is defined in the IEEE 802.15.1. UWB is defined in the IEEE 802.15.3. ZigBee is defined in the IEEE 802.15.4.

Reference

http://standards.ieee.org/getieee802/802.15.html
IEEE 802.15 Specification Download Page

Bluetooth/IEEE 802.15.1 Protocol Stack

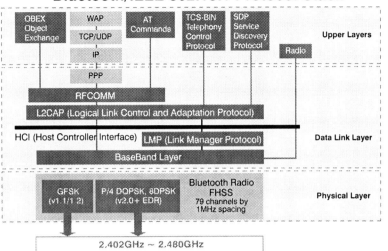

Figure 2-32: Bluetooth/IEEE802.15.1 Protocol Stack

ZigBee/IEEE 802.15.4 Protocol Stack

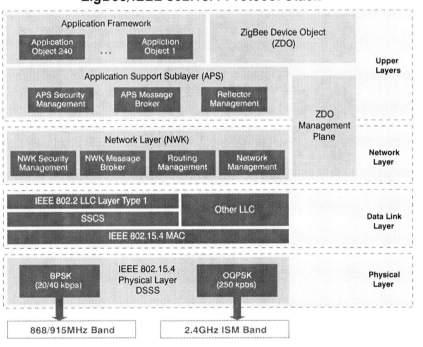

Figure 2-33: ZigBee/IEEE 802.15.4 Protocol Stack

UWB/IEEE 802.15.3 Protocol Stack

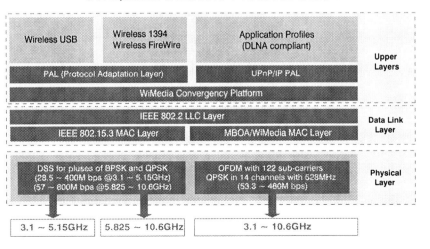

Figure 2-34: UWB/IEEE 802.15.3 Protocol Stack

IEEE 802.15.1 and the Bluetooth for WPAN Communications

Protocol Description

IEEE 802.15.1, a standard defined by IEEE based on the Bluetooth technology, is for wireless personal area network (WPAN) communications. IEEE 802.15.1 has characters such as short-range, low power, low cost, small networks and communication of devices within a Personal Operating Space less than 10 meters.

IEEE 802.15.1 was adapted from the Bluetooth specification and is fully compatible with Bluetooth 1.1. Bluetooth becomes widely used specification for wireless communications among portable digital devices including notebook computers, peripherals, cellular telephones, beepers, and consumer electronic devices. The specification also allows for connection to the Internet. 802.15.1/Bluetooth specify standards in the Physical layer and Data link layer of the OSI model with the following four sub-layers:

RF layer: The air interface is based on antenna power range starting from 0 dBm up to 20 dBm. Bluetooth operates in the 2.4 GHz band and the link range is anywhere from 10 centimeters to 10 meters.

Baseband layer: establishes the Bluetooth physical link between devices forming a piconet -- a network of devices connected in an ad hoc fashion using Bluetooth technology.

Link manager: sets up the link between Bluetooth devices. Other functions of the link manager include security, negotiation of Baseband packet sizes, power mode and duty cycle control of the Bluetooth device, and the connection states of a Bluetooth device in a piconet.

Logical Link Control and Adaptation Protocol (L2CAP): provides the upper layer protocols with connectionless and connection-oriented services.

The IEEE 802.15 Working Groups are making progress to improve the Bluetooth standards. They proposed two general categories of 802.15: the low rate 802.15.4 (TG4, also known as ZigBee) and the high rate 802.15.3 (TG3, also known as Ultra-wideband or UWB). The TG4 ZigBee version provides data speeds of 20 Kbps or 250 Kbps, low power and low cost solutions. The TG3 UWB version supports data speeds ranging from 20 Mbps to 1Gbps, for multi-media applications.

The following chart illustrates the relationship of IEEE802.15.1/ Bluetooth to OSI model.

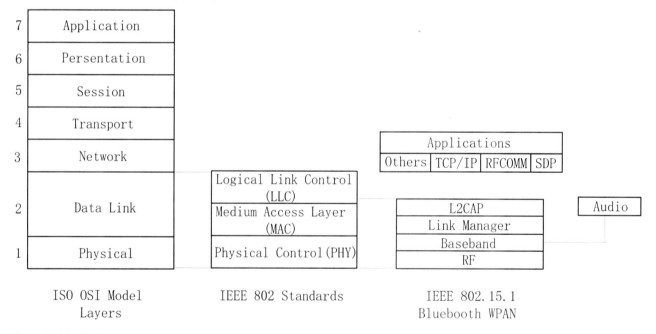

Figure 2-35: IEEE 802.15.1 (Bluetooth) Protocol Stack

Related Protocols

WPAN, WLAN, WMAN, WiMAX, IEEE 802.11, IEEE 802.16, Bluetooth, ZigBee, UWB, IEEE802.15, IEEE802.15.1, IEEE802.15.3, IEEE802.15.4

Sponsor Source

Bluetooth is defined in the IEEE 802.15.1.

Reference

http://standards.ieee.org/getieee802/802.15.html
IEEE 802.15 Specification Download Page

FDDI: Fiber Distributed Data Interface

Protocol Description

Fiber Distributed Data Interface (FDDI) is a set of ANSI protocols for sending digital data over fiber optic cable. FDDI networks are token-passing (similar to IEEE 802.5 Token Ring protocol) and dual-ring networks, and support data rates of up to 100 Mbps. FDDI networks are typically used as backbone technology because of the protocol supports a high bandwidth and a great distance. A related copper specification similar to FDDI protocols, called Copper Distributed Data Interface (CDDI), has also been defined to provide 100-Mbps service over twisted-pair copper.

An extension to FDDI, called FDDI-2, supports the transmission of voice and video information as well as data. Another variation of FDDI, called FDDI Full Duplex Technology (FFDT) uses the same network infrastructure but can potentially support data rates up to 200 Mbps.

FDDI uses dual-ring architecture with traffic on each ring flowing in opposite directions (called counter-rotating). The dual rings consist of a primary and a secondary ring. During normal operation, the primary ring is used for data transmission, and the secondary ring remains idle. As will be discussed in detail later in this chapter, the primary purpose of the dual rings is to provide superior reliability and robustness.

FDDI specifies the physical and media access portions of the OSI reference model. FDDI is not actually a single specification but is a collection of four separate specifications, each with a specific function. Combined, these specifications have the capability to provide high-speed connectivity between upper-layer protocols such as TCP/IP and IPX, and media such as fiber-optic cabling.

FDDI's four specifications are the Media Access Control (MAC), Physical Layer Protocol (PHY), Physical-Medium Dependent (PMD), and Station Management (SMT) specifications. The MAC specification defines how the medium is accessed, including frame format, token handling, addressing, algorithms for calculating cyclic redundancy check (CRC) value, and error-recovery mechanisms. The PHY specification defines data encoding/decoding procedures, clocking requirements, and framing, among other functions. The PMD specification defines the characteristics of the transmission medium, including fiber-optic links, power levels, bit-error rates, optical components, and connectors. The SMT specification defines FDDI station configuration, ring configuration, and ring control features, including station insertion and removal, initialization, fault isolation and recovery, scheduling, and statistics collection.

Protocol Structure

2	6	6	0-30	Variable	4 bytes

Frame control	Destination address	Source address	Route information	Information	FCS

- Frame control -- The frame control structure is as follows:

C	L	F	F	Z	Z	Z	Z

      C -- Class bit: 0 Asynchronous frame; 1 Synchronous frame.

      L -- Address length bit: 0 16 bits (never); 1 48 bits (always).

      FF -- Format bits.

      ZZZZ-- ontrol bits.

- Destination address -- The address structure is as follows:

I/G	U/L	Address bits

- Source address -- The address structure is as follows:

I/G	RII	Address bits

      I/G -- Individual/group address: 0 Group address; 1 Individual address.

      RII -- Routing information indicator: 0 RI absent; 1 RI present.

- Route Information -- The structure of the route information is as follows:

3	5	1	6	1	16	16		16
RT	LTH	D	LF	r	RD1	RD2	...	RDn

      RC -- Routing control (16 bits).
      RDn -- Route descriptor (16 bits).
      RT -- Routing type (3 bits).
      LTH -- Length (5 bits).
      D -- Direction bit (1 bit).
      LF -- Largest frame (6 bits).
      r -- Reserved (1 bit).

- Information -- The Information field may be LLC, MAC or SMT protocol.
- FCS -- Frame check sequence.

Related Protocols

IEEE 802.5 (Token Ring), IEEE 802.2

Sponsor Source

FDDI is defined by ANSI (http://www.ansi.org) X3T9.5 and X3T12.

Reference

http://www.cisco.com/univercd/cc/td/doc/cisintwk/ito_doc/fddi.htm
Fiber Distributed Data Interface

Token Ring: IEEE 802.5 LAN Protocol

Protocol Description

Token Ring is a LAN protocol, defined in IEEE 802.5 where all stations are connected in a ring and each station can directly hear transmissions only from its immediate neighbor. Permission to transmit is granted by a message (token) that circulates around the ring.

Token Ring as defined in IEEE 802.5 is originated from the IBM Token Ring LAN technologies. Both are based on the Token Passing technologies. While they differ in minor ways; they are generally compatible with each other.

Token-passing networks move a small frame, called a token, around the network. Possession of the token grants the right to transmit. If a node receiving the token has information to send, it seizes the token, alters 1 bit of the token (which turns the token into a start-of-frame sequence), appends the information that it wants to transmit, and sends this information to the next station on the ring. While the information frame is circling the ring, no token is on the network, which means that other stations wanting to transmit must wait. Therefore, collisions cannot occur in Token Ring networks.

The information frame circulates the ring until it reaches the intended destination station, which copies the information for further processing. The information frame continues to circle the ring and is finally removed when it reaches the sending station. The sending station can check the returning frame to see whether the frame was seen and subsequently copied by the destination.

Unlike Ethernet CSMA/CD networks, token-passing networks are deterministic, which means that it is possible to calculate the maximum time that will pass before any end station will be capable of transmitting. This feature and several reliability features make Token Ring networks ideal for applications in which delay must be predictable and robust network operation is important.

The Fiber Distributed-Data Interface (FDDI) also uses the Token Passing protocol.

Protocol Structure

1	2	3	9	15bytes
SDEL	AC	FC	Destination address	Source address
Route information 0-30 bytes				
Information (LLC or MAC) variable				
FCS (4 bytes)		EDEL	FS	

• SDEL / EDEL -- Starting Delimiter / Ending Delimiter. Both the SDEL and EDEL have intentional Manchester code violations in certain bit positions so that the start and end of a frame can never be accidentally recognized in the middle of other data.
• AC -- Access Control field contains the priority fields.

• FC -- Frame Control field indicates whether the frame contains data or control information
• Destination address -- Destination station address.
• Source address -- Source station address.
• Route information -- The field with routing control, route descriptor and routing type information.
• Information -- The Information field may be LLC or MAC.
• FCS -- Frame check sequence.
• Frame status -- Contains bits that may be set on by the recipient of the frame to signal recognition of the address and whether the frame was successfully copied.

Related Protocols

IEEE 802.2, 802.3, 802.4, 802.5

Sponsor Source

Token Ring is defined by IEEE (http://www.ieee.org) 802.5.

Reference

http://standards.ieee.org/getieee802/download/802.5-1998.pdf
Token Ring Access Method and Physical Layer Specification
http://www.cisco.com/univercd/cc/td/doc/cisintwk/ito_doc/tokenrng.htm
Token Ring and IEEE 802.5

LLC: Logic Link Control (IEEE 802.2)

Protocol Description

Logic Link Control (LLC) is the IEEE 802.2 LAN protocol that specifies an implementation of the LLC sublayer of the data link layer. IEEE 802.2 LLC is used in IEEE802.3 (Ethernet) and IEEE802.5 (Token Ring) LANs to perform these functions:

a. Managing the data-link communication
b. Link Addressing
c. Defining Service Access Points (SAPs)
d. Sequencing

The LLC provides a way for the upper layers to deal with any type of MAC layer (e.g. Ethernet - IEEE 802.3 CSMA/CD or Token Ring IEEE 802.5 Token Passing).

LLC originated from the High-Level Data-Link Control (HDLC) and uses a subclass of the HDLC specification. LLC defines three types of operation for data communication:

Type 1: Connectionless. The connectionless operation is basically sending with no guarantee of receiving;

Type 2: Connection Oriented. The Type 2 Connection-Oriented operation for the LLC layer provides these 4 services: Connection establishment, Confirmation and acknowledgement that data has been received, Error recovery by requesting received bad data to be resent, Sliding Windows (Modulus: 128), which is a method of increasing the rate of data transfer.

Type 3: Acknowledgement with connectionless service.

The Type 1 connectionless service of LLC specifies a static-frame format and allows network protocols to run on it. Network protocols that fully implement a transport layer will generally use Type 1 service.

The Type 2 connection-oriented service of LLC provides reliable data transfer. It is used in LAN environments that do not invoke network and transport layer protocols.

Protocol Structure

Logic Link Control Layer (LLC) Header:

8	16	24 or 32bit	Variable
DSAP	SSAP	Control	LLC information

• DSAP -- The destination service access point structure is as follows:

1	8bit
I/G	Address bits

    I/G -- Individual/group address may be: 0 Individual DSAP; 1 Group DSAP.

• SSAP -- The source service access point structure is as fol-

lows:

1	8bit
C/R	Address bits

    C/R -- Command/response: 0 Command; 1 Response.

• Control -- The structure of the control field is as follows:

	1		8	9	16bit
Information	0	N(S)		P/F	N(R)
Supervisory	1	0 SS	XXXX	P/F	N(R)
Unnumbered	1	1 MM	P/F MMM		

    N(S) -- Transmitter send sequence number.
    N(R) -- Transmitter receive sequence number.
    P/F -- Poll/final bit. Command LLC PDU transmission/response LLC PDU transmission.
        S -- Supervisory function bits:
        00 -- RR (receive ready).
        01 -- REJ (reject).
        10 -- RNR (receive not ready).
    X -- Reserved and set to zero.
    M -- Modifier function bits.

• LLC information -- LLC data or higher layer protocols.

Related Protocols

IEEE 802.3, 802.5

Sponsor Source

LLC is defined by IEEE (http://www.ieee.org) in the 802.2 specifications.

Reference

http://standards.ieee.org/getieee802/download/802.2-1998.pdf
IEEE 802.2 specification.
https://secure.linuxports.com/howto/intro_to_networking/c5048.htm
IEEE 802.2: Logic Link Control Layer

SNAP: SubNetwork Access Protocol

Protocol Description

The SubNetwork Access Protocol (SNAP) is a standard for the transmission of IP datagrams over IEEE 802 networks. In other words, IP datagrams can be sent on IEEE 802 networks encapsulated within the 802.2 LLC and SNAP data link layers and the 802.3, 802.4 or 802.5 physical network layers.

SNAP is included in an extension of the Logic Link Control (LLC IEEE 802.2) header and is used for encapsulating IP datagrams and ARP requests and replies on IEEE 802 networks. The SNAP header follows the LLC header and contains an organization code indicating that the following 16 bits specify the EtherType code. Normally, all communication is performed using 802.2 type 1 communication. Consenting systems on the same IEEE 802 network may use 802.2 type 2 communication after verifying that it is supported by both nodes. This is accomplished using the 802.2 XID mechanism. However, type 1 communication is the recommended method at this time and must be supported by all implementations.

The mapping of 32-bit Internet addresses to 16-bit or 48-bit IEEE 802 addresses is done via the dynamic discovery procedure of the Address Resolution Protocol (ARP). The IEEE 802 networks may have 16-bit or 48-bit physical addresses. SNAP allows the use of either size of address within a given IEEE 802 network.

With SNAP, the transmission of IP datagrams does not depend on the transmission rate of the under layer LAN technologies (various types of Ethernet and Token Ring), which may have very different transmission rates (from 1 to 20 Mbps).

Protocol Structure

LLC Header:

8	16	24 or 32bit
DSAP	SSAP	Control

For details of the LLC header, please see the LLC page.

SNAP header:

24	40bit
Organization code	EtherType

When SNAP is present the DSAP and SSAP fields within the LLC header contain the value 170 (decimal) each and the Control field is set to 3 (unnumbered information).

- Organization code -- Set to 0.
- EtherType -- Specifies which protocol is encapsulated within the IEEE 802 network: IP = 2048, ARP = 2054.

Related Protocols

IEEE 802.2, 802.3, 802.4, 802.5, IP, ARP

Sponsor Source

SNAP is defined by IEEE (http://www.ieee.org) and IETF (http://www.ietf.org).

Reference

http://standards.ieee.org/getieee802/download/802.2-1998.pdf
IEEE 802.2 specification.
http://www.javvin.com/protocol/rfc1042.pdf
A Standard for the Transmission of IP Datagrams over IEEE 802 Networks

STP: Spanning Tree Protocol (IEEE 802.1D)

Protocol Description

Spanning-Tree Protocol (STP) as defined in IEEE 802.1D is a link management protocol that provides path redundancy while preventing undesirable loops in the network. For an Ethernet network to function properly, only one active path can exist between two stations. Loops occur in networks for a variety of reasons. The most common reason for loops in networks is a deliberate attempt to provide redundancy - in case that one link or switch fails, another link or switch can take over.

STP is a technology that allows bridges to communicate with each other to discover physical loops in the network. The protocol then specifies an algorithm that bridges can use to create a loop-free logical topology. In other words, STP creates a tree structure of loop-free leaves and branches that spans the entire Layer 2 network.

Spanning-Tree Protocol operation is transparent to end stations, which are unaware whether they are connected to a single LAN segment or a switched LAN of multiple segments. Where two bridges are used to interconnect the same two computer network segments, Spanning Tree is a protocol that allows the bridges to exchange information so that only one of them will handle a given message that is being sent between two computers within the network.

Bridge Protocol Data Units (BPDUs) are used by bridges in a network to exchange information regarding their status. The Spanning-Tree Protocol uses the BPDU information to elect the root switch and root port for the switched network, as well as the root port and designated port for each switched segment.

The program in each bridge that allows it to determine how to use the protocol is known as the spanning tree algorithm, which is specifically constructed to avoid bridge loops. The algorithm ensures that a bridge uses only the most efficient path when faced with multiple paths. If the best path fails, the algorithm recalculates the network and finds the next best route.

The spanning tree algorithm determines the network (which computer hosts are in which segment) and this data is exchanged using Bridge Protocol Data Units (BPDUs). It is broken down into two steps:

Step 1: The algorithm determines the best message a bridge can send by evaluating the configuration messages it has received and choosing the best option.

Step 2: Once it selects the top message for a particular bridge to send, it compares its choice with possible configuration messages from the non-root-connections it has. If the best option from step 1 isn't better than what it receives from the non-root-connections, it will prune that port.

Rapid Spanning Tree Protocol (RSTP) defined in IEEE 802.1w is an evolution of the 802.1d standard. RSTP (802.1w) works just like STP (802.1d) in many ways. The key advantage of RSTP is that RSTP improves network convergence when topology changes occur. STP takes a relatively long time to converge: 50 seconds with the default settings, while the RSTP takes less than 10 seconds.

RSTP can be deployed alongside traditional 802.1d STP bridges and switches, with RSTP features working in switches that support it, and STP features working in the switches that support only STP.

Protocol Structure

The Bridge Protocol Data Units (BPDUs).

Protocol ID (2)	Version (1)	Type (1)	Flags (1)	Rood ID (8)	Root Path (4)
Sender BID (8)	Port ID (2)	M-Age (2)	Max Age (2)	Hello (2)	FD (2 Bytes)

• Protocol ID -- Always 0.
• Version -- Always 0.
• Type -- Determines which of the two BPDU formats this frame contains (Configuration BPDU or TCN BPDU).
• Flags -- Used to handle changes in the active topology covered in the next section on Topology Change Notifications.
• Root BID -- Contains the Bridge ID of the Root Bridge. After convergence, all Configuration BPDUs in the bridged network should contain the same value for this field (for a single VLAN). NetXRay breaks out the two BID subfields: Bridge Priority and bridge MAC address.
• Root Path Cost -- The cumulative cost of all links leading to the Root Bridge.
• Sender BID -- The BID of the bridge that created the current BPDU. This field is the same for all BPDUs sent by a single switch (for a single VLAN), but it differs between switches.
• Port ID -- Contains a unique value for every port. Port 1/1 contains the value 0×8001, whereas Port 1/2 contains 0×8002.
• Message Age -- Records the time since the Root Bridge originally generated the information that the current BPDU is derived from.
• Max Age -- Maximum time that a BPDU is saved. Also influences the bridge table aging timer during the Topology Change Notification process (discussed later).
• Hello Time -- Time between periodic Configuration BPDUs.
• Forward Delay -- The time spent in the Listening and Learning states. Also influences timers during the Topology Change Notification process (discussed later).

Related Protocols

IEEE 802.2, 802.3, 802.1P, 802.1Q, RSTP, 802.1W

Sponsor Source

STP is defined by IEEE (http://www.ieee.org) in 802.1D.

Reference

http://standards.ieee.org/getieee802/download/802.1D-1998.pdf
ANSI/IEEE Std 802.1D 1998 Edition
http://www.cisco.com/univercd/cc/td/doc/product/rtrmgmt/sw_ntman/cwsimain/cwsi2/cwsiug2/vlan2/stpapp.htm
Understanding Spanning Tree Protocol
http://www.cisco.com/warp/public/473/146.html
Understand Rapid Spanning Tree Protocol (IEEE 802.1w)

Metropolitan Area Network and MAN Protocols

Description

A Metropolitan Area Network (MAN) is a computer network usually spanning a campus or a city, which typically connect a few local area networks using high-speed backbone technologies. A MAN often provides efficient connections to a wide area network (WAN). There are three important features which discriminate MANs from LANs or WANs:

1. The network size falls intermediate between LANs and WANs. A MAN typically covers an area of between 5 and 50 km range. Many MANs cover an area of the size of a city, although in some cases MANs may be as small as a group of buildings.
2. A MAN (like a WAN) is not generally owned by a single organization. The MAN, its communications links and equipment are generally owned by either a consortium of users or by a network service provider who sells the service to the users.
3. A MAN often acts as a high speed network to allow sharing of regional resources. It is also frequently used to provide a shared connection to other networks using a link to a WAN.

MAN adopted technologies from both LAN and WAN to serve its purpose. Some legacy technologies used for MAN are ATM, FDDI, DQDB and SMDS. These older technologies are in the process of being displaced by Gigabit Ethernet and 10 Gigabit Ethernet. At the physical level, MAN links between LANs have been built on fibre optical cables or using wireless technologies such as microwave or radio.

The Metropolitan Area Network (MAN) protocols are mostly at the data link level (layer 2 in the OSI model), which are defined by IEEE, ITU-T, etc.

Key Protocols

The key MAN protocols are listed as follows:

ATM: Asynchronous Transfer Mode
DQDB: Distributed Queue Dual Bus Defined in IEEE 802.6
Ethernet at data rate 10 Gbps (IEEE 802.3ae)
FDDI: Fiber Distributed Data Interface
Gigabit Ethernet: Ethernet at data rate 1000Mbps (IEEE 802.3z, 802.3ab)
SMDS: Switched Multimegabit Data Service
WiMAX: Broadband Wireless MAN Standard defined in IEEE802.16

Related Protocols

LAN, WAN, TCP/IP

Sponsor Source

MAN protocols are mostly defined by IEEE.

DQDB: Distributed Queue Dual Bus (Defined in IEEE 802.6)

Protocol Description

Distributed Queue Dual Bus (DQDB) is a Data-link layer communication protocol for Metropolitan Area Networks (MANs), specified in the IEEE 802.6 standard and designed for use in MANs. DQDB is designed for data as well as voice and video transmission and is based on cell switching technology (similar to ATM). DQDB, which permits multiple systems to interconnect using two unidirectional logical buses, is an open standard that is designed for compatibility with carrier transmission standards such as SMDS.

For a MAN to be effective it requires a system that can function across long, "city-wide" distances of several miles, have a low susceptibility to error, adapt to the number of nodes attached and have variable bandwidth distribution. Using DQDB, networks can be thirty miles long and function in the range of 34 Mbps to 155 Mbps. The data rate fluctuates due to many hosts sharing a dual bus, as well as to the location of a single host in relation to the frame generator, but there are schemes to compensate for this problem making DQDB function reliably and fairly for all hosts.

The DQDB is composed of two bus lines with stations attached to both and a frame generator at the end of each bus. The buses run in parallel in such a fashion as to allow the frames generated to travel across the stations in opposite directions. Below is a picture of the basic DQDB architecture.

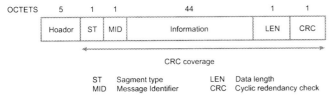

Figure 2-36: DQDB Architecture

Protocol Structure

The DQDB cell has a similar format as to the ATM:

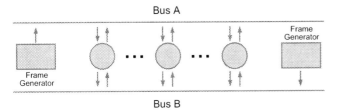

Figure 2-37: DQDB Cell Format

DQDB cell header:

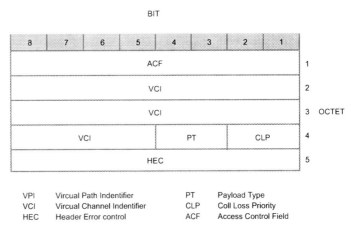

VPI	Vircual Path Indentifier	PT	Payload Type
VCI	Vircual Channel Indentifier	CLP	Coll Loss Priority
HEC	Header Error control	ACF	Access Control Field

Figure 2-38: DQDB cell header

Related Protocols

IEEE 802.6, ATM, SMDS

Sponsor Source

DQDB is defined by IEEE (http://www.ieee.org) 802.6.

Reference

http://standards.ieee.org/getieee802/download/802.6-1994.pdf

Distributed Queue Dual Bus (DQDB) access Method and Physical layer specifications

SMDS: Switched Multimegabit Data Service

Protocol Description

Switched Multimegabit Data Service (SMDS) is a broadband networking technology developed by Bellcore based on the IEEE 802.6 DQDB (Distributed Queue Dual Bus) technology. SMDS can use fiber- or copper-based media. It supports speeds of 1.544 Mbps over DS-1, or 44.736 Mbps over DS-3. In addition, SMDS data units are large enough to encapsulate entire IEEE 802.3, IEEE 802.5, and Fiber Distributed Data Interface (FDDI) frames. SMDS operates by accepting high-speed customer data in increments of up to 9,188 octets, and dividing it into 53-octet cells for transmission through the service provider's network. These cells are reassembled, at the receiving end, into the customer data.

The SMDS Interface Protocol (SIP) is a three-level protocol, based on IEEE 802.6 DQDB, which controls the customer's access to the network. SIP Levels 3 and 2 operate at the Media Access Control (MAC) sublayer of the data link layer of the OSI reference model. SIP Level 1 operates at the physical layer of the OSI reference model. SIP Level 3 receives and transports frames of the upper layer protocol information. SIP Level 2 controls access to the physical medium. SIP Level 1 includes the PLCP and the transmission system.

Protocol Structure

The SIP Level 3 PDU is shown in the following diagram.

36	<= 9188	0-3	0,4	4bytes
Header	Information	PAD	X + CRC32	Trailer

The format of the level 3 header is as follows:

Rsv (1)	BE-tag (1)	BA-size (2)	Destination address (8bytes)				
Source address (8bytes)			X + HLPI (6 bits)	PL (2)	X+ QoS (4 bits)	CIB (1)	HEL (3 bits)	X+Bridging (2bytes)
HE (12 bytes)							

And the format of the level 3 trailer is as follows:

1 byte	1 byte	2 bytes
Reserved	Betag	BAsize

The Level 3 PDU fields are described as follows:

• Rsv -- Reserved. A 1-octet field that the CPE and the SS fill with zeros.
• BE tag -- A 1-octet field that contains a beginning/end tag.
• BA size -- A 2-octet field containing the length in octets of the Level 3 PDU from the beginning of the Destination Address field and including the CRC32 field, if present.

• Destination address -- An 8-octet field containing the address of the intended recipient of the PDU.
• Source address -- An 8-octet field containing the address of the sender of this PDU. This field contains Address Type and Address subfields as described for Destination Address.
• HLPI -- Higher Layer Protocol Identifier. A 6-bit field that aligns the SIP and DQDB protocol formats.
• PL -- PAD Length. A 2-bit field that indicates the number of octets in the PAD field, which aligns the Level 3 PDU on a 32-bit boundary.
• QoS -- Quality of Service. A 4-bit field that aligns the SIP and DQDB protocol formats.
• CIB -- CRC32 Indication Bit. A 1-bit field that indicates the presence (1) or absence (0) of the CRC32 field.
• HEL -- Header Extension Length. A 3-bit field that indicates the number of 32-bit words in the Header Extension field.
• Bridging -- A 2-octet field that aligns the SIP and DQDB Bridging protocol formats.
• HE -- Header Extension. A 12-octet field that contains the version and carrier-selection information .
• Information field -- Variable-length field, up to 9,188 octets in length, which contains user information.
• PAD -- Variable-length field, 1-3 octets in length, filled with zeros aligning the entire PDU on a 32-bit boundary.
• CRC32 -- 2-octet field that performs error detection on the PDU, beginning with the DA field, up to and including the CRC32 field.

The SIP Level 2 PDU contains a 5-octet header, a 44-octet Segmentation Unit (payload) and a 2-octet trailer as shown below.

Access control (8 bits)	Network control info (32 bits)	Segment type (2bits)	Sequence number (4 bits)	Message ID (10 bits)
Segmentation unit (352 bits or 44 bytes)				
Payload length (6 bits)	Payload CRC (10bits)			

The Level 2 PDU fields are described as follows:

• Access control - 8-bit field that indicates whether the Level 2 PDU Access Control contains information (1) or is empty (0).
• Network control info - 4-octet field that determines whether Network Control Information of the Level 2 PDU contains information (FFFFF022H) or is empty (0).
• Segment type - 2-bit field that indicates how the receiver should process non-empty Level 2 PDUs. Sequence number - 4-bit number that verifies that all the Level 2 PDUs belonging to a single Level 3 PDU have been received in the correct order.
• Sequence number -- 4-bit number that verifies that all the Level 2 PDUs belonging to a single Level 3 PDU have been received in the correct order.
• Message identifier -- 10-bit number that allows the various segments to be associated with a single Level 3 PDU.
• Segmentation unit -- 44-octet field that contains a portion of the Level 3 PDU.

• Payload length -- 6-bit field that indicates which of the 44 octets in the Segmentation Unit contain actual data. BOM and COM segments always indicate 44 octets. EOM segments indicate between 4 and 44 octets, in multiples of 4 octets. SSM segments indicate between 28 and 44 octets, in multiples of 4 octets.
• Payload CRC -- 10-bit field that performs error detection on the Segment Type, Sequence Number, Message Identifier, Segmentation Unit, Payload Length and Payload CRC fields.
• Once assembled, SIP Level 2 PDUs are passed to the PLCP and physical functions within SIP Level 1 for transmission.

Related Protocols

IEEE 802.6 (DQDB), ATM, SMDS

Sponsor Source

SMDS is defined by Bellcore (Telcordia) (http://www.telcordia.com).

Reference

http://www.cisco.com/univercd/cc/td/doc/cisintwk/ito_doc/smds.htm
Switched Multimegabit Data Service

WiMAX: Broadband Wireless MAN Standard defined in IEEE802.16

Protocol Description

The IEEE 802.16 defines the wireless metropolitan area network (MAN) technology which is branded as WiMAX. The 802.16 includes two sets of standards, 802.16-2004 (802.16d) for fixed WiMAX and 802.16-2005(802.16e) for mobile WiMAX. In addition to provide the missing link for the "last mile" connection in metropolitan area networks where DSL, T1/T3 and Cable and other broadband access methods are not available or too expensive, WiMAX also offers an alternative to satellite Internet services for rural areas and allows mobility of the customer equipment.

IEEE 802.16 standards are concerned with the air interface between a subscriber's transceiver station and a base transceiver station. The fixed WiMax standard IEEE 802.16-2004 (also known as 802.16d) is approved by the IEEE in June 2004, which provides fixed, point-to-multi point broadband wireless access service and its product profile utilizes the OFDM 256-FFT (Fast Fourier Transform) system profile. The fixed WiMAX 802.16-2004 standard supports both time division duplex (TDD) and frequency division duplex (FDD) services - the latter of which delivers full duplex transmission on the same signal if desired. In Dec. 2005, IEEE approved the mobile WiMax standard, the 802.16-2005 (also known as 802.16e). IEEE 802.16e, based on the early WiMax standard 802.16a, adds mobility features to WiMAX in the 2 to 11 GHz licensed bands. 802.16e allows for fixed wireless and mobile Non Line of Sight (NLOS) applications primarily by enhancing the OFDMA (Orthogonal Frequency Division Multiple Access).

IEEE 802.16 WiMAX is designed as a complementary technology to other wireless communication technologies such as Wi-Fi (WLAN) and Bluetooth (WPAN). The following table provides a quick comparison of 802.16 with 802.11 and the Bluetooth (802.15):

Parameters	IEEE802.16d / 802.16-2004 (Fixed WiMAX)	IEEE802.16e / 802.16-2005 (Mobile WiMAX)	802.11 (WLAN)	802.15.1 (Bluetooth)
Frequency Band	2-66GHz	2 - 11GHz	2.4 – 5.8GHz	2.4GHz
Range	~31 miles	~31 miles	~100 meters	~10meters
Maximum Data rate	~134 Mbps	~15 Mbps	~55 Mbps	~3Mbps
Number of users	Thousands	Thousands	Dozens	Dozens

Protocol Structure

IEEE 802.16 Protocol Architecture has 4 layers: Convergence, MAC, Trnamission and physical, which can be mapped to two OSI lowest layers: the physical and data link layer. The WiMax protocol stack is displayed below:

WiMAX Protocol Stack

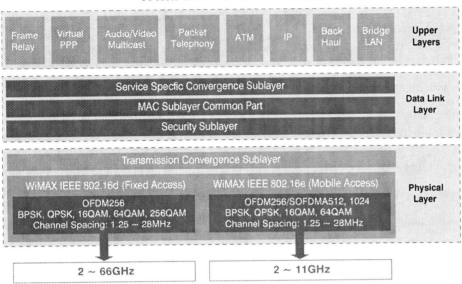

Figure 2-39: WiMax Protocol Stack

Related Protocols

IEEE 802.11, WLAN, Bluetooth, IEEE 802.15, WPAN, WiMAX, WMAN, IEEE802.16d, IEEE802.16-2004, IEEE802.16e, IEEE802.16-2005

Sponsor Source

The WiMAX wireless MAN standards are defined by the IEEE 802.16 working group.

Reference

http://grouper.ieee.org/groups/802/16/published.html
Published 802.16 standards
http://www.intel.com/ebusiness/pdf/wireless/intel/80216_wimax.pdf
IEEE 802.16 and WiMAX

Storage Area Network and SAN Protocols

Description

Storage Area Network (SAN) is a high-speed network or subnetwork whose primary purpose is to transfer data between computer and storage systems. A storage device is a machine that contains nothing but a disk or disks for storing data. A SAN consists of a communication infrastructure, which provides physical connections; and a management layer, which organizes the connections, storage elements, and computer systems so that data transfer is secure and robust.

Typically, a storage area network is part of the overall network of computing resources for an enterprise. A storage area network is usually clustered in close proximity to other computing resources but may also extend to remote locations for backup and archival storage. SANs support disk mirroring, backup and restore, archival and retrieval of archived data, data migration from one storage device to another, and the sharing of data among different servers in a network. SANs can incorporate subnetworks with network-attached storage (NAS) systems.

There are a few SAN technologies available in today's implementations, such as IBM's optical fiber ESCON which is enhanced by FICON architecture, or the newer Fibre Channel technology. High speed Ethernet is also used in the storage Area Network for connection. SCSI and iSCSI are popular technologies used in the Storage Area Network.

A typical SAN architecture is displayed as follows:

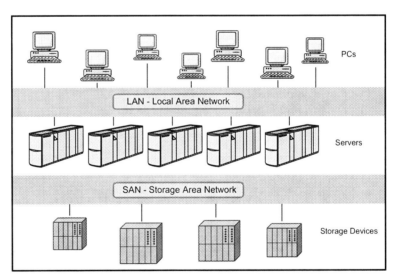

Figure 2-40: Storage Area Network Architecture

Key Protocols

The key SAN protocols are listed as follows:

FCIP: Entire Fibre Channel Frame Over IP
FCP: Fibre Channel Protocol
iFCP: Internet Fibre Channel Protocol
iSCSI: Internet Small Computer System Interface
iSNS: Internet Storage Name Service
NDMP: Network Data Management Protocol

SAS: Serial Attached SCSI
SCSI: Small Computer System Interface

Related Protocols

LAN, WAN, TCP/IP

Sponsor Source

Storage Area Network protocols are defined by IETF, ANSI and ISO.

Reference

http://www.redbooks.ibm.com/redbooks/SG245470.html
Storage Area Network

FC & FCP: Fibre Channel and Fibre Channel Protocol

Protocol Description

The Fibre Channel Standards (FCS) define a high-speed data transfer mechanism that can be used to connect workstations, mainframes, supercomputers, storage devices and displays. FCS addresses the need for very fast transfers of large volumes of information and could relieve system manufacturers of the burden of supporting the variety of channels and networks currently in place, as it provides one standard for networking, storage and data transfer. Fibre Channel Protocol (FCP) is the interface protocol of SCSI on the Fibre Channel. The key Fibre Channel characteristics are as follows:

• Performance from 266 megabits/second to over four gigabits/second
• Supports both optical and electrical media, working from 133 Megabits/sec up to 1062 Megabits/sec with distances up to 10 km.
• Small connectors
• High-bandwidth utilization with distance insensitivity
• Support for multiple cost/performance levels, from small systems to supercomputers
• Ability to carry multiple existing interface command sets, including Internet Protocol (IP), SCSI, IPI, HIPPI-FP, and audio/video.

Fibre Channel consists of the following layers:

• FC-0 -- The interface to the physical media
• FC-1 -- The encoding and decoding of data and out-of-band physical link control information for transmission over the physical media
• FC-2 -- The transfer of frames, sequences and Exchanges comprising protocol information units.
• FC-3 -- Common Services required for advanced features such as striping, hunt group and multicast.
• FC-4 -- Application interfaces that can execute over fibre channel such as the fibre channel protocol for SCSI (FCP).

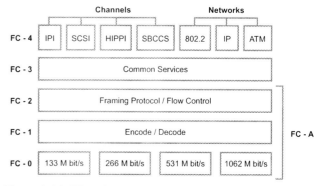

Figure 2-41: Fibre Channel Protocol

The fundamental entity in fibre channel is the fibre channel network. Unlike a layered network architecture, a fibre channel network is largely specified by functional elements and the interfaces between them. These consist, in part, of the following:

a) N_PORTs -- The end points for fibre channel traffic.
b) FC Devices -- The fibre channel devices to which the N_PORTs provide access.
c) Fabric Ports -- The interfaces within a fibre channel network that provide attachment for an N_PORT.
d) The network infrastructure for carrying frame traffic between N_PORTs.
e) Within a switched or mixed fabric, a set of auxiliary servers, including a name server for device discovery and network address resolution.

The principal fibre channel network topologies consist of the following:

a) Arbitrated Loop -- A series of N_PORTs connected together in daisy-chain fashion.
b) Switched Fabric -- A network consisting of switching elements.
c) Mixed Fabric -- A network consisting of switches and "fabric-attached" loops. A loop-attached N_PORT (NL_PORT) is connected to the loop through an L_PORT and accesses the fabric by way of an FL_PORT.

Protocol Structure

Fibre Channel frames are a maximum 2148 bytes long. Fibre Channel Frame Header Structure:

8	16	24	32bit
Routine Control	Destination Address		
Reserve	Source Address		
Upper Level Protocol Type	Frame Control		
Seq_ ID	Data Field Control	Sequence Count	
Parameter			

Related Protocols

SCSI, iFCP, FCP, FCIP, mFCP

Sponsor Source

Fibre Channel (FC) and Fibre Channel Protocol (FCP) are defined by ANSI (www.ansi.org).

Reference

http://www.javvin.com/protocol/rfc3643.pdf
Fibre Channel (FC) Frame Encapsulation
http://hsi.web.cern.ch/HSI/fcs/spec/overview.htm
Fibre Channel Overview

FCIP: Fibre Channel over TCP/IP

Protocol Description

Fibre Channel Over TCP/IP (FCIP) describes mechanisms that allow the interconnection of islands of Fibre Channel storage area networks over IP-based networks to form a unified storage area network in a single Fibre Channel fabric. FCIP relies on IP-based network services to provide the connectivity between the storage area network islands over local area networks, metropolitan area networks, or wide area networks.

The primary function of an FCIP Entity is forwarding FC Frames, employing FC Frame Encapsulation. Viewed from the IP Network perspective, FCIP Entities are peers and communicate using TCP/IP. Each FCIP Entity contains one or more TCP endpoints in the IP-based network. Viewed from the FC Fabric perspective, pairs of FCIP Entities, in combination with their associated FC Entities, forward FC Frames between FC Fabric elements. The FC End Nodes are unaware of the existence of the FCIP Link.

FC Primitive Signals, Primitive Sequences, and Class 1 FC Frames are not transmitted across an FCIP Link because they cannot be encoded using FC Frame Encapsulation. The path (route) taken by an encapsulated FC Frame follows the normal routing procedures of the IP Network.

An FCIP Entity MAY contain multiple FCIP Link Endpoints, but each FCIP Link Endpoint (FCIP_LEP) communicates with exactly one other FCIP_LEP. FCIP Entities do not actively participate in FC Frame routing. The FCIP Control & Services module MAY use TCP/IP quality of service features.

It is necessary to statically or dynamically configure each FCIP entity with the IP addresses and TCP port numbers corresponding to FCIP Entities with which it is expected to initiate communication. If dynamic discovery of participating FCIP Entities is supported, the function SHALL be performed using the Service Location Protocol (SLPv2). Before creating a TCP Connection to a peer FCIP Entity, the FCIP Entity attempting to create the TCP connection SHALL statically or dynamically determine the IP address, TCP port, expected FC Fabric Entity World Wide Name, TCP Connection Parameters, and Quality of Service Information.

FCIP Entities do not actively participate in the discovery of FC source and destination identifiers. Discovery of FC addresses (accessible via the FCIP Entity) is provided by techniques and protocols within the FC architecture.

To support IP Network security, FCIP Entities MUST: 1) implement cryptographically protected authentication and cryptographic data integrity keyed to the authentication process, and 2) implement data confidentiality security features.

On an individual TCP Connection, this specification relies on TCP/IP to deliver a byte stream in the same order that it was sent.

Protocol Structure

Fibre Channel Frame Encapsulation Header Structure – FCIP specific

8	16	24	32bit
Protocol #	Version	-Protocol #	-Version
replication of encapsulation word 0			
pFlags	Reserved	-pFlags	-Reserved
Flags	Frame Length	-Flags	-Frame Length
Time Stamp (integer)			
Time Stamp (fraction)			
CRC			

Common fields:

• Protocol# -- IANA-assigned protocol number identifying the protocol using the encapsulation.
• Version -- Encapsulation version as specified in [ENCAP]
• -Protocol# -- One's complement of the protocol#
• -Version -- One's complement of the version
• Flags -- Encapsulation flags
• Frame Length -- Contains the length of the entire FC Encapsulated frame including the FC Encapsulation Header and the FC frame (including SOF and EOF words) in units of 32-bit words.
• -Flags -- One's complement of the Flags field.
• -Frame Length -- One's complement of the Frame Length field.
• Time Stamp [integer] -- Integer component of the frame time stamp as specified in [ENCAP].
• Time Stamp -- Fractional component of the time stamp [fraction] as specified in [ENCAP].
• CRC -- Header CRC. MUST be valid for iFCP.

FCIP specific fields:

Word 1 of the Protocol Specific field SHALL contain an exact copy of word 0 in FC Frame Encapsulation.

The pFlags (protocol specific flags) field provides information about the protocol specific usage of the FC Encapsulation Header.

Ch	Reserved	SF

The SF (Special Frame) bit indicates whether the FCIP Frame is an encapsulated FC Frame or an FSF (FCIP Special Frame).

The Ch (Changed) bit indicates whether an echoed FSF has been intentionally altered. The Ch bit SHALL be 0 unless the FSF bit is 1.

Related Protocols

SCSI, iFCP, FCP, FCIP, mFCP, iSCSI, TCP

Sponsor Source

FCIP is defined by IETF (www.ietf.org).

Reference

http://www.javvin.com/protocol/rfc3643.pdf
Fibre Channel (FC) Frame Encapsulation
http://www.javvin.com/protocol/rfc3821.pdf
Fibre Channel Over TCP/IP (FCIP)

iFCP: Internet Fibre Channel Protocol

Protocol Description

Internet Fibre Channel Protocol (iFCP) is a gateway-to-gateway protocol, which provides fibre channel fabric services to fibre channel devices over a TCP/IP network. iFCP uses TCP to provide congestion control, error detection and recovery. iFCP's primary objective is to allow interconnection and networking of existing fibre channel devices at wire speeds over an IP network. The protocol and method of frame address translation defined permit the attachment of fibre channel storage devices to an IP-based fabric by means of transparent gateways.

The fundamental entity in Fibre Channel is the fibre channel network. Unlike a layered network architecture, a fibre channel network is largely specified by functional elements and the interfaces between them. These consist, in part, of the following:

a) N_PORTs -- The end points for fibre channel traffic.
b) FC Devices -- The fibre channel devices to which the N_PORTs provide access.
c) Fabric Ports -- The interfaces within a fibre channel network that provide attachment for an N_PORT.
d) The network infrastructure for carrying frame traffic between N_PORTs.
e) Within a switched or mixed fabric, a set of auxiliary servers, including a name server for device discovery and network address resolution.

The iFCP protocol enables the implementation of fibre channel fabric functionality on an IP network in which IP components and technology replace the fibre channel switching and routing infrastructure.

The main function of the iFCP protocol layer is to transport fibre channel frame images between locally and remotely attached N_PORTs. When transporting frames to a remote N_PORT, the iFCP layer encapsulates and routes the fibre channel frames comprising each fibre channel Information Unit via a predetermined TCP connection for transport across the IP network.

When receiving fibre channel frame images from the IP network, the iFCP layer de-encapsulates and delivers each frame to the appropriate N_PORT. The iFCP layer processes the following types of traffic:

a) FC-4 frame images associated with a fibre channel application protocol.
b) FC-2 frames comprising fibre channel link service requests and responses
c) Fibre channel broadcast frames
d) iFCP control messages required to setup, manage or terminate an iFCP session.

Protocol Structure

Fibre Channel Frame Encapsulation Header Structure – iFCP specific:

8	16	24	32bit
Protocol #	Version	-Protocol #	-Version
Reserved (must be zero)			
LS_Command_ACC	IFCP Flags	SOF	EOF
Flags	Frame Length	-Flags	-Frame Length
Time Stamp (integer)			
Time Stamp (fraction)			
CRC			

Common fields:

• Protocol# -- IANA-assigned protocol number identifying the protocol using the encapsulation. For iFCP, the value assigned by [ENCAP] is 2.
• Version -- Encapsulation version as specified in [ENCAP]
• -Protocol# -- One's complement of the protocol#
• -Version -- One's complement of the version
• Flags -- Encapsulation flags
• Frame Length -- Contains the length of the entire FC Encapsulated frame including the FC Encapsulation Header and the FC frame (including SOF and EOF words) in units of 32-bit words.
• -Flags -- One's complement of the Flags field.
• -Frame Length -- One's complement of the Frame Length field.
• Time Stamp [integer] -- Integer component of the frame time stamp as specified in [ENCAP].
• Time Stamp -- Fractional component of the time stamp [fraction] as specified in [ENCAP].
• CRC -- Header CRC. MUST be valid for iFCP.

iFCP specific fields:

• LS_COMMAND_ACC -- For a special link service ACC response to be processed by iFCP, the LS_COMMAND_ACC field SHALL contain a copy of bits 0 through 7 of the LS_COMMAND to which the ACC applies. Otherwise the LS_COMMAND_ACC field SHALL be set to zero.
• iFCP Flags -- iFCP-specific flags:

Reserved	SES	TRP	SPC

• SES: Session control frame
• TRP: Transparent mode Flag
• SPC: Special processing flag

• SOF -- Copy of the SOF delimiter encoding
• EOF -- Copy of the EOF delimiter encoding

Related Protocols

SCSI, iFCP, FCP, FCIP, mFCP, iSCSI, TCP

Sponsor Source

iFCP is defined by IETF (www.ietf.org) RFC 4172.

Reference

http://www.javvin.com/protocol/rfc3643.pdf
Fibre Channel (FC) Frame Encapsulation
http://www.javvin.com/protocol/rfc4172.pdf
iFCP - A Protocol for Internet Fibre Channel Storage Networking

iSCSI: Internet Small Computer System Interface (SCSI)

Protocol Description

Internet Small Computer System Interface (iSCSI) is a TCP/IP-based protocol for establishing and managing connections between IP-based storage devices, hosts and clients, creating a Storage Area Network (SAN). The SAN makes possible to use the SCSI protocol in network infrastructures for high-speed data transfer at the block level between multiple elements of data storage networks.

The architecture of the SCSI is based on the client/server model, which is mostly implemented in an environment where devices are very close to each other and connected with SCSI buses. Encapsulation and reliable delivery of bulk data transactions between initiators and targets through the TCP/IP network is the main function of the iSCSI. iSCSI provides a mechanism for encapsulating SCSI commands on an IP network and operates on top of TCP.

For today's SAN (Storage Area Network), the key requirements for data communication are: 1) Consolidation of data storage systems, 2) Data backup, 3) Server clusterization, 4) Replication, and 5) Data recovery in emergency conditions. In addition, a SAN is likely to have a geographic distribution over multiple LANs and WANs with various technologies. All operations must be conducted in a secure environment and with QoS. iSCSI is designed to perform the above functions in the TCP/IP network safely and with proper QoS.

The iSCSI has four components:

• iSCSI Address and Naming Conventions: An iSCSI node is an identifier of SCSI devices (in a network entity) available through the network. Each iSCSI node has a unique iSCSI name (up to 255 bytes) which is formed according to the rules adopted for Internet nodes.
• iSCSI Session Management: The iSCSI session consists of a Login Phase and a Full Feature Phase which is completed with a special command.
• iSCSI Error Handling: Because of a high probability of errors in data delivery in some IP networks, especially WAN, where the iSCSI can work, the protocol provides a number of measures for handling errors.
• iSCSI Security: As the iSCSI can be used in networks where data can be accessed illegally, the protocol allows different security methods.

Protocol Structure

iSCSI PDU structure:

8	16	24	32bit
Basic Header Structure (BHS)			
Additional Header Structure 1 (AHS) (optional)			
...			
Additional Header Structure n (AHS) (optional)			

Header Digest (optional)
Data Segment (optional)
Data Digest (optional)

iSCSI BHS Format:

	8		16	24	32bit
. I	Op-code	F	Opcode-specific fields		
Total AHS Length		Data Segment length			
Opcode-specific fields or Logic Unit Number (LUN) (8 bytes)					
Initiator Task Tag (4 bytes)					
Opcode-specific fields (28 bytes)					

• I -- For request PDUs, the I bit set to 1 is an immediate delivery marker.
• Opcode -- The Opcode indicates the type of iSCSI PDU the header encapsulates. The Opcodes are divided into two categories: initiator opcodes and target opcodes. Initiator opcodes are in PDUs sent by the initiator (request PDUs). Target opcodes are in PDUs sent by the target (response PDUs).
• Final (F) bit -- When set to 1 it indicates the final (or only) PDU of a sequence.
• Opcode -- specific Fields - These fields have different meanings for different opcode types.
• TotalAHSLength -- Total length of all AHS header segments in units of four byte words including padding, if any.
• DataSegmentLength -- This is the data segment payload length in bytes (excluding padding). The DataSegmentLength MUST be 0 whenever the PDU has no data segment.
• LUN -- Some opcodes operate on a specific Logical Unit. The Logical Unit Number (LUN) field identifies which Logical Unit. If the opcode does not relate to a Logical Unit, this field is either ignored or may be used in an opcode specific way.
• Initiator Task Tag -- The initiator assigns a Task Tag to each iSCSI task it issues. While a task exists, this tag MUST uniquely identify the task session-wide.

Related Protocols

SCSI, iFCP, FCP, FCIP, mFCP, TCP

Sponsor Source

ISCSI is defined by IETF (www.ietf.org).

Reference

http://www.javvin.com/protocol/rfc3347.pdf
Small Computer Systems Interface protocol over the Internet (iSCSI) Requirements and Design Considerations
http://www.javvin.com/protocol/rfc3720.pdf
Internet Small Computer Systems Interface (iSCSI)

iSNS and iSNSP: Internet Storage Name Service and iSNS Protocol

Protocol Description

Internet Storage Name Service (iSNS) facilitates scalable configuration and management of iSCSI and Fibre Channel (FCP) storage devices in an IP network, by providing a set of services comparable to that available in Fibre Channel networks. iSNS thus allows a commodity IP network to function at a comparable level of intelligence to a Fibre Channel fabric. iSNS allows the administrator to go beyond a simple device-by-device management model, where each storage device is manually and individually configured with its own list of known initiators and targets. Using the iSNS, each storage device subordinates its discovery and management responsibilities to the iSNS server. The iSNS server thereby serves as the consolidated configuration point through which management stations can configure and manage the entire storage network, including both iSCSI and Fibre Channel devices.

iSNS can be implemented to support iSCSI and/or iFCP protocols as needed; an iSNS implementation MAY provide support for one or both of these protocols as desired by the implementer. Implementation requirements within each of these protocols are further discussed in section 5. Use of iSNS is OPTIONAL for iSCSI, and REQUIRED for iFCP.

There are four main functions of the iSNS:

1) A Name Service Providing Storage Resource Discovery
2) Discovery Domain (DD) and Login Control Service
3) State Change Notification Service
4) Open Mapping of Fibre Channel and iSCSI Devices

iSNS has the following key Architectural Components:

• iSNS Protocol (iSNSP) -- iSNSP is a flexible and lightweight protocol that specifies how iSNS clients and servers communicate. It is suitable for various platforms, including switches and targets as well as server hosts.
• iSNS Client -- iSNS clients initiate transactions with iSNS servers using the iSNSP. iSNS clients are processes that are co-resident in the storage device, and can register device attribute information, download information about other registered clients in a common Discovery Domain (DD), and receive asynchronous notification of events that occur in their DD(s). Management stations are a special type of iSNS client that have access to all DDs stored in the iSNS.
• iSNS Server -- iSNS servers respond to iSNS protocol queries and requests, and initiate iSNS protocol State Change Notifications. Properly authenticated information submitted by a registration request is stored in an iSNS database.
• iSNS Database -- The iSNS database is the information repository for the iSNS server(s). It maintains information about iSNS client attributes. A directory-enabled implementation of iSNS may store client attributes in an LDAP directory infrastructure.

Protocol Structure

iSNSP message structure:

16	32bit
iSNSP version	Function ID
PDU Length	Flags
Transaction ID	Sequence ID
PDU Payload (variable bytes)	
Authentication Block (variable bytes)	

• iSNSP Version -- the current version is 0x0001. All other values are RESERVED.
• iSNSP Function ID -- defines the type of iSNS message and the operation to be executed. iSNSP PDU Length - specifies the length of the PDU PAYLOAD field in bytes. The PDU Payload contains TLV attributes for the operation.
• iSNSP Flags -- indicates additional information about the message and the type of Network Entity that generated the message.
• iSNSP Transaction ID -- MUST be set to a unique value for each concurrently outstanding request message. Replies MUST use the same TRANSACTION ID value as the associated iSNS request message.
• iSNSP Sequence ID -- The SEQUENCE ID has a unique value for each PDU within a single transaction.
• iSNSP PDU Payload -- The iSNSP PDU PAYLOAD is of variable length and contains attributes used for registration and query operations.
• Authentication Block -- For iSNS multicast and broadcast messages, the iSNSP provides authentication capability. The iSNS Authentication Block is identical in format to the SLP authentication block.

Related Protocols

iFCP, iSCSI, TCP, UDP, NAT, SNMP, SLP, DHCP, DNS, BOOTP

Sponsor Source

iSNS and iSNSP are defined by IET (www.ietf.org).

Reference

http://www.javvin.com/protocol/rfc4171.pdf
Internet Storage Name Service (iSNS)

NDMP: Network Data Management Protocol

Protocol Description

The Network Data Management Protocol (NDMP) is an open protocol for enterprise-wide network-based data management. NDMP defines a network-based mechanism and protocol for controlling backup, recovery, and other transfers of data between primary and secondary storage.

The NDMP (version 5) architecture is based on the client server model. The backup management software is considered the client, namely NDMP data management application (DMA). There is one and only one DMA in an NDMP session. Each additional process participating in the data management session is an NDMP service.

There are three types of NDMP services: Data service, Tape service and Translate service. The NDMP architecture separates the network attached Data Management Application (DMA), Data Servers and Tape Servers participating in archival or recovery operations. NDMP also provides low-level control of tape devices and SCSI media changers.

The DMA is the application that creates and controls the NDMP session. The Client reads, stores and manages all session state: server topology, tape sets and numbering, synchronization points, etc., everything needed to continue the session, or reverse the session, for instance, to restore fully or partially a file system. There is one and only one connection between the DMA and each NDMP service. This is the NDMP Control Connection. The control connection is a bi-directional TCP/IP connection.

If the Client is distributed in such a way that two or more client processes need to communicate to one NDMP service, the client side commands needs to be merged into one command stream and synchronized by the DMA. This command stream is sent to the service over one connection.

The NDMP protocol is based on XDR-encoded messages transmitted over a TCP/IP connection.

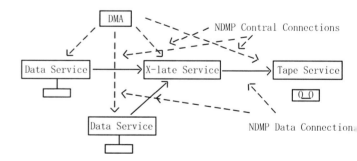

Figure 2-42: NDMP Functional Components

Protocol Structure

An NDMP message consists of a message header optionally followed by a message body. Each message is identified by a message number that is sent as part of the message header.

Each message will be XDR-encoded and sent within a single XDR record.

NDMP_header	message_request
NDMP_header	message_reply

The message headers are defined by the following XDR block

```
enum ndmp_header_message_type
{
        NDMP_MESSAGE_REQUEST,
        NDMP_MESSAGE_REPLY
};
struct ndmp_header
{
        u_long                          sequence;
        u_long                          time_stamp;
        ndmp_header_message_type        message_type;
        enum ndmp_message               message;
        u_long                          reply_sequence;
        ndmp_error                      error;
};
```

Message header data definitions:

• sequence -- The sequence number is a connection local counter that starts at one and increases by one for every message sent.
• time_stamp -- The time_stamp identifies the time, in seconds.
• message_type -- The message_type enum identifies the message as a request or a reply message.
• message -- The message field identifies the message.
• reply_sequence -- The reply_sequence field is 0 in a request message. In reply messages, the reply_sequence is the sequence number from the request message to which the reply is associated.
• error -- The error field is 0 in request messages. In reply messages, the error field identifies any problem that occurred receiving or decoding the message.

Related Protocols

iSCSI, iFCP, FCP, FCIP, mFCP

Sponsor Source

NDMP standards are defined by Storage Networking Industry Association (www.snia.org)

Reference

http://www.ndmp.org
Network Data Management Protocol specifications

SCSI: Small Computer System Interface

Protocol Description

Small Computer System Interface (SCSI), an ANSI standard, is a parallel interface standard used by Apple Macintosh computers, PCs, and many UNIX systems for attaching peripheral devices to computers. SCSI interfaces provide for faster data transmission rates than standard serial and parallel ports. In addition, you can attach many devices to a single SCSI port. There are many variations of SCSI: SCSI-1, SCSI-2, SCSI-3 and the recently approved standard Serial Attached SCSI (SAS).

SCSI-1

SCSI-1 is the original SCSI and is now obsolete. Basically, SCSI-1 used an 8-bit bus, and supported data rates of 4 MBps.

SCSI-2

SCSI-2, an improved version of SCSI-1 based on CCS, is a minimum set of 18 basic commands which work on all manufacture's hardware. SCSI-2 also provides extra speed with options called Fast SCSI and a 16-bit version called Wide SCSI. A feature called command queuing gives the SCSI device the ability to execute commands in the most eficient order. Fast SCSI delivers a 10 MB/sec transfer rate. When combined with a 16-bit bus, this doubles to 20 MB/sec (Fast-Wide SCSI).

SCSI-3

SCSI-3 has many advances over SCSI-2 such as Serial SCSI. This feature will allow data transfer up to 100MB/sec through a six-conductor coaxial cable. SCSI-3 solves many of the termination and delay problems of older SCSI versions. It also eases SCSI installation woes by being more plug-and-play in nature, as by automatic SCSI ID assigning and termination. SCSI-3 also supports 32 devices while SCSI-2 supports only 8.

SCSI-3 changed the document structure. It is not one document dealing with all the different layers and electrical interfaces, but a collection of documents covering the physical layer, the basic protocol specific to that electrical interface, the primary command set layer (SPC) and the specific protocol layer. For example, the specific protocol layer document contains the Hard Disk interface Commands in the Block Commands (SBC), Steam Commands for tape drives (SSC), Controller Commands for RAID arrays (SCC), Multimedia Commands (MMC), Media Changer Commands (MCC) and enclosure services commands (SES). There is an overall architectural model (SAM).

Elements of SCSI-3 are in use today in the forms of Ultra-Wide and Ultra SCSI drives. Ultra SCSI delivers 20MB/sec over the 8-bit bus. Ultra-Wide SCSI incorporates the 16-bit bus, and the speed rises to 40MB/sec.

SAS - Serial Attached SCSI

Serial Attached SCSI (SAS) is an evolutionary replacement for the Parallel SCSI physical storage interface. Serial Attached SCSI offers much faster communication and easier configuration. In addition, Serial Attached SCSI provides device compatibility with Serial ATA and uses similar cabling.

Serial Attached SCSI (SAS) is a point-to-point connection and allows multiple ports to be aggregated into a single controller, either built onto the mother board or as an add-on. Its technology is built upon the robust and tested parallel SCSI communication technology. Serial Attached SCSI (SAS) uses Serial ATA (SATA) cables which are a thin point-to-point connection allowing easy cable routing within a computer system, without the need for daisy-chaining. The first implementation of Serial Attached SCSI provides 1.5 Gb/sec (150MB/sec) of performance for each drive within an array.

Related Protocols

iSCSI, iFCP, FCP, FCIP, mFCP

Sponsor Source

SCSI standards are defined by ANSI (www.ansi.org).

Reference

http://www.danbbs.dk/~dino/SCSI/

SCSI-2 Specification

Protocol Structure

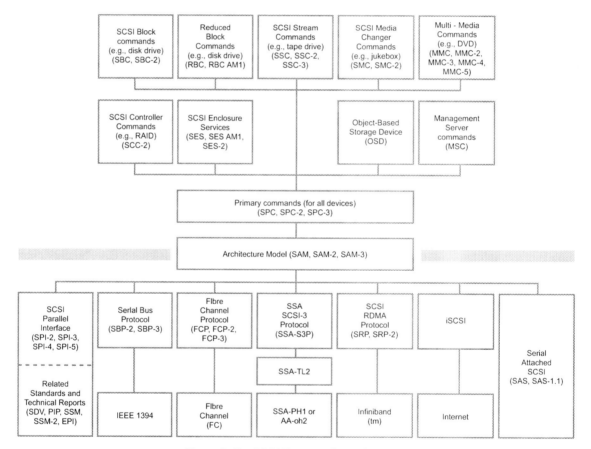

Figure 2-43: SCSI Protocol Stack Structure

ISO Protocols in OSI 7 Layers Reference Model

Description

The Open Systems Interconnection (OSI) model is a reference model developed by ISO (International Organization for Standardization) in 1984, as a conceptual framework of standards for communication in the network across different equipment and applications by different vendors. It is now considered the primary architectural model for inter-computing and internetworking communications. Most of the network communication protocols used today have a structure based on the OSI model. The OSI model defines the communications process into 7 layers, dividing the tasks involved in moving information between networked computers into seven smaller, more manageable task groups. A task or group of tasks is then assigned to each of the seven OSI layers. Each layer is reasonably self-contained so that the tasks assigned to each layer can be implemented independently. This enables the solutions offered by one layer to be updated without adversely affecting the other layers.

ISO defined a group of protocols for internetworking communications based on the OSI model, which are mostly deployed in European countries. ISO protocols are in the layers 3 to 7 and support almost any layer one and two protocols by various standard organizations and major vendors.

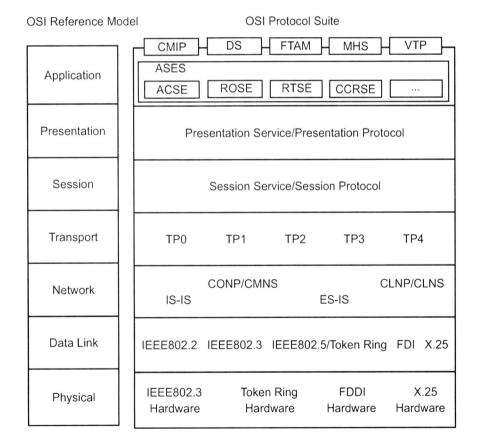

Figure 2-44: ISO Protocols in OSI 7 Layers Reference Model

Key Protocols

Application	ACSE: Association Control Service Element
	CMIP: Common Management Information Protocol
	CMIS: Common Management Information Service
	CMOT: CMIP over TCP/IP
	FTAM: File Transfer Access and Management
	ROSE: Remote Operation Service Element
	RTSE: Reliable Transfer Service Element Protocol
	VTP: ISO Virtual Terminal Protocol
	X.400: Message Handling Service (ISO email transmission service) Protocols
	X.500: Directory Access Service Protocol (DAP)
Presentation Layer	ISO-PP: OSI Presentation Layer Protocol
Session Layer	ISO-SP: OSI Session Layer Protocol
Transport Layer	ISO-TP: OSI Transport Protocols: TP0, TP1, TP2, TP3, TP4
Network Layer	ISO-IP: Connectionless Network Protocol (CLNP)
	CONP: Connection-Oriented Network Protocol
	ES-IS: End System to Intermediate System Routing Exchange protocol
	IDRP: Inter-Domain Routing Protocol
	IS-IS: Intermediate System to Intermediate System

X.800: Security architecture for Open Systems Interconnection for CCITT applications

Sponsor Source

International Organization for Standardization (www.iso.org)

Reference

http://www.doc.ua.pt/arch/itu/rec/product/X.htm
X.200:Information technology - Open Systems Interconnection - Basic Reference Model: The basic model
X.207: Information technology - Open Systems Interconnection - Application layer structure
X.210: Information technology - Open systems interconnection - Basic Reference Model: Conventions for the definition of OSI services
X.211: Information technology - Open systems interconnection - Physical service definition
X.212: Information technology - Open systems interconnection - Data Link service definition
X.213: Information technology - Open Systems Interconnection - Network service definition
X.214: Information technology - Open Systems Interconnection - Transport service definition
X.215: Information technology - Open Systems Interconnection - Session service definition
X.216: Information technology - Open Systems Interconnection - Presentation service definition

ISO ACSE: Association Control Service Element

Protocol Description

The ISO Association Control Service Element (ACSE), an application layer protocol in the OSI model, is designed to establish and release an application-association between two AEIs and to determine the application context of that association. The ACSE supports two modes of communication: connection-oriented and connectionless. For the connection-oriented mode, the application-association is established and released by the reference of ACSE connection-oriented services. For the connectionless mode, the application-association exists during the invocation of the single ACSE connectionless mode service, A UNIT-DATA .

The applications in the OSI reference model represent communication between a pair of application-processes (APs) in terms of communication between their application-entities (AEs) using the presentation-service. The functionality of an AE is factored into a number of application-service-elements (ASEs). The interaction between AEs is described in terms of the use of their ASEs' services. This Service Definition supports the modeling concepts of application-association and application context.

An application-association is a cooperative relationship between two AEIs. It provides the necessary frame of reference between the AEIs in order that they may interwork effectively. This relationship is formed by the communication of application-protocol-control-information between the AEIs through their use of the presentation-service.

An application context is an explicitly identified set of application-service-elements, related options and any other necessary information for the interworking of application-entities on an application association.

The ACSE service-user is that part of an application-entity that makes use of ACSE services. It may be the Control Function (CF) or an ASE or some combination of the two.

The services provided by ACSE are listed as follows:

Communication mode	Service	Type
Connection-oriented	A-ASSOCIATE A-RELEASE A-ABORT A-P-ABORT	Confirmed Confirmed Non-confirmed Provider-initiated
Connectionless	A-UNIT-DATA	Non-confirmed

Protocol Structure

The functions, services and message structure are listed as follows:

Functional Unit	Service	APDU	Field Name
Kernel	A-ASSOCI-ATE	AARQ	Protocol Version Application Context Name Calling AP Title Calling AE Qualifier Calling AP Invocation-identifier Calling AE Invocation-identifier Called AP Title Called AE Qualifier Called AP Invocation-identifier Called AE Invocation-identifier Implementation Information User Information
		AARE	Protocol Version Application Context Name Responding AP Title Responding AE Qualifier Responding AP Invocation-identifier Responding AE Invocation-identifier Result Result Source-Diagnostic Implementation Information User Information
	A-RE-LEASE	RLRQ	Reason User Information
		RLRE	Reason User Information
	A-ABORT	ABRT	Abort Source User Information
Authenti-cation	A-ASSOCI-ATE	AARQ	ACSE Requirements Authentication-mechanism Name Authentication-value
		AARE	Ditto
		ABRT	Diagnostic
Appli-cation Context Negotia-tion	A-ASSOCI-ATE	AARQ	Application Context Name List ACSE Requirements
		AARE	Ditto

Related Protocols

ISO-SP, ISO-PP, ROSE, ISO-VTP

Sponsor Source

ACSE is defined in ISO (www.iso.org) documents 8650, 8649 and ITU (www.itu.org) documents X.227, X.217 andX.237.

Reference

http://www.doc.ua.pt/arch/itu/rec/product/X.htm
X.217: Information technology - Open Systems Interconnection - Service definition for the Association Control Service Element
X.227: Information technology - Open Systems Interconnection - Connection-oriented protocol for the Association Control Service Element: Protocol specification
X.237: Information technology - Open Systems Interconnection - Connectionless protocol for the Association Control Service Element: Protocol specification

ISO CMIP: Common Management Information Protocol

Protocol Description

Common Management Information Protocol (CMIP) is an ISO protocol used with Common Management Information Services (CMIS), supports information exchange between network management applications and management agents. CMIS defines a system of network management information services. CMIP supplies an interface that provides functions which maybe used to support both ISO and user-defined management protocols. The CMIP specification for TCP/IP networks is called CMOT (CMIP Over TCP) and the version for IEEE 802 LAN's is called CMOL (CMIP Over LLC). CMIP/CMIS are proposed as competing protocols to the Simple Network Man-

agement Protocol (SNMP) in the TCP/IP suite.

CMIP uses an ISO reliable connection-oriented transport mechanism and has built in security that supports access control, authorization and security logs. The management information is exchanged between the network management application and management agents through managed objects. Managed objects are a characteristic of a managed device that can be monitored, modified or controlled and can be used to perform tasks.

CMIP does not specify the functionality of the network management application, it only defines the information exchange mechanism of the managed objects and not how the information is to be used or interpreted. The network management system based on the CMIP/CMIS is displayed below:

Network Management Based on the CMIP/CMIS

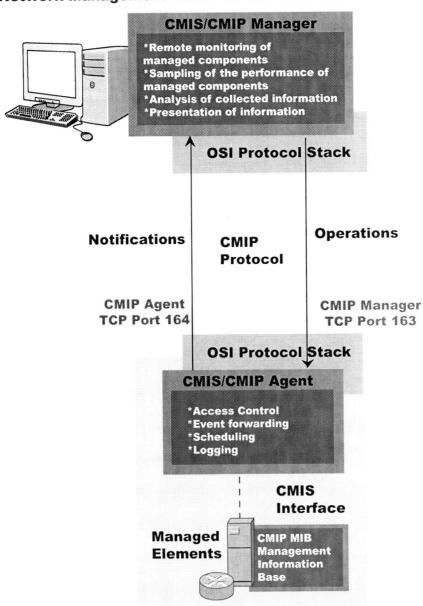

Figure 2-45: Network Management Based on the CMIP/CMIS

The major advantages of CMIP over SNMP are:

• CMIP variables not only relay information, but also can be used to perform tasks. This is impossible under SNMP.
• CMIP is a safer system as it has built in security that supports authorization, access control, and security logs.
• CMIP provides powerful capabilities that allow management applications to accomplish more with a single request.
• CMIP provides better reporting of unusual network conditions

Access to managed information in the managed objects is provided by the Common Management Information Service Element (CMISE) that uses CMIP (Common Management Information Protocol) to issue requests for management services. The management services provided by CMIP/CMISE can be organized into two distinct groups, management operation services initiated by a manager to request that an agent provide certain services or information, and notification services, used by the management agents to inform the managers that some events or set of events have occurred.

Protocol Structure

CMIP is an ASN.1 based protocol, whose PDUs (Protocol Data Units) are based on ROSE. Each service element has its PDUs which are part of the ROSE user data. The CMISE primitives and CMIP operation are listed as follows:

Correspondence between CMISE primitives and CMIP operations

CMIS primitive	Mode	Linked-ID	CMIP operation
M CANCEL GET req/ind	Confirmed	Not applicable	m-Cancel-Get-Confirmed
M CANCEL GET rsp/conf	Not applicable	Not applicable	m-Cancel-Get-Confirmed
M EVENT REPORT req/ind	Non-confirmed	Not applicable	m-EventReport
M EVENT REPORT req/ind	Confirmed	Not applicable	m-EventReport-Confirmed
M EVENT REPORT rsp/conf	Not applicable	Not applicable	m-EventReport-Confirmed
M GET req/ind	Confirmed	Not applicable	m-Get
M GET rsp/conf	Not applicable	Absent	m-Get
M GET rsp/conf	Not applicable	Present	m-Linked-Reply
M SET req/ind	Non-confirmed	Not applicable	m-Set

M SET req/ind	Confirmed	Not applicable	m-Set-Confirmed
M SET rsp/conf	Not applicable	Absent	m-Set-Confirmed
M SET rsp/conf	Not applicable	Present	m-Linked-Reply
M ACTION req/ind	Non-confirmed	Not applicable	m-Action
M ACTION req/ind	Confirmed	Not applicable	m-Action-confirmed
M ACTION rsp/conf	Not applicable	Absent	m-Action-confirmed
M ACTION rsp/conf	Not applicable	Present	m-Linked-Reply
M CREATE req/ind	Confirmed	Not applicable	m-Create
M CREATE rsp/conf	Not applicable	Not applicable	m-Create
M DELETE req/ind	Confirmed	Not applicable	m-Delete
M DELETE rsp/conf	Not applicable	Absent	m-Delete
M DELETE rsp/conf	Not applicable	Present	m-Linked-Reply

Related Protocols

ISO-SP, ISO-TP, ISO-IP, ISO-PP, ROSE, ACSE, CMIP, CMIS, SNMP

Sponsor Source

CMIP/CMIS are defined in ISO (www.iso.org) documents 9595, 9596 and ITU (www.itu.org) X.711.

Reference

http://www.doc.ua.pt/arch/itu/rec/product/X.htm
X.711: Information technology - Open Systems Interconnection - Common management information protocol: Specification
X.700: Management framework for Open Systems Interconnection (OSI) for CCITT applications
X.701: Information technology - Open Systems Interconnection - Systems management overview
X.702: Information technology - Open Systems Interconnection - Application context for systems management with transaction processing
X.703: Information technology - Open Distributed Management Architecture

CMOT: CMIP Over TCP/IP

Protocol Description

Common Management Information Protocol (CMIP), an ISO protocol used with Common Management Information Services (CMIS) for the monitoring and control of heterogeneous networks. CMIS defines a system of network management information services. CMIP was proposed as a replacement for the less sophisticated Simple Network Management Protocol (SNMP) but has not been widely adopted. CMIP provides improved security and better reporting of unusual network conditions.

CMIP Over TCP/IP (CMOT) is a network management protocol using ISO CMIP to manage IP-based networks. CMOT defines a network management architecture that uses the International Organization for Standardization's (ISO) Common Management Information Services/Common Management Information Protocol (CMIS/CMIP) in the Internet. This architecture provides a means by which control and monitoring information can be exchanged between a manager and a remote network element.

Protocol Structure

The following seven protocols comprise the CMOT protocol suite: ISO ACSE, ISO DIS ROSE, ISO CMIP, the lightweight presentation protocol (LPP), UDP, TCP, and IP.

Management Application Processes	
CMISE ISO 9595/9596	
ACSE ISO IS 8649/8650	ROSE ISO DIS 9072-1/2
Lightweight Presentation Protocol (LPP) RFC 1085	
TCP RFC 793	UDP RFC 768
IP/IPv6 RFC 791, RFC 2460	

The following six protocols comprise the CMIP protocol suite: ISO ACSE, ISO DIS ROSE, ISO CMIP, ISO Presentation, ISO Session and ISO Transport.

Management Application Processes	
CMISE ISO 9595/9596	
ACSE ISO IS 8649/8650	ROSE ISO DIS 9072-1/2
ISO Presentation ISO 8822 8823	
ISO Session ISO 8326 8327	
ISO Transportation ISO 8073	

Related Protocols

TCP, UDP, IP, CMIP, CMIS, ACSE, ROSE, CMISE

Sponsor Source

CMOT is defined by ISO (www.iso.org) and IETF (www.itu.org).

Reference

http://www.javvin.com/protocol/rfc1189.pdf
The Common Management Information Services and Protocols for the Internet (CMOT and CMIP)

ISO FTAM: File Transfer Access and Management protocol

Protocol Description

The File Transfer Access and Management protocol (FTAM), an ISO application protocol, offers file transfer services between client (initiator) and server (responder) systems in an open environment. FTAM also provides access to files and management of files on diverse systems. Similar to FTP File Transfer Protocol) and NFS (Network File System) in the TCP/IP environment, FTAM is designed to help users access files on diverse systems that use compatible FTAM implementations.

FTAM is a system in which connection-oriented information about the user and the session is maintained by a server until the session is taken down. Files are transferred between systems by first establishing a connection-oriented session. The FTAM client contacts the FTAM server and requests a session. Once the session is established, file transfer can take place. FTAM uses the concept of a virtual filestore, which provides a common view of files. The FTAM file system hides the differences between different vendor systems. FTAM specifies document types as files with straight binary information or text files in which each line is terminated with a carriage return. Data is interpreted as records and FTAM provides the virtual filestore capabilities that store record-oriented structured files. With FTAM, users can manipulate files down to the record level, which is how FTAM stores files. In this respect, FTAM has some relational database features. For example, users can lock files or lock individual records.

FTAM provides the following FTAM service classes:

• The transfer service class allows the exchange of files or parts of files. It generally includes the simple basic file transfer tasks, allowing single operations with a minimum number of interactions.
• The access service class allows the initiating system to perform several operations on individual FADUs or on the whole file.
• The management service class allows the user control over the virtual filestore in order to create or delete files, read and modify attributes etc..
• The transfer-and-management service class combines the capabilities of the transfer service class with those of the limited file management functional unit to support directory navigation and simple functions. (See below for the functional units.)

Protocol Structure

All commands are in the format of ASN.1 messages. FTAM defines the following functional units :

• kernel functional unit
• read functional unit
• write functional unit
• file access functional unit
• limited file management functional unit
• enhanced file management functional unit
• grouping functional unit
• FADU locking functional unit
• recovery functional unit
• restart functional unit

FTAM has the following key user facilities to operate files locally and remotely:

• FTAM appending facility (APPEND/APPLICATION_PROTOCOL = FTAM) - enables user to append one or more input files to a single output file, within or between FTAM applications.
• FTAM copying facility (COPY/APPLICATION_PROTOCOL = FTAM) - enables user to copy one or more input files to a single output file, within or between FTAM applications.
• FTAM deletion facility (DELETE/APPLICATION_PROTOCOL = FTAM) - enables user to delete files
• FTAM directory facility (DIRECTORY/APPLICATION_PROTOCOL = FTAM) - enables user to display file attributes for one or more files
• FTAM renaming facility (RENAME/APPLICATION_PROTOCOL = FTAM) - enables user to rename files.

Related Protocols

IS-SP, ISO-PP, ROSE, ACSE, FTP, NFS

Sponsor Source

FTAM is defined in ISO (www.iso.org) documents 8571.

Reference

http://www.nhsia.nhs.uk/napps/step/pages/ithandbook/h232-6.htm
OSI File Transfer Access and Management (FTAM) Standard

ISO ROSE: Remote Operations Service Element Protocol

Protocol Description

The ISO Remote Operations Service Element Protocol (ROSE) is a protocol that provides remote operation capabilities, allows interaction between entities in a distributed application, and upon receiving a remote operations service request, allows the receiving entity to attempt the operation and report the results of the attempt to the requesting entity. The ROSE protocol itself is only a vehicle for conveying the arguments and results of the operation as defined by the application.

In the OSI environment, communication between application processes is represented in terms of communication between a pair of application entities (AEs) using the presentation service. Communication between some application-entities is inherently interactive. Typically, one entity requests that a particular operation be performed; the other entity attempts to perform the operation and then reports the outcome of the attempt. The generic structure of an operation is an elementary request/reply interaction. Operations are carried out within the context of an application-association.

Operations invoked by one AE (the invoker) are performed by the other AE (the performer). Operations may be classified according to whether the performer of an operation is expected to report its outcome. Operations may also be classified according to two possible operation modes: synchronous, in which the invoker requires a reply from the performer before invoking another operation; and asynchronous, in which the invoker may continue to invoke further operations without awaiting a reply.

The remote-operation-protocol-machine (ROPM) communicates with its service-user by means of primitives. Each invocation of the ROPM controls a single application-association. The ROPM is driven by ROSE service request primitives from its service-user, and by indication and confirm primitives of the RTSE services, or the presentation-service. The ROPM, in turn, issues indication primitives to its service-user, and request primitives on the RTSE services being used, or on the presentation-service.

The reception of an ROSE service primitive, or of an RTSE service or of a presentation-service primitive, and the generation of dependent actions are considered to be individual. During the exchange of APDUs, the existence of both, the association-initiating AE and the association- responding AE is presumed. During the execution of operations, the existence of an application-association between the peer AEs is presumed.

ROSE services summary

Service	Type

Protocol Structure

ROSE messages:

RO-INVOKE	Non-confirmed
RO-RESULT	Non-confirmed
RO-ERROR	Non-confirmed
RO-REJECT-U	Non-confirmed
RO-REJECT-P	Provider-initiated

ROSE Incoming event list

Abbreviated name	Source	Name and description
AA-ESTAB	RTSE	positive RT-OPEN response primitive or positive RT-OPEN confirm primitive
	ACSE	positive A-ASSOCIATE response primitive or positive A-ASSOCIATE confirm-primitive
RO-INVreq	ROSE-user	RO-INVOKE request primitive
RO-RESreq	ROSE-user	RO-RESULT request primitive
RO-ERRreq	ROSE-user	RO-ERROR request primitive
RO-RJUreq	ROSE-user	RO-REJECT-U request primitive
ROIV	ROPM-peer	valid RO-INVOKE APDU as user data on a TRANSind event
RORS	ROPM-peer	valid RO-RESULT APDU as user data on a TRANSind event
ROER	ROPM-peer	valid RO-ERROR APDU as user data on a TRANSind event
RORJu	ROPM-peer	valid RO-REJECT APDU (user-reject) as user data on a TRANSind event
RORJp	ROPM-peer	valid RO-REJECT APDU (provider-reject with General-problem) as user data on a TRANSind event
APDUua	ROPM-peer	unacceptable APDU as user data on a TRANSind event
TRANSind	ROPM-TR	transfer indication of an APDU
TRANSreq	ROPM	transfer request for an APDU
P-DATAind	PS-provider	P-DATA indication primitive
RT-TRind	RTSE	RT-TRANSFER indication primitive
RT-TRcnf+	RTSE	positive RT-TRANSFER confirm primitive
RT-TRcnf-	RTSE	negative RT-TRANSFER confirm primitive
RT-TPind	RTSE	RT-TURN-PLEASE indication primitive

RT-TGind	RTSE	RT-TURN-GIVE indication primitive
	RTSE	RT-CLOSE response primitive or RT-CLOSE confirm primitive
AA-REL	ACSE	positive A-RELEASE response primitive or A-RELEASE confirm primitive
	ROPM	abort application association
AA-ABreq	ROPM-TR	application association aborted
AA-ABind	RTSE	RT-P-ABORT indication primitive or the RT-U-ABORT indication primitive
ABORTind	ACSE	A-ABORT indication primitive or A-P-ABORT indication primitive

ROSE Outgoing event list

Abbreviated name	Target	Name and description
RO-IN-Vind	ROSE-user	RO-INVOKE indication primitive
RO-RESind	ROSE-user	RO-RESULT indication primitive
RO-ERR-ind	ROSE-user	RO-ERROR indication primitive
RO-RJUind	ROSE-user	RO-REJECT-U indication primitive
RO-RJPind	ROSE-user	RO-REJECT-P indication primitive
ROIV	ROPM-peer	RO-INVOKE APDU as user data on a TRANSreq event
RORS	ROPM-peer	RO-RESULT APDU as user data on a TRANSreq event
ROER	ROPM-peer	RO-ERROR APDU as user data on a TRANSreq event
RORJu	ROPM-peer	RO-REJECT user-reject APDU as user-data on a TRANSreq event
RORJp	ROPM-peer	RO-REJECT provider-reject APDU as user data on a TRANSreq event
TRAN-Sreq	ROPM-TR	transfer request for an APDU
TRAN-Sind	ROPM	transfer indication of an APDU
P-DA-TAreq	PS-provider	P-DATA request primitive
RT-TRreq	RTSE	RT-TRANSFER request primitive
RT-TPreq	RTSE	RT-TURN-PLEASE request primitive
RT-TGreq	RTSE	RT-TURN-GIVE request primitive
AA-ABreq	ROPM-TR	abort application association
AA-ABind	ROPM	application association aborted

ABOR-Treq	RTSE	RT-U-ABORT request primitive
	ACSE	A-ABORT request primitive

Related Protocols
ISO-PP, ISO-SP, ACSE

Sponsor Source
ROSE is defined in ISO (www.iso.org) documents 9072 and ITU (www.itu.org) documents X.229 and X.219.

Reference
http://www.doc.ua.pt/arch/itu/rec/product/X.htm
X.219: Remote Operations: Model, notation and service definition
X.229: Remote Operations: Protocol specification

ISO RTSE: Reliable Transfer Service Element Protocol

Protocol Description

Reliable Transfer Service Element (RTSE), an ISO application layer protocol, provides for the reliable transfer of bulk data by transforming the data into a string of octets, then breaking the string into segments and handing each segment to the Presentation Layer for delivery. Checkpoints are established between segments. Through the services of the Presentation Layer, RTSE uses the activity management services of the Session Layer to manage the transfer of the collection of segments that makes up the bulk data. Activity and minor synchronization facilities of the Session Layer support interruption and possible resumption of data transfer if the underlying network connection is lost.

RTSE is used in the X.400 Message Handling Service (MHS) and is available for use by ROSE when remote operations require reliable transfer. Because of its use in X.400, RTSE is widely available.

Typically the Transport layer is supposed to ensure reliable delivery but this is insufficient for two reasons: 1) No class of transport protocol will recover from a failure of the underlying network, which results in the required QOS (Quality of Service) not being met. Under these circumstances, the underlying connection will be lost. 2) For historical reasons, MHS was designed to operate over TP0 which provides no recovery at all from signalled errors (including X.25 resets). In the event of either an X.25 reset or a disconnect, TP0 terminates the underlying connection.

RTSE is required to re-establish the failed underlying failed connection and to repeat the transmission attempt, transparently to the user. However, RTSE cannot guarantee delivery if success cannot be achieved within a given time, RTSE will report failure. This may occur if there is a catastrophic failure either of the underlying network or of the peer application, which clearly neither RTSE nor any other ASE (Application Service Element) can do anything positive about.

RTSE is not viable on its own. RTSE has no knowledge of the context of the PDU which it is attempting to deliver, nor indeed would it have anything to deliver. There must be an 'RTSE user' which understands what RTSE is being used for, typically a MHS service element using ROSE.

RTSE uses Session Layer Activities for the following reasons: Each PDU (e.g. message) and the response confirming (or otherwise) its successful delivery are encapsulated within dialogue units (major synchronisation points). RTSE may also insert minor synchronization points at suitable intervals during the activity, as it sees fit. An activity may be interrupted in the event of minor errors occurring, and can be resumed later. In the case of more severe errors, such as loss of the application association itself, the activity may need to be discarded and in this case the transaction will start again from scratch at a later time, in a new activity.

Protocol Structure

RTSE Service Summary

Service	Type
RT-OPEN	Confirmed
RT-CLOSE	Confirmed
RT-TRANSFER	Confirmed
RT-TURN-PLEASE	Non-confirmed
RT-TURN-GIVE	Non-confirmed
RT-P-ABORT	Provider-initiated
RT-U-ABORT	Non-confirmed

Related Protocols

ISO-SP, ISO-PP, ROSE, ACSE, X.400

Sponsor Source

RTSE is defined in ISO (www.iso.org) documents 9066 and ITU (www.itu.org) documents X.228 and X.218.

Reference

http://www.doc.ua.pt/arch/itu/rec/product/X.htm
X.218: Reliable Transfer: Model and service definition
X.228: Reliable Transfer: Protocol specification

ISO VTP: ISO Virtual Terminal (VT) Protocol

Protocol Description

The ISO Virtual Terminal (VT) service and protocol (VTP) allows a host application to control a terminal with screen and keyboard and similar devices like printers. In addition, VTP also supports the less common application-application and terminal-terminal communication.

VTP is comparable to Telnet in the TCP/IP suite but more powerful. VTP also includes control of cursor movement, colors, character sets and attributes, access rights, synchronization, multiple pages, facility negotiation, etc. This means that the huge number of classic terminal type definitions (e.g. in UNIX termcap or terminfo) are unnecessary at each host in the net, as the VT protocol includes the corresponding commands for one abstract virtual terminal that only have to be converted by the local implementation to the actual terminal control sequences. Consequently, the use of VT means not every host needs to know every type of terminal.

As with most ISO standards that require general consensus amongst participating members, the OSI VT has many optional capabilities, two modes of operation and an almost infinite number of implementation-specific options. Profiles may help in reducing the optionality present (e.g., there exists a Telnet profile for VT), but it is doubtful if the OSI VT can completely put an end to the 'm x n' terminal incompatibility problem that exists in a heterogeneous computer network.

Related Protocols

ISP-PP, Telnet

Sponsor Source

ISO VTP is defined in ISO (www.iso.org) documents 9040, 9041.

X.400: Message Handling Service Protocol

Protocol Description

X.400 is the Message Handling Service protocol for email transmission specified by the ITU-T and ISO. X.400 is common in Europe and Canada and is an alternative to the more popular email protocol, Simple Mail Transfer Protocol (SMTP), which is defined by IETF. X.400 uses a binary format so it is easy to include binary contents without encoding it for transfer. Also, it is harder for people to fake email addresses and contents than with SMTP, where text messages are used.

X.400 and SMTP have not only similar but also unique features in themselves. Generally speaking, X.400 is a more complex protocol with the following features that are not in the SMTP:

• Delivery notifications -- Delivery notifications are used both about delivery notifications (yes, the message got here) and about non-delivery notifications (no, the message did not get there).
• Receipt notifications -- A receipt notification is passed back to the originating user indicating what happened to the message after it was delivered (for instance that it was read by the recipient). In X.400, receipt and non-receipt notifications may include notifications of something being automatically forwarded, messages deleted, etc.
• Security functions -- X.400 defines a framework for mail transmission securities. It defines the concept of a "security label" and allows using an OID for identifying your security labeling scheme, but no labeling scheme is actually specified in the protocol.
• Priority markers (3 levels) -- This feature is used for ordering the queue of mails to send, so that "important" mails get sent before "less important" mails.
• Deferred delivery -- Schedule delivery time for messages. This feature has not been widely deployed.
• Conversion in the network -- such as converting Teletex to plain text, or fax images to text saying "there was a picture here, but you are not allowed to see it". Conversion never improves a message, and it is impossible to support security functions like signatures or encryption while doing conversion in the network.
• Reliable Transfer Service -- This X.400 feature gives the ability to continue transferring a document after the transfer is interrupted.

SMTP has some functions that X.400 does not, including the following:

• Standard functionality to check each recipient for validity before transferring the message; X.400 requires transferring the complete message before checking recipients.
• Optional functionality for checking whether a message is too large to transfer before sending it.
• Ability to insert any data into the header of a message with a fair probability of it being presented to the user
• Ability (MIME Multipart/Alternative) to send several representations of the same content in the same message, guaranteeing both interoperability with the lowest common denominator

and no loss of information between compatible UAs.

In addition, an X.400 address is different from that of an SMTP. X.400 consists of a set of bindings for country (c), administrative domain (a), primary management domain (p), surname (s) and given name (g). An SMTP e-mail address that looks like this hypothetical address: some.name@javvin.subdomain.us looks like this in an X.400 e-mail message:

G=some; S=name; O=subdomain; OU=javvin; PRMD=attmail; ADMD=attmail; C=US

Protocol Structure

X.400 was designed with attributed addresses. The complete set of attributes is rather large:

Attribute Type	Abbreviation	Label
Given Name	Given Name	G
Initial	Initials	I
Surname	Surname	S
Generation Qualifier	Generation	Q
Common Name	Common Name	CN
Organization	Organization	O
Organizational Unit 1	Org.Unit.1	OU1
Organizational Unit 2	Org.Unit.2	OU2
Organizational Unit 3	Org.Unit.3	OU3
Organizational Unit 4	Org.Unit.4	OU4
Private Management Domain Name	PRMD	P
Administration Management Domain Name	ADMD	A
Country	Country	C
Physical Delivery Personal Name	PD-person	PD-PN
Extension of Postal O/R Address Components	PD-ext. address	PD-EA
Extension of Physical Delivery Address Components	PD-ext. delivery	PD-ED
Physical Delivery Office Number	PD-office number	PD-OFN
Physical Delivery Office Name	PD-office	PD-OF
Physical Delivery Organization Name	PD-organization	PD-O
Street Address	PD-street	PD-S
Unformatted Postal Address	PD-address	PD-A1
(there are individual labels for each line of the address)		PD-A2
		PD-A3
		PD-A4
		PD-A5
		PD-A6

Unique Postal Name	PD-unique	PD-U
Local Postal Attributes	PD-local	PD-L
Postal Restante Address	PD-restante	PD-R
Post Office Box Address	PD-box	PD-B
Postal Code	PD-code	PD-PC
Physical Delivery Service Name	PD-service	PD-SN
Physical Delivery Country Name	PD-country	PD-C
X.121 Network Address	X.121	X.121
E.163/E.164 Network Address	ISDN	ISDN
PSAP Network Address	PSAP	PSAP
User Agent Numeric ID	N-ID	N-ID
Terminal Identifier	T-ID	T-ID
Terminal Type	T-TY	T-TY
Domain Defined AttributE	DDA:	DDA:

Related Protocols

SMTP, MIME, IMAP/IMAP4, POP/POP3

Sponsor Source

X.400 protocol is defined by ISO (www.iso.org) and ITU-T (www.itu.org).

Reference

http://www.itu.int/rec/recommendation.asp?type=products&parent=T-REC-f
X.400 Standards List
http://www.doc.ua.pt/arch/itu/rec/product/X.htm
X.402: Information technology - Message Handling Systems (MHS) - Overall Architecture
X.404: Information technology - Message Handling Systems (MHS): MHS routing - Guide for messaging systems managers

X.500: Directory Access Protocol (DAP)

Protocol Description

X.500, the directory Access Protocol by ITU-T (X.500) and also ISO (ISO/IEC 9594), is a standard way to develop an electronic directory of people in an organization so that it can be part of a global directory available to anyone in the world with Internet access.

In the X.500 directory architecture, the client queries and receives responses from one or more servers in the server Directory Service with the Directory Access Protocol (DAP) controlling the communication between the client and the server.

A Directory System Agent (DSA) is the database in which the directory information is stored. This database is hierarchical in form, designed to provide fast and efficient search and retrieval. The DSAs are interconnected from the Directory Information Tree (DIT). The user interface program for access to one or more DSAs is a Directory User Agent (DUA). DUAs include whois, finger, and programs that offer a graphical user interface.

The Directory System Protocol (DSP) controls the interaction between two or more Directory System Agents, and between a Directory User Agent and a Directory System Agent. This is done in such a way that an end user can access information in the Directory without needing to know the exact location of that specific piece of information.

X.500 offers the following key features:

• Decentralized Maintenance: Each site running X.500 is responsible ONLY for its local part of the Directory, so updates and maintenance can be done instantly.
• Powerful Searching Capabilities: X.500 provides powerful searching facilities that allow users to construct arbitrarily complex queries.
• Single Global Namespace: Much like the DNS, X.500 provides a single homogeneous namespace to users. The X.500 namespace is more flexible and expandable than the DNS.
• Structured Information Framework: X.500 defines the information framework used in the Directory, allowing local extensions.
• Standards-Based Directory Services: As X.500 can be used to build a standards-based directory, applications which require directory information (e-mail, automated resources locators, special-purpose directory tools) can access a planet's worth of information in a uniform manner.

X.500 is criticized as being too complex for most implementations. To address the issue, the University of Michigan developed a simpler TCP/IP-based version of DAP, the Lightweight Directory Access Protocol (LDAP), for use on the Internet. LDAP offers much of the same basic functionality as DAP and can be used to query data from proprietary directories as well as from an open X.500 service. Within the past year, most major suppliers of e-mail and directory-services software have expressed interest in LDAP, which is fast becoming a de facto directory protocol for the Internet.

Protocol Structure

X.500 has a complex data structure in the directory database and for its communication protocols such as DAP. One should read the specification documents from ISO and ITU.

Related Protocols

LDAP, DNS, Finger

Sponsor Source

X.500 (DAP) protocol is defined by ISO (www.iso.org) and ITU-T (www.itu.org).

Reference

http://www.javvin.com/protocol/rfc1308.pdf
Executive Introduction to Directory Services Using the X.500 Protocol
http://www.javvin.com/protocol/rfc1309.pdf
Technical Overview of Directory Services Using the X.500 Protocol

ASN.1: Abstract Syntax Notation One

Protocol Description

Abstract Syntax Notation One (ASN.1), an ISO/ITU-T standard, describes data structures for representing, encoding, transmitting, and decoding data. It provides a set of formal rules for describing the structure of objects regardless of language implementation and physical representation of these data, whatever the application, whether complex or very simple.

ASN.1 sends information in any form (audio, video, data, etc.) anywhere it needs to be communicated digitally. ASN.1 only covers the structural aspects of information. ASN.1 together with specific ASN.1 encoding rules facilitates the exchange of structured data especially between application programs over networks by describing data structures in a way that is independent of machine architecture and implementation language.

Application layer protocols in ISO protocol suite such as X.400 for electronic mail, X.500 for directory services, H.323 (VoIP) and SNMP use ASN.1 to describe the PDUs they exchange. It is also extensively used in the Access and Non-Access Strata of UMTS.

One of the main reasons for the success of ASN.1 is that it is associated with several standardized encoding rules such as the Basic Encoding Rules (BER) - X.209, Canonical Encoding Rules (CER), Distinguished Encoding Rules (DER), Packed Encoding Rules (PER), and XER Encoding Rules (XER). These encoding rules describe how the values defined in ASN.1 should be encoded for transmission, regardless of machine, programming language, or how it is represented in an application program. ASN.1's encodings are more streamlined than many competing notations, enabling rapid and reliable transmission of extensible messages - an advantage for wireless broadband. Because ASN.1 has been an international standard since 1984, its encoding rules are mature and have a long track record of reliability and interoperability.

The compact binary encoding rules (BER, CER, DER, PER, but not XER) are considered alternatives to the more modern XML. However, the ASN.1 allows to describe the data semantics, not only the transfer encoding syntax, so it is a higher level language than XML.

An ASN.1 definition can be readily mapped into a C or C++ or Java data-structure that can be used by application code, and supported by run-time libraries providing encoding and decoding of representations in either an XML or a TLV format, or a very compact packed encoding format.

Protocol Structure

ASN.1 provides a certain number of pre-defined basic types:

• UNIVERSAL 0 -- Reserved for use by the encoding rules
• UNIVERSAL 1 -- Boolean type
• UNIVERSAL 2 -- Integer type
• UNIVERSAL 3 -- Bitstring type
• UNIVERSAL 4 -- Octetstring type
• UNIVERSAL 5 -- Null type
• UNIVERSAL 6 -- Object identifier type
• UNIVERSAL 7 -- Object descriptor type
• UNIVERSAL 8 -- External type and Instance-of type
• UNIVERSAL 9 -- Real type
• UNIVERSAL 10 -- Enumerated type
• UNIVERSAL 11 -- Embedded-pdv type
• UNIVERSAL 12 -- UTF8String type
• UNIVERSAL 13 -- Relative object identifier type
• UNIVERSAL 14-15 -- Reserved for future editions of this Recommendation | International Standard
• UNIVERSAL 16 -- Sequence and Sequence-of types
• UNIVERSAL 17 -- Set and Set-of types
• UNIVERSAL 18-22, 25-30 -- Character string types
• UNIVERSAL 23-24 -- Time types
• UNIVERSAL 31-... -- Reserved for addenda to this Recommendation | International Standard

ASN.1 also makes it possible to define constructed types such as:

• structures (SEQUENCE),
• lists (SEQUENCE OF),
• choice between types (CHOICE),
• etc.

Related Protocols

XML, X.400, X.500, H.323

Sponsor Source

ASN.1 is defined by ITU/ISO in ITU X.680 or ISO/IEC 8824

Reference

http://www.javvin.com/protocol/ASN1X680.pdf
OSI networking and system aspects – Abstract Syntax Notation One (ASN.1)

ISO-PP: OSI Presentation Protocol

Protocol Description

The OSI presentation layer protocol (ISO-PP) is for the information transit between open systems using connection oriented or connectionless mode transmission at the presentation layer of the OSI 7 layer model. An application protocol is specified in terms of the transfer of presentation data values between application entities (PS users), using the User data parameter of presentation service primitives.

The Presentation Layer has two functions it carries out on behalf of PS users:

a) negotiation of transfer syntaxes;
b) transformation to and from transfer syntax.

The function of transfer syntax negotiation is supported by presentation protocols. Transformation of syntax is a function contained within a presentation entity and has no impact on presentation protocol design. For connectionless mode transmission, the sending presentation entity selects the transfer syntaxes. No transfer syntax negotiation occurs.

A set of presentation data value definitions associated with an application protocol constitutes an abstract syntax. For two application entities to communicate successfully they must have an agreement on the set of abstract syntaxes they intend to use. During the course of communication they may decide to modify this agreement. As a consequence, the set of abstract syntaxes in use may be changed. The abstract syntax specification identifies the information content of the set of presentation data values. It does not identify the transfer syntax to be used while presentation data values are transferred between presentation entities, nor is it concerned with the local representation of presentation data values.

The Presentation Layer exists to ensure that the information content of presentation data values is preserved during transfer. It is the responsibility of cooperating application entities to determine the set of abstract syntaxes they employ in their communication and inform the presentation entities of this agreement. Knowing the set of abstract syntaxes to be used by the application entities, the presentation entities are responsible for selecting mutually acceptable transfer syntaxes that preserve the information content of presentation data values. For connectionless mode transmission, the abstract syntaxes used are determined by the sending application entity. For successful communication to take place, these must be acceptable to the receiving application entity.

For connectionless mode transmission, the presentation entities do not negotiate transfer syntaxes. The transfer syntaxes used are determined by the sending application entity. For successful communication to take place, these must be acceptable to the receiving application entity. The abstract syntaxes and the associated transfer syntaxes may be explicitly stated in the "Presentation context definition list" parameter as a user option.

Presentation entities support protocols that enhance the OSI session service in order to provide a presentation service. The PS user is provided with access to the session service which permits full use to be made of that service. This includes negotiation of and access to the session functional units. The role of the Presentation Layer in providing this access includes representation of presentation data values in the User data parameters of session service primitives.

Protocol Structure

The major presentation primitives:

Connection Release Primitive	Token Handling Primitive
P-RELEASE request P-RELEASE indication P-RELEASE response P-RELEASE confirm	P-TOKEN-GIVE request P-TOKEN-GIVE indication P-TOKEN-PLEASE request P-TOKEN-PLEASE indication P-CONTROL-GIVE request P-CONTROL-GIVE indication

Presentation Exception Reporting Primitive	Activity Management Primitive
P-P-EXCEPTION-RE-PORT indication P-U-EXCEPTION-RE-PORT request P-U-EXCEPTION-RE-PORT indication	P-ACTIVITY-START request P-ACTIVITY-START indication P-ACTIVITY-RESUME request P-ACTIVITY-RESUME indication P-ACTIVITY-INTERRUPT request P-ACTIVITY-INTERRUPT indication P-ACTIVITY-NTERRUPT response P-ACTIVITY-INTERRUPT confirm P-ACTIVITY-DISCARD request P-ACTIVITY-DISCARD indication P-ACTIVITY-DISCARD response P-ACTIVITY-DISCARD confirm P-ACTIVITY-END request P-ACTIVITY-END indication P-ACTIVITY-END response P-ACTIVITY-END confirm
Synchronization Services Primitive	
P-SYNC-MINOR request P-SYNC-MINOR indication P-SYNC-MINOR response P-SYNC-MINOR confirm P-SYNC-MAJOR request P-SYNC-MAJOR indication P-SYNC-MAJOR response P-SYNC-MAJOR confirm	

Related Protocols

ISO-TP, ISO-SP, ACSE, ROSE

Sponsor Source

The ISO-PP (OSI Presentation Layer protocol) is defined in ISO (www.iso.org) documents 8823, 8822 and ITU (www.itu.org) documents X.226, X.216 and X.236.

Reference

http://www.doc.ua.pt/arch/itu/rec/product/X.htm
X.226: Information technology - Open Systems Interconnec-

tion - Connection-oriented
Presentation protocol: Protocol specification
X.216: Information technology - Open Systems Interconnection - Presentation service definition
X.236: Information technology - Open Systems Interconnection - Connectionless Presentation protocol: Protocol specification

ISO-SP: OSI Session Protocol

Protocol Description

The OSI Session Protocol (ISO-SP) provides session management, e.g. opening and closing of sessions. In case of a connection loss it tries to recover the connection. If a connection is not used for a longer period, the session layer may close it down and re-open it for next use. This happens transparently to the higher layers. The Session layer provides synchronization points in the stream of exchanged packets.

The Session Protocol Machine (SPM), an abstract machine that carries out the procedures specified in the session layer protocol, communicates with the session service user (SS-user) through an session-service-access-point (SSAP) by means of the service primitives. Service primitives will cause or be the result of session protocol data unit exchanges between the peer SPMs using a transport connection. These protocol exchanges are effected using the services of the transport layer. Session connection endpoints are identified in end systems by an internal, implementation dependent, mechanism so that the SS-user and the SPM can refer to each session connection.

The functions in the Session Layer are those necessary to bridge the gap between the services available from the Transport Layer and those offered to the SS-users.

The functions in the Session Layer are concerned with dialogue management, data flow synchronization, and data flow resynchronization.

These functions are described below; the descriptions are grouped into those concerned with the connection establishment phase, the data transfer phase, and the release phase.

Protocol Structure

ISO Session Layer Protocol Messages:

Functional unit	SPDU code	SPDU name
Kernel	CN OA CDO AC RF FN DN AB AA DT PR	CONNECT OVERFLOW ACCEPT CONNECT DATA OVERFLOW ACCEPT REFUSE FINISH DISCONNECT ABORT ABORT ACCEPT DATA TRANSFER PREPARE
Negotiated release	NF GT PT	NOT FINISHED GIVE TOKENS PLEASE TOKENS

Half-duplex	GT PT	GIVE TOKENS PLEASE TOKENS
Duplex		No additional associated SPDUs
Expedited data	EX	EXPEDITED DATA
Typed data	TD	TYPED DATA
Capability data exchange	CD CDA	CAPABILITY DATA CAPABILITY DATA ACK
Minor synchronize	MIP MIA GT PT	MINOR SYNC POINT MINOR SYNC ACK GIVE TOKENS PLEASE TOKENS
Symmetric synchronize	MIP MIA	MINOR SYNC POINT MINOR SYNC ACK
Data separation		No additional associated SPDUs
Major synchronize	MAP MAA PR GT PT	MAJOR SYNC POINT MAJOR SYNC ACK PREPARE GIVE TOKENS PLEASE TOKENS
Resynchronize	RS RA PR	RESYNCHRONIZE RESYNCHRONIZE ACK PREPARE
Exceptions	ER ED	EXCEPTION REPORT EXCEPTION DATA
Activity management	AS AR AI AIA AD ADA AE AEA PR GT PT GTC GTA	ACTIVITY START ACTIVITY RESUME ACTIVITY INTERRUPT ACTIVITY INTERRUPT ACK ACTIVITY DISCARD ACTIVITY DISCARD ACK ACTIVITY END ACTIVITY END ACK PREPARE GIVE TOKENS PLEASE TOKENS GIVE TOKENS CONFIRM GIVE TOKENS ACK

Related Protocols

ISO-TP, ISO-PP, CONP, CLNP

Sponsor Source

The ISO-SP (OSI Session Layer protocol) is defined in ISO (www.iso.org) documents 8326 and 8327 and ITU (www.itu.org) documents X.215, X.225, X.235.

Reference

http://www.doc.ua.pt/arch/itu/rec/product/X.htm
X.215: Information technology - Open Systems Interconnection - Session service definition
X.225: Information technology - Open Systems Interconnection - Connection-oriented Session protocol: Protocol specification
X.235: Information technology - Open Systems Interconnection - Connectionless Session protocol: Protocol specification

ISO-TP: OSI Transport Layer Protocols TP0, TP1, TP2, TP3, TP4

Protocol Description

The OSI Transport layer protocol (ISO-TP) manages end-to-end control and error checking to ensure complete data transfer. It performs transport address to network address mapping, makes multiplexing and splitting of transport connections, and also provides functions such as Sequencing, Flow Control and Error detection and recover.

Five transport layer protocols exist in the ISO-TP, ranging from Transport Protocol Class 0 through Transport Protocol Class 4 (TP0, TP1, TP2, TP3 & TP4). The protocols increase in complexity from 0-4. TP0-3 works only with connection-oriented communications, in which a session connection must be established before any data is sent; TP4 also works with both connection-oriented and connectionless communications.

Transport Protocol Class 0 (TP0) performs segmentation (fragmentation) and reassembly functions. TP0 discerns the size of the smallest maximum protocol data unit (PDU) supported by any of the underlying networks, and segments the packets accordingly. The packet segments are reassembled at the receiver.

Transport Protocol Class 1 (TP1) performs segmentation (fragmentation) and reassembly, plus error recovery. TP1 sequences protocol data units (PDUs) and will retransmit PDUs or reinitiate the connection if an excessive number of PDUs are unacknowledged.

Transport Protocol Class 2 (TP2) performs segmentation and reassembly, as well as multiplexing and demultiplexing of data streams over a single virtual circuit.

Transport Protocol Class 3 (TP3) offers error recovery, segmentation and reassembly, and multiplexing and demultiplexing of data streams over a single virtual circuit. TP3 also sequences PDUs and retransmits them or reinitiates the connection if an excessive number are unacknowledged.

Transport Protocol Class 4 (TP4) offers error recovery, performs segmentation and reassembly, and supplies multiplexing and demultiplexing of data streams over a single virtual circuit. TP4 sequences PDUs and retransmits them or reinitiates the connection if an excessive number are unacknowledged. TP4 provides reliable transport service and functions with either connection-oriented or connectionless network service. TP4 is the most commonly used of all the OSI transport protocols and is similar to the Transmission Control Protocol (TCP) in the TCP/IP suite.

Both TP4 and TCP are built to provide a reliable connection oriented end-to-end transport service on top of an unreliable network service. The network service may loose packets, store them, deliver them in the wrong order or even duplicate packets. Both protocols have to be able to deal with the most severe problems e.g. a subnetwork stores valid packets and sends them at a later date. TP4 and TCP have a connect, transfer and a disconnect phase. The principles of doing this are also quite similar.

One difference between TP4 and TCP that should be mentioned is that TP4 uses ten different TPDU (Transport Protocol Data Unit) types whereas TCP knows only one. This makes TCP simple but every TCP header has to have all possible fields and therefore the TCP header is at least 20 bytes long whereas the TP4 header maybe as little as 5 bytes. Another difference is the way both protocols react in case of a call collision. TP4 opens two bidirectional connections between the TSAPs whereas TCP opens just one connection. TP4 uses a different flow control mechanism for its messages. It also provides means for quality of service measurement.

Protocol Structure

The OSI transport protocols are quite complicated in terms of their structure, which has 10 different types, each with its own header and PDU structure. The ten types are:

• CR -- Connection Request. The header of this type of message has 7 bytes and the length of the entire TPDU is a variable.
• CC -- Connection Confirm. The header of this type of message has 7 bytes and the length of the entire TPDU is a variable.
• DR -- Disconnect Request. The header of this type of message has 7 bytes and the length of the entire TPDU is a variable.
• DC -- Disconnect Confirm. The header of this type of message has 6 bytes and the length of the entire TPDU is a variable.
• DT -- Data TPDU. The header of this type of message has 3 bytes and the length of the entire TPDU is a variable.
• ED -- Expedited Data TPDU. The header of this type of message has 5 bytes and the length of the entire TPDU is a variable.
• DA -- Data Acknowledgement TPDU. The header of this type of message has 5 bytes and the length of the entire TPDU is a variable.
• EA -- Expedited Data Acknowledgement TPDU. The header of this type of message has 5 bytes and the length of the entire TPDU is a variable.
• RT -- Reject TPDU. The header of this type of message has 5 bytes.
• ER -- Error TPDU. The header of this type of message has 5 bytes and the length of the entire TPDU is a variable.

Related Protocols

IS-IS, CLNP, IDRP, CONP, ES-IS, ISO-SP, ISO-PP

Sponsor Source

CONP is defined in ISO (www.iso.org) 8208 and 8878 and ITU (www.itu.org) X.214, X.224 and X.234.

Reference

http://www.doc.ua.pt/arch/itu/rec/product/X.htm
X.214: Open System Interconnection Protocols Information technology - Open Systems Interconnection - Transport service definition
X.224: Information technology - Open Systems Interconnection - Protocol for providing the connection-mode transport service
X.234: Information technology - Protocol for providing the OSI connectionless-mode transport service

Network Layer

CLNP: Connectionless Network Protocol (ISO-IP)

Protocol Description

Connectionless Network Protocol (CLNP) is an ISO network layer datagram protocol by the layers defined in the Reference Model for Open Systems Interconnection (ISO 7498). CLNP provides fundamentally the same underlying service to a transport layer as IP in the TCP/IP environment. Therefore, CLNP is also called ISO-IP. Another OSI protocol in the network layer is CONP (Connection-Oriented Network Protocol), which provides connection-oriented services at the network layer.

CLNP may be used between network-entities in end systems or in Network Layer relay systems (or both). CLNP provides the Connectionless-mode Network Service. CLNP is intended for use in the Subnetwork Independent Convergence Protocol (SNICP) role, which operates to construct the OSI Network Service over a defined set of underlying services, performing functions necessary to support the uniform appearance of the OSI Connectionless-mode Network Service over a homogeneous or heterogeneous set of interconnected subnetworks. CLNP is defined to accommodate variability where Subnetwork Dependent Convergence Protocols and/or Subnetwork Access Protocols do not provide all of the functions necessary to support the Connectionless-mode Network Service over all or part of the path from one NSAP to another. CLNP may also be used to fulfill other roles and may therefore be used in the context of other approaches to subnetwork interconnection.

CLNP uses NSAP addresses and titles to identify network devices. The Source Address and Destination Address parameters are OSI Network Service Access Point Addresses (NSAP addresses). A network-entity title is an identifier for a network-entity in an end-system or intermediate-system. Network-entity titles are allocated from the same name space as NSAP addresses, and the determination of whether an address is an NSAP address or a network-entity title depends on the context in which the address is interpreted.

CLNP provides the same maximum datagram size as IP, and for those circumstances where datagrams may need to traverse a network whose maximum packet size is smaller than the size of the datagram, CLNP provides mechanisms for fragmentation (data unit identification, fragment/total length and offset). Like IP, a checksum computed on the CLNP header provides a verification that the information used in processing the CLNP datagram has been transmitted correctly, and a lifetime control mechanism ("Time to Live") imposes a limit on the amount of time a datagram is allowed to remain in the Internet system.

Protocol Structure

CLNP has the following PDU structure:

Header Part	Address Part	Segmentation Part	Option Part	Data

CLNP PDU header:

8	16	24	32	35	40	56	72bit
NLP ID	Length ID	Version	Lifetime	Flags	Type	Seg. Length	Checksum

• NLP ID -- Network Layer Protocol Identifier. The value of this field is set to binary 1000 0001 to identify this Network Layer protocol as ISO 8473, Protocol for Providing the Connectionless- mode Network Service. The value of this field is set to binary 0000 0000 to identify the Inactive Network Layer protocol subset.
• Length ID -- Length Indicator is the length in octets of the header
• Version -- Version/Protocol ID Extension identifies the standard Version of ISO 8473
• Lifetime -- PDU Lifetime representing the remaining lifetime of the PDU, in units of 500 milliseconds.
• Flags -- three flags: segmentation permitted, more segments, error report
• Type -- The Type code field identifies the type of the protocol data unit, which could be data PDU or Error Report PDU
• Seg. Length -- The Segment Length field specifies the entire length, in octets, of the Derived PDU, including both header and data (if present).
• Checksum -- The checksum is computed on the entire PDU header.
• Address Part -- It contains information of destination and source addresses, which are defined in OSI 8348/AD2 with variable length.
• Segmentation Part -- If the Segmentation Permitted Flag in the Fixed Part of the PDU Header (Octet 4, Bit 8) is set to one, the segmentation part of the header, illustrated in Figure 6, must be present: If the Segmentation Permitted flag is set to zero, the non-segmenting protocol subset is in use.
• Option Part -- The options part is used to convey optional parameters.
• Data Part -- The Data part of the PDU is structured as an ordered multiple of octets.

Related Protocols

IS-IS, CLNP, IDRP, CONP, ES-IS, ISO-TP

Sponsor Source

CLNP is defined by ISO (www.iso.org) in document 8473 and ITU (www.itu.org) X.213 and X.233.

Reference

http://www.javvin.com/rfc994.pdf
Final Text of DIS 8473, Protocol for Providing the Connectionless-mode Network Service
http://www.doc.ua.pt/arch/itu/rec/product/X.htm
X.213: Information technology – Open Systems Interconnection – Network service definition
X.233: Information technology - Protocol for providing the connectionless-mode network service: Protocol specification

ISO CONP: Connection-Oriented Network Protocol

Protocol Description

Connection-Oriented Network Protocol (CONP) is an OSI network layer protocol that carries upper-layer data and error indications over connection-oriented links. Two types of OSI network layer services are available to the OSI transport layer:

• Connectionless Network Service (CLNS) -- CLNS performs datagram transport and does not require a circuit to be established before data is transmitted.
• Connection-Mode Network Service (CMNS) -- CMNS requires explicit establishment of a path or circuit between communicating transport layer entities before transmitting data.

CONP, based on the X.25 Packet-Layer Protocol (PLP), provides the interface between CMNS and upper layers. It is a network layer service that acts as the interface between the transport layer and CMNS. Six services are provided to transport-layer entities: one for connection establishment, one for connection release, and four for data transfer. Services are invoked by some combination of four primitives: request, indication, response, and confirmation.

There are two types of addresses used in the network layer communication:

• Network Service Access Point (NSAP) -- NSAP addresses identify network layer services, one for each service running.
• Network Entity Title (NET) -- NET addresses identify network layer entities or processes instead of services.

Protocol Structure

The General Format of NSAP:

1byte	2bytes	2-4bytes		0-13bytes	1-8bytes	1byte
IDP		DSP				
AFI	IDI	CDP		CDSP		
AFI	IDI	CFI	CDI	RDAA	ID	SEL

• IDP -- Initial Domain Part
• AFI -- Authority and Format Identifier, a two-decimal-digit, 38 for decimal abstract syntax of the DSP or 39 for binary abstract syntax of the DSP
• IDI -- Initial Domain Identifier, a three-decimal-digit country code, as defined in ISO 3166
• DSP -- Domain Specific Part
• CDP -- Country Domain Part, 2..4 octets
• CFI -- Country Format Identifier, one digit
• CDI -- Country Domain Identifier, 3 to 7 digits, fills CDP to an octet boundary
• CDSP -- Country Domain Specific Part
• RDAA -- Routing Domain and Area Address
• ID -- System Identifier (1..8 octet)
• SEL -- NSAP Selector

While RDIs and RDCIs need not be related to the set of addresses within the domains they depict, RDIs and RDCIs are assigned based on the NSAP prefixes assigned to domains. A subscriber RD should use the NSAP prefix assigned to it as its RDI. A multihomed RD should use one of the NSAP prefixes assigned to it as its RDI.

Related Protocols

IS-IS, CLNP, IDRP, CONP, ES-IS

Sponsor Source

CONP is defined in ISO (www.iso.org) 8208 and 8878 and Itu (www.itu.org) X.213 and X.223.

Reference

http://www.doc.ua.pt/arch/itu/rec/product/X.htm
X.213: Information technology – Open Systems Interconnection – Network service definition
X.223: Use of X.25 to provide the OSI connection-mode Network service for ITU-T applications

ES-IS: End System to Intermediate System Routing Exchange Protocol

Protocol Description

End System to Intermediate System Routing Exchange Protocol (ES-IS), developed by ISO, permits End Systems and Intermediate Systems to exchange configuration and routing information to facilitate the operation of the routing and relaying functions of the Network Layer in the ISO network environment. In an ISO network, there are End Systems, Intermediate Systems, Areas and Domains. End systems are user devices. Intermediate systems are routers. Routers are organized into local groups called 'areas', and several areas are grouped together into a 'domain'. ES-IS, working in conjunction with CLNP, IS-IS, and IDRP, provides complete routing over the entire network.

ES-IS provides solutions for the following practical problems:

1. For end systems to discover the existence and reachability of intermediate systems that can route NPDUs to destinations on subnetworks other than the one(s) to which the end system is directly connected.
2. For end systems to discover the existence and reachability of other end systems on the same subnetwork.
3. For intermediate systems to discover the existence and reachability of end systems on each of the subnetworks to which they are directly connected.
4. For end systems to decide which intermediate system to be used to forward NPDUs to a particular destination when more than one intermediate system is accessible.

ES-IS provides two types of information to Network entities which support its operation: a) Configuration Information, which permits End Systems to discover the existence and reachability of Intermediate Systems and permits Intermediate Systems to discover the existence and reachability of End Systems; and b) Route Redirection Information which allows Intermediate Systems to inform End Systems of (potentially) better paths to use when forwarding NPDUs to a particular destination. A Network Entity may choose to support either the Configuration Information, the Route Redirection Information, neither, or both.

Protocol Structure

ES-IS Protocol Data Unit contains the following:

ES-IS Header	Network address	Subnetwork address	Option

ES-IS Header:

1 byte	1 byte	1 byte	1 byte	1 byte				2 bytes	2 bytes
NL-PID	Length	Version	Reserved	0	0	0	Type	H-Time	Check-sum

• NLPID -- Network Layer Protocol Identification. The value of this field shall be 1000 0010

• Length -- Length Indicator is the length of the entire PDU
• Version -- Protocol ID extension. This identifies a standard version of ISO xxxx, End System to Intermediate System Routing Exchange Protocol for use in conjunction with ISO 8473.
• Reserved -- Must be zero.
• Type -- The Type code field identifies the type of the protocol data unit.
• H-Time -- Holding time field specifies for how long the receiving Network entity should retain the configuration/routing information contained in this PDU.
• Checksum -- Error checking which is computed on the entir PDU header.

Related Protocols

IS-IS, CLNP, IDRP, CONP

Sponsor Source

ES-IS is defined in ISO (www.iso.org).

Reference

http://www.javvin.com/protocol/rfc955.pdf
End System to Intermediate System Routing Exchange Protocol for use in conjunction with ISO 8473

IDRP: Inter-Domain Routing Protocol

Protocol Description

The Inter-Domain Routing Protocol (IDRP), which provides routing for OSI defined network environments, is similar to BGP in the TCP/IP network. In an OSI network, there are End Systems, Intermediate Systems, Areas and Domains. End systems are user devices. Intermediate systems are routers. Routers are organized into local groups called 'areas', and several areas are grouped together into a 'domain'. Inter-Domain Routing Protocol (IDRP) is designed to provide routing among domains. IDRP, working in conjunction with CLNP, ES-IS, and IS-IS, provides complete routing over the entire network.

A router that participates in IDRP is called a Boundary Intermediate System (BIS) and may belong to only one domain. IDRP governs the exchange of routing information between a pair of neighbors, either external or internal. IDRP is self-contained with respect to the exchange of information between external neighbors. Exchange of information between internal neighbors relies on additional support provided by intra-domain routing (unless internal neighbors share a common subnetwork). To facilitate routing information aggregation/abstraction, IDRP allows grouping of a set of connected domains into a Routing Domain Confederation (RDC). A given domain may belong to more than one RDC. The ability to group domains in RDCs provides a simple, yet powerful mechanism for routing information aggregation and abstraction. It allows reduction of topological information by replacing a sequence of RDIs carried by the RD_PATH attribute with a single RDCI. It also allows reduction of the amount of information related to transit policies, and simplifies the route selection policies.

Each domain participating in IDRP is assigned a unique Routing Domain Identifier (RDI), which is basically an OSI network layer address. Each RDC is assigned a unique Routing Domain Confederation Identifier (RDCI). RDCIs are assigned out of the address space allocated for RDIs. RDCIs and RDIs are syntactically indistinguishable. It is expected that RDI and RDCI assignment and management would be part of the network layer assignment and management procedures.

Protocol Structure

The General Format of NSAP:

1byte	2bytes	2-4bytes		0-13bytes	1-8bytes	1byte
IDP		DSP				
AFI	IDI	CDP		CDSP		
AFI	IDI	CFI	CDI	RDAA	ID	SEL

• IDP -- Initial Domain Part
• AFI -- Authority and Format Identifier, a two-decimal-digit, 38 for decimal abstract syntax of the DSP or 39 for binary abstract syntax of the DSP
• IDI -- Initial Domain Identifier, a three-decimal-digit country code, as defined in ISO 3166
• DSP -- Domain Specific Part
• CDP -- Country Domain Part, 2..4 octets

• CFI -- Country Format Identifier, one digit
• CDI -- Country Domain Identifier, 3 to 7 digits, fills CDP to an octet boundary
• CDSP -- Country Domain Specific Part
• RDAA -- Routing Domain and Area Address
• ID -- System Identifier (1..8 octet)
• SEL -- NSAP Selector

While RDIs and RDCIs need not be related to the set of addresses within the domains they depict, RDIs and RDCIs are assigned based on the NSAP prefixes assigned to domains. A subscriber RD should use the NSAP prefix assigned to it as its RDI. A multihomed RD should use one of the NSAP prefixes assigned to it as its RDI.

Related Protocols

ES-IS, CLNP, IDRP, IS-IS, BGP, CONP

Sponsor Source

IDRP is defined in ISO (www.iso.org) 10747 and discussed in IETF (www.ietf.org).

Reference

http://www.javvin.com/protocol/rfc1629.pdf
Guidelines for OSI NSAP Allocation in the Internet
http://www.acm.org/sigcomm/standards/iso_stds/IDRP/10747.TXT
Protocol for the Exchange of Inter-Domain Routing Information among Intermediate Systems to Support Forwarding of ISO 8473 PDUs

IS-IS: Intermediate System to Intermediate System Routing Protocol

Protocol Description

Intermediate System-to-Intermediate System (IS-IS) is a routing protocol developed by the ISO. It is a link-state protocol where ISs (routers) exchange routing information based on a single metric to determine network topology. It behaves similar to Open Shortest Path First (OSPF) in the TCP/IP network.

In an IS-IS network, there are End Systems, Intermediate Systems, Areas and Domains. End systems are user devices. Intermediate systems are routers. Routers are organized into local groups called 'areas', and several areas are grouped together into a 'domain'. IS-IS is designed primarily for providing intra-domain routing or routing within an area. IS-IS, working in conjunction with CLNP, ES-IS and IDRP, provides complete routing over the entire network.

IS-IS routing makes use of two-level hierarchical routing. Level 1 routers know the topology in their area, including all routers and hosts, but they do not know the identity of routers or destinations outside of their area. Level 1 routers forward all traffic for destinations outside of their area to a level 2 router within their area which knows the level 2 topology. Level 2 routers do not need to know the topology within any level 1 area, except to the extent that a level 2 router may also be a level 1 router within a single area.

IS-IS adapted to carry IP network information is called Integrated IS-IS. Integrated IS-IS has the most important characteristic necessary in a modern routing protocol: It supports VLSM and converges rapidly. It is also scalable to support very large networks.

There are two types of IS-IS addresses:

Network Service Access Point (NSAP) -- NSAP addresses identify network layer services, one for each service running. Network Entity Title (NET) - NET addresses identify network layer entities or processes instead of services.

Devices may have more than one of each of the two types of addresses. However, NET's should be unique, and the System ID portion of the NSAP must be unique for each system.

Protocol Structure

IS-IS PDU Header:

8	16 bit
Intradomain routing protocol discriminator	Length indicator
Version/protocol ID extension	ID length
R	R	R	PDU type	Version
Reserved	Maximum area addresses

- Intradomain routing protocol discriminator -- Network layer protocol identifier assigned to this protocol
- Length indicator -- Length of the fixed header in octets.
- Version/protocol ID extension -- Equal to 1.
- ID length -- Length of the ID field of NSAP addresses and NETs used in this routing domain.
- R -- Reserved bits.
- PDU type -- Type of PDU. Bits 6, 7 and 8 are reserved.
- Version -- Equal to 1.
- Maximum area addresses -- Number of area addresses permitted for this intermediate system's area.

Format of NSAP for IS-IS:

< IDP >		< DSP >	
		< HO-DSP >	
AFI	IDI	Contents assigned by authority identified in IDI field	
< Area Address >		< ID >	< SEL >

- IDP -- Initial Domain Part
    - AFI -- Authority and Format Identifier (1-byte); Provides information about the structure and content of the IDI and DSP fields.
    - IDI -- Initial Domain Identifier (variable length)
- DSP -- Domain Specific Part
    - HO-DSP -- High Order Domain Specific Part
    - Area Address (variable)
    - ID -- System ID (1- 8 bytes)
    - SEL -- n-selector (1-byte value that serves a function similar to the port number in Internet Protocol).

Related Protocols

OSPF, ES-IS, CLNP, IDRP, CONP

Sponsor Source

IS-IS is defined in ISO (www.iso.org) 10589 and reviewed by IETF (www.ietf.org) RFC 1629.

Reference

http://www.javvin.com/protocol/rfc1629.pdf
Guidelines for OSI NSAP Allocation in the Internet

Cisco Protocols

Cisco Systems plays an active role in the IETF committees to bring Cisco technology initiatives into the standards track. At the same time, Cisco created many proprietary protocols, which are mostly included in the IOS, the operating system of Cisco products. In this book, we have selected the most frequently used Cisco protocols to introduce.

CDP: Cisco Discovery Protocol
CGMP: Cisco Group Management Protocol
DISL: Dynamic Inter-Switch Link Protocol
DTP: Cisco Dynamic Trunking Protocol
EIGRP: Enhanced Interior Gateway Routing Protocol
HSRP: Hot Standby Router Protocol
IGRP: Interior Gateway Routing Protocol
ISL: Cisco Inter-Switch Link Protocol
NetFlow: Cisco traffic mamagement protocol
RGMP: Cisco Router Port Group Management Protocol
TACACS and TACACS+: Terminal Access Controller Access Control Protocol
VTP: Cisco VLAN Trunking Protocol
XOT: Cisco X.25 Over TCP Protocol

CDP: Cisco Discovery Protocol

Protocol Description

Cisco Discovery Protocol (CDP) is primarily used to obtain protocol addresses of neighboring devices and discover the platform of those devices. CDP can also be used to show information about the interfaces your router uses. CDP is media- and protocol-independent, and runs on all Cisco-manufactured equipment including routers, bridges, access servers, and switches.

Use of SNMP with the CDP Management Information Base (MIB) allows network management applications to learn the device type and the SNMP agent address of neighboring devices, and to send SNMP queries to those devices. Cisco Discovery Protocol uses the CISCO-CDP-MIB.

CDP runs on all media that support Subnetwork Access Protocol (SNAP), including local-area network (LAN), Frame Relay, and Asynchronous Transfer Mode (ATM) physical media. CDP runs over the data link layer only. Therefore, two systems that support different network-layer protocols can learn about each other.

Each device configured for CDP sends periodic messages, known as advertisements, to a multicast address. Each device advertises at least one address at which it can receive SNMP messages. The advertisements also contain time-to-live, or holdtime, information, which indicates the length of time a receiving device should hold CDP information before discarding it. Each device also listens to the periodic CDP messages sent by others in order to learn about neighboring devices and determine when their interfaces to the media go up or down.

CDP Version-2 (CDPv2), the most recent release of the protocol, provides more intelligent device tracking features. These features include a reporting mechanism which allows for more rapid error tracking, thereby reducing costly downtime. Reported error messages can be sent to the console or to a logging server, and cover instances of unmatching native VLAN IDs (IEEE 802.1Q) on connecting ports, and unmatching port duplex states between connecting devices.

Protocol Structure

CDPv2 show commands can provide detailed output on VLAN Trunking Protocol (VTP) management domain and duplex modes of neighbor devices, CDP-related counters, and VLAN IDs of connecting ports. The following table lists the CDP commands:

Command	Purpose
clear cdp counters	Resets the traffic counters to zero.
clear cdp table	Deletes the CDP table of information about neighbors.

show cdp	Displays the interval between transmissions of CDP advertisements, the number of seconds the CDP advertisement is valid for a given port, and the version of the advertisement.
show cdp entry entry-name [protocol | version]	Displays information about a specific neighbor. Display can be limited to protocol or version information.
show cdp interface [type number]	Displays information about interfaces on which CDP is enabled.
show cdp neighbors [type number] [detail]	Displays the type of device that has been discovered, the name of the device, the number and type of the local interface (port), the number of seconds the CDP advertisement is valid for the port, the device type, the device product number, and the port ID. Issuing the detail keyword displays information on the native VLAN ID, the duplex mode, and the VTP domain name associated with neighbor devices.
show cdp traffic	Displays CDP counters, including the number of packets sent and received and checksum errors.
show debugging	Displays information about the types of debugging that are enabled for your router. See the Cisco IOS Debug Command Reference for more information about CDP debug commands.

Related Protocols
SNMP, SNAP

Sponsor Source
CDP is a Cisco protocol.

Reference
http://www.cisco.com/en/US/products/sw/iosswrel/ps1831/products_configuration_guide_chapter09186a00800ca66d.html
Configuring the Cisco Discovery Protocol

CGMP: Cisco Group Management Protocol

Protocol Description

Cisco Group Management Protocol (CGMP) limits the forwarding of IP multicast packets to only those ports associated with IP multicast clients. These clients automatically join and leave groups that receive IP multicast traffic, and the switch dynamically changes its forwarding behavior according to these requests. CGMP provides the following services:

• Allows IP multicast packets to be switched only to those ports that have IP multicast clients.
• Saves network bandwidth on user segments by not propagating unnecessary IP multicast traffic.
• Does not require changes to the end host systems.
• Does not incur the overhead of creating a separate VLAN for each multicast group in the switched network.

When CGMP is enabled, it automatically identifies the ports to which the CGMP-capable router is attached. CGMP is enabled by default and supports a maximum of 64 IP multicast group registrations. Multicast routers that support CGMP periodically send CGMP join messages to advertise themselves to switches within a network. A receiving switch saves the information and sets a timer equal to the router hold time. The timer is updated every time the switch receives a CGMP join message advertising itself. When the last router hold time expires, the switch removes all IP multicast groups learned from CGMP.

CGMP works in conjunction with IGMP messages to dynamically configure Cisco Catalyst switch ports so that IP multicast traffic is forwarded only to those ports associated with IP multicast hosts. A CGMP-capable IP multicast router sees all IGMP packets and therefore can inform the Catalyst switches when specific hosts join or leave IP multicast groups. When the CGMP-capable router receives an IGMP control packet, it creates a CGMP packet that contains the request type (either join or leave), the multicast group address, and the actual MAC address of the host. The router then sends the CGMP packet to a well-known address to which all Catalyst switches listen. When a switch receives the CGMP packet, the switch interprets the packet and modifies the forwarding behavior of the multicast group. From then on, this multicast traffic is sent only to ports associated with the appropriate IP multicast clients. This process is done automatically, without user intervention.

Protocol Structure

CGMP message format:

1 byte	6 bytes	1 byte	6 bytes	1 byte
Count	Group Destination Address	Type	Unicast Source Address	Version

• Count: Unsigned 8 bit integer
• Group Destination Address: The hardware MAC address of the destination device.
• Type: Message Type
• Unicast Source Address: The hardware MAC address of the unicast source device
• Version: CGMP version number

Related Protocols

IPv4, IGMP, PIM-SM, RGMP

Sponsor Source

CGMP is a Cisco protocol.

Reference

http://www.cisco.com/univercd/cc/td/doc/product/lan/28201900/1928v67x/eescg67x/03cgmpl.pdf
Cisco Group Management Protocol

DTP: Cisco Dynamic Trunking Protocol

Protocol Description

Dynamic Trunking Protocol (DTP), a Cisco proprietary protocol in the VLAN group, is for negotiating trunking on a link between two devices and for negotiating the type of trunking encapsulation (802.1Q) to be used.

There are different types of trunking protocols. If a port can become a trunk, it may also have the ability to trunk automatically and, in some cases, even negotiate what type of trunking to use on the port. This ability to negotiate the trunking method with the other device is called dynamic trunking.

The first issue is that both ends of a trunk cable had better agree they're trunking, or they're going to be interpreting trunk frames as normal frames. End stations will be confused by the extra tag information in the frame header, their driver stacks won't understand it, and the end systems may lock up or fail in odd ways. To resolve this problem, Cisco created a protocol for switches to communicate intentions. The first version of it was VTP, VLAN Trunking Protocol, which worked with ISL. The newer version works with 802.1q as well, and is called Dynamic Trunking Protocol (DTP).

The second issue is creating VLAN's. To configure VLAN's individually switch by switch, it is lot of work and easy to cause inconsistency, in which VLAN 100 could be Engineering department on one switch, and Accounting department on another. That would be a source of confusion in troubleshooting, and might also defeat your carefully crafted VLAN security scheme. This issue is also addressed by VTP/DTP. You can create or delete a VLAN on one switch, and have the information propagate automatically to a group of switches under the same administrative control. This group of switches would be a VTP domain.

Protocol Structure

On a Catalyst set-based switch, the syntax for setting up a link as a trunk is:

set trunk mod_num/port_num [on | desirable | auto | nonegotiate] [isl | dot1q | negotiate] [vlan_range]

Use this command to set the specified port or ports to trunking. The first set of keyword arguments govern the DTP modes:

Mode	What the Mode Does
on	Forces the link into permanent trunking, even if the neighbor doesn't agree
off	Forces the link to permanently not trunk, even if the neighbor doesn't agree
desirable	Causes the port to actively attempt to become a trunk, subject to neighbor agreement (neighbor set to on, desirable, or auto)
auto	Causes the port to passively be willing to convert to trunking. The port will not trunk unless the neighbor is set to on or desirable. This is the default mode. Note that auto-auto (both ends default) links will not become trunks.
nonegotiate	Forces the port to permanently trunk but not send DTP frames. For use when the DTP frames confuse the neighboring (non-Cisco) 802.1q switch. You must manually set the neighboring switch to trunking.

The second set of keywords governs the type of VLAN tagging to use: ISL, 802.1q, or negotiate which to use.

Related Protocols

IEEE 802.1Q, VTP, ISL, DISL

Sponsor Source

DTP is a Cisco protocol.

Reference

http://www.cisco.com/en/US/products/hw/switches/ps708/
products_configuration_guide_chapter09186a008019f048.
html#1017196
Understanding and Configuring VLAN Trunking Protocol
http://www.cisco.com/univercd/cc/td/doc/product/lan/cat6000/
sw_5_2/cofigide/e_trunk.htm
configuring VLAN Trunks

EIGRP: Enhanced Interior Gateway Routing Protocol

Protocol Description

Enhanced Interior Gateway Routing Protocol (EIGRP) is an enhanced version of IGRP. IGRP is Cisco's Interior Gateway Routing Protocol used in TCP/IP and OSI internets. It is regarded as an interior gateway protocol (IGP) but has also been used extensively as an exterior gateway protocol for inter-domain routing.

Key capabilities that distinguish Enhanced IGRP from other routing protocols include fast convergence, support for variable-length subnet mask, support for partial updates, and support for multiple network layer protocols.

A router running Enhanced IGRP stores all its neighbors' routing tables so that it can quickly adapt to alternate routes. If no appropriate route exists, Enhanced IGRP queries its neighbors to discover an alternate route. These queries propagate until an alternate route is found.

Its support for variable-length subnet masks permits routes to be automatically summarized on a network number boundary. In addition, Enhanced IGRP can be configured to summarize on any bit boundary at any interface.

Enhanced IGRP does not make periodic updates. Instead, it sends partial updates only when the metric for a route changes. Propagation of partial updates is automatically bounded so that only those routers that need the information are updated. As a result of these two capabilities, Enhanced IGRP consumes significantly less bandwidth than IGRP.

Protocol Structure

8	16	32bit
Version	Opcode	Checksum
Flags		
Sequence number		
Acknowledge number		
Asystem: Autonomous system number		
Type		Length

• Version -- The version of the protocol.
• Opcode -- Operation code indicating the message type: 1 Update. 2 Reserved. 3 Query. 4 Hello. 5 IPX-SAP.
• Checksum -- IP checksum which is computed using the same checksum algorithm as a UDP checksum
• Flag -- Initialization bit and is used in establishing a new neighbor relationship
• Sequence number -- Used to send messages reliably
• Acknowledge number -- Used to send messages reliably
• Asystem -- Autonomous system number. A gateway can participate in more than one autonomous system where each system runs its own IGRP. For each autonomous system, there are completely separate routing tables. This field allows the gateway to select which set of routing tables to use.
• Type -- Value in the type field: 1 EIGRP Parameters. 2 Re-

served. 3 Sequence. 4 Software version. 5 Next Multicast sequence.
• Length -- Length of the frame.

Related Protocols
IP, TCP, IGRP, EGP, BGP, GRE, RIP

Sponsor Source
EIGRP is a Cisco protocol.

Reference
http://www.cisco.com/univercd/cc/td/doc/cisintwk/ito_doc/en_igrp.htm
Enhanced IGRP

HSRP: Hot Standby Router Protocol

Protocol Description

Hot Standby Router Protocol (HSRP) is designed to support non-disruptive failover of IP traffic in certain circumstances and to allow hosts to appear to use a single router and to maintain connectivity even if the actual first hop router they are using fails. In other words, the protocol protects against the failure of the first hop router when the source host cannot learn the IP address of the first hop router dynamically. Multiple routers participate in this protocol and in concert create the illusion of a single virtual router. The protocol insures that one and only one of the routers is forwarding packets on behalf of the virtual router. End hosts forward their packets to the virtual router.

The router forwarding packets is known as the active router. A standby router is selected to replace the active router should it fail. The protocol provides a mechanism for determining active and standby routers, using the IP addresses on the participating routers. If an active router fails a standby router can take over without a major interruption in the host's connectivity.

HSRP runs on top of UDP, and uses port number 1985. Routers use their actual IP address as the source address for protocol packets, not the virtual IP address. This is necessary so that the HSRP routers can identify each other.

Protocol Structure

8	16	24	32bit
Version	Op code	State	Hellotime
Holdtime	Priority	Group	Reserved
Authentication data			
Authentication data			
Virtual IP address			

• Version -- HSRP version number. The current version is 0.
• Op code -- Type of message contained in the packet. Possible values are:

      0 Hello, sent to indicate that a router is running and is capable of becoming the active or standby router.
      1 Coup, sent when a router wishes to become the active router.
      2 Resign, sent when a router no longer wishes to be the active router.
• State -- Internally, each router in the standby group implements a state machine. The State field describes the current state of the router sending the message. Possible values are:

      0 Initial;   1 Learn;   2 Listen;
      4 Speak;   8 Standby;   16 Active.
• Hellotime -- Approximate period between the Hello messages that the router sends (for Hello messages only). If the Hellotime is not configured on a router, then it may be learned from the Hello message from the active router.
• Holdtime -- The amount of time, in seconds, that the current Hello message should be considered valid. (For Hello messages only.)
• Priority -- Used to elect the active and standby routers. When comparing priorities of two different routers, the router with the numerically higher priority wins. In the case of routers with equal priority, the router with the higher IP address wins.
• Group -- Identifies the standby group. For Token Ring, values between 0 and 2 inclusive are valid. For other media, values between 0 and 255 inclusive are valid.
• Authentication data -- Clear-text 8 character reused password. If no authentication data is configured, the recommended default value is 0x63 0x69 0x73 0x63 0x6F 0x00 0x00 0x00.
• Virtual IP address -- Virtual IP address used by this group. If the virtual IP address is not configured on a router, then it may be learned from the Hello message from the active router. An address should only be learned if no address was configured and the Hello message is authenticated.

Related Protocols

IIP, UDP

Sponsor Source

HSRP is a Cisco protocol and circulated by IETF RFC 2281.

Reference

http://www.javvin.com/protocol/rfc2281.pdf
Hot Standby Router Protocol

IGRP: Interior Gateway Routing Protocol

Protocol Description

The Interior Gateway Routing Protocol (IGRP) is a routing protocol to provide routing within an autonomous system (AS). In the mid-1980s, the most popular interior routing protocol was the Routing Information Protocol (RIP). Although RIP was quite useful for routing within small- to moderate-sized, relatively homogeneous internetworks, its limits were being pushed by network growth. The popularity of Cisco routers and the robustness of IGRP encouraged many organizations with large internetworks to replace RIP with IGRP. Cisco developed Enhanced IGRP in the early 1990s to improve the operating efficiency of IGRP.

IGRP is a distance vector Interior Gateway Protocol (IGP). Distance vector routing protocols mathematically compare routes using some measurement of distance. This measurement is known as the distance vector. Distance vector routing protocols are often contrasted with link-state routing protocols, which send local connection information to all nodes in the internetwork.

To provide additional flexibility, IGRP permits multipath routing. Dual equal-bandwidth lines can run a single stream of traffic in round-robin fashion, with automatic switchover to the second line if one line goes down. Multiple paths can have unequal metrics yet still be valid multipath routes. For example, if one path is three times better than another path (its metric is three times lower), the better path will be used three times as often. Only routes with metrics that are within a certain range or variance of the best route are used as multiple paths. Variance is another value that can be established by the network administrator.

Protocol Structure

8	16	24	32bit
Version	Op code	Edition	ASystem
Ninterior	Nsystem	Nexterior	Checksum

• Version -- IGRP version number (currently 1).
• Opcode -- Operation code indicating the message type:
      1 Update;   2 Request.
• Edition -- Serial number which is incremented whenever there is a change in the routing table.
• Asystem -- Autonomous system number. A gateway can participate in more than one autonomous system where each system runs its own IGRP. For each autonomous system, there are completely separate routing tables. This field allows the gateway to select which set of routing tables to use.
• Ninterior, Nsystem, Nexterior -- Indicate the number of entries in each of these three sections of update messages. The first entries (Ninterior) are taken to be interior, the next entries (Nsystem) as being system, and the final entries (Nexterior) as exterior.
• Checksum -- IP checksum which is computed using the same checksum algorithm as a UDP checksum.

Related Protocols
EIGRP, EGP, BGP, GRE, IP, TCP, RIP

Sponsor Source
IGRP is a Cisco protocol.

Reference
http://www.cisco.com/univercd/cc/td/doc/cisintwk/ito_doc/igrp.htm
Interior Gateway routing Protocol

ISL & DISL: Cisco Inter-Switch Link Protocol and Dynamic ISL Protocol

Protocol Description

Inter-Switch Link. Protocol (ISL), a Cisco-proprietary protocol, maintains VLAN information as traffic flows between switches and routers.

Inter-Switch Link (ISL) tagging accomplishes the same task as 802.1Q trunking but uses a different frame format. ISL trunks are Cisco proprietary and define only a point-to-point connection between two devices, typically switches. The name Inter-Switch Link hints at this design. ISL frame tagging uses a low-latency mechanism for multiplexing traffic from multiple VLANs on a single physical path. ISL has been implemented for connections among switches, routers, and network interface cards (NICs) used on nodes such as servers. To support the ISL feature, each connecting device must be ISL-configured. A router that is ISL-configured can allow inter-VLAN communications. A non-ISL device that receives ISL-encapsulated Ethernet frames will most likely consider them protocol errors because of the format and size of the frames.

Like 802.1Q, ISL functions at Layer 2 of the OSI model, but it differs by encapsulating the entire Layer 2 Ethernet frame inside an ISL header and trailer. Because ISL encapsulates the entire frame, it is protocol-independent and can carry any type of Layer 2 frame or upper-layer protocol between the switches. The encapsulated frames may be token-ring or Fast Ethernet, and are carried unchanged from transmitter to receiver. ISL has the following characteristics:

• Performed with application-specific integrated circuits (ASIC)
• Not intrusive to client stations; client does not see the ISL header
• Effective between switches, routers and switches, and switches and servers with ISL NICs

Dynamic Inter-Switch Link Protocol (DISL), also a Cisco protocol, simplifies the creation of an ISL trunk from two interconnected Fast Ethernet devices. Fast EtherChannel technology enables aggregation of two full-duplex Fast Ethernet links for high-capacity backbone connections. DISL minimizes VLAN trunk configuration procedures because only one end of a link needs to be configured as a trunk.

Protocol Structure

ISL header structure:

40	4	4	48	16	8	24	15	1	16	16bits
DA	Type	User	SA	Len	AAA03	HSA	VLAN	BP DU	In- dex	Resv

• DA -- 40-bit multicast destination address.
• Type -- 4-bit descriptor of the encapsulated frame types—Ethernet (0000), Token Ring (0001), FDDI (0010), and ATM (0011).

• User -- 4-bit descriptor used as the type field extension or to define Ethernet priorities. This is a binary value from 0, the lowest priority, to 3, the highest priority.
• SA -- 48-bit source MAC address of the transmitting Catalyst switch.
• LEN -- 16-bit frame-length descriptor minus DA type, user, SA, LEN, and CRC.
• AAAA03 -- Standard SNAP 802.2 LLC header.
• HSA -- First 3 bytes of SA (manufacturer's ID or organizational unique ID).
• VLAN -- 15-bit VLAN ID. Only the lower 10 bits are used for 1024 VLANs.
• BPDU -- 1-bit descriptor identifying whether the frame is a Spanning Tree bridge protocol data unit (BPDU). Also set if the encapsulated frame is a Cisco Discovery Protocol (CDP) frame.
• INDEX -- 16-bit descriptor that identifies the transmitting port ID. Used for diagnostics.
• RES -- 16-bit reserved field used for additional information, such as Token Ring and Fiber Distributed Data Interface (FDDI) frame Frame Check (FC) field.

Related Protocols

IEEE 802.1Q, VTP, DTP, Ethernet, Token Ring

Sponsor Source

ISP and DISL are Cisco protocols.

Reference

http://www.cisco.com/en/US/products/hw/switches/ps708/products_configuration_guide_chapter09186a008019f048.html#1017196
Understanding and Configuring VLAN Trunking Protocol
http://www.cisco.com/univercd/cc/td/doc/product/lan/cat6000/sw_5_2/cofigide/e_trunk.htm
Configuring VLAN Trunks

NetFlow: Cisco Network Traffic Monitoring and Management Protocol

Protocol Description

NetFlow is a Cisco protocol that provides statistics on packets flowing through the routing devices in the network. NetFlow is included in the Cisco IOS for most of the Cisco switches and routers which can be used as a network monitoring, accounting and security technology. NetFlow identifies packet flows for both ingress and egress IP packets. It does not involve any connection-setup protocol, either between routers or to any other networking device or end station. NetFlow does not require any change externally—either to the packets themselves or to any networking device. NetFlow is completely transparent to the existing network, including end stations and application software and network devices like LAN switches. Also, NetFlow capture and export are performed independently on each internetworking device; NetFlow need not be operational on each router in the network.

NetFlow is supported on IP and IP encapsulated traffic over most interface types and encapsulations.However, NetFlow does not support ATM LAN emulation (LANE) and does not support an Inter-Switch Link (ISL)/virtual LAN (VLAN), ATM, or Frame Relay interfaces when more than one input access control list (ACL) is used on the interface.

Cisco routers and switches with NetFlow enabled generate NetFlow records, which are exported from the router in UDP packets and collected using a NetFlow collector. The NetFlow collector will aggregate the NetFlow records from multiple sources and correlate the data and then export them to the NetFlow Analyzer, which is an application that performs the network performance monitoring, traffic profiling, accounting, etc. The NetFlow MIBs can also be sent to the Simple Network Management Protocol (SNMP) based managers for further analysis. The following figure presents a high level network management architecture based on the NetFlow protocol:

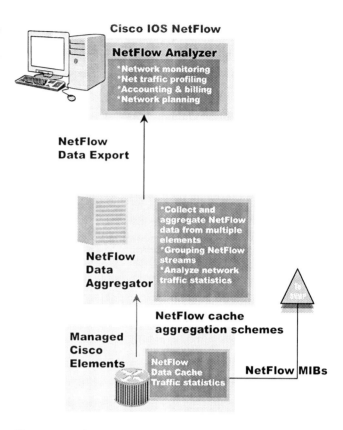

Figure 2-46: Cisco IOS NetFlow Architecture

Other networking hardware vendors also provide similar features in their systems. For example, Juniper Networks provides a similar feature for its routers called cflow.

Protocol Structure

A NetFlow network flow is defined as a unidirectional stream of packets between a given source and destination. A flow is defined by the combination of the seven key fields and the NetFlow information is condensed into a database called the NetFlow cache. The following picture displays the seven flow fields and the cache:

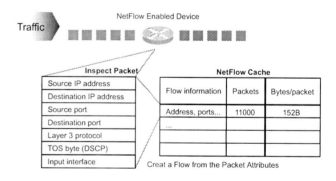

Figure 2-47: NetFlow Seven Flow Fields and the Cache

The NetFlow records are exported via some specifically defined schemes by Cisco. The folllowing table briefly describes post-processing features. User can configure these features to set up the export of NetFlow data.

Post-processing Features	Brief Description
Aggregation schemes	Sets up extra aggregation caches with different combinations of fields that determine which traditional flows are grouped together and collected when a flow expires from the main cache
Export to multiple destinations	Sets up identical streams of NetFlow data to be sent to multiple hosts

Related Protocols

SNMP, cflow, IP, UDP

Sponsor Source

NetFlow is a Cisco protocol.

Reference

http://www.cisco.com/univercd/cc/td/doc/product/software/ios120/12cgcr/switch_c/xcprt3/xcovntfl.htm
Cisco NetFlow Overview

RGMP: Cisco Router Port Group Management Protocol

Protocol Description

The Cisco Router Port Group Management Protocol (RGMP) is defined to address the limitations of Internet Group Management Protocol (IGMP) in its Snooping mechanism. RGMP is used between multicast routers and switches to restrict multicast packet forwarding in switches to those routers where the packets may be needed. RGMP is designed for backbone switched networks where multiple, high-speed routers are interconnected.

The main limitation of IGMP Snooping is that it can only restrict multicast traffic onto switch ports where receiving hosts are connected directly or indirectly via other switches. IGMP Snooping can not restrict multicast traffic to ports where at least one multicast router is connected. It must instead flood multicast traffic to these ports. Snooping on IGMP messages alone is an intrinsic limitation. Through it, a switch can only learn which multicast flows are being requested by hosts. A switch cannot learn through IGMP which traffic flows need to be received by router ports to be routed because routers do not report these flows via IGMP.

The RGMP protocol restricts multicast traffic to router ports. To effectively restrict traffic, it must be supported by both the switches and the routers in the network. Backbone switches use RGMP to learn which groups are desired at each of their ports. Multicast routers use RGMP to pass such information to the switches. Only routers send RGMP messages. They ignore received RGMP messages. When a router no longer needs to receive traffic for a particular group, it sends an RGMP Leave message for the group. A switch enabled for RGMP on a network consumes RGMP messages received from ports of the network and processes them. If enabled for RGMP, the switch must NOT forward/flood received RGMP messages out to other ports of the network.

RGMP is designed to work in conjunction with multicast routing protocols where explicit join/prune to the distribution tree is performed. PIM-SM is an example of such a protocol. The RGMP protocol specifies operations only for IP version 4 multicast routing. IP version 6 is not considered.

Protocol Structure

RGMP message format is the same as the IGMPv2:

8	16	32bit
Type	Reserved	Checksum
Group Address		

• Type -- There are four types of RGMP messages of concern to the router-switch interaction. The type codes are defined to be the highest values in an octet to avoid the re-use of already assigned IGMP type codes: 0xFF = Hello; 0xFE = Bye; 0xFD = Join a group; 0xFC = Leave a group.

• Reserved -- The reserved field in the message MUST be transmitted as zeros and ignored on receipt.
• Checksum -- Checksum covers the RGMP message (the entire IPv4 payload). The algorithm and handling of checksum are the same as those for IGMP messages.
• Group Address -- In an RGMP Hello or Bye message, the group address field is set to zero. In an RGMP Join or Leave message, the group address field holds the IPv4 multicast group address of the group being joined or left.

Related Protocols

IPv4, IGMP, PIM-SM, CGMP

Sponsor Source

RGMP is a Cisco protocol.

Reference

http://www.javvin.com/protocol/rfc3488.pdf
Cisco Systems Router Port Group Management Protocol

TACACS (and TACACS+): Terminal Access Controller Access Control System

Protocol Description

The Terminal Access Controller Access Control System (TACACS) provides access control for routers, network access servers and other networked computing devices via one or more centralized servers. TACACS+ provides separate authentication, authorization and accounting services.

TACACS allows a client to accept a username and password and send a query to a TACACS authentication server, sometimes called a TACACS daemon or simply TACACSD. This server is normally a program running on a host. The host determines whether to accept or deny the request and sends a response back. The TIP then allows access or not, based upon the response. In this way, the process of making the decision is "opened up" and the algorithms and data used to make the decision are under the complete control of whoever is running the TACACS daemon. The extensions to the protocol provide for more types of authentication requests and more types of response codes than were in the original specification.

There are three versions of TACACS and the third version called TACACS+, is not compatible with previous versions.

Protocol Structure

4	8	16	24	32bit
Major	Minor	Packet type	Sequence no.	Flags
Session ID				
Length				

• Major version -- The major TACACS+ version number.
• Minor version -- The minor TACACS+ version number. This is intended to allow revisions to the TACACS+ protocol while maintaining backwards compatibility.
• Packet type -- Possible values are:
    TAC_PLUS_AUTHEN:= 0x01 (Authentication).
    TAC_PLUS_AUTHOR:= 0x02 (Authorization).
    TAC_PLUS_ACCT:= 0x03 (Accounting).
• Sequence number -- The sequence number of the current packet for the current session. The first TACACS+ packet in a session must have the sequence number 1 and each subsequent packet will increment the sequence number by one. Thus clients only send packets containing odd sequence numbers, and TACACS+ daemons only send packets containing even sequence numbers.
• Flags -- This field contains various flags in the form of bitmaps. The flag values signify whether the packet is encrypted.
• Session ID -- The ID for this TACACS+ session.
• Length -- The total length of the TACACS+ packet body (not including the header).

Related Protocols

TCP, TELNET, SMTP, FTP, RADIUS

Sponsor Source

TACACS (and TACACS+) is a Cisco protocol.

Reference

http://www.javvin.com/protocol/rfc1492.pdf
An Access Control Protocol, Sometimes Called TACACS
http://www.javvin.com/protocol/tacacs.html
Introduction to TACACS+

VTP: Cisco VLAN Trunking Protocol

Protocol Description

VLAN Trunking Protocol (VTP) is a Cisco Layer 2 messaging protocol that manages the addition, deletion, and renaming of VLANs on a network-wide basis. Virtual Local Area Network (VLAN) Trunk Protocol (VTP) reduces administration in a switched network. When you configure a new VLAN on one VTP server, the VLAN is distributed through all switches in the domain. This reduces the need to configure the same VLAN everywhere. VTP is a Cisco-proprietary protocol that is available on most of the Cisco Catalyst Family products.

VTP ensures that all switches in the VTP domain are aware of all VLANs. There are occasions, however, when VTP can create unnecessary traffic. All unknown unicasts and broadcasts in a VLAN are flooded over the entire VLAN. All switches in the network receive all broadcasts, even in situations where few users are connected in that VLAN. VTP pruning is a feature used to eliminate (or prune) this unnecessary traffic.

By default, all Cisco Catalyst switches are configured to be VTP servers. This is suitable for small-scale networks where the size of the VLAN information is small and easily stored in all switches (in NVRAM). In a large network, a judgment call must be made at some point when the NVRAM storage needed is wasted, because it is duplicated on every switch. At this point, the network administrator should choose a few well-equipped switches and keep them as VTP servers. Everything else participating in VTP can be turned into a client. The number of VTP servers should be chosen so as to provide the degree of redundancy desired in the network.

There are three version of VTP so far. VTP Version 2 (V2) is not much different from VTP Version 1 (V1). The major difference is that VTP V2 introduces support for Token Ring VLANs. If you are using Token Ring VLANs, you need to enable VTP V2. Otherwise, there is no reason to use VTP V2.

VTP version 3 differs from earlier VTP versions in that it does not directly handle VLANs. VTP version 3 is a protocol that is only responsible for distributing a list of opaque databases over an administrative domain. When enabled, VTP version 3 provides the following enhancements to previous VTP versions:

• Support for extended VLANs.
• Support for the creation and advertising of private VLANs.
• Improved server authentication.
• Protection from the "wrong" database accidentally being inserted into a VTP domain.
• Interaction with VTP version 1 and VTP version 2.
• Provides the ability to be configured on a per-port basis.
• Provides the ability to propagate the VLAN database and other databases.

Protocol Structure

The format of the VTP header can vary depending on the type of VTP message. However, they all contain the following fields in the header:

- VTP protocol version: 1 or 2 or 3
- VTP message types:
  - Summary advertisements
  - Subset advertisement
  - Advertisement requests
  - VTP join messages
- Management domain length
- Management domain name

Summary Advertisements

When the switch receives a summary advertisement packet, it compares the VTP domain name to its own VTP domain name. If the name is different, the switch simply ignores the packet. If the name is the same, the switch then compares the configuration revision to its own revision. If its own configuration revision is higher or equal, the packet is ignored. If it is lower, an advertisement request is sent.

Summary Advert Packet Format:

0	1	2	3
0 1 2 3 4 5 6 7 8	9 0 1 2 3 4 5 6	7 8 9 0 1 2 3 4	5 6 7 8 9 0 1
Version	Code	Followers	MgmtD Len
Management Domain Nance (zero-padded to 32 bytes)			
Configuration Revision Number			
Updater Identity			
Update Timestamp (12 bytes)			
MDS Digest (16 bytes)			

- Followers indicate that this packet is followed by a Subset Advertisement packet.
- The updater identity is the IP address of the switch that is the last to have incremented the configuration revision.
- Update timestamps are the date and time of the last increment of the configuration revision.
- Message Digest 5 (MD5) carries the VTP password if it is configured and used to authenticate the validation of a VTP update.

Subset Advertisements

When you add, delete, or change a VLAN in a switch, the server switch where the changes were made increments the configuration revision and issues a summary advertisement, followed by one or several subset advertisements. A subset advertisement contains a list of VLAN information. If there are several VLANS, more than one subset advertisement may be required in order to advertise them all.

Subset Advert Packet Format:

0	1	2	3
0 1 2 3 4 5 6 7 8	9 0 1 2 3 4 5 6	7 8 9 0 1 2 3 4	5 6 7 8 9 0 1
Version	Code	Sequence Number	MgmtD Len

Management Domain Nance (zero-padded to 32 bytes)
Configuration Revision
VLAN - info field 1
....
VLAN - info field N

The following formatted example shows that each VLAN information field contains information for a different VLAN (ordered with lower valued ISL VLAN IDs occurring first):

V - info - len	Status	VLAN - Type	VLAN - name Len
ISL VLAN - id		MTU Size	
802.10 index			
VLAN - name (padded with zeros to multiple of 4 bytes)			

Most of the fields in this packet are easy to understand. Below are two clarifications:

- Code -- The format for this is 0x02 for subset advertisement.
- Sequence number -- This is the sequence of the packet in the stream of packets following a summary advertisement. The sequence starts with 1.

Advertisement Requests

A switch needs a VTP advertisement request in the following situations:

- The switch has been reset.
- The VTP domain name has been changed.
- The switch has received a VTP summary advertisement with a higher configuration revision than its own.

Upon receipt of an advertisement request, a VTP device sends a summary advertisement, followed by one or more subset advertisements. Below is an example.

0	1	2	3
0 1 2 3 4 5 6 7 8	9 0 1 2 3 4 5 6	7 8 9 0 1 2 3 4	5 6 7 8 9 0 1
Version	Code	Rsvd	MgmtD Len
Management Domain Nance (zero-padded to 32 bytes)			
Start - Value			

- Code -- The format for this is 0x03 for an advertisement request
- Start Value -- This is used in cases where there are several subset advertisements. If the first (N) subset advertisement has been received and the subsequent one (N+1) has not, the Catalyst only requests advertisements from the (N+1)th one.

Related Protocols
IEEE 802.1Q

Sponsor Source
VTP is a Cisco protocol.

Reference

http://www.cisco.com/en/US/products/hw/switches/ps708/
products_configuration_guide_chapter09186a008019f048.
html#1017196
Understanding and Configuring VLAN Trunking Protocol

XOT: X.25 over TCP Protocol by Cisco

Protocol Description

The X.25 over TCP protocol (XOT) is designed by Cisco to transport X.25 over IP internets. The X.25 Packet Level requires a reliable link level below it and normally uses LAPB. XOT is a method of sending X.25 packets over IP internets by encapsulating the X.25 Packet Level in TCP packets.

TCP provides a reliable byte stream. X.25 requires that the layer below it provide message semantics, in particular the boundary between packets. To provide this, a small (4-bytes) XOT header is used between TCP and X.25. The primary content of this header is a length field, which is used to separate the X.25 packets within the TCP stream.

In general, the normal X.25 protocol packet formats and state transition rules apply to the X.25 layer in XOT. Exceptions to this are noted.

Protocol Structure

16	32bit
Version	Length

• Version -- The version number. It must be 0. If no zero number is received, the TCP session must be closed.
• Length -- The length of the packet. Values must be legal X.25 packet lengths. If the length field has an illegal value, then the TCP connection MUST be closed.

Related Protocols

IP, TCP, X.25

Sponsor Source

XOT is a Cisco protocol and circulated in IETF (http://www.ietf.org) RFC1613.

Reference

http://www.javvin.com/protocol/rfc1613.pdf
Cisco Systems X.25 over TCP (XOT)

Novell NetWare and Protocols

Description

NetWare is a Novell network operating system (NOS) that provides transparent remote file access and numerous other distributed network services, including printer sharing and support for various applications such as electronic mail transfer and database access. NetWare specifies the upper five layers of the OSI reference model and runs on any media-access protocol (Layer 2). In addition, NetWare runs on virtually any kind of computer system, from PCs to mainframes. NetWare and its supporting protocols often coexist on the same physical channel with many other popular protocols, including TCP/IP, DECnet, and AppleTalk.

Novell NetWare, introduced in the early 1980s, is based on Xerox Network Systems (XNS) client-server architecture. Clients (sometimes called workstations) request services, such as file and printer access, from servers. NetWare's client/server architecture supports remote access, transparent to users, through remote procedure calls. A remote procedure call begins when the local computer program running on the client sends a procedure call to the remote server. The server then executes the remote procedure call and returns the requested information to the local client.

The most popular protocols in the Novell NetWare suite are:

IPX: Internetwork Packet Exchange protocol- Routing and networking protocol at layer 3. When a device to be communicated with is located on a different network, IPX routes the information to the destination through any intermediate networks. IPX is similar to IP (Internet Protocol) in the TCP/IP suite.

SPX: Sequenced Packet Exchange protocol, control protocol at the transport layer (layer 4) for reliable, connection-oriented datagram transmission. SPX is similar to TCP in the TCP/IP suite.

NCP: Network Core Protocol is a series of server routines designed to satisfy application requests coming from, for example, the NetWare shell. Services provided by NCP include file access, printer access, name management, accounting, security and file synchronization.

NetBIOS: Network Basic Input/Output System (NetBIOS) session-layer interface specification from IBM and Microsoft. NetWare's NetBIOS emulation software allows programs written to the industry-standard NetBIOS interface to run within the NetWare system.

NetWare application-layer services: NetWare Message Handling Service (NetWare MHS), Btrieve, NetWare Loadable Modules (NLMs), and various IBM connectivity features. NetWare MHS is a message delivery system that provides electronic mail transport. Btrieve is Novell's implementation of the binary tree (btree) database access mechanism. NLMs are implemented as add-on modules that attach into the NetWare system. NLMs for alternate protocol stacks, communication services, database services, and many other services are currently available from Novell and third parties.
Since NetWare 5.0, all Novell network services can be run on top of TCP/IP. There, IPS and SPX became Novell legacy network and transport layer protocols.

Architecture

The following figure illustrates the NetWare protocol suite, the media-access protocols on which NetWare runs, and the relationship between the NetWare protocols and the OSI reference model.

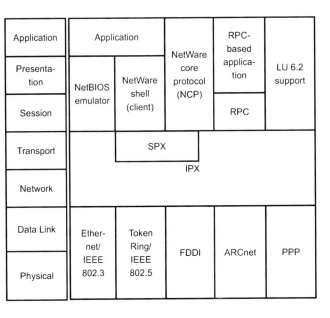

Figure 2-48: Novell Netware Protocol Stack Architecture

Related Protocols

IPX, SPX, Novell NetBIOS, NCP, RPC

Sponsor Source

NetWare is a Novell Operating System.

Reference

http://www.cisco.com/univercd/cc/td/doc/cisintwk/ito_doc/net-warep.htm
NetWare Protocols

IPX: Internetwork Packet Exchange protocol

Protocol Description

Internetwork Packet Exchange (IPX) is the legacy network protocol used by the Novell NetWare operating systems to route packets through an internetwork. IPX is a datagram protocol used for connectionless communications similar to IP (Internet Protocol) in the TCP/IP suite. Higher-level protocols, such as SPX and NCP, are used for additional error recovery services.

To make best-path routing decisions, IPX uses the services of a dynamic distance vector routing protocol such as Routing Information Protocol [RIP]) or NetWare Link-State Protocol [NLSP]).

Novell IPX network addresses are unique and are represented in a hexadecimal format that consists of two parts: a network number and a node number. The IPX network number, which is assigned by the network administrator, is 32 bits long. The node number, which usually is the Media Access Control (MAC) address for one of the system's network interface cards (NICs), is 48 bits long. IPX's use of a MAC address for the node number enables the system to send nodes to predict what MAC address to use on a data link.

Novell NetWare IPX supports four encapsulation schemes on a single router interface:

• Novell Proprietary -- Also called 802.3 raw or Novell Ethernet_802.3, Novell proprietary serves as the initial encapsulation scheme that Novell uses.
• 802.3 -- Also called Novell_802.2, 802.3 is the standard IEEE 802.3 frame format.
• Ethernet version 2 -- Also called Ethernet-II or ARPA, Ethernet version 2 includes the standard Ethernet Version 2 header, which consists of Destination and Source Address fields followed by an EtherType field.
• SNAP -- Also called Ethernet_SNAP, SNAP extends the IEEE 802.2 header by providing a type code similar to that defined in the Ethernet version 2 specification.

The maximum length of the data section of an IPX packet varies from a minimum of 30 bytes (the header only) depending on the lower layer MAC protocol (Ethernet or token ring) that is being used.

Protocol Structure

The NetWare IPX Packet Header:

8	16bit
Checksum	
Packet Length	
Transport control	Packet Type
Destination Network (4 bytes)	
Destination node (6 bytes)	

| Destination socket (2 bytes) |
| Source network (4 bytes) |
| Source node (6 bytes) |
| Source socket (2 bytes) |

• Checksum -- Indicates that the checksum is not used when this 16-bit field is set to 1s (FFFF).
• Packet length -- Specifies the length, in bytes, of a complete IPX datagram. IPX packets can be any length, up to the media maximum transmission unit (MTU) size (no packet fragmentation allowed).
• Transport control -- Indicates the number of routers through which the packet has passed. When this value reaches 16, the packet is discarded under the assumption that a routing loop might be occurring.
• Packet type -- Specifies which upper-layer protocol should receive the packet's information. It has two common values:
        • 5 -- Specifies Sequenced Packet Exchange (SPX)
        • 17 -- Specifies NetWare Core Protocol (NCP)
• Destination network, Destination node, and Destination socket -- Specify destination information.
• Source network, Source node, and Source socket -- Specify source information.

Related Protocols

NetWare, SPX, RIP, NLSP

Sponsor Source

IPX is a Novell protocol.

Reference

http://www.novell.com/documentation/lg/nw65/index.html?page=/documentation/lg/nw65/ipx_enu/data/hc1w6pvi.html
IPX Structure
http://www.cisco.com/univercd/cc/td/doc/cisintwk/ito_doc/netwarep.htm
NetWare Protocols

NCP: NetWare Core Protocol

Protocol Description

The Novell NetWare Core Protocol (NCP) manages access to the primary NetWare server resources. NCP makes procedure calls to the NetWare File Sharing Protocol (NFSP) that services requests for NetWare file and print resources. NCP is the principal protocol for transmitting information between a NetWare server and its clients.

NCP handles login requests and many other types of requests to the file system and the printing system. NCP is a client/server LAN protocol. Workstations create NCP requests and use IPX to send them over the network. At the server, NCP requests are received, unpacked, and interpreted.

NCP services include file access, file locking, security, tracking of resource allocation, event notification, synchronization with other servers, connection and communication, print services and queue and network management.

NCP uses the underlying Internetwork Packet Exchange Layer Services (IPX). More recent NetWare versions (after NetWare 5.0) can also use TCP/IP.

Protocol Structure

The format of the NCP Request header is shown below.

8	16bit
Request type	
Sequence number	Connection number low
Task number	Connection number high
Request code	

• Request type -- Identifies the packet type:
        • 1111H. -- Allocate slot request
        • 2222H -- File server request.
        • 3333H -- File server reply.
        • 5555H -- Deallocate slot request.
        • 7777H -- Burst mode packet (BMP).
        • 9999H -- Positive acknowledge.
        • H signifies hexadecimal notation.
• Sequence number -- Number used by the workstation and file server to identify packets which are sent and received.
• Connection number low -- Low connection ID number assigned to the workstation.
• Task number -- Identifies the operating system e.g., DOS, task.
• Connection number high -- High Connection ID number assigned to the workstation. Used only on the 1000-user version of NetWare, on all other versions will be set to 0.
• Request code -- Identifies the specific request function code.

The structure of the NCP Reply header is the same as the Request header, but the last 2 bytes differ after Connection Number High. This is shown below:

Completion code
Connection status

• Completion code -- The completion code indicates whether or not the Client's request was successful. A value of 0 in the Completion Code field indicates that the request was successful. Any other value indicates an error.
• Connection status -- The fourth bit in this byte will be set to 1 if DOWN is typed at the console prompt, to bring the server down.

Related Protocols

NetWare, SPX, RIP, NLSP, IPX

Sponsor Source

NetWare Core Protocol (NCP) is a Novell protocol.

Reference

http://www.cisco.com/univercd/cc/td/doc/cisintwk/ito_doc/netwarep.htm
NetWare Protocols

NLSP: NetWare Link Services Protocol

Protocol Description

The NetWare Link Services Protocol (NLSP) is a link-state routing protocol in the Novell NetWare architecture. NLSP is based on the OSI Intermediate System-to-Intermediate System (IS-IS) protocol and was designed to replace IPX RIP (Routing Information Protocol) and SAP (Service Advertisement Protocol), Novell's original routing protocols that were designed for small scale internetworks.

Compared with RIP and SAP, NLSP provides improved routing, better efficiency, and scalability. The following are the key features of the NLSP:

• NLSP-based routers use a reliable delivery protocol, so delivery is guaranteed.
• NLSP facilitates improved routing decisions because NLSP-based routers store a complete map of the network, not just next-hop information.
• NLSP is efficient, particularly over a WAN link, because its support of IPX header compression makes it possible to reduce the size of packets. NLSP also supports multicast addressing so that routing information is sent only to other NLSP routers, not to all devices, as RIP does.
• NLSP supports load balancing across parallel paths and improves link integrity. It periodically checks links for connectivity and for the data integrity of routing information.
• NLSP is scalabe because NLSP can support up to 127 hops (RIP supports only 15 hops) and permits hierarchical addressing of network nodes, which allows networks to contain thousands of LANs and servers.
• NLSP-based routers are backward compatible with RIP-based routers.

Similar to IS-IS, NLSP supports hierarchical routing with area, domain, and global internetwork components. Areas can be linked to create routing domains, and domains can be linked to create a global internetwork. NLSP supports three levels of hierarchical routing: Level 1, Level 2, and Level 3 routing.

An NLSP router extracts certain information from the adjacency database and adds locally derived information. Using this information, the router constructs a link-state packet (LSP) that describes its immediate neighbors. All LSPs constructed by all routers in the routing area make up the link-state database for the area. The link-state database is synchronized by reliably propagating LSPs throughout the routing area when a router observes a topology change. Two methods ensure that accurate topology-change information is propagated: flooding and receipt confirmation.

NLSP supports a hierarchical addressing scheme. Each routing area is identified by two 32-bit quantities: a network address and a mask.

Protocol Structure

NLSP WAN Hello Packet:

1	2	3	4		5	6	8			9bytes
Protocol ID	Length Ind.	Minor Version	Rsvd	Rsvd	Packet Type	Major version	Reserved	Rsvd	State	Cct Type
Source ID							Holding Time	Packet Length		
Packet Length	Local Wan Circuit ID	Variable Length Fields								

• Protocol ID -- Identifies the NLSP routing layer with the 0x83 hex number.
• Length indicator -- Determines the number of bytes in the fixed portion of the header.
• Minor version -- Contains one possible decimal value and is ignored on receipt.
• Reserved -- Contains no decimal values and is ignored on receipt.
• Packet type (5 bits) -- Contains 17 possible decimal values.
• Major version -- Contains one possible decimal value.
• Reserved -- Contains no decimal values and is ignored on receipt.
• State (2 bits) -- Sends the router's state associated with the link (0 = up, 1 = initializing, 2 = down).
• Circuit type (Cct type) -- Consists of 2 bits. This field can have one of the following values:

• 0 -- Reserved value; ignore entire packet.
• 1 -- Level 1 routing only.
• 2 -- Level 2 routing only. (The sender uses this link for Level 2 routing.)
• 3 -- Both Level 1 and Level 2. (The sender is a Level 2 router and uses this link for Level 1 and Level 2 traffic.)
• Source ID -- Serves as the system identifier of the sending router.
• Holding time -- Contains the holding timer, in seconds, to be used for the sending router.
• Packet length -- Determines the entire length of the packet, in bytes, including the NLSP header.
• Local WAN circuit ID -- Acts as a unique identifier assigned to this circuit when it is created by the router.
• Variable length field -- Consists of a series of optional fields.

NLSP LAN Hello Packet:

1	2	3	4		5	6	8			9bytes	
Protocol ID	Length Ind.	Minor Version	Rsvd	Rsvd	Packet Type	Major version	Reserved	Rsvd	NM	Res	Cct Type
Source ID							Holding Time	Packet Length			
Packet Length	R	Priority	LAN ID								
Variable Length Fields											

• Protocol ID -- Identifies the NLSP routing layer with the 0x83 hex number.
• Length indicator -- Determines the number of bytes in the fixed portion of the header (up to and including the LAN ID field).
• Minor version -- Contains one possible decimal value and is ignored on receipt.
• Reserved -- Contains no possible decimal values and is ignored on receipt.
• Packet type (5 bits) -- Contains 15 possible decimal values.
• Major version -- Contains one possible decimal value.
• Reserved -- Contains no possible decimal values and is ignored on receipt.
• No multicast (NM) (1 bit) -- Indicates, when set to 1, that the packet sender cannot receive traffic addressed to a multicast address. (Future packets on this LAN must be sent to the broadcast address.)
• Circuit type (Cct Type) (2 bits) -- Can have one of the following values:

• 0 -- Reserved value; ignore entire packet.
• 1 -- Level 1 routing only.
• 2 -- Level 2 routing only. (The sender uses this link for Level 2 routing.)
• 3 -- Both Level 1 and Level 2. (The sender is a Level 2 router and uses this link for Level 1 and Level 2 traffic.)
• Source ID -- Contains the system ID of the sending router.
• Holding time -- Contains the holding timer, in seconds, to be used for the sending router.
• Packet length -- Determines the entire length of the packet, in bytes, including the NLSP header.
• R -- Contains no possible decimal values and is ignored on receipt.
• Priority (7 bits) -- Serves as the priority associated with being the LAN Level 1 designated router. (Higher numbers have higher priority.)
• LAN ID -- Contains the system ID (6 bytes) of the LAN Level 1 designated router, followed by a field assigned by that designated router.
• Variable length fields -- Consists of a series of optional fields.

Related Protocols

NetWare, SPX, RIP, NCP, IPX, SAP

Sponsor Source

NetWare Link Service Protocol (NLSP) is a Novell protocol.

Reference

http://www.cisco.com/univercd/cc/td/doc/cisintwk/ito_doc/nlsp.htm
NetWare Link Services Protocol

SPX: Sequenced Packet Exchange protocol

Protocol Description

The Sequenced Packet Exchange (SPX) protocol is Novell's legacy transport layer protocol providing a packet delivery service for Novell NetWare network. SPX is based on the Xerox Sequenced Packet Protocol (SPP). SPX, operates on top of IPX and is used in Novell NetWare (prior to NetWare 5.0) systems for communications in client/server application programs, e.g. BTRIEVE (ISAM manager). SPX performs equivalent functions to TCP. The newer versions of NetWare services are run on top of TCP/IP.

IPX receives packets from the network and passes on those for SPX to handle. SPX guarantees that packets are received intact, in the order they were sent, and eliminates duplicate packets. SPX prepares the sequence of packets that a message is divided into and manages the reassembly of received packets, confirming that all have been received and requesting retransmission when they haven't. SPX works directly with the Internetwork Packet Exchange (IPX) protocol, which manages the forwarding of packets in the network. SPX does not provide connections to the file server itself, which uses the NetWare Core Protocol (NCP). SPX has been extended as SPX-II (SPX2).

SPX does not provide group broadcast support; packets can only be sent to a single session partner. SPX can detect if its partner has disappeared.

Protocol Structure

The structure of the SPX packet is shown in the following illustration:

8	16bit
Connection control flag	Datastream type
Source connection ID	
Destination connection ID	
Sequence number	
Acknowledge number	
Allocation number	
Data (0-534 bytes)	

• Connection control flag -- Four flags which control the bi-directional flow of data across an SPX connection. These flags have a value of 1 when set and 0 if not set.
    • Bit 4 -- Eom: End of message.
    • Bit 5 -- Att: Attention bit, not used by SPX.
    • Bit 6 -- Ack: Acknowledge required.
    • Bit 7 -- Sys: Transport control.
• Datastream type -- Specifies the data within the packet:
• Source connection ID -- A 16-bit number assigned by SPX to identify the connection.
• Destination connection ID -- The reference number used to identify the target end of the transport connection.
• Sequence number -- A 16-bit number, managed by SPX, which indicates the number of packets transmitted.
• Acknowledge number -- A 16-bit number, indicating the next expected packet.
• Allocation number -- A 16-bit number, indicating the number of packets sent but not yet acknowledged.

The SPX II header is the same as the SPX header described above, except for the following differences:

• Connection control flag -- Bit 2 - Size negotiation. Bit 3 - SPX II type.
• Datastream type - 252 -- Orderly release request. 253 - Orderly release acknowledgment.

There is also an additional 2-byte Extended Acknowledgement field at the end.

Related Protocols

NetWare, SPX, RIP, NLSP, IPX, NCP

Sponsor Source

SPX is a Novell protocol.

Reference

http://www.cisco.com/univercd/cc/td/doc/cisintwk/ito_doc/netwarep.htm
NetWare Protocols
http://docsrv.sco.com/SDK_netware/CTOC-Enhanced_Sequenced_Packet_Exchange_SPXII_Protocol.html
Enhanced Sequenced Packet Exchange protocol (SPXII)

IBM Systems Network Architecture (SNA) and Protocols

Along with the OSI Model, the Systems Network Architecture (SNA) proposed by IBM, is one of the most popular network architecture models. Although the SNA model is now considered a legacy networking model, SNA is still widely deployed. SNA was designed around the host-to-terminal communication model that IBM's mainframes use. IBM expanded the SNA protocol to support peer-to-peer networking. This expansion was deemed Advanced Peer-to-Peer Networking (APPN) and Advanced Program-to-Program Communication (APPC). Advanced Peer-to-Peer Networking (APPN) represents IBM's second-generation SNA. In creating APPN, IBM moved SNA from a hierarchical, mainframe-centric environment to a peer-to-peer (P2P) networking environment. At the heart of APPN is an IBM architecture that supports peer-based communications, directory services, and routing between two or more APPC systems that are not directly attached.

The IBM SNA model has many similarities with the OSI 7 layers model. However, the SNA model has only 6 layers and does not define specific protocols for its physical control layer. The physical control layer is assumed to be implemented via other standards. The functions of each SNA layer are described as follows:

• Data link control (DLC) -- Defines several protocols, including the Synchronous Data Link Control (SDLC) protocol for hierarchical communication, and the Token Ring Network communication protocol for LAN communication between peers. SDLC provided a foundation for ISO HDSL and IEEE 802.2.
• Path control -- Performs many OSI network layer functions, including routing and datagram segmentation and reassembly (SAR)
• Transmission control—Provides a reliable end-to-end connection service (similar to TCP), as well as encrypting and decrypting services
• Data flow control -- Manages request and response processing, determines whose turn it is to communicate, groups messages, and interrupts data flow on request
• Presentation services -- Specify data-transformation algorithms that translate data from one format to another, coordinate resource sharing, and synchronize transaction operations
• Transaction services -- Provides application services in the form of programs that implement distributed processing or management services

The following figure illustrates how the IBM SNA model maps to the OSI 7 layers reference model.

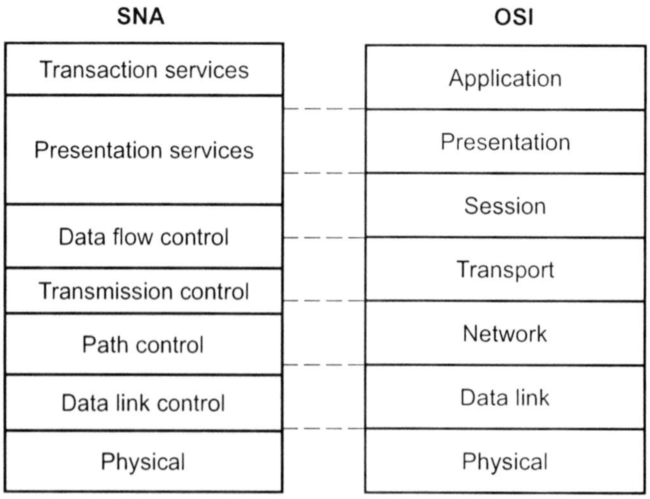

SNA	OSI
Transaction services	Application
Presentation services	Presentation
	Session
Data flow control	Transport
Transmission control	
Path control	Network
Data link control	Data link
Physical	Physical

Figure 2-49: IBM SNA vs. OSI Model

The IBM main protocols are listed as follows:

SNA Layer	IBM Protocols
Transaction Services	SMB: Server Message Block protocol
Presentation Services	IPDS: Intelligent Printer Data Stream
Data Flow Control	APPC: Advanced Program to Program Communication (LU 6.2)
	LU: Logic Units - LU 0, LU 1, LU2, LU 3 LU 6.2
	NetBIOS: Network Basic Input Output System

Reference

http://www-306.ibm.com/software/network
Systems Network Architecture
http://publib-b.boulder.ibm.com/Redbooks.nsf/RedbookAbstracts/
Inside APPN and HPR - The Essential Guide to the Next-Generation SNA
http://publibz.boulder.ibm.com/cgi-bin/bookmgr_OS390/BOOKS/
SNA APPN Architecture Reference

IBM SMB: Server Message Block protocol

Protocol Description

Server Message Block (SMB) protocol is an IBM protocol for sharing files, printers, serial ports, etc. between computers. The SMB protocol can be used over the Internet on top of the TCP/IP protocol or other network protocols such as Internetwork Packet Exchange (Novell IPX) and NetBEUI.

SMB is a client server, request-response protocol, which provides a method for client applications in a computer to read and write to files and to request services from server programs in various types of network environment. Using the SMB protocol, an application can access files as well as other resources including printers, mailslots and named pipes, at a remote server.

In the TCP/IP environment, clients connect to servers using NetBIOS over TCP/IP (or NetBEUI/TCP or SPX/IPX). Once they have established a connection, clients can then send SMB commands to the server that allow them to access shares, open files, read and write files, and generally do all the things that you want to do with a file system.

Microsoft Windows operating systems since Windows 95 include client and server SMB protocol support. Microsoft has offered an open source version of SMB for the Internet, called the Common Internet File System (CIFS), which provides more flexibility than existing Internet applications such as the File Transfer Protocol (FTP). For UNIX systems, a shareware program, Samba, is available.

The Server Message Block (SMB) protocol defines two levels of security:

• Share Level -- Protection is applied at the share level on a server. Each share can have a password, and a client only needs that password to access all files under that share.
• User Level -- Protection is applied to individual files in each share and is based on user access rights. Each user (client) must log in to the server and be authenticated by the server. When it is authenticated, the client is given a UID which it must present on all subsequent accesses to the server.

Protocol Structure

SMB has many variants to handle the complexity of the underneath network environments in which it is employed. The following table displays part of the SBM variants:

SMB Protocol Variant	Protocol Name	Comments
PC NETWORK PROGRAM 1.0	Core Protocol	The original version of SMB as defined in IBM's PC Network Program. Some versions were called PCLAN1.0

MICRO-SOFT NET-WORKS 1.03	Core Plus Protocol	Included Lock&Read and Write&Unlock SMBs with different versions of raw read and raw write SMBs
MICRO-SOFT NET-WORKS 3.0	DOS LAN Manager 1.0	The same as LANMAN1.0, but OS/2 errors must be translated to DOS errors.
LANMAN1.0	LAN Manager 1.0	The full LANMAN1.0 protocol.
DOS LM1.2X002	LAN Manager 2.0	The same as LM1.2X002, but errors must be translated to DOS errors.
LM1.2X002	LAN Manager 2.0	The full LANMAN2.0 protocol.
DOS LANMAN2.1	LAN Manager 2.1	The same as LANMAN2.1, but errors must be translated to DOS errors.
LANMAN2.1	LAN Manager 2.1	The full LANMAN2.1 protocol.
Windows for Workgroups 3.1a	LAN Manager 2.1	Windows for Workgroups 1.0?
NT LM 0.12	NT LAN Manager 1.0	Contains special SMBs for NT
Samba	NT LAN Manager 1.0	Samba's version of NT LM 0.12?
CIFS 1.0	NT LAN Manager 1.0	Really NT LM 0.12 plus a bit

Related Protocols

TCP, SPX, IPX, NetBIOS, NetBEUI

Sponsor Source

Server Message Block (SMB) is an IBM protocol.

Reference

http://samba.anu.edu.au/cifs/docs/what-is-smb.html
What is SMB?

APPC: Advanced Program to Program Communications (SNA LU6.2)

Protocol Description

Advanced Program-to-Program Communications (APPC), a protocol roughly in the OSI resentation and session layer, is a programming interface standard that allows interconnected systems to communicate and share the processing of programs. Originally developed by IBM as a remote transaction processing tool between Logic Units (LUs), APPC is now used to provide distributed services within a heterogeneous computing environment.

APPC software enables high-speed communication to take place between programs residing on different computers, and between workstations and midrange and mainframe computer servers. APPC allows user written programs to perform transactions in a Client-Server network. APPC is a standardized application programming interface which allows an application to use a pre-defined set of VERBS/API for sending and receiving data to/from another program located in a remote node. This set of verbs/API, can only be used with an LU 6.2, which is why the terms APPC, LU 6.2 and PU type 2.1 are very often used interchangeably.

LU 6.2 is the set of SNA parameters used to support APPC when it runs in the SNA network. Basically, LU6.2 acts as an interface, or protocol boundary, between SNA and an end user's application. However, not all APPC communications are based on SNA. APPC also runs between two MVS or CMS program using mainframe system services. Under Anynet, APPC can also run over the TCP/IP protocol used by the Internet.

Protocol Structure

APPC functions and commands:

Sessions, Conversations and Job Management - A client generates a request. It is passed to the subsystem on the client node and is sent through the network to the subsystem on the server node. A subsystem component called the Attach Manager then either queues the request to a running program or starts a new server program.

Attach Manager and Transaction Programs:

• Allocate -- acquires temporary ownership of one of the sessions to the server node.
• Deallocate -- frees the session and ends the conversation.

Sending Data (or Objects)

• Send_Data -- moves a record of data from the application memory to buffers controlled by the subsystem.
• Receive_and_Wait
• Send_Error -- Send_Error breaks the logical chain of incoming records. APPC is responsible for flushing any pending data (from the server node, the network, or the client node). As soon as possible, the client is notified of the problem with a

characteristic return code on the next APPC operation.
• Confirm -- Any pending data is sent, and after the other program receives the data it gets an indication that Confirm is pending. If everything is acceptable, then the correct response is to call the Confirmed verb.

Higher Level Programming:

• Send file (disk to network)
• Send SQL table (DBMS to network)
• Send stack (REXX)
• Send hyperspace (MVS)
• Send clipboard (Windows)

Related Protocols

SNA, APPN

Sponsor Source

APPC (LU6.2) is an IBM protocol.

Reference

http://publib-b.boulder.ibm.com/Redbooks.nsf/RedbookAbstracts/gg242537.html?Open
A CM/2 APPC/APPN Tutorial
http://publib-b.boulder.ibm.com/Redbooks.nsf/RedbookAbstracts/sg243669.html?Open
Inside APPN and HPR - The Essential Guide to the Next-Generation SNA

SNA NAU: Network Accessible Units (PU, LU and CP)

Protocol Description

Network Accessible Units (NAUs), formaerly called "Network Addressable Units", are the IBM Systems Network Architecture (SNA) components to facilitate the communication between a Transaction Program (TP) and the SNA network. NAUs are unique network resources that can be accessed through unique local addresses by other network resources. SNA provides the following types of NAUs:

PU- Physical units

Each SNA node contains a physical unit (PU). The PU manages resources (such as link resources) and supports communication with a host.

LU-Logical Units

Each SNA node contains one or more logical units (LUs). An LU provides a set of functions that are used by TPs and end users to provide access to the network. LUs communicate directly with local TPs and devices.

SNA defines several types of LUs, each optimized for a specific class of applications. LUs of different types cannot communicate with each other, but LUs of the same type can communicate even though they reside on different kinds of systems.

For example, a TP running on a workstation that uses the AIX operating system can communicate with a TP on an AS/400 computer as easily as it can with a TP on another AIX workstation, as long as both TPs use the same LU type.

IBM Communication Server (CS/AIX) supports the following LU types:

LU 6.2 (for APPC, 5250, APPC Application Suite, and CPI-C)

LU 6.2 supports program-to-program communication in a distributed data processing environment. The LU 6.2 data stream is either an SNA general data stream (GDS), which is a structured-field data stream, or a user-defined data stream. LU 6.2 can be used for communication between two type 5 nodes, a type 5 node and a type 2.0 or 2.1 node, or two type 2.1 nodes. (Type 2.1 nodes can serve as APPN nodes.)

This LU type provides more functions and greater flexibility than any other LU type. Unless you are constrained by existing hardware or software, LU 6.2 is the logical choice when developing new applications.

LU 3 (for 3270 printing)

LU 3 supports application programs and printers using the SNA 3270 data stream.

For example, LU 3 can support an application program running under Customer Information Control System (CICS) and sending data to an IBM 3262 printer attached to an IBM 3174 Establishment Controller.

LU 2 (for 3270 displays)

LU 2 supports application programs and display workstations communicating in an interactive environment using the SNA 3270 data stream. Type 2 LUs also use the SNA 3270 data stream for file transfer.

For example, the LU 2 protocol can support 3270 emulation programs, which enable workstations to perform the functions of IBM 3270-family terminals. In addition, LU 2 is used by other programs to communicate with host applications that normally provide output to 3270 display devices. Such TPs enable the workstation to achieve a form of cooperative processing with the host.

LU 1 (for SCS printing and RJE)

LU 1 supports application programs and single- or multiple-device data processing workstations communicating in an interactive, batch-data transfer, or distributed data processing environment. The data streams used by LU type 1 conform to the SNA character string or Document Content Architecture (DCA).

For example, LU type 1 can support an application program running under Information Management System/Virtual Storage (IMS/VS) and communicating with an IBM 8100 Information System. This enables a workstation operator to correct a database that the application program maintains.

Applications that use LU 1 are often described as remote job entry (RJE) applications.

LU 0 (for LUA)

LU 0, an early LU definition, supports primitive program-to-program communication. Certain host database systems, such as IMS/VS (Information Management System/Virtual Storage) and some point-of-sale systems for the retail and banking industries (such as the IBM 4680 Store System Operating System) use LU 0. Current releases of these products also support LU 6.2 communication, which is the preferred protocol for new applications.

CP- Control Points

A control point (CP) is an NAU that manages network resources within its domain, controlling resource activation, deactivation, and status monitoring. The CP manages both physical resources such as links, and logical information such as network addresses.

SNA defines the following types of network control points:

System services control point

On a type 5 node, the CP is called a system services control point (SSCP). It manages and controls the network resources in a subarea network. For example, an SSCP can use a directory of network resources to locate a specific LU under its control, and can establish communication between two LUs in its domain. An SSCP can also cooperate with other SSCPs to establish connectivity between LUs in different subarea do-

mains.

The SSCP also provides an interface to network operators at the host system, who can inspect and control resources in the network.

Physical unit control point

On type 4 nodes and type 2.0 nodes in a subarea network, the control point is called a physical unit control point (PUCP).

Control point

On type 2.1 nodes, the control point provides both PU and LU functions, such as activating local link stations, interacting with a local operator, and managing local resources. It can also provide network services, such as partner LU location and route selection for local LUs.
In a subarea network, the CP on a CS/AIX node acts as a type 2.0 PU. It communicates with an SSCP on a host and does not communicate with other CPs in the subarea network.

When participating in an APPN network, the CP exchanges network control information with the CPs in adjacent nodes. The CP can also function as an independent LU of type 6.2. The CP acts as the default LU for TPs on the local node.

Related Protocols

SNA, APPN, APPC, SSCP, LU0, LU1, Lu2, LU3, LU6.2,

Sponsor Source

NAUs are IBM SNA components.

Reference

http://www-306.ibm.com/software/network/commserver/library/publications/csaix_60/dyvl1m02.htm#ToC_14
Systems Network Architecture

NetBIOS: Network Basic Input Output System

Protocol Description

Network Basic Input Output System (NetBIOS), originally created by IBM, defines a software interface and standard methods providing a communication interface between the application program and the attached medium. NetBIOS, a session layer protocol, is used in various LAN (Ethernet, Token Ring, etc) as well as WAN environments, such as TCP/IP, PPP and X.25 networks.

NetBIOS frees the application from having to understand the details of the network, including error recovery (in session mode). A NetBIOS request is provided in the form of a Network Control Block (NCB) which, among other things, specifies a message location and the name of a destination.

NetBIOS provides the session and transport services described in the Open Systems Interconnection (OSI) model. However, it does not provide a standard frame or data format for transmission. A standard frame format is provided by NetBEUI (NetBIOS Extended User Interface), which provides transport and network layer support of NetBIOS.

NetBIOS provides two communication modes: session or datagram. Session mode lets two computers establish a connection for a "conversation," allows larger messages to be handled, and provides error detection and recovery. Datagram mode is "connectionless" (each message is sent independently), messages must be smaller, and the application is responsible for error detection and recovery. Datagram mode also supports the broadcast of a message to every computer on the LAN.

NetBIOS names are 16 bytes long (padded if necessary) and there are very few restraints on the byte values which can be used. There are three methods of mapping NetBIOS names to IP addresses on small networks that don't perform routing:
1. IP broadcasting -- A data packet with the NetBIOS computer name is broadcast when an associated address is not in the local cache. The host with that name returns its address.
2. The lmhosts file -- This is a file that maps IP addresses and NetBIOS computer names.
3. NBNS -- NetBIOS Name Server. A server that maps NetBIOS names to IP addresses. This service is provided by the nmbd daemon on Linux.

Protocol Structure

NetBIOS packets have many different formats depending on the services and message types as well as on the transport protocols used to carry the NetBIOS packets. NetBIOS has three basic services: NAME, SESSION and DATAGRAM. As an example, we display the NetBIOS name packet format in the TCP/IP environment:

Header (12 bytes)
Question Entry (variable)
Answer Resource Records (variable)
Authority Resource Records (variable)
Additional Resource Records (variable)

The format of the NetBIOS header is shown below:

2	2	1	1	2	2	2 bytes
Length	Delim-inator	Com-mand	Data1	Data2	XMIT Cor	RSP Cor
Destination name (16 bytes)						
Source name (16 bytes)						

• Len -- The length of the NETBIOS header.
• Deliminator -- A delimiter indicating that subsequent data is destined for the NetBIOS function.
• Command -- A specific protocol command that indicates the type of function of the frame.
• Data 1 -- One byte of optional data per specific command.
• Data 2 -- Two bytes of optional data per specific command.
• Xmit/response correlator -- Used to associate received responses with transmitted requests.
• Destination name/num -- In non-session frames this field contains the 16-character name.
• Source name/num -- In non-session frames this field contains the 16-character source name. In session frames this field contains a 1 byte source session number.

Related Protocols

TCP, SMP, Ethernet, Token Ring, X.25, UDP, IPX, NetBEUI, PPP

Sponsor Source

NetBIOS and NetBEUI are IBM protocols.

Reference

http://ourworld.compuserve.com/homepages/TimothyDEvans/contents.htm
NetBios, NetBEUI, NBF, SMB, CIFS Networking
http://www.javvin.com/protocol/rfc1001.pdf
Protocol Standard for a NetBIOS Service on a TCP/UDP Transport: Concepts and Methods
http://www.javvin.com/protocol/rfc1002.pdf
Protocol Standard for a NetBIOS Service on a TCP/UDP Transport: Detailed Specifications

NetBEUI: NetBIOS Extended User Interface

Protocol Description

NetBIOS Extended User Interface (NetBEUI) is an extended version of NetBIOS, that lets computers communicate within a local area network. NetBEUI formalizes the frame format that was not specified as part of NetBIOS, so is sometimes called the NetBIOS frame (NBF) protocol.

NetBEUI provides data transportation but it is not a routable transport protocol. NetBEUI works at the Transport and Network layers of a local area network (LAN). NetBEUI is a good performance choice for communication within a single LAN. For internetwork routing, its interface must be adapted to other protocols such as Internetwork Packet Exchange (IPX) or TCP/IP. Very often, both NetBEUI and TCP/IP are installed in each computer and the server is set up to use NetBEUI for communication within the LAN and TCP/IP for communication beyond the LAN.

NetBIOS and NetBEUI are developed by IBM for its LAN Manager product and have been adopted by Microsoft for its Windows NT, XP and 2000, LAN Manager, and Windows for Workgroups products. Novell, Hewlett-Packard and DEC use them in comparable products.

Protocol Structure

NetBEUI frame header is the same as for NETBIOS:

2	2	1	1	2	2	2 bytes
Length	De-limi-nator	Com-mand	Data1	Data2	XMIT Cor	RSP Cor
Destination name (16 bytes)						
Source name (16 bytes)						

• Length - The length of the header.
• Deliminator -- A delimiter indicating that subsequent data is destined for the NetBIOS function.
• Command -- A specific protocol command that indicates the type of function of the frame.
• Data 1 -- One byte of optional data per specific command.
• Data 2 - Two bytes of optional data per specific command.
• Xmit/response correlator -- Used to associate received responses with transmitted requests.
• Destination name/num -- In non-session frames this field contains the 16-character name.
• Source name/num -- In non-session frames this field contains the 16-character source name. In session frames this field contains a 1 byte source session number.

Related Protocols

TCP, SMP, Ethernet, Token Ring, X.25, UDP, NetBIOS, PPP

Sponsor Source

NetBIOS and NetBEUI are IBM protocols.

Reference

http://ourworld.compuserve.com/homepages/TimothyDEvans/contents.htm
NetBios, NetBEUI, NBF, SMB, CIFS Networking
http://www.javvin.com/protocol/rfc1001.pdf
Protocol Standard for a NetBIOS Service on a TCP/UDP Transport: Concepts and Methods
http://www.javvin.com/protocol/rfc1002.pdf
Protocol Standard for a NetBIOS Service on a TCP/UDP Transport: Detailed Specifications

APPN: Advanced Peer-to-Peer Networking

Protocol Description

Advanced Peer-to-Peer Networking (APPN) is an enhancement to the original IBM SNA architecture. APPN, which includes a group of protocols, handles session establishment between peer nodes, dynamic transparent route calculation, and traffic prioritization. Using APPN, a group of computers can be automatically configured by one of the computers acting as a network controller so that peer programs in various computers will be able to communicate with other using specified network routing.

APPN features include:

• Better distributed network control; because the organization is peer-to-peer rather than solely hierarchical, terminal failures can be isolated
• Dynamic peer-to-peer exchange of information about network topology, which enables easier connections, reconfigurations, and routing
• Dynamic definition of available network resources
• Automation of resouce registration and directory lookup
• Flexibility, which allows APPN to be used in any type of network topology

An APPN network is composed of three types of APPN node:

• Low Entry Networking (LEN) Node -- An APPN LEN node provides peer-to-peer connectivity with all other APPN nodes.
• End Node -- An End Node is similar to a LEN node in that it participates at the periphery of an APPN network. An End Node includes a Control Point (CP) for network control information exchange with an adjacent network node.
• Network Node -- The backbone of an APPN network is composed of one or more Network Nodes which provide network services to attached LEN and End Nodes.
The APPN network has the following major functional processors:

• Connectivity -- The first phase of operation in an APPN network is to establish a physical link between two nodes. When it has been established, the capabilities of the two attached nodes are exchanged using XIDs. At this point, the newly attached node is integrated into the network.
• Location of a Targeted LU -- Information about the resources (currently only LUs) within the network is maintained in a database which is distributed across the End and Network Nodes in the network. End Nodes hold a directory of their local LUs. If the remote LU is found in the directory, a directed search message is sent across the network to the remote machine to ensure that the LU has not moved since it was last used or registered. If the local search is unsuccessful, a broadcast search is initiated across the network. When the node containing the remote LU receives a directed or broadcast search message, it sends back a positive response. A negative response is sent back if a directed or broadcast search fails to find the remote LU.
• Route Selection -- When a remote LU has been located, the originating Network Node server calculates the best route

across the network for a session between the two LUs. Every Network Node in the APPN network backbone maintains a replicated topology database. This is used to calculate the best route for a particular session, based on the required class of service for that session. The class of service specifies acceptable values for such session parameters as propagation delay, throughput, cost and security. The route chosen by the originating Network Node server is encoded in a route selection control vector (RSCV).
• Session Initiation -- A BIND is used to establish the session. The RSCV describing the session route is appended to the BIND. The BIND traverses the network following this route. Each intermediate node puts a session connector for that session in place, which links the incoming and outgoing paths for data on the session.
• Data Transfer -- Session data follow the path of the session connectors set up by the initial BIND. Adaptive pacing is used between each node on the route. The session connectors on each intermediate node are also responsible for segmentation and segment assembly when the incoming and outgoing links support different segment sizes.
• Dependent LU Requestor -- Dependent LUs require a host based System Services Control Point (SSCP) for LU-LU session initiation and management. This means that dependent LUs must be directly attached to a host via a single data link.
• High-performance routing (HPR) -- HPR is an extension to the APPN architecture. HPR can be implemented on an APPN network node or an APPN end node. HPR does not change the basic functions of the architecture. HPR has the following key functions:
    • Improves the performance of APPN routing by taking advantage of high-speed, reliable links
    • Improves data throughput by using a new rate-based congestion control mechanism
    • Supports nondisruptive re-routing of sessions around failed links or nodes
    • Reduces the storage and buffering required in intermediate nodes.

Protocol Structure

A simple APPN network is illustrated in the diagram below:

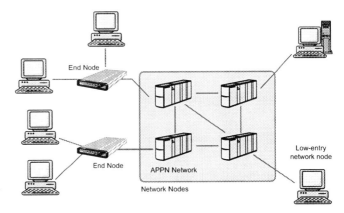

Figure 2-50: IBM APPN Network Illustration.

Related Protocols
SNA, APPC

Sponsor Source

APPN is an IBM network architecture, extended from the IBM SNA.

Reference

http://publib-b.boulder.ibm.com/Redbooks.nsf/RedbookAbstracts/sg243669.html?Open
Inside APPN and HPR - The Essential Guide to the Next-Generation SNA
http://publibz.boulder.ibm.com/cgi-bin/bookmgr_OS390/BOOKS/D50L0000/CCONTENTS
SNA APPN Architecture Reference
http://www.cisco.com/univercd/cc/td/doc/cisintwk/idg4/nd2006.htm#17531
Designing APPN Internetworks
http://www.javvin.com/protocol/rfc2353.pdf
APPN/HPR in IP Networks (APPN Implementers' Workshop Closed Pages Document)

DLSw: Data-Link Switching protocol

Protocol Description

Data-link switching (DLSw) provides a forward mechanism for transporting IBM Systems Network Architecture (SNA) and network basic input/output system (NetBIOS) traffic over an IP network. DLSw does not provide full routing, but instead provides switching at the SNA Data Link layer (i.e., layer 2 in the SNA architecture) and encapsulation in TCP/IP for transport over the Internet.

DLSw, originally a proprietary IBM protocol, was adopted by IETF as a standard. DSLw version 1 (DSLw v1) defines three primary functions:

• The Switch-to-Switch Protocol (SSP) is the protocol maintained between two DLSw nodes or routers.
• The termination of SNA data-link control (DLC) connections helps to reduce the likelihood of link layer timeouts across WANs.
• The local mapping of DLC connections to a DLSw circuit.

DLSw version 2 (DLSw v2), which was introduced in 1997 in IETF, provides the following enhancements to the version 1:

• IP multicast
• UDP unicast responses to DLSw broadcasts
• Enhanced peer-on-demand routing
• Expedited TCP connections

Each of these features enables DLSw as a scalable technology over WANs. In DLSw Version 1, transactions occur with TCP. As a result, many operations in a DLSw environment consume circuits between peers. For example, a multicast requires multiple TCP connections from the source to each peer. With DLSw Version 2, multicast is distributed using unreliable transport following traditional multicast methods.

Cisco supports a third version of DLSw called DLSw+. DLSw+ predates DLSw Version 2 and provides even further enhancements to the basic DLSw.

Protocol Structure

8	16	24	32bit
Version number	Header Length	Message Length	
Remote data link correlator			
Remote DLC port ID			
Reserved Field		Message type	Flow control byte

• Version number -- Set to 0x31 (ASCII 1) indicating a decimal value of 49. This is used to indicate DLSw version 1.
• Header length -- Set to 0x48 for control messages and 0x10 for information and Independent Flow Control messages.
• Message length -- Specifies the number of bytes within the data field following the header.

• Remote data link correlator -- Works in tandem with the remote DLC port ID to form a 64-bit circuit ID that identifies the DLC circuit within a single DLSw node. The circuit ID is unique in a single DLSw node and is assigned locally. An end-to-end circuit is identified by a pair of circuit IDs that, along with the data-link IDs, uniquely identifies a single end-to-end circuit.

• Remote DLC port ID -- Works in tandem with the remote data-link correlator to form a 64-bit circuit ID that identifies the DLC circuit within a single DLSw node. The contents of the DLC and DLC Port ID have local significance only. The values received from a partner DLSw must not be interpreted by the DLSw that receives them and should be echoed "as is" to a partner DLSw in subsequent messages.

• Message type -- Indicates a specific DLSw message type. The value is specified in two different fields (offset 14 and 23 decimal) of the control message header. Only the first field is used when parsing a received SSP message. The second field is ignored by new implementations on reception, but is retained for backward compatibility.

• Flow control byte -- Carries the flow-control indicator, flow-control acknowledgment, and flow-control operator bits.

Related Protocols

SDLC, NetBIOS, TCP, SMP, Ethernet, Token Ring, SNA

Sponsor Source

Data-Link Switching (DSLw) was originated by IBM and adopted as a standard by IETF.

Reference

http://www.javvin.com/protocol/rfc1795.pdf
Data Link Switching: Switch-to-Switch Protocol AIW DLSw RIG: DLSw Closed Pages, DLSw Standard Version 1.0
http://www.javvin.com/protocol/rfc2166.pdf
DLSw v2.0 Enhancements

QLLC: Qualified Logic Link Control

Protocol Description

Qualified Logical Link Control (QLLC) is an IBM-defined data-link-layer protocol that allows SNA data to be transported across X.25 networks. When SNA is used over X.25, it uses the qualifier-bit (Q-bit) in the X.25 packet header to indicate special link control information. This information is relevant for SNA control between the two systems communicating with each other but is of no concern to X.25 link control. These qualified packets help SNA to determine who is calling whom between the two communicating systems and indicate such items as maximum message size.

QLLC commands are implemented in X.25 packets with the use of the Q-bit. X.25 packets containing QLLC primitives are typically 5 bytes, or the length of the X.25 packet header, plus 2 bytes of QLLC control information. After the QLLC connection is established, the X.25 connection's unique virtual circuit is used to forward data traffic. LLC (Logical Link Control) is a subset of HDLC (High Level Data Link Control). SDLC (Synchronous Data Link Control) and QLLC are also subsets of HDLC.

Typical QLLC network architecture is shown below:

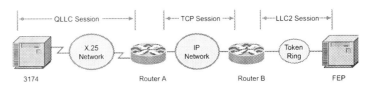

Figure 2-51: QLLC Network Architecture

QLLC supports the following X.25 optional facilities:

• Modulo 8/128 packet sequence numbering
• Closed user groups
• Recognized private operating agencies
• Network user identification
• Reverse charging
• Packet-size negotiation
• Window-size negotiation
• Throughput class negotiation

Protocol Structure

QLLC has the same frame structure as HDLC with the following frame types:

QRR	Receive Ready.
QDISC	Disconnect.
QUA	Unnumbered Acknowledgement.
QDM	Disconnect Mode.
QFRMR	Frame Reject.
QTEST	Test.
QRD	Request Disconnect.
QXID	Exchange Identification.
QSM	Set Mode.

Related Protocols
SNA, APPN, X.25, HDCL, SDCL

Sponsor Source
QLLC is an IBM protocol.

SDLC: Synchronous Data Link Control

Protocol Description

The Synchronous Data Link Control (SDLC) protocol is an IBM data link layer protocol for use in the Systems Network Architecture (SNA) environment.

The data link control Layer provides the error-free movement of data between the Network Addressable Units (NAUs) within a given communication network via the Synchronous Data Link Control (SDLC) Protocol. The flow of information passes down from the higher layers through the data link control Layer and is passed into the physical control Layer. It then passes into the communication links through some type of interface. SDLC supports a variety of link types and topologies. It can be used with point-to-point and multipoint links, bounded and unbounded media, half-duplex and full-duplex transmission facilities, and circuit-switched and packet-switched networks.

SDLC identifies two types of network nodes: primary and secondary. Primary nodes control the operation of other stations, called secondaries. The primary polls the secondaries in a predetermined order, and secondaries can then transmit if they have outgoing data. The primary also sets up and tears down links and manages the link while it is operational. Secondary nodes are controlled by a primary, which means that secondaries can send information to the primary only if the primary grants permission.

SDLC primaries and secondaries can be connected in four basic configurations:

• Point-to-point -- Involves only two nodes, one primary and one secondary.
• Multipoint -- Involves one primary and multiple secondaries.
• Loop -- Involves a loop topology, with the primary connected to the first and last secondaries. Intermediate secondaries pass messages through one another as they respond to the requests of the primary.
• Hub go-ahead -- Involves an inbound and an outbound channel. The primary uses the outbound channel to communicate with the secondaries. The secondaries use the inbound channel to communicate with the primary. The inbound channel is daisy-chained back to the primary through each secondary.

SDLC has a few derivatives which are adopted in different environment:

• HDLC, an ISO protocol for the x.25 network
• LAPB, an ITU-T protocol used in the ISDN network
• LAPF, an ITU-T protocol used in the Frame Relay network
• IEEE 802.2, often referred to as LLC, has three types and is used in the local area network
• QLLC, used to transport SNA data across X.25 networks

Protocol Structure

1 byte	1-2 bytes	1-2 bytes	variable	2 bytes	1 byte

Flag	Ad-dress field	Control field	Data	FCS	Flag

- Flag -- Initiates and terminates error checking.
- Address -- Contains the SDLC address of the secondary station, which indicates whether the frame comes from the primary or secondary.
- Control -- Employs three different formats, depending on the type of SDLC frame used:
    - Information (I) frame -- Carries upper-layer information and some control information.
    - Supervisory (S) frame -- Provides control information. An S frame can request and suspend transmission, report on status, and acknowledge receipt of I frames. S frames do not have an information field.
    - Unnumbered (U) frame -- Supports control purposes and is not sequenced. A U frame can be used to initialize secondaries. Depending on the function of the U frame, its control field is 1 or 2 bytes. Some U frames have an information field.
- Data -- Contains a path information unit (PIU) or exchange identification (XID) information.
- Frame check sequence (FCS) -- Precedes the ending flag delimiter and is usually a cyclic redundancy check (CRC) calculation remainder.

Related Protocols

LAPB, X.25, Frame Relay, HDLC, LAPF, QLLC, LLC

Sponsor Source

SDLC is defined by IBM.

Reference

http://www.cisco.com/univercd/cc/td/doc/cisintwk/ito_doc/sdl-cetc.htm
Synchronous Data Link Control and Derivatives

AppleTalk: Apple Computer Protocols Suite

Description

AppleTalk is a multi-layered protocol suite of Apple Computers providing internetwork routing, transaction and data stream service, naming service and comprehensive file and print sharing among Apple systems using the LocalTalk interface built into the Apple hardware. AppleTalk ports to other network media such as Ethernet by the use of LocalTalk to Ethernet bridges or by Ethernet add-in boards for Apple machines. Many third-party applications exist for the AppleTalk protocols.

An AppleTalk network can support up to 32 devices and data can be exchanged at a speed of 230.4 kilobits per second (Kbps). Devices can be as much as 1,000 feet apart. At the physical level, AppleTalk is a network with a bus topology that uses a trunk cable between connection modules.

The LocalTalk Link Access Protocol (LLAP) must be common to all systems on the network bus and handles the node-to-node delivery of data between devices connected to a single AppleTalk network. Data link layer interfaces to Ethernet, Token ring and FDDI are defined.

The Datagram Delivery Protocol (DDP) is the AppleTalk protocol implemented at the network layer. DDP is a connectionless datagram protocol providing best-effort delivery, which is similar to IP in the TCP/IP suite.

At the Transport Layer, several protocols exist to add different types of functionality to the underlying services. The Routing Table Maintenance Protocol (RTMP) allows bridges and internet routers to dynamically discover routes to the different AppleTalk networks in an internet. The AppleTalk Transaction Protocol (ATP) is responsible for controlling the transactions between requestor and responder sockets.

The Name Binding Protocol (NBP) is for the translation of a character string name into the internet address of the corresponding client. The AppleTalk Echo Protocol (AEP) allows a node to send data to any other node on an AppleTalk internet and receive an echoed copy of that data in return. The AppleTalk Data Stream Protocol (ADSP) is designed to provide byte-stream data transmission in a full duplex mode between any two sockets on an AppleTalk internet. The Zone Information Protocol (ZIP) is used to maintain an internet-wide mapping of networks to zone names.

In the Session Layer, the AppleTalk Session Protocol (ASP) is designed to interact with AppleTalk Transaction Protocol (ATP) to provide for establishing, maintaining and closing sessions.

The AppleTalk Filing Protocol (AFP) is an application or presentation layer protocol designed to control access to remote file systems. A key application using this protocol is the AppleShare for file sharing among a variety of user computers.

Architecture

AppleTalk protocols in the OSI layers:

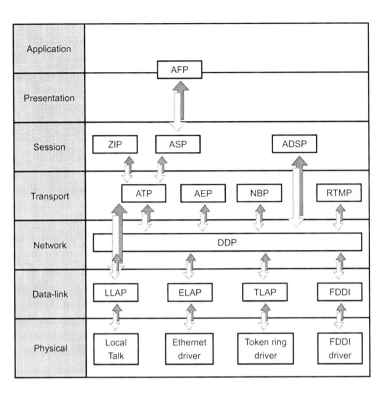

Figure 2-52: AppleTalk Protocol Stack Architecture

Application	AppleShare: for platform sharing of a variety of user computers
Presentation	AFP: AppleTalk Filing Protocol or Apple Filing Protocol
Session	ADSP: AppleTalk Data Stream Protocol
	ASP: AppleTalk Session Protocol
	PAP: Printer Access Protocol
	ZIP: Zone Information Protocol
Transport	AEP: AppleTalk Echo Protocol
	ATP: AppleTalk Transaction Protocol
	NBP: Name Binding Protocol
	RTMP: Routing Table Maintenance Protocol
Network Data Link	DDP: Datagram Delivery Protocol
	AARP: AppleTalk Address Resolution Protocol
	LLAP: LocalTalk Link Access Protocol
	EtherTalk: AppleTalk Ethernet interface
	TokenTalk: AppleTalk Token Ring interface

Related Protocols
Ethernet, Token Ring, FDDI

Sponsor Source
AppleTalk protocols are defined by Apple Computers.

Reference
http://developer.apple.com/macos/opentransport/docs/dev/Inside_AppleTalk.pdf
Inside AppleTalk

DECnet and Protocols

Description

DECnet is a protocol suite developed and supported by Digital Equipment Corporation (Digital or DEC, now part of HP). Several versions of DECnet have been released. The original DECnet allowed two directly attached minicomputers to communicate. Subsequent releases expanded the DECnet functionality by adding support for additional proprietary and standard protocols. Currently, two versions of DECnet are in wide use: DECnet Phase IV and DECnet plus (DECnet V). The DECnet now is part of the HP OpenVMS.

DECnet is developed under the framework of the Digital Network Architecture (DNA), which is a comprehensive layered network architecture that supports a large set of proprietary and standard protocols.

The DECnet Phase IV DNA is similar to the OSI architecture, which utilizes a seven layered approach. However, the Phase IV DNA is comprised of eight layers. The DECnet Phase IV DNA specifies four upper layers to provide user interaction services, network-management capabilities, file transfer, and session management. Specifically, these are referred to as the user layer, network management layer, network application layer, and session control layer.

The DECnet phase V (or DECnet Plus or DECnet/OSI) defines a layered model that implements three protocol suites: OSI, DECnet, and TCP/IP. DECnet plus conforms to the seven-layer OSI reference model and supports many of the standard OSI protocols. DECnet plus provides backward compatibility with DECnet Phase IV and supports multiple proprietary Digital protocols. DECnet plus supports functionality in the application, presentation, and session layers. The TCP/IP implementation of DECnet plus supports the lower-layer TCP/IP protocols and enables the transmission of DECnet traffic over TCP transport protocols.

Key Protocols

DECnet DNA phase IV and V in the OSI model and comparison with the TCP/IP suite , you can see it by figure 2-53.

The key protocols in DECnet protocol suite:

Application	NICE: Network Information and Control Exchange protocol
Presenta-tion	DAP: Data Access Protocol
	CTERM: Command Terminal
Session	SCP: Session Control Protocol
Transport	NSP: Network Service Protocol
Network	DRP: DECnet Routing Protocol
Data Link	MOP: Maintenance Operation Protocol
	DDCMP: Digital Data Communications Message Protocol

Related Protocols

Ethernet, Token Ring, FDDI, TCP, IP, ISO-TP, Frame Relay, LAPB, HDLC, IEEE 802.2

Sponsor Source

DECnet protocols are defined by Digital Equipment Corporation (now part of HP).

Reference

http://ftp.digital.com/pub/DEC/DECnet/PhaseIV/

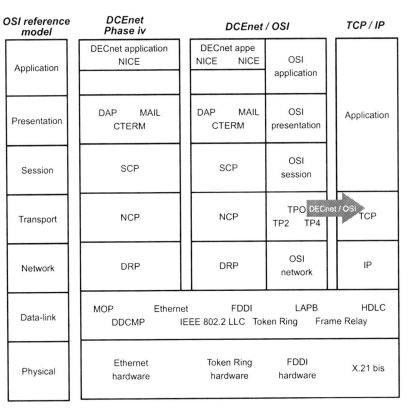

Figure 2-53: DECnet Protocol Suite Architecture

DECnet Phase IV Specifications
http://h71000.www7.hp.com/DOC/73final/6501/6501pro.HTML
DECnet-Plus for OpenVMS Introduction and User's Guide

SS7/C7 Protocols: Signaling System # 7 for Telephony

Protocol Description

Signalling System #7 (SS7) is a telecommunications protocol suite defined by the ITU-T which is used by the telephone companies for interoffice signalling. SS7 uses out of band or common-channel signalling (CCS) techniques, which uses a separated packet-switched network for the signalling purpose. SS7 is known as CCS7 or C7 outside North America and SS7 and C7 are often combined together as SS7/C7 for worldwide audience.

The primary function of SS7/C7 is to provide call control, remote network management, and maintenance capabilities for the inter- office telephone network. SS7 performs these functions by exchanging control messages between SS7 telephone exchanges (signalling points or SPs) and SS7 signalling transfer points (STPs). Basically, the SS7 control network tells the switching office which paths to establish over the circuit-switched network. The STPs route SS7 control packets across the signalling network. A switching office may or may not be an STP.

The SS7/C7 network and protocol are used for providing intelligent network services such as:

- basic call setup, management, and tear down
- wireless services such as personal communications services (PCS), wireless roaming, and mobile subscriber authentication
- local number portability (LNP)
- toll-free (800/888) and toll (900) wireline services
- 911, 411 services
- enhanced call features such as call forwarding, caller ID display, and three-way calling
- efficient and secure worldwide telecommunications

The current SS7 / C7 network, one of the largest data network in the world, connects together local telecoms, cellular, and long-distance networks nationwide and worldwide.

Protocol Structure

The SS7 / C7 protocol suite covers all 7 layers of the OSI model as shown in the following diagram:

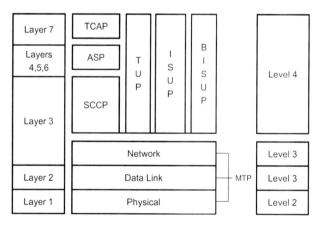

Figure 2-54: SS7/C7 Protocol Suite Architecture

| ASP | Application Service Part | ASP provides the functions of Layers 4 through 6 of the OSI model. |

BICC	Bearer Independent Call Control protocol	BICC is a call control protocol based on ISUP used between serving nodes to support the ISDN services independent of the bearer technology and signalling message transport technology used.
BISUP	B-ISDN User Part	BISUP is an ATM protocol intended to support services such as high-definition television (HDTV), multilingual TV, voice and image storage and retrieval, video conferencing, high-speed LANs and multimedia.
DUP	Data User Part	DUP defines the necessary call control, and facility registration and cancellation related elements for international common channel signalling by use of SS7 for circuit-switched data transmission services.
ISUP	ISDN User Part	ISUP supports basic telephone call connect/disconnect between end offices. ISUP was derived from TUP, but supports ISDN and intelligent networking functions. ISUP also links the cellular and PCS network to the PSTN.
MAP	Mobile Application Part	MAP is used to share cellular subscriber information among different networks.
MTP	Message Transfer Part	MTP crosses physical, data link and network layers. It defines what interface to be used, provides the network with sequenced delivery of all SS7 message packets; and provides routing, message discrimination and message distribution functions.
SCCP	Signalling Connection Control Part	SCCP provides end-to-end routing. SCCP is required for routing TCAP messages to their proper database.
TCAP	Transaction Capabilities Application Part	TCAP facilitates connection to an external database
TUP	Telephone User Part	TUP is an analog protocol that performs basic telephone call connect and disconnect.

Reference

http://www.cisco.com/univercd/cc/td/doc/product/tel_pswt/
vco_prod/ss7_fund/
SS7 Fundamentals
http://www.itu.int/rec/recommendation.asp?type=folders&lang
=e&parent=T-REC-Q.700
Introduction to Signaling System No. 7

Related Protocols

ASP, BICC, BISUP, DUP, ISUP, MTP, SCCP, TCAP, TUP, MAP

Sponsor Source

SS7 / C7 protocols are defined by ITU-T in Q.700 documents series.

BISUP: Broadband ISDN User Part

Protocol Description

Broadband ISDN User Part (BISUP) is a protocol intended to support services such as high-definition television (HDTV), multilingual TV, voice and image storage and retrieval, video conferencing, high-speed LANs and multimedia. Since BISDN is not deployed widely so far, so is not the BISUP.

Protocol Structure

The structure of the B-ISUP protocol is as follows:

8	7	6	5	4	3	2	1	Oc-tets
Message Type								1
Length Indicator								2
								3
Ext.	Broadband/ narrow- band inter- working ind	Pass on not pos- sible ind	Dis- card mes- sage ind	Send notifi- cation ind	Re- lease call ind	Transit at in- termed exch. ind		4

• Message Type -- The different message types. The following message types are available:
• Message Length -- The message length in octets.
• Broadband/narrow-band linterworking Indicator for passing on, discard mesage, release call, etc.
• Pass on not Possible Indicator for release call and discard information
• Discard Message Indicator for dicard or do not discard message
• Send Notification Indicator for sending or do no sending notification
• Release call indicator for release or do not release call
• Transit at intermed exchance Indicator for transit interpretation or end node interpretation

Related Protocols

SS7, ASP, BICC, DAP, ISUP, MTP, SCCP, TCAP, TUP, MAP

Sponsor Source

BISUP is defined by ITU-T Q.2762 and Q.2763.

Reference

http://www.itu.int/rec/recommendation.asp?type=folders&lang=e&parent=T-REC-Q.2762
General Functions of messages and signals of the B-ISUP of Signalling System No. 7

DUP: Data User Part

Protocol Description

Data User Part (DUP), an application protocol in the SS7/C7 protocol suite, defines the necessary call control and facility registration and cancellation related elements for circuit-switched data transmission services. The data signalling messages are divided into two categories:

• Call and circuit related messages: used to set up and clear a call or control and supervise the circuit state.
• Facility registration and cancellation related messages: used to exchange information between originating and destination exchanges to register and cancel information related to user facilities.

While Data User Part (DUP) is still in use currently, but it is fallen out of favor except in certain parts of the world such as China.

Protocol Structure

The pouting label of DUP contains the DPS, OPC, BIC and TSC fields. It is contained in a signalling message and used to identify particulars to which the message refers. This is also used by the message transfer part to route the message towards its destination point.

The general format of the header of call and circuit related messages is shown as follows:

OPC	DPS		
BIC		OPC	
TCS			BIC
Message specific parameters		Heading Code	

The general format of the header of facility registration and cancellation messages is shown as follows:

OPC	DPS	
Spare bits		OPC
Message specific parameters		Heading code

• OPC -- The originating point code (14bits) is the code applicable to the data switching exchange from which the message is sent.
• DPS -- The destination point code (14bits) is the code applicable to the data switching exchange to which the message is to be delivered.
• BIC -- Bearer identification code (12 bits).
• TSC -- Time slot code (8 bits). If the data circuit is derived from the data multiplex carried by the bearer, identified by the bearer identification code:
• Heading code -- The heading code (4 bits) contains the message type code which is mandatory for all messages. It uniquely defines the function and format of each DAP message.
Message specific parameters -- Contains specific fields for • each message.
• Spare bits -- Not used, should be set to "0000".

Related Protocols
SS7, ASP, BICC, BISUP, ISUP, MTP, SCCP, TCAP, TUP, MAP

Sponsor Source
DUP is defined by ITU-T Q.741 (or X.61).

Reference
http://www.itu.int/rec/recommendation.asp?type=folders&lang
=e&parent=T-REC-Q.741
SS7 Data User Part

ISUP: ISDN User Part

Protocol Description
The ISDN User Part (ISUP), a key protocol in the SS7 / C7 signalling system, defines the protocol and procedures used to set-up, manage, and release trunk circuits that carry voice and data calls over the public switched telephone network (PSTN) between different switches. ISUP is used for both ISDN and non-ISDN calls. A simple call flow using ISUP signaling is as follows:

Call set up: When a call is placed to an out-of-switch number, the originating SSP transmits an ISUP initial address message (IAM) to reserve an idle trunk circuit from the originating switch to the destination switch. The destination switch rings the called party line if the line is available and transmits an ISUP address complete message (ACM) to the originating switch to indicate that the remote end of the trunk circuit has been reserved. The STP routes the ACM to the originating switch which rings the calling party's line and connects it to the trunk to complete the voice circuit from the calling party to the called party.

Call connection: When the called party picks up the phone, the destination switch terminates the ringing tone and transmits an ISUP answer message (ANM) to the originating switch via its home STP. The STP routes the ANM to the originating switch which verifies that the calling party's line is connected to the reserved trunk and, if so, initiates billing.

Call tear down: If the calling party hangs-up first, the originating switch sends an ISUP release message (REL) to release the trunk circuit between the switches. The STP routes the REL to the destination switch. If the called party hangs up first, or if the line is busy, the destination switch sends an REL to the originating switch indicating the release cause (e.g., normal release or busy). Upon receiving the REL, the destination switch disconnects the trunk from the called party's line, sets the trunk state to idle, and transmits an ISUP release complete message (RLC) to the originating switch to acknowledge the release of the remote end of the trunk circuit. When the originating switch receives (or generates) the RLC, it terminates the billing cycle and sets the trunk state to idle in preparation for the next call.

Protocol Structure
The ANSI and ITU-T have slightly different ISUP format. ITU-T ISUP message format:

Routing label (5bytes)
Circuit identification code (2 bytes)
Message type code (1 byte)
Parameters – varies according to message type values

• Routing label -- The routing label is used by the relevant user part to identify particulars to which the message refers. It is also used by the Message Transfer Part (MTP) to route the message towards its destination point.
• Circuit identification code -- The allocation of circuit identification codes to individual circuits is determined by bilateral agreement and/or in accordance with applicable predeter-

mined rules.
• Message type code -- The message type code uniquely de-fines the function and format of each ISDN User Part message. Each message consists of a number of parameters. Message types may be:

- Address complete
- Answer
- Blocking
- Blocking acknowledgement
- Call progress
- Circuit group blocking
- Circuit group blocking acknowledgement
- Circuit group query
- Circuit group query response
- Circuit group reset
- Circuit group reset acknowledgement
- Circuit group unblocking
- Circuit group unblocking acknowledgement
- Charge information
- Confusion
- Connect
- Continuity
- Continuity check request
- Facility
- Facility accepted
- Facility reject
- Forward transfer
- Identification request
- Identification response
- Information
- Information request
- Initial address
- Loop back acknowledgement
- Network resource management
- Overload
- Pass-along
- Release
- Release complete
- Reset circuit
- Resume
- Segmentation
- Subsequent address
- Suspend
- Unblocking
- Unblocking acknowledgement
- Unequipped CIC
- User Part available
- User Part test
- User-to-user information

• Parameters -- Each parameter has a name which is coded as a single octet. The length of a parameter may be fixed or variable, and a length indicator for each parameter may be included.

Related Protocols
SS7, ASP, BICC, BISUP, DUP, MTP, SCCP, TCAP, TUP, MAP

Sponsor Source
ISUP is defined by ITU-T Q.763 documents.

Reference
http://www.itu.int/rec/recommendation.asp?type=folders&lang

=e&parent=T-REC-Q.763
SS7 ISDN User Part

MAP: Mobile Application Part

Protocol Description

The Mobile Application Part (MAP), one of the protocols in the SS7 suite, allows for the implementation of the mobile network (GSM) signaling infrastructure. The premise behind MAP is to connect the distributed switching elements, called mobile switching centers (MSCs) with a master database called the Home Location Register (HLR). The HLR dynamically stores the current location and profile of a mobile network subscriber. The HLR is consulted during the processing of an incoming call. Conversely, the HLR is updated as the subscriber moves about the network and is thus serviced by different switches within the network.

MAP has been evolving as wireless networks grow, from supporting strictly voice, to supporting packet data services as well. The fact that MAP is used to connect NexGen elements such as the Gateway GPRS Support node (GGSN) and Serving Gateway Support Node (SGSN) is a testament to the sound design of the GSM signaling system.

MAP has several basic functions:

• Mechanism for a Gateway-MSC (GMSC) to obtain a routing number for an incoming call
• Mechanism for an MSC via integrated Visitor Location Register (VLR) to update subscriber status and routing number.
• Subscriber CAMEL trigger data to switching elements via the VLR
• Subscriber supplementary service profile and data to switching elements via the VLR

Protocol Structure

8	16bit
Operation specifier	Length
MAP Parameters	

• Length -- The length of the packet.
• MAP parameters -- Various parameters depending on the operation.
• Operation specifier -- The type of packet. The following operations are defined:
  • AuthenticationDirective
  • AuthenticationDirectiveForward
  • AuthenticationFailureReport
  • AuthenticationRequest
  • AuthenticationStatusReport
  • BaseStationChallenge
  • Blocking
  • BulkDeregistration
  • CountRequest
  • FacilitiesDirective
  • FacilitiesDirective2
  • FacilitiesRelease
  • FeatureRequest
  • FlashRequest
  • HandoffBack

• HandoffBack2
• HandoffMeasurementRequest
• HandoffMeasurementRequest2
• HandoffToThird
• HandoffToThird2
• InformationDirective
• InformationForward
• InterSystemAnswer
• InterSystemPage
• InterSystemPage2
• InterSystemSetup
• LocationRequest
• MobileOnChannel
• MSInactive
• OriginationRequest
• QualificationDirective
• QualificationRequest
• RandomVariableRequest
• RedirectionDirective
• RedirectionRequest
• RegistrationCancellation
• RegistrationNotification
• RemoteUserInteractionDirective
• ResetCircuit
• RoutingRequest
• SMSDeliveryBackward
• SMSDeliveryForward
• SMSDeliveryPointToPoint
• SMSNotification
• SMSRequest
• TransferToNumberRequest
• TrunkTest
• TrunkTestDisconnect
• Unblocking
• UnreliableRoamerDataDirective
• UnsolicitedResponse

Related Protocols

SS7, ASP, BICC, BISUP, DUP, MTP, SCCP, TCAP, TUP

Sponsor Source

MAP is defined by ITU-T as part of SS7 protocols.

Reference

http://www.cisco.com/univercd/cc/td/doc/product/tel_pswt/vco_prod/ss7_fund/
SS7 Fundamentals
http://www.itu.int/rec/recommendation.asp?type=folders&lang=e&parent=T-REC-Q.700
Introduction to Signaling System No. 7

MTP2 and MTP3: Message Transfer Part level 2 and level 3

Protocol Description

Message Transfer Part (MTP), a protocol in the SS7/C7 protocol suite, transfers signal messages and performs associated functions, such as error control and signaling link security. Message Transfer Part (MTP) also provides reliable routing within a network. MTP has two parts, MTP level 2 (MTP2) and level 3 (MTP3), that respectively perform functions at the layers 2 and 3 of the OSI 7 layers model.

Message Transfer Part Level 2 (MTP2) resides at Layer 2 in the SS7 protocol stack. It is responsible for the reliable transmission of signalling units over an individual Signalling Link. MTP2 reliability is achieved through retransmission techniques.

Message Transfer Part level 3 (MTP3) is the network layer in the SS7 protocol stack. It routes SS7 signalling messages to public network nodes by means of Destination Point Codes, and to the appropriate signalling entity within a node by means of a Service Info Octet. MTP3 is specified as part of the SS7 protocol and is also referred to as part of the B-ICI interface for ATM. MTP3 sits between MTP2 and the user parts (ISUP, TUP, SCCP and TCAP) of the SS7 protocol stack. B-ISUP is an Application Layer protocol run over MTP3.

MTP3 is split into two distinct parts, SMH (Signalling Message Handling) and SNM(Signalling Network Management). The SNM part looks after the general management of MTP, while the SHM part deals with the discrimination, distribution and routing of signalling messages. MTP3 defines the functions and procedures of the signalling system for signalling message handling and signalling network management. Signalling message handling consists of the actual transfer of a signalling message and directing the message to the proper signalling link or user part. Signalling network management consists of controlling the signalling message routing and configuration of the signalling network facilities based on predetermined information and the status of the signalling network facilities.

MTP3 provides a connectionless message transfer system for passing information across a network. MTP3 includes a number of link-protection features, to allow automatic rerouting of signalling messages around broken signalling transfer points. It includes certain management functions for congestion control on signalling links.

MTP2 User Adaptation Layer (M2UA) is used to access MTP2 functions using SCTP (Streaming Control Transmission Protocol). MTP3 User Adaptation Layer (M3UA) is a protocol for supporting the transport of any SS7 MTP3-User signaling (e.g., ISUP, SCCP and TUP messages) over the IP Network.

Protocol Structure

The format of the header of MTP2 is shown as follows:

	7	8bit
	Flag	

BSN (7 bits)	BIB
FSN (7 bits)	FIB
LI (6 + 2 bits)	
SIO	
SIF	
Checksum (16 bits)	
Flag	

• BSN -- Backward sequence number. Used to acknowledge message signal units which have been received from the remote end of the signalling link.
• BIB -- Backward indicator bit. The forward and backward indicator bit together with the forward and backward sequence numbers are used in the basic error control method to perform the signal unit sequence control and acknowledgment functions.
• FSN -- Forward sequence number.
• FIB -- Forward indicator bit.
• LI -- Length indicator. This indicates the number of octets following the length indicator octet.
• SIO -- Service information octet.
• SIF-- Signalling information field.
• Checksum -- Every signal unit has 16 check bits for error detection.

The structure of the MTP-3 header is shown as follows:

4	8bit
Service indicator	Subservice field

• Service indicator -- Used to perform message distribution and in some cases to perform message routing. The service indicator codes are used in international signalling networks for the following purposes:

  • Signalling network management messages
  • Signalling network testing and maintenance messages
  • SCCP
  • Telephone user part
  • ISDN user part
  • Data user part
  • Reserved for MTP testing user part.

• Sub-service field -- The sub-service field contains the network indicator and two spare bits to discriminate between national and international messages.

Related Protocols

SS7, ASP, BICC, BISUP, DUP, ISUP, SCCP, TCAP, TUP

Sponsor Source

MTP level 2 and level 3 protocols are defined by ITU-T documents Q.703 and Q.704.

Reference

http://www.itu.int/rec/recommendation.asp?type=products&parent=T-REC-q
ITU-T Q documents.
http://www.javvin.com/protocol/rfp3331.pdf
Signaling System 7 (SS7) Message Transfer Part 2 (MTP2) - User Adaptation Layer (M2UA)
http://www.javvin.com/protocol/rfp3332.pdf
Signaling System 7 (SS7) Message Transfer Part 3 (MTP3) - User Adaptation Layer (M3UA)

SCCP: Signalling Connection Control Part of SS7

Protocol Description

Signaling Connection Control Part (SCCP), a routing protocol in the SS7 protocol suite (in layer 4), provides end-to-end routing for TCAP messages to their proper databases.

SCCP provides connectionless and connection-oriented network services above MTP Level 3. While MTP Level 3 provides point codes to allow messages to be addressed to specific signaling points, SCCP provides subsystem numbers to allow messages to be addressed to specific applications or subsystems at these signaling points. SCCP is used as the transport layer for TCAP-based services such as free phone (800/888), calling card, local number portability, wireless roaming, and personal communications services (PCS).

SCCP also provides the means by which an STP can perform global title translation (GTT), a procedure by which the destination signaling point and subsystem number (SSN) is determined from digits (i.e., the global title) present in the signaling message. The global title digits may be any sequence of digits, such as 800/888 number, pertinent to the service requested.

Protocol Structure

SCCP messages are contained within the Signaling Information Field (SIF) of an MSU. There are two formats for the SCCP messages. One is defined by ANSI and the other is defined by ITU-T.

Mandatory variable part
Optional part

• Routing label -- A standard routing label – see the picture regarding the ANSI and ITU SCCP message for more information.
• Message type code -- A one octet code which is mandatory for all messages. The message type code uniquely defines the function and format of each SCCP message.
• Mandatory fixed part -- The parts that are mandatory and of fixed length for a particular message type will be contained in the mandatory fixed part.
• Mandatory variable part -- Mandatory parameters of variable length will be included in the mandatory variable part. The name of each parameter and the order in which the pointers are sent is implicit in the message type.
• Optional part -- The optional part consists of parameters that may or may not occur in any particular message type. Both fixed length and variable length parameters may be included. Optional parameters may be transmitted in any order. Each optional parameter will include the parameter name (one octet) and the length indicator (one octet) followed by the parameter contents.

Related Protocols

SS7/C7, ASP, BICC, BISUP, DUP, ISUP, SCCP, TCAP, TUP

Sponsor Source

SCCP is defined by ITU-T documents Q.713.

Reference

http://www.itu.int/itudoc/itu-t/rec/q/q500-999/q713_23786.html
Q.713: SCCP Specification

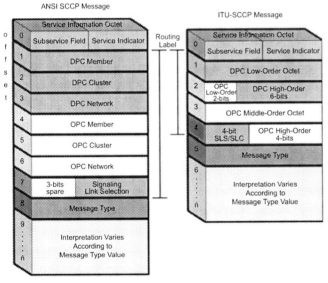

Figure 2-55: SCCP Protocol Structure

The SIF contains the routing label followed by the SCCP message header with the following structure:

Routing label
Message type
Mandatory fixed part

TCAP: Transaction Capabilities Application Part

Protocol Description

Transaction Capabilities Application Part (TCAP), a protocol in the SS7 protocol suite, enables the deployment of advanced intelligent network services by supporting non-circuit related information exchange between signaling points using the Signalling Connection Control Part (SCCP) connectionless service. TCAP also supports remote control-ability to invoke features in another remote network switch.

An SSP uses TCAP to query an SCP to determine the routing number(s) associated with a dialed 800, 888, or 900 number. The SCP uses TCAP to return a response containing the routing number(s) (or an error or reject component) back to the SSP. Calling card calls are also validated using TCAP query and response messages. When a mobile subscriber roams into a new mobile switching center (MSC) area, the integrated visitor location register requests service profile information from the subscriber's home location register (HLR) using mobile application part (MAP) information carried within TCAP messages.

TCAP messages are contained within the SCCP portion of an MSU. A TCAP message is comprised of a transaction portion and a component portion.

Protocol Structure

The TCAP transaction portion contains the package type identifier with the following package types:

- Unidirectional: Transfers component(s) in one direction only (no reply expected).
- Query with Permission: Initiates a TCAP transaction (e.g., a 1-800 query). The destination node may end the transaction.
- Query without Permission: Initiates a TCAP transaction. The destination node may not end the transaction.
- Response: Ends the TCAP transaction. A response to a 1-800 query with permission may contain the routing number(s) associated with the 800 number.
- Conversation with Permission: Continues a TCAP transaction. The destination node may end the transaction.
- Conversation without Permission: Continues a TCAP transaction. The destination node may not end the transaction.
- Abort: Terminates a transaction due to an abnormal situation.

The transaction portion also contains the Originating Transaction ID and Responding Transaction ID fields, which associate the TCAP transaction with a specific application at the originating and destination signaling points respectively.

The TCAP component portion contains components as follows:

- Invoke (Last): Invokes an operation. For example, a Query with Permission transaction may include an Invoke (Last) component to request SCP translation of a dialed 800 number. The component is the "last" component in the query.

- Invoke (Not Last): Similar to the Invoke (Last) component except that the component is followed by one or more components.
- Return Result (Last): Returns the result of an invoked operation. The component is the "last" component in the response.
- Return Result (Not Last): Similar to the Return Result (Last) component except that the component is followed by one or more components.
- Return Error: Reports the unsuccessful completion of an invoked operation.
- Reject: Indicates that an incorrect package type or component was received.

Components include parameters which contain application-specific data carried unexamined by TCAP.

The TCAP header structure:

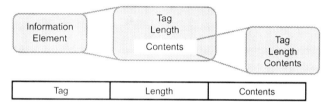

Figure 2-56: TCAP Protocol Structure

- Information Element -- An information element is first interpreted according to its position within the syntax of the message. Each information element within a TCAP message has the same structure. An information element consists of three fields: Tag, Length and Contents.
- Tag -- The Tag distinguishes one information element from another and governs the interpretation of the Contents. It may be one or more octets in length. The Tag is composed of Class, Form and Tag codes.
- Length -- Specifies the length of the Contents.
- Contents -- Contains the substance of the element, containing the primary information the element is intended to convey.

Related Protocols

SS7/C7, ASP, BICC, BISUP, DUP, ISUP, SCCP, TCAP, TUP

Sponsor Source

TCAP is defined by ITU-T documents Q.773.

Reference

http://www.itu.int/itudoc/itu-t/rec/q/q500-999/q773_24880.html
Q.773: TCAP Specification

TUP: Telephone User Part

Protocol Description

The Telephone User Part (TUP) provides the signaling backbone between switching elements for basic call establishment, supervision, and release of circuit switched network connections for telecommunications services. TUP supports analog and digital circuits, and limited call management signaling.

TUP controls the circuits used to carry voice traffic. Also using TUP, the state of circuits can be verified and managed. TUP is good in supporting applications such as switching and voice mail in which calls are routed between endpoints in either fixed or wireless networks.

While Telephone User Part (TUP) is still in use currently, but it is fallen out of favor except certain parts of the world such as China. TUP is replaced by ISUP which adds support for data, advanced ISDN and Intelligent Network.

Protocol Structure

The TUP header structure is as follows:

8	7	6	5	4	3	2	1	Octets
Message Type Code								1

Message Type Code -- It basically contains the label, the heading code and one or more signals and/or indications. The service information octet comprises the service indicator and the subservice field. The service indicator is used to associate signalling information with a particular User Part and is only used with message signal units. The information in the subservice field permits a distinction to be made between national and international signalling messages. In national applications when this discrimination is not required possibly for certain national User Parts only, the subservice field can be used independently for different User Parts.

Related Protocols

SS7, ASP, BICC, BISUP, ISUP, MTP, SCCP, TCAP, DUP, MAP

Sponsor Source

TUP is defined by the ITU-T Q.723 and ISUP is defined in ITU-T Q.763.

Reference

http://www.itu.int/rec/recommendation.asp?type=folders&lang=e&parent=T-REC-Q.723
SS7 Telephone User Part
http://www.itu.int/rec/recommendation.asp?type=folders&lang=e&parent=T-REC-Q.763
SS7 ISDN User Part

Other Protocols

Microsoft CIFS: Common Internet File System

Protocol Description

The Common Internet File System (CIFS), an enhanced version of Microsoft Server Message Block (SMB), is the standard way that computer users share files across intranets and the Internet. CIFS enables collaboration on the Internet by defining a remote file-access protocol that is compatible with the way applications already share data on local disks and network file servers. CIFS runs over TCP/IP, utilizes the Internet's global Domain Naming Service (DNS) for scalability and is optimized to support slower speed dial-up connections common on the Internet. CIFS can be sent over a network to remote devices using the redirector packages. The redirector also uses CIFS to make requests to the protocol stack of the local computer.

Key features that CIFS offers are:

• File Access with integrity: CIFS supports the usual set of file operations; open, close, read, write and seek. CIFS also supports file and record lock and unlocking. CIFS allows multiple clients to access and update the same file while preventing conflicts by providing file sharing and file locking.
• Optimization for Slow Links: The CIFS protocol has been tuned to run well over slow-speed dial-up lines. The effect is improved performance for users who access the Internet using a modem.
• Security: CIFS servers support both anonymous transfers and secure, authenticated access to named files. File and directory security policies are easy to administer.
• Performance and Scalability: CIFS servers are highly integrated with the operating system, and are tuned for maximum system performance. CIFS supports all Microsoft platforms after Windows 95. It also supports other popular operation systems such as UNIX, VMS, Macintosh, IBM LAN server etc.
• Unicode File Names: File names can be in any character set, not just character sets designed for English or Western European languages.
• Global File Names: Users do not have to mount remote file systems, but can refer to them directly with globally significant names, instead of ones that have only local significance.
• CIFS complements Hypertext Transfer Protocol (HTTP) while providing more sophisticated file sharing and file transfer than older protocols, such as FTP.

Protocol Structure

The CIFS and SMB defines many client-and-server types of commands and messages. The commands and messages can be broadly classified as follows:

• Connection establishment messages consist of commands that start and end a redirector connection to a shared resource at the server.
• Namespace and File Manipulation messages are used by the redirector to gain access to files at the server and to read and write them.
• Printer messages are used by the redirector to send data to a print queue at a server and to get status information about the print queue.
• Miscellaneous messages are used by the redirector to write to mailslots and named pipes.

The typical process and architecture of the CIFS message flow is shown as follows:

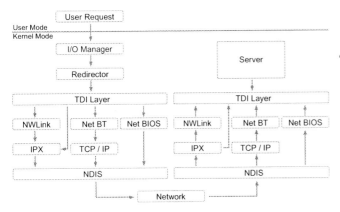

Figure 2-57: Microsoft CIFS Flow Chart

Related Protocols

SMB, HTTP, FTP, DNS

Sponsor Source

CIFS is a Microsoft protocol.

Reference

http://www.microsoft.com/mind/1196/cifs.asp
CIFS: A Common Internet File System
http://www.snia.org/tech_activities/CIFS/CIFS-TR-1p00_FI-NAL.pdf
Common Internet file System (CIFS) Technical Reference

Microsoft SOAP: Simple Object Access Protocol

Protocol Description

The Simple Object Access Protocol (SOAP) is a lightweight and simple XML-based protocol that is designed to exchange structured and typed information on the Web. SOAP can be used in combination with a variety of existing Internet protocols and formats including Hypertext Transfer Protocol (HTTP), Simple Mail Transfer Protocol (SMTP), and Multipurpose Internet Mail Extensions (MIME), and can support a wide range of applications from messaging systems to remote procedure calls (RPCs).

SOAP consists of three parts:

• The SOAP envelope construct defines an overall framework for expressing what is in a message; who should deal with it and whether it is optional or mandatory.
• The SOAP encoding rules define a serialization mechanism that can be used to exchange instances of application-defined data types.
• The SOAP RPC representation defines a convention that can be used to represent remote procedure calls and responses.

SOAP messages are basically one-way transmissions from a sender to a receiver, but SOAP messages are often combined to implement patterns such as request/response. All SOAP messages are encoded using XML. A SOAP message is an XML document that consists of a mandatory SOAP envelope, an optional SOAP header and a mandatory SOAP body.

Binding SOAP to HTTP provides the advantage of being able to use the formalism and decentralized flexibility of SOAP with the rich feature set of HTTP. Carrying SOAP in HTTP does not mean that SOAP overrides existing semantics of HTTP but rather that the semantics of SOAP over HTTP map naturally to HTTP semantics. In the case of using HTTP as the protocol binding, an RPC call maps naturally to an HTTP request and an RPC response maps to an HTTP response. However, using SOAP for RPC is not limited to the HTTP protocol binding.

Protocol Structure

SOAP message format:

SOAP header

<SOAP-ENV: Envelope
Attributes>
<SOAP-ENV:Body
Attributes
</SOAP-ENV:Body>
</SOAP-ENV:Envelope>

Example 1 SOAP Message Embedded in HTTP Request

POST /StockQuote HTTP/1.1
Host: www.stockquoteserver.com
Content-Type: text/xml; charset="utf-8"
Content-Length: nnnn

SOAPAction: "Some-URI"

```
<SOAP-ENV:Envelope
  xmlns:SOAP-ENV="http://schemas.xmlsoap.org/soap/enve-
lope/"
    SOAP-ENV:encodingStyle="http://schemas.xmlsoap.org/
soap/encoding/">
  <SOAP-ENV:Body>
    <m:GetLastTradePrice xmlns:m="Some-URI">
      <symbol>DIS</symbol>
    </m:GetLastTradePrice>
  </SOAP-ENV:Body>
</SOAP-ENV:Envelope>
```

Following is the response message containing the HTTP message with the SOAP message as the payload:

Example 2 SOAP Message Embedded in HTTP Response

```
HTTP/1.1 200 OK
Content-Type: text/xml; charset="utf-8"
Content-Length: nnnn

<SOAP-ENV:Envelope
  xmlns:SOAP-ENV="http://schemas.xmlsoap.org/soap/enve-
lope/"
    SOAP-ENV:encodingStyle="http://schemas.xmlsoap.org/
soap/encoding/"/>
  <SOAP-ENV:Body>
    <m:GetLastTradePriceResponse xmlns:m="Some-URI">
      <Price>34.5</Price>
    </m:GetLastTradePriceResponse>
  </SOAP-ENV:Body>
</SOAP-ENV:Envelope>
```

Related Protocols
HTTP, XML, RPC, MIME, SMTP

Sponsor Source
The Simple Object Access Protocol (SOAP) is proposed by Microsoft.

Reference
http://www.w3.org/TR/2000/NOTE-SOAP-20000508/
Simple Object Access Protocol (SOAP)

NFS: Network File System

Protocol Description
Network File System (NFS), originally developed by Sun Microsystems and then extended by IETF, allows file sharing over network among different types of systems. In other words, NFS was designed for remote file access and sharing over network with various types of machines, operating systems, network architecture and transport protocols.

NFS uses a client/server architecture and consists of a client program and a server program. The server program makes file systems available for access by other machines via a process called exporting. NFS clients access shared file systems mounting them from an NFS server machine. NFS mount protocol is used to communicate between the server and the client for the file access and sharing. NFS mount protocol also allows the server to grant remote access privileges to a restricted set of clients via export control.

NFS Version 2, the first widely implemented version of NFS, originally operated entirely over UDP and was meant to keep the protocol stateless. Several vendors had extended NFSv2 to support TCP as transport. NFS Version 3 introduced support for using TCP as transport. Using TCP as transport made using NFS over a WAN more feasible . Inheritated the good features of the previous versions, the current NFS Version 4 features the following improvements:

• Improved access and performance on the Internet. The protocol is designed to transit firewalls easily, perform well where latency is high and bandwidth is low, and scale to very large numbers of clients per server.
• Strong security with negotiation built into the protocol. The protocol builds on the work of the ONCRPC working group in supporting the Remote Prcedure Call (RPC) RPCSEC_GSS protocol. Additionally, the NFS version 4 provides a mechanism to allow clients and servers to negotiate security and require clients and servers to support a minimal set of security schemes.
• Designed for protocol extensions. The protocol is designed to accept standard extensions that do not compromise backward compatibility.

NFS is strongly associated with UNIX systems, though it can be used on any platform such as Macintosh and Microsoft Windows operating systems. The Server Message Block (SMB) and Common Internet File System (CIFS) are a similar protocol that have equivalent implementation of a network file system under Microsoft Windows.

Protocol Structure
NFS protocol support many basic data types of files. In addition NFS protocol supports the following structured data types:

Name	Structure	Notes

nfstime4	struct nfstime4 {
	int64_t seconds;
	uint32_t nseconds;
	}
		The nfstime4 structure gives the number of seconds and nanoseconds since 0 hour January 1, 1970 Coordinated Universal Time (UTC). This data type is used to pass time and date information.	change_info4	struct change_info4 {
				bool atomic;
				changeid4 before;
				changeid4 after;
				};
					This structure is used with the CREATE, LINK, REMOVE, RENAME operations to let the client know the value of the change attribute for the directory in which the target filesystem object resides.

time_how4	enum time_how4 {
	SET_TO_SERVER_TIME4 = 0,
	SET_TO_CLIENT_TIME4 = 1
	};
		It is used as the attribute definitions to set time values.	clientaddr4	struct clientaddr4 {
				string r_netid<>;
				string r_addr<>;
				};
					It is used as part of the SETCLIENTID operation to either specify the address of the client that is using a clientid or as part of the callback registration.

settime4	union settime4 switch {
	case SET_TO_CLIENT_TIME4:
	nfstime4 time;
	default:
	void;
	};
		It is used as the attribute definitions to set time values.	cb_client4	struct cb_client4 {
				unsigned int cb_program;
				clientaddr4 cb_location;
				};
					This structure is used by the client to inform the server of its call back address; includes the program number and client address.

specdata4	struct specdata4 {
	uint32_t specdata1;
	uint32_t specdata2;
	};
		This data type represents additional information for the device file types NF4CHR and NF4BLK.	nfs_client_id4	struct nfs_client_id4 {
				verifier4 verifier;
				opaque id<NFS4_OPAQUE_LIMIT>;
				};
					This structure is part of the arguments to the SETCLIENTID operation.

fsid4	struct fsid4 {
	uint64_t major;
	uint64_t minor;
	};
		This type is the filesystem identifier that is used as a mandatory attribute.	open_owner4	Struct open_owner4 {
				clientid4 clientid;
				opaque wner<NFS4_OPAQUE_LIMIT>;
				};
					This structure is used to identify the owner of open state.

fs_location4	struct fs_location4 {
	utf8str_cis server<>;
	pathname4 rootpath;
	};
		It is used for the fs_locations recommended attribute which is used for migration and replication support.	lock_owner4	struct lock_owner4 {
				clientid4 clientid;
				opaque owner<NFS4_OPAQUE_LIMIT>;
				};
					This structure is used to identify the owner of file locking state.

fs_locations4	struct fs_locations4 {
	pathname4 fs_root;
	fs_location4 locations<>;
	};
		It is used for the fs_locations recommended attribute which is used for migration and replication support.	open_to_lock_owner4	struct open_to_lock_owner4 {
				seqid4 open_seqid;
				stateid4 open_stateid;
				seqid4 lock_seqid;
				lock_owner4 lock_owner;
				};
					This structure is used for the first LOCK operation done for an open_owner4. It provides both the open_stateid and lock_owner such that the transition is made from a valid open_stateid sequence to that of the new lock_stateid sequence.

fattr4	struct fattr4 {
	bitmap4 attrmask;
	attrlist4 attr_vals;
	};
		The fattr4 structure is used to represent file and directory attributes.			

stateid4	struct stateid4 {
	uint32_t se-
	qid;
	opaque oth-
	er[12];
	};
		This structure is used for various states sharing mechanism between the client and server.

Related Protocols
SMB, CIFS, RPC, TCP, UDP

Sponsor Source
NFS was originally created by Sun Microsystems and now is an IETF protocol.

Reference
http://www.javvin.com/protocol/rfc3530.pdf
NFS Version 4 Protocol Specification
http://www.javvin.com/protocol/rfc1813.pdf
NFS Version 3 Protocol Specification
http://www.javvin.com/protocol/rfc1094.pdf
NFS Version 2 Protocol Specification

Xerox IDP: Internet Datagram Protocol

Protocol Description
Internet Datagram Protocol (IDP) is a simple, unreliable datagram protocol, which is used to support the SOCK_DGRAM abstraction for the Internet Protocol (IP) family. IDP sockets are connectionless and normally used with the sendto and recvfrom subroutines. The connect subroutine can also be used to fix the destination for future packets, in which case the recv or read subroutine and the send or write subroutine can be used.

Xerox protocols (XNS protocol suite) are built vertically on top of IDP. Thus, IDP address formats are identical to those used by the Sequenced Packet Protocol (SPP). The IDP port space is the same as the SPP port space; that is, an IDP port may be "connected" to an SPP port, with certain options enabled. In addition, broadcast packets may be sent (assuming that the underlying network supports this) by using a reserved broadcast address. This address is network interface-dependent.

IDP has been adopted by various other manufacturers. The most popular variant is Novell's IPX.

Protocol Structure
Usage Conventions

The following example illustrates how IDP uses the SOCK_DGRAM mechanism:

```
#include <sys/socket.h>
#include <netns/ns.h>
#include <netns/idp.h>
s = socket(AF_NS, SOCK_DGRAM, 0);
```

Socket Options for IDP

SO_HEADERS_ON_INPUT	When set, the first 30 bytes of any data returned from a read or recvfrom subroutine are the initial 30 bytes of the IDP packet, described as follows:
	struct idp {
	  u_short idp_sum;
	  u_short idp_len;
	  u_char idp_tc;
	  u_char idp_pt;
	  struct ns_addr idp_dna;
	  struct ns_addr idp_sna;
	};
	This allows the user to determine both the packet type and whether the packet was a multicast packet or directed specifically at the local host. When requested by the getsockopt subroutine, the SO_HEADERS_ON_INPUT option gives the current state of the option: NSP_RAWIN or 0.

SO_HEAD-ERS_ON_OUTPUT	When set, the first 30 bytes of any data sent are the initial 30 bytes of the IDP packet. This allows the user to determine both the packet type and whether the packet should be a multicast packet or directed specifically at the local host. You can also misrepresent the sender of the packet. When requested by the getsockopt subroutine, the SO_HEADERS_ON_OUT-PUT option gives the current state of the option: NSP_RAWOUT or 0.
SO_DE-FAULT_HEADERS	The user provides the kernel an IDP header, from which the kernel determines the packet type. When the SO_DEFAULT_HEADERS option is requested by the getsockopt subroutine, the kernel provides an IDP header, showing the default packet type and the local and foreign addresses, if connected.
SO_ALL_PACKETS	When set, this option disables automatic processing of both Error Protocol packets, and SPP packets.
SO_SEQNO	When requested by the getsockopt sub-routine, the S0_SEQNO option returns a sequence number that is not likely to be repeated. It is useful in constructing Packet Exchange Protocol (PEP) packets.

Error Codes

The IDP protocol fails if one or more of the following are true:

EISCONN	The socket already has a connection es-tablished on it.
ENOBUFS	The system ran out of memory for an inter-nal data structure.
ENOTCONN	The socket has not been connected or no destination address was specified when the datagram was sent.
EADDRI-NUSE	An attempt was made to create a socket with a port that has already been allocated.
EADDRNO-TAVAIL	An attempt was made to create a socket with a network address for which no net-work interface exists.

Related Protocols
IPX, XNS

Sponsor Source
IDP is defined by Xerox

Toshiba FANP: Flow Attribute Notification Protocol

Protocol Description
Flow Attribute Notification Protocol(FANP) is a protocol between neighbor modes which manages cut-through packet forwarding functionalities. In cut-through packet forwarding, a router doesn't perform conventional IP packet processing for received packets. FANP indicates mapping information between a datalink connection and a packet flow to the neighbor node. It helps a pair of nodes manage mapping information. By using FANP, routers such as the CSR (Cell Switch Router) can forward incoming packets based on their datalink-level connection identifiers, bypassing usual IP packet processing. FANP has the following characteristics:
• Soft-state, cut-through path (Dedicated-VC) management
• Protocol between neighbor nodes instead of end-to-end
• Applicable to any connection-oriented, datalink platform.

FANP generally runs on ATM networks.

There are 7 FANP control messages. They are encapsulated into IP packets, apart from the PROPOSE message which uses an extended ATM ARP message format. The destination IP address in the IP packet header signifies the neighbor node's IP address. The source IP address is the sender's IP address. The IP protocol ID is 110.

The following message format exists for: Offer, Ready and Error messages. Propose Ack, Remove and Remove Ack messages do not have the flow ID field.

Protocol Structure

8	16	24	32bit
Version	OpCode	Checksum	
VCID type	Flow ID	Reserved/Refresh int./Error code	
VCID			
Flow ID			

• Version -- The Version number. This version is version 1.
• OpCode -- Operation code, the following OpCode values exist: 1. Propose Ack; 2. Offer; 3. Ready; 4. Error; 5. Remove; 6. Remove ACK.
• Checksum -- A 16-bit checksum for the whole message.
• VCID type -- The type of VCID. The current value is 1. The VCID uniquely identifies the datalink connection between neighbor nodes.
• Flow ID -- If the Flow ID is 0, then the flow ID field is null. If the Flow ID is 1, then the Flow ID field described below is present.
• Reserved -- In Offer messages the Refresh Timer field appears here. In error messages, the Error code field appears here.
• Refresh timer -- The interval of the Refresh timer, in seconds. (Only appears in Offer messages.) The recommended value is 120.
• Error code -- Only appears in Error Messages.

• VCID -- Virtual Connection Identification.
• Flow ID -- The Flow ID field does not appear in propose ACK, Remove and Remove Ack messages. When there is a flow ID type value of 1, this field contains the source and destination IP addresses of the flow.

Sponsor Source

FANP is a Toshiba protocol circulated by IETF (www.ietf.org) in RFC 2129.

Reference

http://www.javvin.com/protocol/rfc2129.pdf
Toshiba's Flow Attribute Notification Protocol (FANP) Specification

TCP and UDP Port Numbers

Description

TCP and UDP are both transport protocols above the IP layer, which are interfaces between IP and upper-layer processes. TCP and UDP protocol port numbers are designed to distinguish multiple applications running on a single device with one IP address from one another.

Since many network applications may be running on the same machine, computers need something to make sure the correct software application on the destination computer gets the data packets from the source machine, and to make sure replies get routed to the correct application on the source computer. This is accomplished through the use of the TCP or UDP "port numbers". In the TCP and UDP header, there are "Source Port" and "Destination Port" fields which are used to indicate the message sending process and receiving process identities defined. The combination of the IP address and the port number is called "socket".

There are three port ranges defined by IETF IANA: the Well Known Ports, the Registered Ports, and the Dynamic and/or Private Ports.

• The Well Known Ports are in the range of 0 to 1023, which are assigned by the IANA. In most cases, they can only be used by system (or root) processes or by programs executed by privileged users.
• The Registered Ports are in the range of 1024 to 49151, which are not controlled by IANA. They are commonly used by ordinary user processes or programs executed by ordinary users.
• The Dynamic and/or Private Ports are in the range of 49152 to 65535, which are typically used as source port by a TCP or UDP client, to communicate with a remote TCP or UDP server, using a well-known port as destination port.

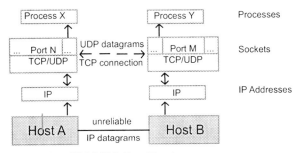

Figure 3-1: TCP/UDP Port Numbers

Partial TCP UDP Port Numbers (Well-Known Ports)

Port No.	Protocol	Service Name	Aliases	Comment
1	TCP	tcpmux		TCP Port Service Multiplexer
2	TCP/UDP	compress-net		Management Utility
3	TCP/UDP	compress-net		Compression Process
7	TCP/UDP	echo		Echo
13	TCP/UDP	daytime		Daytime
19	TCP/UDP	chargen	ttytst source	Character generator
20	TCP	ftp-data		File Transfer
21	TCP	ftp		FTP Control
22	TCP	ssh		SSH remote login protocol
23	TCP	telnet		Telnet
25	TCP	smtp	mail	Simple Mail Transfer
37	TCP/UDP	Time		Time
39	UDP	RLP	resource	Resource Location Protocol
42	TCP/UDP	nameserver	name	Host Name Server
43	TCP	nicname	whois	Who Is
49	UDP	TACACS		TACACS: Login Host Protocol
53	TCP/UDP	domain	DNS	Domain Name Server
67	UDP	bootps	dhcps	Bootstrap Protocol Server
68	UDP	bootpc	dhcpc	Bootstrap Protocol Client
69	UDP	TFTP		Trivial File Transfer Protocol
70	TCP	gopher		Gopher
79	TCP/UDP	finger		Finger
80	TCP/UDP	http	www, http	World Wide Web
88	TCP/UDP	kerberos	krb5	Kerberos
101	TCP	hostname	hostnames	NIC Host Name Server
102	TCP	iso-tsap		ISO-TSAP Class 0
107	TCP	rtelnet		Remote Telnet Service

110	TCP	Pop3	postof-fice	Post Office Protocol - Version 3
111	TCP/UDP	sunrpc	rpcbind portmap	SUN Remote Procedure Call
113	TCP	Auth	ident tap	Authentication Sevice
117	TCP	Uucp-path		UUCP Path Service
118	TCP	sqlserv		SQL Services
119	TCP	nntp	usenet	Network News Transfer Protocol
123	UDP	Ntp		Network Time Protocol
135	TCP/UDP	epmap	loc-srv	DCE endpoint resolution
137	TCP/UDP	netbios-ns	nbname	NETBIOS Name Service
138	UDP	netbios-dgm	nbdata-gram	NETBIOS Datagram Service
139	TCP	netbios-ssn	nbses-sion	NETBIOS Session Service
143	TCP	Imap	imap4	Internet Message Access Protocol
158	TCP	pcmail-srv	reposi-tory	PC Mail Server
161	UDP	snmp	snmp	SNMP
162	UDP	snmp-trap	snmp-trap	SNMP TRAP
170	TCP	Print-srv		Network PostScript
179	TCP	BGP		Border Gateway Protocol
194	TCP	irc		Internet Relay Chat Protocol
213	UDP	ipx		IPX over IP
389	TCP	ldap		Lightweight Directory Access Protocol
401	TCP/UDP	UPS		Uninterruptible Power Supply
443	TCP/UDP	https	MCom	http protocol over TLS/SSL
445	TCP/UDP	CIFS		Microsoft-ds (CIFS)
464	TCP/UDP	kpass-wd		Kerberos (v5)
500	UDP	isakmp	ike	Internet Key Exchange (IPSec)
513	TCP	login		Remote Login
513	UDP	who	whod	Database of who's logged on, average load
514	TCP	cmd	shell	Automatic Authentication
514	UDP	syslog		

515	TCP	printer	spooler	Listens for incoming connections
517	UDP	talk		Establishes TCP Connection
520	TCP	efs		Extended File Name Server
520	UDP	Routing	router routed	RIPv.1, RIPv.2
521	UDP	Routing	router routed	RIPng
525	UDP	Timed	timeserver	Timeserver
526	TCP	Tempo	newdate	Newdate
530	TCP/UDP	Courier	rpc	RPC
531	TCP	conference	chat	IRC Chat
532	TCP	net-news	read-news	Readnews
533	UDP	Netwall		For emergency broadcasts
540	TCP	Uucp	uucpd	Uucpd
543	TCP	Klogin		Kerberos login
544	TCP	Kshell	krcmd	Kerberos remote shell
550	UDP	new-rwho	new-who	New-who
554	UDP	rtsp		Real Time Stream Control Protocol
556	TCP	re-motefs	rfs rfs_server	Rfs Server
560	UDP	rmoni-tor	rmoni-tord	Rmonitor
561	UDP	monitor		
636	TCP	Ldaps	sldap	LDAP over TLS/SSL
749	TCP/UDP	kerbe-ros-adm		Kerberos administration
750	UDP	Kerbe-ros-iv		Kerberos version IV
1080	TCP/UDP	socks		socks
1812	TCP	RA-DIUS		RADIUS
1813	TCP	RA-DIUS		RADIUS accounting

Reference Links

http://www.iana.org/assignments/port-numbers
TCP and UDP port numbers

Major Networking and Telecom Standard Organizations

ANSI: American National Standards Institute

25 west 43rd Street, 4th FL
New York NY 10036 USA
Tel: 212-642-4900
http://www.ansi.org

CEN: European Committee for Standardizations

36 rue de Stassart,
B - 1050 Brussels
Tel: 32 2 550 08 11
http://www.cen.eu

Ethernet Alliance

PO Box 200757
Austin, TX 78720-0757 USA
Tel: 512-363-9932
http://www.ethernetalliance.org

ETSI: European Telecommunications Standards Institute

650, Route des Lucioles
06921 Sophia Antipolis Cedex, France
Tel: 33 (0)4 92 94 42 00
http://www.etsi.org

FCC: Federal Communications Commission

445 12th Street SW
Washington DC 20554 USA
Tel: 888-225-5322
http://www.fcc.gov

IEC: International Electro-technical Commission

3, rue de Varembe
P.B. Box 131
CH-1211 Geneva 20, Switzerland
Tel: 41 22 919 02 11
http://www.iec.ch

IEEE: Institute of Electrical and Electronics Engineers, Inc.

445 Hoes Lane
Piscataway, NJ 08855-1331 USA
Tel: 732-981-0060
http://www.ieee.org

ISOC: Internet Society

http://www.isoc.org

IETF: Internet Engineering Task Force

1775 Wiehle Ave. Suite 102
Reston VA 20190 USA
Tel: 703-326-9880

http://www.ietf.org

ITU: International Telecommunications Union

ITU - Place des Nations
CH-1211 Geneva 20, Switzerland
Tel: 41 22 99 51 11
http://www.itu.ch

ISO: International Organization for Standardization

One rue de Varembe CH-1211
Case Postale 56
Geneva 20, Switzerland
Tel: 41 22 749 0111
http://www.iso.ch

MFA Forum

48377 Fremont Blvd., Suite 117
Fremont, CA 94538
Tel: 510-492-4056
http://www.mfaforum.org

NIST: National Institute of Standard and Technology

100 Bureau Drive, Stop 1070, Gaithersburg, MD 20899-1070
Tel: 301-975-6478
http://www.nist.gov

OMA: Open Mobile Alliance

4275 Executive Square
Suite 240
La Jolla, Ca 92037
Tel: 858-623-0742
http://www.openmobilealliance.org

W3C: World Wide Web Consortium

32 Vassar Street
Room 32-G515
Cambridge, MA 02139 USA
Tel: 617-253-2613
http://www.w3.org

Network Protocols Dictionary: From A to Z and 0 to 9

A B C D E F G H I J K L M N O P Q R S T U V W X Y Z Numbers

A

AAL: ATM Adaptation Layer 137

The ATM Adaptation Layer (AAL) relays ATM cells between the ATM Layer and higher layers. When relaying information received from the higher layers, it segments the data into ATM cells. When relaying information received from the ATM Layer, it must reassemble the payloads into a format the higher layers can understand. This operation, which is called Segmentation and Reassembly (SAR), is the main task of AAL. Different AALs (AAL0, AAL1, AAL2, AAL3/4 and AAL5) were defined in supporting different traffic or services expected to be used.
ATM Forum and ITU-T Specification: ITU-T I.363

AAL0: ATM Adaptation Layer Type 0

ATM Adaptation Layer Type 0 (AAL0) refers to raw ATM cells. AAL0 payload consists of 48 bytes without a special field.
ATM Forum and ITU-T Specification: ITU-T I.366.2

AAL1: ATM Adaptation Layer Type 1 137

ATM Adaptation Layer Type 1 (AAL1) supports constant bit rates, time-dependent traffic such as voice and video. AAL1 is used for connection-oriented, delay-sensitive services requiring constant bit rates (CBR), such as video and voice traffic.
ATM Forum and ITU-T Specification: ITU-T I.366.2

AAL2: ATM Adaptation Layer Type 2 137

ATM Adaptation Layer Type 2 (AAL2) is designed for variable bit rate video transfer. AAL2 is perfect for low-rate voice traffic, with compression, silent and idle channel suppression. AAL type 2 is subdivided into the Common Part Sublayer (CPS) and the Service Specific Convergence Sublayer (SSCS).
ATM Forum and ITU-T Specification: ITU-T I.366.2

AAL3/4: ATM Adaptation Layer Type 3/4 137

ATM Adaptation Layer Type 3/4 (AAL3/4) is designed for variable bit rate, delay-tolerant data traffic requiring some sequencing and/or error detection support. AAL 3/4 supports both connectionless and connection-oriented links, but is primarily used for the transmission of SMDS packets over ATM networks.
ATM Forum and ITU-T Specification: ITU-T I.366.2

AAL5: ATM Adaptation Layer Type 5 137

ATM Adaptation Layer Type 5 (AAL5) is designed for variable bit rate, delay-tolerant connection-oriented data traffic requiring minimal sequencing or error detection support. AAL5 supports connection-oriented, VBR services. AAL5 is used predominantly for the transfer of classic IP over ATM and LANE traffic. AAL5 uses SEAL and is the least complex of the current AAL recommendations. AAL5 has no per-cell length or per-cell CRC fields, and offers low bandwidth overhead and simpler processing requirements in exchange for reduced bandwidth capacity and error-recovery capability.
ATM Forum and ITU-T Specification: ITU-T I.366.2

AARP: AppleTalk Address Resolution Protocol 272

AppleTalk Address Resolution Protocol (AARP), similar to the Address Resolution Protocol (ARP), maps AppleTalk nodes addresses at the network layer to the physical layer (usually MAC) addresses. The AARP table allows for management of the Address Mapping Table on the managed device.
Apple Protocol

ACSE: Association Control Service Element 219

Association Control Service Element (ACSE), an application layer protocol in the OSI model defined by ISO, is designed to establish and release an application-association between two AEIs and to determine the application context of that association. The ACSE supports two modes of communication: connection-oriented and connectionless. For the connection-oriented mode, the application association is established and released by the reference of ACSE connection-oriented services. For the connectionless mode, the application association exists during the invocation of the single ACSE connectionless mode service, a UNIT-DATA.
ISO / ITU-T Specification: ISO 8650 / X.227

ADCCP: Advanced Data Communications Control Protocol

Advanced Data Communications Control Protocol(ADCCP) is a bit-oriented data link control protocol that places data on a network and ensures proper delivery to a destination. ADCCP is based on the IBM's SDLC (Synchronous Data Link Control) protocol. The HDLC (High Level Data Link Control) by ISO and the LAPB(Link Access Protocol-Balanced) by ITU/CCITT are based on the ADCCP.
ANSI Specification: ANSI X3.66

ADSL Lite 152

ADSL Lite, also known as universal ADSL, splitterless ADSL or G.lite, is one of the Digital Subscriber Line technologies that allows broadband data access over normal phone lines (twisted pair cables, also called POTS). ADSL Lite offers a maximum of 1.5 Mbit/s downstream and 512 kbit/s upstream and does not require the use of phone line splitters.
ANSI/ITU-T Protocol

ADSL: Asynchronous Digital Subscriber Line 152

Asynchronous Digital Subscriber Line (ADSL) is one of the Digital Subscriber Line technologies that allows broadband data access over normal phone lines (twisted pair cables, also called POTS). ADSL allows higher speed for data downstream than upstream, and this is why the word "Asynchronous" is there. For conventional ADSL, downstream rates start at 256 kbit/s and typically reach 8 Mbit/s within 1.5 km (5000 ft) of the DSLAM-equipped central office or remote terminal. Upstream rates start at 64 kbit/s and typically reach 256 kbit/s but can go as high as 1024 kbit/s. The name ADSL Lite is sometimes used for the slower versions.
ANSI/ITU-T Protocols

ADSP: AppleTalk Data Stream Protocol 272

AppleTalk Data Stream Protocol (ADSP) is a session-level protocol that provides symmetric, connection-oriented, full-duplex communication between two sockets on the AppleTalk network. In addition, it handles flow-control and reliability and provides a data channel for the hosts, which is a simple trans-

port method for data accross a network. ADSP is a connection-oriented protocol that guarantees in-sequence data delivery with flow control.
Apple Protocol

AEP: AppleTalk Echo Protocol   272

AppleTalk Echo Protocol (AEP) is a transport layer protocol in the AppleTalk protocol suite designed to test the reachability of network nodes. AEP generates packets to be sent to the network node and is identified in the Type field of a packet as an AEP packet. The packet is first passed to the source DDP. After it is identified as an AEP packet, it is forwarded to the node where the packet is examined by the DDP at the destination. After the packet is identified as an AEP packet, the packet is then copied and a field in the packet is altered to create an AEP reply packet, and is then returned to the source node.
Apple Protocol

AES: Advanced Encryption Standard

The Advanced Encryption Standard (AES), also known as Rijndael, is a block cipher adopted as an encryption standard developed by NIST. AES is intended to specify an unclassified, publicly-disclosed, symmetric encryption algorithm. AES has a fixed block size of 128 bits and a key size of 128, 192 or 256 bits.
NIST Specification: Federal Information Processing Standards Publication 197

AES-CMAC

AES-CMAC, abbreviation of Advanced Encryption Standard-Cipher-based Message Authentication Code, is an authentication algorithm based on CMAC with the 128-bit Advanced Encryption Standard (AES). AES-CMAC achieves a security goal similar to that of HMAC. Since AES-CMAC is based on a symmetric key block cipher, AES, and HMAC is based on a hash function, such as SHA-1, AES-CMAC is appropriate for information systems in which AES is more readily available than a hash function.
IETF Specification: RFC 4493

AES-CMAC-PRF-128

AES-CMAC-PRF-128, abbreviation of Advanced Encryption Standard-Cipher-based Message Authentication Code-Pseudo-Random Function-128, is an authentication algorithm based on AES-CMAC. AES-CMAC-PRF-128 is identical to AES-CMAC except that the 128-bit key length restriction is removed.
IETF Specification: RFC 4615

AFP: Apple Filling Protocol   272

Apple Filing Protocol (AFP), formerly AppleTalk Filing Protocol, is the protocol for communicating with AppleShare file servers. Built on top of ASP, it provided services for authenticating users (extensible to different authentication methods including two-way random-number exchange) and for performing operations specific to the Macintosh HFS filesystem.
Apple Protocol

AFP: AppleTalk Filing Protocol   272

AppleTalk Filing Protocol (AFP), renamed to Apple Filing Protocol now, is the protocol for communicating with AppleShare file servers. Built on top of ASP, it provided services for authenticating users (extensible to different authentication methods including two-way random-number exchange) and for performing operations specific to the Macintosh HFS file system.
Apple Protocol

AH: Authentication Header   97

Authentication Header, a protocol in the IPsec (Internet Security) suite, is used to provide connectionless integrity and data origin authentication for IP datagrams, and to provide protection against replays. This protection service against replay is an optional service to be selected by the receiver when a Security Association is established. AH provides authentication for as much of the IP header as possible, as well as for upper level protocol data. However, some IP header fields may change in transit and the value of these fields, when the packet arrives at the receiver, may not be predictable by the sender. The values of such fields cannot be protected by AH. Thus the protection provided to the IP header by AH is only partial in some cases.
IETF Specification: RFC 2402

Airline protocol

Airline protocol refers to the airline reservation system data and the protocols, such as P1024B (ALC), P1024C (UTS), and MATIP, that transport the data between the mainframe and the Agent Set Control Unit (ASCU).

AKE: Augmented Key Exchange

Augmented Key Exchange(AKE) is a key exchange protocol for public key cryptography systems.
IETF Protocol

ALC: Airline Control Protocol

Airline Control Protocol (ALC) is a data link layer polled protocol that runs in full-duplex mode over synchronous serial (V.24) lines and uses the binary-coded decimal (BCD) character set.
ANDNA: Abnormal Netsukuku Domain Name
Anarchy Abnormal Netsukuku Domain Name Anarchy (ANDNA), similar to the Domain Name System (DNS), is the distributed, non-hierarchical and decentralised system of hostname management in Netsukuku. The ANDNA database is scattered inside all the Netsukuku and works in the following way: in order to resolve a hostname, we just have to calculate its hash. The hash is nothing more than a number (IP), and the node related to that IP is called andna_hash_node. The hash_node will keep a small database, which associates all the hostnames related to it with the IP of the node, which has registered the same hostnames.

APON: ATM Passive Optical Network

ATM Passive Optical Network (APON), or ATM PON, is the initial PON specification defined by the FSAN (Full Service Access Network) group using ATM as their layer 2 signaling protocol. Use of the term APON led users to believe that only ATM services could be provided to end-users, so the FSAN decided to broaden the name to Broadband PON (BPON). BPON systems offer numerous broadband services including Ethernet access and video distribution.
FSAN Group Protocol

APPC: Advanced Program-to-Program Communications   262

Advanced Program-to-Program Communications (APPC), a protocol roughly in the OSI presentation and session layers, is a programming interface standard in the IBM SNA system that allows interconnected systems to communicate and share the processing of programs. Originally developed by IBM as a remote transaction processing tool between Logic Units (LUs), APPC is now used to provide distributed services within a heterogeneous computing environment. APPC establishes and

tears down connections between communicating programs, and consists of two interfaces, a programming interface and a data-exchange interface. The former replies to requests from programs requiring communication; the latter establishes sessions between programs.
IBM Protocol

AppleTalk 272

AppleTalk is a multi-layered protocol suite of Apple Computers, providing internetwork routing, transaction and data stream service, naming service and comprehensive file and print sharing among Apple systems using the LocalTalk interface built into the Apple hardware. AppleTalk ports to other network media such as Ethernet by the use of LocalTalk to Ethernet bridges or by Ethernet add-in boards for Apple machines. Many third-party applications exist for the AppleTalk protocols.
Apple Protocol

APPN: Advanced Peer-to-Peer Networking 267

Advanced Peer-to-Peer Networking (APPN) is an enhancement to the original IBM SNA architecture. APPN, which includes a group of protocols, handles session establishment between peer nodes, dynamic transparent route calculation and traffic prioritization. Using APPN, a group of computers can be automatically configured by one of the computers acting as a network controller so that peer programs in various computers will be able to communicate with each other using specified network routing.
IBM Protocol

ARP: Address Resolution Protocol 83

Address Resolution Protocol (ARP) performs mapping of an IP address to a physical machine address (MAC address for Ethernet) that is recognized in the local network. For example, in IP Version 4, an address is 32 bits long. In an Ethernet local area network, however, addresses for attached devices are 48 bits long.
IETF Specification: RFC 826

ASCII: American Standard Code for Information Interchange

American Standard Code for Information Interchange (ASCII) is 8-bit code for character representation (7 bits plus parity). ASCII codes represent text in computers, communications equipment, and other devices that work with text. Most modern character encodings have a historical basis in ASCII. It defines codes for 33 non-printing, mostly obsolete control characters that affect how text is processed, plus 95 printable characters as follows: !"#$%&'()*+,-./0123456789:;<=>? @ABCDEF-GHIJKLMNOPQRSTUVWXYZ[\]^_ `abcdefghijklmnopqrstu-vwxyz{|}~
ANSI Protocol

ASE: Application Service Element

Application Service Element (ASE), defined by ISO, is a protocol in the presentation layer of the OSI seven layer model which provides an abstracted interface layer to service application protocol data units (APDU). Because applications and networks vary, ASEs are split into common application service element (CASE) and Specific-application service elements (SASEs).
ISO Protocol

ASN.1: Abstract Syntax Notation One 230

Abstract Syntax Notation One (ASN.1), an ISO/ITU-T standard, describes data structures for representing, encoding, transmit-

ting, and decoding data. It provides a set of formal rules for describing the structure of objects regardless of language implementation and physical representation of these data, whatever the application, whether complex or very simple.
ISO Specification: X.680

ASP: AppleTalk Session Protocol 272

AppleTalk Session Protocol (ASP), a protocol developed by Apple Computers, provides session establishment, maintenance, and teardown, as well as request sequencing. ASP is built on top of AppleTalk Transaction Protocol (ATP) which is the original reliable session-level protocol for AppleTalk.
Apple Protocol

ATCP: AppleTalk Control Protocol 272

AppleTalk Control Protocol (ATCP) is the protocol that establishes and configures AppleTalk over PPP. ATCP is responsible for configuring, enabling, and disabling the AppleTalk protocol modules on both ends of the point-to-point (PPP) link. ATCP uses the same packet exchange mechanism as the Link Control Protocol (LCP). ATCP packets may not be exchanged until PPP has reached the Network-Layer Protocol phase. ATCP packets received before this phase is reached should be silently discarded.
Apple Protocol

ATIP: AppleTalk Tunneling Through IP

AppleTalk Tunneling Through IP (ATIP) is a protocol that allows an AppleTalk WAN with two or more native AppleTalk networks to be connected through a tunnel built on a TCP/IP internet. This protocol is replaced by AppleTalk Update-based Routing Protocol (AURP).
IETF Protocol

ATM Layer 136

The ATM layer, the layer 2 in the ATM reference model, provides an interface between the ATM adaptation layer (AAL) and the physical layer. This layer is responsible for relaying cells from the AAL to the physical layer, such as SONET, for transmission, and from the physical layer to the AAL for use at the end systems.
ATM Forum and ITU-T Specification: ITU-T I.361

ATM UNI 140

The ATM User-to-Network Interface (UNI) signaling protocols within the Signalling ATM Adaptation Layer (SAAL) are responsible for ATM call and connection control, including call establishment, call clearing, status enquiry and point-to-multipoint control between ATM end users and a private ATM switch, or between a private ATM switch and the public carrier ATM network. ATM UNI signaling message uses the Q.931 message format, which is made up of a message header and a variable number of Information Elements.
ATM Forum and ITU-T Specification: ITU-T I.432

ATM: Asynchronous Transfer Mode 134

The Asynchronous Transfer Mode (ATM) comprises a protocol suite under the ATM reference model, which establishes a mechanism to carry all traffic on a stream of fixed 53-byte packets (cells). A fixed-size packet can ensure that the switching and multiplexing function is carried out quickly and easily. ATM is a connection-oriented technology, i.e. two systems on the network should inform all intermediate switches about their service requirements and traffic parameters in order to establish communication.
ATM Forum and ITU-T Protocol

ATMARP: ATM Address Resolution Protocol

ATM Address Resolution Protocol (ATMARP) is a specialised variant of ARP used to resolve layer-three (IP) addresses to layer-two (ATM NSAP or E.164) addresses in the Classical IP (CLIP) over ATM network environment. The main difference to traditional ARP is that - because ATM lacks a broadcast facility - there is a single designated ATMARP server whose layer-two address has to be configured statically in each client.

IETF / ITU-T Protocol

ATP: ALPS Tunneling Protocol

ALPS Tunneling Protocol is a protocol used to transport ALPS data across a TCP/IP network between an ALC/UTS router and an AX.25/EMTOX router. It consists of a set of messages (or primitives) to activate and deactivate ALPS ATP circuits and to pass data.

ALPS Protocol

ATP: AppleTalk Transaction Protocol   272

AppleTalk Transaction Protocol (ATP), built on top of Datagram Delivery Protocol (DDP), is a transport-level protocol that provides a loss-free transaction service between sockets. The service allows exchanges between two socket clients in which one client requests the other to perform a particular task and to report the results. ATP binds the request and the response together to ensure the reliable exchange of request-response pairs.

Apple Protocol

AURP: AppleTalk Update-Based Routing Protocol

272

The AppleTalk Update-Based Routing Protocol (AURP) is a transport layer protocol in the AppleTalk protocol suite that allows two or more AppleTalk internetworks to be interconnected through a TCP/IP network to form an AppleTalk WAN. AURP is a method of encapsulating AppleTalk traffic in the header of a foreign protocol, allowing the connection of two or more discontiguous AppleTalk internetworks. This connection is called an AURP tunnel. In addition to its encapsulation function, AURP maintains routing tables for the entire AppleTalk WAN by exchanging routing information between exterior routers.

Apple Protocol

B

BACP: Bandwidth Allocation Control Protocol   160

The Bandwidth Allocation Control Protocol (BACP) is the associated control protocol for Bandwidth Allocation Protocol. BACP provides Multilink PPP peers with the ability to govern link utilization. Once peers have successfully negotiated using BACP, they can use the Bandwidth Allocation Protocol (BAP) to negotiate bandwidth allocation.

IETF Specification: RFC 2125

Banyan VINES Protocols

Banyan Virtual Integrated Network Service (VINES) is a protocol stack defined by Banyan Company, derived from the Xerox Network Systems (XNS) protocols. VINES is based on the UNIX operating system and uses a client/server architecture. The Banyan suite includes the following protocols: VARP (VINES Address Resolution Protocol); VIP (VINES Internet Protocol); ICP (Internet Control Protocol); RTP (Routing Update Protocol); IPC (InterProcess Communications Protocol); SPP (Sequenced Packet Protocol); NetRPC (NetRemote Procedure Call); SteetTalk.

In October 1999 Banyan became ePresence, an internet service provider. At the same time, it announced the obsolescence of VINES and other Banyan products.

Banyan Protocol

BAP: Bandwidth Allocation Protocol   160

The Bandwidth Allocation Protocol (BAP) can be used to manage the number of links in a multi-link bundle. BAP defines datagrams to coordinate adding and removing individual links in a multi-link bundle, as well as specifying which peer is responsible for various decisions regarding managing bandwidth during a multi-link connection. BAP provides a set of rules governing dynamic bandwidth allocation through call control. Bandwidth Allocation Control Protocol (BACP) is the associated control protocol for BAP to connect two peers.

IETF Specification: RFC 2125

Basic NAT: Basic Network Address Translation   22

Basic Network Address Translation (Basic NAT) is a method by which IP addresses are mapped from one group to another, transparent to end users. Network Address Port Translation, or NAPT, is a method by which many network addresses and their TCP/UDP ports are translated into a single network address and its TCP/UDP ports. Together, these two operations, referred to as traditional NAT, provide a mechanism to connect a realm with private addresses to an external realm with globally unique registered addresses.

IETF Specification: RFC 3022

BCAST: Broadcast Protocol

Broadcast Protocol (BCAST), a Novell protocol in the NetWare suite, deals with announcements from the network running Netware to inform the user when receiving a message.

Novell Protocol

BCP: Bridging Control Protocol   161

The Bridging Control Protocol (BCP), a protocol in the Point-Point Protocol (PPP) suite, is responsible for configuring the bridging protocol parameters on both ends of the point-to-point link. BCP uses the same packet exchange mechanism as the Link Control Protocol. BCP packets cannot be exchanged until PPP has reached the Network-Layer Protocol phase. BCP packets received before this phase is reached are discarded.

IETF Specification: RFC 3518

BEEP: Blocks Extensible Exchange Protocol

Blocks Extensible Exchange Protocol(BEEP) is a framework for creating network application protocols, that is intended to abstract out the common features that have traditionally been duplicated in each protocol implementation. BEEP is a generic application protocol kernel for connection-oriented, asynchronous interactions. BEEP permits simultaneous and independent exchanges within the context of a single application user-identity, supporting both textual and binary messages.

IETF Specification: RFC 3080

BFD: Bidirectional Forwarding Detection

Bidirectional Forwarding Detection (BFD) is a network protocol used to detect faults between two forwarding engines. BFD provides low-overhead, low-latency detection of faults even on physical media that don't support failure detection of any kind, such as ethernet, virtual circuits, tunnels and MPLS LSPs. BFD establishes a session between two endpoints over a particular link. If more than one link exists between two systems, multiple BFD sessions may be established to monitor each one of them. The session is established with a three-way handshake,

and is torn down the same way.
IETF Protocol

BGMP: Border Gateway Multicast Protocol   67

Border Gateway Multicast Protocol (BGMP) is a protocol for inter-domain multicast routing. BGMP natively supports "source-specific multicast" (SSM). To also support "any-source multicast" (ASM), BGMP builds shared trees for active multicast groups and allows domains to build source-specific, inter-domain distribution branches where needed. Building upon concepts from PIM-SM and CBT, BGMP requires that each global multicast group be associated with a single root. However, in BGMP, the root is an entire exchange or domain, rather than a single router.
IETF Specification: RFC 3913

BGP: Border Gateway Protocol   51

The Border Gateway Protocol (BGP) runs over TCP and is an inter-Autonomous System routing protocol. BGP is the only protocol that is designed to deal with a network of the Internet's size and the only protocol that can deal well with having multiple connections to unrelated routing domains. It is built on experience gained with EGP. The primary function of a BGP system is to exchange network reachability information with other BGP systems.
IETF Specification: RFC 1771

BGP-4: Border Gateway Protocol version 4   51

The Border Gateway Protocol (BGP) is the routing protocol used to exchange routing information across networks. BGP runs over TCP and is an inter-Autonomous System routing protocol. Border Gateway Protocol version 4 (BGP-4), the current version of BGP, provides a set of mechanisms for supporting Classless Inter-Domain Routing (CIDR). These mechanisms include support for advertising a set of destinations as an IP prefix and eliminating the concept of network "class" within BGP. BGP-4 also introduces mechanisms which allow aggregation of routes, including aggregation of AS paths.
IETF Specification: RFC 4271

BIC: Broadband Inter Carrier

Broadband Inter-Carrier (BIC), also known as Broadband Inter-Carrier Interface (BICI) or BISDN Inter-Carrier Interface, is an ITU-T standard that defines the protocols and procedures needed for establishing, maintaining, and terminating broadband switched virtual connections between public networks.
ITU-T Protocol

BICC: Bearer Independent Call Control

Bearer Independent Call Control (BICC) is a signaling protocol based on N-ISUP that is used to support narrowband ISDN service over a broadband backbone network without interfering with interfaces to the existing network and end-to-end services. BICC was designed to be fully compatible with existing networks and any system capable of carrying voice messages.
ITU-T Specification: Q.1901

B-ICI: BISDN Inter Carrier Interface

BISDN Inter Carrier Interface (B-ICI), also known as Broadband Inter-Carrier Interface (BCI), is based on Broadband ISDN User Part (B-ISUP) signaling messages and parameters. BICI is an interface connecting two different ATM based public network providers or carriers. B-ICI is used to facilitate end-to-end national and international ATM/BISDN services. The B-ICI specification also includes service specific functions above the

ATM layer required to transport, operate and manage a variety of intercarrier services across the B-ICI.
ITU-T Protocol

BIDIR-PIM: Bi-directional PIM

Bi-directional PIM (BIDIR-PIM) is one of the Protocol Independent Multicast (PIM) protocols based on PIM-SM. The main difference of BIDIR-PIM from PIM-SM is in the method used to send data from a source to the RP. Whereas in PIM-SM data is sent using either encapsulation or a source-based tree, in BIDIR-PIM the data flows to the RP along the shared tree, which is bi-directional. The main advantage of BIDIR-PIM is that it scales very well when there are many sources for each group. However, the lack of source-based trees means that traffic is forced to remain on the possibly inefficient shared tree. BIDIR-PIM is not used often in real world.
IETF Protocol

BISDN: Broadband Integrated Services Digital Network   153

Broadband Integrated Services Digital Network (BISDN or Broadband ISDN) is designed to handle high-bandwidth applications. BISDN currently uses ATM technology over SONET-based transmission circuits to provide data rates from 155 to 622 Mbps and beyond, in contrast to the traditional narrowband ISDN (or N-ISDN), which is only 64 kps basically and up to 2 Mbps maximum.
ITU-T Protocol

BISUP: Broadband ISDN User Part   278

Broadband ISDN User Part (BISUP) is a protocol intended to support services such as high-definition television (HDTV), multilingual TV, voice and image storage and retrieval, video conferencing, high-speed LANs and multimedia. Since BISDN is not deployed widely so far, so is not the BISUP.
ITU-T Specification: Q.2763

BISYNC

BISYNC, also known as Binary Synchronous Communication (BSC), is an old IBM protocol that was originally designed for batch transmissions between the IBM S/360 mainframe family and IBM 2780 and 3780 terminals. BISYNC establishes rules for transmitting binary-coded data between a terminal and a host computer's BISYNC port. While BISYNC is a half-duplex protocol, it will synchronize in both directions on a full-duplex channel. BISYNC supports both point-to-point (over leased or dial-up lines) and multipoint transmissions. BISYNC was replaced by SDLC (Synchronous Data Link Control).
IBM Protocol

Bluetooth   196

Bluetooth, defined in IEEE 802.15, is for wireless personal area networks (WPANs), which has characters such as short-range, low power, low cost, small networks and communication of devices within a Personal Operating Space. Bluetooth is for wireless transmission between a wide variety of devices such as PCs, cordless phone, headsets and PDAs within 10-meter range.
IEEE Specification: IEEE 802.15.1

BMP: Burst Mode Protocol   252

The Burst Mode Protocol (BMP), a protocol in the Novell NetWare suite, was designed to allow multiple responses to a single request for file reads and writes. Burst Mode increases the efficiency of client/server communications by allowing workstations to submit a single file read or write request and receive

up to 64 kilobytes of data without submitting another request. BMP is actually a type of NetWare Core Protocol (NCP) packet (Request type = 7777H).
Novell Protocol

BOOTP: Bootstrap Protocol   10

The Bootstrap Protocol (BOOTP) is a UDP/IP-based protocol which allows a booting host to configure itself dynamically and without user supervision. BOOTP provides a means to notify a host of its assigned IP address, the IP address of a boot server host and the name of a file to be loaded into memory and executed. Other configuration information, such as the local subnet mask, the local time offset, the addresses of default routers and the addresses of various Internet servers, can also be communicated to a host using BOOTP.
IETF Specification: RFC 951

BPDU: Bridge Protocol Data Unit

Bridge Protocol Data Unit (BPDU), a protocol in the PPP suite, refers to some of "hello packets" of the spanning tree protocol sent out at intervals to exchange information among bridges in the network. BPDUs help describe and identify attributes of a switch port and allow for switches to obtain information about each other.
 IETF Protocol

BPON: Broadband Passive Optical Network

Broadband Passive Optical Network (BPON) is renamed from the ATM PON (APON) which is defined by the Full Service Access Network (FSAN) group. Since using of the term APON led users to believe that only ATM services could be provided to end-users, the FSAN decided to broaden the name to Broadband PON (BPON). BPON systems offer numerous broadband services including Ethernet access and video distribution.
FSAN Group Protocol

BSC: Binary Synchronous Communication

Binary Synchronous Communication (BSC), also known as bisync, is an old IBM protocol that was originally designed for batch transmissions between the IBM S/360 mainframe family and IBM 2780 and 3780 terminals. BISYNC establishes rules for transmitting binary-coded data between a terminal and a host computer's BISYNC port. While BISYNC is a half-duplex protocol, it will synchronize in both directions on a full-duplex channel. BISYNC supports both point-to-point (over leased or dial-up lines) and multipoint transmissions. BISYNC was replaced by SDLC (Synchronous Data Link Control).
IBM Protocol

BVCP: Banyan VINES Control Protocol

Banyan VINES Control Protocol(BVCP), as defined in IETF RFC 1763, is responsible for configuring, enabling, and disabling the VINES protocol modules on both ends of the point-to-point (PPP) link. In order to establish communications over a point-to-point link, each end of the PPP link must first send LCP packets to configure and test the data link. After the link has been established and optional facilities have been negotiated as needed by the LCP, PPP must send BVCP packets to choose and configure the VINES network-layer protocol. Once BVCP has reached the Opened state, VINES datagrams can be sent over the link. The link will remain configured for communications until explicit LCP or BVCP packets close the link down, or until some external event occurs (such as an inactivity timer expires or network administrator intervention).
IETF Specification: RFC 1763

C

C7: Common Channel Signaling 7   276

Common Channel Signaling 7 (CCS7 or C7), also known as Signaling System #7 (SS7), is a telecommunications protocol suite defined by the ITU-T which is used by the telephone companies for interoffice signalling SS7 uses out of band or common-channel signalling (CCS) techniques. SS7/C7 uses a separated packet-switched network for the signalling purpose. SS7 is known as C7 outside North America.
ITU-T Protocol

CCMP: Counter mode with Cipher-block chaining Message authentication code Protocol

Counter mode with Cipher-block chaining Message authentication code Protocol(CCMP) is an encryption protocol in the 802.11i standard. The CCMP is based upon the CCM mode of the AES encryption algorithm and utilizes 128-bit keys, with a 48-bit initialization vector (IV) for replay detection.
IEEE Specification: 802.11i

CCP: Compression Control Protocol

Compression Control Protocol (CCP), a protocol in the Point-to-Point Protocol suite, configures, enables, and disables data compression algorithms on both ends of the point-to-point link.
IETF Protocol

CCS7: Common Channel Signaling 7   276

Common Channel Signaling 7 (CCS7 or C7), also known as Signaling System #7 (SS7), is a telecommunications protocol suite defined by the ITU-T which is used by the telephone companies for interoffice signalling SS7 uses out of band or common-channel signalling (CCS) techniques. SS7/C7 uses a separated packet-switched network for the signalling purpose. SS7 is known as C7 outside North America.
ITU-T Protocol

CDDI: Copper Distributed Data Interface

Copper Distributed Data Interface (CDDI), a version of FDDI using twisted pair cables, provides data rates of 100 Mbps and uses dual-ring architecture to provide redundancy. CDDI supports distances of about 100 meters from desktop to concentrator. The CDDI standard is officially named as the Twisted-Pair Physical Medium-Dependent (TP-PMD) standard. It is also referred to as the Twisted-Pair Distributed Data Interface (TP-DDI).
ANSI Protocol

CDMA: Code Division Multiple Access

Code Division Multiple Access (CDMA) is a second generation (2G) cellular technology defined by Qualcomm in IS-95 and IS-2000. Other widely used multiple access techniques for cellular are Time Division Multiple Access (TDMA) and Frequency Division Multiple Access (FDMA). CDMA technologies are evolving into CDMA2000 to meet the challenges. CDMA2000 is the 3rd Generation solution based on IS-95.
Qualcomm Protocol

CDMA2000: Code Division Multiple Access 2000

Code Division Multiple Access 2000 (CDMA2000) is the 3rd Generation solution based on CDMA IS-95, which supports 3G services as defined by the ITU 3G standards IMT-2000. CDMA2000 defines both an air interface and a core network. CDMA2000 has already been implemented as an evolutionary step from cdmaOne as CDMA2000 provides full backward

compatibility with IS-95B.
Qualcomm Protocol

cdmaOne

cdmaOne is the commercial name for a CDMA (Code Division Multiple Access) system defined by the consortium including Qualcomm, AT&T Wireless and Motorola. The IS-95 standard is part of cdmaOne as the air interface.
Qualcomm Protocol

CDP: Cisco Discovery Protocol 241

Cisco Discovery Protocol (CDP) is primarily used to obtain protocol addresses of neighboring devices and discover the platform of those devices. CDP can also be used to show information about the interfaces your router uses. CDP is media- and protocol-independent and runs on all Cisco-manufactured equipment, including routers, bridges, access servers and switches.
Cisco Protocol

CEP: Certificate Enrollment Protocol

Certificate Enrollment Protocol (CEP) is a certificate management protocol jointly developed by Cisco Systems and VeriSign, Inc. CEP is an early implementation of Certificate Request Syntax (CRS), which is a standard of IETF under the PKIX group. CEP specifies how a device communicates with a CA, including how to retrieve the public key of the CA, how to enroll a device with the CA, and how to retrieve a certificate revocation list (CRL). CEP uses Public Key Cryptography Standard (PKCS) 7 and PKCS 10 as key component technologies.
Cisco Protocol

CGMP: Cisco Group Management Protocol 242

Cisco Group Management Protocol (CGMP) limits the forwarding of IP multicast packets to only those ports associated with IP multicast clients. These clients automatically join and leave groups that receive IP multicast traffic, and the switch dynamically changes its forwarding behavior according to these requests.
Cisco Protocol

CHAP: Challenge Handshake Authentication Protocol 163

Challenge Handshake Authentication Protocol (CHAP) is used to periodically verify the identity of the peer using a 3-way handshake. This is done upon initial link establishment and may be repeated any time after the link has been established. CHAP uses a challenge/response authentication mechanism where the response varies every challenge to prevent replay attacks.
IETF Specification: RFC 1994

CIF: Cells in Frames

Cells in Frames (CIF) is an ATM Protocol for ATM over LAN but with Variable Length Packets. CIF allows ATM to be embedded into various frame based legacy protocols (Ethernet & Token Ring), using only one ATM header for up to 31 cells from the same virtual circuit in a packet. The specification of CIF over PPP and Sonet is underway. A significant feature of CIF is that ATM can be transported to workstations without changing the legacy NIC card because the necessary processing is done in simple downloaded software "SHIM" on the workstation.
ETSI & ECSA Protocol

CIFS: Common Internet File System 286

The Common Internet File System (CIFS), an enhanced version of Microsoft Server Message Block (SMB), is the standard way that computer users share files across intranets and the Internet. CIFS enables collaboration on the Internet by defining a remote file-access protocol that is compatible with the way applications already share data on local disks and network file servers. CIFS runs over TCP/IP and utilizes the Internet's global Domain Naming Service (DNS) for scalability, and is optimized to support slower speed dial-up connections common on the Internet. CIFS can be sent over a network to remote devices using the redirector packages. The redirector also uses CIFS to make requests to the protocol stack of the local computer.
Microsoft Protocol

CLAW: Common Link Access for Workstations

Common Link Access for Workstations (CLAW) is a Data link layer protocol to transport data between the IBM mainframe and the Channel Interface Processor (CIP) in TCP/IP environments. CLAW improves efficiency of channel use and allows the CIP to provide the functionality of a 3172 in TCP/IP environments and support direct channel attachment. The output from TCP/IP mainframe processing is a series of IP datagrams that the router can switch without modifications.
IBM Protocol

CLDAP: Connectionless Lightweighted Directory Access Protocol

Connectionless Lightweighted Directory Access Protocol (CLDAP) is defined in RFC 3352. CLDAP is not deployed in real network.
IETF Specification: RFC 3352

CLNP: Connectionless Network Protocol 235

Connectionless Network Protocol (CLNP) is an ISO network layer datagram protocol by the layers defined in the Reference Model for Open Systems Interconnection (ISO 7498). CLNP provides fundamentally the same underlying service to a transport layer as IP in the TCP/IP environment. Therefore, CLNP is also called ISO-IP. Another OSI protocol in the network layer is CONP (Connection-Oriented Network Protocol), which provides connection-oriented services at the network layer.
ISO Specification: X.213

CLTP: Connectionless Transport Protocol

Connectionless Transport Protocol (CLTP) provides for end-to-end Transport data addressing (via Transport selector) and error control (via checksum), but cannot guarantee delivery or provide flow control. It is the OSI protocol stack, equivalent of UDP of TCP/IP protocol stack.
ISO Protocol

CMAC: Cipher-based Message Authentication Code

Cipher-based Message Authentication Code (CMAC) is an authentication algorithm defined by the National Institute of Standards and Technology (NIST). Also called NIST-CMAC, it is a keyed hash function that is based on a symmetric key block cipher, such as the Advanced Encryption Standard [NIST-AES]. CMAC is equivalent to the One-Key CBC MAC1 (OMAC1) submitted by Iwata and Kurosawa [OMAC1a, OMAC1b]. OMAC1 is an improvement of the eXtended Cipher Block Chaining mode (XCBC) submitted by Black and Rogaway [XCBCa, XCBCb], which itself is an improvement of the basic Cipher Block Chaining-Message Authentication Code (CBC-MAC). XCBC efficiently addresses the security deficiencies of CBC-MAC, and OMAC1 efficiently reduces the key size of XCBC. There are a few variations of CMAC available, such as AES-

CMAC and AES-CMAC-PRF-128 defined by IETF.
NIST Specification: Special Publication 800-38B

CMIP: Common Management Information Protocol
220

Common Management Information Protocol (CMIP), an ISO protocol used with the Common Management Information Services (CMIS), supports information exchange between network management applications and management agents. CMIS defines a system of network management information services. CMIP supplies an interface that provides functions which may be used to support both ISO and user-defined management protocols.
ITU-T/ISO Specification: ITU-T X.700, X.711 and ISO 9595, 9596

CMIS: Common Management Information Service
220

Common Management Information Service (CMIS), an ISO protocol used with the Common Management Information Protocol (CMIP), supports information exchange between network management applications and management agents. CMIS defines a system of network management information services. CMIP supplies an interface that provides functions which may be used to support both ISO and user-defined management protocols.
ITU-T/ISO Specification: ITU-T X.700, X.711 and ISO 9595, 9596

CMOT: CMIP Over TCP/IP   222

CMIP Over TCP/IP (CMOT) is a network management protocol using ISO CMIP to manage IP-based networks. CMOT defines a network management architecture that uses the International Organization for Standardization's (ISO) Common Management Information Services/Common Management Information Protocol (CMIS/CMIP) in the Internet.
IETF Specification: RFC 1189

CONP: OSI Connection-Oriented Network Protocol
236

OSI Connection-Oriented Network Protocol (CONP) is an OSI network layer protocol that carries upper-layer data and error indications over connection-oriented links. Two types of OSI network layer services are available: Connectionless Network Service (CLNS) and Connection-Mode Network Service (CMNS). CONP, based on the X.25 Packet-Layer Protocol (PLP), provides the interface between CMNS and upper layers.
ISO Protocol

COPS: Common Open Policy Service   128

The Common Open Policy Service (COPS) protocol is a simple query and response protocol that can be used to exchange policy information between a policy server (Policy Decision Point or PDP) and its clients (Policy Enforcement Points or PEPs). One example of a policy client is a RSVP router that must exercise policy-based admission control over RSVP usage. At least, one policy server exists in each controlled administrative domain. The COPS protocol has a simple but extensible design.
IETF Specification: RFC 2748

CR-LDP: Constraint-based LDP   81

Constraint-based LDP (CR-LDP) is one of the protocols in the MPLS architecture. It contains extensions for LDP to extend its capabilities, such as setup paths, beyond what is available for the routing protocol. For instance, a LSP (Label Switched Path) can be set up based on explicit route constraints, QoS constraints and other constraints.
IETF Specification: RFC 3212

CRS: Certificate Request Syntax

Certificate Request Syntax (CRS) describes syntax for certification requests. A certification request consists of a distinguished name, a public key, and optionally a set of attributes, collectively signed by the entity requesting certification. Certification requests are sent to a certification authority, which transforms the request into an X.509 public-key certificate.
IETF Specification: RFC 2986

CSMA/CA: Carrier Sense Multi-Access/Collision Avoidance   179

Carrier Sense Multi-Access Collision Avoidance (CSMA/CA) is one of the methods in CSMA. CSMA is a network access method used on shared network topologies such as Ethernet for a node to verify the absence of other traffic before transmitting on a shared physical medium. In Collision Avoidance (CA), collisions are avoided because each node signals its intent to transmit before actually doing so. This method is not popular because it requires excessive overhead that reduces performance. CA is used in wireless LAN communications.
IEEE Specification: IEEE 802.3

CSMA/CD: Carrier Sense Multi-Access/Collision Detection   179

Carrier Sense Multi-Access (CSMA) is a network access method used on shared network topologies such as Ethernet for a node to verify the absence of other traffic before transmitting on a shared physical medium. Collision Detection (CSMA/CD) is one of the methods often used in Ethernet to avoid possible collision, in which when a collision occurs, and both devices stop transmission, wait for a random amount of time, then retransmit.
IEEE Specification: IEEE 802.3

CSMA: Carrier Sense Multi-Access   179

Carrier Sense Multi-Access (CSMA) is a network access method used on shared network topologies such as Ethernet for a node to verify the absence of other traffic before transmitting on a shared physical medium. CSMA devices attached to the network cable listen (carrier sense) before transmitting. If the channel is in use, devices wait before transmitting. Multiple Access(MA) indicates that many devices can connect to and share the same network. All devices have equal access to use the network when it is clear. Even though devices attempt to sense whether the network is in use, there is a good chance that two stations will attempt to access it at the same time. There are two methods for avoiding these so-called collisions: Carrier Sense Multi-Access/Collision Avoidance and Carrier Sense Multi-Access/Collision Detection.
IEEE Specification: IEEE 802.3

CSLIP: Compressed Serial Link Internet Protocol

Compressed Serial Link Internet Protocol (CSLIP), also known as Van Jacobsen TCP header compression, is an extension of SLIP that, when appropriate, allows just header information to be sent across a SLIP connection, reducing overhead and increasing packet throughput on SLIP lines. CSLIP can reduce the TCP header from 40 bytes to seven bytes but with no effects on UDP.

IETF Specification: RFC 1114
CTERM: Command Terminal

Command Terminal (CTERM) is a protocol in the Digital Network Architecture for the terminal emulation. CTERM uses DECnet to provide a command terminal connection between DEC terminals and DEC operating systems such as VMS and RSTS/E.
DEC/HP Protocol

D

DAP: Data Access Protocol

Data Access Protocol (DAP) is a protocol in the Digital Network Architecture to provide remote file access to systems supporting the DECnet.
DEC/HP Protocol

DAP: Directory Access Protocol

Directory Access Protocol (DAP), defined in ISO X.500, is a global directory service. Its components cooperate to manage information about objects such as countries, organizations, people, machines, and so on in a worldwide scope. It provides the capability to look up information by name (a white-page service) and to browse and search for information (a yellow-page service). A subset of X.500 is used to define the Lightweight Directory Access Protocol (LDAP), which supports TCP/IP. LDAP is more popular in real implementation.
ISO&ITU Specification: ISO

DCAP: Data Link Switching Client Access Protocol

11

The Data Link Switching Client Access Protocol (DCAP) is an application layer protocol used between workstations and routers to transport SNA/NetBIOS traffic over TCP sessions. DCAP was introduced to address a few deficiencies in the Data Link Switching Protocol (DLSw). The implementation of the Data Link Switching Protocol (DLSw) on a large number of workstations raises the important issues of scalability and efficiency.
IETF Specification: RFC 2114

DCE/RPC: Distributed Computing Environment / Remote Procedure Calls

Distributed Computing Environment / Remote Procedure Calls (DCE/RPC), commissioned by the Open Software Foundation in a "Request for Technology, includes a group of technologies to call procedures from one application in another application over the network, without having to know about what computer the other application is running on. The usual underlying concerns of a Remote Procedure Call system, such as how, where, who, security and encryption are all hidden behind an extremely well-defined interface. DCE/RPC's reference implementation (version 1.1) is available under the BSD-compatible (Free Software) OSF/1.0 license, and is available for at least Solaris, AIX and VMS.
Open Software Foundation Protocol

DCOP: Desktop COmmunication Protocol

Desktop COmmunication Protocol(DCOP) is a light-weight interprocess and software componentry communication system. DCOP allows applications to interoperate, and to share complex tasks. Essentially, DCOP is a "remote control" system, which allows an application or a script to enlist the help of other applications. It is built on top of the X Window System's Inter-Client Exchange protocol. K Desktop Environment (KDE) applications and the KDE libraries make heavy use of DCOP,

and most of the KDE applications can be controlled by scripts via the DCOP mechanism.

DCP: Data Compression Protocol over Frame Relay

Data Compression Protocol (DCP), defined in FRF.9, defines data compression over Frame Relay. The compression mechanisms can be implemented on both switched virtual circuits (SVC) and permanent virtual circuits (PVC). Their use is negotiated at the time the Frame Relay data link connection identifier (DLCI) is initiated. It applies to unnumbered information (UI) frames encapsulated using Q.933 Annex E and FRF.3.1. It may be used on Frame Relay connections that are interworked with ATM using FRF.5. DCP is logically decomposed into two sublayers: the DCP Control sublayer, and the DCP Function sublayer.
ITU-T Specification: FRF.9

DCPCP: Data Compression Protocol Control Protocol

Data Compression Protocol Control Protocol (DCPCP) is used to enable, disable, and optionally configure Data Compression Protocol (DCP). DCPCP has two modes of operation: Mode-1 operation is required; Mode-2 operation is optional. Mode-2 provides full negotiation capabilities to enable, disable, and configure DCP using the Point-to-Point Protocol (PPP) Link Control Protocol (LCP) negotiation procedures. Mode-1 uses a subset of the Mode-2 negotiation primitives with simplified procedures to enable and disable DCP with the default DCFD and default parameter values.
IETF Protocol

DDDS: Dynamic Delegation Discovery System

The Dynamic Delegation Discovery System (DDDS) defines a mechanism for using Domain Name System (DNS) as the database for arbitrary identifier schemes. DDDS is used to implement lazy binding of strings to data, in order to support dynamically configured delegation systems. The DDDS functions by mapping some unique string to data stored within a DDDS Database by iteratively applying string transformation rules until a terminal condition is reached. Enum(E164 NUmber Mapping) is defines as a DDDS application to resolve phone numbers into data stored in DNS.
IETF Specification: RFC 3401

DDP: Datagram Delivery Protocol

Datagram Delivery Protocol (DDP), a protocol in the AppleTalk suite, is for socket-to-socket delivery of datagrams over an AppleTalk network. DDP was the lowest-level data-link-independent transport protocol. It provided a datagram service with no guarantees of delivery. All application-level protocols in the AppleTalk suite, including the infrastructure protocols NBP, RTMP and ZIP, were built on top of DDP.
Apple Protocol

DECnet
274

DECnet is a protocol suite developed and supported by Digital Equipment Corporation (Digital or DEC, now part of HP). Several versions of DECnet have been released. The original DECnet allowed two directly attached minicomputers to communicate. Subsequent releases expanded the DECnet functionality by adding support for additional proprietary and standard protocols. Currently, two versions of DECnet are in a wide use: DECnet Phase IV and DECnet plus (DECnet V). The DECnet now is part of the HP OpenVMS.
DEC/HP Protocol

DHCP: Dynamic Host Configuration Protocol   *11*

Dynamic Host Configuration Protocol (DHCP) is a communications protocol enabling network administrators to manage centrally, and to automate, the assignment of IP addresses in a network. In an IP network, each device connecting to the Internet needs a unique IP address. DHCP lets a network administrator supervise and distribute IP addresses from a central point and automatically sends a new IP address when a computer is plugged into a different place in the network.
IETF Specification: RFC 2131 and RFC 3396

DIAG: Diagnostic Responder protocol

Diagnostic Responder protocol (DIAG), a protocol in the Novell NetWare suite, is used for connectivity testing and information gathering. By default, Novell NetWare clients use the Diagnostic Responder to reply to diagnostic requests.
Novell Protocol

DiffServ   *94*

DiffServ defines an architecture for implementing scalable service differentiation in the Internet. A "Service" defines some significant characteristics of packet transmission in one direction across a set of one or more paths within a network. These characteristics may be specified in quantitative or statistical terms of throughput, delay, jitter and/or loss, or may otherwise be specified in terms of some relative priority of access to network resources.
IETF Specification: RFC 2474 and RFC 2475

DISL: Dynamic Inter-Switch Link Protocol   *247*

Dynamic Inter-Switch Link Protocol (DISL), a Cisco protocol, simplifies the creation of an ISL trunk from two interconnected Fast Ethernet devices. Fast EtherChannel technology enables aggregation of two full-duplex Fast Ethernet links for high-capacity backbone connections. DISL minimizes VLAN trunk configuration procedures because only one end of a link needs to be configured as a trunk.
Cisco Protocol

DLSw: Data-link switching   *268*

Data-link switching (DLSw) provides a forward mechanism for transporting IBM Systems Network Architecture (SNA) and network basic input/output system (NetBIOS) traffic over an IP network. DLSw does not provide full routing, but instead provides switching at the SNA Data Link layer (i.e., layer 2 in the SNA architecture) and encapsulation in TCP/IP for transport over the Internet.
IBM Protocol

DMDP: DNSIX Message Deliver Protocol

DNSIX Message Deliver Protocol(DMDP) provides a basic message-delivery mechanism for all DOD Network Security for Information Exchange (DNSIX) elements.

DNA: Digital Network Architecture   *274*

Digital Network Architecture (DNA), defined by Digital Equipment Corporation (now part of HP), is essentially a set of documents which define the network architecture in general, states the specifications for each layer of the architecture, and describes the protocols which operate within each layer.
DEC/HP Protocol

DNCP: DECnet (DNA) Phase IV Control Protocol *274*

DECnet Phase IV Control Protocol (DNCP), also known as DNA Phase IV Routing Control Protocol (DNCP), is responsible for configuring, enabling, and disabling the DNA Phase

IV Routing protocol modules on both ends of the point-to-point link (PPP). DNCP uses the same packet exchange mechanism as the Link Control Protocol (LCP). DNCP packets may not be exchanged until PPP has reached the Network-Layer Protocol phase. DNCP packets received before this phase is reached should be silently discarded.
DEC/HP Protocol

DNS: Domain Name System or Service   *12*

Domain Name System or Service (DNS) is a distributed Internet directory service. DNS is used mostly to translate between domain names and IP addresses and to control Internet email delivery. Most Internet services rely on DNS to work, and if DNS fails, web sites cannot be located and email delivery stalls.
IETF Specification: RFC 1034

DOCSIS: Data Over Cable Service Interface Specification   *157*

Data Over Cable Service Interface Specification (DOCSIS), developed by CableLabs and approved by the ITU, defines interface requirements for cable modems involved in high-speed data distribution (both MPEG and IP data) over cable television system networks. Other devices that recognize and support the DOCSIS standard include HDTVs and Web-enabled set-top boxes for regular televisions.
CableLab Specification: ITU J.112

DQDB: Distributed Queue Dual Bus   *203*

Distributed Queue Dual Bus (DQDB) is a Data-link layer communication protocol for Metropolitan Area Networks (MANs), specified in the IEEE 802.6 standard and designed for use in MANs. DQDB is designed for data as well as voice and video transmission and is based on cell switching technology (similar to ATM). DQDB, which permits multiple systems to interconnect using two unidirectional logical buses, is an open standard that is designed for compatibility with carrier transmission standards such as SMDS.
IEEE Specification: IEEE 802.6

DRARP: Dynamic Reverse Address Resolution Protocol

Dynamic Reverse Address Resolution Protocol (DRARP), an extensions to the Reverse Address Resolution Protocol (RARP), is used to acquire (or allocate) a protocol level address given the fixed hardware address for a host. Its clients are systems being installed or reconfigured, and its servers are integrated with other network administration services. The protocol, along with adjunct protocols as briefly described here, supports several common styles of "Intranet" administration including networks which choose not to support the simplified installation and reconfiguration features enabled by DRARP.
IETF Protocol

DRIP: Duplicate Ring Protocol

Duplicate Ring Protocol (DRIP), a Cisco protocol, runs on Cisco routers and switches that support Virtual LAN networking, and is used to identify active Token Ring VLANs. DRIP information is used for all-routes explorer filtering and detecting the configuration of duplicate Token ring Concentrator Relay Function (TrCRF) across routers and switches, which would cause a TrCRF to be distributed across ISL trunks. DRIP sends advertisements to a multicast address so the advertisements are received by all neighboring devices. The advertisement includes VLAN information for the source device only.

Cisco Protocol
DRP: Director Response Protocol

The Director Response Protocol (DRP) is a simple User Datagram Protocol (UDP)-based application developed by Cisco Systems. It enables Cisco's DistributedDirector product to query routers (DRP Server Agents) in the field for Border Gateway Protocol (BGP) and Interior Gateway Protocol (IGP) routing table metrics between distributed servers and clients.

Cisco Protocol
DS0: Digital Signal level 0

Digital Signal level 0 (DS0) is a basic digital signaling rate of 64 kbit/s, corresponding to the capacity of one voice-frequency-equivalent channel. The DS0 forms the basic unit for the digital multiplex transmission hierarchy in both the European and North American systems. The DS0 rate may support twenty 2.4 kbit/s channels, ten 4.8 kbit/s channels, five 9.67 kbit/s channels, one 56 kbit/s channel, or one 64 kbit/s clear channel.

ANSI Protocol
DS1: Digital Signal level 1

Digital Signal level 1 (DS1) is a T-carrier signaling scheme devised by Bell Labs. Technically, DS1 is the data transmitted over a physical T1 line, however, the terms DS1 and T1 are often used interchangeably. A DS1 circuit is made up of twenty-four 8-bit channels (DS0's), each channel being a 64 kbit/s DS0 multiplexed pseudo-circuit. A DS1 is also a full-duplex circuit, meaning you can (in theory) send 1.536 Mbit/s and receive 1.536 Mbit/s simultaneously. A total of 1.536 Mbit/s of bandwidth is achieved by sampling each of the twenty-four 8-bit DS0's 8000 times per second. It is a widely used standard in telecommunications in North America and Japan to transmit voice and data between devices. E1 is used in place of T1 outside of North America and Japan.

ANSI Protocol
DS3: Digital Signal level 3

Digital Signal level 3 (DS3) is a digital signal level 3 T-carrier and it is also called T3. The data rate for this type of signal is 44.736 Mbit/s. DS3 can transport 28 DS1 level signals or transport 672 DS0 level channels within its payload. DS3 is a standard for North America and Japan. Other part of the world uses a similar standard called E3.

ANSI Protocol
DSL: Digital Subscribe Line 158

Digital Subscriber Line(DSL) is a modem technology for broadband data access over ordinary copper telephone lines (POTS) from homes to businesses. There are many flavors of DSL, collectively called xDSL, such as ADSL (and G.Lite), HDSL, SDSL, IDSL and VDSL etc. xDSLs sometimes are referred to as last-mile (or first mile) technologies because they are used only for connections from a telephone switching station to a home or office, not between switching stations.

ANSI Protocol
DSMCC: Digital Storage Media Command and Control

Digital Storage Media Command and Control (DSM-CC), Part 6 of MPEG-2, is an ISO/IEC standard developed to provide the control functions and operations specific to managing MPEG-1 and MPEG-2 bitstreams. These protocols may be used to support applications in both stand-alone and heterogeneous network environments. In the DSM-CC model, a stream is sourced by a Server and delivered to a Client. Both the Server and the Client are considered to be Users of the DSM-CC network. DSM-CC defines a logical entity called the Session and Resource Manager (SRM) which provides a (logically) centralized management of the DSM-CC Sessions and Resources.]\

ANSI/ITU Protocol
DSn: Digital Signal Level n

Digital Signal Level n (DSn), also known as Tn, is a group of classification of digital circuits, which is a time division multiplexed hierarchy of standard digital signals used in telecommunications systems. The DS technically refers to the rate and the format of the signal, whereas the T designation refers to the equipment providing the signals. In practice, DS and T are used synonymously; for example, DS1 and T1, DS3 and T3.

ANSI Protocol
DTP: Dynamic Trunking Protocol 243

Dynamic Trunking Protocol (DTP), a Cisco proprietary protocol in the VLAN group, is for negotiating trunking on a link between two devices and for negotiating the type of trunking encapsulation (802.1Q) to be used. There are different types of trunking protocols. If a port can become a trunk, it may also have the ability to trunk automatically and, in some cases, even negotiate what type of trunking to use on the port. This ability to negotiate the trunking method with the other device is called dynamic trunking.

Cisco Protocol
DUP: Data User Part 278

Data User Part (DUP), an application protocol in the SS7/C7 protocol suite, defines the necessary call control and facility registration and cancellation related elements for circuit-switched data transmission services.

ANSI/ITU-T Protocol
DUNDi: Distributed Universal Number Discovery

Distributed Universal Number Discovery (DUNDi) is a Peer-to-Peer (P2P) protocol for providing services equivalent to those provided by Electronic Numbering (ENUM). DUNDi has an advantage above ENUM because that it is far more resilient, as it lacks a central point of failure. DUNDi can be used to augment DNS and it is developed with Voice over IP (VOIP) services.

IETF Protocol
DVMRP: Distance Vector Multicast Routing Protocol 68

Distance Vector Multicast Routing Protocol (DVMRP) is an Internet routing protocol that provides an efficient mechanism for connectionless message multicast to a group of hosts across an internetwork. DVMRP is an "interior gateway protocol" (IGP), suitable for use within an autonomous system but not between different autonomous systems.

IETF Specification: RFC 1075
Dynamic IISP: Dynamic Interim-Interswitch Signaling Protocol

Dynamic Interim-Interswitch Signaling Protocol (Dynamic IISP) is a dynamic version of the ATM Forum standard Interim Inter-Switch Signaling Protocol, that automatically reroutes ATM connections in the event of link failures. Dynamic IISP was an interim solution until PNNI Phase 1 was completed.

E

E1 or E-1

E1 or E-1 is the European/China format for digital signal trans-

mission, while T1/DS1 is for the North America/Japan. E1 carries signals at 2 Mbps with 32 channels at 64Kbps each, where 30 DS0 channels for voice/data and 2 channels for signaling and controlling. For T1, it carries signals at 1.544 Mbps with 24 channels at DS0 64Kbps each. E1 and T1 lines may be interconnected for international use.
ITU-T Protocol

E3 or E-3

E3 or E-3 is the European/China format for digital signal transmission, while T3/DS3 is for the North America/Japan. E3 carries data at a rate of 34.368 Mbps. E3 can carry 16 E1 channels. E3 and T3 lines may be interconnected for international use.
ITU-T Protocol

EAP: PPP Extensible Authentication Protocol   162

The PPP Extensible Authentication Protocol (EAP) is for PPP authentication. EAP supports multiple authentication mechanisms. EAP does not select a specific authentication mechanism at Link Control Phase, but rather postpones this until the Authentication Phase. This allows the authenticator to request more information before determining the specific authentication mechanism. This also permits the use of a "back-end" server which actually implements the various mechanisms while the PPP authenticator merely passes through the authentication exchange.
IETF Specification: RFC 2284

EAP-TLS: Extensible Authentication Protocol - Transport Layer

Security Extensible Authentication Protocol - Transport Layer Security(EAP-TLS) is an encrypted authentication scheme based on Extensible Authentication Protocol (EAP). EAP-TLS was created by Microsoft and accepted by the IETF.
IETF Specification: RFC 2716

EAP-TTLS: Extensible Authentication Protocol–Tunneled Transport Layer Security

Extensible Authentication Protocol–Tunneled Transport Layer Security (EAP-TTLS) is an encrypted authentication scheme based on Extensible Authentication Protocol (EAP) and easier to manage than Extensible Authentication Protocol–Transport Layer Security (EAP-TLS). EAP-TTLS is a proprietary protocol which was developed by Funk Software and Certicom, and is supported by Agere Systems, Proxim, and Avaya.
Funk Software Protocol

EAPOL: EAP over LAN

EAP over LAN (EAPOL), defined in the IEEE 802.1X, offers an effective framework for authenticating and controlling user traffic to a protected network, as well as dynamically varying encryption keys. EAPOL is a standard for passing Extensible Authentication Protocol (EAP) over a wired or wireless LAN. In the wireless environment, 802.1X also describes a way for the access point and the wireless user to share and change encryption keys, and adds some messages which help smooth operations over wireless. The key change messages help solve the major security vulnerability in 802.11, the management of WEP keys. With 802.1X, WEP is brought up to an acceptable level of security for most companies.
IEEE Specification: IEEE 802.1x

ECHO: Echo Protocol

Echo Protocol (ECHO) is defined in RFC 862 for testing and measurement purposes in an IP network. A host may connect to a server that supports the ECHO protocol, on either TCP or UDP port 7. The server then sends back any data it receives. Current testing and measurement of IP networks is more commonly done with ping and traceroute defined in the ICMP.
IETF Specification: RFC 862

ECP: Encryption Control Protocol

Encryption Control Protocol (ECP), a protocol in the PPP suite, can be used to ensure that only authorized devices can establish a PPP connection. ECP is responsible for negotiating and managing the use of encryption on a PPP link.
IETF Specification: RFC 1968

EGP: Exterior Gateway Protocol   51

Exterior Gateway Protocol (EGP) is for exchanging routing information between two neighbor gateway hosts in a network of autonomous systems. EGP is commonly used between hosts on the Internet to exchange routing table information. The protocol is based on periodic polling using Hello/I-Heard-You (I-H-U) message exchanges to monitor neighbor reachability and Poll commands to solicit Update responses.
IETF Specification: RFC 904

EIGRP: Enhanced Interior Gateway Routing Protocol   244

Enhanced Interior Gateway Routing Protocol (EIGRP) is an enhanced version of IGRP. IGRP is Cisco's Interior Gateway Routing Protocol used in TCP/IP and OSI internets. It is regarded as an interior gateway protocol (IGP) but has also been used extensively as an exterior gateway protocol for inter-domain routing.
Cisco Protocol

ELAP: EtherTalk Link Access Protocol

EtherTalk Link Access Protocol (ELAP) is a link-access protocol used in an AppleTalk over Ethernet network. ELAP is built on top of the standard Ethernet data link layer.

ENUM: E164 NUmber Mapping

Electronic Numbering (ENUM or Enum), also refered to as "E164 NUmber Mapping", is a suite of protocols to unify the telephone system with the Internet by using E.164 addresses with Dynamic Delegation Discovery System (DDDS) and Domain Name System (DNS). ENUM is a standard adopted by the Internet Engineering Task Force (IETF) that uses the domain name system (DNS) to map telephone numbers to Web addresses or uniform resource locators (URL). The goal of the ENUM standard is to provide a single number to replace the multiple numbers and addresses for an individual's home phone, business phone, fax, cell phone, and e-mail.
IETF Specification: RFC 3761

EoS: Ethernet over SONET/SDH   151

Ethernet over SONET/SDH (EoS) refers to a group of industry standard specifications for optimal transport of Ethernet through SONET/SDH, because Ethernet is not directly supported over the SONET/SDH network traditionally. Basically, EoS capability turns the Sonet/SDH MAN/WAN infrastructure backbone into a transparent Ethernet segment for attached servers and clients.
ITU-T Protocol

EPON: Ethernet Passive Optical Network

Ethernet Passive Optical Network (EPON), defined by IEEE 802.3ah, is a point to multipoint (Pt-MPt) network topology implemented with passive optical splitters, along with optical fiber PMDs that support this topology. EPON is based upon

a mechanism named MPCP (Multi-Point Control Protocol), which uses messages, state machines, and timers, to control access to a P2MP topology. Each ONU in the P2MP topology contains an instance of the MPCP protocol, which communicates with an instance of MPCP in the OLT. On the basis of the EPON/MPCP protocol lies the P2P Emulation Sublayer, which makes an underlying P2MP network appear as a collection of point-to-point links to the higher protocol layers (at and above the MAC Client). It achieves this by prepending a Logical Link Identification (LLID) to the beginning of each packet, replacing two octets of the preamble. In addition, a mechanism for network Operations, Administration and Maintenance (OAM) is included to facilitate network operation and troubleshooting.
IEEE Specification: IEEE 802.2ah

ES-IS: End System to Intermediate System Routing Exchange Protocol 237

End System to Intermediate System Routing Exchange Protocol (ES-IS), developed by ISO, permits End Systems and Intermediate Systems to exchange configuration and routing information to facilitate the operation of the routing and relaying functions of the Network Layer in the ISO network environment. In an ISO network, there are End Systems, Intermediate Systems, Areas and Domains. End systems are user devices. Intermediate systems are routers. Routers are organized into local groups called "areas" and several areas are grouped together into a "domain".
ISO Specification: ISO 8473

ESMTP: Extended Simple Mail Transfer Protocol

Extended Simple Mail Transfer Protocol (ESMTP) is the extended version of the original Simple Mail Transfer Protocol (SMTP), which includes additional functionality, such as delivery notification and session delivery. All the features of ESMTP are included in the latest version of SMTP as defined in RFC 2821 and the ESMTP is no longer necessary.
IETF Specification: RFC 2821

ESP: Encapsulating Security Payload 98

Encapsulating Security Payload (ESP), a key protocol in the IPsec (Internet Security) architecture, is designed to provide a mix of security services in IPv4 and IPv6. The IP Encapsulating Security Payload (ESP) seeks to provide confidentiality and integrity by encrypting data to be protected and by placing the encrypted data in the data portion of the IP ESP. Depending on the user's security requirements, this mechanism may be used to encrypt either a transport-layer segment (e.g., TCP, UDP, ICMP, IGMP) or an entire IP datagram. Encapsulating the protected data is necessary to provide confidentiality for the entire original datagram.
IETF Specification: RFC 2406

Ethernet 179

Ethernet protocols refer to the family of local area networks (LAN) covered by a group of IEEE 802.3 standards. In the Ethernet standard, there are two modes of operation: half-duplex and full-duplex. In the half-duplex mode, data are transmitted using the popular Carrier-Sense Multiple Access/Collision Detection (CSMA/CD) protocol on a shared medium. The main disadvantages of the half-duplex are the efficiency and distance limitation, in which the link distance is limited by the minimum MAC frame size. This restriction reduces the efficiency drastically for high-rate transmission. Therefore, the carrier extension technique is used to ensure the minimum frame size of 512 bytes in Gigabit Ethernet to achieve a reasonable link distance.
IEEE Specification: IEEE 802.3

EtherTalk

EtherTalk, full named as EtherTalk Link Access Protocol (ELAP), places AppleTalk's DDP formatted packets in Ethernet frames. EtherTalk enables the implementation of AppleTalk using Ethernet as a delivery system.
Apple Protocol

F

FANP: Flow Attribute Notification Protocol 291

Flow Attribute Notification Protocol (FANP) is a protocol between neighbor modes which manages cut-through packet forwarding functionalities. In cut-through packet forwarding, a router doesn't perform conventional IP packet processing for received packets. FANP indicates mapping information between a datalink connection and a packet flow to the neighbor node. It helps a pair of nodes manage mapping information. By using FANP, routers such as the CSR (Cell Switch Router) can forward incoming packets based on their datalink-level connection identifiers, bypassing usual IP packet processing. FANP generally runs on ATM networks.
Toshiba Protocol

Fast Ethernet 181

Fast Ethernet (100BASE-T) offers a speed increase ten times that of the 10BaseT Ethernet specification, while preserving such qualities as frame format, MAC mechanisms and MTU. Such similarities allow the use of existing 10BaseT applications and network management tools on Fast Ethernet networks. Officially, the 100BASE-T standard is IEEE 802.3u.
IEEE Specification: IEEE 802.3u

FC-0 Layer

FC-0, also known as FC-PH(the physical layer), is the lowest level of Fibre Channel. FC-0 defines the physical links in the system, including the fibre, connectors, optical and electrical parameters for a variety of data rates.
ANSI Protocol

FC-1 Layer

FC-1, also known as FC-PH, is the data link layer in the Fibre Channel protocols. FC-1 implements the 8b/10b encoding and decoding of signals. FC-1 defines the transmission protocol including serial encoding and decoding rules, special characters and error control. The transmission code must be DC balanced to support the electrical requirements of the receiving units. The Transmission Characters ensure, that short-run lengths and enough transitions are present in the serial bit stream to make clock recovery possible
ANSI Protocol

FC-2 Layer

FC-2, also known as FC-PH, is the network layer protocol in the Fibre Channel suite. FC-2 is defined by the FC-PI-2 standard, which consists of the core of FC. The framing rules of the data to be transferred between ports, the different mechanisms for controlling the three service classes and the means of managing the sequence of a data transfer are defined by FC-2.
ANSI Protocol

FC-3 Layer

FC-3 is the common services layer in the Fibre Channel protocol suite, a thin layer that could eventually implement functions like encryption or RAID. The FC-3 level of the FC standard is intended to provide the common services required for advanced features such as: Striping to multiply bandwidth using multiple N_ports in parallel to transmit a single information unit across multiple links; Hunt groups for more than one Port to respond to the same alias address; and Multicast to deliver a single transmission to multiple destination ports.

ANSI Protocol

FC-4 Layer

FC-4, the highest level in the Fibre Channel structure, defines the application interfaces that can execute over Fibre Channel. FC-4 specifies the mapping rules of upper layer protocols using the FC levels below. FC-4 is a layer in which other protocols, such as SCSI, are encapsulated into an information unit for delivery to FC2.

ANSI Protocol

FCIP: Fibre Channel Over TCP/IP   209

Fibre Channel Over TCP/IP (FCIP) describes mechanisms that allow the interconnection of islands of Fibre Channel storage area networks over IP-based networks to form a unified storage area network in a single Fibre Channel fabric. FCIP relies on IP-based network services to provide the connectivity between the storage area network islands over local area networks, metropolitan area networks or wide area networks.

IETF Specification: RFC 3821

FCP: Fibre Channel Protocol   208

Fibre Channel Protocol (FCP) is the interface protocol of SCSI on the Fibre Channel. FCP maps the SCSI commands to the Fibre Channel transport layer.

ANSI Protocol

FCS: Fibre Channel Standards

The Fibre Channel Standards (FCS) define a high-speed data transfer mechanism that can be used to connect workstations, mainframes, supercomputers, storage devices and displays. FCS addresses the need for very fast transfers of large volumes of information and could relieve system manufacturers of the burden of supporting the variety of channels and networks currently in place, as it provides one standard for networking, storage and data transfer. Fibre Channel Protocol (FCP) is the interface protocol of SCSI on the Fibre Channel.

ANSI Protocol

FDDI: Fiber Distributed Data Interface   197

Fiber Distributed Data Interface (FDDI) is a set of ANSI protocols for sending digital data over fiber optic cable. FDDI networks are token-passing (similar to IEEE 802.5 Token Ring protocol) and dual-ring networks and support data rates of up to 100 Mbps. FDDI networks are typically used as backbone technology because the protocol supports a high bandwidth and a great distance. A related copper specification similar to FDDI protocols, called Copper Distributed Data Interface (CDDI), has also been defined to provide 100 Mbps service over twisted-pair copper.

ANSI Specification: X3T9.5 and X3T12

FDDI II: Fiber Distributed Data Interface II

Fiber Distributed Data Interface II (FDDI II or FDDI-2) is an ANSI standard that enhances FDDI. FDDI II provides isochronous transmission for connectionless data circuits and connection-oriented voice and video circuits.

ANSI Protocol

Fibre Channel   208

Fibre Channel is a group of multi-gigabit speed network tech-

nology primarily used for Storage Networking using both coaxial cable or fiber. There are three major Fibre Channel topologies: Point-to-Point (FC-P2P) in which two devices are connected back to back; Arbitrated Loop (FC-AL), in which all devices are in a loop or ring; and Switched Fabric (FC-SW), in which all devices are connected to Fibre Channel switches. Fibre Channel is a layered protocol. It consists of 5 layers, namely: FC0, FC1, FC2, FC3 and FC4.

ANSI Protocol

Finger User Information Protocol   13

The Finger user information protocol provides an interface to a remote user information program (RUIP). Finger is a protocol, based on the Transmission Control Protocol, for the exchange of user information using TCP port 79. The local host opens a TCP connection to a remote host on the Finger port. A RUIP becomes available on the remote end of the connection to process the request. The local host sends the RUIP a one line query based upon the Finger query specification and waits for the RUIP to respond.

IETF Specification: RFC 1288

FLAP: FDDITalk Link Access Protocol

FDDITalk Link Access Protocol (FLAP) is the AppleTalk protocol used for the FDDI interface. The FLAP protocol resides in the Data Link Layer of the OSI Reference Model.

Apple Protocol

Frame Relay   171

Frame Relay is a WAN protocol for LAN internetworking which operates at the physical and data link layer to provide a fast and efficient method of transmitting information from a user device to another across multiple switches and routers. Frame Relay is based on packet-switched technologies similar to x.25, which enables end stations to dynamically share the network medium and the available bandwidth. It employs the following two packet techniques: a) Variable-length packets and b) Statistical multiplexing. It does not guarantee data integrity and discards packets when there is network congestion. In reality, it still delivers data with high reliability.

ITU-T Protocol

FreeDCE

FreeDCE is the Open Group's reference implementation of Distributed Computing Environment/Remote Procedure Calls (DCE/RPC) updated to be interoperable with Free Software development practices. FreeDCE is DCE 1.1 reworked, and it includes an up-to-date implementation of DCEThreads that actually works with the Linux 2.4 and 2.6 kernels on x86 hardware and also on AMD64 processors.

Open Group Protocol

FSSRP: Fast Simple Server Redundancy Protocol

Fast Simple Server Redundancy Protocol (FSSRP), an improvement of the ATM LAN Emulation (LANE) Simple Server Replication Protocol (SSRP), creates fault-tolerance using standard LANE protocols and mechanisms. FSSRP differs from LANE SSRP in that all configured LANE servers of an Emulated LAN (ELANE) are always active. FSSRP-enabled LANE clients have virtual circuits (VCs) established to a maximum of four LANE servers and broadcast and unknown servers (BUSs) at one time. If a single LANE server goes down, the LANE client quickly switches over to the next LANE server with BUS resulting in no data or LE-ARP table entry loss and no extraneous signalling.

Cisco Protocol

FST: Fast Sequenced Transport

Fast Sequenced Transport (FST) is a connectionless, sequenced transport protocol that runs on top of the IP protocol. Source-Route Bridging (SRB) traffic is encapsulated inside of IP datagrams and is passed over a FST connection between two network devices (such as routers). FST speeds up data delivery, reduces overhead, and improves the response time of SRB traffic.

FTAM: File Transfer Access Management Protocol

223

The File Transfer Access and Management protocol (FTAM), an ISO application protocol, offers file transfer services between client (initiator) and server (responder) systems in an open environment. FTAM also provides access to files and management of files on diverse systems. Similar to FTP (File Transfer Protocol) and NFS (Network File System) in the TCP/IP environment, FTAM is designed to help users access files on diverse systems that use compatible FTAM implementations.

ISO Protocol

FTP: File Transfer Protocol

14

File Transfer Protocol (FTP) enables file sharing between hosts. FTP uses TCP to create a virtual connection for controlling information and then creates a separate TCP connection for data transfers. The control connection uses an image of the TELNET protocol to exchange commands and messages between hosts.

IETF Specification: RFC 959

FUNI: Frame-based User-to-Network Interface

Frame-based User-to-Network Interface (FUNI), developed by the ATM Forum, is for users with the ability to connect between ATM networks and existing frame-based equipment such as routers and switches. FUNI uses a T1/E1 interface and offers a relatively easy and cost-effective method for users to take advantage of ATM infrastructure or an ATM backbone, while not having to replace existing equipment with more expensive ATM equipment.

ITU-T Protocol

G

G.703

G.703, a standard based on PCM standard, specifies voice over digital networks. Voice to digital conversion according to PCM requires a bandwidth of 64 kbps (+/- 100 ppm), resulting in the basic unit for G.703. G.703 specifies the physical and electrical characteristics of hierarchical digital interfaces at a rate up to 140Mbit/s.

ITU-T Specification: G.703

G.704

G.704 defines the synchronous frame structure used at primary and secondary hierarchy levels on G.703 interfaces up to 45Mbit/s. The conventional use of G.704 on a 2Mbit/s primary rate circuit provides 30 discrete 64kbit/s channels, with a further 64kbit/s channel available for common channel signalling.

ITU-T Specification: G.704

G.707

G.707 defines the Synchronous Digital Hierarchy (SDH) Bit Rates.

ITU-T Specification: G.707

G.708

G.708 defines the Network Node Interface (NNI) for Synchronous Digital Hierarchy (SDH).

ITU-T Specification: G.708

G.709

G.709 defines the Synchronous Multiplexing Structure.

ITU-T Specification: G.709

G.711

120

G.711 is an ITU-T standard for audio companding released in 1972. It is primarily used in telephony. G.711 represents 8-bit compressed pulse code modulation (PCM) samples for signals of voice frequencies, sampled at the rate of 8000 samples/second. G.711 encoder will create a 64 kbit/s bitstream. There are two main algorithms defined in the standard: mu-law algorithm (used in North America & Japan) and a-law algorithm (used in Europe and other countries).

ITU-T Specification: G.711

G.721

120

G.721 is a 32 kbps Adaptive Differential Pulse Code Modulation (ADPCM) speech compression algorithm. The sampling rate is 8 KHz. G.721 produces toll quality speech. With transmission error rates higher than 10.4, the perceived quality of G.721 is better than G.711. G.721 is the first ADPCM standard. Later came the standards of G.726 and G.727 for 40, 32, 24 and 16 kbps.

ITU-T Specification: G.721

G.722

120

G.722 is a wideband speech coding algorithm supporting bit rates of 64, 56 and 48 kbps. In G.722, the speech signal is sampled at 16000 samples/second. G.722 can handle speech and audio signal bandwidth upto 7 kHz, compared with 3.6 kHz in narrow band speech coders. G.722 coder is based on the principle of Sub Band - Adaptive Differential Pulse Code Modulation (SB-ADPCM). The signal is split into two subbands and samples from both bands are coded using ADPCM techniques.

ITU-T Specification: G.722

G.723 or G.723.1

120

G.723, also known as G.723.1 in more precise terms, is a standard-based voice codec providing voice quality (300 Hz to 3400 Hz) at 5.3 / 6.3 kbps. It was designed for video conferencing/telephony over standard phone lines, and is optimized for real-time encoding & decoding. G.723.1 is part of the H.323 (IP) and H.324 (POTS) standards for video conferencing.

ITU-T Specification: G.723

G.726

120

G.726 is a ITU-T speech codec based on ADPCM operating at bit rates of 16-40 kbit/s. The most commonly used mode is 32 kbit/s, since this is half the rate of G.711, thus increasing the usable network capacity by 100%. G.726 specifies how a 64 kbps A-law or μ-law PCM signal can be converted to 40, 32, 24 or 16 kbps ADPCM channels where the 24 and 16 kbps channels are used for voice in Digital Circuit Multiplication Equiment (DCME) and the 40 kbps is for data modem signals (especially modems doing 4800 kbps or higher) in DCME.

ITU-T Specification: G.726

G.727

120

G.727 is an embedded Adaptive Differential Pulse Code Mod-

ulation (ADPCM) algorithms at rates of 40, 32, 24 and 16 kbit/s. G.727 defines the transcoding law when the source signal is a pulse-code modulation signal at a pulse rate of 64 kbit/s developed from voice frequency analog signals as fully specified by G.711.
ITU-T Specification: G.727

G.728   120

G.728, based on the Low-Delay Code Excited Linear Prediction (LD-CELP) compression principles, is a 16 kbps compression standard. G.728 has an algorithmic coding delay of 0.625 ms. G.728 normally compresses toll quality speech at 8000 samples/second. G.728 Annex G (G.728 G) is a fixed point specification of the coder working at a bit rate of 16000 bits/second. G.728 Annex I (G.728 I) is the packet loss concealment (PLC) technique used along with G.728 G. G.728 coders are widely used for applications of telephony over packet networks, especially voice over cable and VoIP, where low delay is required.
ITU-T Specification: G.728

G.729   120

G.729 is an audio data compression algorithm for voice that compresses voice audio in chunks of 10 milliseconds. G.729 does coding of speech at 8 kbit/s using Conjugate-Structure Algebraic-Code-Excited Linear-Prediction(CS-ACELP). G.729 is mostly used in Voice over IP (VoIP) applications for its low bandwidth requirement. Standard G.729 operates at 8 kbit/s, but there are extensions, which provide also 6.4 kbit/s and 11.8 kbit/s rates for marginally worse and better speech quality respectively. Also very common is G.729a which is compatible with G.729, but requires less computation.
ITU-T Specification: G.729

G.780

G.780 defines the terms for SDH Networks and Equipment.
ITU-T Specification: G.780

G.781

G.781 defines the structure of Recommendations on Equipment for the Synchronous Digital Hierarchy (SDH).
ITU-T Specification: G.781

G.782

G.782 defines types and characteristics of Synchronous Digital Hierarchy (SDH) Equipment.
ITU-T Specification: G.782

G.783

G.783 defines characteristics of Synchronous Digital Hierarchy (SDH) Equipment Functional Blocks.
ITU-T Specification: G.783

G.7xx   120

G.7xx is a suite of ITU-T standards for audio compressions and de-commmpressions. It is primarily used in telephony. In telephony, there are 2 main algorithms defined in the standard, mu-law algorithm (used in America) and a-law algorithm (used in Europe and the rest of the world). Both are logarithmic, but the later a-law was specifically designed to be simpler for a computer to process. G.7xx codec suite includes G.712, G.721, G.722, G.723, G.726, G.727, G.728, G.729 etc.
ITU-T Specification: G.7xx

G.803

G.803, an ITU-T standard, defines the architecture of transport networks based on the Synchronous Digital Hierarchy (SDH).

ITU-T Specification: G.803

G.804

G.804 is the ITU-T framing standard that defines the mapping of ATM cells into the physical medium.
ITU-T Specification: G.804

G.832

G.832, an ITU-T standard, defenes the transport of SDH elements on PDH networks, the trame and multiplexing structures.
ITU-T Specification: G.832

G.Lite   158

G.Lite, also known as ADSL Lite and Splitterless ADSL, is one of the Digital Subscriber Line technologies that allows broadband data access over normal phone lines (twisted pair cables, also called POTS). G.Lite offers a maximum of 1.5 Mbit/s downstream and 512 kbit/s upstream and does not require the use of phone line splitters.
ITU-T Protocol

GARP: Generic Attribute Registration Protocol   187

The Generic Attribute Registration Protocol (GARP) provides a generic framework whereby devices in a bridged LAN, e.g. end stations and switches, can register and de-register attribute values, such as VLAN Identifiers, with each other. In doing so, the attributes are propagated to devices in the bridged LAN, and these devices form a "reachability" tree that is a subset of an active topology. GARP defines the architecture, rules of operation, state machines and variables for the registration and de-registration of attribute values.
IETF Specification: IEEE 802.1q

GDP: Gateway Discovery Protocol

Gateway Discovery Protocol (GDP) is a Cisco protocol based on UDP that allows hosts to dynamically detect the arrival of new routers as well as determine when a router goes down.
Cisco Protocol

GFP: Generic Framing Procedure   151

Generic Framing Procedure (GFP), an encapsulation scheme for Ethernet over SONET/SDH, is defined by ITU-T G.7041. GFP allows mapping of variable length, higher-layer client signals over a transport network like SDH/SONET. The client signals can be protocol data unit (PDU) oriented (like IP/PPP or Ethernet Media Access Control [MAC]) or can be block-code oriented (like fiber channel). GFP has two modes: GFP-F and GFP-T. GFP-F maps each client frame into a single GFP frame. GFP-T allows mapping of multiple 8B/10B client data frames into an efficient 64B/65B block code for transport within a GFP frame.
ITU-T Specification: G.7041

GGP: Gateway-to-Gateway Protocol

Gateway-to-Gateway Protocol (GGP) is a MILNET protocol specifying how core routers (gateways) should exchange reachability and routing information. GGP uses a distributed shortest-path algorithm. The Gateway-to-Gateway Protocol is obsolete.

Gigabit Ethernet Protocol   182

The Gigabit Ethernet protocol, based on the Ethernet protocols, has a theoretical maximum data rate of 1000 Mbps, using shorter frames with carrier Extension. It is published as the IEEE 802.3z and 802.3ab supplements to the IEEE 802.3 base standards.

IEEE Specification: IEEE 802.3z, 802.3ab

GIOP: General Inter-ORB Protocol

General Inter-ORB Protocol(GIOP) is the abstract protocol by which Object Request Brokers (ORBs) communicate. Standards associated with the protocol are maintained by the Object Management Group (OMG). GIOP is implmented in various environment and Internet Inter-ORB Protocol (IIOP) is the implementation of GIOP for TCP/IP, which is used in the CORBA framework for accessing objects across the Internet.

OMG Protocol

GMM/SM: GPRS Mobility Management/Session Management

GPRS Mobility Management/Session Management (GMM/SM) protocol supports mobility management functionality of a mobile such as GPRS attach, GPRS detach, security, routing area update, location update. The main function of the Session Management (SM) layer is to support PDP context handling of the user terminal. SM comprises of procedures for the PDP context activation, deactivation, and modification. The GMM layer uses the services of the Radio Access Network Application Protocol (RANAP) over the Iu interface to provide these services.

ETSI Protocol

GMM: GPRS Mobility Management

GPRS Mobility Management (GMM) is a GPRS signaling protocol that handles mobility issues such as roaming, authentication, and selection of encryption algorithms. GPRS Mobility Management, together with Session Management (GMM/SM) protocol support the mobility of user terminal so that the SGSN can know the location of a mobile station (MS) at any time and to activate, modify and deactivate the PDP sessions required by the MS for the user data transfer.

ETSI Protocol

GMPLS: Generalized Multiprotocol Label Switching

80

Generalized Multiprotocol Label Switching (GMPLS) enhances MPLS architecture by the complete separation of the control and data planes of various networking layers. GMPLS enables a seamless interconnection and convergence of new and legacy networks by allowing end-to-end provisioning, control and traffic engineering even when the start and the end nodes belong to heterogeneous networks.

IETF Specification: RFC 3945

GMRP: GARP Multicast Registration Protocol 188

GARP Multicast Registration Protocol (GMRP) is a Generic Attribute Registration Protocol (GARP) application that provides a constrained multicast flooding facility similar to IGMP snooping. GMRP and GARP are industry-standard protocols defined by the IEEE 802.1P.

IEEE Specification: IEEE 802.1q

Gopher

Gopher is a distributed document search and retrieval network protocol designed for the Internet. Its goal was similar to that of the World Wide Web, and it has been almost completely displaced by the Web. The Gopher protocol offers some features not natively supported by the Web and imposes a much stronger hierarchy on information stored in it. Its text menu interface is well-suited to computing environments that rely heavily on remote computer terminals, common in universities at the time of its creation.

IETF Specification: RFC 1436

GPON: Gigabit Passive Optical Network

Gigabit Passive Optical Network (GPON), an extension of BPON, is a PON technology operating at bit rates of above 1 Gb/s. Apart from the need to support higher bit rates, the overall protocol has been opened for re-consideration and the sought solution should be the most optimal and efficient in terms of support for multiple services, OAM&P functionality and scalability.

ITU-T Protocols

GPRS: General Packet Radio Service

General Packet Radio Service (GPRS) technology runs at speeds up to 115Kbit/sec., compared with the 9.6Kbit/sec. of older GSM systems. It enables high-speed wireless Internet and other communications such as e-mail, games and applications. It supports a wide range of bandwidths and is an efficient use of limited bandwidth. It's particularly suited for sending and receiving small amounts of data, such as e-mail and Web browsing, as well as large volumes of data.

ETSI Protocol

GRE: Generic Routing Encapsulation 95

Generic Routing Encapsulation (GRE) is a protocol for encapsulation of an arbitrary network layer protocol over another arbitrary network layer protocol.In the most general case, a system has a packet, namely a payload, which needs to be encapsulated and delivered to some destination. The payload is first encapsulated in a GRE packet. The resulting GRE packet can then be encapsulated in some other protocol and then forwarded. This outer protocol is called the delivery protocol.

IETF Specification: RFC 2784

GSM: Global Service for Mobile Communication

Global System for Mobile Communications (GSM), origionally known as Groupe Spécial Mobile, is a digital cellular system defined by ETSI based on TDMA narrowband technology. GSM allows up to eight simultaneous communications on the same frequency. GSM is widely deployed in Europe and some Asian Countries, competing with CDMA which was developed by Qualcomm and deployed mainly in the US.

ETSI Protocol

GSMP: General Switch Management Protocol

General Switch Management Protocol (GSMP) is designed to control a label switch. GSMP allows a controller to establish and release connections across the switch, to add and delete leaves on a multicast connection, to manage switch ports, to request configuration information, to request and delete reservation of switch resources, and to request statistics. The protocol is asymmetric, the controller being the master and the switch being the slave. Multiple switches may be controlled by a single controller and a switch may be controlled by more than one controller.

ITU-T Protocol

GTP: GPRS Tunnelling Protocol

GPRS Tunnelling Protocol (GTP) allows end users of a GSM or UMTS network to move from place to place whilst continuing to connect to the internet as if from one location at the GGSN. It does this by carrying the subscriber's data from the subscriber's current SGSN to the GGSN which is handling the subscriber's session. GTP version zero supports both signalling and user data under one generic header. It can be used with UDP (User Datagram Protocol) or TCP (Transmission

Control Protocol) on the registered port 3386. GTP version one is used only on UDP. The control plane protocol GTP-C (Control) uses the registered port 2123 and the user plane protocol GTP-U (User) uses the registered port 2152.
ETSI Protocol

GVRP: GARP VLAN Registration Protocol   189

Generic Attribute Registration Protocol(GARP) VLAN Registration Protocol (GVRP) defines a GARP application that provides 802.1Q-compliant VLAN pruning and dynamic VLAN creation on 802.1Q trunk ports. GVRP is an application, defined in the IEEE 802.1P standard, which allows for the control of 802.1Q VLANs.
IEEE Specification: IEEE 802.11q and 802.1p

H

H.225   106

H.225, a key protocol in the H.323 VOIP architecture defined by ITU-T, is a standard to cover narrow-band visual telephone services defined in H.200/AV.120-Series Recommendations. It specifically deals with those situations where the transmission path includes one or more packet-based networks, each of which is configured and managed to provide a non-guaranteed QoS, which is not equivalent to that of N-ISDN, such that additional protection or recovery mechanisms beyond those mandated by Rec.
ITU-T Specification: H.225

H.225.0   106

H.225.0 is the specific document number for RAS, use of Q.931, and use of RTP under the H.323 VOIP architecture. It is also called as H.225.
ITU-T Specification: H.225.0

H.235   108

H.235 is the security recommendation for the H.3xx series systems. In particular, H.235 provides security procedures for H.323-, H.225.0-, H.245- and H.460-based systems. H.235 is applicable to both simple point-to-point and multipoint conferences for any terminals which utilize H.245 as a control protocol.
ITU-T Specification: H.235

H.245   109

H.245, a control signaling protocol in the H.323 multimedia communication architecture, is for the exchange of end-to-end H.245 messages between communicating H.323 endpoints/terminals. The H.245 control messages are carried over H.245 control channels. The H.245 control channel is the logical channel 0 and is permanently open, unlike the media channels. The messages carried include messages to exchange capabilities of terminals and to open and close logical channels.
ITU-T Specification: H.245

H.248   110

H.248, also known as Media Gateway Control protocol (Megaco), is for the control of elements in a physically decomposed multimedia gateway, enabling the separation of call control from media conversion. Megaco is a result of joint efforts of the IETF and the ITU-T Study Group 16. Therefore, the IETF defined Megaco is the same as ITU-T Recommendation H.248.
ITU-T Specification: H.248

H.261   122

H.261 is the video coding standard of the ITU. It was designed for data rates which are multiples of 64Kbit/s and is sometimes

called p x 64Kbit/s (p is in the range 1-30). These data rates suit ISDN lines, for which this video codec was originally designed. H.261 transports a video stream using the real-time transport protocol, RTP, with any of the underlying protocols that carry RTP.
ITU-T Specification: H.261

H.263   123

The H.263, by the International Telecommunications Union (ITU), supports video compression (coding) for video-conferencing and video-telephony applications. H.263 was developed to stream video at bandwidths as low as 20K to 24K bit/sec and was based on the H.261 codec. As a general rule, H.263 requires half the bandwidth to achieve the same video quality as in the H.261. As a result, H.263 has largely replaced H.261. H.263 uses RTP to transport video streams.
ITU-T Specification: H.263

H.264   124

The H.264, also named Advanced Video Coding (AVC), is the MPEG-4 Part 10. H.264 is jointly developed by ITU and ISO. H.264 supports video compression (coding) for video-conferencing and video-telephony applications. The H.264 video codec has a very broad rang of applications that covers all forms of digital compressed video from, low bit-rate Internet streaming applications to HDTV broadcast and Digital Cinema applications with nearly lossless coding. H.264 is designed as a simple and straightforward video coding with enhanced compression performance, to provide a "network-friendly" video representation.
ITU-T Specification: H.264

H.323   105

H.323, a protocol suite defined by ITU-T, is for voice transmission over internet (Voice over IP or VOIP). In addition to voice applications, H.323 provides mechanisms for video communication and data collaboration, in combination with the ITU-T T.120 series standards. H.323 is one of the major VOIP standards, on a par with Megaco and SIP.
ITU-T Specification: H.323

H.450.2

H.450.2 is the call transfer supplementary service in the H.323 VOIP architecture.
ITU-T Specification: H.450.2

H.450.3

H.450.3 is the call diversion supplementary service in the H.323 VOIP architecture.
ITU-T Specification: H.450.3

HDLC: High Level Data Link Control   174

The High Level Data Link Control (HDLC) protocol, an ISO data link layer protocol based on the IBM SDLC, ensures that data passed up to the next layer has been received exactly as transmitted (i.e. error free, without loss and in the correct order). Another important function of HDLC is flow control, which ensures that data is transmitted only as fast as the receiver can receive it. There are two distinct HDLC implementations: HDLC NRM (also known as SDLC) and HDLC Link Access Procedure Balanced (LAPB). The later is the more popular implementation. HDLC is part of the X.25 stack.
IBM Protocol

HDSL: High Data Bit Rate DSL   158

High Data Bit Rate Digital Subscriber Line (HDSL), also known as High Speed DSL or High data-rate DSL, provides equal

bandwidth for both downloads and uploads. HDSL is one of oldest DSL technologies. HDSL can carry as much on a single wire of twisted-pair cable as can be carried on a T1 line (up to 1.544 Mbps) in North America or an E1 line (up to 2.048 Mbps) in Europe over a somewhat longer range and is considered an alternative to a T1 or E1 connection.
ETSI/ITU-T Protocol

HDSL2: 2nd generation HDSL

HDSL2, the 2nd generation HDSL (High Data Bit Rate Digital Subscriber Line), is a variant of HDSL which delivers 1.5 Mbps service each way, supporting voice, data, and video using either ATM (asynchronous transfer mode), private-line service or frame relay over a single copper pair. This ATIS standard (T1.418) for this symmetric service gives a fixed 1.5 Mbps rate both up and downstream. HDSL2 does not provide standard voice telephone service on the same wire pair. HSDL2 differs from HDSL in that HDSL2 uses one pair of wires to convey 1.5 Mbps whereas ANSI HDSL uses two wire pairs.
ATIS Protocol

HDSL4: 4th generation HDSL

HDSL4, the 4th generation HDSL (High Data Bit Rate Digital Subscriber Line), is an enhanced version of HDSL2 which achieves about 30% greater distance than HDSL or HDSL2 by using two pairs of wire (thus, 4 conductors), whereas HDSL2 uses one pair of wires.
ATIS Protocol

HELLO

HELLO protocol is an early version of routing protocol for TCP/IP network using a distance-vector algorithm. HELLO does not use hop count as a metric. Instead, it attempts to select the best route by assessing network delays and choosing the path with the shortest delay. HELLO protocols also contain routing information in the form of a set of destinations that the sending router is able to reach and a metric for each. The HELLO protocol was developed in the early 1980s and documented in RFC 891. The name "HELLO" is capitalized and it should not be confused with the hello process used by a few protocols.
IETF Specification: RFC 891

HPR-APPN: High Performance Routing for Advanced Peer-to-Peer Network

High Performance Routing for Advanced Peer-to-Peer Network (HPR-APPN), an IBM SNA component for dynamic routing across arbitrary network topologies, is an extension of the SNA APPN network. Two new components (Rapid Transport Protocol (RTP) and Automatic Network Routing (ANR)) in HPR-APPN provides some key advancements such as: Non-disruptive path switching; Better utilization of high-speed communication paths; An advanced congestion control methodology.
IBM Protocol

HSRP: Hot Standby Router Protocol 245

Hot Standby Router Protocol (HSRP) is designed to support non-disruptive failover of IP traffic in certain circumstances and to allow hosts to appear to use a single router and to maintain connectivity even if the actual first hop router they are using fails. In other words, the protocol protects against the failure of the first hop router when the source host cannot learn the IP address of the first hop router dynamically. Multiple routers participate in this protocol and, in concert, create the illusion of a single virtual router.
IETF and Cisco Specification: RFC 2281

HTML: HyperText Markup Language

HyperText Markup Language (HTML) is a markup language designed for the creation of web pages with hypertext and other information to be displayed in a web browser. HTML is used to structure information — denoting certain text as headings, paragraphs, lists and so on — and can be used to describe, to some degree, the appearance and semantics of a document.
IETF Specification: RFC 1866

HTTP: Hypertext Transfer Protocol 16

The Hypertext Transfer Protocol (HTTP) is an application level protocol with the lightness and speed necessary for distributed, collaborative, hypermedia information systems. HTTP has been in use by the World-Wide Web global information initiative since 1990.
IETF Specification: RFC 2616

HTTPS: Hypertext Transfer Protocol Secure 16

Hypertext Transfer Protocol Secure (HTTPS) refers to the HTTP running on top of TLS or SSL for secured transactions. HTTPS is not to be confused with S-HTTP, a security-enhanced version of HTTP developed and proposed as a standard by IETF.

HVPLS: Hierarchical Virtual Private LAN Service

Hierarchical Virtual Private LAN Service (HVPLS) is introduced to improve the scalability of VPLS, which is a layer 2 Virtual Private Network (VPN) services over Ethernet networks. The HVPLS standards allow the creation of hierarchies with a hub-and-spoke arrangement. The full mesh of tunnels is maintained between the hub sites (designated as PEs). The CE equipment is connected to an MTU-s router, which is connected to a PE router, thus providing the hierarchy.
IETF Protocol

I

IBM Systems Network Architecture (SNA) 5

The IBM Systems Network Architecture (SNA) is one of the most popular network architecture models. Although now considered a legacy networking model, SNA is still widely deployed. SNA was designed around the host-to-terminal communication model that IBM's mainframes use.
IBM Protocol

ICMP: Internet Control Message Protocol 52

Internet Control Message Protocol (ICMP) is an integrated part of the IP suite. ICMP messages, delivered in IP packets, are used for out-of-band messages related to network operation or mis-operation. ICMP packet delivery is unreliable, so hosts can't count on receiving ICMP packets for any network problems.
IETF Specification: RFC792 and 950

ICMPv6: ICMP for IPv6 52

ICMP for IPv6 (ICMPv6) is a revision of ICMP for IPv6. The original Internet Control Message Protocol (ICMP) is designed for IP version 4. ICMPv6 is used by IPv6 nodes to report errors encountered in processing packets, and to perform other internet-layer functions, such as diagnostics (ICMPv6 "ping"). ICMPv6 is an integral part of IPv6 and must be fully implemented by every IPv6 node. In addition, the multicast control functions of the IPv4 Group Membership Protocol (IGMP) are now incorporated in the ICMPv6.
IETF Specification: RFC 2461, 2463

ICP: Internet Control Protocol in VINES

Internet Control Protocol(ICP), a network layer protocol in the Banyan VINES protocol stack, defines exception-notification and metric-notification packets. Exception-notification packets provide information about network layer exceptions; metric-notification packets contain information about the final transmission used to reach a client node.

Banyan Protocol

IDP: Internet Datagram Protocol

Internet Datagram Protocol (IDP), a protocol in the Xerox protocol stack, is a simple, unreliable datagram protocol which is used to support the SOCK_DGRAM abstraction for the Internet Protocol (IP) family. IDP sockets are connectionless and normally used with the sendto and recvfrom subroutines. The connect subroutine can also be used to fix the destination for future packets, in which case the recv or read subroutine and the send or write subroutine can be used.

Xerox Protocol

IDPR: Interdomain Policy Routing

Interdomain Policy Routing (IDPR) is an OSI exterior routing protocol that dynamically exchanges policies between autonomous systems. IDPR encapsulates interautonomous system traffic and routes it according to the policies of each autonomous system along the path.

IETF Specification: RFC 1479

IDRP: Inter-Domain Routing Protocol   238

The Inter-Domain Routing Protocol (IDRP), which provides routing for ISO defined network environments, is similar to BGP in the TCP/IP network. In an ISO network, there are End Systems, Intermediate Systems, Areas and Domains. End systems are user devices. Intermediate systems are routers. Routers are organized into local groups called "areas", and several areas are grouped together into a "domain". Inter-Domain Routing Protocol (IDRP) is designed to provide routing among domains. IDRP, working in conjunction with CLNP, ES-IS, and IS-IS, provides complete routing over the entire network.

ISO Specification: ISO 10747

IDSL: ISDN Digital Subscriber Line   158

ISDN Digital Subscriber Line (IDSL) is a technology allowing existing ISDN subscribers to access the Internet using POTS dial service. Similar to ISDN, IDSL uses a single-wire pair to transmit full-duplex data at 128 kbps and at distances of up to RRD range, and IDSL uses a 2B1Q line code to enable transparent operation through the ISDN "U" interface. Also, the user can use existing ISDN CPE to make the CO connections. However, unlike ISDN, ISDL is terminated at the Service Provider by a data equipment instead of through the voice switch.

ANSI/ITU Protocol

FCP: Internet Fibre Channel Protocol

Internet Fibre Channel Protocol (iFCP) is a gateway-to-gateway protocol which provides fiber channel fabric services to fiber channel devices over a TCP/IP network. iFCP uses TCP to provide congestion control, error detection and recovery. iFCP's primary objective is to allow interconnection and networking of existing fiber channel devices at wire speeds over an IP network. The protocol and method of frame address translation defined permit the attachment of fiber channel storage devices to an IP-based fabric by means of transparent gateways.

IETF Specification: RFC 4172

IFMP: Ipsilon Flow Management Protocol

Ipsilon Flow Management Protocol (IFMP) is a protocol for allowing a node to instruct an adjacent node to attach a layer 2 label to a specified IP flow. The label allows more efficient access to cached routing information for that flow. The label can also enable a node to switch further packets belonging to the specified flow at layer 2 rather than forwarding them at layer 3.

IETF Protocol

IGMP: Internet Group Management Protocol   69

Internet Group Management Protocol (IGMP), a multicasting protocol in the internet protocols family, is used by IP hosts to report their host group memberships to any immediately neighboring multicast routers. IGMP messages are encapsulated in IP datagrams, with an IP protocol number of 2. IGMP has versions IGMP v1, v2 and v3.

IETF Specification: RFC1112, RFC2236 and RFC3376

IGRP: Interior Gateway Routing Protocol   246

The Interior Gateway Routing Protocol (IGRP) is a routing protocol to provide routing within an autonomous system (AS). In the mid-1980s, the most popular interior routing protocol was the Routing Information Protocol (RIP). Although RIP was quite useful for routing within small- to moderate-sized, relatively homogeneous internetworks, its limits were being pushed by network growth. The popularity of Cisco routers and the robustness of IGRP encouraged many organizations with large internetworks to replace RIP with IGRP.

Cisco Protocol

IIOP: Internet Inter-ORB Protocol

Internet Inter-ORB Protocol (IIOP) is a protocol used in the CORBA framework for accessing objects across the Internet. IIOP is the implementation of General Inter-ORB Protocol (GIOP) for TCP/IP. It is a concrete realization of the abstract GIOP definitions.

OMG Protocol

IISP: Interim Inter-switch Signaling Protocol

Interim Inter-switch Signaling Protocol (IISP) is an ATM signaling protocol that provides static routing in ATM networks. It is a subset of the ATM NNI (Network-to-Network Interface) specification in which administrators need to manually configure routes. IISP, formerlly called PNNI 0, was an interim solution until PNNI Phase 1 is completed.

ITU-T Protocol

IKE: Internet Key Exchange Protocol   99

Internet Key Exchange (IKE) Protocol is a key protocol in the IPsec architecture. IKE processes can be used for negotiating virtual private networks (VPNs) and also for providing a remote user from a remote site (whose IP address need not be known beforehand) access to a secure host or network. IKE is a hybrid protocol using part of Oakley and part of SKEME in conjunction with ISAKMP to obtain authenticated keying material for use with ISAKMP, and for other security associations such as AH and ESP for the IPsec DOI.

IETF Specification: RFC 2409

IKEv2: Internet Key Exchange version 2   99

Internet Key Exchange version 2 (IKEv2), a replacement for Internet Key Exchange (IKE), is an IPsec (Internet Protocol Security) standard protocol used to ensure security for virtual private network (VPN) negotiation and remote host or network access.

IETF Specification: RFC 4306

ILMI: Interim Local Management Interface

Interim Local Management Interface (ILMI) is an interim speci-fication used to provide network management functions be-tween end users and networks and between private and public networks in an ATM network. ILMI allows bi-direction exchange of management information between UNI Management Enti-ties (UMEs) within UNI peers. Management information relat-ed to the Physical Layer, ATM Layer, Virtual Path Connections, Virtual Channel Connections, Address Registration, as well as ATM Layer Statistics, is represented in a standard MIB struc-ture called the ATM UNI ILMI MIB.
ITU-T Protocol

IMA: Inverse multiplexing over ATM

Inverse multiplexing over ATM (IMA) defines a sublayer-1 pro-tocol for building a virtual link that consists of multiple physical T1 or E1 links. The IMA protocol handles link failure and au-tomatic link recovery, and it also adds and deletes links while keeping the IMA group in service.
ATM Forum Protocol

IMAP: Internet Message Access Protocol   18

Internet Message Access Protocol (IMAP) is a method of ac-cessing electronic mail or bulletin board messages that are kept on a mail server. IMAP permits a "client" email program to access remote message stores as if they were local. Email stored on an IMAP server can be manipulated from a desktop computer remotely, without the need to transfer messages or files back and forth between these computers. The current ver-sion of IMAP is IMAP version 4.
IETF Specification: RFC 3501

IMAP4: Internet Message Access Protocol version 4   18

Internet Message Access Protocol version 4 (IMAP4) is the current verson of IMAP, a method of accessing electronic mail or bulletin board messages that are kept on a mail server. IMAP permits a "client" email program to access remote message stores as if they were local. Email stored on an IMAP server can be manipulated from a desktop computer remotely, without the need to transfer messages or files back and forth between these computers. The Key features for IMAP4 include:· Fully compatible with Internet messaging standards, e.g. MIME. · Allows message access and management from more than one computer. · Allows access without reliance on less efficient file access protocols. · Provides support for "online", "offline" and "disconnected" access modes. · Supports concurrent access to shared mailboxes · Client software needs no knowledge about the server's file store format.
IETF Specification: RFC 3501

IMT-2000

International Mobile Telecommunication 2000 (IMT-2000) is a group of technologies defined by ITU-T for the third generation mobile telephony. It can also be applied to mobile telephone standards that meet a number of requirements in terms of transmission speed and other factors.
ITU-T Protocol

INAP: Intelligent Network Application Part

Intelligent Network Application Part (INAP) is a signaling proto-col used in the intelligent network architecture. It is part of the SS7/C7 protocol suite, typically layered on top of the TCAP protocol. INAP, a European parallel definition of IN standards based on the American AIN 0.1, is used to query databases for a variety of functions not related to call setup and tear down. The INAP messages are encoded using ASN.1. SCCP is used for the INAP message routing. TCAP is used to separate the transactions apart.
ITU-T Protocol

InARP: Inverse Address Resolution Protocol   83

Inverse Address Resolution Protocol (InARP), also known as Inverse ARP, is an addition to ARP to provide address map-ping in Frame Relay environment. Basic InARP operates essentially the same as ARP with the exception that InARP does not broadcast requests, since the hardware address of the destination station is already known in the Frame Relay network.
IETF Specification: RFC 2390

Integrated IS-IS: Integrated Intermediate System-to-Intermediate System

Integrated Intermediate System-to-Intermediate System (Inte-grated IS-IS), also known as Dual IS-IS, is a routing protocol based on the OSI routing protocol IS-IS but with support for IP and other protocols, in addition to OSI protocols. Integrated IS-IS implementations send only one set of routing updates, making it more efficient than two separate implementations.
IETF Specification: RFC 1195

IP: Internet Protocol   54

The Internet Protocol (IP) is a network layer (Layer 3 in the OSI model) protocol that contains addressing information and some control information to enable packets to be routed in a network. IP is the primary network layer protocol in the TCP/IP protocol suite. Along with the Transmission Control Protocol (TCP), IP represents the heart of the Internet protocols. IP is equally well suited for both LAN and WAN communications.
IETF Specification: RFC 791

IPBCP: IP Bearer Control Protocol

IP Bearer Control Protocol (IPBCP) is used for the exchange of media stream characteristics, port numbers and IP addresses of the source and sink of a media stream to establish and allow the modification of IP bearers. IPBCP is also known as BICC (Bearer Independent Call Control) IP Bearer Control Protocol, because it is suitable for use in IP network environments where the BICC protocol is deployed. The information exchanged with IPBCP is done during BICC call establishment. IPBCP can be used also in other environments.
ITU-T Specification: Q.1970

IPC: InterProcess Communications protocol

Interprocess Communication Protocol (IPC), a transport layer (layer 4) protocol in the VINES protocol stack, provides both datagram and reliable message delivery service.
Banyan Protocol

IPCP: IP Control Protocol   84

IP Control Protocol (IPCP) define the Network Control Proto-col for establishing and configuring the Internet Protocol (IPv4) over PPP, and a method to negotiate and use Van Jacobson TCP/IP header compression with PPP.
IETF Specification: RFC 1332

IPHC: IP Header Compression

IP Header Compression (IPHC) is a scheme to compress IP, TCP and UDP headers to increase bendwidth efficiency. It is necessary over low and medium bandwidth links such as dial up and wireless communications. The IP Header Compres-sion defined in the IETF RFC 2507 supports compression of

multiple IP headers including IPv4 and IPv6, UDP and TCP headers on a per hop basis. This header compression scheme compresses the UDP and TCP headers typically down to 2 to 5 bytes (without UDP or TCP checksum).
IETF Protocol

IPsec AH: IPsec Authentication Header 97

IPsec Authentication Header (IPsec AH), a key protocol in the IPsec (Internet Security) architecture, is used to provide connectionless integrity and data origin authentication for IP datagrams, and to provide protection against replays. This latter (optional) service may be selected by the receiver when a Security Association is established. AH provides authentication for as much of the IP header as possible, as well as for upper level protocol data. However, some IP header fields may change in transit and the value of these fields when the packet arrives at the receiver may not be predictable by the sender.
IETF Specification: RFC 2402

IPsec IKE: Internet Key Exchange 99

IPsec Internet Key Exchange (IKE) Protocol is a key protocol in the IPsec architecture. IKE processes can be used for negotiating virtual private networks (VPNs) and also for providing a remote user from a remote site (whose IP address need not be known beforehand) access to a secure host or network. IKE is a hybrid protocol using part of Oakley and part of SKEME in conjunction with ISAKMP to obtain authenticated keying material for use with ISAKMP, and for other security associations such as AH and ESP for the IPsec DOI.
IETF Specification: RFC 2409

IPsec: IP Security 96

IP Security (IPsec) provides security services at the network layer by enabling a system to select required security protocols, determine the algorithm(s) to use for the service(s) and put in place any cryptographic keys required to provide the requested services. IPsec can be used to protect one or more "paths" between a pair of hosts, between a pair of security gateways or between a security gateway and a host.
IETF Specification: RFC 2401

IPv4: Internet Protocol version 4 54

Internet Protocol version 4 (IPv4), defined in the RFC 791, is the most widely deployed networking technology. When people talk about IP, most likely it refers to the IPv4. IPv6 is the new version of Internet Protocol (IP) based on IPv4. The Internet Protocol (IP) is a network-layer (Layer 3) protocol in the OSI model that contains addressing information and some control information to enable packets being routed in network. IP is the primary network-layer protocol in the TCP/IP protocol suite. Along with the Transmission Control Protocol (TCP), IP represents the heart of the Internet protocols.
DARPA/IETF Specification: RFC 791

IPv6: Internet Protocol version 6 55

Internet Protocol version 6 (IPv6) is the new version of Internet Protocol (IP) based on IPv4. It is a network-layer (Layer 3) protocol that contains addressing information and some control information enabling packets to be routed in the network. IPv6 is also called the next generation IP or IPng.
IETF Specification: RFC 2460

IPv6CP: IPv6 Control Protocol 84

IPv6 Control Protocol (IPv6CP) defines the Network Control Protocol for establishing and configuring the IPv6 over PPP, and a method to negotiate and use Van Jacobson TCP/IP

header compression with PPP.
IETF Specification: RFC 2472

IPX: Internetwork Packet Exchange 255

Internetwork Packet Exchange (IPX) is the legacy network protocol used by the Novell NetWare operating systems to route packets through an internetwork. IPX is a datagram protocol used for connectionless communications—similar to IP (Internet Protocol) in the TCP/IP suite. Higher-level protocols, such as SPX and NCP, are used for additional error recovery services.
Novell Protocol

IPXCP: IPX PPP Control Protocol

IPX PPP Control Protocol (IPXCP), a protocol in the Novell NetWare stack, is for the configuration of the IPX network-layer protocol over PPP.
Novell Protocol

IPXWAN: Novell IPX over Various WAN Media

IPXWAN is a protocol of Novell IPX over Various WAN Media that negotiates end-to-end options for new links. When a link comes up, the first IPX packets sent across are IPXWAN packets negotiating the options for the link. When the IPXWAN options have been successfully determined, normal IPX transmission begins.
IETF Specification: RFC 1634

IRCP: Internet Relay Chat Protocol 19

Internet Relay Chat Protocol (IRCP), which is well-suited to running on many machines distributely, enables teleconferencing on the Internet. The IRC protocol has been developed on systems using the TCP/IP network protocol, although there is no requirement that this remains the only environment in which it operates. The IRC protocol is a text-based protocol, with the simplest client being any socket program capable of connecting to the server.
IETF Specification: RFC 1459

IRDP: ICMP Router Discovery Protocol 57

ICMP Router Discovery Protocol (IRDP) enables a host to determine the address of a router that it can use as a default gateway. IRDP is similar to ES-IS in the OSI network but used with IP.
IETF Specification: RFC 1256

ISAKMP: Internet Security Association and Key Management Protocol 100

Internet Security Association and Key Management Protocol (ISAKMP), a key protocol in the IPsec (Internet Security) architecture, combines the security concepts of authentication, key management and security associations to establish the required security for government, commercial and private communications on the Internet.
IETF Specification: RFC 2408

iSCSI: Internet Small Computer System Interface

212

Internet Small Computer System Interface (iSCSI) is a TCP/IP-based protocol for establishing and managing connections between IP-based storage devices, hosts and clients, for creating a Storage Area Network (SAN). The SAN makes possible to use the SCSI protocol in network infrastructures for high-speed data transfer at the block level between multiple elements of data storage networks.
IETF Specification: RFC 3347 and RFC 3720

ISDN: Integrated Services Digital Network   154

Integrated Services Digital Network (ISDN) is a system with digitized phone connections. For decades, telephony has used purely analogue connections. This is the first protocol to define a digital communications line that allows for the transmission of voice, data, video and graphics, at high speeds, over standard communication lines. The various media are simultaneously carried by bearer channels (B channels) occupying a bandwidth of 64 kbits per second (some switches limit bandwidth to 56 kb/s). A defined data channel (D channel) handles signaling at 16 kb/s or 64 kb/s, depending on the service type.
ITU-T Protocol

IS-IS: Intermediate System-to-Intermediate System   239

Intermediate System-to-Intermediate System (IS-IS) is a routing protocol developed by the ISO. It is a link-state protocol where ISs (routers) exchange routing information based on a single metric to determine network topology. It behaves similarly to Open Shortest Path First (OSPF) in the TCP/IP network.
ISO Protocol

ISL: Inter-Switch Link Protocol   247

Inter-Switch Link Protocol (ISL), a Cisco proprietary protocol, maintains VLAN information as traffic flows between switches and routers. Inter-Switch Link (ISL) tagging accomplishes the same task as 802.1Q trunking but uses a different frame format. ISL trunks are Cisco proprietary and define only a point-to-point connection between two devices, typically switches. The name Inter-Switch Link hints at this design. ISL frame tagging uses a low-latency mechanism for multiplexing traffic from multiple VLANs on a single physical path.
Cisco Protocol

iSNS: Internet Storage Name Service   213

Internet Storage Name Service (iSNS) facilitates scalable configuration and management of iSCSI and Fibre Channel (FCP) storage devices in an IP network, by providing a set of services comparable to that available in Fibre Channel networks. iSNS thus allows an IP network to function at a comparable level of intelligence to a Fibre Channel fabric. iSNS allows the administrator to go beyond a simple device-by-device management model, where each storage device is manually and individually configured with its own list of known initiators and targets.
IETF Specification: RFC 4171

iSNSPL: Internet Storage Name Service Protocol

Internet Storage Name Service Protocol (iSNSP) is a flexible and lightweight protocol that specifies how Internet Storage Name Service (iSNS) clients and servers communicate. It is suitable for various platforms, including switches and targets as well as server hosts.
IETF Specification: RFC 4171

ISO Protocols   217

ISO Protocols are a group of protocols defned by the nternational Organization for Standardization (ISO based on the Open Systems Interconnection (OSI) model. The OSI model defines the communications process into 7 layers, dividing the tasks involved in moving information between networked computers into seven smaller, more manageable task groups.
ISO Protocool

ISO VTP: ISO Virtual Terminal service and protocol   227

The ISO Virtual Terminal (VT) service and protocol (ISO VTP) allows a host application to control a terminal with screen and keyboard and similar devices, like printers. In addition, VTP also supports the less common application-application and terminal-terminal communication.
ISO Specification: ISO 9040

ISO-IP: ISO Internetworking Protocol   235

ISO Internetworking Protocol refers to the Connectionless Network Protocol(CLNP) as the primary network layer protocol in an OSI network. It is similar to the IP (Internet Protocol) in the TCP/IP network.
ISO / ITU-T Specification: X.213

ISO-PP: ISO Presentation Protocol   231

The ISO Presentation Protocol (ISO-PP) is for information transit between open systems using connection oriented or connectionless mode transmission at the presentation layer of the OSI 7 layer model. An application protocol is specified in terms of the transfer of presentation data values between application entities (PS users), using the User data parameter of presentation service primitives.
ISO / ITU-T Specification: X.216

ISO-SP: OSI Session Layer Protocol   232

The OSI Session Layer Protocol (ISO-SP) provides session management, e.g. opening and closing of sessions. In case of a connection loss, it tries to recover the connection. If a connection is not used for a longer period, the session layer may close it down and re-open it for next use. This happens transparently to the higher layers. The Session layer provides synchronization points in the stream of exchanged packets.
ISO / ITU-T Specification: X.215

ISO-TP: OSI Transport Protocol   233

The OSI Transport Protocol (ISO-TP) manages end-to-end control and error checking to ensure complete data transfer. It performs transport address to network address mapping, makes multiplexing and splitting of transport connections and also provides functions such as Sequencing, Flow Control and Error detection and recover.
ISO / ITU-T Specification: X.214

ISUA: SS7 ISUP-User Adaptation Layer

SS7 ISUP-User Adaptation Layer (ISUA), an integral part of the OpenSS7 SIGTRAN stack, is an SS7 Signalling User Adaptation Layer for providing ISUP-User signalling over SCTP. ISUA is intended to be used on a Provider/User basis where ISUP resides on a Signalling Gateway (SG) and ISUP call control applications reside on an Application Server (AS).
IETF Specification: RFC 4233

ISUP: ISDN User Part   279

The ISDN User Part (ISUP), a key protocol in the SS7/C7 signaling system, defines the protocol and procedures used to set-up, manage and release trunk circuits that carry voice and data calls over the public switched telephone network (PSTN) between different switches. ISUP is used for both ISDN and non-ISDN calls.
ITU-T Protocol

ITOT: ISO Transport Service on top of TCP   44

ISO Transport Service on top of TCP (ITOT) is a mechanism that enables ISO applications to be ported to a TCP/IP network. There are two basic approaches which can be taken

when "porting" ISO applications to TCP/IP (and IPv6) environments. One approach is to port each individual application separately, developing local protocols on top of TCP. A second approach is based on the notion of layering the ISO Transport Service over TCP/IP.
ISO Protocol

IUA: ISDN Q.921-User Adaptation Layer

ISDN Q.921-User Adaptation Layer(IUA), a protocol in the SIGTRAN protocol suite, defines a method for backhauling of ISDN Q.921 User messages over IP using the Stream Control Transmission Protocol (SCTP). IUA is used between a Signaling Gateway (SG) and Media Gateway Controller (MGC). It is assumed that the SG receives ISDN signaling over a standard ISDN interface.
IETF Specification: RFC 4233

J

JMODEM

JMODEM is a file transfer protocol developed by Richard Johnson in 1988. It is similar to the seminal XMODEM in most ways, but uses a variable-sized packet in order to make better use of the available bandwidth on high-speed modems.

JFIE: JPEG File Interchange Format

JPEG File Interchange Format (JFIE) is a standard created by the Independent JPEG Group. JFIE specifies how to produce a file suitable for computer storage and transmission (such as over the Internet) from a JPEG stream.
JPEG Protocol

JNG: JPEG Network Graphics

JPEG Network Graphics (JNG) is a JPEG-based graphics file format. JNG is a lossy single-image member of the PNG (Portable Network Graphics) format family. It encapsulates a JPEG datastream in PNG-style chunks, along with an optional alpha channel and ancillary chunks that carry color-space information and comments. While JNG is primarily intended as a subformat of the MNG (Multiple-image Network Graphics) format, standalone JNG files are also possible. Unlike JFIF (the usual JPEG file format), JNG supports transparency. The structure of JNG files is essentially the same as that of PNG files, differing only in the slightly different signature and the use of different chunks.
W3C Protocol

JPEG: Joint Photographic Experts Group

Joint Photographic Experts Group (JPEG) is a commonly used standard method of lossy compression for photographic images. The file format which employs this compression is also called JPEG. The common file extensions for this format are .jpeg, .jfif, .jpg, .JPG, or .JPE. JPEG itself specifies only how an image is transformed into a stream of bytes, but not how those bytes are encapsulated in any particular storage medium. A further standard, created by the Independent JPEG Group, called JFIF (JPEG File Interchange Format), specifies how to produce a file suitable for computer storage and transmission (such as over the Internet) from a JPEG stream. In common usage, when one speaks of a "JPEG file" one generally means a JFIF file, or sometimes an Exif JPEG file. There are, however, other JPEG-based file formats, such as JNG, and the TIFF format can carry JPEG data as well.
JPEG Protocol

K

Kerberos   88

Kerberos is a network authentication protocol. Kerberos is designed to provide strong authentication for client/server applications by using secret-key cryptography. This is accomplished without relying on authentication by the host operating system, without basing trust on host addresses, without requiring physical security of all the hosts on the network, and under the assumption that packets traveling along the network can be read, modified and inserted at will.
MIT / IETF Specification: RFC 1510

Kermit

Kermit is a very slow telecom data-transfer protocol developed at Columbia University, and used primarily in VAX environments, although widely ported. Like any other telecom data-transfer protocol, it's purpose is to break a data stream into blocks, and provide flow-control, error detection, and re-transmission on the transfer of the blocks.
Columbia University Protocol

L

L2CAP: Logical Link Control and Adaptation Protocol   196

LogicalLink Control and Adaptation Protocol, typically short as L2CAP, is used within the Bluetooth protocol stack at the data link layer. It passes packets to either the Host Controller Interface (HCI) or on a hostless system, directly to the Link Manager.
IEEE Specification: IEEE 802.15.1

L2F: Layer 2 Forwarding protocol   91

Layer 2 Forwarding (L2F) protocol, originally developed by Cisco, uses tunneling of PPP over IP to create a virtual extension of a dial-up link across a network, initiated by the dial-up server and transparent to the dial-up user. L2F is used to establish a secure tunnel across a public infrastructure (such as the Internet) that connects an ISP POP to an enterprise home gateway. This tunnel creates a virtual point-to-point connection between the user and the enterprise customer's network.
Cisco Specification: RFC 2341

L2TP: Layer 2 Tunneling Protocol   92

The Layer 2 Tunneling Protocol (L2TP), defined by IETF based on the Microsoft Point-to-Point Tunneling Protocol (PPTP) and Cisco Layer 2 Forward Protocol (L2F), is used for integrating multi-protocol dial-up services into Internet Service Provider's Point of Presence. L2TP defines an encapsulation mechanism for transporting multiprotocol packets across layer 2 point-to-point links and it enables the operation of a virtual private network over the Internet.
IETF Specification: RFC 2661

LANE NNI: LAN Emulation NNI   142

The LAN Emulation NNI (LNNI), a protocol in the ATM suite, defines the behavior of these LANE service components as seen by each other, the procedures necessary to provide a distributed and reliable LAN Emulation Service. A single ELAN may be served by multiple LECSs, LESs, BUSs and SMSs. Each LES, BUS and SMS serves a single ELAN, while an LECS may serve multiple ELANs. LANE service components interconnect with multiple VCCs for Configuration, Status, Database Synchronization, Control and Data forwarding. The LNNI specification provides multivendor interoperability among the components serving an ELAN so that consumers

may mix and match the LANE Service implementations of different vendors.
ITU-T Protocol

LANE UNI: LAN Emulation UNI 144

The LAN Emulation UNI (LANE), a protocol in the ATM suite, defines the protocols and interactions between LAN Emulation Clients (LE Clients) and the LAN Emulation Service, including initialization, registration, address resolution, and data transfer procedures. Each LE Client connects across the LUNI to a single LES and BUS, may connect to a single LECS, and may have connections to multiple SMSs.
ITU-T and ATM Forum Protocol

LAPB: Link Access Procedure, Balanced 175

Link Access Procedure, Balanced (LAPB) is a data link layer protocol used to manage communication and packet framing between data terminal equipment (DTE) and the data circuit-terminating equipment (DCE) devices in the X.25 protocol stack. LAPB, a bit-oriented protocol derived from HDLC, is actually the HDLC in BAC (Balanced Asynchronous Class) mode. LAPB makes sure that frames are error free and properly sequenced.
ITU-T Protocol

LAP-D: Link Access Procedure, D-Channel 155

Link Access Procedure, D-Channel (LAP-D), a Layer 2 protocol in the ISDN suite, is used to do call setup and other signaling over the D Channel. Data transmissions take place on B channels. LAP-D is almost identical to the X.25 LAP-B protocol. LAPD is defined in the ITU Q.921 protocol.
ITU-T Protocol

LAPF: Link Access Procedure for Frame Mode Services 173

Link Access Procedure for Frame Mode Services (LAPF), as defined in ITU Q.922, is an enhanced LAPD (Q.921) with congestion control capabilities for Frame Mode Services in the Frame Relay network. LADF is used in the Frame Relay network for end-to-end signaling. LAPF conveys data link service data units between DL-service users in the User Plane for frame mode bearer services across the ISDN user-network interface on B-, D- or H-channels.
ITU-T Specification: Q.922

LAP-H: Link Access Procedure for H-Channel

Link Access Procedure for H-Channel (LAP-H) performs the same function as B-Channel (LAPB) but operates at rates exceeding DS-0 (64 Kbps). The H-Channel is good for fast facsimile, video, high-speed data, high-quality audio, and multiple info streams at lower data rates.
ITU-T Protocol

LAP-M: Link Access Procedure for Modems

Link Access Procedure for Modems (LAP-M) is the data link protocol used by V.32 error-correcting modems. When two LAPM modems establish a session, they transmit data in frames using bit-oriented synchronous techniques. An attached computer still sends data to the LAPM modems as standard asynchronous input, but the modem transmits it as frames.
ITU-T Protocol

LAPS: Link Access Procedure-SDH

Link Access Procedure - SDH (LAPS), a variant of the original LAP protocol, is an encapsulation scheme for Ethernet over SONET/SDH. LAPS includes data link service and protocol specification used in transporting IP packets over SDH networks. LAPS provides a point-to-point unacknowledged connectionless service over SONET/SDH. LAPS enables the encapsulation of IPv6, IPv4, PPP, and other higher-layer protocols. X.86 Defines Ethernet over LAPS.
ITU-T Protocol

LAT: Local Area Transport protocol 274

Local Area Transport (LAT) protocol, a protocol in the DECnet, is designed to handle multiplexed terminal traffic to/from time-sharing hosts. Local Area Transport is a non-routable networking technology to provide connection between the DECserver 90, 100, 200, 300, 700 and DECserver 900 Terminal Servers and Digital's VAX and Alpha host computers via Ethernet, giving communication between those hosts and serial devices such as video terminals and printers. The protocol itself was designed in such a manner as to maximize packet efficiency over ethernet by bundling multiple characters from multiple ports into a single packet for Ethernet transport. Over time, other host implementations of the LAT protocol appeared allowing communications to a wide range of Unix and other non-DECnet operating systems using the LAT protocol.
DEC/HP Protocol

LAVC: Local Area VAX Cluster protocol

Local Area VAX Cluster protocol (LAVC) belongs to the DECnet protocol suite for communications between DEC VAX computers in a cluster.
DEC/HP Protocol

LCAS: Link Capacity Adjustment Scheme

Link Capacity Adjustment Scheme (LCAS) is a method of using SONET/SDH overhead to communicate the status of a Virtually Concatenation (VC) connections. LCAS allows re-adjust of link capacity without traffic loss or network error. LCAS is a key enabler of Ethernet over SONET/SDH (EoS) networks. The LCAS mechanism can also automatically decrease the capacity if a VC/SPE in a VCG experiences a failure in the network, and increase the capacity when the fault is repaired.
ITU-T Protocol

LCP: Link Control Protocol 164

The Link Control Protocol (LCP), a protocol in the Point-to-Point protocol (PPP) suite, is used to automatically agree upon the encapsulation format options, handle varying limits on sizes of packets, detect a looped-back link and other common misconfiguration errors and terminate the link. Other optional facilities provided are authentication of the identity of its peer on the link and determination when a link is functioning properly and when it is failing. LCP is versatile and portable to a wide variety of environments.
IETF Specification: RFC 1570

LDAP: Lightweight Directory Access Protocol 20

Lightweight Directory Access Protocol (LDAP) is designed to provide access to the X.500 Directory while not incurring the resource requirements of the Directory Access Protocol (DAP). LDAP is specifically targeted at simple management applications and browser applications that provide simple read/write interactive access to the X.500 Directory and is intended to be a complement to the DAP itself.
IETF Specification: RFC 3377

LDCELP: Low-delay CELP

Low-delay CELP (LSCELP) is a CELP voice compression algorithm providing 16 kbps, or 4:1 compression. LSCELP has

been standardized in ITU-T Recommendation G.728.
ITU-T Specification: G.728

LDP: Label Distribution Protocol   81

Label Distribution Protocol (LDP) is a signaling protocol in the MPLS (Multi Protocol Label Switching) architecture. In the MPLS network, 2 label switching routers (LSR) must agree on the meaning of the labels used to forward traffic between and through them. LDP defines a set of procedures and messages by which one LSR (Label Switched Router) informs another of the label bindings it has made.
IETF Specification: RFC 3036

LE_ARP: LAN Emulation Address Resolution Protocol

LAN Emulation Address Resolution Protocol (LE_ARP) provides the ATM address that corresponds to a MAC address.
ATM Forum Protocol

LEAP: Lightweight Extensible Authentication Protocol

Lightweight Extensible Authentication Protocol (LEAP), also known as Cisco-Wireless EAP, is a Cisco security technology that builds on Wi-Fi's WEP encryption. Basically, it changes the WEP key dynamically during a session to make it less likely that a snooper will be able to derive the key. LEAP provides username/password-based authentication between a wireless client and a RADIUS server like Cisco ACS or Interlink AAA. LEAP is one of several protocols used with the IEEE 802.1X standard for LAN port access control.
Cisco Protocol

LLAP: LocalTalk Link Access Protocol   272

LocalTalk Link Access Protocol (LLAP) is a link-level protocol that manages node-to-node delivery of data on a LocalTalk/AppleTalk network. LLAP manages bus access, provides a node-addressing mechanism, and controls data transmission and reception, ensuring packet length and integrity.
Apple Protocol

LLC: Logic Link Control   198

Logic Link Control (LLC) is the IEEE 802.2 LAN protocol that specifies an implementation of the LLC sublayer of the data link layer. IEEE 802.2 LLC is used in IEEE802.3 (Ethernet) and IEEE802.5 (Token Ring) LANs to perform some functions.
IEEE Specification: IEEE 802.2

LLC2: Logical Link Control, type 2

Logical Link Control,type 2 (LLC2) is a connection-oriented LLC-sublayer protocol. LLC2 (IEEE 802.2) is widely used in LAN environments, particularly among IBM communication systems connected by Token Ring.
IEEE Specification: IEEE 802.2

LMP: Link Manager Protocol

Link Manager Protocol (LMP) is a data link layer protocol in the Bluetooth protocol stack. LMP carries out link setup, authentication, link configuration and other protocols. It discovers other remote Link Manager (LM) and communicates with them via the Link Manager Protocol (LMP). To perform its service provider role, the LM uses the services of the underlying Link Controller (LC).
IEEE Specification: IEEE 802.15.1

LocalTalk   272

LocalTalk is a particular implementation of the data link and physical layer of the AppleTalk networking system from Apple Computer. LocalTalk uses CSMA/CD and specifies a system of shielded twisted pair cabling, plugged into self-terminating transceivers, running at a rate of 230.4 kbit/s.
Apple Protocol

LPP: Lightweight Presentation Protocol   42

Lightweight Presentation Protocol (LPP) describes an approach for providing "streamlined" support of OSI application services on top of TCP/IP-based network for some constrained environments. LPP was initially derived from a requirement to run the ISO Common Management Information Protocol (CMIP) in TCP/IP-based networks.
IETF Specification: IETF 1085

LQR: Link Quality Report

Link Quality Report (LQR), a protocol in the Point-to-Point Protocol (PPP) suite, specifies the mechanism for link quality monitoring and reporting for PPP communications. Data communications links are rarely perfect. Packets can be dropped or corrupted for various reasons (line noise, equipment failure, buffer overruns, etc.). To determine when, and how often, the link is dropping data. Routers, for example, may want to temporarily allow another route to take precedence. An implementation may also have the option of disconnecting and switching to an alternate link. The process of determining data loss is called "Link Quality Monitoring".
IETF Protocol

LU: Logic Unit   263

Logical Units (LUs) are functions in the IBM Systems Network Architecture including LU0, LU1, LU2, LU3, LU6.2, for communication session management. Each SNA node contains one or more logical units (LUs). An LU provides a set of functions that are used by Transaction Programs (TPs) and end users to provide access to the network. LUs communicate directly with local TPs and devices. For example, a TP running on a workstation that uses the AIX operating system can communicate with a TP on an AS/400 computer as easily as it can with a TP on another AIX workstation, as long as both TPs use the same LU type.
IBM Protocol

LU 6.2: Logical Unit 6.2   262

Logical Unit 6.2 (LU 6.2) is a term in the IBM SNA network, which provides peer-to-peer communications between programs in a distributed computing environment. The IBM APPC also runs on LU 6.2 devices.
IBM Protocol

M

M2PA: MTP2 Peer-to-peer user Adaptation   129

MTP2 Peer-to-peer user Adaptation layer (M2PA), a protocol in the SIGTRAN protocol suite, enables SS7 signaling messages over IP using Stream Control Transmission Protocol (SCTP). M2PA is intented to be used on a Peer-to-Peer basis and replace the functionality provided by a traditional SS7 link. M2PA is for an OpenSS7 Network Device.
IETF Specification: RFC 4165

M2UA: MTP2-User Adaptation layer   129

MTP2-User Adaptation layer (M2UA), a protocol in the SIGTRAN protocol suite, is for backhauling of SS7 MTP2-User signaling messages over IP using Stream Control Transmission Protocol (SCTP). M2UA is intended to be used on a Provider/User basis where MTP Level 2 resides on a Signalling

Gateway (SG) and MTP Level 3 resides on an Application Server (AS). It is not intended for peer-to-peer operation: that is, it is not intended to emulate a signalling link between two SCTP endpoints.

IETF Specification: RFC 3331

M3UA: MTP3-User Adaptation layer   129

MTP3-User Adaptation layer (M3UA), a protocol in the SIG-TRAN protocol suite, supports transport of SS7 MTP3-User signaling over IP using Stream Control Transmission Protocol (SCTP). M3UA is intented to be used on a Provider/User basis where MTP Level 3 resides on a Signalling Gateway (SG) and MTP Users reside on an Application Server (AS).

IETF Specification: RFC 3332

MacIP: Macintosh Internet Protocol

Macintosh Internet Protocol (MacIP) tunnels IP datagrams inside AppleTalk for a Macintosh client communicating over an AppleTalk network to a MacIP server. The MacIP server pulls the IP packet out of the AppleTalk datagram and forwards it as Native IP. MacIP is ideal for Macs using LocalTalk or AppleTalk Remote Access (ARA) at the Data Link Layer (OSI Layer 2). These data links only support AppleTalk. By tunneling IP inside of AppleTalk packets, IP connectivity can be gained through the MacIP server.

Apple Protocol

MAP: Manufacturing Automation Protocol

Manufacturing Automation Protocol (MAP) is a network architecture created by General Motors to meet the specific needs of the factory floor. MAP specifies a token-passing LAN similar to IEEE 802.4.

GM Protocol

MAP: Mobile Application Part   281

The Mobile Application Part (MAP), one of the protocols in the SS7 suite, allows for the implementation of the mobile network (GSM) signaling infrastructure. The premise behind MAP is to connect the distributed switching elements, called mobile switching centers (MSCs), with a master database, called the Home Location Register (HLR). The HLR dynamically stores the current location and profile of a mobile network subscriber. The HLR is consulted during the processing of an incoming call.

ITU-T Protocol

MAPOS: Multiple Access Protocol over SONET / SDH

Multiple Access Protocol over SONET/SDH (MAPOS) is a protocol extension to SONET/SDH that has high performance, supports multiple access, broadcast and multicast transmission. MAPOS is connection-less, like IP, with simple design and seamless interconnectivity for LAN and WAN.

ITU-T and MAPOS Org Protocol

MARS: Multicast Address Resolution Server   70

Multicast Address Resolution Server (MARS) is a mechanism for supporting IP multicast over an ATM network. A MARS serves a group of nodes (known as a cluster); each node in the cluster is configured with the ATM address of the MARS. The MARS supports multicast through multicast messages of overlaid point-to-multipoint connections or through multicast servers. ATM-based IP hosts and routers use a MARS to support IP multicast over the ATM Forum's UNI 3.0/3.1 point-to-multipoint connection service. Clusters of endpoints share a MARS and use it to track and disseminate information identifying the

nodes listed as receivers for given multicast groups.

IETF Specification: RFC 2022

MATIP: Mapping of airline traffic over IP

Mapping of airline traffic over IP (MATIP) is a protocol for transporting airline reservation, ticketing, and messaging traffic over TCP/IP.

IETF Specification: RFC 2351

MBGP: Multiprotocol BGP   71

The multiprotocol BGP (MBGP) adds capabilities to BGP to enable multicast routing policy throughout the Internet and to connect multicast topologies within and between BGP autonomous systems. In other words, multiprotocol BGP (MBGP) is an enhanced BGP that carries IP multicast routes. BGP carries two sets of routes: one set for unicast routing and one set for multicast routing. The routes associated with multicast routing are used by the Protocol Independent Multicast (PIM) to build data distribution trees.

IETF Specification: RFC 2858

Megaco: Media Gateway Control Protocol   110

The Media Gateway Control Protocol (Megaco), is for the control of elements in a physically decomposed multimedia gateway, enabling the separation of call control from media conversion. The Media Gateway Control Protocol (Megaco) is a result of joint efforts of the IETF and the ITU-T Study Group 16. Therefore, the IETF-defined Megaco is the same as ITU-T Recommendation H.248.

ITU-T Specification: H.248

MEL CAS: Mercury Exchange Limited Channel Associated Signaling

Mercury Exchange Limited Channel Associated Signaling (MEL CAS) is a voice signaling protocol used primarily in the United Kingdom.

MFTP: Multisource File Transfer Protocol

Multisource File Transfer Protocol (MFTP) is designed for the purpose of file sharing. This is the communication protocol used by such clients as eMule and eDonkey and, in its extended implementation, by the Overnet network.

MGCP: Media Gateway Control Protocol   111

Media Gateway Control Protocol (MGCP) is a VOIP protocol, used between elements of a decomposed multimedia gateway, which consists of a Call Agent containing the call control "intelligence" and a media gateway containing the media functions, e.g., conversion from TDM voice to Voice over IP.

Cisco/ Telcordia Specification: IETF RFC 3435

MHS: Message Handling Service

Message Handling Service, defined in ISO X.400 specifications, is for email transmission specified by the ITU-T. ISO. X.400 is common in Europe and Canada, and is an alternative to the more popular email protocol, Simple Mail Transfer Protocol (SMTP), which is defined by IETF. X.400 uses a binary format so it is easy to include binary contents without encoding it for transfer. Also, it is harder for people to fake email addresses and contents than with SMTP, where text messages are used.

ISO Specification: ISO X.400

Microsoft CIFS: Common Internet File System   286

The Common Internet File System (Microsoft CIFS), an enhanced version of Microsoft Server Message Block (SMB), is the standard way that computer users share files across in-

tranets and the Internet. CIFS enables collaboration on the Internet by defining a remote file-access protocol that is compatible with the way applications already share data on local disks and network file servers. CIFS runs over TCP/IP, utilizes the Internet's global Domain Naming Service (DNS) for scalability and is optimized to support slower speed dial-up connections common on the Internet.
Microsoft Protocol

Microsoft SOAP: Simple Object Access Protocol

287

The Simple Object Access Protocol (Microsoft SOAP) is a lightweight and simple XML-based protocol that is designed to exchange structured and typed information on the Web. SOAP can be used in combination with a variety of existing Internet protocols and formats, including Hypertext Transfer Protocol (HTTP), Simple Mail Transfer Protocol (SMTP) and Multipurpose Internet Mail Extensions (MIME), and can support a wide range of applications from messaging systems to remote procedure calls (RPCs).
Microsoft Protocol

MIME: Multipurpose Internet Mail Extensions   21

Multipurpose Internet Mail Extensions (MIME) specifies how messages must be formatted so that they can be exchanged between different email systems. MIME is a very flexible format, permitting one to include virtually any type of file or document in an email message. MIME messages can contain text, images, audio, video, or other application-specific data.
IETF Specification: RFC 2049

MISTP: Multiple Instances Spanning Tree Protocol

Multiple Instances Spanning Tree Protocol (MISTP) is a Cisco standard which allows several VLANs to be mapped to a reduced number of spanning-tree instances. This is possible since most networks do not need more than a few logical topologies. Each instance handles multiple VLANs that have the same Layer 2 topology. The Multiple Spanning Tree (MST) Protocol defined in IEEE 802.1s is based on the Cisco MISTP.
Cisco Protocol

MLP: Multilink Procedure

Multilink Procedure (MLP), added upper sublayer of the LAPB, operates between the packet layer and a multiplicity of single data link protocol functions (SLPs) in the data link layer (X.25).
ISO Specification: ISO 7776

MNG: Multiple-image Network Graphics

Multiple-image Network Graphics (MNG) is a public file format for animated images. MNG is closely related to the PNG image format as an animation-supporting version of PNG.
W3C Protocol

MNP: Microcom Networking Protocol

Microcom Networking Protocol (MNP) is a type of error correcting/compression protocol. MNP were commonly used on early high-speed (2400 bit/s and higher) modems. Originally developed for use on Microcom's own family of modems, the protocol was later openly licensed and used by most of the modem industry, notably Telebit, USRobotics and Hayes. MNP was later supplanted by v.42bis, which was used almost universally on the first v.32bis modems in the early 1990s. MNP has many versions, MNP 1 to MNP 10. Each class/version generally improved performance over earlier versions, which were retained only for backward-compatibility reasons.

Microcom Protocol

Mobile IP   59

Mobile IP is the key protocol to enable mobile computing and networking, which brings together two of the world's most powerful technologies, the Internet and mobile communication. In Mobile IP, two IP addresses are provided for each computer: home IP address which is fixed and care-of IP address which is changing as the computer moves. When the mobile moves to a new location, it must send its new address to an agent at home so that the agent can tunnel all communications to its new address timely.
IETF Specification: RFC 3344 and RFC 3775

MODEM7

MODEM7, also known as MODEM7 batch or Batch XMODEM, is a protocol for file transfer capable of batch transfers. MODEM7 was used only for a short time, replaced by more capable batching protocols such as YMODEM.

MOP: Maintenance Operation Protocol

Maintenance Operation Protocol(MOP), a protocol in the DECnet suite, is a utility services such as uploading and downloading system software, remote testing and problem diagnosis. For example, MOP can be used to download a system image to a diskless station.
DEC/HP Protocol

MOSPF: Multicast Extensions to OSPF   72

Multicast Extensions to OSPF (MOSPF) provides enhancements to OSPF Version 2 to support IP multicast routing. The enhancements have been added in a backward-compatible fashion; routers running the multicast additions will interoperate with non-multicast OSPF routers when forwarding regular (unicast) IP data traffic.
IETF Specification: RFC 1584

MOUNT

MOUNT is a Netowrk File System protocol used to initiate client access to a server supporting NFS. The NFS mount protocol facilitates the fucntions that allow NFS clients to attach remote directory trees to a mount point in the local file system. A mount point is an empty directory or subdirectory, created as place to attache a remote file system. In order to mount a file system from an NFS server, a user needs an account on the machine where the file system resides. The NFS client passes the UID and GID of the process requesting the mount to the NFS server. The server then validates the request. Mount protocol also allows the server to grant remote access privileges to a restricted set of clients via export control.
SUN Specification: NFS

MP: Multilink Point-to-Point Protocol   165

MultiLink Point-to-Point Protocol (MultiPPP, MP or MLP), also known as PPP Multilink protocol, is a method for splitting, recombining and sequencing datagrams across multiple logical data links. This work was originally motivated by the desire to exploit multiple bearer channels in ISDN, but is equally applicable to any situation in which multiple PPP links connect two systems, including async links. MP is based on an LCP option negotiation that permits a system to indicate to its peer that it is capable of combining multiple physical links into a "bundle".
IETF Specification: RFC 1990

MPEG: Motion Pictures Experts Group

Motion Pictures Experts Group (MPEG) is a working group of ISO/IEC charged with the development of video and audio encoding standards. MPEG includes hundreds of members worldwide from various industries, universities, and research institutions. MPEG's official designation is ISO/IEC JTC1/SC29 WG11. MPEG has defined a group of standards over the years including MPEG-1, MPEG-2, MPEG-3, MPEG-4, MPEG-7 and MPEG-21.

ISO/IEC Protocol

MPEG-1

MPEG-1 is a group of audio and video coding standards defined by Moving Picture Experts Group(MPEG). MPEG-1 video is used by the Video CD format. MPEG-1 consists of several "parts": Part 1, Synchronization and multiplexing of video and audio; Part 2, Compression codec for non-interlaced video signals; and Part 3, Compression codec for perceptual coding of audio signals. MP3 is the MPEG-1 audio layer 3 in MPEG-1 Part 3.

ISO/IEC Protocol

MPEG-2

MPEG-2 is a group of coding standards for digital audio and video, agreed upon by Moving Pictures Experts Group(MPEG). MPEG-2 is typically used to encode audio and video for broadcast signals, including direct broadcast satellite and Cable TV. MPEG-2, with some modifications, is also the coding format used by standard commercial DVD movies. MPEG-2 includes a few parts: Systems part (part 1) defines Transport Stream to carry digital video and audio over somewhat-unreliable media, and are used in broadcast applications. The Video part (part 2) provides support for interlaced video. The MPEG-2 Audio part (Part 3) enhances MPEG-1's audio by allowing the coding of audio programs with more than two channels. In MPEG-2 AAC (Part 7), audio can alternatively be coded in a non-backwards-compatible way, which allows encoders to make better use of available bandwidth.

ISO/IEC Specification: ISO/IEC 13818

MPEG-21

The MPEG-21 standard defines an open framework for multimedia applications by Moving Picture Experts Group (MPEG). Specifically, MPEG-21 defines a "Rights Expression Language" standard as means of sharing digital rights/permissions/restrictions for digital content from content creator to content consumer. As an XML-based standard, MPEG-21 is designed to communicate machine-readable license information and do so in a "ubiquitous, unambiguous and secure" manner.

ISO/IEC Specification: ISO 21000

MPEG-3

MPEG-3 is a group of audio and video coding standards agreed upon by Moving Picture Experts Group(MPEG). MPEG-3 was designed to handle HDTV signals in the range of 20 to 40 Mbit/s. It was soon discovered that similar results could be obtained through slight modifications to the MPEG-2 standard. Shortly thereafter, work on MPEG-3 was discontinued.

ISO/IEC Protocol

MPEG-4   124

MPEG-4 is a video CODEC for web (streaming media) and CD distribution, conversational (videophone), and broadcast television. MPEG-4 absorbs many of the features of MPEG-1 and MPEG-2 and other related standards, adding new features such as (extended) VRML support for 3D rendering, object-oriented composite files (including audio, video and VRML objects), support for externally-specified Digital Rights Management and various types of interactivity. MPEG-4 consists

of several standards—termed "parts". Profiles are also defined within the individual "parts", so an implementation of a part is ordinarily not an implementation of an entire part.

ISO/IEC Protocol

MPEG-47

MPEG-47 is a nickname of the combination of MPEG-4 and MPEG-7, which refers to use MPEG-4 to do the content CODEC and distribution and use MPEG-7 to facilitate the distribution with metadata.

ISO/IEC Protocol

MPEG-7

MPEG-7 is a multimedia content description standard defined by Moving Picture Experts Group(MPEG). It is very different from other MPEG CODEC standards like MPEG-1, MPEG-2 and MPEG-4. It uses XML to store metadata, and can be attached to timecode in order to tag particular events, or synchronise lyrics to a song.

ISO/IEC Protocol

MPLS: Multiprotocol Label Switching   78

Multiprotocol Label Switching (MPLS), an architecture for fast packet switching and routing, provides the designation, routing, forwarding and switching of traffic flows through the network. More specifically, it has mechanisms to manage traffic flows of various granularities. It is independent of the layer 2 and layer 3 protocols, such as ATM and IP. MPLS is used as the protocol for the core network for the next generation networking (NGN).

IETF Specification: RFC 3031

MPOA: Multi Protocol Over ATM   146

The Multi Protocol Over ATM (MPOA) deals with the efficient transfer of inter-subnet unicast data in a LANE environment. MPOA integrates LANE and NHRP to preserve the benefits of LAN Emulation, while allowing inter-subnet, internetwork layer protocol communication over ATM VCCs without requiring routers in the data path. MPOA provides a framework for effectively synthesizing bridging and routing with ATM in an environment of diverse protocols, network technologies and IEEE 802.1 virtual LANs.

ITU-T Protocol

MPP: Multichannel Point-to-Point Protocol

Multichannel Point-to-Point Protocol (MPP) supports inverse multiplexing, session management, and bandwidth management. MPP enables the combination of up to 30 individual channels into a single high-speed connection. MPP consists of two components: a low-level channel identification, error monitoring, and error recovery mechanism, and a session management level for supporting bandwidth modifications and diagnostics. MPP enables the Ascend unit to add or remove channels from a connection as bandwidth needs change without disconnecting the link. This capability is called Dynamic Bandwidth Allocation, or DBA.

Ascend Communication Protocol

MPPC: Microsoft Point-to-Point Compression Protocol

Microsoft Point-to-Point Compression Protocol (MPPC) is a scheme of representing arbitrary Point-to-Point Protocol (PPP) packets in a compressed form. The MPPC algorithm is designed to optimize processor utilization and bandwidth utilization in order to support a large number of simultaneous connections. The MPPC algorithm is also optimized to work

efficiently in typical PPP scenarios (1500 byte MTU, etc.). The MPPC algorithm uses an LZ [3] based algorithm with a sliding window history buffer. The MPPC algorithm keeps a continous history so that after 8192 bytes of data has been transmitted compressed, there is always 8192 bytes of history to use for compressing, except when the history is flushed.
IETF / Microsoft Specification: RFC 2118 and RFC 3078

MSDP: Multicast Source Discovery Protocol   73

The Multicast Source Discovery Protocol (MSDP) describes a mechanism to connect multiple PIM Sparse Mode (PIM-SM) domains together. Each PIM-SM domain uses its own independent RP(s) and does not have to depend on RPs in other domains.
IETF Specification: RFC 3618

MS-RDP: Microsoft's Remote Desktop Protocol

Microsoft's Remote Desktop Protocol (MS-RDP) is designed to provide remote display and input capabilities over network connections for Windows-based applications running on a server. When TS 4.0 was released, RDP was a new protocol based on an existing ITU T.120 family of protocols with limited features and performances. Windows 2000 Terminal Services and the RDP 5.0 protocol includes several critical new features together with some significant performance improvements over all types of network connections, including LAN, WAN, and dial-up.
Microsoft Protocol

MSRPC: Microsoft Remote Procedure Call

Microsoft Remote Procedure Call (MSRPC) is the Microsoft implementation of the DCE RPC mechanism. Additions include support for Unicode strings, implicit handles, inheritance of interfaces (which are extensively used in DCOM), and complex calculations in the variable-length string and structure paradigms already present in DCE/RPC. Microsoft also added new transport protocols for DCE RPC, the ncacn_np transport, which use named pipes carried into the SMB protocol. MSRPC was used by Microsoft to seamlessly create a client/server model in Windows NT/2000/2003. For example, the Windows Server domains protocols are entirely MSRPC based, as is Microsoft's DNS administrative tool. Microsoft Exchange Server 5.5's administrative front-ends are all MSRPC client/server applications, and its MAPI was made more secure by "proxying" MAPI over a set of simple MSRPC functions that enable encryption at the MSRPC layer without involving the MAPI protocol.
Microsoft Protocol

MST: Multiple Spanning Tree Protocol

Multiple Spanning Tree (MST) Protocol defined in the IEEE 802.1s was based on the Cisco's Multiple Instances Spanning Tree Protocol (MISTP). MST combines the best aspects from both the Cisco Per-VLAN Spanning Tree (PVST+) and the 802.1q. The idea is that several VLANs can be mapped to a reduced number of spanning tree instances because most networks do not need more than a few logical topologies.
IEEE Specification: IEEE 802.1s

MTP: Message Transfer Part   282

Message Transfer Part (MTP), a protocol in the SS7/C7 protocol suite, transfers signal messages and performs associated functions, such as error control and signaling link security. Message Transfer Part (MTP) also provides reliable routing within a network. MTP has has three layers: Layers 1 (physical), 2 (data), and 3 (network).

ITU-T Specification: Q.7XX-series

MTP1: Message Transfer Part Level 1

Message Transfer Part Level 1 (MTP1), a SS7 physical layer unit, defines the physical, electrical, and functional characteristics of the digital signaling link.
ITU-T Specification: Q.7XX-series

MTP2: Message Transfer Part level 2   282

Message Transfer Part Level 2 (MTP2) is the signalling protocol at the data link layer of SS7/C7 protocol suite. MTP2 provides error detection, sequence checking, and initiates retransmission in case of erroneous reception of messages. MTP Level 2 uses packets called signal units to transmit SS7 messages. There are three types of signal units: Fill-in Signal Unit (FISU), Link Status Signal Unit (LSSU), Message Signal Unit (MSU).
ITU-T Specification: Q.7XX-series

MTP3: Message Transfer Part level 3   282

Message Transfer Part level 3 (MTP3) is the signalling protocol at the network layer of SS7/C7 protocol suite. MTP3 provides routing functionality to transport signaling messages through the SS7 network to the requested endpoint. Each network element in the SS7 network has a unique address, the Signaling Point Code (SPC). Message routing is performed according to this address.
ITU-T Specification: Q.7XX-series

MultiPPP: MultiLink Point to Point Protocol   165

MultiLink Point-to-Point Protocol (Multilink PPP, MultiPPP or MP), also known as PPP Multilink protocol, is a method for splitting, recombining and sequencing datagrams across multiple logical data links. This work was originally motivated by the desire to exploit multiple bearer channels in ISDN, but is equally applicable to any situation in which multiple PPP links connect two systems, including async links. MultiPPP is based on an LCP option negotiation that permits a system to indicate to its peer that it is capable of combining multiple physical links into a "bundle".
IETF Specification: RFC 1990

MZAP: Multicast-Scope Zone Announcement Protocol   74

Multicast-Scope Zone Announcement Protocol (MZAP) is for the discovery of the multicast administrative scope zones that are relevant at a particular location. MZAP also provides mechanisms to discover common misconfigurations of administrative scope zones.
IETF Specification: RFC 2776

N

NARP: NBMA Address Resolution Protocol   60

The NBMA Address Resolution Protocol (NARP) allows a source terminal (a host or router), wishing to communicate over a Non-Broadcast, Multi-Access (NBMA) link layer network, to find out the NBMA addresses of a destination terminal if the destination terminal is connected to the same NBMA network as the source.
IETF Specification: RFC 1735

NAT: Network Address Translation   22

Network Address Translation (NAT) is a method by which IP addresses are mapped from one group to another, transparent to end users. The need for IP Address translation arises when a network's internal IP addresses cannot be used outside the network either for privacy reasons or because they are invalid for use outside the network. Network topology outside a local domain can change in many ways.

IETF Specification: RFC 3022

NAUs: Network Accessible Units 263

Network Accessible Units (NAUs) are the IBM Systems Network Architecture (SNA) components to facilitate the communication between a Transaction Program (TP) and the SNA network, formerly called "network addressable units". NAUs are unique network resources that can be accessed through unique local addresses by other network resources. SNA provides the following types of NAUs: Physical units (PU), Logical units (LU) and Control points (CP).

IBM Protocol

NBFCP: NetBIOS Frames Control Protocol

NetBIOS Frames Control Protocol (NBFCP) is a network control protocol for establishing and configuring the NBF protocol over Point-to-Point Protocol (PPP) links. The NBF Control Protocol (NBFCP) is responsible for configuring, enabling, and disabling the NBF protocol modules on both ends of the point-to-point link. NBFCP uses the same packet exchange mechanism as the Link Control Protocol. NBFCP packets MUST NOT be exchanged until PPP has reached the Network-Layer Protocol phase. NBFCP packets received before this phase is reached should be silently discarded. NBFCP is only applicable for an end system to connect to a peer system or the LAN that peer system is connected to. It is not applicable for connecting two LANs together due to NetBIOS name limitations and NetBIOS name defense mechanisms.

IETF Specification: RFC 2097

NBMA: Non-Broadcast Multi-Access

Non-Broadcast Multi-Access (NBMA) network allows only data transfer from one computer to another over a virtual circuit or across a switching device. The NBMA network is the opposite of a broadcast network, on which multiple computer devices are connected through a shared cable. The typical NBMA networks are Frame Relay, ATM and X.25 networks.

Novell Protocol

NBP: Name Binding Protocol

Name Binding Protocol (NBP) is the AppleTalk transport-level protocol used for translating network device names to addresses and manages the use of names on AppleTalk networks. NBP enables AppleTalk protocols to understand user-defined zones and device names by providing and maintaining translation tables that map names to their corresponding socket addresses.

Apple Protocol

NBSS: NetBIOS Session Service 265

The NetBIOS Session Service (NBSS) is one of two ways by which applications may communicate with each other, the alternative being the NetBIOS Datagram service. NetBIOS Session Service is for connection-oriented communications. NBSS lets two computers establish a connection for a "conversation", allows larger messages to be handled, and provides error detection and recovery. The bulk of all NetBIOS traffic generated on a network occurs using the NetBIOS Session service, which utilizes TCP port 139. File and printer services are the primary user of the NetBIOS Session service. Another common use for NBSS is the networked application: Server Manager, User Manager, Event Viewer, Registry Editor, and Performance Monitor.

IBM Protocol

NCP: NetWare Core Protocol 256

The Novell NetWare Core Protocol (NCP) manages access to the primary NetWare server resources. NCP makes procedure calls to the NetWare File Sharing Protocol (NFSP) that services requests for NetWare file and print resources. NCP is the principal protocol for transmitting information between a NetWare server and its clients.

Novell Protocol

NCP: Network Control Protocols

The Network Control Protocol (NCP), a protocol in the Point-to-Point Protocol (PPP) suite, provides services in the PPP link connection process to establish and configure different network-layer protocols such as IP, IPX or AppleTalk. After a NCP has reached the opened state, PPP will carry the corresponding network-layer protocol packets. Any supported network-layer protocol packets, received when the corresponding NCP is not in the opened state, must be silently discarded. The most commonly used NCPs are IP Control Protocol (IPCP) and IPv6CP.

IETF Specification: RFC 3435

NCS: Network-based Call Signaling 112

Network-based Call Signaling (NCS), based on the Media Gateway Control Protocol (MGCP), is the VOIP signaling protocol adopted by the CableLab as a standard for PacketCable embbed clients, which is a network element that provides:

• Two or more traditional analog (RJ11) access lines to a voice-over-IP (VoIP) network.

• Optionally, one or more video lines to a VoIP network

IETF Protocol

NDMP: Network Data Management Protocol 214

The Network Data Management Protocol (NDMP) is an open protocol for enterprise-wide network based data management. NDMP defines a network-based mechanism and protocol for controlling backup, recovery, and other transfers of data between primary and secondary storage.

SNIA Protocol

NDS: NetWare Directory Services

NetWare Directory Services (NDS), based on X.400, is the Novell's directory services for Netware, Windows NT, and Unix. The NDS directory represents each network resource (user, hardware, or application) as an object of a certain class, where each class has certain properties. The directory is hierarchical, divided into branches by rules of containment.

Novell Protocol

NetBEUI: NetBIOS Extended User Interface 266

NetBIOS Extended User Interface (NetBEUI) is an extended version of NetBIOS that lets computers communicate within a local area network. NetBEUI formalizes the frame format that was not specified as part of NetBIOS, so is sometimes called the NetBIOS frame (NBF) protocol.

IBM Protocol

NetBIOS Datagram Service 265

The NetBIOS Datagram Service is one of two ways by which applications may communicate with each other, the alternative being the NetBIOS Session service. The NetBIOS Datagram Service provides connectionless and broadcast-oriented communications, making use of the UDP transport-layer protocol, port number 138. The Datagram service, because it uses UDP, is faster and more efficient but does not provide guaranteed

delivery of packets.
IBM Protocol

NetBIOS Session Service   265

The NetBIOS Session Service (NBSS) is one of two ways by which applications may communicate with each other, the alternative being the NetBIOS Datagram service. The bulk of all NetBIOS traffic generated on a network occurs using the NetBIOS Session service, which utilizes TCP port 139. File and printer services are the primary user of the NetBIOS Session service. Another common use for NBSS is the networked application: Server Manager, User Manager, Event Viewer, Registry Editor, and Performance Monitor.
IBM Protocol

NetBIOS: Network Basic Input Output System   265

Network Basic Input Output System (NetBIOS), created by IBM originally, defines a software interface and standard methods providing a communication interface between the application program and the attached medium. NetBIOS, a session layer protocol, is used in various LAN (Ethernet, Token Ring, etc) as well as WAN environments, such as TCP/IP, PPP and X.25 networks.
IBM Protocol

NetRPC: NetRemote Procedure Call

The NetRemote Procedure Call (NetRPC) protocol, a protocol in the session/presentation layer of the VINES protocol stack, is used to access VINES applications such as StreetTalk and VINES Mail. A program number and version identify all VINES applications. Calls to VINES applications must specify the program number, program version, and the specific procedure within the program, where applicable.
Banyan Protocol

NetWare   254

NetWare is a Novell network operating system (NOS) that provides transparent remote file access and numerous other distributed network services, including printer sharing and support for various applications such as electronic mail transfer and database access. NetWare specifies the upper five layers of the OSI reference model, and runs on any media-access protocol (Layer 2). In addition, NetWare runs on virtually any kind of computer system, from PCs to mainframes. NetWare and its supporting protocols often coexist on the same physical channel with many other popular protocols, including TCP/IP, DECnet, and AppleTalk.
Novell Protocol

Network Protocol   6

Network Protocols define the rules and procedures for the network communications. A protocol is a formal set of rules, conventions and data structure that governs how computers and other network devices exchange information over a network. In other words, a protocol is a standard procedure and format that two data communication devices must understand, accept and use to be able to talk to each other.

NFS: Network File System   288

Network File System (NFS), originally developed by Sun Microsystems and then extended by IETF, allows file sharing over network among different types of systems. In other words, NFS was designed for remote file access and sharing over network with various types of machines, operating systems, network architecture and transport protocols.
SUN Specification: RFC 3530

NHRP: NBMA Next Hop Resolution Protocol   61

NBMA Next Hop Resolution Protocol (NHRP) is used by a source station (host or router) connected to a Non-Broadcast, Multi-Access (NBMA) subnetwork to determine the internetworking layer address and NBMA subnetwork addresses of the "NBMA next hop" towards a destination station. If the destination is connected to the NBMA subnetwork, then the NBMA next hop is the destination station itself. Otherwise, the NBMA next hop is the egress router from the NBMA subnetwork that is "nearest" to the destination station.
IETF Specification: RFC 2332

NIS: Network Information Service

Network Information Service (NIS), previously known as Yellow Page protocol, is a directory service used for name look-up and general table enumeration. Each NIS database consists of key-value pairs, maps, and domains. NIS defines a set of key-value pairs as a map. Each map belongs to a domain that is a category of maps. This hierarchy of key-value pairs, maps, and domains provides a generic structure for modeling a database of information. An optional component to a NIS server database implementation is the NIS binder (YPbind) server. NIS uses YPbinder servers to provide addressing information about NIS database servers to potential clients.
Sun Protocol

NLSP: NetWare Link Services Protocol   257

The NetWare Link Services Protocol (NLSP) is a link-state routing protocol in the Novell NetWare architecture. NLSP is based on the OSI Intermediate System-to-Intermediate System (IS-IS) protocol and was designed to replace IPX RIP (Routing Information Protocol) and SAP (Service Advertisement Protocol), Novell's original routing protocols that were designed for small-scale internetworks.
Novell Protocol

NLSP: Network Layer Security Protocol

Network Layer Security Protocol (NLSP) is an OSI protocol for end-to-end encryption services at the top of OSI layer 3. NLSP is derived from the Secure Data Network System (SDNS) protocol but is much more complex.
ISO Specification: ISO 11577

NNI: Network Node Interface

Network Node Interface (NNI), also known as Network-to-Network Interface, is the standard interface between ATM switches. The term is also used with frame relay. NNI makes network routing possible.
ITU-T Protocol

NNI: Network-to-Network Interface

Network-to-Network Interface (NNI), also known as Network Node Interface, is an internal interface within a network linking two or more elements. Many technologies such as ATM (ATM PNNI), Frame Relay (Frame RElay NNI) require this type of interface for the communication between network devices.
ITU-T Protocol

NNTP: Network News Transfer Protocol   22

Network News Transfer Protocol (NNTP) specifies a protocol for the distribution, inquiry, retrieval and posting of news articles, using a reliable stream (such as TCP port 119) server-client model. NNTP is designed so that news articles need only be stored on one (presumably central) server host, and subscribers on other hosts attached to the network may read news articles using stream connections to the news host. The

Network News Transfer Protocol (NNTP) established the technical foundation for the widely used Newsgroups.
IETF Specification: RFC 977

Novell NetWare 254

Novell NetWare is a Novell network operating system (NOS) that provides transparent remote file access and numerous other distributed network services, including printer sharing and support for various applications, such as electronic mail transfer and database access. NetWare specifies the upper five layers of the OSI reference model and runs on any media access protocol (Layer 2). In addition, NetWare runs on virtually any kind of computer system, from PCs to mainframes. NetWare and its supporting protocols often coexist on the same physical channel with many other popular protocols, including TCP/IP, DECnet and AppleTalk.
Novell Protocol

NPAT: Network Port Address Translation 22

Network Port Address Translation (NPAT), also known as Port Address Translation (PAT), is a feature of a Network Address Translation (NAT) device that translates not only IP addresses but also TCP or UDP ports between a host and port on an outside network to a host and port on an inside network. NPAT allows one single IP address to be used for many internal hosts. With NPAT one outside IP address can account for over 64000 inside hosts.
IETF Protocol

NSP: Network Services Protocol

Network Services Protocol (NSP), a protocol in the DECnet suite, provides reliable virtual connection services with flow control to the network layer Routing Protocol.
DEC/HP Protocool

NTP: Network Time Protocol 23

Network Time Protocol (NTP) is a time synchronization system for computer clocks through the Internet network. It provides the mechanisms to synchronize time and coordinate time distribution in a large, diverse internet operating at rates from mundane to light wave. It uses a returnable time design in which a distributed sub-network of time servers, operating in a self-organizing, hierarchical master-slave configuration, synchronizes logical clocks within the sub-network and to national time standards via wire or radio. The servers can also redistribute reference time via local routing algorithms and time daemons.
IETF Specification: RFC 1305

OAKLEY Key Determination Protocol

The OAKLEY Key Determination Protocol is based on the Diffie-Hellman algorithm and designed to be a compatible component of ISAKMP. OAKLEY was proposed as a protocol "by which two authenticated parties can agree on secure and secret keying material.
IETF Specification: RFC 2412

OC: Optical Carrier

Optical Carrier (OC) is a group of signal bandwidth in a SONET fiber optic network with many defined levels. It is typically denoted as OC-n, where n is the multiplexing factor of the basic rate of 51.8 Mbit/s. The currently defined levels are:
OC-1 -- 51.8 Mbit/s
OC-3 -- 155.52 Mbit/s
OC-12 -- 622.08 Mbit/s
OC-24 -- 1.244 Gbit/s
OC-48 -- 2.488 Gbit/s
OC-96 -- 4.976 Gbit/s
OC-192 -- 9.953 Gbit/s
OC-256 -- about 13 Gbit/s
OC-384 -- about 20 Gbit/s
OC-768 -- about 40 Gbit/s
OC-1536 -- about 80 Gbit/s
OC-3072 -- about 160 Gbit/s
ANSI/ITU-T Protocol

OC1: Optical Carrier One

Optical Carrier One (OC1 or OC-1) is a SONET line with a transmission speed of 51.84 Mbit/s (payload: 50.112 Mbit/s; overhead: 1.728 Mbit/s) using optical fiber. OC-1 is the basic rate for the SONET optical fiber lines and the other rate levels of SONET are multipled based on the OC-1 speed. OC-1 is equivalent to STS-1 (Electrical level) and STM-0 (SDH).
ANSI/ITU-T Protocol

OC12: Optical Carrier 12

Optical Carrier 12 (OC12 or OC-12) is a fiber optic network line with a SONET rate of 622.08 Mbit/s (payload: 601.344 Mbit/s; overhead: 20.736 Mbit/s) or 12 times the basic SONET signal transmitting rate of 51.84 Mbit/s (OC-1). OC-12 lines are commonly used by Service Providers as WAN connections. This connection speed is often used by mid-sized (below Tier 2) internet customers, such as web hosting companies or smaller ISPs buying service from larger ones. OC-12 is equivalent to STS-12 (Electrical level) and STM-4 (SDH).
ANSI/ITU-T Protocol

OC192: Optical Carrier 192

Optical Carrier 192 (OC192 or OC-192) is a SONET rate of 9953.28 Mbit/s (payload: 9621.504 Mbit/s; overhead: 331.776 Mbit/s) over optic fiber lines, or 192 times the basic 51.84 Mbit/s SONET signal (OC-1). The WAN version of 10 Gigabit Ethernet is designed to interoperate with OC-192. As of 2006, OC-192 connections are the most common for use on the backbones of large ISPs. OC-192 is equivalent to STS-192 (Electrical level) and STM-64 (SDH).
ANSI/ITU-T Protocol

OC3: Optical Carrier 3

Optical Carrier 3 (OC3 or OC-3) is a optic fiber line using SONET with a transmission speed of 155.52 Mbit/s (payload: 150.336 Mbit/s; overhead: 5.184 Mbit/s), or 3 times the basic 51.84 Mbit/s SONET signal (OC-1). OC-3 is equivalent to STS-3 (Electrical level)and STM-1 (SDH).
ANSI/ITU-T Protocol

OC48: Optical Carrier 48

Optical Carrier 48 (OC48 or OC-48) is a fiber optic line with a SONET rate of 2488.32 Mbit/s (payload: 2405.376 Mbit/s; overhead: 82.944 Mbit/s) or 48 times the basic SONET signal transmitting at 51.84 Mbit/s. OC-48 connections are used as the backbones of many regional ISPs. OC-1 is equivalent to STS-48 (Electrical level) and STM-16 (SDH).
ANSI/ITU-T Protocol

OC768: Optical Carrier 768

Optical Carrier 768 (OC768 or OC-768) is a fiber optic line with a SONET rate of 39,813.12 Mbit/s (payload: 38,486.016 Mbit/s; overhead: 1327.104 Mbit/s), or 768 times the basic SONET rate of 51.84 Mbit/s (OC-1). It's often referred to as "40 Gbit".

OC-768 is equivalent to STS-768 (Electrical level) and STM-256 (SDH).
ANSI/ITU-T Protocol

OC96: Optical Carrier 96

Optical Carrier 96 (OC96 or OC-96) is a fiber optic line with a SONET rate of 4976 Mbit/s, or 96 times the basic SONET rate of 51.84 Mbit/s (OC-1). It's not used much in the real world.
ANSI/ITU-T Protocol

OC-n: Optical Carrier level n

Optical Carrier level n (OC-n) is a group of signal bandwidth in a SONET fiber optic network with many defined levels. It is typically denoted as OC-n, where n is the multiplexing factor of the basic rate of 51.8 Mbit/s. The currently defined levels are:

OC-1 -- 51.8 Mbit/s
OC-3 -- 155.52 Mbit/s
OC-12 -- 622.08 Mbit/s
OC-24 -- 1.244 Gbit/s
OC-48 -- 2.488 Gbit/s
OC-96 -- 4.976 Gbit/s
OC-192 -- 9.953 Gbit/s
OC-256 -- about 13 Gbit/s
OC-384 -- about 20 Gbit/s
OC-768 -- about 40 Gbit/s
OC-1536 -- about 80 Gbit/s
OC-3072 -- about 160 Gbit/s
ANSI/ITU-T Protocol

OpenSS7

OpenSS7, also known as LinuxSS7, is an open-source development project to provide robust and GPL'ed SS7 stack for Linux and other UN*X operation systems. The website of this organization is: http://www.openss7.org.
Open Group Protocol

OpenSSL

The OpenSSL is a collaborative project to develop a robust, commercial-grade, full-featured, and Open Source toolkit implementing the Secure Sockets Layer (SSL v2/v3) and Transport Layer Security (TLS v1) protocols as well as a full-strength general purpose cryptography library. The project is managed by a worldwide community of volunteers that use the Internet to communicate, plan, and develop the OpenSSL toolkit and its related documentation. The OpenSSL toolkit is licensed under an Apache-style licence, which means that you are free to get and subject to some simple license conditions.
OpenSSL Protocol

OSI Model: OSI Network Architecture 7 Layers Model 2

OSI Network Architecture 7 Layers Model (OSI Model or OSI 7 Layers Model) is a reference model developed by ISO (International Organization for Standardization) in 1984, as a conceptual framework of standards for communication in the network across different equipment and applications by different vendors. It is now considered the primary architectural model for inter-computing and inter-networking communications. Most of the network communication protocols used today have a structure based on the OSI model.
ISO Protocol

OSI NLCP: OSI Network Layer Control Protocol

OSI Network Layer Control Protocol (OSI NLCP), a protocol in the Point-to-Point Protocol (PPP) suite, is responsible for configuring, enabling and disabling the OSI protocol modules on both ends of the PPP link.
IETF Specification: RFC 1337

OSI 7-Layer Reference Model 2

Open Systems Interconnection (OSI) 7-Layer Reference Model, also known as OSI model or 7 layers model or OSI reference model, is a reference model developed by ISO (International Organization for Standardization) in 1984, as a conceptual framework of standards for communication in the network across different equipment and applications by different vendors. It is now considered the primary architectural model for inter-computing and inter-networking communications. Most of the network communication protocols used today have a structure based on the OSI model. The OSI model defines the communications process into 7 layers, dividing the tasks involved with moving information between networked computers into seven smaller, more manageable task groups. A task or group of tasks is then assigned to each of the 7 OSI layers. Each layer is reasonably self-contained, so that the tasks assigned to each layer can be implemented independently. This enables the solutions offered by one layer to be updated without adversely affecting the other layers.

OSP: Open Settlement Protocol

Open Settlement Protocol(OSP) is a client/server protocol defined by the ETSI TIPHON to establish authenticated connections between gateways, and to allow gateways and servers to transfer accounting and routing information securely. OSP allows service providers to roll out VoIP services without establishing direct peering agreements with other ITSPs.
ETSI Protocol

OSPF: Open Shortest Path First 62

Open Shortest Path First (OSPF) is an interior gateway protocol which is used for routing between routers belonging to a single Autonomous System. OSPF uses link-state technology in which routers send each other information about the direct connections and links which they have to other routers. Each OSPF router maintains an identical database describing the Autonomous System's topology. From this database, a routing table is calculated by constructing a shortest path tree. OSPF recalculates routes quickly in the face of topological changes, utilizing a minimum of routing protocol traffic. OSPF has two primary versions OSPFv2, which is designed for IPv4 and OSPFv3 for IPv6.
IETF Specification: RFC 2328

OSPFv3: Open Shortest Path First version 3 62

Open Shortest Path First version 3 (OSPFv3), also known as OSPF for IPv6, is an interior gateway protocol for routing between routers belonging to a single Autonomous System in IPv6 networks. OSPFv3, based on the widely deployed OSPFv2, has maintained many fundamental mechanisms of OSPFv2. Changes between OSPFv2 for IPv4 and OSPFv3 include the following: 1) Addressing semantics have been removed from OSPF packets and the basic LSAs. 2) New LSAs have been created to carry IPv6 addresses and prefixes. 3) OSPF now runs on a per-link basis, instead of on a per-IP-subnet basis. 4) Flooding scope for LSAs has been generalized. 5) Authentication has been removed from the OSPF protocol itself, instead relying on IPv6's Authentication Header and Encapsulating Security Payload.
IETF Specification: RFC 2740

P3P: Platform for Privacy Preferences

The Platform for Privacy Preferences (P3P) is a protocol allowing Websites to declare their intended use of information they collect about browsing users. Designed to give users more control of their personal information when browsing, P3P was developed by the World Wide Web Consortium (W3C) and officially recommended on April 16, 2002.
W3C Protocol

PAgP: Port Aggregation Protocol

Port Aggregation Protocol (PAgP) aids in the automatic creation of Fast EtherChannel links. PAgP packets are sent between Fast EtherChannel-capable ports in order to negotiate the forming of a channel.
Cisco Protocol

PAP: Password Authentication Protocol   167

The Password Authentication Protocol (PAP), a Link Control Protocol in the PPP suite, provides a simple method for the peer to establish its identity using a 2-way handshake. This is done only upon initial link establishment. Unlike CHAP, PAP passes the password and the host name or username in the clear (unencrypted). PAP does not itself prevent unauthorized access but merely identifies the remote end. The router or access server then determines whether that user is allowed access.
IETF Specification: RFC 1994

PAP: Printer Access Protocol

Printer Access Protocol (PAP), a protocol in the AppleTalk suite, manages the virtual connection to printers and other servers in an AppleTalk network.
Apple Protocol

PDCP: Packet Data Convergence Protocol

Packet Data Convergence Protocol (PDCP) is used in UMTS 3G network to map higher-level protocol characteristics onto the characteristics of the underlying radio-interface protocols, providing protocol transparency for higher-layer protocols. PDCP also provides protocol control information compression.
3GPP Specification: 3GPP TS 25.323

PEAP: Protected Extensible Authentication Protocol

Protected Extensible Authentication Protocol(PEAP), a protocol developed by Microsoft, Cisco and RSA Security as an open standard, is used to authenticate wireless LAN clients without requiring them to have certificates. PEAP is a method to securely transmit authentication information, including passwords, over wireless networks. PEAP utilizes Transport Layer Security (TLS) to set up an end-to-end tunnel to transfer the user's credentials without having to use a certificate on the client. PEAP uses only server-side public key certificates to authenticate clients by creating an encrypted SSL/TLS tunnel between the client and the authentication server, which protects the ensuing exchange of authentication information from casual inspection.
IETF Draft Protocol

PEP: Packet Exchange Protocol

Packet Exchange Protocol(PEP), an Xerox protocol, provides a semi-reliable packet delivery service that orients towards single-packet exchanges.
Xerox Protocol

PGM: Pragmatic General Multicast   75

Pragmatic General Multicast (PGM) is a reliable transport protocol for applications that require ordered or unordered, duplicate-free, multicast data delivery from multiple sources to multiple receivers. PGM is specifically intended as a workable solution for multicast applications with basic reliability requirements rather than as a comprehensive solution for multicast applications with sophisticated ordering, agreement and robustness requirements. Its central design goal is simplicity of operation with due regard for scalability and network efficiency.
IETF Specification: RFC 3208

PIC: Pre-IKE Credential Provisioning Protocol

Pre-IKE Credential (PIC) Provisioning Protocol is a proposed replacement for the Internet Key Exchange (IKE) protocol. PIC presents a method to bootstrap IPSec authentication via an "Authentication Server" (AS) and legacy user authentication (e.g., RADIUS). The client machine communicates with the AS using a key exchange protocol where only the server is authenticated, and the derived keys are used to protect the legacy user authentication. Once the user is authenticated, the client machine obtains credentials from the AS that can be later used to authenticate the client in a standard IKE exchange with an IPSec-enabled security gateway. The later stage does not require user intervention. The proposed server-authenticated key exchange uses an ISAKMP-based protocol, similar to a simplified IKE exchange, and arbitrary legacy authentication is supported via the use of the EAP protocol.
IETF Protocol

PIM: Protocol Independent Multicast   77

Protocol Independent Multicast (PIM) refers to a group of multicast routing protocols, each optimized for a different environment. There are two main PIM protocols: PIM Sparse Mode and PIM Dense Mode. A third PIM protocol, Bi-directional PIM(BIDIR-PIM), is less widely used. All PIM protocols share a common control message format. PIM control messages are sent as raw IP datagrams, either multicast to the link-local ALL PIM ROUTERS multicast group, or unicast to a specific destination.
IETF Specification: RFC 2362

PIM-DM: PIM Dense Mode   76

PIM Dense Mode (PIM-DM), one of Protocol Independent Multicast protocols, is mainly designed for multicast LAN applications, while the PIM-SM is for wide area, inter-domain networks. PIM-DM implements the same flood-and-prune mechanism that Distance Vector Multicast Routing Protocol (DVMRP) and other dense mode routing protocols employ. The main difference between DVMRP and PIM-DM is that PIM-DM introduces the concept of protocol independence. PIM-DM can use the routing table populated by any underlying unicast routing protocol to perform reverse path forwarding (RPF) checks.
IETF Specification: RFC 3973

PIM-SM: PIM Sparse Mode   77

PIM Sparse Mode (PIM-SM), one of Protocol Independent Multicast protocols, is for efficiently routing to multicast groups that may span wide-area (WAN and inter-domain) internets, while PIM-DM is mainly for LAN. The protocol is not dependent on any particular unicast routing protocol and is designed to support sparse groups. It uses the traditional IP multicast model of receiver-initiated membership, supports both shared and shortest-path trees and uses soft-state mechanisms to adapt to changing network conditions. It can use the route informa-

tion that any routing protocol enters into the multicast Routing Information Base (RIB).
IETF Specification: RFC 2362

PMAP: Port Mapper

The Port Mapper (PMAP) protocol manages the allocation of transport layer ports to network server applications, which eliminates the need to reserve permanently a port number for each application because only the PMAP application itself requires a reserved port. Server applications obtain a port by requesting a port assignment using PMAP. Clients wanting to access an application first call the PMAP program through a well-known port to obtain the transport port registered to the application. The client then calls the application directly using the registered port.
Sun Protocol

PLP: Packet Level Protocol

Packet Level Protocol (PLP), also known as X.25 Level 3 protocol, is a network layer protocol in the X.25 protocol stack.
ITU-T Protocol

PNG: Portable Network Graphics

Portable Network Graphics (PNG) is an extensible file format for the lossless, portable, well-compressed storage of raster images. PNG provides a patent-free replacement for GIF and can also replace many common uses of TIFF. Indexed-color, grayscale, and truecolor images are supported, plus an optional alpha channel. Sample depths range from 1 to 16 bits. PNG is designed to work well in online viewing applications, such as the World Wide Web, so it is fully streamable with a progressive display option. PNG is robust, providing both full file integrity checking and simple detection of common transmission errors. Also, PNG can store gamma and chromaticity data for improved color matching on heterogeneous platforms.
IETF Specification: RFC 2083

PNNI: ATM Private Network-Node Interface   147

Private Network-Node Interface (PNNI), a critical ATM network-to-network signaling protocol, provides mechanisms to support scalable, QoS-based ATM routing and switch-to-switch switched virtual connection (SVC) interoperability. The PNNI is a hierarchical, dynamic link-state routing protocol. It is designed to support large-scale ATM networks. PNNI is based on UNI 4.0 and Q.2931.
ITU-T Protocol

POP: Post Office Protocol   24

The Post Office Protocol(POP) is designed to allow a workstation with an email client to dynamically access a mail drop on a server host over the TCP/IP network. POP3 is the version 3 (the latest version) of the Post Office Protocol, which has obsoleted the earlier versions of the POP protocol: POP1 and POP2. POPs are not intended to provide extensive manipulation operations of mail on the server; normally, mail is downloaded and then deleted.
IETF Specification: RFC 1939

POP1: Post Office Protocol version 1

The Post Office Protocol version 1 (POP1) is designed to allow a workstation with an email client to dynamically access a mail drop on a server host over the TCP/IP network. POP1 has been obsoleted by the latest version POP3.
IETF Specification: RFC 918

POP2: Post Office Protocol version 2

The Post Office Protocol version 2 (POP2) is designed to al-low a workstation with an email client to dynamically access a mail drop on a server host over the TCP/IP network. POP2 has been obsoleted by the latest version POP3.
IETF Specification: RFC 937

POP3: Post Office Protocol version 3   24

The Post Office Protocol version 3 (POP3) is designed to allow a workstation with an email client to dynamically access a mail drop on a server host. POP3 is the version 3 (the latest version) of the Post Office Protocol. POP3 transmissions appear as data messages between stations. The messages are either command or reply messages. POP3 is not intended to provide extensive manipulation operations of mail on the server; normally, mail is downloaded and then deleted.
IETF Specification: RFC 1939

Port Number   293

Port numbers are associated with TCP and UDP protocols designed to distinguish multiple applications running on a single device with one IP address from one another. Since many network applications may be running on the same machine, computers need something to make sure the correct software application on the destination computer gets the data packets from the source machine, and to make sure replies get routed to the correct application on the source computer. This is accomplished through the use of the TCP or UDP "port numbers". In the TCP and UDP header, there are "Source-Port" and "DestinationPort" fields which are used to indicate the message sending process and receiving process identities defined. The combination of the IP address and the port number is called "socket".

PoS: Packet over SONET/SDH   168

Packet Over SONET/SDH (PoS) is a technology that maps IP datagrams into the SONET frame payload using Point-to-Point Protocol (PPP). Packet over SONET (PoS) is a highly scalable protocol that overcomes many of the inefficiencies of ATM, while providing legacy support to internetworks with existing SONET architectures. PoS provides a mechanism to carry packets directly within the SONET synchronous payload envelope (SPE) using a small amount of High-Level Data Link Control (HDLC) or PPP framing. PoS has three layers:
Top layer: IP encapsulation into PPP
Mid layer: Framing of PPP with HDLC
Bottom layer: Mapping into SONET
IETF Specification: RFC 2615

PP: ISO Presentation Protocol   231

The ISO Presentation Protocol (PP), also known as ISO-PP, is for information transit between open systems using connection-oriented or connectionless mode transmission at the presentation layer of the OSI 7 layer model. An application protocol is specified in terms of the transfer of presentation data values between application entities (PS users), using the User data parameter of presentation service primitives.
ISO Protocol

PPP Multilink Protocol   165

The PPP Multilink protocol, also known as Multilink PPP (Multilink PPP, MultiPPP or MP), is a method for splitting, recombining and sequencing datagrams across multiple logical data links. This work was originally motivated by the desire to exploit multiple bearer channels in ISDN, but is equally applicable to any situation in which multiple PPP links connect two systems, including async links. PPP MultiLink protocol is based on an LCP option negotiation that permits a system to indicate to its peer that it is capable of combining multiple physical links into a "bundle".

IETF Specification: RFC 1990

PPP NCP: Network Control Protocol in PPP   166

The Network Control Protocol (NCP), a protocol in the Point-to-Point Protocol (PPP) suite, provides services in the PPP link connection process to establish and configure different network-layer protocols such as IP, IPX or AppleTalk. After an NCP has reached the opened state, PPP will carry the corresponding network-layer protocol packets. Any supported network-layer protocol packets received when the corresponding NCP is not in the opened state must be silently discarded. The most commonly used NCPs are IP Control Protocol (IPCP) and IPv6CP.

IETF Specification: RFC 1661

PPP: Point-to-Point Protocol   159

The Point-to-Point Protocol (PPP) suite provides a standard method for transporting multi-protocol datagrams over point-to-point links. PPP was originally devised as an encapsulation protocol for transporting IP traffic between two peers. It is a data link layer protocol (layer 2 in the OSI model) in the TCP-IP protocol suite for synchronous modem links, as a replacement for the non-standard layer 2 protocol, SLIP. However, other protocols other than IP can also be carried over PPP, including DECnet and Novell's Internetwork Packet Exchange (IPX).

IETF Specification: RFC 1661

PPP-BPDU: PPP Bridge Protocol Data Unit

Bridge Protocol Data Unit (BPDU), a protocol in the PPP suite, is some "hello packets" of the spanning tree protocol sent out at intervals to exchange information among bridges in the network. BPDUs help describe and identify attributes of a switch port and allow for switches to obtain information about each other.

IETF Protocol

PPPoA: PPP over ATM AAL5   169

PPP over ATM AAL5 (PPPoA) describes the use of ATM Adaptation Layer 5 (AAL5) for framing PPP encapsulated packets. The Point-to-Point Protocol (PPP) provides a standard method for transporting multi-protocol datagrams over point-to-point links.

IETF Specification: RFC 2364

PPPoE: PPP over Ethernet   170

PPP over Ethernet (PPPoE) provides the ability to connect a network of hosts over a simple bridging access device to a remote Access Concentrator. With this model, each host utilizes its own PPP stack, and the user is presented with a familiar user interface. Access control, billing and type of service can be done on a per-user, rather than per-site, basis.

IETF Specification: RFC 2516

PPTP: Point-to-Point Tunneling Protocol   93

Point-to-Point Tunneling Protocol (PPTP), defined originally by Microsoft, is a protocol that allows corporations to extend their corporate network through private "tunnels" over the public Internet, which is known as a virtual private network (VPN). VPN enables a company not to lease private lines but to use the public networks for wide-area communication securely. PPTP is replaced by an IETF standard called Layer 2 Tunneling Protocol (L2TP).

Microsoft Protocol

PVST: Per-VLAN Spanning Tree

Per-VLAN Spanning Tree (PVST) maintains a spanning tree instance for each VLAN configured in the network. It uses ISL Trunking and allows a VLAN trunk to be forwarding for some VLANs while blocking for other VLANs. Since PVST treats each VLAN as a separate network, it has the ability to load balance traffic (at layer-2) by forwarding some VLANs on one trunk and other VLANs on another trunk without causing a Spanning Tree loop.

Cisco Protocol

PVST+: Per-VLAN Spanning Tree Plus

Per VLAN Spanning Tree Plus (PVST+), an enhancement to the 802.1Q specification and unsupported on non-Cisco devices, maintains a spanning tree instance for each VLAN configured in the network. PVST+ is a new version of PVST, uses ISL Trunking and allows a VLAN trunk to be forwarding for some VLANs while blocking for other VLANs. Since PVST treats each VLAN as a separate network, it has the ability to load balance traffic (at layer-2) by forwarding some VLANs on one trunk and other Vlans on another trunk without causing a Spanning Tree loop.

Cisco Protocol

PUP: PARC Universal Protocol

PARC Universal Protocol (PUP), also known as PARC Universal Packet, developed at Xerox PARC, is an early internetworking protocol suite for network routing and packet delivery. In the 1980s, Xerox used PUP as the base for the Xerox Network Services (XNS) protocol suite; some of the protocols in the XNS suite (e.g. the Internetwork Datagram Protocol) were lightly modified versions of the ones in the PUP suite, but others are quite different, reflecting the experience gained with PUP.

Xerox Protocol

Q

Q.2931   148

Q.2931, based on Q.931, is a signaling protocol, which specifies the procedures for the establishment, maintenance and clearing of network connections at the B-ISDN user network interface. The PNNI and the UNI specifications are based on Q.2931. The procedures are defined in terms of messages exchanged.

ITU-T Specification: Q.2931

Q.730

Q.730, an ITU-T specification, defines the ISDN User Part (ISUP) supplementary services.

ITU-T Specification: Q.730

Q.700

Q.700, an ITU-T specification, provides an introduction to CCITT Signalling System No. 7 (SS7).

ITU-T Specification: Q.700

Q.703

Q.703, an ITU-T specification, defines the Signalling System No. 7 (SS7) - Message Transfer Part, Signalling Link.

ITU-T Specification: Q.703

Q.704

Q.704, an ITU-T specification, defines the Signalling System No. 7 (SS7) - Message Transfer Part, Signalling System No. 7 - Signalling Network Functions and Messages.

ITU-T Specification: Q.704

Q.705

Q.705, an ITU-T specification, defines the System No. 7 - Signalling network structure.
ITU-T Specification: Q.705

Q.706

Q.706, an ITU-T specification, defines the Signalling System No. 7 - Message Transfer Part Signalling Performance.
ITU-T Specification: Q.706

Q.712

Q.712, an ITU-T specification, defines the Signalling System No. 7 (SS7) - Definition and Function of SCCP Messages.
ITU-T Specification: Q.712

Q.713

Q.713, an ITU-T specification, defines the Signalling System No. 7 - SCCP Formats and Codes.
ITU-T Specification: Q.713

Q.716

Q.716, an ITU-T specification, defines the Signalling System No. 7 - Signalling connection control part (SCCP) performance.
ITU-T Specification: Q.716

Q.725

Q.725, an ITU-T specification, defines Signalling System No. 7 - Signalling performance in the telephone application.
ITU-T Specification: Q.725

Q.731

Q.731, an ITU-T specification, provides the Stage 3 description for numbering identification supplementary services using Signalling System No. 7 (SS7).
ITU-T Specification: Q.731

Q.732

Q.732, an ITU-T specification, provides the Stage 3 description for call offering supplementary services using Signalling System No. 7(SS7).
ITU-T Specification: Q.732

Q.733

Q.733, an ITU-T specification, provides the Stage 3 description for call completion supplementary services using No. 7 Signalling System (SS7).
ITU-T Specification: Q.733

Q.734

Q.734, an ITU-T specification, provides the Stage 3 description for multiparty supplementary services using Signalling System No. 7.
ITU-T Specification: Q.734

Q.735

Q.735, an ITU-T specification, provides the Stage 3 description for community of interest supplementary services using SS7.
ITU-T Specification: Q.735

Q.736

Q.736, an ITU-T specification, provides the Stage 3 description for charging supplementary services using Signalling System No. 7 (SS7).
ITU-T Specification: Q.736

Q.737

Q.737, an ITU-T specification, provides the Stage 3 description for additional information transfer supplementary services using Signalling System No. 7 (SS7).

ITU-T Specification: Q.737

Q.761

Q.761, an ITU-T specification, provides Signalling System No.7 (SS&) – ISDN user part (ISUP) functional description.
ITU-T Specification: Q.761

Q.762

Q.762, an ITU-T specification, defines the general function of messages and Signals of the ISDN User Part (ISUP) of Signalling System No. 7 (SS7).
ITU-T Specification: Q.762

Q.763

Q.763, an ITU-T specification, defines the formats and codes of the ISDN User Part (ISUP) of Signalling System No. 7 (SS7).
ITU-T Specification: Q.763

Q.764

Q.764, an ITU-T specification, defines the Signalling System No. 7 - ISDN User Part (ISUP) Signalling Procedures.
ITU-T Specification: Q.764

Q.766

Q.766, an ITU-T specification, defines the Signalling System No.7 - Performance Objectives in the Integrated Services Digital Network Application.
ITU-T Specification: Q.766

Q.772

Q.772, an ITU-T specification, defines the Signalling System No. 7 (SS7) - Transaction Capabilities Information Element Definition.
ITU-T Specification: Q.772

Q.773

Q.773, an ITU-T specification, defines the Signalling System No. 7 (SS7) - Transaction Capabilities Formats and Encoding.
ITU-T Specification: Q.773

Q.774

Q.774, an ITU-T specification, defines the Signalling System No. 7 - Transaction Capabilities Procedures.
ITU-T Specification: Q.774

Q.850

Q.850, an ITU-T specification, defines the usage of cause and location in the Digital Subscriber Signalling System No. 1 and the Signalling System No. 7 ISDN User Part.
ITU-T Specification: Q.850

Q.920

Q.920, an ITU-T specification, together with Q.921, defines the ISDN UNI data link layer.
ITU-T Specification: Q.921

Q.921

Q.921, an ITU-T specification, together with Q.920, defines ISDN user-network interface - Data link layer - General aspects.
ITU-T Specification: Q.921

Q.922

Q.922, an ITU-T specification, defines the Link Access Procedure/Protocol (LAPF), which is an enhanced LAPD (Q.921) with congestion control capabilities for Frame Mode Services in the Frame Relay network. LADF is used in the Frame Relay network for end-to-end signaling. LAPF conveys data link service data units between DL-service users in the User Plane for frame mode bearer services across the ISDN user-network

interface on B-, D- or H-channels.
ITU-T Specification: Q.922

Q.922A

Q.922A is an ITU-T specification for Frame Relay encapsulation.
ITU-T Specification: Q.922A

Q.930

Q.930, an ITU-T specification, defines the Digital Subscriber Signalling System No 1 (DSS1) - ISDN user - network interface layer 3 - General aspects.
ITU-T Specification: Q.930

Q.931   156

Q.931, the network layer protocol in the telecommunication architecture, is used in ISDN for call establishment and the maintenance and termination of logical network connections between two devices. Q.931 is one of the network layer (layer 3) protocols in the telecommunication architecture specified by the ITU Q series documents Q.930 through Q.931.
ITU-T Specification: Q.931

Q.932

Q.932, an ITU-T specification, defines the generic procedures applicable for the control of supplementary services at the user-network interface. These procedures expand on the basic call-control functions defined in Q.931.
ITU-T Specification: Q.932

Q.933

Q.933, an ITU-T specification, defines Digital subscriber Signalling System No.1 (DSS 1) - Signalling specification for frame mode basic call control.
ITU-T Specification: Q.933

Q.939

Q.939, an ITU-T specification, defines service indicator coding examples.
ITU-T Specification: Q.939

Q.93B

Q.93B, an evolution of ITU-T recommendation Q.931, is an ITU-T specification for signaling to establish, maintain, and clear BISDN network connections.
ITU-T Specification: Q.93B

Q.950

Q.950, an ITU-T specification, defines ISDN supplementary services.
ITU-T Specification: Q.950

Q.951

Q.951, an ITU-T specification, provides stage 3 description for number identification supplementary services using DSS1, such as Calling line identification presentation (CLIP); Calling line identification restriction (CLIR); Connected line ID and Malicious Call Identification (MCID).
ITU-T Specification: Q.951

Q.952

Q.952, an ITU-T specification, provides stage 3 description for additional information transfer supplementary services using DSS1 (Digital subscriber Signalling System No.1), including Diversion supplementary services and Explicit Call Transfer (ECT).
ITU-T Specification: Q.952

Q.953

Q.953, an ITU-T specification, defines Stage 3 description for call completion supplementary services using DSS 1 such as Call waiting, Call hold, Completion of Calls to Busy Subscribers (CCBS), Terminal Portability (TP) and Call Completion on No Reply (CCNR).
ITU-T Specification: Q.953

Q.954

Q.954, an ITU-T specification, provides the Stage 3 description for multiparty supplementary services using DSS 1, such as Conference calling and Three-party service.
ITU-T Specification: Q.954

Q.955

Q.955, an ITU-T specification, provides Stage 3 description for community of interest supplementary services using DSS 1, such as Closed user group and Multi-level precedence and preemption.
ITU-T Specification: Q.955

Q.956

Q.956, an ITU-T specification, defines Integrated services digital network (ISDN) - Stage 3 service description for charging supplementary services using DSS 1 such as Clause 2 - Advice of charge (AOC) and Clause 3 - Reverse charging.
ITU-T Specification: Q.956

Q.957

Q.957, an ITU-T specification, provides Stage 3 description for additional information transfer supplementary services using DSS 1: User-to-User Signalling (UUS).
ITU-T Specification: Q.957

QLLC: Qualified Logical Link Control   269

Qualified Logical Link Control (QLLC) is an IBM-defined data-link layer protocol that allows SNA data to be transported across X.25 networks. When SNA is used over X.25, it uses the qualifier-bit (Q-bit) in the X.25 packet header to indicate special link control information. This information is relevant for SNA control between the two systems communicating with each other but is of no concern to X.25 link control.
IBM Protocol

QSPN: Quantum Shortest Path Netsukuku

Quantum Shortest Path Netsukuku(QSPN) is the routing algorithm used by Netsukuku to find the best routes in the network. It is optimised to run on a real network, i.e. cannot be used on a map without simulating the nodes which send each other the QSPN packets.

QSIG: Q Signaling

Q Signaling(QSING) is a common channel signaling protocol based on ISDN Q.931 standards and used by many digital PBXs.
ITU-T Protocol

R

RADIUS: Remote Authentication Dial In User Service   89

Remote Authentication Dial In User Service (RADIUS) is a protocol for carrying authentication, authorization and configuration information between a Network Access Server which desires to authenticate its links and a shared Authentication Server. RADIUS uses UDP as the transport protocol. RADIUS also carries accounting information between a Network Access Server and a shared Accounting Server.

IETF Specification: RFC 2865 and 2866

RADSL: Rate Adaptive DSL

Rate-adaptive Asymmetric Digital Subscriber Line (RADSL) is a variation of ADSL which automatically adjusts the connection speed depanding on the quality and length of the telephone line. In RADSL, the broadband modem is configured at startup to test the phone line and adjust the data rate. RADSL typically operates at a lower date rate than regular ADSL. Like ADSL, RADSL provides relatively more bandwidth for downloads and less for uploads.

ITU-T Protocol

RANAP: Radio Access Network Application Part

Radio Access Network Application Part (RANAP) is the Radio Network Layer signaling protocol used in a UMTS system on the Iu interface. It is responsible for functions including the setting up of a RAB (Radio Access Bearer) between the CN (Core Network) and the RNC (Radio Network Controller).

ITU-T Protocol

RARP: Reverse Address Resolution Protocol   85

Reverse Address Resolution Protocol (RARP) allows a physical machine in a local area network to request its IP address from a gateway server's Address Resolution Protocol (ARP) table or cache. A network administrator creates a table in a local area network's gateway router that maps the physical machines'(or Media Access Control [MAC]) addresses to corresponding Internet Protocol addresses.

IETF Specification: RFC 903

RAS: Registration, Admission and Status   106

Registration, Admission and Status (RAS), defined in the ITU-T H.225.0/RAS, is the protocol between endpoints (terminals and gateways) and gatekeepers. The RAS is used to perform registration, admission control, bandwidth changes, status, and disengage procedures between endpoints and gatekeepers. An RAS channel is used to exchange RAS messages. This signaling channel is opened between an endpoint and a gatekeeper prior to the establishment of any other channels.

ITU-T Specification: H.225

RCP: Remote Copy Protocol

Remote Copy Protocol (RCP), a command on the Unix operating systems, is a protocol that allows users to copy files to and from a file system residing on a remote host or server on the network. RCP uses TCP to ensure the reliable delivery of data. But RCP can use kerberos for authentication. This command has been largely superseded by more secure methods, such as the scp and sftp commands based on SSH.

Unix Protocol

RDP: Reliable Data Protocol   45

Reliable Data Protocol (RDP) is a connection-oriented transport protocol designed to efficiently support the bulk transfer of data for such host monitoring and control applications as loading/dumping and remote debugging. It attempts to provide only those services necessary, in order to be efficient in operation and small in size.

IETF Specification: RFC 1115

RDP: Remote Desktop Protocol

Remote Desktop Protocol (RDP) is a Microsoft protocol designed to provide remote display and input capabilities over network connections for Windows-based applications running on a server. RDP was first released with Windows Terminal Services (TS) 4.0 based on an existing ITU T.120 family of protocols with limited features and performances. Windows 2000 TS and the RDP 5.0 protocol include several critical new features together with some significant performance improvements over all types of network connections, including LAN, WAN, and dial-up.

Microsoft Protocol

RFC: Request for Comments

Request for Comments (RFC), a series of documents about the Internet technologies, started in 1969 (when the Internet was the ARPANET). The documents discuss many aspects of computing and computer communication focusing in networking protocols, procedures, programs, and concepts, but also including meeting notes, opinion, and sometimes humor. The specification documents of the Internet protocol suite, as defined by the Internet Engineering Task Force (IETF) and its steering group (the IESG), are published as RFCs. Many of the TCP/IP protocols and PPP protocols are defined by rfc's.

IETF Protocol

RGMP: Router Port Group Management Protocol

249

The Router Port Group Management Protocol (RGMP) is defined by Cisco Systems to address the limitations of Internet Group Management Protocol (IGMP) in its Snooping mechanism. RGMP is used between multicast routers and switches to restrict multicast packet forwarding in switches to those routers where the packets may be needed. RGMP is designed for backbone switched networks where multiple, high-speed routers are interconnected.

Cisco Protocol

RIP: Routing Information Protocol   63

Routing Information Protocol (RIP) is a standard for exchange of routing information among gateways and hosts. This protocol is most useful as an "interior gateway protocol". In a nationwide network such as the current Internet, there are many routing protocols used for the whole network. The network will be organized as a collection of "autonomous systems". Each autonomous system will have its own routing technology, which may well be different for different autonomous systems. The routing protocol used within an autonomous system is referred to as an interior gateway protocol, or "IGP".

IETF Specification: RFC 1058

RIP2: Routing Information Protocol version 2   63

Routing Information Protocol version 2 (RIP2) is an extension of the Routing Information Protocol (RIP), intended to expand the amount of useful information carried in the RIP2 messages and to add a measure of security. RIP2 is a UDP-based protocol. Each host that uses RIP2 has a routing process that sends and receives datagrams on UDP port number 520. RIP and RIP2 are for the IPv4 network while the RIPng is designed for the IPv6 network.

IETF Specification: RFC 2453

RIPng: Routing Information Protocol for the IPv6

64

Routing Information Protocol for the IPv6 (RIPng), is based on protocols and algorithms used extensively in the IPv4 Internet. In an international network such as the Internet, there are many routing protocols used for the entire network. The network will be organized as a collection of Autonomous Systems (AS). Each AS will have its own routing technology, which may differ among AS's. The routing protocol used within an AS is

referred to as an Interior Gateway Protocol (IGP). A separate protocol, called an Exterior Gateway Protocol (EGP), is used to transfer routing information among the AS's.
IETF Specification: RFC 2080

RIPX: Routing Information Protocol for IPX

Routing Information Protocol for IPX (RIPX), a Novell NetWare protocol, is used to collect, maintain and exchange correct routing information among gateways within the Internet for NetWare nodes.
Novell Protocol

rlogin: remote login   25

Remote login (rlogin) is a UNIX remote login command that allows an authorized user to log in to other UNIX machines (hosts) on a network and to interact as if the user were physically at the host computer. Once logged in to the host, the user can do anything that the host has given permission for, such as read, edit or delete files.
IETF Specification: RFC 1282

RLP: Radio Link Protocol

Radio Link Protocol (RLP) is a link layer protocol used for 2G(GSM and cdmaOne) and CDMA-2000 (3G) network-based error correction to ensure robust data transmission. RLP terminates at the Mobile Station(MS) and the Interworking Function(IMF) generally located at the Mobile Switching Centre(MSC). Cellular networks such as GSM and CDMA and CDMA-2000 use different variations of RLP.
IEEE Specification: IEEE 802.20

RM Cell: Resource Management Cell

Resource Management (RM) cell is a protocol in the ATM suite for Available Bit Rate (ABR) services. RM Cells are used to convey ATM network status (available bandwidth, congestion levels) and request peak cell rates for ATM blocks. RM cells are standard 53-byte ATM cells with the payload type field in the header set to a binary value of 110. Forward RM cells are sent to the destination end-system on the same VC as data cells and at an interval defined by the number of RM cells (NRM) parameter. By default, a source ABR device sends one forward RM cell for every 32 data cells.
ITU-T Protocol

RMON: Remote Monitoring   26

Remote Monitoring (RMON) is a standard monitoring specification that enables various network monitors and console systems to exchange network-monitoring data. RMON provides network administrators with more freedom in selecting network-monitoring probes and consoles with features that meet their particular networking needs. RMON has two versions: RMON1 and RMON2.
IETF Specification: RFC 2819 and RFC 2021

RMON1: Remote Network Monitoring version 1

Remote Network Monitoring version 1 (RMON1 or RMONv1) can now be found on most modern network hardware, defined 9 MIB groups for basic network monitoring.
IETF Specification: RFC 2819

RMON2: Remote Network Monitoring version 2

Remote Network Monitoring version 2 (RMON2 or RMONv2) is an extension of RMON that focuses on higher layers of traffic above the medium access control (MAC) layer. RMON2 has an emphasis on IP traffic and application level traffic. RMON2 allows network management applications to monitor packets on all network layers.

IETF Specification: RFC 2021

ROSE: Remote Operations Service Element Protocol   224

The Remote Operations Service Element Protocol (ROSE), an ISO protocol, is a protocol that provides remote operation capabilities, allows interaction between entities in a distributed application and, upon receiving a remote operations service request, allows the receiving entity to attempt the operation and report the results of the attempt to the requesting entity. The ROSE protocol itself is only a vehicle for conveying the arguments and results of the operation as defined by the application.
ISO Protocol

RP: DECnet Routing Protocol   274

DECnet Routing Protocol (RP), similar to Routing Information Protocol in the IP network, distributes routing information among DECnet hosts.
DEC/HP Protocol

RPC Mount Procedures

RPC Mount Procedures are the services for the Remote Procedure Call (RPC) to initiate client access to a server supporting RPC.
Sun Protocol

RPC NFS Procedures

RPC NFS Procedures refer to the Network File System (NFS) implementation using the RPC Protocol. All NFS operations are implemented as RPC procedures.
Sun Protocol

RPC: Remote Procedure Call   43

Remote Procedure Call (RPC) is a protocol for requesting a service from a program located in a remote computer through a network, without having to understand the underlayer network technologies. RPC presumes the existence of a low-level transport protocol, such as TCP or UDP, for carrying the message data between communicating programs.
Sun / IETF Specification: RFC 1831

RPC-PMP: RPC Port Mapper Procedures

RPC Port Mapper Procedures are the Port Mapper (PMAP) protocol which manages the allocation of transport layer ports to network server applications, which eliminates the need to reserve permanently a port number for each application because only the PMAP application itself requires a reserved port.
Sun Protocol

RPR: Resilient Packet Ring

Resilient Packet Ring (RPR), defined by the IEEE's 802.17 working group, is a Layer 2 MAC-based technology to bring SONET-like abilitites to metro Ethernet networks, by adding support for a ring topology and fast recovery from fiber cuts and link failures at Layer 2. RPR uses Ethernet switching and a dual counter-rotating ring topology to provide SONET-like network resiliency and optimized bandwidth usage, while delivering multipoint Ethernet/IP services. RPR maintains its own protection scheme and uses physical-layer alarm information and Layer 2 protocol communications to detect node and/or link failures. When a failure is detected, the RPR switching mechanism restores networks in less than 50 milli-seconds.
IEEE Specification: IEEE 802.17

rsh: Remote Shell Protocol

Remote Shell Protocol (rsh) is a protocol that allows a user to execute commands on a remote system without having to log in to the system. For example, rsh can be used to remotely examine the status of a number of access servers without connecting to each communication server, executing the command, and then disconnecting from the communication server. rsh originated as part of the BSD Unix operating system as part of the rlogin package on 4.2BSD in 1983. rsh has since been ported to other operating systems. rsh is mostly replaced by a more secured protocol called Secure Shell protocol(SSH) in today's environment.

RSS: Really Simple Syndication

Really Simple Syndication (RSS) is a lightweight XML format designed for sharing headlines and other Web content. RSS becomes a popular means of sharing content between sites. RSS solves myriad problems webmasters commonly face, such as increasing traffic, and gathering and distributing news. RSS can also be used for additional content distribution services.

W3C Protocol

RSTP: Rapid Spanning Tree Protocol

Rapid Spanning Tree Protocol (RSTP), defined in the IEEE 802.1w, is an evolution of the Spanning Tree Protocol (STP) defined in IEEE 802.1d. RSTP provides for faster spanning tree convergence after a topology change. RSTP provides a loop free topology for any LAN or bridged network.

IEEE Specification: IEEE 802

RSVP: Resource Reservation Protocol   65

Resource Reservation Protocol (RSVP) is a resource reservation setup protocol designed for quality integrated services over the Internet. RSVP is used by a host to request specific qualities of service from the network for particular application data streams or flows. RSVP is also used by routers to deliver quality-of-service (QoS) requests to all nodes along the path(s) of the flows and to establish and maintain state to provide the requested service. RSVP requests will generally result in resources being reserved in each node along the data path.

IETF Specification: RFC 2205

RSVP-TE: Resource Reservation Protocol - Traffic Extension   82

The Resource Reservation Protocol – Traffic Extension (RSVP-TE) is an addition to the RSVP protocol for establishing label switched paths (LSPs) in MPLS networks. The extended RSVP protocol supports the instantiation of explicitly routed LSPs, with or without resource reservations. It also supports smooth rerouting of LSPs, preemption and loop detection.

IETF Specification: RFC 3209

RSUP: Reliable SAP Update Protocol

Reliable SAP Update Protocol (RSUP) is a bandwidth-saving protocol developed by Cisco for propagating services information. RSUP allows routers to reliably send standard Novell SAP packets only when the routers detect a change in advertised services. RSUP can transport network information either in conjunction with or independently of the Enhanced IGRP routing function for IPX.

Cisco Protocol

RTCP: RTP Control Protocol   127

The RTP control protocol (RTCP) is based on the periodic transmission of control packets to all participants in the session, using the same distribution mechanism as the data packets. The underlying protocol must provide multiplexing of the data and control packets, for example using separate port numbers with UDP.

IETF Specification: RFC 3350

RTMP: Real Time Messaging Protocol

Real Time Messaging Protocol (RTMP) is a proprietary protocol developed by Adobe Systems (formerly Macromedia) that is primarily used with Macromedia Flash Media Server to stream audio and video over the internet to the Macromedia Flash Player client. The default connection port is port 1935.

Adobe Protocol

RTMP: Routing Table Maintenance Protocol

Routing Table Maintenance Protocol (RTMP), based on Routing Information Protocol (RIP), is a communication protocol used by AppleTalk to ensure that all routers on the network have consistent routing information. RTMP establishes and maintains the routing information that is required to route datagrams from any source socket to any destination socket in an AppleTalk network. Using RTMP, routers dynamically maintain routing tables to reflect changes in topology.

Apple Protocol

RTP: Rapid Transport Protocol

Rapid Transport Protocol (RTP) provides pacing and error recovery for IBM APPN data as it crosses the APPN network. With RTP, error recovery and flow control are done end-to-end rather than at every node. RTP prevents congestion rather than reacts to it.

IBM Protocol

RTP: Real-Time Transport Protocol   126

The Real-Time Transport Protocol (RTP) provides end-to-end delivery services for data with real-time characteristics, such as interactive audio and video or simulation data, over multicast or unicast network services. Applications typically run RTP on top of UDP to make use of its multiplexing and checksum services; both protocols contribute parts of the transport protocol functionality. However, RTP may be used with other suitable underlying network or transport protocols.

IETF Specification: RFC 3550

RTP: VINES Routing Table Protocol

VINES Routing Table Protocol (RTP), a network layer protocol in the VINES protocol stack, distributes network topology information. Routing update packets are broadcast periodically by both client and service nodes. These packets inform neighbors of a node's existence and also indicate whether the node is a client or a service node. In each routing update packet, service nodes include a list of all known networks and the cost factors associated with reaching those networks.

Banyan Protocol

RTSE: Reliable Transfer Service Element   226

Reliable Transfer Service Element (RTSE), an ISO application layer protocol, provides for the reliable transfer of bulk data by transforming the data into a string of octets, then breaking the string into segments and handing each segment to the Presentation Layer for delivery. Checkpoints are established between segments. Through the services of the Presentation Layer, RTSE uses the activity management services of the Session Layer to manage the transfer of the collection of segments that make up the bulk data.

ISO Protocol

RTSP: Real-Time Streaming Protocol   113

The Real-Time Streaming Protocol (RTSP) establishes and

controls either a single or several time-synchronized streams of continuous media, such as audio and video. RTSP does not typically deliver the continuous streams itself, although interleaving of the continuous media stream with the control stream is possible. In other words, RTSP acts as a "network remote control" for multimedia servers. RTSP provides an extensible framework to enable controlled, on-demand delivery of realtime data, such as audio and video.
IETF Specification: RFC 2326

RUDP: Reliable UDP 46

Reliable UDP (RUDP) is a simple packet-based transport protocol which was intended as a reliable transport protocol to transport telephony signaling across IP networks. RUDP is designed to allow characteristics of each connection to be individually configured so that a number of protocols with different transport requirements can be implemented simultaneously not on the same platform.
IETF Specification: draft

S

S/MIME: Secure Multipurpose Internet Mail 21

Secure Multipurpose Internet Mail (S/MIME), a secure version of MIME, is defined to support encryption of email messages. S/MIME provides the following cryptographic security services for electronic messaging applications: authentication, message integrity and non-repudiation of origin and privacy and data security. S/MIME can be used by traditional mail user agents (MUAs) to add cryptographic security services to mail that is sent, and to interpret cryptographic security services in mail that is received. However, S/MIME is not restricted to mail; it can be used with any transport mechanism that transports MIME data, such as HTTP.
IETF Specification: RFC 2632 and RFC 2633

SABP: Service Area Broadcast Protocol

Service Area Broadcast Protocol (SABP) is a 3G UMTS protocol for information broadcasting services, which allows cellular operators to deliver information such as stock prices, traffic information, weather reports and emergency alerts to mobile users within selected cells of the network.
3GPP TS 25.419 Specification: 3GPP

SAN: Storage Area Network 207

Storage Area Network (SAN) is a high-speed network or subnetwork whose primary purpose is to transfer data between computer and storage systems. A storage device is a machine that contains nothing but a disk or disks for storing data. A SAN consists of a communication infrastructure, which provides physical connections, and of a management layer, which organizes the connections, storage elements and computer systems so that data transfer is secure and robust.

SAP: Service Advertising Protocol 114

Service Advertising Protocol (SAP), a protocol in the Novell's Netware suite, provides information about what servers are available on the network. SAP is used to inform network clients, via routers and servers, of available network resources and services.
Novell Protocol

SAP: Session Announcement Protocol 114

Session Announcement Protocol (SAP) is an announcement protocol that is used to assist the advertisement of multicast multimedia conferences and other multicast sessions and to communicate the relevant session setup information to prospective participants.
IETF Specification: RFC 2974

SAS: Serial Attached SCSI 215

Serial Attached SCSI (SAS) is an evolutionary replacement for the Parallel SCSI physical storage interface. Serial Attached SCSI offers much faster communication and easier configuration. In addition, Serial Attached SCSI provides device compatibility with Serial ATA and uses similar cabling.
ANSI Protocol

SCCP: Signaling Connection Control Part 283

Signaling Connection Control Part (SCCP), a routing protocol in the SS7 protocol suite (in layer 4), provides end-to-end routing for TCAP messages to their proper databases. SCCP offers enhancements to MTP level 3 to provide connectionless and connection-oriented network services, as well as to address translation capabilities.
ITU-T Protocol

SCCP: Skinny Client Control Protocol 118

Skinny Client Control Protocol (SCCP or Skinny) is a Cisco proprietary protocol used between Cisco Call Manager and Cisco VOIP phones. It is also supported by some other vendors. For VOIP solutions, the end station of a LAN or IP-based PBX must be simple to use, familiar and relatively cheap. SCCP defines a simple and easy to use architecture, while the H.323 recommendations produce quite an expensive system. An H.323 proxy can be used to communicate with the Skinny Client using the SCCP.
Cisco Protocol

SCP: Session Control Protocol

Session Control Protocol (SCP), a DECnet protocol, manages logical links for DECnet connections.
DEC/HP Protocol

SCSI: Small Computer System Interface 215

Small Computer System Interface (SCSI), an ANSI standard, is a parallel interface standard used by Apple Macintosh computers, PCs and many UNIX systems for attaching peripheral devices to computers. SCSI interfaces provide for faster data transmission rates than standard serial and parallel ports. In addition, you can attach many devices to a single SCSI port.
ANSI Protocol

SCSP: Server Cache Synchronization Protocol

Server Cache Synchronization Protocol (SCSP) is designed to solve the generalized cache synchronization/cache-replication problem for distributed protocol entities. SCSP synchronizes caches (or a portion of the caches) of a set of server entities of a particular protocol which are bound to a Server Group (SG). The client/server protocol which a particular server uses is identified by a Protocol ID (PID). SGs are identified by a SGID. The combination PID/SGID identifies both the client/server protocol for which the servers of the SG are being synchronized as well as the instance of that protocol. An example of types of information that must be synchronized can be seen in NHRP using IP where the information includes the registered clients' IP to NBMA mappings in the SG LIS. The algorithm used in SCSP is quite similar to that used in Open Shortest Path First (OSPF) protocol.
IETF Specification: RFC 2334

SCTP: Stream Control Transmission Protocol 130

Stream Control Transmission Protocol (SCTP), a part of the

Signalling Transport (SIGTRAN) protocol family, was designed to transport PSTN signaling messages (SS7/C7) over IP networks but is capable of broader applications. SCTP is a reliable transport protocol operating on top of a connectionless packet network such as IP. SCTP is designed to address the limitations and complexity of TCP while transporting real time signaling and data such as SS7/C7 over an IP network. SCTP can also run on top of the UDP layer.
IETF Specification: RFC 2960

SDCP: Serial Data Control Protocol

Serial Data Control Protocol (SDCP), a link control protocol in the PPP suite, is responsible for configuring, enabling and disabling the Serial Data Transport Protocol (SDTP) modules on both ends of the point-to-point link. SDTP together with its associated protocol SDCP was developed for using PPP's many features to provide a standard method for synchronous data compression. STDP and SDTP represent a component of a proposal to use PPP to provide compression of synchronous data in DSU/CSUs.
IETF Specification: RFC 1963

SDH: Synchronous Data Link Hierarchy

Synchronous Data Link Hierarchy (SDH) is a European standard for data transmission over optical fiber network equivalent to SONET of North America. SDH's basic unit, the STM-1 (Synchronous Transport Module-level 1), operates at 155.52 Mbit/s. Transmission rates of up to 10 Gbit/s can be achieved in today's SDH systems, and the 40 Gbit/s systems are possible. SDH systems are fully compatiable to SONET systems.
ITU-T Specification: G.707, G. 708 and G.709

SDLC: Synchronous Data Link Control   270

The Synchronous Data Link Control (SDLC) protocol is an IBM data link layer protocol for use in the Systems Network Architecture (SNA) environment.The data link control Layer provides the error-free movement of data between the Network Addressable Units (NAUs) within a given communication network via the Synchronous Data Link Control (SDLC) Protocol. The flow of information passes down from the higher layers through the data link control Layer and is passed into the physical control Layer.
IBM Protocol

SDP: Session Description Protocol   115

The Session Description Protocol (SDP) describes multimedia sessions for the purpose of session announcement, session invitation and other forms of multimedia session initiation.Session directories assist the advertisement of conference sessions and communicate the relevant conference setup information to prospective participants. SDP is designed to convey such information to recipients.
IETF Specification: RFC 2327

SDP: Service Discovery Protocol

The Service Discovery Protocol (SDP or Bluetooth SDP) in the Bluetooth protocol stack provides special means for applications in the Bluetooth environment to discover which services are available and to determine the characteristics of those available services. The SDP defines how a Bluetooth client's application shell acts to discover available Bluetooth servers' services and their characteristics. The protocol defines how client can search for a service based on specific attributes without the client knowing anything of the available services. The SDP provides means for discovery of new services become becoming available when the client enters an area where a Bluetooth server is operating. The SDP also provides functionality for detecting when a service is no longer available.
IEEE Specification: IEEE 802.15.1

SDSL: Single-line Digital Subscriber Line   158

Single-line Digital Subscriber Line (SDSL), also known as Symmetric Digital Subscriber Line, is one variaton of DSL technologies that provides equal bandwidth for both uploads and downloads. SDSL delivers 1.544 Mbps both downstream and upstream over a single copper twisted pair. The use of a single twisted pair limits the operating range of SDSL to 10,000 feet (3048.8 meters).
ANSI/ITU Protocol

SDSL: Symmetric Digital Subscriber Line   158

Symmetric Digital Subscriber Line (SDSL), also known as Single-line Digital Subscriber Line, is one variaton of DSL technologies that provides equal bandwidth for both uploads and downloads. SDSL delivers 1.544 Mbps both downstream and upstream over a single copper twisted pair. The use of a single twisted pair limits the operating range of SDSL to 10,000 feet (3048.8 meters).
ANSI/ITU Protocol

SDTP: Serial Data Transport Protocol

Serial Data Transport Protocol (SDTP), a network-level protocol in the PPP suite, is used for synchronous serial data compression over a PPP link, provides encapsulation and an associated Serial Data Control Protocol (SDCP) for transporting serial data streams over a PPP link. SDTP together with its associated protocol SDCP were developed for the purpose of using PPP's many features to provide a standard method for synchronous data compression. STDP and SDTP represent a component of a proposal to use PPP to provide compression of synchronous data in DSU/CSUs.
IETF Specification: RFC 1963

SER: Serialization packet

Serialization packet (SER), a protocol in the Novell NetWare suite, ensures that a single version of NetWare is not being loaded on multiple servers.
Novell Protocol

SGCP: Simple Gateway Control Protocol

Simple Gateway Control Protocol (SGCP), a Cisco protocol for VOIP, is designed for media gateway control and signaling. SGCP controls Voice over IP gateways by an external call control element (called a call-agent). SGCP is not deployed in the real world and is obsoleted by the Media Gateway Control Protocol (MGCP) and Megaco.
Cisco & Telcordia Protocol

SGML: Standardized Generalized Markup Language

Standardized Generalized Markup Language (SGML) is an international standard for the definition of system-independent, device-independent methods of representing text in electronic form. SGML is a metalanguage in which one can define markup languages for documents. XML is derived from SGML and now dwarfs SGML in terms of breadth of application. XML is a profile—a specific subset of SGML—designed to be simpler to parse and process than full SGML, and to have more lightweight internationalization. XML is a simplification of SGML for general-purpose applications.
ISO Specification: ISO 8879

SGMP: Simple Gateway Monitoring Protocol

Simple Gateway Monitoring Protocol (SGMP) is a network

management protocol that was considered for Internet standardization and later evolved into SNMP.
IETF Specification: RFC 1028

SHDSL: Symmetric High-speed DSL

Symmetric High-speed DSL (SHDSL), also known as G.shdsl, achieves 20% better loop-reach than older versions of symmetric DSL. SHDSL causes much less crosstalk into other transmission systems in the same cable, and multi-vendor interoperability is facilitated by the standardization of this technology. SHDSL systems may operate at many bit-rates, from 192 kbps to 5.7 Mbps, thereby maximizing the bit-rate for each customer. G.shdsl specifies operation via one pair of wires, or for operation on longer loops, two pairs of wire may be used. For example, with two pairs of wire, 1.2 Mbps can be sent over 20,000 feet of 26 AWG wire. SHDSL is best suited to data-only applications that need high upstream bit-rates. Though SHDSL does not carry voice like ADSL, new voice-over-DSL techniques may be used to convey digitized voice and data via SHDSL.
ITU-T Specification: G.991.2 or "Symmetric HDSL"

Single-pair high-speed digital subscriber line

Single-pair high-speed digital subscriber line (SHDSL) is a form of Digital Subscriber Line similar to HDSL but providing T1 or E1 connections over a single twisted-pair copper line. See SHDSL.

S-HTTP: Secure HTTP   17

Secure HTTP (S-HTTP) is a secure message-oriented communications protocol designed for use in conjunction with HTTP. S-HTTP is designed to coexist with HTTP's messaging model and to be easily integrated with HTTP applications.
IETF Specification: RFC 2660

Signaling System #7 (SS7)   276

Signaling System #7 (SS7) is a telecommunications protocol suite, defined by the ITU-T, which is used by telephone companies for interoffice signaling. SS7 uses out-of-band or common-channel signaling (CCS) techniques, which use a separated packet-switched network for the signaling purpose. SS7 is also known as Common Channel Signaling System 7 (CCS7 or C7) outside North America.
AT-T Protocol

SIGTRAN: Signaling Transport   129

Signaling Transport (SIGTRAN) refers to a protocol stack for the transport of Switched Circuit Network (SCN) signaling protocols (such as SS7/C7 an Q.931) over an IP network. SIGTRAN, an evolution of the PSTN signaling, defines adaptors and a core transport capabilities that blend SS7 and packet protocols to provide users with the best both technologies have to offer. Applications of SIGTRAN include: Internet dial-up remote access, IP telephony interworking with PSTN and other services as identified.
IETF Specification: RFC 2719

SIMPLE: Session Initiation Protocol for Instant Messaging and Presence Leveraging Extensions

Session Initiation Protocol for Instant Messaging and Presence Leveraging Extensions(SIMPLE) is an open standard instant messaging (IM) and presence protocol suite based on Session Initiation Protocol (SIP). SIMPLE applies the SIP to the problems of: 1) Registering for presence information and receiving notifications when such events occur, for example when a user logs-in or comes back from lunch. 2) Managing a session of real-time messages between two or more participants.
IETF Specification: RFC 3428

SIP: Session Initiation Protocol   116

Session Initiation Protocol (SIP) is an application layer control protocol that can establish, modify and terminate multimedia sessions such as Internet telephony calls. SIP can also invite participants to already existing sessions, such as multicast conferences. Media can be added to (and removed from) an existing session. SIP transparently supports name mapping and redirection services, which supports personal mobility; users can maintain a single externally visible identifier regardless of their network location.
IETF Specification: RFC 3261

SIP: SMDS Interface Protocol

SMDS Interface Protocol(SIP) is used for communications between CPE and SMDS carrier equipment. SIP provides connectionless service across the subscriber network interface (SNI), allowing the CPE to access the SMDS network. SIP is based on the IEEE 802.6 Distributed Queue Dual Bus (DQDB) standard for cell relay across metropolitan-area networks (MANs). SIP consists of three levels. SIP Level 3 operates at the Media Access Control (MAC) sublayer of the data link layer of the OSI reference model. SIP Level 2 operates at the MAC sublayer of the data link layer. SIP Level 1 operates at the physical layer of the OSI reference model.
Bellcore

SIP-T: SIP for Telephones

Session Initiation Protocol (SIP) for Telephones (SIP-T), previously known as SIP-BCP-T, is a mechanism that uses SIP to facilitate the interconnection of the PSTN with IP. SIP-T allows traditional IN-type services to be seamlessly handled in the Internet environment. It is essential that SS7 information be available at the points of PSTN interconnection to ensure transparency of features not otherwise supported in SIP. SS7 information should be available in its entirety and without any loss to the SIP network across the PSTN-IP interface. SIP-T defines SIP functions that map to ISUP interconnection requirements.
IETF Specification: RFC 3372

Skinny   118

Skinny, also known as Skinney Client Control Protocol (SCCP), is a Cisco proprietary protocol used between Cisco Call Manager and Cisco VOIP phones. It is also supported by some other vendors. For VOIP solutions, the end station of a LAN or IP-based PBX must be simple to use, familiar and relatively cheap. SCCP defines a simple and easy to use architecture, while the H.323 recommendations produce quite an expensive system. An H.323 proxy can be used to communicate with the Skinny Client using the SCCP.
Cisco Protocol

SLIP: Serial Line IP   86

Serial Line IP (SLIP) is a protocol used for point-to-point serial connections running TCP/IP. SLIP is commonly used on dedicated serial links, and, sometimes, for dialup purposes, and is usually used with line speeds between 1200bps and 19.2Kbps. SLIP is useful for allowing mixes of hosts and routers to communicate with one another (host-host, host-router and router-router are all common SLIP network configurations).
IETF Specification: RFC 1055

SLP: Service Location Protocol   28

The Service Location Protocol (SLP) provides a scalable framework for the discovery and selection of network services. Using this protocol, computers using the Internet no longer need so much static configuration for network services and network-based applications. This is especially important as computers become more portable, and users less tolerant or less able to fulfill the demands of network system administration.
IETF Specification: RFC 2165

SMB: Sever Message Block   261

Server Message Block (SMB) protocol is an IBM protocol for sharing files, printers, serial ports, etc between computers. The SMB protocol can be used over the Internet on top of the TCP/IP protocol or other network protocols, such as Internetwork Packet Exchange (Novell IPX) and NetBEUI.
IBM Protocol

SMDS: Switched Multimegabit Data Service   204

Switched Multimegabit Data Service (SMDS) is a broadband networking technology, developed by Bellcore and based on the IEEE 802.6 DQDB (Distributed Queue Dual Bus) technology.
IEEE Specification: IEEE 802.6

SMLCPP: Serving Mobile Location Center Peer to Peer Protocol

Serving Mobile Location Center Peer to Peer Protocol (SMLCPP) is a transport protocol for the communication between the Serving Mobile Location Centers (SMLCs). The main functions of SMLCPP are: 1) allowing an SMLC to ask for and obtain information about Radio Interface Timing (RIT), as known from measurements done by LMUs not under its direct control; 2) allowing an SMLC, that controls deciphering keys in the location area, to sent them to other SMLCs in the same location area.
ETSI Specification: ETSI GSM 08.31

SMPP: Short Message Peer to Peer

Short Message Peer to Peer (SMPP) is a protocol for exchange short messages between SMS peer entities such as short message service centers. SMPP is often used to allow third parties (e.g. value-added service providers like news organisations) to submit messages, often in bulk.
Aldiscon/Logica Protocol

SMRP: Simple Multicast Routing Protocol

The Simple Multicast Routing Protocol (SMRP) is a transport layer protocol developed to route multimedia data streams over AppleTalk networks. It supports Apple Computer's QuickTime Conferencing (QTC) technology. SMRP provides connectionless, best-effort delivery of multicast datagrams and relies on underlying network layer protocols for services. In particular, SMRP facilitates the transmission of data from a single source to multiple destinations.
Apple Protocol

SMS: Short Message Service

Short Message Services is a mechanism of delivery of short messages over the mobile networks. SMS was originally designed as part of GSM, but is now available on a wide range of networks, including 3G networks. There are two forms of SMS: Short Message Service - Point-to-Point (SMS-PP) and Short Message Service - Cell Broadcast (SMS-CB). The message length is 140 bytes. Larger contents (known as long SMS or concatenated SMS) can be sent segmentedly over multiple messages, in which case each message will start with a user

data header (UDH) containing segmentation information.
3GPP Specification: GSM 03.40 and GSM 03.41

SMS-CB: Short Message Service - Cell Broadcast

Short Message Service - Cell Broadcast (SMS-CB), a form of Short Message Service for the delivering of short messages over the mobile networks, allows messages (advertising, public information, etc.) to be broadcast to all mobile users in a specified geographical area.
3GPP Specification: GSM 03.40

SMS-PP: Short Message Service - Point to Point

Short Message Service - Point to Point (SMS-PP), a form of Short Message Service for the delivering of short messages over the mobile networks, provides, allows messages to be sent from an individual to another.
3GPP Specification: GSM 03.40

SMTP: Simple Mail Transfer Protocol   29

Simple Mail Transfer Protocol (SMTP) is a protocol designed to transfer electronic mails reliably and efficiently. SMTP is a mail service modeled on the FTP file transfer service. SMTP transfers mail messages between systems and provides notification regarding incoming mail.
IETF Specification: RFC 2821

SNA NAU: Network Accessible Units   263

Network Accessible Units (NAUs), formerly called "network addressable units", are the IBM Systems Network Architecture (SNA) components to facilitate the communication between a Transaction Program (TP) and the SNA network. NAUs are unique network resources that can be accessed through unique local addresses by other network resources.
IBM Protocol

SNA: System Network Architeture   5

The Systems Network Architecture (SNA) defined by IBM is one of the most popular network architecture models. Although now considered a legacy networking model, SNA is still widely deployed. SNA was designed around the host-to-terminal communication model that IBM's mainframes use.
IBM Protocol

SNACP: SNA PPP Control Protocol

SNA PPP Control Protocol (SNACP), is responsible for configuring, enabling and disabling SNA on both ends of the point-point link (PPP). SNACP uses the same packet exchange mechanism as the Link Control Protocol (LCP). SNACP packets may not be exchanged until PPP has reached the Network-Layer Protocol phase. SNACP packets received before this phase is reached should be silently discarded. There are two SNA Network Control Protocols; one for SNA over LLC 802.2 and the other for SNA without LLC 802.2.
IETF Specification: RFC 2043

SNAP: SubNetwork Access Protocol   199

The SubNetwork Access Protocol (SNAP) is a standard for the transmission of IP datagrams over IEEE 802 networks. In other words, IP datagrams can be sent on IEEE 802 networks encapsulated within the 802.2 LLC and SNAP data link layers and the 802.3, 802.4 or 802.5 physical network layers.
IEEE Specification: IEEE 802.2

SNDCP: Sub Network Dependent Convergence Protocol

The Sub Network Dependent Convergence Protocol (SNDCP) provides services to the higher layers which may include

connectionless and connection-oriented mode, compression, multiplexing and segmentation. SNDCP is used in a number of different technologies. The General Packet Radio Service (GPRS) uses the SNDCP layer services. SNDCP can operate within the Mobile Station (MS) or Serving GPRS Support Node (SGSN) depending on the option selected by the customer.
ETSI Protocol

SNI: Subscriber Network Interface

Subscriber Network Interface (SNI) refers to the TDM access links such as DS0, DS1/T1, DS3/T3, E1, E3 that connects CPE and an SMDS switch of the PSTN network.
ANSI Protocol

SNMP MIB: Simple Network Management Protocol Management Information Base

Simple Network Management Protocol Management Information Base (SNMP-MIB) is managed objects that could be accessed via a virtual information store through the Simple Network Management Protocol (SNMP). Objects in the MIB are defined using the mechanisms defined in the Structure of Management Information (SMI).
IETF Specification: RFC 3418

SNMP-OID: SNMP Object Identifiers

SNMP Object Identifiers (SNMP-OID) are the sequences of integers on the path leading from the root of the tree to a named object. SNMP uses an Object Identifier (OID) to specify the exact parameter to set or get in the tree.
IETF Protocol

SNMP-RMON: SNMP Remote Network Monitoring

SNMP Remote Network Monitoring (SNMP-RMON), also known as Remote Monitoring (RMON), is a standard monitoring specification that enables various network monitors and console systems to exchange network-monitoring data. RMON provides network administrators with more freedom in selecting network-monitoring probes and consoles with features that meet their particular networking needs. RMON has two versions: RMON1 and RMON2.
IETF Specification: RFC 2819 and RFC 2021

SNMP-RMON1: SNMP Remote Network Monitoring version 1

SNMP Remote Network Monitoring version 1 (SNMP-RMON1), also known as RMON1, RMONv1, which can now be found on most modern network hardware, defined 9 MIB groups for basic network monitoring.
IETF Specification: RFC 2819

SNMP-RMON2: SNMP Remote Network Monitoring version 2

SNMP Remote Network Monitoring version 2 (SNMP-RMON2), also known as RMON2, is an extension of RMON that focuses on higher layers of traffic above the medium access control (MAC) layer. RMON2 has an emphasis on IP traffic and application level traffic. RMON2 allows network management applications to monitor packets on all network layers.
IETF Specification: RFC 2021

SNMP-SMI: SNMP Structure of Management Information

SNMP Structure of Management Information (SNMP-SMI) is a collection of managed objects, residing in a virtual information store. The SMI is divided into three parts: module definitions, object definitions, and notification definitions. There are two

types of SMI: SMIv1 and SMIv2.
IETF Specification: RFC 1155 v1 and RFC 2578 v2

SNMP: Simple Network Management Protocol   30

Simple Network Management Protocol (SNMP) is the standard protocol developed to manage nodes (servers, workstations, routers, switches and hubs, etc) on an IP network. SNMP enables network administrators to manage network performance, find, solve network problems and plan for network growth. Network management systems learn of problems by receiving traps or change notices from network devices implementing SNMP.
IETF Specification: RFC 1157, 1441, 3410

SNMPv1: Simple Network Management Protocol version 1   31

Simple Network Management Protocol version 1 (SNMPv1) is a simple request/response protocol. The network management system issues a request to the managed devices that return responses. This behavior is implemented by using one of four protocol operations: Get, GetNext, Set and Trap. The Get operation is used by the NMS to retrieve the value of one or more object instances from an agent. If the agent responding to the Get operation cannot provide values for all the object instances in a list, it does not provide any values.
IETF Specification: RFC 1157

SNMPv2: Simple Network Management Protocol version 2   32

Simple Network Management Protocol version 2 (SNMPv2) is an evolution of SNMPv1. The Get, GetNext, and Set operations used in SNMPv1 are exactly the same as those used in SNMPv2. However, SNMPv2 adds and enhances some protocol operations. The SNMPv2 Trap operation, for example, serves the same function as that used in SNMPv1 but uses a different message format and is designed to replace the SNMPv1 Trap.
IETF Specification: RFC 1441

SNMPv3: Simple Network Management Protocol version 3   34

Simple Network Management Protocol version 3 (SNMPv3) adds security and remote configuration capabilities to the previous versions. The SNMPv3 architecture introduces the User-based Security Model (USM) for message security and the View-based Access Control Model (VACM) for access control. The architecture supports the concurrent use of different security, access control and message processing models.
IETF Specification: RFC 3410

SNTP: Simple Network Time Protocol   35

The Simple Network Time Protocol (SNTP) is an adaptation of the Network Time Protocol (NTP) used to synchronize computer clocks on the Internet. SNTP can be used when the ultimate performance of the full NTP implementation is not needed or justified. When operating with current and previous NTP and SNTP versions, SNTP involves no changes to the NTP specification or known implementations, but rather a clarification of certain design features of NTP which allow operation in a simple, stateless remote-procedure call (RPC) mode with accuracy and reliability expectations similar to the UDP/TIME protocol.
IETF Specification: RFC 2030

SOAP: Simple Object Access Protocol   287

Simple Object Access Protocol (SOAP) is a lightweight protocol intended for exchanging structured information in a decentralized, distributed environment. It uses XML technologies to define an extensible messaging framework providing a message construct that can be exchanged over a variety of underlying protocols. The framework has been designed to be independent of any particular programming model and other implementation specific semantics.

W3C Protocol

SOCKS   *102*

The SOCKS protocol, also known as authenticated firewall traversal (AFT), provides a framework for client-server applications in both the TCP and UDP domains to conveniently and securely use the services of a network firewall. SOCKS enables a proxy server to accept requests from client users in a company's network so that it can forward them across the Internet. SOCKS uses sockets to represent and keep track of individual connections. The client side of SOCKS is built into certain Web browsers and the server side can be added to a proxy server.

IETF Specification: RFC 1928

SOCKS v5   *102*

The SOCKS v5 is the latest version of the SOCKS protocol, which provides a framework for client-server applications in both the TCP and UDP domains to conveniently and securely use the services of a network firewall. SOCKS v5 provides stronger authentication than the SOCKS Version 4. SOCKS v5 extends the SOCKS v4 model to include UDP, and extends the framework to include provisions for generalized strong authentication schemes. It also adapts the addressing scheme to encompass domain-name and IPv6 addresses.

IETF Specification: RFC 1928

SONET/SDH: Synchronous Optical Network (SONET) and Synchronous Digital Hierarchy (SDH)   *150*

The Synchronous Optical Network (SONET) and Synchronous Digital Hierarchy (SDH), often combined as SONET/SDH, are a set of related standards for synchronous data transmission over fiber optic networks that are often used for framing and synchronization at the physical layer. SONET is the United States version of the standard published by the American National Standards Institue (ANSI). SDH is the international version of the standard published by the International Telecommunications Union (ITU). Transmission rates of up to 10 Gbit/s can be achieved in today's SONET/SDH systems and the 40 Gbit/s systems are possible. SONET/SDH systems are fully compatiable with each other.

ANSI / ITU-T Protocol

SONET: Synchronous Optical Network   *150*

The Synchronous Optical Network (SONET), the US version of the standard published by the American National Standards Institue (ANSI), is a set of standards for synchronous data transmission over fiber optic networks that are often used for framing and synchronization at the physical layer. SONET is based on transmission at speeds of multiples of 51.840 Mbps, or STS-1. SDH is the international version of the standard published by the International Telecommunications Union (ITU). Transmission rates of up to 10 Gbit/s can be achieved in today's SONET systems, and the 40 Gbit/s systems are possible. SONET systems are fully compatiable to SDH systems.

ANSI Specification: ANSI T1.105

SPANS: Simple Protocol for ATM Network Signaling

Simple Protocol for ATM Network Signaling (SPANS) was de-

veloped by FORE Systems for use in ATM networks. The protocol specifies the signaling messages that are exchanged between hosts and the ATM network to perform functions such as opening and closing connections. These functions allow hosts and routers to use an ATM LAN as a subnet of a larger internet. In what follows, the term "network" is used to refer to the network of ATM switches, and is distinct from the end systems that communicate with the network.

FORE Systems Protocol

SPP: Sequenced Packet Protocol in VINES

The Sequenced Packet Protocol (SPP), a transport layer protocol in the VINES protocol stack, provides a reliable virtual connection service for private connections.

Banyan Protocol

SPP: Sequenced Packet Protocol (Xerox)

Sequenced Packet Protocol (SPP), a transport layer protocol in the Xerox protocol stack, provides a reliable virtual connection service for private connections.

Xerox Protocol

SPX: Sequenced Packet Exchange   *259*

The Sequenced Packet Exchange (SPX) protocol is Novell's legacy transport layer protocol providing a packet delivery service for Novell NetWare network. SPX is based on the Xerox Sequenced Packet Protocol (SPP). SPX operates on top of IPX and is used in Novell NetWare (prior to NetWare 5.0) systems for communications in client/server application programs, e.g. BTRIEVE (ISAM manager). SPX performs equivalent functions to TCP. The newer versions of NetWare services are run on top of TCP/IP.

Novell Protocol

SRB: Source Routing Bridging

Source Routing Bridging (SRB) is a method of bridging originated by IBM and popular in Token Ring networks. In an SRB network, the entire route to a destination is predetermined; in real time, prior to the sending of data to the destination. SRBs store and forward the frames as indicated by the route appearing in the appropriate frame field. Since its initial proposal, IBM has offered a new bridging standard: the source-route transparent (SRT) bridging solution. Although SRT bridging has achieved support, SRBs are still widely deployed.

IBM Protocol

SRCP: Simple Resource Control Protocol

Simple Resource Control Protocol(SRCP) is a set of extensions to MGCP to allow the VSC to poll the gateway about its current configuration.

Cisco Protocol

SRP: Spatial Reuse Protocol

Spatial Reuse Protocol (SRP) is the underpinning of Cisco's proprietary metropolitan IP offerings, and will be a key component of the IEEE 802.17 Resilient Packet Ring (RPR).

Cisco Protocol

SRTP: Sequenced Routing Update Protocol

Sequenced Routing Update Protocol (SRTP) is VINES protocol that assists VINES servers in finding neighboring clients, servers, and routers.

VINES Protocol

SS7: Signaling System 7   *276*

Signaling System #7 (SS7) is a telecommunications protocol suite, defined by the ITU-T, which is used by telephone com-

panies for interoffice signaling. SS7 uses out-of-band or common-channel signaling (CCS) techniques, which use a separated packet-switched network for the signaling purpose. SS7 is also known as Common Channel Signaling System 7 (CCS7 or C7) outside North America.
ITU-T Protocol

SSCOP: Service Specific Connection Oriented Protocol

Service Specific Connection Oriented Protocol (SSCOP) is a data link layer protocol in the B-ISDN suite that guarantees the delivery of ATM signaling packets. SSCOP is responsible for providing mechanisms for the establishment, release and monitoring of signaling information exchanged between peer signaling entities. SSCOP is positioned within the AAL architecture.
ITU-T Specification: ITU Q.2110

SSH: Secure Shell Protocol   90

Secure Shell Protocol(SSH) is a Unix-based command interface and protocol for secure remote login and other secure network services over an insecure network. It is widely used by network administrators to control Web and other kinds of servers remotely. SSH is actually a suite of utilities - slogin, ssh, and scp - that are secure versions of the earlier UNIX utilities, rlogin, rsh, and rcp. SSH consists of three major components : (1) Transport Layer Protocol [SSH-TRANS]; (2) User Authentication Protocol [SSH-USERAUTH]; (3) Connection Protocol [SSH-CONNECT].
IETF Specification: RFC 4251

SSL/TLS: Secure Socket Layer (SSL) and Transport Layer Security (TLS) Protocol   101

Secure Socket Layer (SSL) and Transport Layer Security (TLS) Protocol provided privacy and data integrity between two communicating applications. The protocol is composed of two layers: the TLS Record Protocol and the TLS Handshake Protocol. At the lowest level, layered on top of some reliable transport protocol (TCP) is the TLS Record Protocol. SSL was renamed to TLS by IETF. But the SSL name has gained enough popularity, and people still call the protocol SSL or SST/TLS.
IETF Specification: RFC 2246

SSL: Secure Socket Layer   101

The Secure Sockets Layer (SSL), a protocol originally defined by Netscape, is a commonly-used protocol for managing the security of a message transmission on the Internet. SSL has been succeeded by Transport Layer Security (TLS). But the SSL name has gained enough popularity, and people still call the protocol SSL or SST/TLS. The protocol is composed of two layers: the TLS Record Protocol and the TLS Handshake Protocol. At the lowest level, layered on top of some reliable transport protocol (TCP) is the TLS Record Protocol. SSL is included as part of both the Microsoft and Netscape browsers and most Web server products.
IETF Specification: RFC 2246

SSM: Source Specific Multicast

Source Specific Multicast(SSM) is a datagram delivery model that supports one-to-many applications, also known as broadcast applications. SSM is intended to provide unambiguous semantics to the designers of the protocols and host interfaces used in conjunction with source-specific multicast.
IETF Specification: RFC 3569

SSP: Switch-to-Switch Protocol

Switch-to-Switch Protocol (SSP), specified in the DLSw standard, allows routers to establish DLSw connections, locate resources, forward data, and handle flow control and error recovery.
IBM Protocol

SSRP: Simple Server Replication Protocol

Simple Server Replication Protocol (SSRP), also known as Simple Server Redundancy Protocol, is an ATM LANE Services redundancy protocol. With SSRP, it is possible to have more than one LES/BUS running in a LANE cloud and creates fault-tolerance using standard LANE protocols and mechanisms.
ATM Forum Protocol

STM: Synchronous Transmission Module

Synchronous Transmission Module (STM), also known as Synchronous Transfer Mode, is the basic rate of transmission of the SDH ITU-T fiber optic network transmission standard. It has a bit rate of 155.52 Mbit/s and is the SDH equivalent of an OC-3 (SONET).
ITU-T Protocol

STM-0: Synchronous Transmission Module level zero

Synchronous Transmission Module level zero (STM-0) is the SDH ITU-T fiber optic network transmission standard. It has a bit rate of 51.84 Mbit/s and is the SDH equivalent of an OC-1 (SONET).
ITU-T Protocol

STM-1: Synchronous Transmission Module level one

Synchronous Transmission Module level one (STM-1) is the basic rate of transmission of the SDH ITU-T fiber optic network transmission standard. It has a bit rate of 155.52 Mbit/s and is the SDH equivalent of an OC-3 (SONET).
ITU-T Protocol

STM-4: Synchronous Transmission Module level 4

Synchronous Transmission Module level 4 (STM-4) is one of the transmission mode of the SDH ITU-T fiber optic network transmission standard. It has a bit rate of 622.08 Mbit/s and is the SDH equivalent of an OC-12 (SONET).
ITU-T Protocol

STM-n: Synchronous Transmission Module level n

Synchronous Transmission Module n (STM-n), also known as Synchronous Transfer Mode n, refers to a group of the transmission modes of the SDH ITU-T fiber optic network transmission standard, which is the multiplexing "n" of the STM-1 frames.
ITU-T Protocol

STP: Spanning-Tree Protocol   200

Spanning-Tree Protocol (STP), as defined in IEEE 802.1D, is a link management protocol that provides path redundancy while preventing undesirable loops in the network. For an Ethernet network to function properly, only one active path can exist between two stations. Loops occur in networks for a variety of reasons. The most common reason for loops in networks is a deliberate attempt to provide redundancy—in case that one link or switch fails, another link or switch can take over.
IEEE Specification: IEEE 802.1D

StreetTalk

StreetTalk is an application protocol in the VINES protocol stack which maintains a distributed directory of the names of network resources. In VINES network, names are global across the Internet and independent of the network topology.
Banyan Protocol

STS-1: Synchronous Transport Signal level 1

Synchronous Transport Signal level 1(STS-1) is the basic building block signal of SONET, operating at 51.84 Mbps. Faster SONET rates are defined as STS-n, where n is a multiple of 51.84 Mbps.

STS-3c: Synchronous Transport Signal level 3, concatenated

Synchronous Transport Signal level 3, concatenated(STS-3c) is the SONET format that specifies the frame structure for the 155.52-Mbps lines used to carry ATM cells.

SUA: SS7 SCCP-User Adaptation Layer

SS7 SCCP User Adaptation Layer (SUA), a protocol in the SIGTRAN protocol stack, provides SCCP-User signalling over SCTP. SUA is intended to be used on a Provider/User basis where SCCP resides on a Signalling Gateway (SG) and SCCP Users reside on an Application Server (AS).
IETF Specification: RFC 3868

syslog 36

syslog, also known as syslog protocol, is a standard for forwarding log messages in an IP network. The term "syslog" is often used for both the actual syslog protocol, as well as the application or library sending syslog messages.
IETF Specification: RFC 3164

T

T.120 119

The T.120, an ITU-T standard, is made up of a suite of communication and application protocols. T.120 protocols are designed for multipoint Data Conferencing and real time communication, including multilayer protocols which considerably enhance multimedia, MCU and codec control capabilities. Depending on the type of T.120 implementations, the resulting product can make connections, transmit and receive data and collaborate using compatible data conferencing features, such as program sharing, whiteboard conferencing and file transfer.
ITU-T Specification: T.120

T.30

The T.30, an ITU-T standard, describes the overall procedure for establishing and managing communication between two fax machines.
ITU-T Specification: T.30

T.38

The T.38, an ITU-T standard, defines procedures for real-time Group 3 facsimile communication over IP networks.
ITU-T Specification: T.38

TABS: Telemetry Asynchronous Block Serial

Telemetry Asynchronous Block Serial (TABS) is an AT&T polled point-to-point or multipoint communication protocol that supports moderate data transfer rates over intra-office wire pairs.
AT&T Protocol

TACACS: Terminal Access Controller Access Control System 250

The Terminal Access Controller Access Control System (TACACS) provides access control for routers, network access servers and other networked computing devices via one or more centralized servers. TACACS provides separate authentication, authorization and accounting services. There are three versions of TACACS and the third version is called TACACS+, which is not compatible with previous versions.
Cisco Protocol

TACACS+: Terminal Access Controller Access Control System (version 3) 250

Terminal Access Controller Access Control System (version 3), also known as TACACS+, provides access control for routers, network access servers and other networked computing devices via one or more centralized servers. TACACS provides separate authentication, authorization and accounting services. TACACS+ is not compatible with previous versions of TACACS.
Cisco Protocol

TALI: Tekelec's Transport Adapter Layer Interface 47

Tekelec's Transport Adapter Layer Interface (TALI), a protocol in the SIGTRAN suite, is the interface of a Signaling Gateway, which provides interworking between the Switched Circuit Network (SCN) and an IP network. Since the Gateway is the central point of signaling information, not only does it provide transportation of signaling from one network to another, but can also provide additional functions such as protocol translation, security screening, routing information and seamless access to Intelligent Network (IN) services on both networks.
IETF Specification: RFC 3094

TAP: Telocator Alphanumeric Protocol

Telocator Alphanumeric Protocol (TAP) is a simple protocol dedicated to the forwarding of alphanumeric pages. Although the features and capabilities of TAP are in TDP, the TAP protocol may co-exist with TDP. The TAP protocol may be utilized to forward binary data to RF-linked computers if input is formatted and processed.

TARP: TID Address Resolution Protocol

TID Address Resolution Protocol (TARP) is a protocol defined in Telcordia (a.k.a Bellcore) GR-253 standard document for SONET and used in OSS to resolve a TL1 TID to a CLNP address (NSAP). Many legacy SONET systems still use TARP to translate Target Identifier of a SONET node.
Telcordia Protocol

TBOS: Telemetry Byte Oriented Serial Protocol

Telemetry Byte Oriented Serial(TBOS) protocol is an open standard for network management, originally developed by Bellcore for AT&T. TBOS transmits alarm, status, and control points between NE and OSS. TBOS defines one physical interface for a direct connection between the telemetry equipment and the monitored equipment.
AT&T Protocol

TCAP: Transaction Capabilities Application Part 284

Transaction Capabilities Application Part (TCAP), a protocol in the SS7 protocol suite, enables the deployment of advanced intelligent network services by supporting non-circuit-related information exchange between signaling points, using the Signaling Connection Control Part (SCCP) connectionless service. TCAP also supports remote control—ability to invoke

features in another remote network switch.
ITU-T Specification: Q.773

TCP Port Numbers 293

TCP Port Numbers are designed to distinguish multiple applications running on a single device with one IP address from one another. In the TCP header, there are "SourcePort" and "DestinationPort" fields which are used to indicate the message sending process and receiving process identities defined. The combination of the IP address and the port number is called "socket".
IANA Protocol

TCP/IP 8

The TCP/IP protocol suite establishes the technical foundation of the Internet. Development of the TCP/IP started as DOD projects. Now, most protocols in the suite are developed by the Internet Engineering Task Force (IETF) under the Internet Architecture Board (IAB), an organization initially sponsored by the US government and now an open and autonomous organization. The IAB provides the coordination for the R&D underlying the TCP/IP protocols and guides the evolution of the Internet. The TCP/IP protocols are well-documented in the Request For Comments (RFC), which are drafted, discussed, circulated and approved by the IETF committees. All documents are open and free and can be found online in the IETF site listed in the reference.
IETF Protocol

TCP/IP Four Layers Architecture Model 4

TCP/IP architecture does not exactly follow the OSI model. Unfortunately, there is no universal agreement regarding how to describe TCP/IP with a layered model. It is generally agreed that TCP/IP has fewer levels (from three to five layers) than the seven layers of the OSI model. We adopt a four layers model for the TCP/IP architecture.

TCP: Transmission Control Protocol 48

Transmission Control Protocol (TCP) is the transport layer protocol in the TCP/IP suite which provides a reliable stream delivery and virtual connection service to applications through the use of sequenced acknowledgment, with retransmission of packets when necessary. Along with the Internet Protocol (IP), TCP represents the heart of the Internet protocols.
IETF Specification: RFC 793

TCS: Telephony Control Protocol Specification

The Telephony Control Protocol Specification (TCS) is a protocol in the Bluetooth protocol stack that defines ways to send audio calls between Bluetooth devices. It also controls the device mobility management procedures. It can be used to create a three-in-one phone:
1) On the move, a mobile phone connected to a cellular network;
2) At home, a cordless phone connected to a PSTN via a gateway or base station;
3) At the office, an intercom.
IEEE Specification: 802.15.1

TDP: Tag Distribution Protocol

Tag Distribution Protocol (TDP), a two-party protocol defined by Cisco originally, runs over a connection-oriented transport layer with guaranteed sequential delivery. The MPLS protocol, based on the TDP, has gained popularity among service providers as the protocol for next generation multiple service networks.

Cisco Protocol

TDP: Telocator Data Protocol

Telocator Data Protocol (TDP) is a suite of protocols used for sending messages from a computer, through a paging system, to a mobile receiving computer. Together, these protocols define the flow of messages from input devices through several processing steps until the entire message is received by an RF-linked computer. The set is compromised of several protocols, including TME, TRT, and TMC.

TELNET: Terminal Emulation Protocol in a TCP/IP environment 37

TELNET is the terminal emulation protocol in a TCP/IP environment for the remote access of a terminal (client) to a server. TELNET uses the TCP as the transport protocol to establish connection between server and client. After connecting, TELNET server and client enter a phase of option negotiation that determines the options that each side can support for the connection. Each connected system can negotiate new options or renegotiate old options at any time. In general, each end of the TELNET connection attempts to implement all options that maximize performance for the systems involved.
IETF Specification: RFC 854

TFTP: Trivial File Transfer Protocol 38

Trivial File Transfer Protocol (TFTP) is a simple protocol to transfer files. It has been implemented on top of the User Datagram Protocol (UDP) using port number 69. TFTP is designed to be small and easy to implement and, therefore, lacks most of the features of a regular FTP. TFTP only reads and writes files (or mail) from/to a remote server. It cannot list directories and currently has no provisions for user authentication.
IETF Specification: RFC 1350

THDR: Transport Layer Header

Transport Layer Header (THDR), a protocol in the IBM SNA suite, is used by RTP endpoints to provide correct processing of the packet.
IBM Protocol

TIFF: Tagged Image File Format

Tagged Image File Format (TIFF) is a file format mainly for storing images, including photographs and line art. Originally created by the company Aldus, now part of Adobe Systems for use with PostScript printing, TIFF is a popular format for high color-depth images, along with JPEG and PNG. TIFF format is widely supported by image-manipulation applications such as Photoshop by Adobe, GIMP, and Paint Shop Pro by Jasc, by desktop publishing and page layout applications, such as QuarkXPress and Adobe InDesign, and by scanning, faxing, word processing, optical character recognition, and other applications.
Adobe Protocol

Time Protocol

Time Protocol allows time clients to obtain the current time-of-day within one-second resolution from Time servers.
IETF Specification: RFC 868

Timeplex BRE: Bridge Relay Encapsulation

Bridge Relay Encapsulation (BRE) is a proprietary Ascom Timeplex protocol that extends bridging across WAN links by means of encapsulation. The BRE version 2 (BRE2) sits directly on the link layer protocol, requires less configuration and provides its own routing protocol.
Ascom Timeplex Protocol

TKIP: Temporal Key Integrity Protocol

Temporal Key Integrity Protocol (TKIP) is part of the IEEE 802.11i encryption standard for wireless LANs security. TKIP utilizes RC4 stream cippher with 128 bit key for encryption and 64 bit key for authentication. TKIP is the next generation of WEP (Wired Equivalency Protocol). TKIP provides per-packet key mixing, a message integrity check and a re-keying mechanism, thus fixing the flaws of WEP.
IEEE Specification: IEEE 802.11i

TLAP: TokenTalk Link Access Protocol

TokenTalk Link Access Protocol (TLAP) is a link-access protocol used in an AppleTalk network. TLAP is built on top of the standard Token Ring data-link layer.
Apple Protocol

TLS: Transport Layer Security Protocol   101

Transport Layer Security (TLS) protocol, based on SSL developed by Netscape, provides privacy and data integrity between two communicating applications. TLS is used extensively by web browsers to provide secure connections for transferring credit cards numbers and other sensitive data. Though SSL was superseeded to TLS by IETF, but the SSL name has gained enough popularity and people still call the protocol SSL or SST/TLS. The protocol is composed of two layers: the TLS Record Protocol and the TLS Handshake Protocol. At the lowest level, layered on top of some reliable transport protocol (TCP) is the TLS Record Protocol.
IETF Specification: RFC 2246

TMC: Telocator Mobile Computer Protocol

Telocator Mobile Computer Protocol (TMC) is the protocol that operates between the Radio Frequency (RF) receiver and the mobile computer, which is the ultimate recipient of data sent from the Message Entry Device (MED).
TME: Telocator Message Entry Protocol
Telocator Message Entry Protocol (TME) defines the protocol operating between the Message Entry Device (MED) and Paging Message Processor (PMP).

Token Ring   198

Token Ring is a LAN protocol, defined in IEEE 802.5, where all stations are connected in a ring and each station can directly hear transmissions only from its immediate neighbor. Permission to transmit is granted by a message (token) that circulates around the ring.
IEEE Specification: IEEE 802.5

TOP: Technical Office Protocol

Technical Office Protocol (TOP) is an applications layer network application and protocol stack for office automation developed by Boeing. TOP is very similar to MAP except at the lowest levels, where it uses Ethernet (IEEE 802.3) rather than Token Bus (IEEE 802.4).
Boeing Protocol

Toshiba FANP: Flow Attribute Notification Protocol

Flow Attribute Notification Protocol is a protocol between neighbor modes which manages cut-through packet forwarding functionalities. In cut-through packet forwarding, a router does not perform conventional IP packet processing for received packets. FANP indicates mapping information between a datalink connection and a packet flow to the neighbor node. It helps a pair of nodes manage mapping information.
Toshiba Protocol

TP: ISO Transport Protocol   233

The OSI Transport layer protocol (ISO-TP or TP) manages end-to-end control and error checking to ensure complete data transfer. It performs transport address to network address mapping, makes multiplexing and splitting of transport connections, also provides functions such as Sequencing, Flow Control and Error detection and recover. Five transport layer protocols exist in the OSI suite, ranging from Transport Protocol Class 0 through Transport Protocol Class 4 (TP0, TP1, TP2, TP3 & TP4). The protocols increase in complexity from 0-4. TP0-3 work only with connection-oriented communications, in which a session connection must be established before any data is sent; TP4 also works with both connection-oriented and connectionless communications.
ISO Specification: ISO Document 8073

TP0: ISO Transport Protocol Class 0   233

Transport Protocol Class 0 (TP0), one of the five transport layer protocols existing in the OSI suite, performs segmentation (fragmentation) and reassembly functions. TP0 discerns the size of the smallest maximum protocol data unit (PDU) supported by any of the underlying networks, and segments the packets accordingly. The packet segments are reassembled at the receiver.
ISO Specification: ISO Document 8073

TP1: ISO Transport Protocol Class 1   233

Transport Protocol Class 1 (TP1), one of the five transport layer protocols existing in the OSI suite, performs segmentation (fragmentation) and reassembly, plus error recovery. TP1 sequences protocol data units (PDUs) and will retransmit PDUs or re-initiate the connection if an excessive number of PDUs are unacknowledged.
ISO Specification: ISO Document 8073

TP2: ISO Transport Protocol Class 2   233

Transport Protocol Class 2 (TP2), one of the five transport layer protocols existing in the OSI suite, performs segmentation and reassembly, as well as multiplexing and demultiplexing of data streams over a single virtual circuit.
ISO Specification: ISO Document 8073

TP3: ISO Transport Protocol Class 3   233

Transport Protocol Class 3 (TP3), one of the five transport layer protocols existing in the OSI suite, offers error recovery, segmentation and reassembly, and multiplexing and demultiplexing of data streams over a single virtual circuit. TP3 also sequences PDUs and retransmits them or re-initiates the connection if an excessive number is unacknowledged.
ISO Specification: ISO Document 8073

TP4: ISO Transport Protocol Class 4   233

Transport Protocol Class 4 (TP4), one of the five transport layer protocols existing in the OSI suite, offers error recovery, performs segmentation and reassembly, and supplies multiplexing and demultiplexing of data streams over a single virtual circuit. TP4 sequences PDUs and retransmits them or re-initiates the connection if an excessive number are unacknowledged. TP4 provides reliable transport service and functions with either connection-oriented or connectionless network service. TP4 is the most commonly used of all the OSI transport protocols, which is similar to the Transmission Control Protocol (TCP) in the TCP/IP suite.
ISO Specification: ISO Document 8073

TRIP: Telephony Routing over IP   132

Telephony Routing over IP (TRIP) is a policy-driven inter-ad-

ministrative domain protocol for advertising the reachability of telephony destinations between location servers and for advertising attributes of the routes to those destinations. TRIP's operation is independent of any signaling protocol; hence TRIP can serve as the telephony routing protocol for any signaling protocol.
IETF Specification: RFC 3219

TRISL: Token Ring Inter-Switch Link

Token Ring Inter-Switch Link(TRISL) is a Cisco protocol for interconnecting multiple routers and switches and maintaining VLAN information as traffic goes between routers and switches. The TRISL feature provides a method to transport native Token Ring frames from multiple VLANs across a 100-MB Fast Ethernet link.
Cisco Protocol

TUA: TCAP-User Adaptation Layer

TCAP-User Adaptation Layer (TUA) TUA is an SS7 Signalling User Adaptation Layer for providing TCAP-User signalling over SCTP. TUA is intended to be used on a Provider/User basis where TCAP resides on a Signalling Gateway (SG) and TCAP Users reside on an Application Server (AS). TUA is an integral part of the OpenSS7 SIGTRAN stack.
IETF Protocol

TUD: Trunk up-down

Trunk up-down(TUD) is a protocol used in ATM networks that monitors trunks and detects when one goes down or comes up. ATM switches send regular test messages from each trunk port to test trunk line quality. If a trunk misses a given number of these messages, TUD declares the trunk down. When a trunk comes back up, TUD recognizes that the trunk is up, declares the trunk up, and returns it to service.

TULIP: TCP and UDP over Lightweight IP

TCP and UDP over Lightweight IP (TULIP) is a protocol for running TCP and UDP applications over ATM, in which only the IP protocol field is carried in each packet, and everything else being bound at call set-up time. In this case, the implicit binding is between the IP entities in each host. Since there is no further routing problem once the binding is established, since AAL5 can indicate packet size, since fragmentation cannot occur, and since ATM signaling will handle exception conditions, the absence of all other IP header fields and of ICMP should not be an issue. Entry to TULIP mode would occur as the last stage in SVC signaling, by a simple extension to the encapsulation negotiation. TULIP changes nothing in the abstract architecture of the IP model, since each host or router still has an IP address which is resolved to an ATM address. It simply uses the point-to-point property of VCs to allow the elimination of some per-packet overhead. The use of TULIP could, in principle, be negotiated on a per-SVC basis or configured on a per-PVC basis.
IETF Specification: RFC 1932

TUNIC: TCP and UDP over Nonexistent IP Connection

TCP and UDP over Nonexistent IP Connection(TUNIC) is a protocol for running TCP and UPD applications over ATM. In this case, no network-layer information is carried in each packet and everything is bound at virtual circuit set-up time. The implicit binding is between two applications using either TCP or UDP directly over AAL5 on a dedicated VC. If this can be achieved, the IP protocol field has no useful dynamic function. However, in order to achieve binding between two appli-

cations, the use of a well-known port number in classical IP or in TULIP mode may be necessary during a call set-up.
IETF Specification: RFC 1932

TUP: Telephone User Part   285

The Telephone User Part (TUP) provides the signaling backbone between switching elements for basic call establishment, supervision, and release of circuit switched network connections for telecommunications services. TUP supports analog and digital circuits, and limited call management signaling.
TU-T Specification: Q.763

U

UA: User Adaptation Layers

User Adaptation Layers (UA) are a collection of the Signaling User Adaptation Layers in the SIGTRAN protocol suite. UA includes: SS7 TCAP-User Adaptation Layer (TUA), SS7 SCCP-User Adaptation Layer (SUA), SS7 ISUP-User Adaptation Layer (ISUA), SS7 MTP3-User Adaptation Layer (M3UA), SS7 MTP2-User Adaptation Layer (M2UA), SS7 MTP2-User Peer-to-Peer Adaptation Layer (M2PA), ISDN-User Adaptation Layer (IUA), and Tekelec's Transport Adapter Layer Interface (TALI).
IETF Protocol

UB Net/One: Ungermann-Bass Net/One

Ungermann-Bass Net/One (UB Net/One) is a routing protocol developed by UB Networks, that uses hello packets and a path-delay metric, with end nodes communicating using the XNS protocol. There are a number of differences between the manner in which Net/One uses the XNS protocol and the usage common among other XNS nodes.
UB Networks Protocol

UDLP: UniDirectional Link Protocol

UniDirectional Link Protocol (UDLP) is used by inexpensive, receive-only antennas to receive data via satellite.

UDP Port Numbers   293

UDP Port Numbers are designed to distinguish multiple applications running on a single device with one IP address from one another. In the UDP header, there are "SourcePort" and "DestinationPort" fields which are used to indicate the message sending process and receiving process identities defined. The combination of the IP address and the port number is called "socket".
IANA Protocol

UDP: User Datagram Protocol   49

User Datagram Protocol (UDP) is a connectionless transport layer (layer 4) protocol in the OSI model which provides a simple and unreliable message service for transaction-oriented services. UDP is basically an interface between IP and upper-layer processes. UDP protocol ports distinguish multiple applications running on a single device from one another.
IETF Specification: RFC 768

UMTS: Universal Mobile Telecommunication System

Universal Mobile Telecommunications System (UMTS) is a 3G cellular network technology that uses WCDMA (Wideband Code Division Multiple Access), which was operating in 25 countries as of mid-2005. The transmission rates range from a theoretical 384K bit/sec. for phones that are moving up to 2M bit/sec. for stationary devices.
ETSI Protocol

UNI: User Network Interface

The User-to-Network Interface (UNI) signaling protocol within the Signalling ATM Adaptation Layer (SAAL) are responsible for ATM call and connection control, including call establishment, call clearing, status enquiry and point-to-multipoint control between ATM end users and a private ATM switch, or between a private ATM switch and the public carrier ATM network. ATM UNI signaling message uses the Q.931 message format, which is made up of a message header and a variable number of Information Elements.
ITU-T Protocol

URL: Uniform Resource Locator   39

Uniform Resource Locator (URL) is the global address of documents and other resources on the World Wide Web. The first part of the address indicates what protocol used, and the second part specifies the IP address or the domain name where the resource is located.
IETF Specification: RFC 1738

UTS: Universal Terminal Support

Universal Terminal Support(UTS) is a data link layer protocol (P1024C) that runs in full-duplex mode over synchronous serial (V.24) lines and uses the ASCII character set.

UWB: Ultra-Wide-Band   194

Ultra-Wide-Band (UWB), also called digital pulse, is a wireless technology defined in IEEE 802.15.3 for transmitting digital data over a wide swath of the radio frequency spectrum with very low power. Because of the low power requirement, it can carry signals through doors and other obstacles that tend to reflect signals at more limited bandwidths and a higher power. It can carry large amounts of data (maximum bandwidth of 1Gbps) and can be used for multimedia content transfer, high-resolution radar, ground-penetrating radar, and radio locations systems.
IEEE Specification: 802.15.3

V

V.24

V.24 is an ITU-T standard for a physical layer interface between DTE and DCE. V.24 is essentially the same as the EIA/TIA-232 standard.
ITU-T Specification: V.24

V.25bis

V.25bis is an ITU-T specification describing procedures for call setup and tear-down over the DTE-DCE interface in a PSDN.
ITU-T Specification: V.25bis

V.32

V.32 is an ITU-T standard serial line protocol for bidirectional data transmissions at speeds of 4.8 or 9.6 kbps.
ITU-T Specification: V.32

V.32bis

V.32bis is an ITU-T standard that extends V.32 to speeds up to 14.4 kbps.
ITU-T Specification: V.32bis

V.34

V.34 is an ITU-T standard that specifies a serial line protocol. V.34 offers improvements to the V.32 standard, including higher transmission rates (28.8 kbps) and enhanced data compression.
ITU-T Specification: V.34

V.35

V.35 is an ITU-T standard describing a synchronous, physical layer protocol used for communications between a network access device and a packet network. V.35 is most commonly used in the United States and in Europe, and is recommended for speeds of up to 48 kbps.
ITU-T Specification: V.35

V.42

V.42 is an ITU-T standard protocol for error correction using Link Access Procedure for Modems (LAPM).
ITU-T Specification: V.42

V5UA: V5.2-User Adaptation Layer

V5.2-User Adaptation Layer (V5UA) is a protocol in the SIGTRAN protocol stack for the backhauling of V5.2 messages over IP using the Stream Control Transmission Protocol (SCTP). This protocol may be used between a Signaling Gateway (SG) and a Media Gateway controller (MGC). It is assumed that the SG receives V5.2 signaling over a standard V5.2 interface.
IETF Specification: RFC 3807

Van Jacobson   50

Van Jacobson is a compressed TCP protocol which improves the TCP/IP performance over low speed (300 to 19,200 bps) serial links and solves problems in link-level framing, address assignment, routing, authentication and performance.
IETF Specification: RFC 1144

VARP: VINES Address Resolution Protocol

VINES Address Resolution Protocol (VARP), similar to the ARP in an IP network, is responsible for the mapping of VINES network address with the Data Link layer address of devices. VARP entities are classified as either address-resolution clients or address-resolution services. Address-resolution clients usually are implemented in client nodes, whereas address-resolution services typically are provided by service nodes.
Banyan Protocol

VC: Virtual Concatenation

Virtual Concatenation (VC), an encapsulation scheme for Ethernet over SONET/SDH, allows for non-standard SONET/SDH multiplexing in order to address the bandwidth mismatch problem. Using virtual concatenation, the SONET/SDH transport pipes may be "right-sized" for Ethernet transport. Virtual Concatenation is a technique that allows SONET channels to be multiplexed together in arbitrary arrangements. This permits custom-sized SONET pipes to be created that are any multiple of the basic rates. Virtual concatenation is valid for STS-1 rates as well as for Virtual Tributary (VT) rates. All the intelligence to handle virtual concatenation is located at the endpoints of the connections, so each SONET channel may be routed independently through the network without it requiring any knowledge of the virtual concatenation. In this manner, virtually concatenated channels may be deployed on the existing SONET/SDH network with a simple endpoint upgrade. All the equipment currently in the center of the network need not be aware of the virtual concatenation.
ITU-T / IEEE Protocol

VCI: Virtual Channel Identifier

Virtual Channel Identifier (VCI) is a label used in Asynchronous Transfer Mode (ATM). VCI has 12 bits in length and is used for routing from end user to end user and functions as service access point. The VCI labels are owned by network nodes, and get randomized quite quickly as connections come and go.

ITU-T Protocol
VDSL: Very-high-data rate Digital Subscriber Line

158

Very-High-Data-Rate Digital Subscriber Line (VDSL) is one of the DSL technologies with asymmetric upstream and down-stream. VDSL transmits high-speed data over short reaches of twisted-pair copper telephone lines, with a range of speeds depending on actual line length. The maximum downstream rate under consideration is between 51 and 55 Mbps over lines up to 1000 feet (300 m) in length. Downstream speeds as low as 13 Mbps over lengths beyond 4000 feet (1500 m) are also common. Upstream rates are at speeds from 1.6 to 2.3 Mbps and maybe higher with enhancement.
ANSI/ITU Specification: G.993

VDSL2: Second Generation VDSL

Second Generation VDSL (VDSL2), an enhanced version of VDSL, specifies 8 profiles that address a range of applications including up to 100 Mb/s symmetric transmission on loops about one hundred meters long (using a bandwidth of 30 MHz), symmetric bit-rates in the 10-30 Mb/s range on intermediate length loops (using a bandwidth of 12 MHz), and asymmetric operation with downstream rates in the range of 10-40Mb/s on loops of lengths ranging from 3km to 1km (using a bandwidth of 8.5 MHz). VDSL2 includes most of the advanced feature from ADSL2. The rate/reach performance of VDSL2 is better than VDSL.
ITU-T Specification: G.993.2

VINES IPC: VINES Interprocess Communication Protocol

VINES Interprocess Communication Protocol (IPC), a transport layer (layer 4) protocol in the VINES protocol stack, provides both datagram and reliable message delivery service.
Banyan Protocol

VINES NetRPC: NetRemote Procedure Call

The VINES NetRemote Procedure Call (NetRPC) protocol, a protocol in the session/presentation layer of the VINES prtocol stack, is used to access VINES applications such as Street-Talk and VINES Mail. A program number and version identify all VINES applications. Calls to VINES applications must specify the program number, program version, and the specific procedure within the program, where applicable.
Banyan Protocol

VINES RTP: VINES Routing Table Protocol

VINES Routing Table Protocol (RTP), a network layer protocol in the VINES protocol stack, distributes network topology information. Routing update packets are broadcast periodically by both client and service nodes. These packets inform neighbors of a node's existence and also indicate whether the node is a client or a service node. In each routing update packet, service nodes include a list of all-known networks and the cost factors associated with reaching those networks.
Banyan Protocol

VINES SPP: Sequenced Packet Protocol

The VINES Sequenced Packet Protocol (SPP), a transport layer protocol in the VINES protocol stack, provides a reliable virtual connection service for private connections.
Banyan Protocol

VINES StreetTalk

VINES StreetTalk is an application protocol in the VIENS proto-col stack which maintains a distributed directory of the names of network resources. In VINES network, names are global across the Internet and independent of the network topology.
Banyan Protocol

VINES: Virtual Integrated Network Service

Virtual Integrated Network Service (VINES) is a protocol stack defined by Banyan Company, derived from the Xerox Network Systems (XNS) protocols. VINES is based on the UNIX operating system and uses a client/server architecture. The Banyan suite includes the following protocols: VARP (VINES Address Resolution Protocol); VIP (VINES Internet Protocol); ICP (Internet Control Protocol); RTP (Routing Update Protocol); IPC (InterProcess Communications Protocol); SPP (Sequenced Packet Protocol); NetRPC (NetRemote Procedure Call); StreetTalk. In October 1999, Banyan became ePresence, an internet service provider. At the same time, it announced the obsolescence of VINES and other Banyan products.
Banyan Protocol

VIP: VINES Internet Protocol

VINES Internet Protocol (VIP), the key protocol in the Banyan VINES protocol stack, performs the network layer (Layer 3) activities such as internetwork routing. VINES network layer addresses, similar to the IP addresses, are 48-bit entities subdivided into network (32 bits) and subnetwork (16 bits) portions.
Banyan Protocol

VLAN: Virtual LAN

185

Virtual LAN (VLAN) refers to a logical network in which a group of devices on one or more LANs that are configured so that they can communicate as if they were attached to the same wire, when in fact they are located on a number of different LAN segments. Because VLANs are based on logical, instead of physical, connections, they are very flexible for user/host management, bandwidth allocation and resource optimization.
IEEE Specification: IEEE 802.1q

VOIP Protocols

103

Voice over IP (VOIP) uses the Internet Protocol (IP) to transmit voice as packets over an IP network. Using VOIP protocols, voice communications can be achieved on any IP network regardless of whether it is Internet, Intranet or Local Area Network (LAN). In a VOIP-enabled network, the voice signal is digitized, compressed and converted to IP packets and then transmitted over the IP network. VOIP signaling protocols are used to set up and tear down calls, carry information required to locate users and negotiate capabilities.
ITU-T / IETF Protocol

VOIP: Voice over IP

103

Voice over IP (VOIP) uses the Internet Protocol (IP) to transmit voice as packets over an IP network. Using VOIP protocols, voice communications can be achieved on any IP network regardless it is Internet, Intranets or Local Area Networks (LAN). In a VOIP-enabled network, the voice signal is digitized, compressed and converted to IP packets and then transmitted over the IP network. VOIP signaling protocols are used to set up and tear down calls, carry information required to locate users and negotiate capabilities. The key benefits of Internet telephony (voice over IP) are the very low cost, the integration of data, voice and video on one network, the new services created on the converged network and the simplification of management of end users and terminals.

VPCI: Virtual Path Channel Identifier

In an ATM cell, the Virtual Path Identifier (VPI) and the Virtual Channel Identifier (VCI) together form the routing field, also called VPCI, which associates each cell with a particular channel or circuit. The VCI is a single-channel identifier; the VPI allows grouping of VCs with different VCIs and allows the group to be switched together as an entity. However, the VPIs and VCIs have significance only on the local link; the contents of the routing field will generally change as the cell traverses from link to link. These fields, in UNI, can support up to 16 million users to network sessions.

ITU-T Protocol

VPI: Virtual Path Identifier

Virtual Path Identifier (VPI) is a routing label used in the Asynchronous Transfer Mode (ATM) header. The VPI, together with the Virtual Channel Identifier (VCI), identifies the next destination of a cell as it passes through a series of ATM switches on its way to its destination. VPI field has 8 to 12 bits: 8 in the case of user-network interface and 12 in the case of network-network interface. The 4 extra bits in the network-network interface allows support for an expanded number of VPC internal to the network, which can be used for network management. A VPI of 0 indicates that this PVC is a virtual channel connection (VCC). A nonzero value indicates that this is a virtual path connection (VPC).

ITU-T Protocol

VPLS: Virtual Private LAN Service

Virtual Private LAN Service (VPLS) is an MPLS application defined by IETF. It allows geographically dispersed sites to share an ethernet broadcast domain by connecting each site to an MPLS-based network, as if they were in the same local area network (LAN). The wide area network (WAN) and metropolitan area network (MAN) become transparent to all customer locations. Ethernet VPN, based on VLPS and MPLS, provides more benefits than other alternative layer 2 or 3 VPN technologies.

IETF Protocol

VRML: Virtual Reality Modeling Language

Virtual Reality Modeling Language(VRML) is a language defined by the W3C for displaying three-dimensional objects on the World Wide Web. It is the 3-D equivalent of HTML. VRML allows Web developers to create three-dimensional (3-D) space and 3-D objects in full color with special texture, animation, and lighting effects. This means users can move in three dimensions on a VRML Web page as they do with a video game or flight simulator.

W3C Protocol

VRRP: Virtual Router Redundancy Protocol   66

Virtual Router Redundancy Protocol (VRRP) specifies an election protocol that dynamically assigns responsibility for a virtual router to one of the VRRP routers on a LAN. The VRRP router controlling the IP address(es) associated with a virtual router is called the Master and forwards packets sent to these IP addresses. The election process provides dynamic fail-over in the forwarding responsibility should the Master become unavailable. This allows any of the virtual router IP addresses on the LAN to be used as the default first hop router by end hosts.

IETF Specification: RFC 2338

VTP: VLAN Trunking Protocol   251

VLAN Trunking Protocol (VTP) is a Cisco Layer 2 messaging protocol that manages the addition, deletion and renaming of VLANs on a network-wide basis. Virtual Local Area Network (VLAN) Trunk Protocol (VTP) reduces the administration in a switched network. When you configure a new VLAN on one VTP server, the VLAN is distributed through all switches in the domain. This reduces the need to configure the same VLAN everywhere. VTP is a Cisco proprietary protocol that is available on most of the Cisco Catalyst Family products.

Cisco Protocol

W

WAE: Wireless Application Environment

The Wireless Application Environment (WAE) is the top-most level in the Wireless Application Protocol (WAP) suite, which combines both the WWW and Mobile Telephony technologies. WAE provides the operators and service providers with an interoperable environment on which they can build applications and services for hand-held client devices. WAE includes the micro-browser that contains functionality for using not only WML and WML Script as previously stated, but also Wireless Telephony Application, namely (WTA and WTAI) -- telephony services and programming interfaces as well as content formats including well-defined data formats, images, phone book records and calendar information.

WAP Forum Protocol

WAIS: Wide Area Information Server

Wide Area Information Server(WAIS) is a distributed database protocol developed to search for information over a network. WAIS supports full-text databases, which allow an entire document to be searched for a match. WAIS system has been replaced by the Web based search engines. There are few, if any, WAIS servers in existence on the Internet today.

ANSI Specification: ANSI Z39.50

WAP: Wireless Application Protocol

The Wireless Application Protocol (WAP) refers to a group of related technologies and protocols widely used as a de facto standard protocol in providing Internet access to mobile phones or other thin-client devices. Typical use of the WAP protocol involves a website transmitting scaled-down versions of normal web pages specifically optimized for use by wireless telecommunications devices. When used with Wireless Markup Language (WML), for example, hyperlinks can be accessed by the numbers of 0 through 9 in addition to assigned hotkeys on a user's phone.

WAP Forum / OMA Protocol

WaRP: Wavelength Routing Protocol

Wavelength Routing Protocol (WaRP) is a protocol that enables the provisioning, routing, protection, and restoration of virtual wavelength paths (VWP) through an optical network based on intelligent communication between Cisco 15900 Series Wavelength Routers.

Cisco Protocol

WCCP: Web Cache Communication Protocol

Web Cache Communication Protocol (WCCP), a Web-caching protocol developed by Cisco and then standardized by IETF, specifies interactions between one or more routers and one or more Web caches to establish and maintain the transparent redirection of selected types of traffic flowing through a group of routers. The selected traffic is redirected to a group of Web caches with the aim of optimizing resource usage and lowering response time.

IETF/Cisco Protocol

W-CDMA: Wideband-Code Division Multiple Access

Wideband Wideband-Code Division Multiple Access(W-CDMA or WCDMA), also known as UMTS in Europe, is a 3G standard for GSM in Europe, Japan and the United States. It's also the principal alternative being discussed in Asia. It supports very high-speed multimedia services such as full-motion video, Internet access and video conferencing. It uses one 5-MHz channel for both voice and data, offering data speeds of up to 2 Mbps.

ITU-T Specification: IMT-2000 direct spread

WDOG: Watchdog protocol

Watchdog protocol (WDOG) provides constant validation of active workstation connections and notifies the NetWare operating system when a connection may be terminated as a result of lengthy periods without communication.

Novell Protocol

WDP: Wireless Datagram Protocol

The Wireless Datagram Protocol(WDP), a protocol in WAP architecture, covers the Transmission Layer Protocols in an Internet model. As a general transport service, WDP offers to the upper layers an invisible interface independent of the underlying network technology used. In consequence of the interface common to transport protocols, the upper layer protocols of the WAP architecture can operate independent of the underlying wireless network. By letting only the transport layer deal with physical network-dependent issues, global interoperability can be acquired using mediating gateways.

WAP Forum / OMA Protocol

Wellfleet BOFL: Wellfleet Breath of Life

Wellfleet Breath of Life (Wellfleet BOFL) is a proprietary header of Bay Networks (now part of Nortel) used as a line sensing protocol on Ethernet LANs to detect transmitter jams. Synchronous lines run WFLT STD protocols to determine if the line is up and Dial backup PPP lines.

BAY Networks / Nortel Protocol

Wellfleet SRB: Source Routing Bridging

Wellfleet Source Routing Bridging (Wellfleet SRB) is a proprietary header of Bay Networks (now part of Nortel) which passes Token Ring information over WAN lines.

BAY Networks / Nortel Protocol

WEP: Wired Equivalent Privacy

Wired Equivalent Privacy (WEP) is a security protocol, specified in the IEEE Wireless Fidelity (Wi-Fi) standard, 802.11b, that is designed to provide a wireless local area network (WLAN) with a level of security and privacy comparable to what is usually expected of a wired LAN. WEP is based on a security scheme called RC4 that utilizes a combination of secret user keys and system-generated values. The original implementations of WEP supported the so-called 40-bit encryption, having a key of length 40 bits and 24 additional bits of system-generated data (64 bits total). Research has shown that 40-bit WEP encryption is too easy to decode, and consequently product vendors today employ 128-bit encryption (having a key length of 104 bits, not 128 bits) or better.

IEEE Specification: IEEE 802.11b

Whois   39

The whois protocol retrieves information about domain names from a central registry. The whois service is provided by the organizations that run the Internet. Whois is often used to retrieve registration information about an Internet domain or server. It can tell you who owns the domain, how their technical contact can be reached, along with other information.

IETF Specification: RFC 954

WiFi: Wireless Fidelity   190

Wireless Fidelity (WiFi or Wi-Fi), originally Nick named for 802.11b for wireless LAN with bandwith up to 11 Mbps, now refers to the entire wireless LAN technologies including 802.11a, 802.11b, 802.11g and 802.11n etc. Wi-Fi is actually the industry name for wireless LAN (WLAN) communication technology related to the IEEE 802.11 family of wireless networking standards.

IEEE Specification: IEEE 802.11

WINS: Windows Internet Name Service

Windows Internet Name Service (WINS) provides a distributed database for registering and querying dynamic NetBIOS names to IP address mapping in a routed network environment. WINS supports name resolution, the automated conversion of computer names to network addresses, for Windows networks. Specifically, WINS converts NetBIOS names to IP addresses on a LAN or WAN. WINS is to NetBIOS names as what Domain Name Service (DNS) is to domain names - a central mapping of host names to network addresses.

Microsoft Protocol

WiMax: Worldwide Interoperability for Microwave Access   205

WiMax, abreviated from Worldwide Interoperability for Microwave Access, is a popular name of the 802.16 wireless metropolitan-area network standard, including both 802.16-2004 for fixed WiMAX and 802.16-2005 for mobile WiMAX. WiMax has a range of up to 31 miles. Data rates for WiMax can reach up to 75 Mbps (Fixed) or 15 Mbps (Mobile). A number of wireless signaling options exist ranging anywhere from the 2 GHz range up to 66 GHz. WiMax is primarily aimed at making broadband network access widely available without the expense of stringing wires (as in cable-access broadband) or the distance limitations of Digital Subscriber Line. WiMax technology can deliver high-speed Internet access to rural areas and other locations. WiMax also offers an alternative to satellite Internet services.

IEEE Specification: IEEE 802.16

WLAN: Wireless Local Area Network   190

Wireless local-area networks (WLAN or wireless LAN) use radio waves to connect a user device to a LAN, which extends an existing wired local area network. WLAN provides Ethernet connections over the air and operate under the 802.11 family of specifications developed by the IEEE. WLANs are built by attaching a device called the access point (AP) to the edge of the wired network. Clients communicate with the AP using a wireless network adapter similar in function to a traditional Ethernet adapter. The WLAN technology is defined by the IEEE 802.11 family of specifications, namely, 802.11, 802.11a, 802.11b, 802.11g and 802.11n. All use the Ethernet protocol and CSMA/CA (carrier sense multiple access with collision avoidance instead of CSMA/CD) for path sharing.

IEEE Specification: IEEE 802.11

WML: Wireless Markup Language

Wireless Markup Language (WML), based on HTML and XML, delivers Internet content to small wireless devices, such as browser-equipped cellular phones and handheld devices, which typically have very small displays, slow CPUs, limited memory capacity, low bandwidth and restricted user-input capabilities. WML demands less memory and processing power from browsers than HTML and JavaScript. WML also includes features that tailor it for the relatively small display sizes of today's wireless devices. WML and HTML differ in significant ways. Although WML strips some features from HTML and co-opts others, WML also incorporates some powerful programming constructs not found in HTML like variables, tasks, and events. WML implements a stricter tag syntax than HTML and includes a DTD for use with XML parsers.

W3C Protocol

WSP: Wireless Session Protocol

The Wireless Session Protocol (WSP), a protocol in the Wireless Application Protocol (WAP) suite, provides the Wireless Application Environment a consistent interface with two services: connection-oriented service to operate above the Transaction Layer Protocol (WTP) and a connectionless service that operates above either secure or non-secure datagarm service (WDP). Currently, the protocols of the WSP family provide HTTP/1.1 functionality and semantics in a compact encoding, long lived session state with session suspend-and-resume capabilities, a common facility for reliable and unreliable data push as well as a protocol feature negotiation. These protocols are optimised to be used in low-bandwith bearer networks with relative long latency in order to connect a WAP client to a HTTP server.

WAP Forum / OMA Protocol

WTLS: Wireless Transport Layer Security

The Wireless Transport Layer Security (WTLS) protocol, a protocol in the Wireless Application Protocol (WAP) suite, is based on Transport Layer Security (TLS) or formely known as Secure Sockets Layer (SSL). It is designed to be used with other WAP protocols and to support narrow-band networks. It uses data encryption with a method that is negotiated at the start of the session to provide privacy, data integrity, authentication and denial-of-service protection. The latter is needed in cases when data is replayed or not properly verified. When that happens, WTLS detects the misuse and rejects the data in order to make many typical denial-of-service attacks harder to accomplish.

WAP Forum / OMA Protocol

WTP: Wireless Transaction Protocol

The Wireless Transaction Protocol (WTP), a protocol in the Wireless Application Protocol (WAP) suite, operates efficiently over either secure or non-secure wireless datagram networks. It provides three different kinds of transaction services, namely unreliable one-way, reliable one-way and reliable two-way transactions. This layer also includes optional user-to-user reliability by triggering the confirmation of each received message. To reduce the number of messages sent, the feature of delaying acknowledgements can be used.

WAP Forum / OMA Protocol

X

X Protocol 41

The X Window System Protocol, also known as X Window or X Protocol, is a graphics architecture used as the graphical system on UNIX systems (primarily) and Linux systems. The X Window System is also used, less commonly, on VMS, MVS, and MS-Windows systems. X Window System (X Protocol) provides an inherently client/server-oriented base for displaying windowed graphics. X Window provides a public protocol by which client programs can query and update information on X servers.

X.org Protocol

X Window 41

The X Window System Protocol, also known as X Window or X Protocol, is a graphics architecture used as the graphical system on UNIX systems (primarily) and Linux systems. The X Window System is also used, less commonly, on VMS, MVS, and MS-Windows systems. X Window System (X Protocol) provides an inherently client/server-oriented base for displaying windowed graphics. X Window provides a public protocol by which client programs can query and update information on X servers.

X.Org Protocol

X.121

X.121 is an ITU-T address format of the X.25 protocol suite used as part of call setup to establish a switched virtual circuit between Public Data Networks (PDNs), connecting two network user addresses (NUAs). It consists of just fourteen digits and is sent over the Packet Layer Protocol (PLP) after the packet type identifier (PTI). IP addresses can be mapped to X.121 as described in RFC 1236.

ITU-T Specification: X.121

X.21

X.21 is an ITU-T standard for serial communications over synchronous digital lines. The X.21 protocol is used primarily in Europe and Japan.

ITU-T Specification: X.25

X.21bis

X.21bis is an ITU-T standard that defines the physical layer protocol for communication between DCE and DTE in an X.25 network.

ITU-T Specification: X.25

X.25 176

X.25, an ISO and ITU-T protocol for wide area network (WAN) communications, is a packet-switched data network protocol which defines the exchange of data as well as the control of information between a user device, called Data Terminal Equipment (DTE), and a network node, called Data Circuit Terminating Equipment (DCE). X.25 specifies LAPB, a data-link-layer protocol, and PLP, a network-layer protocol. Frame Relay has, to some degree, superseded X.25.

ITU-T Specification: X.25

X.28

X.28 is an ITU-T recommendation that defines the terminal-to-PAD interface in X.25 networks.

ITU-T Specification: X.25

X.29

X.29 is an ITU-T recommendation that defines the form for control information in the terminal-to-PAD interface used in X.25 networks.

ITU-T Specification: X.25

X.3

X.3 is an ITU-T recommendation that defines various PAD parameters used in X.25 networks.

ITU-T Specification: X.25

X.400 227

X.400 is the Message Handling Service protocol for email transmission specified by the ITU-T and ISO. X.400 is common in Europe and Canada and is an alternative to the more popular email protocol, Simple Mail Transfer Protocol (SMTP), which is defined by IETF. X.400 uses a binary format so it is easy to include binary contents without encoding it for transfer. Also, it is harder for people to fake email addresses and contents than with SMTP, where text messages are used.

OSI / ITU-T Specification: X.400

X.500   229

X.500, the directory Access Protocol by ITU-T (X.500) and also ISO (ISO/IEC 9594), is a standard way to develop an electronic directory of people in an organization so that it can be part of a global directory available to anyone in the world with Internet access.

OSI / ITU-T Specification: X.500

X.509

X.509 is an ITU-T standard for public key infrastructure (PKI). X.509 specifies, amongst other things, standard formats for public key certificates and a certification path validation algorithm. X.509 was initially issued in 1988 and was begun in association with the X.500 standard and assumed a strict hierarchical system of certificate authorities (CAs) for issuing the certificates. The X.500 system has never been fully implemented, and the IETF's public-key infrastructure working group has adapted the standard to the more flexible organization of the Internet. In fact, the term X.509 certificate usually refers to the IETF's PKI Certificate and CRL Profile of the X.509 v3 certificate standard, as specified in RFC 3280, commonly referred to as PKIX.

ITU-T Specification: X.509

X.75

X.75 is the signaling protocol for X.25, which defines the signaling system between two PDNs. X.75 is essentially an Network-to-Network Interface (NNI).

ITU-T Specification: X.75

X.86

X.86 is a physical interface sublayer (PHY) for 802.3 Ethernet Media Access Control (MAC) frames, which provides for the encapsulation of 802.3 MAC frames in a sublayer-level address and control frame, LAPS. X.86 allows 802.3 Ethernet switches and Hubs to interface directly with SDH (Recommendation G.707) transmission infrastructure for point-to-point data-link communications over Wide Area Networks (WANs). The data transfer rates for this new PHY reflect the various concatenated and non-concatenated payload rates in the SDH standard.

ITU-T Specification: X.86

X3T9.5: X Display Manager Control Protocol

X Display Manager Control Protocol (X3T9.5) isused to communicate between X terminals and workstations running the UNIX operating system.

X.Org Protocol

XCAP: XML Configuration Access Protocol

Extensible Markup Language (XML) Configuration Access Protocol (XCAP) allows a client to read, write and modify application configuration data, stored in XML format on a server. XCAP maps XML document sub-trees and element attributes to HTTP URIs, so that these components can be directly accessed by HTTP. XCAP is a set of conventions for mapping XML documents and document components into HTTP URIs, rules for how the modification of one resource affects another,

data validation constraints, and authorization policies associated with access to those resources.

IETF Protocol

XDR: eXternal Data Representation

eXternal Data Representation(XDR) is a standard for the description and encoding of data. XDR is useful for transferring data between different computer architectures, and it has been used to communicate data between such diverse machines as the SUN WORKSTATION*, VAX*, IBM-PC*, and Cray*. XDR fits into the ISO presentation layer and is roughly analogous in purpose to X.409, ISO Abstract Syntax Notation. The major difference between these two is that XDR uses implicit typing, while X.409 uses explicit typing.

IETF Specification: RFC 4506

xDSL: Digital Subscriber Line   158

xDSL refers to a collection of Digital Subscriber Line(DSL) technologies, which is a modem technology for broadband data access over ordinary copper telephone lines (POTS) from homes to businesses. xDSL refers collectively to all types of DSL, such as ADSL (and G.Lite), HDSL, SDSL, IDSL and VDSL etc. They are sometimes referred to as last mile (or first mile) technologies because they are used only for connections from a telephone switching station to a home or office, not between switching stations.

ANSI/ITU-T Protocol

Xerox IDP: Internet Datagram Protocol   290

Internet Datagram Protocol (IDP), a protocol in the Xerox protocol stack, is a simple, unreliable datagram protocol which is used to support the SOCK_DGRAM abstraction for the Internet Protocol (IP) family. IDP sockets are connectionless and normally used with the sendto and recvfrom subroutines. The connect subroutine can also be used to fix the destination for future packets, in which case the recv or read subroutine and the send or write subroutine can be used.

Xerox Protocol

XGCP: eXternal Media Gateway Control Protocols

eXternal Media Gateway Control Protocols(XGCP) refers to a group of VOIP media gateway control protocols, including SGCP and MGCP.

XMPP: Extensible Messaging and Presence Protocol   40

Extensible Messaging and Presence Protocol (XMPP) is designed to stream XML elements for near-real-time messaging, presence, and request-response services. XMPP is based on the Jabber protocol, an open and popular protocol for instant messaging.

IETF Specification: RFC 3920

XML: Extensible Markup Language

Extensible Markup Language (XML), a subset of SGML, defines a syntax that lets you create markup languages to specify information structures. Information structures define the type of information, for example, subscriber name or address, not how the information looks (bold, italic, and so on). External processes can manipulate these information structures and publish them in a variety of formats. Text markup language designed to enable the use of SGML on the World Wide Web. XML allows you to define your own customized markup language. XML tags are not predefined. You must define your own tags. XML uses a Document Type Definition (DTD) or an XML Schema to describe the data. XML is not a replacement

for HTML. Actually, XML and HTML are complimentary to each other.
W3C Protocol

XMLDSIG: XML Digital Signatures

XML Digital Signatures (XMLDSIG) is a standard for creating and managing digital signatures using Extensible Markup Language (XML).
IETF Specification: RFC 3275

XKMS: XML Key Management Specification

XML Key Management Specification (XKMS) is a standard for encrypting information based on Extensible Markup Language (XML). XKMS comprises two services: the XML Key Information Service (X-KISS) and the XML Key Registration Service Specification (X-KRSS).
W3C Protocol

XNS: Xerox Network System

Xerox Network System (XNS) is a suite of protocols, providing routing capability and support for both sequenced and connectionless packet delivery. Many PC networking companies, such as 3Com, Banyan, Novell, and UB Networks used a variation of XNS as their primary transport protocol.
Xerox Protocol

XON/XOFF

XON/XOFF is software data flow communications protocol for controlling the flow of data between computers and other devices. X stands for transmitter. XON/XOFF is frequently referred to as "software flow control". Typically, the receiver will send an XOFF character, when it can't take any more data (e.g. it may need time to process something), and when it can once again take more data, will send an XON character to the transmitter.

XOT: X.25 Over TCP   253

X.25 Over TCP(XOT) is developed by Cisco to transport X.25 over IP internets. The X.25 Packet Level requires a reliable link level below it and normally uses LAPB. XOT is a method of sending X.25 packets over IP internets by encapsulating the X.25 Packet Level in TCP packets.
IETF Specification: RFC 1613

Xmodem

XMODEM is a simple file transfer protocol in 1977 which became extremely popular in the early bulletin board system (BBS) market, largely because it was so simple to implement. It was also fairly inefficient, and as modem speeds increased, this problem led to the development of a number of modified versions of XMODEM to improve performance or address other problems with the protocol. The later versions of XMODEM: YMODEN, especially the ZMODEN protocol developed based on the XMODEM, had much better performance and replaced XMODEM in the early 1990s.

Y

Ymodem

YMODEM is a protocol for file transfer used between modems. YMODEM was developed by Chuck Forsberg as the successor to XMODEM and MODEM7. The original YMODEM was essentially the same as XMODEM except that it sent the file's name, size, and timestamp in a regular XMODEM block before actually transferring the file. Sending the file size solved XMODEM's problem of superfluous padding at the end of the file.

YP: Yellow Pages protocol

The Yellow Pages (YP) protocol, now known as Network Information Service (NIS), is a directory service used for name lookup and general table enumeration. Each YP database consists of key-value pairs, maps, and domains. YP defines a set of key-value pairs as a map. Each map belongs to a domain that is a category of maps. This hierarchy of key-value pairs, maps, and domains provides a generic structure for modeling a database of information. An optional component to a YP server database implementation is the YP binder (YPbind) server. YP uses YP-binder servers to provide addressing information about YP database servers to potential clients.
Sun Protocol

Z

ZigBee   194

ZigBee, defined in the IEEE 802.15.4, is the technology used in the low data rate Wireless Personal Area Network (WPAN) for home control, building automation industrial automation. ZigBee covers up to 330 feet (about 100 meters) in the bandwidth of 20 to 250 kbps.
IEEE Specification: IEEE 802.15.4

ZIP: Zone Information Protocol

Zone Information Protocol (ZIP), an AppleTalk session layer protocol, manages the relationship between network numbers and zone names. ZIP is used by NBP to determine which networks contain nodes that belong to a zone.
Apple Protocol

Zmodern

ZMODEM is a file transfer protocol, developed by Chuck Forsberg in 1986, to improve file transfers over X.25 network. In addition to dramatically improved performance compared to older protocols XMODEM and YMODEM, ZMODEM also offered restartable transfers, auto-start by the sender, an expanded 32-bit CRC, and control character quoting, allowing it to be used on networks that might "eat" control characters. ZMODEM became extremely popular on bulletin board systems in the early 1990s, displacing earlier protocols such as XMODEM, YMODEM and JMODEM.

Numbers

802.1

802.1 is the IEEE protocol suite for internetworking of LAN, MAN, WAN, LAN security, and management. 802.1 protocol suites include 802.1D, 802.1P, 802.1Q, 802.1S, 802.1W, 802.1X, etc.
IEEE Specification: IEEE 802.1

802.11   190

802.11 is a group of wireless specifications developed by the IEEE for wireless local area network (WLAN) communications. It details a wireless interface between devices to manage packet traffic to avoid collisions. Some common specifications include the following: 802.11a, 802.11b, 802.11g, 802.11n, etc.
IEEE Specification: IEEE 802.11

802.12

802.12 is an IEEE standard which defines the 100 VG-Any LAN standard. 808.12 specifies the physical layer and the MAC sublayer of the data link layer. IEEE 802.12 uses the demand priority media-access scheme at 100 Mbps over a variety of physical media.

IEEE Specification: IEEE 802.12

802.15
194

IEEE 802.15, a group of standards of wireless communicatoins defined by IEEE, is for wireless personal area networks (WPANs). IEEE 802.15 has characters such as short-range, low power, low cost, small networks and communication of devices within a Personal Operating Space. The current technologies included in the IEEE 802.15 family are: 802.15.1 (Bluetooth), 802.15.2 (UWB) and 802.15.4 (ZigBee).
IEEE Specification: IEEE 802.15

802.16
205

The IEEE 802.16 refers to a group of standards that defines wireless communications between a subscriber site and a core network such as the public telephone network (PSTN) and the Internet. It is called Wireless MAN technology, which is also branded as WiMAX. This wireless broadband access standard provides the missing link for the "last mile" connection in metropolitan area networks where DSL, Cable and other broadband access methods are not available or too expensive.
IEEE Specification: IEEE 802.16

802.2

IEEE 802.2 LAN protocol specifies an implementation of the LLC sublayer of the data link layer. IEEE 802.2 LLC is used in IEEE802.3 (Ethernet) and IEEE802.5 (Token Ring) LANs to perform these functions:
a. Managing the data-link communication
b. Link Addressing
c. Defining Service Access Points (SAPs)
d. Sequencing
IEEE Specification: IEEE 802.2

802.3
179

802.3 is a group of IEEE standards which defines the Ethernet LAN protocols. Four data rates are currently defined for operation over optical fiber and twisted-pair cables:
10 Mbps -- 10Base-T Ethernet (IEEE 802.3)
100 Mbps -- Fast Ethernet (IEEE 802.3u)
1000 Mbps -- Gigabit Ethernet (IEEE 802.3z)
10 Gbps -- 10Gigabit Ethernet (IEEE 802.3ae).
IEEE Specification: IEEE 802.3

802.4

IEEE 802.4 defines the media access control (MAC) layer for bus networks that use a token-passing mechanism (token bus networks). This is an application of the concepts used in token ring networks. The main difference is that the endpoints of the bus do not meet to form a physical ring. The IEEE 802.4 Working Group is disbanded.
IEEE Specification: IEEE 802.4

802.5
198

802.5 is an IEEE standard for Token Ring technologies where all stations are connected in a ring, and each station can directly hear transmissions only from its immediate neighbor. Permission to transmit is granted by a message (token) that circulates around the ring. Token Ring as defined in IEEE 802.5 is originated from the IBM Token Ring LAN technologies. Both are based on the Token Passing technologies. While they differ in minor ways, but they generally compatible with each other.
IEEE Specification: IEEE 802.5

802.6
203

802.6 is an IEEE standard which defines Distributed Queue Dual Bus (DQDB) protocol for Metropolitan Area Networks (MANs). DQDB is designed for data as well as voice and video transmission based on cell switching technology (similar to ATM). DQDB, which permits multiple systems to interconnect using two unidirectional logical buses, is an open standard that is designed for compatibility with carrier transmission standards such as SMDS, which is based on the DQDB standards.
IEEE Specification: IEEE 802.6

1000BaseCX or 1000Base-CX
182

1000BaseCX, also known as 1000Base-CX, is a physical layer specification for Gigabit Ethernet transmission over a special balanced 150 ohm cable shorter than 25m. This cable is a type of shielded cable. In order to minimize safety and interference concerns caused by voltage difference, both transmitters and receivers will share a common ground. The return loss for each connector is limited to 20db to minimize transmission distortions. The connector type for 1000Base-CX will be a DB-9 connector or HSSDC.
IEEE Specification: IEEE 802.3z

1000BaseF or 1000Base-F
182

1000BaseF, also known as 1000Base-F, is a physical layer baseband specification for Ethernet communications over optical fibers. 1000Base-F uses 8B/10B ANSI X3T11 Fibre Channel FC-1 frame encoding, serializer/deserializer (SERDES) and NRZ on the fiber, clocked at 1250 Mbaud. 1000BaseF can support a fiber cable length of 500m full duplex on multimode fiber fiber, and of 2-3km full duplex on single mode fiber.
IEEE Specification: IEEE 802.3z

1000BaseLH or 1000Base-LH
182

1000BaseLH, also known as 1000Base-LH, is a physical layer specification for Gigabit Ethernet over fiber optic cabling as defined in IEEE 802.3z. LH stands for long haul, and 1000Base-LH uses long wavelength laser (1310nm) over multimode and single-mode fiber. 1000BaseLH can support a maximum distance of 550m for multimode fiber, and of 10km for single mode fiber.
IEEE Specification: IEEE 802.3z

1000BaseLX or 1000Base-LX
182

1000BaseLX, also known as 1000Base-LX, is a physical layer specification for Gigabit Ethernet over fiber optic cabling as defined in IEEE 802.3z. LX stands for long wavelength, and 1000Base-LX uses long wavelength laser (1310nm) over multimode and single-mode fiber as opposed to 1000Base-SX, which uses short wavelength laser over multimode fiber. The maximum distance of fiber is 550m for multi mode and 5km for single mode.
IEEE Specification: IEEE 802.3z

1000BaseSX or 1000Base-SX
182

1000BaseSX, also known as 1000Base-SX, is a physical layer specification for Gigabit Ethernet over fiber optic cabling as defined in IEEE 802.3z. SX stands for short wavelength, and 1000Base-SX uses short wavelength laser (850nm) over multimode fiber as opposed to 1000Base-LX, which uses long wavelength laser over both multimode and single mode fiber. The maximum distance of (multimode) fiber, based on 1000BaseSX, is 550m.
IEEE Specification: IEEE 802.3z

1000BaseT or 1000Base-T
182

1000BaseT, also known as 1000Base-T, is a physical layer standard that supports data transfer rates up to 1000 Mbps (1 Gbps) over twisted pair cables up to 100m. The 1000BASE-

T standard is defined in the IEEE 802.3ab. Like Ethernet, 1000BaseT is based on the CSMA/CD LAN access method.
IEEE Specification: IEEE 802.3ab

1000BaseX or 1000Base-X 182

1000BaseX identifies various Gigabit Ethernet physical layer standards as defined in IEEE802.3z, such as 1000BaseLX, 1000BaseSX, 1000BaseCX and 1000BaseLH. Basically, all standards included in 1000BaseX uses 8B/10B coding scheme with 8 bits of data and 2 bits of error-correction data. Each specification allows various cable (fiber or copper) lengthes, and uses different cable media.
IEEE Specification: IEEE 802.3z

1000BaseZX

1000BaseZX (or 1000Base-ZX) is a Cisco specified standard for gigabit Ehternet communication. 1000BaseZX operates on ordinary single-mode fiber-optic link spans up to 43.5 miles (70 km). Link spans up to 62.1 miles (100 km) are possible using premium single-mode fiber or dispersion-shifted single-mode fiber. 1000BaseZX uses a long wavelength laser (1550 nm). The 1000BASEZX GBIC is intended to be used as a Physical Medium Dependent (PMD) component for Gigabit Ethernet interfaces found on various switch and router products. It operates at a signaling rate of 1250 Mbaud, transmitting and receiving 8B/10B encoded data.
Cisco Protocol

100BaseFX or 100Base-FX 181

100BaseFX, also known as 100Base-FX, is a 100-Mbps baseband Fast Ethernet specification. 100BaseFX, a part of 100BaseX defined in the IEEE 802.3 standard, uses 4B/5B block encoding for Fast Ethernet over fiber-optic cabling. The fiber distance that the 100BaseFX can support is: 412m half duplex on Multi Mode fiber, 2km full duplex on Multi Mode fiber, and 15-20km full duplex on Single Mode fiber.
IEEE Specification: IEEE 802.3

100BaseT or 100Base-T 181

100BaseT, also known as 100Base-T or fast Ethernet, is a physical layer standard that supports data transfer rates up to 100 Mbps (100 megabits per second). 100BASE-T is based on Manchester signal encoding transmitted over Category 3 or better twisted-pair cable. The 100BASE-T standard is defined in the IEEE 802.3u. Like Ethernet, 100BaseT is based on the CSMA/CD LAN access method.
IEEE Specification: IEEE 802.3u

100BaseT4 or 100Base-T4 181

100BaseT4, also known as 100Base-T4, is a 100-Mbps baseband Fast Ethernet specification using four pairs of Category 3, 4, or 5UTP wiring. To guarantee proper signal timing and quality, a 100BaseT4 segment cannot exceed 100 meters in length. 100BaseT4 is part of the IEEE 802.3 standard.
IEEE Specification: IEEE 802.3

100BaseTX or 100Base-TX 181

100BaseTX, also known as 100Base-TX, is a 100-Mbps baseband Fast Ethernet specification using two pairs of either UTP or STP wiring, based on 4B/5B signal encoding. The first pair of wires is used to receive data, and the second to transmit data. To guarantee proper signal timing and quality, a 100BaseTX segment cannot exceed 100 meters in length. 100BaseTX is part of the 100BaseX as defined in the IEEE 802.3u standard.
IEEE Specification: IEEE 802.3u

100BaseX or 100Base-X 181

100BaseX, including 100BaseFX and 100BaseTX, is a 100-Mbps baseband Fast Ethernet specification based on IEEE 802.3 standard using 4B/5B block encoding for Fast Ethernet over fiber-optic cabling (FX) and two pairs (TX).
IEEE Specification: IEEE 802.3u

100VG-AnyLAN

100VG-AnyLAN, originally developed by Hewlett-Packard, is a 100-Mbps Fast Ethernet and Token Ring media technology using four pairs of Category 3, 4, or 5 UTP cabling. 100VG-AnyLAN can be made to operate on existing 10BaseT Ethernet networks. 100VG-AnyLAN is defined in the IEEE 802.12 standard.
IEEE Protocol

10Base2 (10Base-2 or 10Base2 Thin) 179

10Base2, also called Cheapernet or ThinNet, is a 10-Mbps baseband Ethernet specification using a 50-ohm thin coaxial cable. 10Base2, defined in the IEEE 802.3a specification, has a distance limit of 185 meters per segment. 10Base2 is based on Manchester signal encoding transmitted over a thin coaxial cable.
IEEE Specification: IEEE 802.3

10Base5 (10Base-5 or 10Base Thick) 179

10Base5, also called ThickNet, is a 10-Mbps baseband Ethernet specification using a standard (thick) 50-ohm baseband coaxial cable. 10Base5, which is part of the IEEE 802.3 baseband physical layer specification, has a distance limit of 500 meters per segment. 10Base5 is based on Manchester signal encoding transmitted.
IEEE Specification: IEEE 802.3

10BaseF or 10Base-F 179

10BaseF, also known as 10Base-F, is 10 Mbps Ethernet system based on Manchester signal encoding transmitted over fiber optic cable. 10BaseF includes 10BaseFL, 10BaseFB and 10BaseFP and is defined in IEEE 802.3j specification.
IEEE Specification: IEEE 802.3

10BaseFB or 10Base-FB 179

10BaseFB, also called as 10Base-FB, is a 10-Mbps baseband Ethernet specification using fiber-optic cabling. 10BaseFB is part of the IEEE 10BaseF specification. It is not used to connect user stations, but instead provides a synchronous signaling backbone that allows additional segments and repeaters to be connected to the network. 10BaseFB segments can be up to 2,000 meters long (1.24 miles).
IEEE Specification: IEEE 802.3

10BaseFL or 10Base-FL 179

10BaseFL, also called as 10Base-FL, is a 10-Mbps baseband Ethernet specification using fiber-optic cabling. 10BaseFL is part of the 10BaseF specification and, while able to interoperate with FOIRL, is designed to replace the FOIRL specification. 10BaseFL segments can be up to 1,000 meters long if used with FOIRL, and up to 2,000 meters if 10BaseFL is used exclusively.
IEEE Specification: IEEE 802.3

10BaseFP or 10Base-FP 179

10BaseFP, also called 10Base-FP, is a 10-Mbps fiber-passive baseband Ethernet specification using fiber-optic cabling. 10BaseFP is part of the 10BaseF specification. It organizes a number of computers into a star topology without the use of re-

peaters. 10BaseFP segments can be up to 500 meters long.
IEEE Specification: IEEE 802.3

10BaseT or 10Base-T   179

10BaseT, also known as 10Base-T, is a transmission medium specified by IEEE 802.3i that carries information at rates up to 10Mbps in baseband form using unshielded twisted pair (UTP) conductors with low cost Level 3 or better UTP wiring up to 100 meters (328 ft.). 10BaseT uses RJ45 connectors and sometimes 50-pin AMP connectors to a patch panel.
IEEE Specification: IEEE 802.3

10GBase   183

10GBase is a set of standards as defined by IEEE 802.3ae for Gigabit Ethernet system to operate in full-duplex mode only, over fiber optic media. There are a few media types, which are designed for use in either local or wide-area networking. This provides the 10 Gigabit Ethernet system with the flexibility needed to operate in local area networks (LAN), metropolitan area networks (MAN), regional area networks (RAN) and wide area networks (WAN). IEEE 802.3ae provides support to extend the 802.3 protocol and MAC specification to an operating speed of 10 Gb/s. Several Physical Coding Sublayers known as 10GBASE-X, 10GBASE-R and 10GBASE-W are specified, as well as significant additional supporting material for a 10 Gigabit Media Independent Interface (XGMII), a 10 Gigabit Attachment Unit Interface (XAUI), a 10 Gigabit Sixteen-Bit Interface (XSBI) and management. The 10GBase includes 10GBASE-S, a 850nm wavelength serial transceiver which uses two multimode fibers; 10GBASE-L4, a 1310nm wavelength division multiplexing (WDM) transceiver which uses two multi-mode or single mode fibers; 10GBASE-L, a 1310nm wavelength serial transceiver which uses two single mode fibers; and 10GBASE-E, a 1550nm wavelength serial transceiver which uses two single mode fibers.
IEEE Specification: IEEE 802.3ae

10GBASE-CX4   183

10GBase-CX4 is a 10-gigabit Ethernet protocol using 4-laned copper InfiniBand connectors. 10GBase-CX4, developed by IEEE 802.3ak working group, is a lower-cost switch interface. 10GBase-CX4 uses the XAUI (10 Gigabit Attachment Unit Interface) specified in 802.3ae, and the 4X connector used for InfiniBand. Rather than attempt to transmit 10 gigabits over a single copper link, the 802.3ak specification uses four transmitters and four receivers operating differentially over a bundle of very thin twin-axial cables to transmit 2.5G bit/sec each at a baud rate of 3.125 GHz per channel with 8B10B coding. This requires four differential pairs in each direction for a total of eight twin-axial channels per assembly. 10GBase-CX4 can support a cable length up to 25-meter.
IEEE Specification: IEEE 802.3ak

10GBASE-E or 10GbE   183

10Gbase-E, as defined by IEEE 802.3ae, is for single mode fiber (SMF based on G.652) with 1550 nm laser transceiver with a bandwidth of 10 Gbps. 10GBase-E allows optical signal transmission up to 40km. The 10GBASE-ER media types is designed for use over dark fiber, while the 10GBASE-EW media type is designed to connect to SONET equipment.
IEEE Specification: IEEE 802.3ae

10GBase-ER   183

10GBase-ER is a mode of 10GBase-E supporting a link length of up to 40 kilometers on single mode fiber (SMF based on G.652) using optical wavelength 1550nm. The 10GBASE-ER

media types is designed for use over dark fiber.
IEEE Specification: IEEE 802.3ae

10GBase-EW   183

10GBase-EW is a mode of 10GBase-E supporting a link length of up to 40 kilometers on single mode fiber (SMF based on G.652) using optical wavelength 1550nm. 10GBASE-EW media type is designed to connect to SONET equipment.
IEEE Specification: IEEE 802.3ae

10GBASE-L   183

10GBase-L, as defined by IEEE 802.3ae, is for single mode fiber (SMF based on G.652) with 1310 nm laser transceiver with a bandwidth of 10 Gbps. 10GBase-E allows optical signal transmission up to 10km. The 10GBASE-LR media type is designed for use over dark fiber, while the 10GBASE-LW media type is designed to connect to SONET equipment.
IEEE Specification: IEEE 802.3ae

10GBASE-LR   183

10GBase-LR is a mode of 10GBase-L supporting a link length of 10 kilometers on standard single-mode fiber (SMF) (G.652). 10GBASE-LR media type is designed for use over dark fiber.
IEEE Specification: IEEE 802.3ae

10GBase-LW   183

10GBase-LW is a mode of 10GBase-L supporting a link length of 10 kilometers on standard single-mode fiber (SMF) (G.652). 10GBASE-LW media type is designed to connect to SONET equipment.
IEEE Specification: IEEE 802.3ae

10GBASE-LX4   183

10GBase-LX4, as defined by IEEE 802.3ae, uses wave division multiplexing technology to send signals over four wavelengths of light carried over a single pair of fiber optic cables. The 10GBASE-LX4 system is designed to operate at 1310 nm over multi-mode or single-mode dark fiber. The design goal for this media system is from 2 meters up to 300 meters over multimode fiber or from 2 meters up to 10 kilometers over singlemode fiber, with longer distances possible depending on cable type and quality.
IEEE Specification: IEEE 802.3ae

10GBASE-S   183

10GBase-S, as defined by IEEE 802.3ae, is for multimode fiber (MMF) with a 850-nm laser transceiver with a bandwidth of 10 Gbps. It can support up to a 300-meter cable length. The 10GBASE-SR media type is designed for use over dark fiber, while the 10GBASE-SW media type is designed to connect to SONET equipment.
IEEE Specification: IEEE 802.3ae

10GBase-SR   183

10GBase-SR, as defined by IEEE 802.3ae, is a mode of 10GBase-S for multimode fiber (MMF) with a 850-nm laser transceiver with a bandwidth of 10 Gbps. It can support up to a 300 meters cable length. The 10GBASE-SR media type is designed for use over dark fiber.
IEEE Specification: IEEE 802.3ae

10GBase-SW   183

10GBase-SW, as defined by IEEE 802.3ae, is mode of 10GBase-S for multimode fiber (MMF) with a 850-nm laser transceiver with a bandwidth of 10 Gbps. It can support up to a 300 meters cable length. The 10GBASE-SW media type is designed to connect to SONET equipment.

IEEE Specification: IEEE 802.3ae

10GBASE-T   *183*

10GBASE-T is a standard proposed by the IEEE 802.3an committee to provide 10 Gigabit/second connections over conventional unshielded twisted pair cables (Category 5e or Category 6 or Category 7 cables). 10GBASE-T allows the conventional RJ-45 used for Ethernet LANs. 10GBASE-T can support signal transmision at the full 100m distance specified for LAN wiring.
IEEE Specification: IEEE 802.3an

10GBase-ZR   *183*

10GBASE-ZR, supporting link lengths of up to about 80 kilometers on SMF, is a 10 Gigabit Ethernet specification that is not part of the IEEE 10 Gb Ethernet standard but is built according to Cisco optical specifications. 10GBase-ZR uses the 1550nm laser wavelength.
IEEE Specification: IEEE 802.3ae

10Broad36

10Broad36 is an obsolete standard for carrying 10 Mbit/s Ethernet signals over a standard 75-ohm CATV cable with a 3600 meter range.
IEEE Specification: IEEE 802.3

1Base5

1Base5 refers to an obsolete standard to carry 1 Mbps over a unshielded twisted pair for StarLAN Ethernet.
IEEE Protocol

2B1Q: 2 Binary 1 Quaternary

2 Binary 1 Quaternary (2B1Q) is a full duplex physical layer encoding method used in ISDN and other digital communication technologies. In 2B1Q, two binary bits are encoded into one quaternary signal, doubling the effectiveness of transmission.
ANSI Specification: T1.601

802.11a   *190*

802.11a is an extension to IEEE 802.11 that applies to wireless LANs and provides up to 54 Mbps in the 5GHz band. 802.11a uses an orthogonal frequency division multiplexing (OFDM) encoding scheme rather than FHSS or DSSS. 802.11a, actually newer than 802.11b, offers significantly more radio channels than the 802.11b and has a shorter range than 802.11g. It isn't compatible with 802.11b.
IEEE Specification: IEEE 802.11a

802.11b   *190*

802.11b, also referred to as 802.11 High Rate or Wi-Fi, is an extension to IEEE 802.11 that applies to wireless LANS and provides 11 Mbps transmission (with a fallback to 5.5, 2 and 1 Mbps) in the 2.4 GHz band. 802.11b uses only DSSS. 802.11b was a ratification to the original 802.11 standard, allowing wireless functionality comparable to Ethernet.
IEEE Specification: IEEE 802.11b

802.11e

802.11e, an IEEE standard, is the quality-of-service specification over a LAN, in particular, the 802.11 Wi-Fi standard. The standard is considered of critical importance for delay-sensitive applications, such as Voice over Wireless IP and Streaming Multimedia. The protocol enhances the IEEE 802.11 Media Access Control (MAC) layer.
IEEE Specification: IEEE 802.11e

802.11g   *190*

802.11g is an extension to IEEE 802.11 which offers wireless transmission over relatively short distances at 20 – 54 Mbps in the 2.4 GHz band. The 802.11g also uses the orthogonal frequency division multiplexing (OFDM) encoding scheme. 802.11g is compatible with older 802.11b.
IEEE Specification: IEEE 802.11g

802.11i   *191*

802.11i, also called Wi-Fi Protected Access 2 (WPA 2), is the standard for WLAN security. IEEE 802.11i enhances the WEP (Wireline Equivalent Privacy), a technology used for many years for the WLAN security, in the areas of encryption, authentication and key management. WPA 2 supports the 128-bit-and-above Advanced Encryption Standard, along with 802.1x authentication and key management features. It also uses TKIP (Temporal Key Integrity Protocol) which rotates key periodically to improve WLAN security.
IEEE Specification: IEEE 802.11i

802.11j

802.11j is the IEEE standard to the 802.11 family of standards for wireless local area networks (WLANs) for 4.9 GHz - 5 GHz frequency use of WLAN systems in Japan.
IEEE Specification: IEEE 802.11j

802.11k

The 802.11k is the Radio Resource Management standard to provide measurement information for access points and switches to make wireless LANs run more efficiently. It may, for example, better distribute traffic loads across access points or allow dynamic adjustments of transmission power to minimize interference.
IEEE Specification: IEEE 802.11k

802.11n   *190*

802.11n is the IEEE Standard for WLAN enhancements for higher throughput designed to raise effective WLAN throughput to more than 100Mbit/sec. and to cover a range up to 400 meters. IEEE 802.11n technology is also known as Multiple Input, Multiple Output (MIMO).
IEEE Specification: IEEE 802.11n

802.11r

The 802.11r is the Fast Roaming standard to address-maintaining connectivity as a user moves from one access point to another. This is especially important in applications that need low latency and high quality.
IEEE Specification: IEEE 802.11r

802.11s

802.11s, an IEEE standard, is designed to deal with mesh networking in wireless communication. It is predicted to be ratified in mid-2008.
IEEE Specification: IEEE 802.11s

802.11x   *190*

802.11x refers to a group of evolving wireless local area network (WLAN) standards that are elements of the IEEE 802.11 family of specifications. 802.11x should not be mistaken for any one of its elements because there is no single 802.11x standard. The 802.11 family currently includes six over-the-air modulation techniques that all use the same protocol. The most popular (and prolific) techniques are those defined by the b, a, and g amendments to the original standard; security was originally included and was later enhanced via the 802.11i amendment. 802.11n is another new modulation technique. Other standards in the family (c–f, h, j) are service enhancements and extensions or corrections to previous specifications. 802.11b was the first widely accepted wireless networking standard, followed by 802.11a and 802.11g.

IEEE Protocol

802.15.1 195

802.15.1 is an IEEE wireless technology standard based on the Bluetooth technology. It is used for short range network monitoring and control applications, which is called wireless personal area network (WPAN).

IEEE Specification: IEEE 802.15.1

802.15.3 194

802.15.3 is an IEEE wireless technology standard that is used for short range network monitoring and control applications, which is called wireless personal area network (WPAN). 802.15.3 is also called UWB.

IEEE Specification: IEEE 802.15.3

802.15.4 194

802.15.4 is an IEEE wireless technology standard that is used for short range network monitoring and control applications, which is called wireless personal area network (WPAN). 802.15.4 is also called Zigbee.

IEEE Specification: IEEE 802.15.4

802.16-2004 205

802.16-2004, also known as 802.16d, is an IEEE standard for the fixed wireless broadband (WiMax). IEEE 802.16-2004 product profile utilizes the OFDM 256-FFT (Fast Fourier Transform) system profile. The Fixed WiMAX 802.16-2004 standard supports both time division duplex (TDD) and frequency division duplex (FDD) services -- the latter of which delivers full duplex transmission on the same signal if desired. Mobile WiMAX will do the same.

IEEE Specification: IEEE 802.16-2004

802.16-2005 205

802.16-2005, also known as 802.16e, is an IEEE standard addressing mobility of wireless broadband (WiMax). IEEE 802.16-2005 is sometimes called "Mobile WiMAX", after the WiMAX forum for interoperability. 802.16-2005, based on an existing WiMax standard 802.16a, adds WiMax mobility in the 2 to 6 GHz licensed bands.

IEEE Specification: IEEE 802.16-2005

802.16a 205

802.16a is an IEEE wireless communications specification for metropolitan area networks (MANs) as part of a set of standards known as 802.16 or WiMAX. The 802.16a standard was developed for wireless MANs operating between 2 GHz and 11 GHz, at data speeds of up to 75 megabits per second (Mbps). 802.16a has been replaced by later standards in the family 802.16d (802.16-2004) and 802.16e (802.16-2005).

IEEE Specification: IEEE 802.16a

802.16d

802.16d, also known as 802.16-2004, is an IEEE standard for the fixed wireless broadband (WiMax). IEEE 802.16d product profile utilizes the OFDM 256-FFT (Fast Fourier Transform) system profile. The Fixed WiMAX 802.16-2004 standard supports both time division duplex (TDD) and frequency division duplex (FDD) services -- the latter of which delivers full duplex transmission on the same signal if desired.

IEEE Specification: IEEE 802.16-2004

802.16e 205

802.16e, also known as 802.16-2005, is an IEEE standard

addressing mobility of wireless broadband (WiMax). IEEE 802.16e is sometimes called "Mobile WiMAX", after the WiMAX forum for interoperability. 802.16e, based on an existing WiMax standard 802.16a, adds WiMax mobility in the 2 to 6 GHz licensed bands. 802.16e allows for fixed wireless and mobile Non Line of Sight (NLOS) applications primarily by enhancing the OFDMA (Orthogonal Frequency Division Multiple Access).

IEEE Specification: IEEE 802.16-2005

802.1ad

802.1ad, an IEEE standard also referred to as "Q-in-Q" tag stacking, builds on the IEEE's 802.1Q (Virtual LANs) to enable stacked VLANs. IEEE 802.1ad is an amendment to IEEE standard IEEE 802.1Q-1998, intended to develop an architecture and bridge protocols to provide separate instances of the MAC services to multiple independent users of a Bridged Local Area Network in a manner that does not require cooperation among the users, and requires a minimum of cooperation between the users and the provider of the MAC service.

IEEE Specification: IEEE 802.1ad

802.1D

802.1D is an IEEE specification which defines Spanning-Tree Protocol (STP). STP is a link management protocol that provides path redundancy while preventing undesirable loops in the network. For an Ethernet network to function properly, only one active path can exist between two stations. Loops occur in networks for a variety of reasons. The most common reason for loops in networks is a deliberate attempt to provide redundancy -- in case that one link or switch fails, another link or switch can take over.

IEEE Specification: IEEE 802.1d

802.1P 186

IEEE 802.1p specification enables Layer 2 switches to prioritize traffic and perform dynamic multicast filtering. The prioritization specification works at the media access control (MAC) framing layer. The 802.1p standard also offers provisions to filter multicast traffic to ensure it does not proliferate over layer 2-switched networks.

IEEE Specification: IEEE 802.1p

802.1Q 185

802.1Q is an IEEE standards, also known as virtual LAN (VLAN), which allows multiple bridged networks to transparently share the same physical network link without leakage of information between networks. IEEE 802.1Q also defines the meaning of a virtual LAN or VLAN with respect to the specific conceptual model underpinning bridging at the MAC layer and to the IEEE 802.1D spanning tree protocol.

IEEE Specification: IEEE 802.1q

802.1s

802.1s is an IEEE standard for the Multiple Spanning Tree (MST) Protocol, which was based on the Cisco's Multiple Instances Spanning Tree Protocol (MISTP). MST combines the best aspects from both the Cisco Per-VLAN Spanning Tree (PVST+) and the 802.1q. The idea is that several VLANs can be mapped to a reduced number of spanning tree instances because most networks do not need more than a few logical topologies.

IEEE Specification: IEEE 802.1s

802.1w

802.1w is an IEEE standard which defines the Rapid Span-

ning Tree Protocol (RSTP), an evolution of the Spanning Tree Protocol. RSTP provides for faster spanning tree convergence after a topology change. RSTP provides a loop free topology for any LAN or bridged network.
IEEE Specification: IEEE 802.1w

802.1x   193

802.1x is an IEEE standard for port-based network access control, particularly useful for securing 802.11 wireless local area networks (WLANs). The IEEE 802.1X offers an effective framework for authenticating and controlling user traffic to a protected network, as well as dynamically varying encryption keys. 802.1X ties a protocol called EAP (Extensible Authentication Protocol) to both the wired and wireless LAN media and supports multiple authentication methods, such as token cards, Kerberos, one-time passwords, certificates and public key authentication. Therefore, 802.1X is also known as EAP over LAN (EAPOL).
IEEE Specification: IEEE 802.1x

802.20

802.20 is an IEEE standard of Mobile Broadband Wireless Access (MBWA) by specifying new mobile air interfaces for wireless broadband. 802.20 is a competing standard with 802.16e. 802.16e, based on 802.16a, adds mobility in the 2 to 6 GHz licensed bands, while 802.20, a brand new standard, aims for operation in licensed bands below 3.5GHz and with a peak data rate of over 1 Mbit/s.
IEEE Specification: IEEE 802.20

802.22

802.22 is an IEEE standard for Wireless Regional Area Networks (WRAN). IEEE 802.22 specifies a cognitive air interface for fixed, point-to-multipoint, wireless regional area networks that operate on unused channels in the VHF/UHF TV bands between 54 and 862 MHz. Signals at these frequencies can propagate 40 km or more from a well-sited base station, depending on terrain.
IEEE Specification: IEEE 802.22

802.3ab   182

IEEE 802.3ab, also known as 1000BaseT, is a standard for gigabit ethernet over copper wiring cable (Cat 5e or better). 1000BASE-T uses all four cable pairs for simultaneous transmissions in both directions through the use of echo cancellation and a 5-level pulse amplitude modulation (PAM-5) technique.
IEEE Specification: IEEE 802.3ab

802.3ad

IEEE 802.3ad defines the technology called Ethernet link aggregation. Link aggregation is a computer networking term which describes using multiple Ethernet network cables/ports in parallel to increase the link speed beyond the limits of any single cable or port. Other terms for this also include "ethernet trunk", "NIC teaming", "port teaming", "port trunking", "NIC bonding" and "link aggregate group" (LAG).
IEEE Specification: IEEE 802.3ad

802.3ae   183

802.3ae is an IEEE 10-Gigabit Ethernet standard, which offers data speeds up to 10 billion bits per second but preserves similar benefits to those of the preceding Ethernet standard. 10-Gigabit Ethernet is used to interconnect local area networks (LANs), wide area networks (WANs), and metropolitan area networks (MANs). 10-Gigabit Ethernet uses the familiar IEEE

802.3 Ethernet media to access control (MAC) protocol and its frame format and size. However, it supports the full duplex mode but not the half-duplex operation mode, and it only functions over optical fiber. So it does not need the carrier-sensing multiple-access with Collision Detection (CSMA/CD) protocol as it is used in other Ethernet standards.
IEEE Specification: IEEE 802.3ae

802.3af

802.3af (often erroneously called 802.11af) is an IEEE standard which describes a mechanism for Power over Ethernet (PoE). The standard provides the capability to deliver both power and data over standard Ethernet cabling. Power over Ethernet enables remote devices (such as VoIP phones or Wireless Access Points) to operate without a separate power source. The elimination of line voltage AC power simplifies equipment installation and fosters safety in most areas.
IEEE Specification: IEEE 802.3af

802.3ah

802.3ah, an IEEE Data-link OAM specification, provides utilities for monitoring and troubleshooting Ethernet links, which are vital for carrier deployment. The IEEE 802.3ah EFM specification defines OAM as an optional sublayer just above the Ethernet media access controller (MAC). The OAM sublayer consists of a parser block, a multiplexer block, and a control block. All three blocks communicate with an OAM client, which is the "brains of the IEEE 802.3ah management architecture.
IEEE Specification: IEEE 802.3ah

802.3u   181

802.3u is an IEEE standard for the Fast Ethernet (100BASE-T). Fast Ethernet has the same frame format, MAC mechanisms, and MTU as the original Ethernet. Such similarities allow the use of existing 10BaseT applications and network management tools on Fast Ethernet networks.
IEEE Specification: IEEE 802.3u

802.3z   182

802.3z is an IEEE standard for the Gigabit Ethernet over fiber and cable, which has a physical media standard 1000Base-X (1000BaseSX -- short wave covers up to 500m, and 1000BaseLX -- long wave covers up to 5km). The IEEE 802.3ab defines the Gigabit Ethernet over the unshielded twisted pair wire (1000Base-T covers up to 75m).
IEEE Specification: IEEE 802.3z

Javvin Networking Technology Series

Network Dictionary

Networking, Internet, telecom, wireless, computer, hardware and software - multiple dictionaries in one. A "Must have" reference for IT/Networking professionals and students!

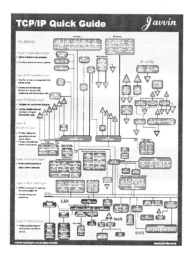

TCP/IP Quick Guide

Practical TCP/IP information extracted from hundreds of pages of TCP/IP books. A comprehensive and clear map of all TCP/IP protocols in OSI 7 layers model. A portable tool for you to carry, insert into a folder or put on your desk.

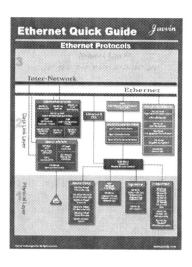

Ethernet Quick Guide

Practical Ethernet information extracted from hundreds of pages of Ethernet books. A comprehensive and clear map of all Ethernet protocols. A portable tool for you to carry, insert into a folder or put on your desk.

The Network Protocols Map Poster

All network protocols illustrated on one Chart. A "must have" for all networking, IT and Telecom professionals and students.

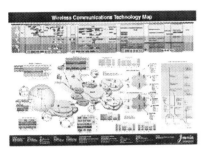

Wireless Communications Technology Map Poster

All major wireless technologies displayed in one chart: WLAN, WiMAX (WMAN), WPAN and mobile wireless technologies (WWAN)...

Network Security Map

All you must know about network security on one chart! A unique gift for yourself, your colleagues, partners and customers.

www.NetworkDictionary.com

Free networking technology library, comprehensive network protocol and network security knowledge, telecom encyclopedia, computer hardware and software terms and white-papers.

DATE DUE

Printed in the United States
129023LV00001B/39/A